Communist—Christian Encounter
in
East Europe

BY

ROBERT TOBIAS

SCHOOL OF RELIGION PRESS

INDIANAPOLIS, USA

1956

COMMUNIST—CHRISTIAN ENCOUNTER IN EAST EUROPE

Copyright, 1956, by Robert Tobias

Printed in the United States of America
MITCHELL-FLEMING PRINTING, INC.,
Greenfield, Indiana

ACKNOWLEDGEMENTS

Several personal friends and acquaintances, both Communist and Christian, were involved in the sharp conflicts between Communism and Christianity in East Europe which elevated some to high positions and sent others to prison or to death. They were the first inspiration for this book. The suggestion of friends in the West that I undertake such a study encouraged me to begin.

To these and others, many of whom must be un-named, I am greatly indebted for this book's completion: the individuals, libraries and information offices of government and private organizations which have provided invaluable information; the authors and publishers who have permitted me to use excerpts from their works; the translators who have helped with documents in nearly a dozen languages; the former colleagues in Europe who have given expert counsel at many points; and, in particular, Dr. W. A. Visser't Hooft of the World Council of Churches, Dean Jaques Courvoisier of the University of Geneva, Dr. H. H. Wolf of the Graduate School of Ecumenical Studies, Dr. George Walker Buckner, Jr., of the Council on Christian Unity, Dean O. L. Shelton of the School of Religion, and members of my family who have given encouragement, counsel and material assistance to make this volume possible. The conclusions I have drawn are my own, and I take full responsibility for them.

ROBERT TOBIAS
Indianapolis, 1956

CONTENTS

C. THE CHURCH UNIVERSAL

PART II—A CHRONICLE OF EVENTS

vi *Contents*

COMMUNIST-CHRISTIAN ENCOUNTER

Preface

The purpose of this study is to set forth in as objective manner as possible the inter-action of Communist governments and Christian churches in East Europe in the period from 1917 to 1951, their effect upon one another's purposes, policies and structures, and the relevance of these developments for the Church Universal.

This study is therefore limited (a) to those countries of East Europe presently governed by Communist administrations (commonly called "Satellites") closely allied with the Soviet (U.S.S.R.) Government, (b) to the respective periods since those Communist administrations came into control until 1951, and (c) to the specific developments in church-state relations which appear to have affected the purposes, policies or structure of either or both.

This does not, therefore, embrace a study of the Marx-Lenin ideology, nor, in general, of the theory of church-state relations, nor, in comprehensive detail, of the theologies of Christians in East Europe.[1] Nor has any attempt been made to describe the detailed political, military, and social developments which paralleled and affected church-state developments. These will already be well known to the reader, or will be found in other documents. This study is principally concerned with the way Christians in a given area have been confronted by the proponents of the Communist ideology, and the effect they have had one on the other, and may ultimately have for the Church Universal. It is recognized that the subject is still too vast for comprehensive treatment in one volume. In some instances, therefore, questions can only be posed, and left to another time and place for proper examination.

Several serious handicaps involved in a study of this nature will be apparent. In point of time, the events under consideration are too near to be appraised properly, while anyone in the West is too distant to comprehend their deepest meaning. Those concerned about Christians in East Europe are likely to be too involved to think objectively, or too concerned for the welfare of friends to reveal, or perhaps even to face some pertinent data. Sources of information are limited, being either too meager or too biased to be entirely dependable. And pre-conceived notions of the subject in question may preclude objectivity.

Nevertheless, it is a subject which needs urgent and careful study. Perhaps ultimately some objectivity will be achieved. What follows is intended as a contribution to that end by one who, over a period of seven years, has visited most of the countries concerned

---

1. A comparative study of theological trends as indicated in the writings of Bp. Bereczky, Prof. Hromadka, Bp. Nicolai, and others is being made by another colleague.

and conferred with many church and government leaders involved. He has observed how propagandists, by selective reporting, have been able to speak no falsehood and yet grossly distort truth, with unfortunate consequences. The writer has therefore begun with a meticulous and comprehensive survey of actual conflicts, negotiations, decisions and other pertinent relationships between churches and states in East Europe. He has gone through all sorts of propaganda, the books and journals listed in the bibliography, official government documents, church reports and various unpublished materials. A principal source of information has been private correspondence and personal conferences with people in the areas concerned (In this document no precise source is indicated for such information).

The summary result of these findings is set forth in Part II of this volume. Within Part II no effort has been made to interpret, evaluate or relate one incident to another. It is therefore a sourcebook or *chronicle of events* in which facts of varying degrees of relevance are left to stand for themselves as they occurred in each country and have been recorded by various interests. These "facts" and their selection may not be free from error, and will require further correcting as additional information is brought to light.

Part I describes the writer's analysis and principal conclusions from these facts. Where precise documentation has seemed necessary to substantiate the writer's conclusions, excerpts have been copied from the *Chronicle*. However, an attempt has been made to hold repetition to a minimum by using cross-references between the two parts.

In organizing Part I, the writer considered the possibility of treating each country and each confession separately before dealing with East Europe in general. The merits of such a comparative study are evident: there have been differences in Communist strategy from country to country, and from confession to confession. There have also been differences as between different age groups, professions, ethnic groups, and other categories of people.

As the study progressed, however, it became evident that varieties of Communist strategy in relation to such groups were circumstantial results which pointed to more central, determinative purposes. This interpretation therefore begins with a description of Communist purposes as the writer sees them. Within that larger determinative framework, various attitudes towards special groups, and the responses of these groups, have been considered: e.g., youth (page 42 ff.), confessional groups (page 146 ff.). Differences of implementation of Communist policy as between countries are evident in the *Chronicle of Events* and have been summarized at the end of that section.

Abbreviations Used in This Work

Bp.—Bishop

Cf.—*confer* (compare)

Chron.—Chronicle of Events; Part II of this work

EPS—Ecumenical Press Service (ICPIS prior to 1947)

FCCC—Information Service, Federal Council of Churches of Christ in America

Ff.—following

Ibid.—*ibidem* (in the same place)

ICPIS—International Christian Press and Information Service (EPS after 1946)

Loc. cit.—*loco citato* (in the place cited)

NCC—National Council of Churches of Christ in the U. S. A.

NYT—New York Times

Op. cit.—*opere citato* (in the work cited)

P.—page

Pp.—pages

Pr.—Pastor

Prof.—Professor

R. C.—Roman Catholic

Ref.—Reference or refer to

Rev.—Reverend

RNS—Religious News Service

RNC—Rumanian National Committee publication, *Persecution of Religion in Rumania*

USA—United States of America

USSR—Union of Soviet Socialist Republics

WCC—World Council of Churches

Foreword

On the Action of Faith

This must be said at the outset. Christians in East Europe did not develop an advance strategy for dealing with Communism. But as one looks back on what has happened, it is clear that the churches were not left alone. And if they had no plan calculated to deflect or reform or restrain Communism, it is nonetheless evident that Communists have often been restrained and their purposes deflected and re-considered because of the churches.

When Communists created neat laws and constitutions which they subsequently disregarded, Christians challenged them to live up to their own highest ideals and protestations.

When Communists instituted an aggressive program against religion, Christians challenged them to public debate and so embarrassed those who accepted that the anti-religious organization (USSR) instructed its members to avoid discussion with Christians.

When Communists thought to take over the churches by taking over their central administrative offices, the churches scattered their administration to the local congregational level; and when Communists sought to divide the churches to rule them, Christians intensified their sense of solidarity and mutual assistance.

When Communists restricted religious publications to practical non-existence, Christians passed news from person to person until "more people were being confronted with the gospel than in many years."

When Communists spread a tide of hate, fear and distrust, Christians responded with such love that Communist youth were deserting their ranks, and Communists eventually sought to impregnate their own program with love.

When Communists concealed behind attractive promises their ultimate aims regarding the churches, churches acted on the basis of promises made, and so confused the people and many Communists that Communist leaders were forced to reveal ultimate intentions, and then be exposed by the churches.

When Communists demanded that churches make statements favoring government policies, churches quoted back to the governments the noble promises and guarantees set forth in their state constitutions.

When Communists forbade religious instruction in the schools, religious instruction was taken up in many homes, thereby instructing also the parents.

(5)

When Communist governments cut off the support of theological schools, the response of local congregations was so solid and generous that governments found ways again to bring the schools into their purview.

When Communists severed the international contacts of Christians, interest in the ecumenical fellowship was increased.

When Communist governments rebuilt churches as historic monuments with hopes of government glorification, Christians who worshipped there continued to glorify God.

This is part of the story of East Europe. Not all Communists have acted this way, nor all Christians so responded, but their number has been great enough to affect the course of history in East Europe.

COMMUNIST—CHRISTIAN ENCOUNTER

in

EAST EUROPE

PART I

An Interpretation

"The abolition of religion as an illusory happiness of the people is a requisite of their real happiness."[1]

A. COMMUNIST PURPOSES

Chapter I

INTRODUCTION

The Christianization of East Europe, from Constantine to the present century, cannot be dissociated from the political and economic strategies of ambitious rulers. The Christian faith and the Christian community have frequently been distorted, exploited, attacked or defended to serve the interests of those whose purposes had little or nothing in common with that faith and community. This was part of the "Christianization" process. The church and political powers, religion and social practices, evangelism and propaganda, moralism and economic exploitation—all were inextricably entangled in a total society called "Christian."

Long before the Russian Revolution the process of "de-Christianization" was under way. At its worst, oppressed laborers came to think of the Church as opposed or indifferent to their welfare. Landless peasants could regard the Church as their extortionist landlord. Scientists could accuse religion of promoting superstition. And many other ills of a society in travail could be blamed on the "Christian" component of a "Christian Civilization" which could not be accepted as Christian.

Not least involved in that de-Christianization process were concerned Christians themselves who recognized the secular nature of their pseudo-Christian society and sought to call it by appropriate secular titles in order that what was of Christ could stand in its own right and draw people to Him, not to a society falsely called by His name. But the most articulate exponents of de-Christianization have been the Communists.

An Ultimate Objective

From the outset, leaders in the Marx-Engels-Lenin-Stalin tradition have left little doubt as to their ultimate aim with regard to religion: idealistic religion must "die out," churches should disappear.

---

1. Karl Marx, *Critique of Hegel's Philosophy of Law* (cf. N. Berdyaev, *The Origin of Russian Communism*, Charles Scribner's Sons, N.Y., 1937, p. 192).

Marx considered religion to be the product of "pre-socialist man's" fears, ignorance and suffering.

It is not religion that creates man, but man who creates religion.[2] . . . Religion is the groan of the downtrodden creature. . . . It is the opium of the people. . . . The abolition of religion as an illusory happiness of the people is a requisite of their real happiness.[3]

If religion was produced by misery, it was no less the perpetrator of prolonged misery. So long as man was miserable, he would have religion. So long as he had religion he would be resigned to his miserable estate.

As Marx-Leninism began to take practical form in movements and government, the underlying philosophical point on religion was and has been the same: religion must disappear. How that would come about has been an open question.

Engels prophesied that religion would simply disappear:

When society, taking in hand the whole range of the means of production and using them systematically, liberating thereby itself and all its members from slavery . . . only then will the last external force vanish, which up to that time expressed itself in religion, and with it *there will vanish the religious image itself,* for the simple reason that there will be nothing to reflect.[4]

In 1908, Lenin, less content to wait for the "Perfect Man" in a "Perfect Society" who would no longer need or be interested in religion, called for an aggressive program to exorcise religion itself:

Marxism as materialism is absolutely atheistic and resolutely hostile to all religion. We must combat religion: this is the rudiment of all materialism and consequently of Marxism. The fight against religion must not be confined to abstract ideological preaching. The fight

---

2. Lenin, in *Socialism and Religion*, Vol. VIII, further elaborated:
The impotence of the exploited classes in struggle with the exploiters inevitably gives birth to faith in a better life beyond the grave, just as the impotence of primitive people in struggle with nature gives birth to gods, devils, miracles, etc. To him who all his life works and suffers need, religion teaches humility and patience in earthly life, comforting him with the hope of heavenly reward. And to those who live by the toil of others, religion teaches philanthrophy in earthly life, offering them very cheap justification for all their exploiting existence, and selling at low price tickets to heavenly bliss. Religion is opium for the people. Religion is a sort of spiritual moonshine (bad homemade liquor) in which the slaves of capital drown their human figure, their demands for even any sort of worthy human life (as quoted by Anderson in *People, Church and State in Modern Russia*, p. 48).
3. Karl Marx, *Critique of Hegel's Philosophy of Law.*
4. Engels, *Anti-Duhring*, p. 261, as quoted by Paul Anderson, *op. cit.*, p. 47.

must be linked with the concrete practical work of the class movement, which aims at eliminating the social roots of religion.[5]

In 1918, in the debate over Article XIII of the Constitution, moderate Socialists who believed that religion would eventually crumble away, proposed the formula "religion is a private affair of the citizens." They were overruled by Lenin, who insisted on a more aggressive formula.[6]

Very early, then, as the Communist idea took on organizational form, Communists agreed to one ultimate aim: idealistic religion must disappear. But the differences among Communists as to how that should happen have greatly affected subsequent developments.

Experimental Phases in the USSR

The rise and decline of the League of Militant Atheists, the creation of the U.S.S.R. commissions on religious affairs, along with other church-state developments to be examined later, indicate that the emphasis in Communist strategy has fluctuated between the two extremes of *laisser mourir* and *faire mourir*. However, one thing is clear: that *some* strategy and program was eventually seen to be necessary and was therefore developed.

What was that strategy?

There has been no single, pre-conceived, unchanging strategy over the entire period from 1917 to 1951. Rather, there appear to have evolved at least four major stages by the process of trial and error.[7] Each phase suggests not only some change of emphasis or tactics, but also the shifting of responsibility for religious matters among Communists of differing viewpoints, and changes in the ultimate objectives of the Government, if not of the Communist Party. These phases can be identified (in the Soviet Union) in succeeding, but partly overlapping periods:

(1) Obliteration of churches,
    toleration of religion—1917-1918;

(2) Nationalization of churches,
    adaptation of religion—1918-1938;[8]

---

5. Lenin, "Attitude of Worker's Party toward Religion," *Selected Works*, International Publishers, N. Y., 1943, Vol. XI, p. 666.

6. Timasheff, *Religion in Soviet Russia*, p. 22 (*Chron.*, p. 230).

7. Paul Anderson speaks of three stages of political development—Revolutionary, Socialist, and Communist—corresponding in general to the writer's Obliteration, Nationalization and New Religion stages (*op. cit.*, p. 107).

8. Anti-religious education got well under way after 1929, reached a peak in the mid-thirties, and, except for a brief come-back in the 1938-39 suppression, rapidly waned until its re-creation in a different form during the past five years.

(3) Cooperation with nationalized churches, materialization of religion—1941-1950;
(4) Transformation of churches, creation of a new, "realistic" religion—1947-?.

What occurred in each phase and what brought about the progression from one phase to the next will be examined in detail in the following four chapters. Mention should be made here, however, of two factors fundamental to all these changes. One was the tenacity of Christians for their churches and their faith. This the Communists had grossly underestimated. Time after time they were deflected in their pursuits by the unexpected response of Christians. The other factor was the interplay between two wings of the Communist Party itself, and consequent ambivalence with regard to the churches.[9]

A Coordinated Strategy Abroad

If at the outset there was no singleness of strategy for the decades ahead, it does not follow that by 1944 there was no over-all plan for satellite countries. Already in 1946 in the Balkans, and later in other East European countries, the writer was astonished to see how similar were the approaches of the several governments to the religious question. What was happening in one country was not an isolated experiment. Public speeches, news releases, decrees, constitutional articles on religion, all had the ring of a common origin. In Rumania there was talk of a "Vishinsky Plan"[10] for the re-orientation of the churches in areas scheduled for Soviet occupation. Documents or directives of a similar nature cropped up elsewhere. It became obvious that there was a common, recently conceived plan, probably based on earlier experience in the U. S. S. R.,[11] some center of consultation and sharing of information, and some body thinking out current strategy in broad lines, with flexibility allowed for, or created by factors peculiar to a given area, or even for differences of opinion within Communist ranks.

---

9. See Chapter V.

10. The "Plan" provided for control of the clergy by controlling their stipends and compromising the most reluctant, liquidation of undesirable leaders in key places and replacing them with Soviet-trained leaders, prohibition of all religious activities except worship, and creation of a loyal Orthodox front under Moscow leadership and against Western Churches (*Chronicle*, Rumania, August 23, 1944, p. 321).

11. The Program of the Communist International was described by Lenin as follows: "The first round against religion, the opium of the people, occupies an important position among the tasks of the cultural revolution. This fight must be carried on persistently and systematically. The proletarian power must withdraw all State support from the Church, and abolish the influence exercised by the Church in the system of education and training organized by the State; it must ruthlessly suppress the counter-revolutionary activities of ecclesiastical organizations.

As new Communist governments came into power, domestic religious matters were kept closely related to "foreign affairs," and presumably thereby to the central planning group. In Bulgaria, for example, religious affairs were dealt with by the Ministry of Foreign Affairs and Cults. From a domestic viewpoint, this already seemed so unnatural as to suggest that foreign powers were determining the policy on religion. Later, following the U. S. S. R. pattern, Ministries or Commissions of Religious Affairs were created. This did not mean that religious matters would be dealt with domestically.

Recently the fact has come to light that the Cominform established a department of religious affairs, called the "Orginform." Sometime before 1951,[12] the Orginform and the Association of Atheists were reported to have met at Karlsbad, Czechoslovakia, for consultation and instruction. Later, in April, 1951, special representatives were sent to Hungary to speed up the liquidation of "clerical reaction."[13] This was probably not an isolated case of joint international action on a religious problem in a national setting.

There was, then, a tried pattern—the Soviet pattern—and an international strategy board to put it into operation. Russian Communism had stumbled through the steps of its struggle with religion over a period of thirty-six years. For new Communist countries the Russian pattern was modified in the light of later developments there, and the last three phases were crowded into the space of five or six years with consequent overlapping and frequently conflicting results.

In the working out of details, as will be seen in later chapters and in the *Chronicle* there has been great variety as between countries, confessions, nations, professions, ages and sexes. But in general, all three phases are there, country by country, church by church, believer by believer, and if later phases are not yet felt in certain countries or churches, e.g., East Germany, they can probably be expected.

"The proletarian power acknowledges freedom of conscience, but at the same time uses all the means at its disposal to conduct anti-religious propaganda, abolishes the privileged position of the established Church and reforms the entire educational system on the basis of the scientific materialist conception of the world." Lenin, *Religion*, Lawrence and Wishart, as quoted by D. Hyde, *The Answer to Communism*, p. 33.

12. Possibly July, 1948, when a fuller document defining Communist strategy towards churches first appeared (*Chron.*, p. 494).

13. MacEoin, *The Communist War on Religion*, p. 139.

"You ask what we want. Gentlemen, we want to break your necks!"[1]

Chapter II

OBLITERATION

If, as Lenin proposed, the Communist Party was to combat religion in more concrete ways than "abstract ideological preaching," where was it to take hold, on the Church or on religion itself?

Leading Communists have recently asserted[2] that the Communist Party does not seek directly to obliterate or suppress churches. Today, this may be true. But the Communist Party did not in fact foresee the inadvisability of a direct attack on the churches without first having tried it—and lost. It was tried in Russia on two occasions, once for a very short period immediately after the Communist Government came into power, and again during the political purges of 1937. In Central Europe attempts have been made more recently to dissolve a number of smaller churches (Seventh-Day Adventist, Pentecostal, Salvation Army, Mormon).

Obliteration During Internal Revolution

The nature and scope of the early "obliteration" measures is well-known. Numerous books have been written on the subject.[3] In general, the procedure[4] was (a) to imprison or execute, or otherwise incapacitate clergymen and active laymen, (b) to close church buildings and take over church property for secular, often anti-religious purposes, and (c) to destroy or desecrate parish and private icons, religious equipment and symbols.[5]

What idea lay behind such action?

The Communist ideology was concerned in the first place with *religion* as a phenomenon which must be eliminated, not with the institutional church. But religion, as Marx taught, was the creation of the down-trodden proletariat. And the Communist Party was seeking to identify itself with the proletariat. If a direct at-

---

1. Comment of C. Gottwald, General Secretary of the Czechoslovakian Party, before the Czechoslovakian Parliament, 1929.
2. USSR—*Chron.*, pp. 234, 235, 242, 245, 246, 294; Estonia, *Chron.*, p. 313.
3. Valentinoff, *The Assault of Heaven;* Chernavin, *I Speak for the Silent;* Father George, *God's Underground*, and others.
4. Timasheff, *Religion in Soviet Russia*, p. 143.
5. The disruption of the home and family life, although undertaken for "scientific" reasons, played some part in the obliteration program, and ultimately its demise.

tack were launched at religion, the laboring people might well assume that they, or something they held dear was being attacked. Therefore, any attack must be oblique, not direct.

The Church, however, represented something else. It was not religion. It was not the creation of the proletariat.[6] In fact, there was widespread bitterness among the people towards certain aspects of institutional church life: hierarchical tyranny, land-holding, compulsory religious instruction, corruption. Popular feeling by mid-1917 was such[7] that it could be reasonably assumed by the Communists that the proletariat would not only not oppose a general attack on the Church, but would enter heartily into such an attack. This would suit Communist purposes remarkably well. For, although they believed that the downtrodden had created religion, it was the bourgeoisie who maintained religion through the Church and the clergy.

The logical conclusion therefore was to attack the "bourgeois" Church while at the same time assuring freedom of religion to the proletariat. The logic of it was convincing; churches were attacked.

Whether it was the Communists or the people who took greater initiative in the 1917-18 persecution is a moot question. The whole country was in turmoil; people were aiming their long pent-up indignation at many presumed adversaries. Whatever happened to the Church, as in the French Revolution, was part of the revolutionary process. The Communist Party may conceivably have had little more to do with the original attack on the churches than to capitalize on existing anti-clericalism, blaming present ills on the churches, and preparing on the same grounds long range programs of anti-religious propaganda and education.

On the other hand, some lessons were learned, notably that overt attacks on religion which over-stepped the bounds of popular dissatisfaction with church administration rather revived than overcame religion. Party leaders became aware that when private religious instruction groups were limited to a maximum of three children (no public instruction was permitted), religious instruction units of three persons sprang up everywhere. When publication of religious literature was curtailed, books were copied by hand and circulated. Church choirs organized community singing fests, and priests became sports leaders. Forbidden monastic or-

---

6. Communist theory distinguished between the exploiting classes (bourgeoisie and foreign groups), indigenous churches (organizers of religious propaganda and tools of the exploiting classes), and the masses (victims of the exploiting classes). See *Program and Rules of the Eighth Congress*, page 15 (cf. p. 56).

7. Landless peasants, under the slogan "land, bread and peace" were seizing large estates and church farms. Church administration was left largely in the hands of those least sympathetic towards the proletariat after liberal churchmen were driven from responsible posts, accused of being Bolsheviks (*Chron.*, p. 228).

ders formed themselves into "Labor Communes." Villagers organized special religious processions and speeches in frank defiance of Government orders. The churches had proved to be neither an effective scape-goat for Communist failures, nor a whipping post for the people's frustrations.[8]

At the next meeting of the Communist Party a statement was approved which set forth clearly that the Church and religion must be tackled differently, and that in no case should religion be inadvertently strengthened through excessive violence:

> "The aim of the Party is finally to destroy the ties between the exploiting classes and the organization of religious propaganda, at the same time helping the toiling masses actually to liberate their minds from religious superstitions, and organizing on a wide scale scientific-educational and anti-religious propaganda.

> "It is however, necessary to *avoid offending the religious sensibilities of believers* which leads only to the strengthening of religious fanaticism."[9]

After such a clear directive from the Party one might assume that no Communist would dare instigate further suppressions. There were, however, recurrent attempts (and frequent verbal campaigns which were checked) to "obliterate" the churches by "administrative measures."[10] The second major attempt was during the persecutions of 1937-38. The new Constitution established in November, 1936, was considered more liberal towards religion, and rescinded several control measures. Religion appeared to take heart. At the end of 1936 the census revealed, and the League of Militant Atheists confirmed that great numbers of people were still Christian. Thereupon, elements in the Communist Party, through *Pravda* (Communist Party organ), *Izvestia* (Soviet Government organ), Comsomol (Communist youth movement), and other channels demanded a new, intensive anti-religious drive.[11] The Government, through the League of Militant Atheists, resisted overt anti-church measures. Experience had taught that such action would only embitter and in the end strengthen the believers.

---

8. *Chronicle*, pp. 229, 230.

9. VIII Congress, March 18-23, 1919, included in the *Program and Rules of the Communist Party of the Soviet Union, 1932*, as quoted in *Notes on Soviet Affairs*, June 23, 1952, p. 3 (italics mine).

10. In 1929, at a conference of the Godless Society, Comsomol (Communist Youth) representatives introduced a motion which would compel trade union members to withdraw from membership in religious associations. The Commissar of Education explained (*Chron.*, p 238) that such action would only intensify religious feeling, and the motion was defeated.

11. *Chronicle*, p. 242.

Obliteration and Changes in Communist Policy

The matter would probably have gone little further than an appeal to excessive anti-religionists for moderation had it not been for the conflict between Russian Communists and "international" Communists[12] which broke in 1937. In that struggle Russian Communists gained control and determined to displace or destroy "international" Communists who did not put the Soviet Union first.[13] Thereupon, any person with international leanings, or contacts, or the possibility of contacts abroad became suspect.

Political trials and purges swept the country into chaos. Normal restraints exercised by the Communist combination of abstract ideology and practical government gave way through fear and revenge to unchecked terrorism. In that atmosphere, few distinctions were made between politician and churchman. In any case, theoretical distinctions would have mattered little. The ideology had maintained that in case of counter-revolution, the partly-defeated bourgeoisie would exploit the remnants of religion, the bourgeois clergy, to regain control, and the Church, or its clergy, had had international contacts. Therefore, church leaders were no less suspect than outright politicians. Clergymen were charged with espionage, sabotage, arson, terrorism, theft, immorality and similar crimes, and were "liquidated" or given severe sentences. The purges, aimed at leaders, quickly swept beyond church leaders and into the realm of religion itself. Lay believers and youth were subjected to oppressive measures. During the year 1937-38, ten thousand religious associations were suppressed, and some two thousand churches closed.[14]

However, suppressive measures had scarcely reached full swing before *Bezboznik*, official organ of the League of Militant Atheists, recognized that they were succeeding only in driving Christians underground. Christians were meeting in all kinds of places and groups (e.g., "ravine worshippers") had organized a "League for the Revival of the Church," were instructing believers in the organization of secret "home" churches, were training priests in secret theological seminaries, assisting travelling "espionage" priests, and engaging in other "catacomb" activities. There was sufficient renewal of religious activity among children for the Commissariat of Education to call for an anti-religious campaign

---

12. The Comintern (Communist Internationale) sought equilateral socialist progress on a world-wide scale; the new nationalist policy called for the establishment of pure socialism first in one country.
13. The adoption of the 1936 Constitution appeared to be an initial step calculated to prepare the Soviet Union to be the laboratory for the nationalizing of Communism.
14. Timasheff, *Religion in Soviet Russia*, p. 52.

at that level. And popular interest in anti-religious films, clubs and publications was practically non-existent.[15]

If it was the Communist Party which suggested a renewed anti-religious drive, it was probably also the Communist Party which, when it saw to what detrimental excesses the suppressive measures had gone, was instrumental in stopping them. Suddenly at the beginning of 1939, with the replacement of Yezhoff by Beria in the Ministry of Interior, persecution ceased. Followers of Trotsky and Bukharin were accused of instigating the persecutions of churchmen "in order to increase the hostility to the Soviet Government."[16] An olive branch was extended to the churches, and the Christian religion was heralded as a beneficial factor in man's development.[17]

It is doubtful that direct supppressive measures of such scope and brutality will be repeated so long as new generations of Communists learn and remember the lessons learned by their predecessors.

Suppression of the "Non-nationalized" Sects

Obliteration of minor sects is, however, a different matter, and efforts toward their suppression can hardly be expected to cease. The reason is not that they are religious, but that they will not make their religion conform to new social patterns. They refuse to be made innocuously "respectable," to accept government support. They will not be exclusively nationalistic patriots. Many of them refuse military service. They have their own independent way of working for "Peace." They shun compromises, moral or political. Since, to the Communist mind, they are already fanatics, suppressive measures would make them no more determined; and since they are small in number, their suppression would not likely affect the "religious sensibilities" of the majority of believers. Indeed, there has been some untimely approval or lack of expressed

15. *Chronicle*, pp. 244, 245.
16. Timasheff, *op. cit.*, p. 97. *Chronicle*, p. 245.
17. The League of Militant Atheists distributed a circular to anti-religious propagandists including the following statement:
"Christianity should not be identified with capitalism. Early Christians were not rich, and they did not pay much attention to wealth. Christianity should not be identified with other religions: for it is a cult of the 'abstract man' and emphasizes his ideal properties. The beneficial role Christianity played in the development of family relations should not be denied, for it helped to establish monogamy. Christianity has contributed to the improvement of folkways and customs; it has eliminated bloody and orgiastic rites; it insisted on the abolition of harmful customs such as fights between gladiators and the coursing of men by beasts in the circus."
(As quoted in Timasheff, *Religion in Soviet Russia*, p. 115, *Chronicle*, p. 245).

disapproval by some members of larger churches at the suppression of these fellow Christians.[18]

One can conclude that there are two sets of circumstances under which attempts may be made to obliterate the churches. One is the revolutionary situation in which matters get out of control and fall into the hands of enraged masses, or inexperienced Communists, or those whose formation in Communist tactics goes back to the pre-1918 ideological era in the U.S.S.R. (as, e.g., Dimitrov in Bulgaria, Rakosi in Hungary). The other is in relation to those churches or groups of believers which cannot or will not conform to Communist desires through the "nationalization" process.

Outside of these circumstances, a determined effort has been made since 1918 not to drive people to religion by heavy-handed suppression. The obliteration strategy, though the churches lost 45,000 priests and nearly as many places of worship in the process, from the Communist viewpoint was a failure. Communists came to recognize that "Religion is like a nail. The harder you hit it, the deeper it goes."[19] The new strategy, therefore, was to nationalize the churches while allowing freedom of religious worship. Subsequent statements of Communist planners have consistently reiterated the Lenin axiom: "Avoid offending the religious sensibilities of believers, which leads only to the strengthening of religious fanaticism."[20]

---

18. E.g., Bulgaria, p. 360 ff. of *Chronicle*.
19. U.S.S.R. Commissar of Education Lunacharsky, as quoted by Pares in *Russia, Its Past and Present*, p. 110.
20. VIII Congress of the Communist Party, March 18-23, 1919, as quoted in *Notes on Soviet Affairs*, June 23, 1952, p. 3.

"To close churches is easy; but the peasants build churches in their souls."[1]

Chapter III

NATIONALIZATION OF CHURCHES

There have been three distinct, but not unrelated elements in the nationalization phase:

(1) nationalization or domestication of the churches;
(2) toleration of religious worship and belief;
(3) experimentation with anti-religious propaganda and education.

In the U.S.S.R., this phase spread over a period of twenty-three years, from 1918 to 1941, though it was probably not recognized as such before the introduction of the Socialist program in 1925. It began when the Government realized the futility of trying to overcome religion and the Church by persecution.[2] It ended, if indeed it has ended, when the Government was convinced that the Church was fully loyal to the Government's program and recognized that the Church had possibilities for a positive contribution to the Government's interests.

In other countries the process was accelerated, and in some, e.g., Rumania, Bulgaria and Albania, has been accomplished in three or four years. In Poland, East Germany, and to some extent Hungary and Czechoslovakia, this phase is not yet (1951) completed.

Why a "nationalized" church? Stalin put it simply: "To close churches is easy, but the peasants build churches in their souls."[3]

If the Church or religion could not be obliterated, it was better to have it organized under an orderly, legalized administration with tangible offices and leaders with whom one could deal, than to have a movement of unknown proportions and purposes operat-

---

1. J. Stalin, reported address to the Central Executive of the League of Militant Atheists.
2. A church under state control was not without precedent in the USSR. Tsar Peter, in 1722 succeeded in placing the Russian Orthodox Church under government control by replacing the Patriarchate with a Holy Synod directed by an appointee of the Tsar—a relationship which continued nearly two hundred years (*Chron.*, p. 223).
3. J. Stalin, reported address to the Central Executive of the League of Militant Atheists.

ing underground as "ravine worshippers" or "Leagues for the Revival of the Church." Further, if the place of religion as a historic phenomenon could be discreetly recognized, believers would be in a psychological condition more conducive to cooperation in technical developments and to conversion to the "progress" ideology.

What were the minimum requriements of a "contained" or nationalized church? Believers would obviously be satisfied with no less than access to church buildings, possibilities of worship, facilities for receiving the sacraments, some voice in the selection of leaders, freedom of private religious life, and freedom to convey their faith to their children.

The Government, on the other hand, to be true to its ideology, should be solely responsible for the following: the administration of politics, of the national economy, and all productive capital, including land; the maintenance of civil records; the control of labor and therefore of public holidays and celebrations; the "proper" education of the masses, and therefore control of all media of communication; the care of the needy, and therefore the administration of all welfare; international affairs, and therefore all contacts of any citizens with foreign countries; and the "scientific" formation of the future generations.

A national church, therefore, must be one which would not exceed the framework prescribed for performing its religious functions, and, secondly, would be loyal to the Government in the Government's administration of governmental responsibilities—or at least not oppose the Government. Within that framework there would be freedom, even assistance. Said Foreign Minister Kolarov of Bulgaria: "Our state will lend help and support to all religious denominations in the country which observe the constitution and loyally collaborate with the People's Government."[4]

How should Communist governments go about creating loyal national churches? This was bound to be a painful process, as Central European churches had far to go, and much to lose before they could fit the role cut out for "national" churches. That task, of re-shaping and re-orienting the churches, fell to the various Commissions of Religious Affairs, or of Education and Religion or of the Interior. Guided by whatever master-plan had been worked out, and by consultation one with another, they ran through a succession of secret directives, Party instructions and speeches, governmental decrees, negotiations and agreements with churches until, when the fulfillment of the nationalization process was relatively assured, post-facto codifications of prior decrees were incorporated into national constitutions, and new church statutes

---

4. Foreign Minister V. Kolarov, Address to the National Assembly, Feb. 2, 1949, News release from the Bulgarian Legation, London, March, 1949.

were drawn up. Nearly every aspect of church life as it is known in the West was affected in the process. The following summary of significant points will indicate the scope of their effect on the Church. The sequence has varied in different countries according to local conditions.

Vital Statistics

Until the introduction of Communist reforms, records of births, marriages and deaths were kept by the churches. Prior to the Middle Ages, the churches had undertaken this responsibility because records were needed, the Church was concerned, and in many communities only clergymen could read and write. In most countries there were no other statistical records.

Later, when statistics-conscious governments were established, many were content to have the clergy continue this time-consuming and often annoying function. It was a task which became increasingly difficult for the clergy when, for example, non-believers or Free-churchmen came to be married by the State Church priest, who, for ecclesiastical reasons, should refuse to marry them, and for legal reasons must marry them. It was hardly a job local clergy coveted. Even so, there was some resistance against nationalization of statistical records.[5] In Russia the Orthodox Synod and Patriarch instructed Orthodox clergy to continue their recording of births, baptisms, marriages and deaths as usual, and to permit Government officers to copy such records under the supervision of church members, but not to possess the church's records. There was difficulty particularly over the introduction of compulsory civil vows to replace church marriages, not so much because of the new system of records as for the materialistic concept of marriage and procreation accompanying it.

Marx had made it clear in *The Origin of the Family* that there would be no place for the home and family life in the scientific society. Children would be brought up in scientifically-operated state institutions. Engels "wrote a book to show that the family belonged only to a certain, backward stage of man's development and that he would, by the aid of Communism, ultimately outgrow it."[6] And a new law on marriage bluntly asserted that "Birth itself shall be the basis of the family . . . whether in or out of wedlock."[7]

The Church was only slightly placated later when the Government conceded that the Church might perform religious ceremonies in addition to the prescribed civil vows.

5.   *Chronicle*, p. 284, items 32, 33.
6.   Douglas Hyde, *The Answer to Communism*, p. 63.
7.   Government decree of Dec. 18, 1917, as quoted by Pares, *Russia, Its Past and Present*, p. 210 (*Chron.*, p. 229).

In all East European countries the transfer of vital statistics has now been made to government offices, and it is unlikely that the churches would elect to take up such a task again even if the opportunity should arise. They do, however, maintain that the Church must have the right to perform the sacrament of marriage (Orthodox) or to pronounce Divine blessing on the institution of marriage (Protestant). So long as provision is made for both civil vows and religious ceremonies there is no serious conflict.

Land Reform

In 1917, the Russian Orthodox Church owned more than 2,000,000 acres of monastery lands, plus a thousand church farms and 2,000 buildings used or rented for non-religious purposes. When, in the general chaos of the 1917 uprisings, land-hungry peasants and soldiers took over many church farms and large private estates, the Church identified its interests with those of the private landholders.[8]

One of the first acts which the Communist Government undertook after coming into power was to provide for the systematic nationalization of lands, farms and buildings, including those of the churches. The Orthodox Church hierarchy retaliated by urging local congregations to set up lay holding societies, which would become "owners" of church property and thereby protect it from confiscation. Believers were called upon to resist all attempts at sequestration. Those who aided the Government were excommunicated.[9]

The Roman Catholic Church declared that its properties had been given exclusively to the Church and that therefore only the Church could negotiate the sale or transfer of its property.

Nonetheless, all church property was declared national property by the Government. Local congregations could be accorded use of places of worship by contractual agreement between the Government and twenty or more believers. The congregation was then responsible for upkeep and insurance on the buildings.

In 1946 some small properties were returned to Orthodox parishes and monasteries, exempt from taxation.

In other countries, with the exception of Latvia and Estonia where personal funds, homes and cars of clergymen were ordered to be nationalized, land reform has been undertaken more gradually.

---

8. The final session of the All-Russian Conference of Clergy and Laymen condemned the seizure of estates, and two months later (Aug. 1917) Bishop Arseny asserted before the Orthodox Sobor that "the landlords and the Church stand together" (*Chron.*, p. 228).

9. *Chron.*, p. 230.

The general pattern has been, first, to re-distribute large estates, capitalizing on popular feeling against large land-holders, and granting plots to each land-hungry peasant; later, to reduce middle-sized estates, cutting out certain categories of owners entirely, and turning considerable lands to state administration; and finally, to nationalize all lands.

When the first step was introduced in Lithuania, parish priests were permitted to keep eighty acres of land, or were given eight acres if they had no land. In Poland, farms up to 250 acres could be kept for the support of priests, sanctuaries and inhabited monasteries. In Hungary, where the Roman Catholic Church had 10,000,000 acres of land, the first agrarian law in 1945 permitted churches to keep 1,100 acres each, and in Czechoslovakia the Agrarian Reform Law of 1947 did not touch estates of less than two hundred acres.

In the second stage, maximum holdings were cut in Czechoslovakia to 125 acres. In Hungary, provision was made for the churches to sell remaining holdings to the Government at fixed prices. Parish houses, and some small garden properties were exempted in Rumania.

In the final stage, or near, land has been either simply confiscated or given over to the state "voluntarily." When Evangelicals in Transylvania found it too difficult to administer their lands and meet Government harvest quotas, they turned over all lands to the State, except for garden plots (2½ acres) retained for the clergy. In Czechoslovakia, the Government decreed in 1950 that all church estates, palaces and institutions were nationalized.

In East Germany, where in spite of the Land Reform Law of 1945, ninety-five percent of the arable land was still in private hands, another factor entered in: the churches' ownership of lands has provided an effective means of nationalizing their liquid assets.[10] The churches have long had small holdings, and since 1933 received more land from private bequests. The Land Reform Law of 1945, which should have nationalized church estates, was not implemented. Indeed, the State often refused to take the lands even on insistence from the churches. The State then fixed quotas for production from church lands. These could not be met by the churches except by purchasing produce in the expensive State-owned "Handel's Organization" stores with church funds. If quotas were not met, responsible church leaders could be tried for "sabotage of production"—punishable by death!

---

10. In the USSR the same end was accomplished by fixing high premiums for insurance (which congregations must pay), by collecting "Drama Union" dues from church choristers and ministers of religion, and high taxes or production quotas (Letter of Metropolitan Sergius to the Government; Anderson, *op. cit.*, pp. 32-84; *Chron.*, pp. 291-293).

While it may be reasonably assumed that Communist administrators in East Germany will eventually discover, as did the Soviet Union in 1930,[11] that such a policy works against them, the threat is no less real for many churchmen today.

In all of East Europe, something over 15,000,000 acres of land once held by the churches has now been redistributed or nationalized. Few people in East Europe would maintain that the nationalization of land has been undertaken as an anti-church measure. In fact, there has been some expression of popular disapproval when churches protested against the reform in its early stages.

The aim of property redistribution has ostensibly been to provide for more efficient production. While many churchmen have questioned the churches' involvement in the business of production, they have also indicated that, owing to poor technical organization, poor handling of human relations and poor incentives, production has been lower under Communist than under church administration.

The principal complaint of the churches against their loss of lands was that it impoverished the churches and prevented the fulfillment of their administrative responsibilities. So long as governments were interested only in obliterating churches, they were little bothered by this objection. Effective nationalization of the churches, however, required that as friendly relations as possible be maintained with church authorities, which in turn necessitated some provision for meeting the churches' administrative responsibilities. The governments of every country concerned have therefore replaced former church income from estates with direct or semi-direct financial subsidies. In Poland, the income from nationalized church estates was to go into a central church fund to provide for the maintenance and reconstruction of church buildings, for salaries of the clergy and the charitable work of the churches. In Hungary, there was no direct compensation for lands; but the Government is subsidizing the churches' budgets over a period of eighteen years. Similarly, in Czechoslovakia, the Government now underwrites the churches' total administrative costs. Presently the churches are less concerned about their loss of lands and wealth, than about their loss of independence.

Church Buildings

"When the time comes, the churches will be used as stables for the horses of the victorious Communist armies." Thus R. Horn, of the Socialist Union Party (Communist) of East Germany dis-

---

11. The Soviet People's Commissariat of Finance decreed on Jan. 5, 1930, that individual believers could not be held responsible for taxes, insurance or other debts of their church (*Chron.*, p. 238 ff.).

closed an ultimate Communist objective. The time he referred to seems to have come for nearly 100,000 churches and chapels in East Europe (many of which, however, were destroyed in the war and could not be rebuilt). But for the remaining 70,000, it seems a long way off.

Communist governments, intent on the nationalization of church life, are alert to the desires of believers: believers should not be unduly offended. If believers want buildings for worship, they should have some buildings. Mr. Horn apparently had not yet understood that.

On June 9, 1923, the Central Committee of Trade Unions (USSR) declared that "the struggle against religion will not be terminated by casual decrees and administrative coercion. . . ."[12] Ten days later the Government decreed that church buildings previously sequestered by the Government should be re-distributed to existing religious groups.

In 1924, the Thirteenth Congress of the Communist Party declared that "it is necessary to liquidate all attempts to uproot religion by administrative measures, such as the closing of churches."[13]

In the same year a member of the Central Committee of the Communist Party in Georgia stated:[14] "Today there is no intelligent Party member who would not agree that our anti-religious activity has been overdone. All talk that peasants do not want their churches and voluntarily close them is self-delusion. We must make up for our mistake and give the peasants back the keys of their churches . . ."

In May, 1929, the Soviet Assembly was reported to have declared that by May, 1937, "No church is to be left in the Soviet Union";[15] but less than a year later the Government decreed that the closing of churches by local authorities was against the will of the people and should be stopped.[16] When in 1937, Smolensk Communist officials tried to get people to sign petitions for the closing of churches, *Pravda* labeled them provacateurs and demanded their punishment.[17] Similarly, in Vologda, it was the League of Militant Atheists which suppressed a mass campaign to close churches, on grounds that it would only embitter the believers.[18] And this occurred in the midst of wildest attacks against church leaders.

In 1945 the Soviet Government passed decrees restoring to the Orthodox Church a large part of the properties confiscated

---

12.   Timasheff, *Religion in Soviet Russia*, p. 95 (*Chron.*, p. 234).
13.   *Ibid.*, p. 37 (*Chron.*, p. 235).
14.   Timasheff, *Religion in Soviet Russia*, p. 96 (*Chron.*, p. 235).
15.   *Ibid.*, p. 38 (*Chron.*, p. 238).
16.   *Ibid.*, p. 45 (*Chron.*, p. 239).
17.   *Ibid.*, p. 122 (*Chron.*, p. 243).
18.   *Ibid.*, p. 46 (*Chron.*, p. 242).

some fifteen years earlier, and in 1948, Andrei Vishinsky added this note to his summary *Laws of the Soviet State*: "The State does not intrude in the internal affairs of organizations of church folk. . . . Closing churches is appropriate only if the toilers themselves have passed a directive concerning it."[19]

Communists no longer intend "administratively" to do away with church buildings. But they have insisted on government planning as to where, how and when there should be places of worship, particularly in areas where most buildings were destroyed in the war or where new communities are being established. This they accomplish in accordance with several "scientific" factors and by several means.

Some of these factors were listed by M. Karpoff, Chairman of the USSR Commission on Orthodox Religious Affairs, in defining the functions of that Commission: "We place absolutely no barriers to church expansion. . . ." He added that petitions for church buildings were rarely refused, and when refused it was because there was no building available, or there were too many churches in the area already, or too few people to maintain a church.[20]

Government planning as related to church buildings has generally been based on one or more of these factors:

Shared buildings: Where there had been church buildings and there was a continuing demand for them, church buildings might be provided. This did not mean, however, that every congregation of every confession in a given area must have its own exclusive church building. A young Communist whom the writer saw in Rumania put it this way:

"Thousands of our homes, factories and schools were blown to bits in the war. Our re-construction problem is enormous, building materials are limited, and people are clamoring for homes and places to work. To provide each congregation at this time with its own exclusive church building, which would be used only a very short part of one day a week, is a luxury which we cannot afford, and which the people would not accept. The churches must learn to share their buildings."

---

19. As quoted by Barron and Waddams, *op. cit.*, p. 21 (*Chron.*, p. 266). This principle, as indicated above, had been applied many years previously, and on one occasion (1930) Metropolitan Sergius had written the Government concerning abuses of it: "Before closing a church the decisive factor should not be the desire of the unbelieving part of the population, but the existence of believers who desire and are able to use the given building. . . ." (Letter of Feb. 19, 1930; Anderson, *op. cit.*, pp. 82-84; *Chronicle*, pp. 292-293.

20. *New York Times*, Aug. 12:13:3, 1944 (*Chron.*, p. 258).

In Lithuania a decree forbade the maintenance of more than one church within a radius of seven miles.[21] In principle, when two or more congregations were "merged" (e.g., Uniate and Orthodox parishes in Rumania or two congregations within one confession which cannot separately keep up rental payments on buildings now owned by the Government) one building was freed for "priority" purposes.

Unnecessary buildings: In newly developed industrial areas, where industrial workers were expected to be "enlightened materialists," no churches were considered necessary. If church buildings existed they would be used for "priority" housing, storehouses or educational purposes. If they did not exist, none was included in city planning. But, as one civic official in a new industrial city remarked privately when asked where the church would be located, "We do not need a church. But in case we ever should, we have this lovely park located in the center of the city!"

Undesirable buildings: Many church buildings not destroyed in the war have since been removed, particularly in villages, allegedly to improve town planning or to broaden public highways, or in response to "popuar feeling."

Desirable buildings: In almost every country the Government has at one time or another assisted various churches in rebuilding some historic structure or in providing for its upkeep as a national monument.

Old cathedrals in conspicuous places, churches of a unique architecture, or buildings related to some important historic event have received special attention. This show of concern has been received with considerable interest among the churches.

Church buildings and scientific education: Places of worship related to active congregational life were expected to be kept as inconspicuous as possible. Symbols, reminders of the existence of religion, have been occasionally suppressed. A skyline of church steeples and crosses apparently causes considerable discomfort to government leaders. In the course of a public procession in Warsaw, the President suddenly became aware of a cross which had been erected on top of a recently repaired church dome. A man was quickly dispatched to saw it off. In other places, troops, whether out of vandalism or on instructions, have used crosses on church spires for their target practice—an act which, apparently they have not realized as did Lenin and his followers in Russia, only makes the religious more religious.[22]

---

21. *Chronicle*, p. 310.
22. Timasheff, *Religion in Soviet Russia*, p. 124 (*Chron.*, p. 245).

In the USSR, church buildings became the property of the State. They have been rented or lent to congregations "for prayer purposes and no other."[23] In Czechoslovakia, the Government prepared a law in 1950 which would give the Government custody over religious treasures, relics, paintings, castles, etc. Church buildings, after the law of October, 1949, are *de facto* property of the State. But whether the Government holds title to church buildings and asks a nationalized church to maintain them, or whether a national church retains title and maintains them in accordance with government specifications is of little importance. In either case the result is that church buildings in lands where there are nationalized churches are nationalized.

But many are still used for the worship of God, as is evident, said Yaroslavsky, leader of the Militant Atheists, from the way church buildings are cared for—an indication "of the joy of the believers in making sacrifices. . . ."[24]

Monasteries and Convents

The religious Orders presented the Communists with a formidable obstacle on the way to a scientifically-planned society. Monasteries owned land—much land; they engaged in production, welfare, education, evangelization and their own philosophical pursuits. Their members numbered well over 150,000. They had a strong spiritual discipline and solidarity in action. Their loyalty to a Divine calling and plan rather than a governmental "Five-Year Plan" made them particularly undesirable as elements in the new social order. So long as they existed, they constituted a major denial of, and real threat to the Government's exclusive claims to plan the economy, establish production, direct all labor, determine community order and discipline, and control public thought. They were sufficiently independent of the churches as to require direct consideration.

Through the nationalization of land, welfare and education, their economic and social basis for existence was eliminated. Buildings were converted to hospitals, social institutions, rest homes or apartments. Members who considered these aspects of their work as their *raison d'etre* were given opportunity to continue in the same type of work under government auspices. What was left, evangelism, contemplation and liturgical services, was the function of normal church life. Those who cared to pursue

---

23. 1944 statement of M. Polyansky, Chairman of the Soviet Government's Commission on Religious Affairs (non-Orthodox), *ICPIS* and *N. Y. Times*, Oct. 3:12:5, 1944 (*Chron.*, p. 259).

24. Report on the status and work of the League of Militant Atheists, *Anti-religioznik*, May, 1941, as reported in *ICPIS*, No. 25, June 1941 (*Chron.*, p. 252).

these services were to find their place within the normal church framework. Those who resisted were tried (as spies, Nazi collaborators, etc.), along with other "difficult" church leaders, or were ousted. Many, however, continued their religious vocation in secret, while performing some professional function amenable to it, e.g., traveling cobblers, tailors, knife grinders, house servants, doctors, and teams of agricultural workers.[25]

Later, rather than have them continue underground, the U.S.S.R. saw the possibility and the desirability of having the Orders recreated within the framework of the new social structure. In 1946 approval was given for their re-organization. As "nationalized" Orders, they could participate in the liturgical work of nationalized churches, or, as in Rumania, they might form *kolkhozes* under the economic guidance of the State.[26] Similar developments can be expected in Hungary and Poland.

Their new status, however, can be regarded as hardly more than a concession to some 30,000 aging individual adherents of the old Orders. There is very little place for the Orders to perpetuate themselves as religious communities. Nationalization, therefore, means total re-adaptation and integration into the life of the Church.

Social Welfare

The nationalization of welfare programs is based on three pre-suppositions. In the ultimate, ideal Communist state, no welfare program will be required. The "planned economy" will eliminate chronic needs, and every emergency will be provided for by social security and national reserves. Secondly, in the transition period, some relief may be necessitated by local misfortunes or national disasters. And, thirdly, such relief must be administered in the best interests of the total national life. Relief must therefore develop confidence in, and loyalty to the State. This rules out administration by any international organization, or by any unofficial domestic body such as the Church. Distribution must be efficient, based on a knowledge of all needs, and distributed selectively—in the interest of the nation. This really means that no independent body could be trusted to administer nationwide welfare services. And, finally, relief must not propagate an idea or loyalty foreign to Communism.

Communist governments have therefore shown little interest in the churches' possibilities for relief work on an international scale. Even in time of major disaster, as in Rumania in 1946 and later, they have preferred to do without than to have aid from

---

25. *ICPIS*, No. 17, May, 1941 (*Chron.*, p. 251).
26. *Chron.*, p. 386.

abroad come through the churches. The reason is evident: international church relief nurtures loyalties above and beyond unquestioning fidelity to the national Government, and undermines the absoluteness of State control over the people.

Within Communist countries, church institutions, homes, orphanages, hospitals and relief programs have gradually been absorbed by government agencies, or, as in the case of the Roman Catholic C.A.R.I.T.A.S. in Poland, Government-appointed leadership has been put in charge. In the transition period towards the "perfect society," congregations may continue works of mercy on a more localized, individual scale, especially for abnormal children and old people.[27] Or they may contribute to government-sponsored relief efforts.

In certain fields, such as medical services, if measured on the basis of strictly mechanical criteria, mankind—the mass—has benefited from the leveling-off process. More people have access to a modicum of physical care than under former *laisser-faire* systems. But the warmth of individual concern, of spiritual values, of comfort and encouragement has largely disappeared.

Welfare programs, one concludes, are to the Communists a matter of political expediency. The emphasis is on persuasion, not assuasion.[28] And they take precautions that the persuaded are directed toward the Communist State and not towards the Church.

Education

Education in East Europe was the child of the Church. Long before governments were concerned about education, churches had established an extensive system of schools in several countries, and scattered educational enterprises in others.

Nevertheless, East European governments have been able to present a fairly strong case for nationalization of the educational system, based on evident ills of the parochial system.

Unification of structure. Educational facilities were not uniform in different parts of various countries; textbooks and curricula varied, transfers from schools in one area to those in another were difficult. Nationalization would provide a unified structure throughout the country.

Freedom of religion. Communists charged that all pupils at confessional schools were required to receive religious instruction in that confession, whether parents were members of that confes-

---

27. Protestant churches in Hungary still maintain a very effective hospital and medical service, independent of, but encouraged by the Government, according to *Hungarian Press Service*, May 15, 1953, p. 100.

28. To some degree they may have learned this lesson from some church groups which, in the past, have exploited the people's need and used their own ministrations to add to their own numbers.

sion or of none.   Nationalized schools would provide for the various religious convictions and desires of the parents.

Equal rights.   It was said that confessional schools discriminated against some children for reasons of class origin or disfavor of parents by ecclesiastical authorities.   Nationalized schools would make education equal and compulsory for all children.

Scientific content and method.   Confessional schools were accused of being medieval in method and content,[29] of propagating superstition and fear, and opposing scientific progress.   Nationalized schools would liberate children from "ignorance and religious tyranny."

Economy.   In small villages, the maintenance of several small schools to accommodate several confessions was economically impracticable.   Nationalized education would re-group education facilities in such a way as to provide maximum facilities for every child.

Whatever weight these ostensible reasons carried for nationalization, the principal concern of Communist theorists was the purpose of education itself.

The Moscow *Anti-Religious Magazine* characterized religion in education as follows:

> "The influence of religion on the mind and will of the child is devastating.   Religion implants in the growing personality inferior qualities such as humility, patience, submissiveness, passivity, lack of will power, contempt for life, rejection of science, and enmity towards Communism, collective work, and socialistic collective property.   Religion brings the child up as a slave of God."[30]

In Bulgaria, teachers were instructed not to teach forgiveness, love, kindness, and humility, as these created sheep-mindedness, but rather to teach revenge and hatred.[31]

A clear definition of the aim of Communist education was given by Oleshchuk, head of the Department for Agitation and Propaganda of the Soviet Communist Party, namely, "to educate the young generation in the spirit of Marxist-Leninist science, in the spirit of a materialist and truly scientific world outlook, which is incompatible with any religion."[32]

---

29.   Czechoslovakian Vice-Premier Fierlinger, July, 1949 (*Chron.*, p. 501). Statistics from the USSR suggest the "scientific effectiveness" of the nationalized system: illiteracy dropped from 70-80% in 1913 to 19% in 1939 (NCC, *Christian's Handbook on Communism*, p. 28).

30.   *Anti-religioznik*, No. 7, 1940, as quoted by *ICPIS*, No. 2, 1941 (*Chron.*, p. 250).

31.   *Chronicle*, p. 358.

32.   Barron and Waddams, *Communism and the Churches*, p. 32 (*Chron.*, p. 270).

The *Anti-religious Magazine* indicated in more concrete terms what this meant: "The whole Soviet public must make a determined effort to ensure that the Soviet school produces convinced atheists, courageous Communist fighters for the great cause of Marx, Engels, Lenin and Stalin."[33]

In East Germany, as well as in the U.S.S.R. and other countries, echoes of that policy have been heard in terms of "inculcating a burning patriotism and belief in the creative forces of the nation, instilling hatred for the enemies of progress, inculcating love for the Socialist Fatherland, friendship, comradship, humanism, honesty and cooperation in work, respect for the Soviet Government and love for Comrade Stalin."[34]

In effect, unswerving loyalty and political indoctrination came first, a kind of scientific formation next, and ability to think, evaluate, decide and act last, if at all.

If this was the kind of student and citizen "education" was to produce, obviously, church schools were not suitable to such a task![35] It was clear what body was, and nationalization was the formula prescribed.

How should nationalization be achieved? "We shall have to commence some propaganda . . . but we must not take administrative steps, and any threat of national disadvantage is not allowed," said Ortutay, Hungarian Minister of Education and Cults.[36] He proceeded to elaborate, in total disregard for any consistency, with his famous four introductory points: (1) nationalize the schools; (2) edit school-books jointly with the churches; (3) make religious education obligatory; and (4) assimilate all teachers under Government employment and require them to declare their allegiance to the Government.[37]

---

33. *Anti-religioznik*, No. 7, 1940, from *ICPIS*, No. 2, January, 1941 (*Chron.*, p. 250).

34. *Chron.*, p. 537.

35. National Council of Churches, *A Christian's Handbook on Communism*, p. 28.
Stalin is reported to have said, "Education is a weapon whose effect depends upon who holds it in his hands and at whom it is aimed."

36. Address before the Communist Party Committee, June 7, 1950, as reported in *Uj Harangszo*, June 18, 1950, and *Die Protestantischen Kirchen in Ungarn*, 1939-1950 (*Chron.*, pp. 481-482).

37. *News Behind the Iron Curtain*, Feb., 1953, p. 19 (*Chron.*, p. 439). The implementation of the nationalization of schools in Hungary is an interesting study in Communist strategy.
On November 6, 1946, the Government offered to print school textbooks. The offer was not accepted (*Chron.*, p. 436). On March 12, 1947, Right and Left Wing parties of the coalition government introduced a bill which would change compulsory religious instruction in the schools to optional. After loud general protest, the bill was defeated. The Communist Party declared that the Small Landholders' Party had introduced the bill to embarrass the Communists and that the Communist Party had had nothing to do with it (*Chron.*, p. 437). On Feb. 23, 1948, Minister of Religion and Education Ortutay, addressing the National Assembly, praised the Roman Catholic Church for its contribution to

education and assured the churches that the Hungarian Democracy did not wish to deprive the churches of their schools (*Chron.*, p. 439). Three weeks later Minister Ortutay proposed his four-point program for the nationalization of schools and the elimination of religious instruction (*Chron.*, p. 439).

On April 5, Deputy Prime Minister Rakosi advised Protestant Churches to relinquish their schools voluntarily (*Chron.*, p. 440). Shortly thereafter they were assured that after nationalization, religious education would be compulsory (*Chron.*, p. 442). Few were persuaded.

Then, publications and organizations began urging the nationalization of schools, including, among others, a Catholic youth organization (*Chron.*, p. 441). Clergy were asked to make formal declarations of loyalty to the Government, and in an atmosphere of riots, charges and counter-charges between Government and Roman Catholic leaders, a bill approving nationalization was approved by Parliament on June 16 (*Chron.*, p. 443). An attempt had been made first to persuade the people of the merits of a modified nationalization, then to proceed anyway, but not to "offend the sensibilities" of Protestant Churches and of the populace in general. No such gentility was accorded Roman Catholic leaders after they gave evidence of being unsusceptible to nationalization.

If one were to chart a composite of the steps taken in several countries and the relative involvement of Church and State, the pattern would be somewhat as follows:

Christian Education	Communist Education
1. Parochial schools and church curriculum.	1. Few secular schools; children of Communists attend church schools.
2. Nationalization.	2. Nationalization.
3. Church-Government joint curriculum.	3. Teachers of religion paid by government.
4. Obligatory religious instruction (except on parental objection).	4. Religious education texts prepared by Government (Czechoslovakia) or taught by "scientific" teachers.
5. Optional religious instruction (on application of parents).	5. Materialist curriculum, Christian teachers purged.
6. Free-time religious instruction (off school grounds).	6. Stalinist hymns, pictures, slogans, statues introduced.
7. Private religious education permitted.	7. Anti - religious curriculum.
8. No religious instruction permitted.	8. Parent - teacher councils aid anti-religious formation in school and home.
9. Church attendance restricted.	9. Extra-curricular Sunday excursions, political activities.
10. Children curious about religion.	10. Patriotic, scientific education.
11. ?	11. ?

Further comments should be made on several of these steps.

Step 1. Parochial schools. Prior to the advent of the Communist regime in the U.S.S.R., the greatest reproach against the churches' relationship to education was that "religious dogmatics

—which are incompatible with the principles of materialistic ideology—were *forced* upon the students by religious instruction."[38]

Under the near-total parochial school system of a country like Poland, Communist families were instructed by the Party to keep their children away from church schools. Many other families resisted the confessionalistic, doctrinaire teaching received at church schools. A few private schools had been established simply to avoid the totalitarian nature of the confessional system.

Step 2. Nationalization. At the time of nationalization, in Hungary, for example, all church-appointed teachers who could be were assimilated in the State schools. Many others were retired on pension. Where schools could not be nationalized immediately, the Government often provided subsidies and supervision. In Poland, nationalization is being achieved by an "indirect" process in which the church is handing over its schools (some 1,000 by 1950) to the "Children's Friends Association." In either case the church relinquishes its buildings, equipment and funds.

In all of East Europe the total number of church schools has been reduced from *circa* 22,000 to something less than 1,000.[39] No new schools may be built by private organizations except with Government approval. The resentment with which such a radical change was received was temporarily eased for some churchmen by the promise of obligatory religious education in the public schools.

Step 3. Joint Curriculum. In connection with obligatory religious education, the churches were expected to prepare new textbooks "which would take into account new economic, social and political realities,"[40] or were to conduct such instruction jointly with the State.[41] Teachers of religion became government employees and received their orders from government-appointed educators.

Step 4. Obligatory Religious Instruction from State Texts or Teachers. Where compulsory religious instruction was continued, the Government had a new advantage through its provision of textbooks or appointment of teachers of religion. This story came from a Czechoslovakian schoolroom. After the customary group repetition of the Lord's Prayer, the teacher said to the pupils:

> "You have just asked God to give you your daily bread. (Pause.) You can see for yourself God does not exist, because there is no response to your request. Now let us pray to our father Stalin and see if he won't hear

38. Statement of Kolossow, *Theologische Literaturzeitung*, 1950, No. 8, p. 502 (*Chron.*, p. 229).

39. P. 89 and *Chron.*, p. 427.

40. Hungary, October, 1948 (*Chron.*, p. 446).

41. Poland, Provisional Pact between Roman Catholic leaders and the Government, April, 1950 (*Chron.*, p. 399).

our prayer. (Two people enter the classroom with candy
and gifts.) You see, my dear children, we owe everything
to the leader of the workers, the great Stalin."

*Step 5. Optional Religious Instruction and Materialistic Cur-
riculum.* Parents might elect to have their children receive religious instruction. But, warned the Hungarian Minister of Education, "to send children to a reactionary pastor for religious instruction is a political movement against the People's Democracy,
whether intentional or not. Optional religious instruction in the
schools is in this connection not yet the last possibility of realizing
the democratic principles."[42] It was a courageous parent who
dared apply for religious instruction for his children in the face
of that warning.

It was precisely at this point that conflict between the State
and Church broke out in Hungary. By Governmental decree parents were given the right to apply for the religious education of
their children in the public schools.[43] The Catholic Board of
Bishops therefore sent out a pastoral letter to all Roman Catholic
parents telling them to file applications. In rural areas nearly
100% of the people applied. Deputy Premier Rakosi called the
pastoral letter bellicose, accused the Church of persecuting parents
and children, and warned that in view of such terrorism the Government would "fill in the gap on the spiritual front . . . we shall
change our methods."[44]

Teachers and religious leaders were thereupon accused of violating State-guaranteed freedom of conscience and religion in urging parents to apply for their children's religious instruction. The
axiom "do not offend the sensibilities . . ." was over-ruled.

School rooms and facilities for religious instruction classes
were also to have been provided by the Government, but a Governmental decree (February 11, 1949) stipulated that such facilities
could not exceed those already in use for such purposes before
nationalization.[45] In fact, much less was provided.

On the secular side, the curriculum included not only obligatory "scientific" courses and Marxist doctrine, but every course
was to be presented with an anti-religious bias. Paul Anderson
has carefully documented the way in which, in the U.S.S.R., courses
ranging from mathematics to diseases were slanted to disprove the
"myths and legends" of religion.[46]

---

42. Address by Hungarian Minister of Education and Cults Revai to the
Communist Party Committee, June 7, 1950 (*Chron.*, p. 481).
43. *Die Protestantischen Kirchen in Ungarn,* 1939-1950, enclosure 69
(*Chron.*, p. 451).
44. *London Times* 5:10, 1949 (*Chron.*, p. 452).
45. *Die Protestantischen Kirchen, op. cit.,* p. 23 (*Chron.*, pp. 476-477).
46. Anderson, *People, Church and State in Modern Russia,* p. 91 ff.

Religious teachers were to be ousted. "A believing teacher in a Soviet school is an awkward contradiction. . . . The Departments of Popular Education are bound to use every opportunity to replace such teachers with new ones of anti-religious sentiment."[47]

"The new democratic school demands teachers possessed of political awareness and political training."[48] In Poland 500 Roman Catholic teachers were removed in September, 1950, for not signing the Stockholm Appeal.[49] However, where it was necessary to keep some Christian teachers, they were to have no other work than their teaching, and were to have no contacts with the pupils outside the classrooms. Students were to be specially assigned to observe teaching procedures and advise school authorities whether teachers were acceptable.

> In East Germany, an applicant for a teaching post "must prove that he is whole-heartedly for peace and for the democratic unity of Germany; that he upholds those views both in and out of school; that he is a partisan of peace and of friendship with all freedom-loving peoples, especially the Soviet Union and the People's Democracies; that he is prepared to organize his work of instruction and education jointly with the F. D. J. (Communist - Free German Youth) and the Young Pioneers."[50]

Special care is given through courses, conferences, publications, and other media, to the ideological indoctrination of the teachers themselves.

Step 6. Religious Instruction in Free Time—"Hero-Worship" in School. With the reduction of religious instruction from optional courses in the school curriculum to release of children for instruction under church auspices, "Joseph Stalin Corners," with "altars," "ikons" and statues of Stalin and short inscriptions were created on school premises for meditation "on the Russian example." Hymns, letters and other special forms of veneration addressed to Stalin became a part of the educational program. "Every teacher (in East Germany) must be a genuine friend of the Soviet Union, and work as a propaganda agent among his pupils and parents for true friendship with the Soviet Union."[51] Religious symbols were removed from public school premises.

---

47. USSR Minister of Education Lunacharsky in a published article, as reported by Timasheff, *op. cit.*, 44 (*Chron.*, p. 237).
48. *Tribune de Geneve* report of Berlin Union of Masters and Teachers in *Preuves*, Oct. 1951.
49. MacEoin, *The Communist War on Religion*, p. 210 (*Chron.*, p. 400).
50. *Tribune de Genève*, report of Berlin Union of Masters and Teachers in *Preuves*, Oct., 1951.
51. *Loc cit.*

Step 7. Religious Instruction Private—Anti-religious Curriculum in School. When "private" religious instruction was introduced in the U.S.S.R. in 1918, a court interpretation stated that the maximum number of children which could be considered "private" would be three. Subsequently, large numbers of units of three were formed by priests and lay leaders.

Later, "private religious instruction" was effectively restricted to the family circle. M. Polyansky, Chairman of the U.S.S.R. Commission on Religious Affairs (non-Orthodox), stated in 1944[52] that instruction could not be given inside a church as "this would be against our established laws, which maintain that the Church is given to the congregation for prayer purposes and no other."

Any religious instruction of any kind without the consent of the parents was, by Supreme Court order,[53] a crime punishable by imprisonment and confiscation of property. While this extreme has not yet been reached by Communists in Central Europe, neither do they claim to have reached "the last possibility of realizing the democratic principles."[54] In Lithuania an extremist action was taken; clergymen were requested to sign statements that they would not give instruction to children "in churches . . ., in the homes of children or in my own apartment or elsewhere. Thus I have no right to talk to them about religious matters."[55]

In the public schools, the curriculum became openly and aggressively anti-religious. In East Germany, Grotewohl, in an address before the Congress of the Social Unity Party (July 22, 1950) warned church leaders that "further interference with curriculi in schools will not be tolerated and only the State will dictate subjects and courses."[56]

Step 8. Religious Instruction Forbidden in Private—Parents Recruited for Anti-Religious Activity. Finally, various actions were taken to prevent children from receiving any religious formation. In Bulgaria the Fatherland Front demanded, and succeeded in getting from the Orthodox Holy Synod an assurance that the Church was not carrying on any religious propaganda among children and that there were no organizations of a church character for children.[57] This was from a church which only a few months previously had protested against the Government's ob-

---

52. *New York Times*, Oct. 3:12:5, 1944 (*Chron.*, p. 259).
53. *New York Times*, June 3:1:2, 1935 (*Chron.*, p. 240).
54. Address of Hungarian Minister of Education and Cults to the Communist Party Committee, June 7, 1950 (*Chron.*, p. 455).
55. *News Behind the Iron Curtain*, Feb., 1953, Vol. 2, No. 2, p. 27 (*Chron.*, p. 309).
56. *New York Times*, July 22:5:5, 1950 (*Chron.*, pp. 532-533).
57. *Tserkoven Vestnic*, Oct. 23, 1948 (*Chron.*, p. 370).

structionism toward newly-opened Sunday Schools, and against anti-religious propaganda in the schools.

But the most effective way of prohibiting religious instruction seems to have been the organization of anti-religious activities in connection with the parents. Under names such as "Friends of the New Schools" or "Children's Friends Association"[58] central planning councils have been formed. These are responsible for creating local parent-teacher sub-councils, for conducting parent seminars, evening meetings, and conferences. Teachers are expected to see that the program for the "anti-religious enlightenment of the parents" is carried out. Children help by reporting to the teachers or to their Pioneer leaders concerning the religious attitudes of their parents. There are many tragic stories of children's betrayal of their parents' religious life.

Parentless children, whether actual orphans or of parents declared "incompetent," are given special indoctrination as young Communist elite in government boarding schools where they are free from the restraints and influence of normal family life.

Step 9. Church Attendance Restricted—Scientific Education Free. To the writer's knowledge, no decrees have ever been passed forbidding children to exercise their constitutional "right" of freedom of worship, except for the children of Communist Party members. This would only provoke religious "fanaticism." However, attempts have been made to restrain children from worship by indirect means such as discrimination against Christian children in the schools and youth organizations, systematic ridicule and even violence against Christian children by other children, or arranging for other activities and interests which would occupy children at hours of worship.

The negative techniques of discrimination and ridicule were largely abandoned in the U.S.S.R. in 1939 in favor of the latter, positive approach. Newer Communist States seem not yet to have evolved so far.

However, organized activities are being rapidly introduced, including the following: Sunday outings, excursions and visits to museums; volunteer clean-up work or other public services; mass parades and processions in the Catholic pattern with poles, flags, drums, bands; group tours for musical presentations, drama, demonstrations and athletics; class visits and services to "adopted" projects; essay contests on "Peace," "American Aggression in Korea," "Stalin" or other political figures, etc.

In connection with the 1950 elections in East Germany, *Tägliche Rundschau* stated that

---

58.   Poland, Sept., 1950 (*Chron.*, p. 400).

"Pupils absolutely must be responsible for wall newspapers . . . in order to stir up the neighboring streets . . .
"Two pupils will form the staff for the big black-
board to be put up in the street where the school is. To
ensure a surprise effect, it is hoped to do publicity work
by means of lighted signs. A dove and the word 'peace'
will be shown in this way until October 13, when the elections are held."[59]

Special days to be celebrated included Peace Day, Resistance
Fighters Day, Founding Day of the Democratic Republic, World
Youth Day, Young Pioneers' Day, Stalin's, Marx's, Lenin's and
President Pieck's Birthdays, Liberation Day, International Wo-
men's Day.

Step 10. Religious Curiosity—Scientific Training. The life
of a child is filled with "patriotic," "scientific" education. He is
nonetheless curious about this forbidden idea of "religion" which
seems to require so much attention—a fact recognized in U.S.S.R.
in 1940:

"fighting the religious outlook . . . must be done carefully, so as not to awaken in children an unhealthy curiosity about the church, church customs, ikons, etc., by ex-
aggerating the anti-religious propaganda."[60]
"Skillfully and calmly, tactfully and persistently, the
Soviet teacher must expose and overcome religious prejudices in the course of his activity in school and outside
school, day in and day out."[61]

Nationalization of education has been accomplished. Step after step along the way the Church has resisted, but found no effective front where nationalization could be stopped, and no workable compromise.

The most achieved, and that in the U.S.S.R., has been the
privilege of giving religious instruction in the home, or of sending
children to be taught by the priest.[62] This has not been achieved
by the battling or bargaining of leaders at high echelons, but by
parents and kin who have doggedly continued to impress upon
children something of their own faith.

---

59. *Tribune de Genève* report of Berlin Union of Masters and Teachers in
Preuves, Oct., 1951.
60. *Anti-religioznik*, No. 7, 1940, as quoted by *ICPIS*, No. 2, Jan., 1941
(*Chron.*, p. 250. Related statements, *Chron.*, pp. 240, 245).
61. Statement of F. N. Oleshchuk, Department for Agitation and Propaganda of Communist Party Central Committee, to Soviet teachers, *Uchitelskaya
Gazeta*, as quoted by Barron and Waddams, *op. cit.*, p. 32 (*Chron.*, p. 270).
62. Statement of Chairman Karpoff of the Commission on Orthodox Religious Affairs, *N. Y. Times*, Sept. 15:5:2, 1944 (*Chron.*, p. 258).

It is too early to assess the lasting results of the new education in Central Europe, though some further comments will be given in a later chapter. One thing is clear. In the transition, children have quickly seen that authority supercedes right, that a double life is possible—is necessary—by knowing double sets of prescribed answers.

But even authority has become relative and the child's world insecure. If the child must "spy" on parental authority, if *he* must decide what is right or desired in the home or in the school curriculum today, on what new authority must he spy tomorrow? Children may learn that and may withstand it some years. But many youth are breaking. In East Germany it is reported that nearly two-thirds of all cases in mental institutions are young people.

If schools have been re-grouped in an over-all orderly pattern, the mind of youth still seeks some consistent pattern of order.

Youth

"Youth" as a distinct category in the social structure is a product of an economy of abundance. The phenomenon of "youth" is in a sense a western luxury.[63]

In East Europe, except for the aristocracy, people passed directly from childhood to adulthood in field, factory or work shop. "Youth" has been a very recent phenomenon of which East Europe was only beginning to become aware by 1940. The churches were at the fore in this growing consciousness. Indeed, a major determinative factor in the nature and scope of the growing youth work was the different confessional attitudes.

Protestant churches generally had active youth groups in local congregations but little or no regional or national organizations, staff or planning. (There had been a nation-wide structure in Germany but this was seriously curtailed during the Nazi period.)

Roman Catholic churches had carefully organized national or regional offices, with staff, equipment and funds, but local congregational activities were spotty, in some areas only beginning, in few others well established.

Orthodox churches had no over-head youth organization, and little or no organized work for youth as such in the local parishes. Young people simply participated in the normal life and activities of the local congregations.

---

63. It is possible where the standard of living is sufficiently high not to require children to be productively employed as soon as they are physically able. It has generally been preceded by a broad democratization of the social and economic structure. It embodies a period of "leisure time" between the ages of childhood and parental responsibility for independence of thought and action, i.e., relatively free from parental authority and economic demands.

Hence, the prevailing pattern in predominantly Orthodox Russia, Rumania and Bulgaria was no church youth work, in Catholic Poland, Slovakia and West Hungary youth work organized from the top down, and in East Germany and Transylvania active local groups.

The Student Christian Movement, YMCA and YWCA, although introduced into these areas early in the century were still embryonic. Secular youth organizations were scarcely known except in East Germany and Czechoslovakia.

But the "youth" phenomenon was developing rapidly among youth, particularly in urban areas. Independent, energetic, ambitious youth were ready for any leadership of an imaginative nature. Communist leaders have claimed exclusive right to that role. As they saw it, youth were not only part of contemporary national life, they were the nation of tomorrow. If the Communist nation was to persist tomorrow, youth must be appropriately trained. The purpose of Communist youth work must be, therefore, "the education, training and indoctrination of present day youth . . . according to Communist morals."[64]

Four major steps have been involved in the nationalization of youth and youth organizations.

First, organize unorganized youth. In 1946 the writer visited Communist-run youth brigades in the Balkans, where a year before there had been no organized youth work. It was not obvious to the young people that they were in Communist work camps. What they knew was that, as in the liberation of their countries from Nazism, they were joined together in a cause for which they could work, fight and die. All the inherent capacities of youth— their energy, zeal, idealism, altruism, universalism, self-discipline —all were channeled into a gigantic effort. As the young people saw it, they had gained their freedom, they were now building not only an irrigation dam or railroad, but a new world. They were working with and on behalf of all the down-trodden people of the world. They responded enthusiastically to the idea of one world, of solidarity with all people. Through their newly-gained franchise they felt responsible for their government and society. Discipline and morality was practically without blemish, although in one brigade several thousand young men and women worked and lived together. In few Christian enterprises has the writer seen such purposefulness, consecration, discipline and selflessness. In fact, the significance of the youth's response, the needs of their part of the world and the results of their labor were so overwhelming as to make any questioning of manifest objectives and tactics at that time appear petty. Certainly it would have been premature.

---

64. Lenin, *Marx-Engels Marxism.*

Urban youth joined-up by the hundreds of thousands. Peasant young people gladly left the drudgery of their plows or work shops for the adventure of working with other young people to "change the world." In their "liberation" to the status of "youth" one could see in miniature the uprising of the down-trodden, a test-tube revolution of the masses. Almost any young person with any spirit desired to participate; and woe to the reluctant—regarded by these enthusiasts as "traitors" to the new Utopia. In the process youth were organized, taught to read, indoctrinated, trained and disciplined, and given a job to do. Among them were great numbers of Christian youth, at the outset probably the majority, who considered this new life a fulfillment of their religious idealism. Leaders were carefully picked, meticulously trained and enviably competent. Eventually youth were to discover that the movement they had joined was Communist.

A second measure has been to unify organized youth. Neither new youth activities nor new organizations for youth were initiated under the Communist label. Rather, existing youth organizations were called upon to join together in some national youth federation, "United Youth Front," "National Youth for Democracy," "Anti-Fascist Youth League," etc., for some national effort. As at the level of their seniors in government, leadership of the "Front" organizations was controlled by disciplined Communists, with various innocuous responsibilities carried by representatives of the participating non-Communist bodies.

Reasons for which independent youth organizations joined the federations varied. The constructive work in rebuilding and reform appealed to idealistic movements, including many religious groups. In Hungary, for example, leaders of several Christian youth movements, after condemning the church for its adherence to the class system and earthly power, asserted that Christian youth should collaborate with "democratic, progressive youth" to eliminate social injustice and reconstruct the country.[65]

A number of leaders, both in non-Communist political parties and in religious bodies felt that by participating in the federations they could maintain a broad democratic basis for cooperation and prevent the whole federation from being excessively influenced by the Communist minority.

Social pressure brought in many organizations. Propaganda made it clear that it was the patriotic thing to do, and that organizations which did not participate in the unions were not participating in the nation's life, its reconstruction and future, ergo, they were unpatriotic, disloyal, reactionary, and traitorous.

---

65. *Chronicle*, p. 441.

Organizations which were still reluctant to participate fully were infiltrated by Communist agents, and eventually the whole leadership, objectives and nature of the organizations were changed. A notable case was the YMCA in Poland. After a short period of infiltration, the General Meeting of the YMCA was able to declare that the YMCA had previously been promoting the imperialistic ideology, and proceeded to transform itself into a new umbrella "association" in which the Central Trade Union Council, Polish Youth Association, Polish University Youth Association, Polish Scout's Association, and others were federated.[66]

Techniques used by experienced elders in political life were also used in the struggle for control of youth organizations: falsification of ballots, innuendo and misleading statements.[67] In Hungary a published declaration, allegedly by Catholic students at Papa, that Christian youth should collaborate with "democratic, progressive youth," was flatly disowned by the students.[68] Other Christian youth elected to positions of highest responsibility in their organizations reported that they no longer had anything to say about the conduct of their organizations.

As a last resort, governments simply gave instructions that all youth organizations were to be unified. This happened in Poland,[69] in Czechoslovakia,[70] Hungary, and, directly or indirectly, in the other countries.

The final measure in nationalizing youth activities was to suppress remaining organizations which did not elect to lose their identity in a nation-wide secular youth movement. Vice-Premier Seroky of Czechoslovakia, in announcing his Government's decision to unify youth organizations, called Christian youth groups "unnecessary" and "undesirable." Almost immediately Lutheran youth groups in Slovakia were dissolved and their publication banned.[71] In Hungary the decision of Soviet authorities in 1946 to suppress certain Catholic youth organizations which had allegedly collaborated with the Nazis was tabled for a time and finally implemented in November, 1949.[72] At about the same time, organized Protestant youth work in East Germany was forbidden, Christian symbols were not to be worn by youth in public.

With few exceptions, the work of independent youth organizations as such technically disappeared, either by assimilation into official youth movements, or by dissolution, or, as in the case

---

66. *Zycie Warszawy*, Oct. 25, 1949 (*Chron.*, pp. 419-420).
67. Report of German Lutheran Bp. Dibelius (*Chron.*, p. 529).
68. Mindszenty, *Four Years' Struggle of the Church in Hungary*, p. 151 (*Chron.*, p. 441).
69. *Chronicle*, p. 390.
70. *Chronicle*, p. 496.
71. *EPS*, Jan. 24, 1949 (*Chron.*, p. 496).
72. *Chronicle*, p. 453.

of Christian youth, by assimilation into the life of local congregations.

A "nationalized" youth program was established and related to the Government's educational, cultural or other ministries dealing especially with youth. No child was too young to begin participating in the national youth program. The purpose of its work was fixed by Lenin. Its activities must above all contribute towards discipline of a military intensity, indoctrination of a political nature, and secondarily, should contribute to the economic, educational and social life of the nation, as well as the physical wellbeing of the young people.

Individual Christians have had serious difficulties. They were under heavy pressure to join Communist youth organizations, and a high percentage have done so, while at the same time trying to remain Christian. Youth recognized for their Christian convictions have been discriminated against in school entrance examinations, in seeking work, housing or other facilities of livelihood under government control.[73] Under such pressure many youth have been driven from the faith, and under the same pressure others formed small cells from which they could go out into the society about them to manifest the Good News, apostolic style.

Within the congregation, however, Christian young people in many places have shown an increasing interest in Bible study, prayer and singing, charitable work and evangelization and counseling together. In many instances youth groups, where they could not meet openly, still meet privately. And in several countries, Christian leaders of youth, when they come together, are able to make plans and relate their several groups across provincial and even national boundaries. In 1950 forty youth leaders in Czechoslovakia came together to study problems of ecumenical work and to discuss world Christian youth meetings held in Oslo (1947) and Amsterdam (1948).[74]

Worship and Holy Days

Communists do not like religious worship—they tolerate it. Belief in God is considered a mark of ignorance and lack of social evolvement, but it has been recognized that to forbid worship is to encourage its practice,[75] and at least in later stages of nationaliza-

---

73. *Chronicle*, p. 537.
74. *EPS*, Feb. 24, 1950 (*Chron.*, p. 506).
75. In 1949, Oleshchuk, in an article in *Science and Life, op. cit.*, wrote that "the Bolshevik Party and the Soviet Government have never embarked on the path of banning . . . the exercise of religious ceremonies. This path is organically alien to the Marxist and Leninist conception of the way to defeat religion. It is necessary to reform the mind of the believer and this cannot be achieved by a mere ban. . . ." As quoted by *Church Times*, London, 24.2. 1950 (*Chron.*, p. 301).

tion, that to place obstacles in the way of worship can be almost as disastrous to Communist interests as outright prohibition of worship. Possibilities of worship are therefore permitted, but, particularly in early stages, not without attempts at limitations,[76] conditions and distractions. Obstructionist measures which occurred in the early stages of nationalization included the intimidation of worshippers, limitations on worship facilities, and censorship.

Intimidation. According to Czechoslovakian Minister of Information Kopecky,[77]

> "People who go to church demonstrate their opposition to the People's Democracy and Socialism, gain courage in church to invoke American imperialism . . . In the struggle against such enemies, we stop at nothing. We do not hesitate even to enter upon the so-called holy ground of the churches, monasteries and convents. Nor are we stopped by the so-called sacred cloth of priestly surplices."

Following such a statement, a law requiring believers to register could be, and in many cases has been very effective in curtailing attendance at worship and in scattering records of membership.

People attending church have felt that they were observed, their frequency of attendance recorded, and their "loyalty" classified acordingly. In the U.S.S.R. in 1925 the "Friends of the Godless" set as one of its aims the indoctrination of people with the idea that religious belief was a form of disloyalty to the Socialist State.[78] In many communities discrimination, depending upon one's occupation and status, has followed, including loss of work.[79] Children and youth have been particularly discouraged by their clubs, schools and other groups, from church attendance.[80] Members of the Communist Party and their families have been forbidden to take part in religious services in several countries,[81]

---

76. *News Behind the Iron Curtain*, National Committee for Free Europe, Feb., 1953, Vol. 2, No. 2, p. 16.

77. *Loc. cit.*

78. Timasheff, *Religion in Soviet Russia*, p. 35 (*Chron.*, p. 235).

79. Ex-Prime Minister Nagy of Hungary reported (March, 1949) that Government agents kept lists of names of church-goers, and that students and civil servants were promoted or ousted depending on their religious interest. FCCC., March 19, 1949 (*Chron.*, p. 450).

80. *Chronicle*, p. 265.

81. *Chron.* references: USSR, pp. 237, 238, 265:
      Baltics, pp. 304, 306, 307, 310, 315;
      Bulgaria, pp. 360, 370;
      Hungary, pp. 450, 455, 481, 482;
      East Germany, pp. 528, 530.
Whereas in these countries and at this stage it was a "crime" for Communists to participate in religious activities, in Poland and Czechoslovakia

except by special dispensation and for special reasons. Said Beltcho Nicolov to the Communist Congress in Bulgaria: "I propose that everyone who attends church services or protects the church be punished at once—be expelled from the Party and persecuted more intensely than any other Fascist."[82]

Limited possibilities for worship. Limitations on the provision of buildings for worship have already been discussed. Regularly scheduled services of worship have often been cancelled suddenly on the pretext that they endanger health, or create fire and other hazards. Obligatory work programs and political rallies have been scheduled at hours of worship. Seasonally urgent work is not to be obstructed by worship.[83] In the Soviet Union the seven-day week was at one time cut to five working days followed by one rest-day to avoid the seventh as a non-working holy day. A law made absence from work punishable by dismissal. Special excursions, hikes and sports for children and youth were organized, and, as in many countries of the anti-Communist world, adults did not lack for opportunities to participate in legion parades, band concerts, ball games and races when they might be at Sunday morning worship services. In addition to these competitive demonstrations, which test the quality rather than prevent the exercise of religious conviction, worship services from Bulgaria to Poland have been interrupted by "failures" of electric current, untimely ringing of church bells, noisy intrusion of youth into or around the churches,[84] political rallies just outside the church,[85] breaking of windows, or "loss" of hymnals and liturgical books. Supplies for worship have been sometimes procurable, sometimes unprocurable, and often churches have not been able to provide their own supplies.

Censorship. In Czechoslovakia a Communist Party aide announced in 1949 that "observers" would be sent to all religious meetings, including the confessional.[86] This was not untypical. Sermons were generally not censored before preaching, but copious notes were taken by local militia or Party agents.

(*Chron.*, p. 507) Catholic clergy were tried and sentenced for refusing to provide religious ministrations for Communists.

82. *Free Independent Bulgaria*, July 27, 1949 (*Chron.*, pp. 370, 371).

83. "Church leaders are responsible that the life in the community (of Christians) does not interfere with their public duties, for example in rural areas, worship services may not be held at a time when there is agricultural work to do" (Statutes of Russian Orthodox Church Organization, approved Jan. 31, 1945, article 36; *Dokumente Zur Ordnung der Kirche; Chron.* p. 300).

84. In at least one instance of juvenile vandalism at a Protestant church in Poland, the Government police arrested the young people involved, and reported that the Catholic Church was organizing or stimulating such acts against Protestantism as in the pre-Revolutionary era.

85. Latvia, *Chron.*, p. 304.

86. *New York Times*, Sept. 14:8:2, 1949 (*Chron.*, p. 502).

If, in the early stages of the nationalization process, worship services were tolerated so long as they had no relevance to the social, economic or political situation, or rather no content of an anti-Communist socialist, political or economic nature, later in the process they were welcomed if they were related to the social, economic and political situation, i.e., in support of the prevailing national position. In Bulgaria, where Prime Minister Dimitrov warned the churches in 1946 to "stick to your spiritual work,"[87] two years later the Minister of Foreign Affairs and Cults was trying to instruct the pastors how they should support nationalization, preach that the State was above the Church, counter-act anti-Communist propaganda, and preach love for the State leaders.[88] In Rumania, Poland and other countries, clergymen were also expected to contribute to a better understanding of the Government's policy and program through their sermons; or at least they must not be critical.

There has been the suggestion that even the symbols of worship must contribute to the new national goals. In Rumania, church symbols must be approved by the Government before use.[89] Soviet flags have been raised in many chancels in other countries than the U.S.S.R. as an indication of these nations' foreign ties.

In spite of obstructions, however, worship services have been attended, often better than in pre-Revolution days. Worship attendance has in fact become a barometer of Church-State relationships. Attendance at worship frequently varies in direct proportion to the intensity of the Government's repressive measures, as will be seen in a later chapter. It is understandable, therefore, that in Russia, attempts to disturb worship by over-zealous Communists were denounced as contributing to anti-Soviet feeling.[90]

And beyond formal worship, worship as the constant experience of corporate Christian life has taken on new realism. A story from one country is nearly legend. A pastor "volunteered" with members of the community to do road repairs on Sunday morning. As they trudged into the country, the pastor remarked that there was no regulation against singing as they walked. So they sang a hymn. During a rest period he suggested that the Government encouraged reading whenever possible. So they read the Bible. Under such circumstances, a crust of black bread from a lunch sack, and a bottle of wine passed from person to person bring a stark realism into the celebration of the Lord's Supper scarcely known in heated cathedrals.

---

87. *Chron.*, p. 356.
88. *Chron.*, p. 358.
89. Law of August 4, 1948, *Monitorul Official*, Art. 19 (*Chron.*, p. 341).
90. Timasheff, *Religion in Soviet Russia*, p. 123 (*Chron.*, p. 245).

Holy Days. At the outset holy days were tampered with perhaps more than Sunday worship. Religious holidays from time to time have been suppressed completely as "disturbances of the democratic order," or shifted to other dates or transformed into secular celebrations, or, once again, encouraged and abetted. In Czechoslovakia an unsuccessful attempt was made in 1949 to move all religious holidays from week-days to Sundays.[91] The public celebration of Christmas as a religious holiday was prohibited in almost every country that year. Singing of Christmas carols, telling of Christmas stories, erection of Christmas trees and exchanging of gifts were forbidden. The Christmas vacation in schools in East Germany was renamed "winter" vacation. "Soliman," a secular version of Santa Claus, or the Soviet "Grandfather Frost" was to replace the Christ-Child at the center of the "winter" festivities.[92] In Hungary, after forbidding Christmas celebrations, the Government extended the observance of Stalin's birthday through Christmas Eve. The Communist publishing house distributed thousands of cards depicting the Nativity, with the text overprinted in red: "Christmas is their holiday, ours is the First of May. Christ is their superstition; our hope is Socialism."[93]

Again the following year "Christmas" was forbidden, and celebrations of Stalin's birthday anniversary on December 21 became the focus of public festivities. In Rumania, Orthodox Patriarch Justinian called the priests' attention to the regulations covering "winter celebrations" and advised them that sermons on this occasion should be in keeping with the Government's position and propaganda in the struggle for peace.[94] The "Winter tree" or "Peace tree" was intended to replace Christmas tree festivities. Winter school vacations (Rumania 1952) did not begin until after Christmas and ran from December 31 to January 10.

"Easter" vacation was replaced by "spring" vacation. In the spring of 1950 special (Comenius) celebrations planned by the Reformed Churches of Hungary were taken over by the Government as a cultural festival.[95] Many Catholic celebrations entailed public processions, permission for which was secured irregularly and after considerable difficulties, if at all.

Quite apart from religious or anti-religious considerations, the multitude of processions, holidays, celebrations, spectacles, and masquerades which cluttered the calendar year, disrupting work

91. *Chronicle*, p. 501.
92. *Chronicle*, p. 528.
93. *Chronicle*, p. 453.
94. *La Natione Roumaine*, Jan. 1, 1951 (*Chron.*, p. 337).
95. *Chronicle*, p. 455.

schedules and economic reconstruction,[96] was a serious problem to governments concerned with reconstruction and industrialization. But the way East European Governments went about changing holidays did not indicate that their main concern was working hours or economics. It was the religious nature of such celebrations that they opposed. And it was also for religious considerations that they ceased overt opposition.

The conclusion was reached in the U.S.S.R. already in 1939 that attempts at disturbing worship were only increasing anti-Soviet feeling, and not decreasing religious "prejudices";[97] if believers were to be constituted in loyal "national" churches, they must have opportunity for worship.

It is surprising that later Communist governments did not remember and profit from the Russian experiment. For, in the end, Communist governments have had to give in to many medieval festival practices verging on superstition and social escapism. It may be for these reasons that religious celebrations are more freely permitted now than five years ago: younger Communist governments have realized not only that the people should not be offended to the point of fanaticism, but also that ultimately materialistic or scientific governments have little to lose if superstition and medieval excesses are closely identified with religion.

And in any case public celebrations, religious or otherwise, conducted within the nationalized framework have provided governments with fresh opportunities for mass "education" and propaganda.

Publications and Radio

If Communist governments were to be responsible for the "scientific" formation and direction of the masses, they must control the media of mass communication. Church publications, once a major channel for disseminating information, for guiding public opinion and maintaining the allegiance of believers, proved to be one of the tangibles of church life which was relatively easily nationalized. Several measures have been used.

Banning. Some religious publications were banned on charges of anti-government or other illegal activities. In Hungary, the Roman Catholic *Magyar Kurir* was banned for reporting Mindszenty's charges that the Government was persecuting the church.[98]

---

96. The *Agitators' Guide, 1937* included this statement: "Religious customs, especially religious holidays bring vast material loss to socialist economy, and put a brake on the rise of culture in the masses," as quoted by Anderson, *op. cit.*, pp. 104-105 (*Chron.*, p. 296).

97. Timasheff, *op. cit.*, p. 123 (*Chron.*, p. 245).

98. *Chronicle*, p. 440.

Acta Curiae in Czechoslovakia was banned in March, 1949.[99] Religious publications in general were banned by Government occupation authorities in East Germany in April of the same year. *Petrus Blatt,* Roman Catholic publication in West Berlin was banned from East Germany "since there is no demand for it." Offenders against the ban were warned that "addressees might find themselves in trouble."[100]

Censorship. Secondly, content of religious publications has been censored. As early as 1946 religious publications in Rumania and Bulgaria were subjected to censorship by their respective Ministries of Cults and of Information and Propaganda.[101] In Albania, Church Law no. 745 ruled that "All religious communities are obliged to send immediately to the Council of Ministers pastoral letters, messages, speeches, memoranda and everything to be printed or made public. The Council of Ministers has the right to annul . . ."[102] In Hungary, Roman Catholic Archbishop Mindszenty refused to comply with a similar bill, Number 16 R.C., requiring all printed matter and circulars to be approved by the Government before circulation.[103]

Religious radio broadcasts were also subject to Government censorship prior to emission. When official church leaders refused to comply, not without attempts to reach some understanding, "cooperative" pastors were put in charge of the radio programs, or programs were discontinued.[104] Foreign religious radio programs, especially Roman Catholic, have frequently been jammed.[105]

Mechanical Restrictions. Mechanical disabilities have further limited the churches' channels of communication. Unwanted church publications often found that they were not on the government's priority list for paper rations. Printer's unions frequently refused or delayed the setting of type and printing of religious materials, although cleared by government censors.[106] A typical example occurred in the U.S.S.R.: the Godless Society voted not to make a direct attack on membership in religious associations lest religious feeling be intensified, but indirect strategies were introduced whereby printers' unions refused to print religious pub-

99.   *Chronicle,* p. 497.
100. *Chronicle,* p. 527.
101. *Chronicle,* p. 322.
102. *News Behind the Iron Curtain,* Feb., 1953, Vol. 2, No. 2 (*Chron.,* p. 382).
103. He added: "We are compelled to descend into the catacombs . . . we shall henceforth speak less frequently and only briefly." Mindszenty, *Four Years' Struggle of the Church in Hungary,* p. 122 ff. (*Chron.,* p. 438).
104. Hungary, *Chron.,* p. 438; East Germany, *Chron.,* p. 534.
105. *Chronicle,* p. 444.
106. Timasheff, *op. cit.,* p. 43 (*Chron.,* p. 238).

lications, transport workers would not carry religious supplies, and postal workers would not handle communications for the clergy.

Editors or editorial staff of church journals have been occasionally "detained" or imprisoned on various charges,[107] and church printing presses were nationalized along with other industries. This meant, of course, that churches would have to find other ways of disseminating information. And they have.

In the most difficult periods, whether during "obliteration," or before "nationalization" had made provision for "approved" materials, books have been copied by hand and circulated, important messages have been carried by "runners" and pastoral letters by specially organized Orders, and general information passed from person to person with extraordinary speed.[108] This was, of course, not entirely satisfactory to Communist governments. It meant that the content passed through such clandestine news channels was decidedly not pro-Government.

Government printing. More recently government printing has figured largely in the churches' communications. After East European governments had nationalized an estimated one hundred church-owned printing establishments, they began to make printing facilities available for *approved* church publications. In Czechoslovakia in March 1949, the Government ruled that the Government would be sole publisher and printer in Czechoslovakia, but that Government printing presses would be available for printing church books.[109] Similarly in the U.S.S.R., Rumania, Bulgaria and other countries, documents prepared by the churches and approved by the governments are printed on government presses.

Government publication. Finally, governments or government-related organizations are intended to prepare and distribute publications dealing with religion. In Czechoslovakia the *Gazette of the Catholic Clergy,* published through close collaboration of the Government and Catholic Action, an allegedly Communist-sponsored clerical organization, appeared shortly after the official ecclesiastical journal *Acta Curiae* was banned.[110] The Government ruled that no ecclesiastical instructions should be considered valid until their publication in the *Gazette.* Religious publications in this stage become the voice of a nationalized church whose role in a national situation seems mutually tolerable both to government and to church leaders.

---

107.   *Chronicle,* p. 391.
108.   *Chronicle,* p. 305.
109.   *Chronicle,* p. 497.
110.   Abp. Beran retaliated by forbidding Catholics to read the Gazette. *Loc. cit.*

As churches have progressed in their nationalization and Communist governments could accord them a greater degree of confidence, religious publications have reappeared in increasing numbers (though still fewer than before the Revolution) in the U.S.S.R., in Rumania, Hungary and other countries. Among them are found theological books and journals, seminary and mission reports, hymnals and liturgical books, religious calendars, devotional booklets, Bible study materials, news services, pastors' journals and evangelistic tracts. Bibles are being printed and even translations of well-known and respected Western theologians. Most noticeably lacking is any considerable amount of objective, prophetic work on social and political life apart from the "nationalized" line. Nonetheless, as the Communist cycle moves on beyond "nationalization," publications are not without serious and dynamic evangelistic and theological content. Indeed, in spite of the volume of politically-slanted religious matter, the basic theological content compares not unfavorably with the kernel of religious truth mixed with the chaff of religious publications in the West, or in pre-"Revolutionary" East Europe.[111]

Church Leadership

A nationalized church must be led by a nationalized clergy. Here was the crux of the nationalization process. The so-called "Orginform Instructions to Communists" in 1948[112] stipulated that the program of denunciation of religion should be discontinued, and the "fight" leveled at "unworthy" leaders, i.e., unacceptable or unnationalized religious leaders. Shortly thereafter a program to collect information on the political beliefs of all clergy was initiated.[113] In addition to conclusions one can draw from general developments in the total East European scene, or from the charges brought against religious leaders as listed on page 63 there is considerable evidence that Communist leaders had to spell out in precise detail for their own followers the kind of church leaders they wanted.

Qualifications for nationalized leaders. The qualifications which follow have been drawn largely from documents intended for that purpose.[114]

---

111. E.g., compare pre-Evanston studies in Hungary with studies in American or British journals.

112. *Chronicle*, pp. 516, 517.

113. In Lithuania this was undertaken almost immediately after Communist occupation. MacEoin, *The Communist War on Religion*, p. 177 (*Chron.* p. 309).

114. Especially from the circumstances surrounding the inception of the Vvedensky "Living Church" in Russia and the reinstatement of Patriarch Tikhon (pp. 233, 234 of *Chronicle*); the law on religion of the Rumanian Government (p. 340 ff. of *Chronicle*); the Bulgarian Ministry of Foreign Affairs' instruction to all clergy (p. 358 of *Chronicle*); the circular on State-Church rela-

The "nationalized church leader must be loyal to the State." In the U.S.S.R Patriarch Tikhon, after his reinstatement in 1923, requested Orthodox Christians "to submit to the Soviet power . . . remembering the words of the Apostle 'Let every soul be subject to the higher powers . . .' "[115] Similarly his successor, Metropolitan Sergius, in 1929 stated that he had assured the Soviet Government of Orthodox Christians' "sincere willingness to become law-abiding citizens . . ."[116] By 1950 the Russian Church went so far as to demand pledges of loyalty to the Mother Church and to the Soviet Government from Russian Orthodox priests outside the U.S.S.R.[117] In Bulgaria, Foreign Minister Kolarov declared that "the Church is under the people's sovereignty, it is subordinate to the Constitution . . ." A circular letter from the Ministry of Foreign Affairs and Cults to church leaders stated boldly that the State stands above the Church.[118] In Rumania, Czechoslovakia and Hungary every clergyman was expected to take a special oath of allegiance. And in Poland the Workers' (Communist) Party, in a statement defining the Party position towards the Churches, noted that "the Party demands unconditional loyalty of the clergy of all confessions to the People's State."[119] Final authority for the "nationalized" minister rests in the "State." It should be noted, however, that his loyalty is to the Communist "State," not to the "nation": "whoever publicly incites to, or approves nationalistic . . . strife, shall be punished. . . ." (Polish decree of June 13, 1946).[120]

Secondly, the "nationalized" church leader should not introduce any foreign ("Western," "International") or non-Communist influence into the community. This point has received perhaps greater attention than any other in dealing with religious leaders. It signalled the turning point in the U.S.S.R. from the policy of "obliteration" to "Nationalization" when the Eighth Congress of

---

tions of the Bulgarian Orthodox Church (p. 370 of *Chronicle*); Bulgarian Minister of Religion Kolarov's comments on the law on the Churches entitled "What is Inadmissable in Our Country?" (p. 376 of *Chronicle*); the report of the Minister of Education to the Workers' Party in Hungary (*Chronicle*, p. 455); the "Instructions to Communists" of the Czechoslovakian Party's Central Committee (*Chron.*, p. 516) and Law no. 218 (*Chron.*, p. 518); Polish President Bierut's report to Roman Catholic clergy on the Communist Party's terms for peace with the Church (*Chron.*, p. 396); the "Accord between the Roman Catholic Church and the Polish Republic" (*Chron.*, pp. 410 ff.); and the "Instructions to Communist Party Members" printed by *Neues Deutschland* (*Chron.*, p. 548).

115.   The Moscow Patriarchate, *The Truth About Religion in Russia*, p. 28 (*Chron.*, p. 235).

116.   Barron and Waddams, *Communism and the Churches*, p. 22 (*Chron.*, p. 236).

117.   Anderson, *People, Church and State in Modern Russia*, p. 130 (*Chron.*, p. 239).

118.   *Chronicle*, p. 358.

119.   *Polish Facts and Figures*, Polish Embassy, London, March 26, 1949 (*Chron.*, p. 416).

120.   *Yearbook of Human Rights*, 1946, p. 236 (*Chron.*, p. 405).

the Communist Party declared that its aim was "to destroy the ties between the exploiting classes and the organization of religious propaganda . . ."[121] Religion, if it was to be tolerated in order not to "offend the sensibilities of the believers,"[122] must be a "safe" local movement, not a channel of infection for foreign ideas and practices. Russian Orthodox Patriarch Tikhon, in his "confession" before reinstatement, declared, ". . . I completely and resolutely severed connections with the foreign and domestic monarchists . . ."[123] And in Bulgaria, Minister Kolarov bespoke the phobia of Communist leaders when he warned the National Assembly on February 17, 1949, that "the high clergy had merged with the ruling (foreign) reactionary classes . . . (to) transform the Church into an instrument of political oppression of the people."[124] Every other Communist Government, through accusations, trials, laws, threats or ousters has left no doubt that there is no place for religious leaders who have loyalties, channels of information and instruction, obligations or responsibilities to Western powers.

Thirdly, church leaders should treat only with "religious" and ethical matters from the pulpit. As has been pointed out in the section on Worship, in the early stages of nationalization this meant steering clear of any intimation of criticism of the Government. Later it came to mean support of the Government.[125]

The Church leader in the process of nationalization should not retain leadership and confidence of the community by virtue of his spiritual or ecclesiastical authority. This posed a real problem, as clergymen were often the only educated people in the villages, and were looked to for leadership on all kinds of civil as well as religious matters. It was the Communists' desire that the pastor's position as leader in the community should be in direct proportion to his adherence to, and support of Government policy.

Ultimately, he should not propagate religion among children. One of the charges against thirty-eight churchmen on trial in the U.S.S.R. in 1937 was that they were attracting youth to church and baptizing them.[126] And in Bulgaria, the Orthodox Holy Synod stated that "Because of the demands of the Fatherland Front that the Church not carry out religious propaganda among children,

---

121. *Notes on Soviet Affairs*, No. 138, June 23, 1952 (*Chron.*, p. 231).

122. *Ibid.*

123. As quoted by Paul Anderson, *People, Church and State in Modern Russia*, p. 66 (*Chron.*, p. 284).

124. Press Service of the Bulgarian Legation, London, Feb., 1949 (*Chron.*, p. 376 ff.).

125. *Chronicle*, p. 530.

126. *Orlovskaia*, as quoted by Anderson, *op. cit.*, p. 115 (*Chron.*, p. 243).

the Holy Synod announces that the Church is not undertaking such propaganda . . ."[127]

Church leaders must show respect for Government leaders. In the U.S.S.R. the "Living Church" showed "respect" in 1922 by declaring that "the Soviet authority is the only one . . . which will realize . . . the ideals of the Kingdom of God."[128] In Bulgaria Mr. Illiev of the Ministry of Foreign Affairs and Religions instructed churchmen to "display portraits of Government leaders in the churches and preach love for State Leaders."[129] Subsequently the Holy Synod declared "that it lawfully fulfills the Constitution by paying due respect to the leaders of the People's Republic."[130] In Poland this stipulation was the first of many in the accord signed between the Roman Catholic Bishops and the Government.[131]

The loyal minister should cooperate in national welfare projects. Very early in the nationalization process "cooperation" meant no opposition. In Hungary, Rakosi warned the churches in the midst of the education reform: "anyone who opposes the democratic laws of the country will be smashed by the fist of democracy."[132] When a year and a half later Catholics were opposing the loyalty pledge and compulsory teaching of Marx-Leninism in the schools, Minister of Religion and Education Ortutay warned it was "time they (Catholic leaders) supported the cause of the people."[133]

Cooperation also meant that nothing should be done which would undermine the confidence of the people in their own strength "just at a time when this confidence is necessary in order that a new and prosperous society be built."[134]

Cooperation came to mean, not neutrality, but active support. In the U.S.S.R., the "Living Church" Sobor of 1922 declared that "every faithful churchman must . . . fight . . . with the Soviet authority for the realization of the Kingdom of God on earth."[135] Petru Groza, while Prime Minister of Rumania, declared to the writer that he was a militant Christian himself, the son of an Orthodox clergyman, and expected the Christian leaders to engage actively in creative projects of the State. In Poland the "Workers' Congress" called on the clergy to support the Government "in all

127. *Tserkoven Vestnic*, Oct. 23, 1948 (*Chron.*, p. 370).
128. Anderson, *op. cit.*, pp. 63-64 (*Chron.*, p. 284).
129. *Chronicle*, p. 358.
130. *Tserkoven Vestnic*, Oct. 23, 1948 (*Chron.*, p. 370).
131. Article I, *Accord, Religious Freedom and the State Church Agreement*, Polish Research and Information Service, pp. 4-8 (*Chron.*, p. 410 ff.).
132. *London Times*, June 14, 1948 (*Chron.*, p. 443).
133. *New York Times*, Dec. 21, 11:2, 1949 (*Chron.*, p. 453).
134. *Bulgarian Communist Directives to Local Committees*, CCIA, London (*Chron.*, p. 368).
135. Anderson, *loc cit.* (*Chron.*, p. 284).

its measures aimed at full social liberation, prosperity, progress and the happiness of all."[136] In Bulgaria, Minister Illiev (Foreign Affairs and Cults) asked the clergy to "support the nationalization of private industries and mines . . . (and) all Government measures . . ."[137] The Orthodox Holy Synod announced that it would "continue to cooperate with the State in achieving its social projects . . ."[138] In Hungary, Rev. Darvas, on the occasion of his installation as inspector in the district of former Bishop Ordass, declared "we consider it right that the Church should not enter politics . . . But at the same time . . . we do not hold it incompatible that our Church not only recognize but approve and with every means at its disposal help the mighty transformation of society . . ."[139]

The acceptable pastor should counter-act anti-Communist and anti-Russian feeling and propaganda. This was specifically included with other instructions delivered to the clergy by Mr. Illiev of Bulgaria.[140] Similar inferences may be found in laws or speeches from Poland[141] and Czechoslovakia. Here was tacit acknowledgment that there was considerable anti-Communist feeling (in some countries as high as 97% of the population), but also that church leaders were in a position to do something about it if they could be brought to do so. When East European governments were attacked for their "persecution" of religion, churchmen were found who declared "We enjoy complete religious freedom. Religious leaders are being prosecuted for crimes, not persecuted for their religious belief."[142]

The "nationalized" churchman should take an active part in national, political life. This entailed participation in political demonstrations, parades, pronouncements, labor brigades, elections and propaganda. The reason lay in that properly oriented religious collaborators could help sell the Communist program and politic to balky masses. This obviously was considered a very important point to the Communists for they have gone to great trouble and expense to get or to extort from church leaders permission for the lower clergy to take an active role in politics. The Holy Synod of the Bulgarian Orthodox Church reported that it had given permission for priests to participate in the Fatherland

---

136. *Poland Today*, Feb., 1949 (*Chron.*, p. 415).
137. *Chronicle*, p. 358.
138. *Tserkoven Vestnic, op. cit.* (*Chron.*, p. 370).
139. *Chronicle*, pp. 450, 454.
140. *Chronicle*, p. 358.
141. *Chronicle*, pp. 399, 410 ff.
142. Metropolitan Sergius, USSR, Feb., 1930 (*Chron.*, p. 239); Orthodox Ch. publication *The Truth About Religion in Russia* (*Chron.*, p. 255); Rumania (*Chron.*, p. 349); Bulgaria (*Chron.*, p. 360); Poland (*Chron.*, p. 392); Latvia (*Chron.*, p. 307).

Front *"under strong pressure* from the Government . . . which had been resisted for some time . . ."[143] And in at least one country representatives of the united "Front" party contacted clergymen in their homes, seeking, often with threats, their membership in the Party. East German Premier Grotewohl declared that "according to the text and spirit of the Constitution, every citizen (also each clergyman) not only has the right, but also the duty of cooperation and identification with the Government. . . . Whoever tries to hinder a clergyman in the exercise of (these) . . . rights and duties acts against . . . the Constitution."[144] So also in Poland, Czechoslovakia and Rumania.

These are some of the requisites for Church leadership which Communist leaders were driving at as they swung into the nationalization process. If, at the outset, they were happy enough when churchmen simply did not oppose them, by the end of this phase churchmen were expected to be actively engaged in national pursuits prescribed by the Government. It will be seen later that the trials of thousands of clergy focused on various of these "standards" which the accused did not measure up to.

The nationalizing of church leaders. How were the Communists to achieve a "nationalized" church leadership?

Church leaders represented a cross-section of the whole population. Among them would be found men of conviction and courage, stubborn warriors, ambitious collaborators, naive idealists, realistic reformers, shrewd politicians, prophets and weaklings. "Nationalization" would obviously require a multifarious, comprehensive program. Any cataloging of methods in this document cannot deal adequately with the complexities involved. However, the "instructions" or strategies for dealing with the clergy, which Communist Party organs or governments have listed from time to time are worth careful study, viz., instructions in the U.S.S.R. *Agitators' Guide, No. 23,*[145] the "Vishinsky Plan" in Rumania;[146] "Directives for Local Agitators" in Bulgaria,[147] "Instructions of the Karlsbad Meeting of Orginform and the Association of Godless."[148]

From these and other documents, and still more conclusively from events, one can summarize a variety of inter-related measures as follows:

(a) re-orient or displace difficult leaders;
(b) disrupt spiritual solidarity among the clergy;

---

143. *Tserkoven Vestnik,* Oct. 23, 1948 (*Chron.,* p. 359).
144. *New York Times,* June 17, 4:2, 1950 (*Chron.,* p. 549).
145. *Chronicle,* p. 243.
146. *Chronicle,* p. 321.
147. *Chronicle,* p. 367.
148. *Chronicle,* pp. 494, 516.

(c) cultivate a "patriotic" body of clergy;

(d) sever or control international contacts;

(e) assure an orientation program for the new clergy;

(f) take over administrative authority.

(a) *Re-orientation* or *displacement* of difficult leaders. "Difficult" leaders were those who would block, either directly or indirectly as a symbol of resistance, any of the measures of "nationalization" already discussed: youth, education, property, social welfare, civil records, etc. The "Vishinsky Plan" simply called for their liquidation and the placing of Soviet-trained religious leaders in key positions.[149] As it has worked out, a variety of methods has been developed including intimidation, compromise, discrediting, detention and replacement, public trial and death.

By acts of discrimination and intimidation of the clergy, it was assumed many clergymen would be displaced. In the U.S.S.R. churchmen were classified with non-productive labor and thereupon practically lost their citizenship, rations, housing, education for their children, and possibilities for employment.[150] A similar measure was taken in Czechoslovakia in 1949 with regard to clothing rations.[151]

In the Baltics, as in Poland, Hungary, Bulgaria and East Germany, clear warnings were sounded by government officials with the apparent purpose of getting "difficult" pastors to flee.[152] And in particular cases, notably Archbishop Mindszenty and Bishop Ordass[153] in Hungary, Pastor Hamel in East Germany, and countless others, direct attempts or suggestions were made to get church leaders to go abroad and stay abroad, or be transferred by their ecclesiastical superiors to non-Communist areas. In the case of Mindszenty, the Vatican rejected the Government's request to transfer him elsewhere. Bishop Ordass was determined not to vacate his office while abroad and be accused of espionage, thereby giving the Government an excuse for making even more radical changes in the leadership of the Church. Hundreds of other faithful pastors have courageously refused to abandon their flocks when an easy road of escape was opened to them.

Secondly, attempts were made to compromise church leaders in order to re-orient or oust them. Few mortals have never erred. East European churchmen, with fast-changing and inconsistent governments, occupiers, laws and currencies were no exception. But there, a blot on one's past record, a minor court sentence, fi-

---

149. *Chronicle*, p. 321.

150. Art. 69, 1918 Constitution; reiterated in 1929 Constitution (*Chron.*, pp. 230, 238); also Latvia (*Chron.*, p. 305) and Czechoslovakia (*Chron.*, p. 496).

151. *Chronicle*, p. 496.

152. USSR, *Chron.*, pp. 230, 263; Czechoslovakia, *Chron.*, pp. 496, 497.

153. *Chronicle*, pp. 445, 450.

nancial irregularities, social misconduct, contact with the Nazis or Western Allies, or family members in trouble, became suitable occasion for blackmail. Services to the Communist cause could be extorted by threats of exposure or prosecution. It was the job of special agents to ascertain where a marked leader's "compromise" spots were. And if there were none, active measures were recommended for forcing "compromise," including, as listed in the Czech Communist Party's instructions, "if necessary, by means of woman agents."[154] The *Lithuanian Bulletin* reported that priests were frequently summoned "to give the last rites to a dying person," who would turn out to be an alleged anti-Communist guerilla. The priest was then "compromised" for association with "bandits."[155] Once "compromised," the clergyman who feared exposure or prosecution was at the mercy of his new political or moral lords.

The spiritual authority of church leaders was discredited. Presumably the theory was that if difficult leaders could be compromised and discredited in the minds of believers, the believers themselves would rise up and oust them or abandon them along with the religion they bespoke. The *Agitator's Guide*, No. 23, instructed agitators to "illustrate the reactionary, counter-revolutionary role of . . . the clergy from actual events; show . . . from past and present life the vile moral image of ministers of religious cults."[156] The *Guide* accused Orthodox Metropolitan Sergius of having amassed more than 300,000 rubles . . . "often has drunken parties." Other churchmen were accused of becoming rich "magnates" and of immoral conduct. In other countries, extensive propaganda campaigns were launched to undermine the confidence of the people in religious leaders. The Catholic Church particularly was to be intensively worked over. Said the Czech Communist Party's *Instructions to Communists*s "Attack the Catholic Church with all the usual weapons: celibacy, economic questions, the church as a capitalist institution, moral delinquents, etc. . . ."[157] Caricatures, stories, cartoons and poetry portraying religious leaders as gangsters, the "black enemy of the people," moral degenerates, despised animals, etc., appeared in official Government and popular publications.[158] In Lithuania priests were reportedly forced to disrobe in MVD offices where they were photographed with MVD "girls." The photographs were then circulated among the people.[159] In Czechoslovakia priests and monks were infected

154. *Chronicle*, p. 516.
155. *Lithuanian Bulletin*, Nos. 1-3, Jan.-March, 1949, p. 4.
156. As quoted by Anderson, *op. cit.*, p. 118 (*Chron.*, p. 243).
157. Barron and Waddams, *op. cit.*, pp. 48-49; MacEoin, *The Communist War on Religion*, p. 30 (*Chron.*, p. 516).
158. Bulgaria, *Chron.*, p. 359; Rumania, *Chron.*, p. 327; East Germany, *Chron.*, p. 553.
159. *Lithuanian Bulletin*, Jan.-March, 1949.

by medical treatment with venereal diseases, then "exposed" to the public as immoral criminals.[160]   Government leaders, the press and fellow clergymen accused religious leaders of opposing the teaching of science in the schools and of discouraging parents from sending children to school, of opposing the Government's "progressive" programs and plotting to overthrow the Government and the Red Army, of supporting imperialists and war-mongers, of preventing priests and believers from performance of their political convictions.   Direct links of contact between clergy and people were curtailed or broken.   Larger groups were enlisted to secure denunciations.   In Hungary, through mass meetings and solicitation people were urged or compelled to sign petitions denouncing Cardinal Mindszenty.   The Government offered to negotiate with other Roman Catholic leaders if they would denounce him.[161]   And in Poland, where a key issue between the Roman Catholic Church and the Government was over the Church's refusal to set up a permanent ecclesiastical administration for the Oder-Neisse area annexed from Germany (and by implication, refusal to accept the peace settlement as valid or permanent), the Government appealed to the Poles' nationalism, accusing the Catholic leaders of pro-Germanism, in order to separate the people from the clergy and lay the foundations of a national Catholic Church.[162]

A fourth method of getting difficult leaders out of the way was to detain and replace them.   A number of clergymen were "taken into custody" for "questioning" with regard to their activities, or were allegedly "writing books" in their homes (Abp. Beran, Czechoslovakia), were "suspended" by the Government for "anti-democratic attitudes," were deposed by "special disciplinary courts" of the churches (Bishop Ordass), resigned for "reasons of health" (Exarch Stefan, Bulgaria), or simply disappeared (Hungarian pastors who allegedly opposed the election of Dezséry to succeed Ordass).   Whatever the reason given[163]—and in no case was "religious activity" the ostensible reason for detention—unless the detained leaders could conform to government desires, their offices, as in the case of Bishop Ordass, were considered vacant, and should be filled—often by government-nominated or approved men.   After Cardinal Mindszenty in Hungary was imprisoned, two men nominated and elected to his office by the Church were imprisoned before one acceptable to the Government was elected.[164]

---

160.   *Chron.*, pp. 509, 517.
161.   *Chronicle*, pp. 447-448.
162.   *Chronicle*, pp. 391, 416.
163.   Other reasons, *Chron.*, pp. 328, 329, 359, 361, 391, 512.
164.   *Christian Century*, Sept. 6, 1950 (*Chron.*, p. 456). Similarly, Lutheran Bishop Ordass, *Die Protestantischen Kirchen in Ungarn*, p. 22 (*Chron.*, p. 455).

The most spectacular "re-orientation" of church leadership has been in connection with the public court-room. While it is not our purpose here to do an elaborate review of several hundred trials—there are numerous books on the subject—a brief overall consideration of the charges against churchmen, trial methods, confessions and net results is pertinent to this analysis.

Church leaders were tried for "crimes," not religious activities. This was an axiom: "prosecution, not persecution."[165]

In the U.S.S.R., Patriarch Tikhon referred in his "confession" to his past hostility towards the Soviet authorities, his anathematizing Soviet authorities, his opposition to the Government's decree for the removal of church treasures, and to connections with foreign and domestic monarchists and White-Guard counter-revolutionaries; *ergo*, he had been prosecuted for these "crimes," not persecuted for his religious work.[166] In 1937, a group of thirty churchmen was sentenced on charges of joining a counter-Revolutionary Fascist organization of churchmen, seeking to strengthen the Church as an anti-Soviet spirit, derogating the Soviet Constitution, opposing the census, preaching counter-Revolutionary sermons, attracting youth to church and baptizing children.[167]

A year later, "great numbers" of churchmen were convicted of espionage, arson, establishing a "miracle factory," instructing believers to organize secret "home" churches, collaboration with foreign Fascist organizations, assisting traveling "espionage" priests and stealing church property.[168]

There has been somewhat less variety in the indictments of churchmen in other East-European countries. Although the wording has varied, criminal charges generally could be classified in one of four categories: Fascist war collaboration, subversive activities, currency violations, infringement of religious rights.[169]

165. USSR, *Chron.*, pp. 239, 255; Bulgaria, *Chron.*, pp. 360, 378; Poland, *Chron.*, p. 392; Hungary, *Chron.*, p. 445.
166. Anderson, *op. cit.*, p. 66 (*Chron.*, p. 234).
167. *Orlovskaia*, from Anderson, *op. cit.*, p. 115 (*Chron.*, p. 243).
168. *Chronicle*, p. 244.
169. (1) *Fascist war collaboration*:
"supporting the Nazi war and anti-Soviet propaganda,"—Lutheran Bishop Turoczy, Hungary;
"assisting Polish (Fascist) refugees"—Czech Roman Catholic clergy;
"Collaborating with Germans, hoping for early return of the Nazis"—Czech Roman Catholic clergy;
"war crimes, Fascist collaboration"—Albanian Roman Catholic clergy;
(2) *Subversive activities*:
"leading an organization seeking to overthrow the Government and restore the Hapsburg monarchy"—Archbishop Mindszenty, Hungary;
"plotting with the Vatican and the U. S. A. against the Government,"

There were also various charges of immoral conduct.

Were churchmen guilty of the "crimes" as charged? Secondary charges of immoral conduct, Fascist collaboration, currency violations may be dealt with first. Where these charges were made in the fields of the writer's particular competence, especially the Bulgarian Protestant pastors, they were untrue. Financial and material aid transactions carried out between these churchmen and the World Council of Churches were not "illegal" unless illegality consists of consultation with and transmission through government channels. And in Hungary, the judges would have acquitted Bishop Ordass when similar charges against him were refuted had they not received instructions to find him guilty. All such charges and alleged evidence therefore become suspect. But, admittedly, some churchmen had been collaborators, voluntarily or involuntarily. Some may have been involved in illegal currency traffic. Some were convicted on these charges. But there were countless numbers of people in high positions, including Communist positions, whose war crimes and immoral acts were popularly known to exceed alleged acts of church leaders. It was therefore

---

"distributing funds to support anti-Government activities, inciting peasants against the Government"—Hungarian Roman Catholic clergy;
"imperialist agents and war incendiaries"—Bulgarian Roman Catholic clergy;
"treason and espionage on behalf of the Americans"—Bulgarian Orthodox clergy;
"receiving instructions from, and collecting information for American Intelligence"—Jehovah's Witnesses, Poland;
"subversive political activities"—Salvation Army, Czechoslovakia;
"plotting rebellions against the State"—Czechoslovak Roman Catholic clergy;
"when faced with two authorities, chose the foreign (Vatican) authority"—Czech Roman Catholic clergy;
"unfriendly acts towards the U. S. S. R. and anti-Communist attacks, activities against peace and democracy"—Polish Roman Catholic clergy;
"obedience to church law and the Vatican above civil law,"
"forming a network of spies and agitators directed by the Vatican,"
"espionage for the Vatican,"
"concealing arms in the monasteries"—Czech Roman Catholic clergy;

(3) *Currency violations*:
"illegal traffic in foreign monies"—Bishop Ordass, Hungary;
"black-marketing"—Cardinal Mindszenty, Hungary;
"stealing jewelry from monasteries to smuggle abroad"—Roman Catholic monks, Czechoslovakia;

(4) *Infringement of religious rights of others*:
"preventing clergy from joining 'Catholic Action' "—Roman Catholic Bishop Buzalka, Czechoslovakia;
"refusing to administer sacraments to Communists,"
"advising parents not to select Communists as God-parents, and not to read (the Government-encouraged) *Catholic News*"—Czech Roman Catholic clergy.

a risky business to the Communists' own position to focus public attention on war crimes and immorality!

Further, if churchmen were convicted of these "domestic" crimes, sentence would require simple imprisonment and would risk making martyrs of the condemned men on incidental issues. The purpose of the trials has not been, with few exceptions, simply to put church leaders in prison, but to effect a nationalized church leadership. This required an absolute break with international allegiances. All churchmen could be imprisoned on various charges of immorality or black marketing, and still not clarify their positions *vis-a-vis* international affiliations. The central issue, therefore, must of necessity be, and has been, the international one. Churchmen must be accused in such a way as to force them either to recant of and denounce foreign contacts, and become "loyal" nationalists—in which case it would not be necessary to hold them indefinitely—or else they must receive, particularly as a public warning, severest punishment for "treason."

During the nationalization process trials of churchmen have therefore been focused principally on whether their loyalties were to foreign or to national authority. Even "Fascist collaboration," "currency violations," and "infringements of religious rights," where these were mentioned, will, on careful scrutiny and with few exceptions, be found to mean subversive activity or plotting for foreign powers.

Have churchmen, then, been guilty of "subversive" activities? By Communist definition, yes, and so convicted. But it is important to record the ambiguity of some indictments, which allowed the press to interpret accusations with sinister overtones to the populace, and the accused to confess on the basis of entirely different connotations. For example, the Bulgarian pastors confessed to having conversations with foreigners, to having been friendly to the Anglo-American culture (where they received their education), to having received instructions, to having given information and to having received money.[170] To the extent cited here, and insofar as the writer was involved on behalf of the World Council of Churches, the confessions are true—if interpreted in the context of fact. There was conversation, it was friendly, information concerning church life was given, and aid was sent to the churches for their material reconstruction and spiritual tasks. By shrewd insinuations, however, the confessions were used to mean espionage, black marketing and treason.

According to Roman Catholic sources, a Roman Catholic abbott in Czechoslovakia was asked if he was faithful to the Vatican. His affirmative reply brought the charge, "You confess therefore

---

170. Tobias, *Fifteen Bulgarian Pastors*, pp. 59, 95, 96 (*Chron.*, p. 361).

to having relations abroad, and with adversaries of the regime."
Another, a Jesuit leader, acknowledged having discussed prospects
for opening Roman Catholic schools with the Papal Internuncio,
and was thereupon charged with indulging secrets to an enemy
government.[171] In Poland, the Jehovah's Witnesses' correspondence with Jehovah's Witnesses in America was interpreted to mean
collecting of espionage information for American intelligence services; the defendants were accused of "criminal subversive activity
aimed at overthrowing the system of people's democracy."[172] And
in Hungary Cardinal Mindszenty's ambiguous confession to "guilt
in principle and currency speculation"[173] is subject to two vastly
differing interpretations.

This is not to suggest that there were no straight-forward confessions to specific charges of disloyalty, nor that there was no
subversive activity among churchmen, no opposition to the government, that churchmen were not deliberately involved in underground movements. Many were. But whether they were or not,
if they were blocking nationalization on whatever grounds, they
were so charged and convicted.

Of what were they guilty? Certainly church leaders were involved in international relations—they could hardly be true to
their calling if they were not. But often as not, they were simply
caught between the narrow Communist concept of "state" and
their own supra-national concept. As in Bulgaria, pastors were
concerned about things universal and eternal. They exhorted the
people to adhere to an inflexible code of ethics whereas their governments desired relative mores determined by what best served
the Party's devious purposes.

To the pastors, liberty involved Eternal Design and universal
concern; exception might be taken to the ideas of fellow man with
the possibility of beneficial results. To the Government liberty
existed only within and according to the Party's delineation; exception might not be taken. Freedom of conscience was accorded
only to those whose consciences were "properly educated."

The pastors preached of man's shortcomings, of his dependence on God, of unfailing justice, of society as based on the principle "love thy neighbor," of righteousness and daily religious living, of forgiveness, meekness and humility. They instructed their
children, their youth and their parishes in this kind of religion.
Such doctrines when cast against any totalitarian background
would be conspicuously non-Marxist, or perhaps "Western."

---

171. *New York Times*, April 6, 7, 1950 (*Chron.*, p. 509).
172. *Trybuna Ludu*, as reported in *Christian Century*, Sept. 27, 1950
(*Chron.*, p. 400).
173. *New York Times*, Feb. 4:1:1, 1949 (*Chron.*, p. 449).

It is not surprising, therefore, that Communist governments should find that "under the veil of various doctrines, (the churches) introduce the policies of foreign influence . . . destroy the people's confidence, demoralize the people (and) divert them from the (Communist) path to salvation."[174]

The Bulgarian pastors were found "guilty" of "spreading malicious rumors and creating an opposition among the people."[175] In the eyes of the Communist Government this probably consisted not so much in *what* the pastors may have said to Allied Control Commission representatives or to other Bulgarian people as in the fact that they were an extremely conspicuous living example that all was not going well under the Communist regime. Since the pastors were not in the Party, then it would be obvious to all that they were against it (or so reasoned the Bulgarian Communist). Therefore, they became a last remaining symbol, and perhaps a potential leadership of the stubborn resistance of the Bulgarian people against giving up their individual freedom to a collective, highly centralized society. (Should there be a showdown, the Government could probably not count on the support of more than five percent of the people.) The pastors also stood as a symbol to the West that all in Bulgaria was not totally "Stalinized," and that there might be some chance of redeeming the situation according to Western patterns. The Government did not want pastors or anyone else in a position to "create confusion, distrust and uncertainty"[176] among the Bulgarian people, or to prejudice other nations against full acceptance of the Bulgarian Communist Government as the unanimously acclaimed representative government of the Bulgarian people.

The pastors were therefore "subversive internationals" who must be "nationalized." And as silent leaders of a resistant spirit, they must be brought to capitulate to national authority in such a manner as would best break the spirit of any other resisters.

One point remains concerning trials of churchmen: what brought them to confess, whether unequivocally or by innuendo, to things they had not done; what brought them to "repent" and to beg for a chance to "dedicate themselves" to the new nation? It is not our purpose here to re-examine what little details are known of several hundred cases. Risking over-simplification, one may surmise that in general the processes ranged from simple questioning to physical and mental torture, depending on the accused's degree of innocence and resistance. In the interrogation process, the accused have often been subjected to incessant series of extreme

---

174. *Communist Directives to Local Committees*, Bulgaria, CCIA, London (*Chron.*, pp. 367-368).
175. Tobias, *op. cit.*, p. 25 ff.
176. *Communist Directives, op. cit.* (*Chron.*, p. 368).

contrasts: cold, bare cells then luxurious suites, starvation then feasts, sleepless torment and wracking interrogation followed by hours of solitude, threats to self or loved ones then promises, bringing the accused to the point of death then reviving him—this, interspersed with round after round of questioning and instruction in painful circumstances, until the will is broken, mental processes are confused, facts become distorted and the accused finds some peace or security in capitulation to the authority of his interrogator. The confession is drawn up, signed, and presented to the court. The defendant may be presented as mentally unstable, morally corrupt and wholly untrustworthy. To show its "generosity" (and to avoid making him a martyr) the court sentences the convict to something less than the maximum penalty, or because of his confession and change of mind, and plea to work for the "new order," may even turn him "free" for constructive work as a "regenerated" citizen.

The net result is, theoretically, a nationalized church leadership; a discredited and displaced symbol of resistance; a subtle suggestion that one has no "right" to life except by the grace of the regime.

A final method of displacing difficult church leaders has been murder. There have been instances, e.g., Hungary, in which church leaders have been protected and sustained by Communist troops or government officers. It must not be forgotten that great numbers of clergymen labored together with Communists in the anti-Nazi resistance and in liberation armies. On the other hand, numerous instances can be cited in which obviously deliberate plans were made to dispose by "accident" of church leaders who might prove indomitably anti-Communist.[177] Among these were some who, in their resistance against the Nazis, had collaborated closely with the Communists who later slew them.

In the whole of East Europe an estimated 80,000 clergymen, plus half that many monks and nuns and an inestimable number of lay leaders have been displaced from positions of leadership by depositions, imprisonment, deportation or death under Communist regimes.

(b) A second development in the nationalization of church leadership was the *disruption of spiritual solidarity* among church leaders. Lower clergy were separated from higher clergy, churchmen denounced and betrayed fellow churchmen, age-old rivalries between confessions were kindled, denomination opposed denomi-

---

177 Roman Catholic Msgr. Glaser, Rumania, after opposing a move to create of the Roman Catholic Church in Rumania a "democratic Rumanian Catholic Church," was arrested and "died of heart failure." *New York Times,* June 7, 1950 (*Chron.*, p. 335).

nation, churches took conflicting positions over political issues and further fanned flames of distrust, until finally "Communist governments should emphasize the frustration in the religious situation of today and the necessity for unity, (and) . . . use . . . (a National) Church as the instrument for unity."[178]

It is difficult to establish whether the Communists, in their plans, foresaw and exploited inherent frictions, historic conflicts, rivalries and personal grudges in inter-church relations. In dealing with Uniate churches, they obviously did. But whether they did or not, the result was the same: internal strains in church relations hastened the breaking of spiritual solidarity.

In the Roman Catholic and Orthodox Churches the separation of lower clergy from the hierarchy began with governments championing the interests of disgruntled priests versus their superiors. The hierarchy was accused of exploiting the peasants, of intimidating the lower clergy, preventing free expression of their political convictions, and preventing negotiations between the Church and the Government. In Poland, where the hierarchy had not yet been displaced and was blocking a Church-State agreement, the Minister of Public Administration called on "patriotic" priests to make a concordat with the Government over the heads of the Episcopate.[179] At times little contact was permitted among the clergy or between clergy and hierarchy. Among Protestants ambitious young men have often been aided in their scramble for power, pitting their minority factions against the body of the Church. Their opponents have often been labeled "reactionary Roman Catholic collaborators."[180]

Within and across denominational lines, churchmen have been brought to spy on and "denounce" or condemn fellow clergymen. Loyalty oaths have required clergy to keep State secrets. "What secrets?" a fellow-clergyman wonders. The director of the Catholic People's League in Hungary reported after fleeing to Austria that the Secret Police had tried to force him to spy on and denounce Abp. Mindszenty. As early as 1947, several Protestant leaders dissociated themselves from Roman Catholic Archbishop Mindszenty for his "political Catholicism."[181] Lutheran Bishop Ordass refused an offer for immediate release if he would denounce Mindszenty.[182] In Bulgaria statements were issued by Protestant, Orthodox, Catholic, and non-Christian religious organizations, in some instances frankly condemning the Protestant pas-

---

178. Orginform *Instructions to Communists, op. cit.* (*Chron.*, pp. 516, 517).
179. *The Tablet*, Feb. 25, 1950 (*Chron.*, p. 397).
180. *Chronicle*, pp. 439, 445.
181. Mindszenty, *Four Years Struggle*, p. 121 (*Chron.*, p. 448; other denunciations, p. 448).
182. *L.W.F. Newsbulletin*, Geneva, May 1, 1950 (*Chron.*, p. 448).

tors on trial, in others denouncing spying and treason in general.[183]
Court "confessions" of lower clergy frequently included denunciations of higher clergy.[184]

There have been other instances of evasive condemnation of
crime in general which indicate that some form of statement had
been demanded, but that some church leaders would not stand in
judgment over other churchmen. Some denunciations are known
to have been prepared by government agents for signature; others
were never seen by the alleged signatories.

Between the churches there has been rivalry over political
position and material power. The *Instructions to Communists*
in Czechoslovakia[185] called for close cooperation of Communists
with the Czech National Church, praising their bishops and giving
them highest honors in all State functions and celebrations. Such
favoritism or rumors of favoritism drove a sharp and quick wedge.
The Roman Catholic *Orbis Catholicus* carried an article in its
March, 1949, issue claiming that

> "only one single (the Roman Catholic) organization
> (stood) outside and in contrast to this (Communist na-
> tionalization) scheme. In the years of resistance against
> Germany . . . the Czechoslovakian (National) Church has
> become unimportant in view of the Catholic renewal;
> Protestant communities under the spiritual leadership of
> Hromadka make no further difficulties and the Orthodox
> Church has subjected itself to the Moscow Patriarchate."

This scarcely could better Protestant, Orthodox and Roman
Catholic relations. In Poland the Protestant churches protested
vehemently when, shortly after the war, the Government seemed
to be favoring the Roman Catholic Church, as it had for generations, in the redistribution of ownerless land and churches.[186]
Within the same year Protestant churches acknowledged that they
were receiving special Government attention in opposition to Roman Catholicism.[187] When State support of churches was first
proposed in Czechoslovakia, Czech Brethren, Lutheran, Free
Churches and Roman Catholics opposed the bill. The Czech National Church, Orthodox Church, Unitarian Church and Lutheran
Church of East Silesia approved.[188] In Rumania, display of the
Russian flag and singing of the national anthem in one church

---

183. Tobias, *op. cit.* (*Chron.*, p. 360 ff.). Similarity of text indicated a common origin of the denunciations.
184. U.S.S.R., *Chron.*, pp. 233, 244; Bulgaria, *Chron.*, pp. 360, 361; Hungary,
Chron., p. 449.
185. *Chronicle*, pp. 516-517.
186. *Chronicle*, pp. 385-387, *passim*.
187. *Chronicle*, p. 388.
188. *Chronicle*, pp. 504 ff.

shattered the trust of and fellowship with other churches.[189] Within various faiths and communions there has been considerable haggling and discontent over alleged preferential treatment in the distribution of funds and relief supplies.

Historic conflicts between confessional bodies and ethnic groups were re-opened. After a Prague journal reported that Roman Catholic leaders had slandered reformer Jan Hus, the Government's Deputy Premier, at the (Protestant) Jan Hus Memorial Day services in 1949, declared: "Hus fought not only against the immorality of the Catholic Church but also against the increasing German influence . . . which was backed by the corrupt Catholic hierarchy and the Pope."[190] Similar inflammatory speeches were delivered before Protestants by other Communist leaders on the same occasion.

In Rumania, the fact that Roman Catholics were of German and Hungarian origin, Orthodox of Rumanian, Reformed of Hungarian, and Lutheran of German origins was no small factor in weakening the solidarity of the Churches as churches.

Czech Roman Catholic bishops irritated Orthodox and Protestant churches by referring to non-Catholics as "sects."[191] Slovak Lutherans in turn estranged lesser Protestants with the same epithet.

Whether out of fear, lack of concern, or a sense of helplessness, when Communist governments were liquidating Jehovah's Witnesses and similar groups there was no evidence of intervention from strong church bodies.[192]

One noteworthy attempt was made to undo one age-old interchurch controversy. In the re-integration of Uniate (Eastern rite Roman-Catholic) believers into Orthodox churches in Rumania, Poland and Czechoslovakia, care was taken to point out that the Uniates had once been Orthodox, and had been forced into union with Rome by the connivance of the Pope and political rulers some centuries before.

Conflicting positions which different churches took on crucial and incidental issues further estranged them from each other. This will be particularly evident in chapters on the churches' response. One example will suffice here: The *Tribune de Genève* (Switzerland) published a "letter from Berlin" in August, 1950, touching on Roman Catholic-Protestant relationships. The letter declared that many Protestants in predominantly Protestant East Germany were becoming Roman Catholics because Roman Catholicism had taken a firm stand against Communism while Protes-

---

189. *Chronicle*, p. 323.
190. MacEoin, *The Communist War on Religion*, p. 40 (*Chron.*, p. 500).
191. *Chronicle*, p. 495.
192. Poland, *Chron.*, p. 400; East Germany, *Chron.*, p. 534.

tantism had tried to be neutral; Roman Catholic leaders were suffering martyrdom while Protestant pastors retained their official status; the Roman Catholic Church had an authoritative, uniform political position while Protestants wavered without uniformity or authority.[193]

The facts were that in the same year Roman Catholic students were given special ecclesiastical dispensations to participate in Communist youth organizations, in singing of hymns to Stalin and other political activities, while many Protestants faced expulsion from East German universities for conscientiously refusing to do so. In the "National Front" elections, Roman Catholic priests were advised by the Bishop of Bautzen and by Western officials to vote, and did so, resulting momentarily in more favorable treatment. Many Protestants did not vote and suffered for it. They were astonished that Catholics could vote in view of the Vatican order ex-communicating Communist collaborators, and the fact that their fellow Roman Catholics in neighboring Czechoslovakia were on trial for non-collaboration in similar circumstances.

No source was given for the letter, but if Communists had cared to, they could hardly have chosen a better time, place or method of inciting Protestants against Catholics. Or, Protestants could well wonder, was this a shrewd trick of anti-Communist origin to try to get Protestant Churches to declare themselves on the anti-Communist bandwagon? In any case the letter did not contribute to the solidarity of Protestant and Roman Catholic Christians.

In the pre-Communist era, there were diversities of opinions, policies and purposes among churchmen, but here and there church leaders manifested degrees of spiritual solidarity in their own way. Communist regimes, having seen to the atomization of that kind of unity, were ready to "emphasize the frustration in the religious situation today and the necessity for unity"[194] and to remake it according to their own patterns.

(c) The third measure in effecting a nationalized church leadership has been the development of a loyal, "patriotic" clergy. In Russia, immediately after the arrest of Orthodox Patriarch Tikhon in 1922 an archpriest who had been active in organizing an "All Russian Union of Democratic Orthodox Clergy and Laymen" in opposition to the Patriarchate, was able with Governmental assistance to secure control of the Orthodox Church administration.[195] In Rumania, one of the first acts of the Ministry of

193. *Tribune de Genève*, Augt. 30, 1950 (*Chron.*, p. 533).
194. Orginform, *Instructions to Communists, op. cit.* (*Chron.*, pp. 516-517). 03).
195. Bolshakoff, *Russian Non-Conformity*, p. 160 and Anderson, *op. cit.*, pp. 61-63 (*Chron.*, p. 233 ff.).

Cults under the "Popular Front" (1945) was to organize a "Union of Democratic Clergy."[196] Immediately after the liberation Polish Communists were instructed to create a "patriotic priests' " and a "progressive lay Catholics' " organization.[197] A "commission of priests" was to be attached to the "Union of Defenders of Fighters for Freedom and Democracy," using the Army chaplains corps for leaders. Similarly, in every other country special attention was given to the organization of associations of lower clergy under governmental direction or control. Those clergy participated who were already considered loyal, fully "nationalized." Membership was encouraged through deliberate programs of compromise, conciliation or governmental subsidies. In Rumania, for example, the first adherents to the "Patriotic Defense" were largely clergymen who had formerly been in the Iron Guard, or who were on trial before church courts and were assured of livelihood and rehabilitation if they collaborated in the organization. Conciliation was clearly called for when, in 1944, the Patriotic Defense was instructed to overcome clerical resistance by exempting parish houses from requisition, restoring land and other confiscated property and granting churches aid for repairs.[198] In Poland, "patriotic" clergy were to receive special support, tax exemptions, and property.[199]

A central point in the "Vishinsky Plan" (Rumania) stipulated that church leaders should be controlled by "controlling or providing stipends."[200] As early as 1946 the Rumanian Government was subsidizing "loyal" priests, and promising better salaries for those who would give better support to the Government.[201]

Other incentives must be mentioned: social and political pressure, fear that their children could not continue their education, fear that facilities for simple existence could not be secured, gullible willingness to take political phrases at their face value, hopes of making a constructive impact from within "patriotic" organizations. Whatever the reason, great numbers of clergy did join.

In some instances, government-aligned clerical organizations were established by taking over the leadership of existing clerical bodies. In Bulgaria there had long been an Association of Orthodox Priests. In 1946, though the Association was more aggressive than the Synod in its social concern and program, it stood fully behind the Holy Synod on issues involving Government relationships. In May, 1947, at the annual meeting of the Association, G. B. Georgiev, the leader of the minority pro-Government faction

196. *Chronicle*, p. 322.
197. *Chronicle*, pp. 397, 422.
198. *Chronicle*, pp. 321, 322.
199. *Chronicle*, pp. 394, 416, 425.
200. *Chronicle*, p. 321.
201. *Chronicle*, p. 323.

in the Association, shouted angrily, "Now we are twenty, next year we shall be two hundred."[202] A few months later the leader of the Association was replaced by Georgiev, who succeeded in having other important offices filled by his associates. In any conflict the Association thereafter took the side of the Government against the official Church administration.[203]

Similarly in Hungary, a meeting of lower Catholic clergy was held in Budapest to "declare that the attitude of our church towards the People's Republic has to change, in order to get it out of the *cul-de-sac* into which some of the bishops have got it as a result of . . . their prejudice against progress and their desire for the old order to return."[204] The Ministry of Religion and Education assured the priests of the approval and support of the Government for their movement. The priests then passed resolutions (a) declaring their fidelity to the State and its five-year plan (one speaker noted that the Bench of Bishops had approved the five-year plan prior to the election of the "People's Front"!); (b) promising their support in the fight for peace; (c) condemning the "war-mongering imperialists," their action in Korea, and the atom bomb; and (d) expressing the desirability of the State's supporting those clergy "true to the people."

While governments maintained a facade of non-interference in strictly religious affairs, it was clear that the associations turned to governments, not to ecclesiastical offices as their authority.

"Patriotic" clergy were expected not only to support the national effort as a group, but as indicated earlier, were to participate actively in politics as individuals. Political activities included special declarations of loyalty to the government, work in brigades and "volunteer" projects, participation in elections and public offices and other activities supporting the government, as e.g., in Hungary, preaching special sermons of praise of the constitution.[205] In effect "politically active" meant to indicate by their activities that the church's purposes were identified with those of the state.

A storm of protests against government meddling in church affairs arose, particularly from the Roman Catholic Church hierarchy, and orders were issued forbidding clergy to participate in politics or to seek election to government offices.[206] This provided

202. "Religious Freedom in Bulgaria," *New Central European Observer*, No. 2 (*Chron.*, p. 357).

203. *Tserkoven Vestnik*, Oct. 23, 1948 (*Chron.*, p. 359).

204. *State and Church in Hungary*, Hungarian News and Information Service, Oct., 1950 (*Chron.*, pp. 483-484).

205. *Chronicle*, pp. 456-457.

206. Poland, *Chron.*, pp. 397, 400, 418; Hungary, *Chron.*, p. 435; Czechoslovakia, *Chron.*, pp. 494, 507; East Germany, *Chron.*, pp. 529, 532.

many clergy with an excuse for non-participation: "it was against church regulations." Governments then enacted laws to punish church leaders and prelates who obstructed participation of priests in political activities.[207] Priests who defied ecclesiastical decrees of excommunication and supported the governments were promised special bonuses and support.[208] In Czechoslovakia Roman Catholic clergy were at one time offered salaries three times as high as those of civil servants (15,000 crowns versus 5,000) if they would subscribe to the Government's program and oath.

While the ultimate purpose of the "Patriotic" associations, from the government's point of view, may have been to provide a nucleus for undermining "reactionary" clergy and ultimately creating a nationalized church, the Patriotic Associations have often focused on real issues and done good work along with their support of the government. They have secured various benefits for the families of clergy such as hospitalization and social security, have established special training facilities, refresher courses and conferences for the clergy (not wholly unmixed with political indoctrination), have encouraged social concern and action among the clergy, exchanged evangelistic and other ideas or techniques, and have espoused the causes of the lower clergy versus the hierarchy, many of which pre-date the Communist regimes.[209]

(d) As an important step towards clerical nationalization, undesirable international contacts have been severed or controlled. It appears that the Communists were motivated in this action by genuine fear of an international, anti-Communist combine working through the churhes, maintaining "agents" within their borders bearing local citizenship.

The governments were determined that every citizen's loyalty should be to some focal point within the Communist orbit, and therefore controllable. Churchmen's contacts abroad raised suspicion as to their supreme loyalty. This was at the root of the trials and the controversy over loyalty oaths: could a priest be loyal both to a national and to an opposing world body.

Foreign sources were ready to provide funds for indigenous churches to carry on intensive evangelistic and educational campaigns independent of governmental direction and alien to governmental purposes.

Foreign contacts would provide channels for information or instructions to leak in and out of East Europe, threatening the

207. Bulgaria, *Chron.*, p. 358; Poland, *Chron.*, pp. 394, 397, 408 ff.; Czechoslovakia, *Chron.*, pp. 496, 499; East Germany, *Chron.*, p. 549.

208. U.S.S.R., *Chron.*, p. 233; Rumania, *Chron.*, pp. 323, 335; Bulgaria, *Chron.*, p. 359; Poland, *Chron.*, pp. 394, 425; Czechoslovakia, *Chron.*, pp. 498, 500, 508, 512; East Germany, *Chron.*, pp. 533, 534, 549-550.

209. E.g., re-marriage of clerical widowers, modernizing of priest's dress, direct representation in official church governing bodies.

effectiveness of an intensive propaganda program abroad and thought-control program at home. "Western orientation," the Czech Minister of Education called it. The conscience and actions of people might be determined or at least affected on the basis of broader interests than provincial or Communist. Was a rival authority over a regime's "subjects" to be tolerated? Could Communist governments permit persons in their orbits to be tempted by foreign contacts to activities of sabotage? Foreign contacts must be absolutely controlled.[210]

Roman Catholics would obviously be hit hardest. Since a center of Orthodoxy was in Moscow, within the Communist orbit, Orthodox leaders would suffer least. Once East European Orthodox Churches gave evidence of their independence from the World Council of Churches, from the Ecumenical Patriarchate (Constantinople) or other Western entanglements,[211] Orthodoxy was regarded as a relatively safe risk, internationally speaking, and it was necessary to deal only with international contacts of local Orthodox leaders which led westward.

Larger independent Protestant bodies, e.g., Reformed in Hungary, were early regarded as being relatively loyal national groups, free from foreign control and authority. Insofar as government leaders understood that participation in ecumenical activities involved no national disloyalty, local churches were able to participate in ecumenical conversations with limited supervision. In Poland, however, non-Roman Churches were exhorted by the Minister of Justice to re-direct their ecumenical focus from Geneva towards ecumenical traditions of the past among Slavic nations;[212] and in Germany, Protestant Churches were called upon to develop "ecumenicity" with the Orthodox Church of Moscow.[213]

Smaller Protestant groups, which seemed to look to parent churches in the West for their authority and support were either dissolved or abruptly severed from their Western church contacts, e.g., Czechoslovakian Salvation Army and Mormons,[214] Bulgarian Protestants,[215] or Slovak Lutherans (the Lutheran World Federation representative in Slovakia was expelled as a "threat to the national security").[216] Uniate Churches were transferred from Roman Catholic to Orthodox jurisdiction.[217]

---

210. In October, 1945, Polish Vice-Minister Chajn declared that his Government was opposed to any church receiving its directives from abroad (*New York Times*, October 26, 1945; *Chron.*, p. 386).
211. Moscow Conference, 1948.
212. *Chronicle*, pp. 390, 391.
213. *Chronicle*, p. 533.
214. *Chronicle*, pp. 505-508, 510.
215. Tobias, *Fifteen Bulgarian Pastors*, p. 55 (*Chron.*, p. 360).
216. *Chronicle*, p. 505.
217. Ukraine, *Chron.*, p. 262; Rumania, *Chron.*, p. 329 ff.

But Roman Catholicism involved both a religious authority and a political State situated in a Western country with a "Western" anti-Communist approach to the revolution and subsequent reforms. Roman Catholic leaders in East Europe had no power to make or approve administrative, economic, political or spiritual changes involving the Church without reference back to Rome. Roman Catholicism, as a foreign State (the Vatican), within East European states, was directing its prelates, ambassadors and agents in what appeared to be a definite attempt to control and direct the people's loyalty towards the Vatican—in any case away from and external to Communism.

Had Vatican City been situated within the Communist orbit, the situation of Roman Catholics in East Europe might conceivably have been little different from that of Orthodox Christians in East Europe. It is not at all unthinkable that Roman Catholic Churches would then have been able to maintain concordats with Eastern governments simultaneously with allegiance to the authority of their Pope.

In reality, the Vatican has had two (perhaps theoretical) alternatives: it could regard itself as a political power and be dealt with by Communist governments on a par with other governments, but have no religious contacts within Communist countries; or it could maintain contacts of a strictly spiritual nature with nationalized Catholic Churches, but engage in no political, economic or administrative affairs in East Europe. It could not do both, and in fact has been able to do virtually neither. It has not succeeded in the role of political state: political concordats and exchanges of envoyees has practically ceased. Roman Catholics in East Europe must of necessity become "patriotic" citizens of the country in which they live and not of Vatican City, and their churches must become "loyal" national churches. Severance of administrative, economic and political contacts with the Vatican was inevitable. That has been a long and bloody battle. But a strictly religious relationship was also impossible for reasons inherent in Roman Catholicism, as well as in the East European situation. In October, 1944, M. Polyansky, Chairman of the Soviet Government's Commission on Religious Affairs (for non-Orthodox Churches) stated that Roman Catholic Churches in the USSR had the same rights as other churches and might communicate with the Vatican so long as they dealt only with purely religious matters. However, it was so inconceivable that such communications could be kept on a purely religious plane that they have been practically non-existent.[218] And in other countries severance or control of foreign contacts has also been effected by the ousting of

---

218. *New York Times*, Oct. 3:12:5, 1944 (*Chron.*, p. 259).

foreign religious representatives, censoring mails, and intimidation.

When difficult church leaders were either out of the way or re-oriented, clerical solidarity and potential resistance was shattered and replaced by a strong body of "patriotic" clergy to back up government-church action. When international contacts were severed, and indigenous church leadership was "liberated" from foreign control, church leadership was in effect "nationalized."

"Nationalized" clergymen declared their loyalty to and were accepted by the governments as devoted to the ultimate good of the nation.[219] If they had criticism or suggestions concerning domestic practices, such suggestions were to be directed in a constructive spirit to appropriate offices of the government where they would be considered and acted upon. Criticism was not to be placed in the hands of foreign powers or underground movements interested in overthrowing the government. In short, national church leaders must accept their governments as their *de facto*, if not legitimate authority, responsible for and seeking after the welfare of the country. If there was a conflict between civil law and church law, they should obey civil law.[220] On these conditions they received the rights and facilities of full citizenship. Thereafter, as will be seen in a later chapter, international contacts were not only welcomed, but greatly desired by Communist governments.

(e) One final step remained: ensuring the continuity of the nationalized clergy by providing appropriate orientation and training facilities.

Series of conferences organized by governments or by church or priests' associations were held to help the clergy adapt to the new situation and fulfil their responsibilities as loyal clergymen. Attendance was poor except where required. In Rumania an Orthodox Theological Institute was established and special "missionary courses" to guide priests "in the service of the people and of peace" were offered.[221] An examination at the close of the course would "qualify and evaluate (priests) . . . calling some to higher posts, reducing others to lower places." Publications, ec-

---

219. Rumania, *E.P.S.*, No. 4, 1948, *Chron.*, pp. 324, 328; Hungary, *Chron.*, pp. 441, 452, 453, 479; Czechoslovakia, *Chron.*, p. 504; East Germany, *Chron.*, p. 534; Poland, Decree of National Council of Poland, Feb. 10, 1953 (*R.N.S.*, 6:2:53). The loyalty pledge was not a Communist innovation. In Rumania and other countries Church leaders formally pledged allegiance to nation, King or Constitution under previous regimes (*Chron.*, p. 319).

220. Russian Patriarch Tikhon was tried and sentenced for maintaining that canon law stood above civil law. Laws of other countries: Bulgaria, Law on the Churches, Articles 5, 6, *Chron.*, p. 371; Poland, Workers Party Statements, *Chron.*, pp. 391, 414; Czechoslovakia, *Chron.*, pp. 505, 508, 516; East Germany, *Chron.*, p. 541.

221. *Persecution of Religion in Rumania*, p. 34 (*Chron.*, p. 331).

clesiastical and secular, counselled, instructed and warned the clergy as to appropriate conduct in their new situation.

While theological seminaries were still under independent church control, or until nationally-oriented professors could be readied, many were closed or requisitioned for other uses. In Hungary two of four Reformed Church seminaries were closed and the remaining two combined. The reason given was "lack of financial support," whereas there were three possibilities of total support. According to the Church-State agreement the Government should have been supporting all of them, or local churches would have supported them had they been given the opportunity, or churches abroad would have provided support had they been permitted to do so.

Gradually special instructors were introduced into seminary faculties to teach courses on socialism, history, and politics. When the independent theological institutions of Czechoslovakia were abolished and re-organized, rectors appointed by the Deputy Premier were "to have power of decision in all matters pedagogical and theological" and would head faculty councils. The Deputy Premier was also to decide "spheres of work," appoint instructors and decide who should be admitted. Students were to "work to become patriotic priests or preachers, who would sincerely help the population."[222] Similar practices were followed elsewhere, the degree of "independence" varying with the degree of government confidence in church leadership. If the church administration was considered loyally "national," it might administer its own theological seminaries. If not, the seminaries were run under more direct government supervision. In Bulgaria, the organization and programs of (theological) educational institutions are drawn up according to special regulations approved by the Minister of Foreign Affairs.[223] In Albania, most Roman Catholic priests were to be trained in seminaries "created and administered" under Government supervision.[224]

All over East Europe, as in Bulgaria, "only (national) subjects—honest citizens of good reputation who have not been deprived of rights by a sentence in a court of law—may be ministers or hold office in any church. . . . Ministers, as well as all other officials of the churches, who break the law, offend against public order or public morality or who work against the democratic institutions of the State, may, at the proposal of the Minister of For-

---

222. *Chronicle*, p. 511.
223. Article 14, *Law on the Churches*, Press Service of Bulgarian Legation, London (*Chron.*, p. 373).
224. Associated Press, Aug. 3, 1950 (*Chron.*, p. 382).

eign Affairs be temporarily suspended or dismissed. . . .
If the minister is not suspended by the leadership of the
church concerned, he is suspended by administrative order."[225]

Church leadership has theoretically been nationalized. Occasionally communications come from Christian leaders in East
Europe saying that "never has the world-wide ecumenical fellowship seemed so real!"

Church Administration

Communist governments moved into the nationalization phase
with the assumption that churches could and would be formed
into "nationalized" churches. Russian and Bulgarian Orthodox
Churches had cultural and historical affinities to national life and
even a theology conducive to the concept of national churches.
Orthodox and Uniate Churches of Rumania were to be combined
to form *the* Rumanian Church to which a nationalized Catholic
Church would be added later.[226] In 1946 Communist leaders in
Poland were planning for a Polish National (Catholic) Church
created from the Roman Church.[227] Protestants, Old Catholics,
and Orthodox were to become a part of a larger ecumenical fellowship related to Moscow.[228]

The Czech National Church and Czechoslovakian Orthodox
Church were to be combined as the nucleus for a National Orthodox Church under Moscow's jurisdiction.[229] The Roman Church in
Hungary was to become a National Church, "liberated" from
Rome.[230] All Orthodox Churches, with varying degrees of autonomy, were to look to the Moscow Patriarchate as the new Constantinople and new Rome. These were the long-range goals of an era.

But nationalization of church administration (with few exceptions, and those were already "State" churches) as the final
step towards nationalization has not yet been taken in several
countries. The reason is clear. Statistics, property, buildings, religious orders, social welfare, education, youth, worship and holy
days, publications and radio, church leadership—when these have
been nationalized, the church is a nationalized church. It is necessary then only to codify and set in order a *fait accompli*. And not

---

225. Articles 10, 11, 12, Bulgarian *Law on the Churches, op. cit.* (*Chron.*,
p. 373).
226. *Notes on Soviet Affairs*, No. 138, June, 1952, and *N. Y. Times*, July 10,
1950 (*Chron.*, p. 335).
227. *Chronicle*, p. 397.
228. Also in Lithuania, *Chron.*, p. 310, and Czechoslovakia, *Chron.*, pp. 492,
494, 511, 516.
229. *Instructions to Communists. op. cit.* (*Chron.*, p. 516).
230. *Chronicle*, pp. 442, 449, 456, 458.

all of these steps have as yet been achieved in all East European countries.

"Separation of Church and State." Four nations, the U.S.S.R., Bulgaria, Albania and Hungary, include "Separation of Church and State" in their laws.[231] This is misleading.

In the "obliteration" phase of church-state relations, there was a reason for separation of church and state. The Russian Church was in a relatively strong position. The anti-clerical element in the Revolution demanded separation to protect the State from Church meddling. Later (1927), when the State was in the dominant position Orthodox Church leaders in the U.S.S.R. urged the Government to implement the law intended to separate Church and State so that the Church could get on with its religious work.[232] More important, however, was the assumption by Communist theorists in that period that the Church and religion deprived of political and bourgeois (State) economic support would simply crumble away. When this assumption proved false, a new line was taken, but the expression "separation" lingered.[233] Its recurrence in Bulgaria, long after the U.S.S.R. had given up actual separation as desirable, can hardly reflect more than Bulgarian Premier Dimitrov's Communist formation and training in the U.S.S.R. during those early years. Kolarov, his Foreign Minister, and subsequent Bulgarian history interpreted "separation" to mean that the Government was not to interfere with religious dogma, heresies, etc., that the Church was not to interfere in Government affairs, that the Church *per se* was not to be concerned with the direction of education, welfare and such activities, though individual believers and clergy should participate as citizens under governmental direction, and that "the Church is neither outside the State, nor a state within a state . . . (and) is subordinate to the Constitution." Within this framework the State defines activities permissable to the Church and supports the Church as it sees fit.[234]

---

231. U.S.S.R., Art. 13, 1918 Constitution, *Chron.*, p. 230; Art. 124, 1936 and 1947 Constitution, *Chron.*, p. 294; Bulgaria, *Chron.*, p. 361; Art. 78 of Constitution, *Chron.*, p. 367; Art 2, 1949 Constitution, *Chron.*, p. 371; Albania, Art. 16, 1946 Constitution, *Chron.* p. 381; Hungary, Constitution of 1949, Art. 54, *Chron.*, pp. 451, 478.

232. "Solovetsk Document," as quoted by Anderson, *People, Church and State in Modern Russia*, pp. 70-74 (*Chron.*, pp. 285-287).

233. Soviet Communists recognized that "bourgeois democracy" also professed "separation," but made the distinction that in bourgeois states no actual attempt was made to "carry out (separation) to the end owing to the diverse and actual ties which bind capital and religious propaganda"; whereas the Communist state combined an active program of anti-religious or scientific education with separation (Program of the All-Soviet Communist Party, 1932, Article 13; Anderson, *op. cit.*, p. 50, *Chron.*, pp. 293-294).

234. Kolarov interpretation of the 1949 Law on Churches, Press Service of the Bulgarian Legation, London, Feb., 1949 (*Chron.*, pp. 376-378).

In short, what "separation" seems to mean is that where church and state once claimed inter-dependent co-existence (there was a church-sanctioned regime and an official regime-appointed church), the state is now independent of any religion and the churches are "subordinate to the Constitution"[235] in all things except doctrine. In Rumania, Orthodox leaders regard the Church as not separated from the State, but separated from the schools.[236] In East Germany it is simply stated that "there is no State Church."[237] The constitutions or laws of other countries provide a similar framework by "guaranteeing religious freedom" (doctrine and worship) and requiring state recognition and approval of ecclesiastical constitutions, governments and leaders before a communion may function.

Concordats and Agreements. Existing concordats were abrogated before or during the early processes of nationalization. Obviously they were no longer relevant in a situation so radically changed by war and by reforms in social, educational, property and political practices. The purpose of the church was regarded differently; so, therefore, were relationships between church and state. Concordats with the foreign Vatican State could not be considered valid when the Vatican was no longer to be recognized as a religio-political entity.

Still, Communist governments in the early stages of nationalization made a show of seeking agreements with churches, especially Roman Catholic Churches. If it was the ultimate desire of Communism to see the churches wane and disappear, why should Communists bother about negotiations for new agreements at all? Apparently the negotiations were only stop-gap: between warring church and state, a kind of truce; between cooperative church and state, a definition of scope of work and responsibility.

Essentially, agreements were desired by the governments as a sign that the churches accepted governmental reforms and were ready to continue in the nationalized framework. Agreement negotiations would force the issue on the churches; they must decide either to work with, or declare themselves against the Communist governments. If church leaders would not come to agreement, they could be held responsible for blocking agreement and dealt with as "reactionaries" or "traitors." If they did come to terms, it would be of enormous value to the governments in their domestic and foreign relationships.

---

235. *Ibid.*

236. *Moscow Patriarchal Journal* No. IV, 1949; *E.P.S.*, Sept. 8, 1950 (*Chron.*, p. 333).

237. Constitution of Oct. 7, 1949, Art. 43 (*Chron.*, p. 541).

Negotiations were generally conducted in secret, probably to avoid publicizing basic conflicts and risking public support of the church's position.

General content of the agreements between churches and states, as discussed or ratified, was similar in the several Central European states. (There appear to have been no major negotiations for concordats in Rumania and Bulgaria except as contained in governmental and ecclesiastical laws.) Clauses and compromises dealing with special local conditions differed, but were incidental to the overall purpose. Churches were expected to recognize the government, to pray for, or in other ways, support governmental leaders, to accept and support governmental reforms and programs, and to counteract anti-government activities.[238]

These clauses closely resemble the expectations laid down by Communist governments for a nationalized church leadership.[239] The governments, on their part, were to guarantee religious freedom, to concur in and support the religious activities of the churches, to provide for or approve of specified facilities for religious training and to ensure a prescribed basis of church support.

Key issues on which negotiations got hung up were authority and religious activities. Protestants, particularly Hungarian Lutherans prior to the arrest of Bishop Ordass, sought to have restrictions on welfare, youth, educational and other church activities lifted.[240] In Germany, because of such restrictions, negotiations got no further than the churches' assertion that they were concerned with the reconstruction of a life of peace and freedom, and the Government's assurance that "the churches can fulfill their work on the basis of the Constitution. . . ."[241]

Negotiations with Roman Catholic leaders, however, snagged both on "restrictions" and on "authority." Governments did not wish to deal with the Vatican, but with national leaders of Catholic churches. They sought agreements independently of Rome with churches independent of Rome. Roman Catholic leaders, on the other hand, themselves acknowledged and sought government recognition of the supremacy of the Pope in Catholic affairs. Ultimately, the quarrel between the Polish Government and the Polish hierarchy over the establishment of a permanent ecclesiastical administration in the "Western Territories" was one of authority. The Government ordered a permanent arrangement, the Vatican refused a permanent arrangement. The hierarchy took the side of

---

238. Rumania, *Chron.*, p. 333; Poland, *Chron.*, pp. 387, 399, 410; Hungary, *Chron.*, p. 457; Czechoslovakia, *Chron.*, p. 497.
239. Cf., p. 54, ff.
240. *Chron.*, p. 440.
241. *Chron.*, p. 531.

the Vatican in opposition to the Government.[242]   Until the hierarchy was "re-oriented," or the Government changed its position,
final agreement was impossible.

Where agreement has been impossible, e.g., negotiations in
Czechoslovakia between the State and Roman Catholicism, the
Government's desires have ultimately been incorporated in new
laws and the Church brought to conform. "It is the law!" Church-
State relations from that moment have been considered resolved.
Offenders against the law are subject to prosecution as criminals:
"Resistors will be broken as enemies of the State."[243]

In the light of the East German Evangelical Church's refusal
to enter into an accord with the Government which would provide
a legal framework for prescribing the scope of their religious activities, the statement of the East German Government that "the
churches could fulfill their work on the basis of the Constitution"
probably implies that a new church law is being readied which will
be far more effective in bringing the Church to conform than
would be any mutual agreement.

The Role of Religious Affairs Commissions. As "nationalization" progressed through the effects of Revolution or the efforts
of occupation leaders, governmental offices and the Communist
Party, official government offices were established to deal with
religious affairs on a more permanent and respectable basis. In
the U.S.S.R. there is a "Council for the Affairs of the Russian
Orthodox Church," and another for "religious cults" (Protestant,
Jewish, Roman Catholic, etc.). In Bulgaria it is the "Ministry of
Foreign Affairs and Cults (or Religions)," in Rumania, "Ministry
of Cults," in Czechoslovakia, "Ministry of Religious (alternative-
ly, Church) Affairs."

These are not simply liaison offices between the churches and
governments to which the churches turn when occasion arises,
although these offices do refer relevant questions to other departments of governments on behalf of the churches. Their first
task has been to codify and tidy-up relationships between nationalized or nearly-nationalized churches and states. Once that
is done, the trend has been toward making religion a department
of government along with education, welfare and other departments. This will be dealt with more fully in a later chapter.

An indication of the purposes of the commissions can be

---

242. *Poland Today*, Dec., 1950 (*Chron.*, p. 401).

243. Statement of Czechoslovakian Minister of Justice Cepicka in final
discussions of the church law by the Church Commission of the Central Action
Committee (*Chron.*, p. 503).

gathered from a composite of purposes as set forth when they were established:[244]

Authority—To "acquire authority" (Czechoslovakia) ;

Laws—To propose laws and regulations re. religious affairs and church order (U.S.S.R.) ;
To assure observance of laws on religious matters (U. S. S. R.) ;
To provide liaison between churches and other ministries (U.S.S.R.) ;

Church constitutions—To ratify statutes (Bulgaria) ;
To approve the founding of new parishes, communities, etc. (Rumania) ;
To establish administrative boundaries of dioceses, etc. (Rumania) ;

Church leaders—To investigate eligibility, approve and suspend clerical appointments (Bulgaria, Rumania, Czechoslovakia) ;
To control relationships abroad (Bulgaria, Rumania) ;
To supervise theological education (Bulgaria, Rumania) ;

Church administration—To control budgets (Bulgaria), funds and possessions (Rumania, Czechoslovakia) ;
To control use of symbols, letters and contacts abroad (Bulgaria, Rumania) ;
To study and make recommendations to the government concerning practical church needs: paper, printing, premises (U.S.S.R.).

State Laws and Church Government. Governments have taken action to bring into one master church law all relevant bills, decrees, instructions, court decisions and agreements. Such laws exist in the U.S.S.R., Rumania, Bulgaria,[245] Albania, and, only in part, in Hungary, Poland, Czechoslovakia and East Germany.

Those in existence are very similar; laws in other countries can be expected to follow their pattern. In general, they deal with such matters as religious rights of citizens,[246] religious rights of churches (communities or associations), relations between church and state, relations between churches and foreign bodies, church government and activities, church leaders, church property, relations between religions, religious instruction, church support, punishment for violation of the church law.

---

244. USSR, *Chron.*, pp. 256, 258; Rumania, *Chron.*, p. 332; Czechoslovakia, *Chron.*, pp. 493, 503, 517-518; East Germany, *Chron.*, p. 555.
245. Texts of church laws, *Chron.*, pp. 340 ff., 371 ff.
246. Significantly, these derive as "rights" from the law, not from inherent rights or natural law.

Once new laws have been adopted, churches have been expected to re-draft their constitutions, governments and administration in harmony with State laws, and apply for recognition and approval as church bodies.

Financial Support. Churches of East Europe, prior to the Revolution, were supported by proceeds from church property, voluntary gifts of believers, occasional gifts from abroad, regular government grants, or a scheme of church "taxes" collected by governments for the churches. With some exceptions, notably the Free churches, their sustenance was assured through their close relationship to governmental offices. In the Soviet Union after Church and State were separated in 1918, Government support of the Church was discontinued. As the Church no longer had income from properties, an extremely difficult financial period followed. After Germany attacked the U.S.S.R. in 1941, the Soviet Government, as will be described in the next chapter, welcomed the co-operation of the churches, and was prepared to extend various material concessions in order to seal that cooperation. On what exact basis and to what extent financial support has been given it is impossible to know. Unlike other Communist governments which have made much propaganda of their support of churches, the Soviet Government has apparently tried to maintain before its progeny an air of integrity on the state-church separation principle. The idea that they should support churches at all may have been suggested, not by the practices of the Communists' predecessors (which they revolted against) but by their experiences with Nazi Germany. In April, 1940, the Soviet League of Militant Atheists—puritans on the church-state question—asked Molotov to try to get the Soviets' Nazi ally to cease supporting churches in Germany.[247] But the Nazis were political realists on the church-state question. Some very difficult experiences of churches in Soviet-occupied Germany since 1945 may be attributed to the failure of that mission, and the fact that, as German armies in 1941-42 swept into Russia, they re-opened churches previously closed by Russian Communists and provided fiscal support.[248] At that point the Soviet Union began supporting churches.

In other East European countries, because of the historic relationship between church and state on financial matters, Communist nationalization of material support has not been the most heated issue among church-state controversies. Governments have changed and the degree of church autonomy altered, but the underlying principle has not been brought to focus or clarified. In several instances churches desired continuation of state sup-

247. *New York Times*, April 28, 1940 (*Chron.*, p. 249).
248. *Chronicle*, p. 252.

port.[249] Indeed, so far as the continuation, scope and policy of the institutional life of the Church was concerned, the churches are, if anything, less independent financially than before.

In a typical situation,[250] the government has underwritten the churches' financial obligations. The church budget must then be approved by the state. Any voluntary gifts of believers, or contributions from abroad, reduce the government's obligation by that amount. In Rumania aid from abroad is forbidden,[251] and in other countries it can be received only after government approval and through government channels.[252]

Theoretically, there is no independent income from church properties since the nationalization of property. An exception might be cited in Poland where a "Church Fund" was created to receive the proceeds from nationalized church lands. The "Church Fund," however, is little different from other Government budgets for church support. It is administered by a "nationalized" committee "to ensure the material welfare of meritorious priests . . .," and is subsidized by the Government.[253]

The Rumanian Government simply provides subsidies for "democratic leaders,"[254] the Bulgarian Government for churches "which observe the Constitution and loyally collaborate with the People's Government,"[255] the Czech Government for "approved clergy." Subsidies or outright support are also provided for "approved" clerical training, and travel and other expenses. In Rumania, insurance and pensions are also provided through the General Confederation of Labor.[256]

What is the ultimate aim? In Hungary the Government has made rather elaborate agreements with the churches providing for support on a diminishing scale over a period of twenty years.[257] It is assumed that by the end of that period the churches will be self-supporting. Voluntary gifts are said to be increasing, but there is fear that the Government will eventually take over the support of "approved" or nationalized churches and clergy on a permanent basis.

Whatever administrative relationship may evolve regarding finances, whether the government supports the church direct, or the people support the nationalized church through registered

---

249. Bulgaria, *Chron.*, p. 356; Hungary, *Chron.*, p. 433; Czechoslovakia, *Chron.*, p. 492.
250. Czechoslovakia, *Law No. 218 For the Economic Security of Churches* (*Chron.*, pp. 518 ff.).
251. *Chronicle*, p. 323.
252. E.g., Bulgaria, Article 24 of *Law on the Churches* (*Chron.*, p. 374).
253. *Chronicle*, pp. 397-398, 413.
254. *Chronicle*, p. 323.
255. Kolarov, "Interpretation of the Church Law" (*Chron.*, p. 376 ff.).
256. *Chronicle*, p. 323.
257. *Chronicle*, pp. 468-471, 474.

"voluntary" contributions, it is clear that nationalized churches will not become independent of national purposes and politics. Conversely, the East German churches, which are as yet somewhat independent, are subjected to considerable financial pressure. Voluntary gifts can be made with difficulty. Liquid assets of the churches, which enable them to be independent are being used up, as once in the U.S.S.R. and the Baltics, to cover Government taxes, quotas and assessments on church farms and properties.[258]   Payment of church "taxes" by believers, now optional, is discouraged.

The objective of Communist governments has not been to secure the material welfare of the Church as independent religious associations, but to ensure their dependence on and allegiance to the government.   Once the churches were nationalized, their support was assured.   Czechoslovakian Minister of Justice Cepicka expressed it this way: "We want *living* churches.   We want *them* to grow."[259]

So, the Nationalized Church—"the place of worship of the faithful; the place where they exercise freely their religious beliefs."[260]

Minimum requisites (page 21) have been met: believers have access to sanctuaries, possibilities of worship,[261] facilities for the sacraments, some voice in the selection of their leaders, freedom of conscience or private religious thought, and possibilities for conveying religious faith to their children.

Administratively, the nationalized church is a department of the government.   Church property is *de facto* property of the state.   Roll books, budgets and elections are supervised by the state.   Leaders are appointed by government approval.   Sermons are subject to censorship.   Support is underwritten by the state.[262]

The government has exclusive authority in relation to education, youth work, publications, social welfare, charities, civil records, economics, law and international relations.   There is freedom, but "full religious freedom is dependent on the full recognition of the State interests."[263]

---

258. Cf. p. 24.
259. *Chronicle*, p. 503.
260. Rumania, "Official Statement in the Matter of Religious Liberties," *Scanteia*, February 22, 1949 (*Chron.*, p. 348).
261. "Religious freedom" is still a variable concept. In one extreme case in Hungary (*Chron.*, p. 452) a priest was accused of violating religious freedom because he scheduled masses at the same hour the meetings of the "Pioneers" (Communist children's organization) were held.
262. Parallels on several points may be found in non-Communist states. In Denmark, for example, an 18th century law forbids pastors to preach against the laws of the King. Church delegates to official conferences abroad must be appointed by the State.
263. Official Statement on Church-State relations by Polish Press Agency, *Poland Today*, April, 1950 (*Chron.*, pp. 424-425).

Or, as President Bierut of Poland put it, for a price the Church may have peace. The price—

"complete support of all social, educational, economic and religious changes which the regime seeks to introduce; active support . . . for . . . socializing . . .; weakening of ties (abroad or) with the Vatican; the use of the pulpit for propaganda of the achievements of the People's Democracy; democratization of the . . . church in such a manner that the priests and not the hierarchy rule."[264]

Measured in figures the price has been high. The following figures indicate part of the cost in the whole of East Europe, including destruction during World War II:

	Pre-Revolution	1945-50	Gone
Population	251,581,000	279,966,000	over 20,000,000[265]
Believers	230,754,000	212,814,000	17,940,000[266]
Sanctuaries and Chapels	167,300	73,300	94,000
Clergy	126,400	46,000	80,400
Monks, nuns, Deaconesses	152,100	under 28,600	over 123,500
Schools, Institutions	22,000	under 600	over 21,400
Theological Schools	152	34	118
Land (acres)	14,300,000	under 150,000	over 14,150,000
Publications	1,050	50	1,000

However, nationalization, at whatever price, or static "peace" was hardly the final possibility either to Communist governments or to churches. Vital elements in both made further encounter at deeper levels inevitable.

---

264. Markham, *Communists Crush the Churches*, p. 115 (*Chron.*, p. 396).
265. Pre-Revolution and 1945-50 population figures include U.S.S.R., which, owing to annexations, etc., showed an increase of nearly 50,000,000 during this period. The 20,000,000 "gone" represents death rate over birth rate in the same period, but excluding the USSR. Among these twenty million would have been war victims plus those deported, imprisoned or escaped exclusive of U.S.S.R. If the U.S.S.R. were included as of 1945 the figure would be nearer 70,000,000 (p. 225 of *Chronicle*).
266. This figure also excludes the U.S.S.R. Since the estimate on the number of believers presently in the U.S.S.R. is approximately the same as in 1917, believers who have "disappeared" in the U.S.S.R. have presumably been fully replaced by those from annexed territories or by conversions. However the author could find no reliable estimate as to what that figure might be. It would probably exceed that of the rest of East Europe combined.

"We expect the church to cooperate, as in Russia, with the forces of progress, truth, justice and nationalism."[1]

Chapter IV

COOPERATION OF CHURCHES

Almost immediately after the Communists came into power in the Soviet Union, they faced problems so acute that cooperation with any possible succor, even their worst enemy, had to be seriously considered. The years from 1918 to 1930 are sprinkled with instances of attempts at cooperation with individual religious leaders or specific churches.[2] But "cooperation" during that period was not the dominant characteristic, nor was it the Communist purpose, in the State-Church relationship. State and Church were still separate entities with distinct purposes and methods.

Later, during the nationalization process, when the Church was technically regarded as a necessary evil, there were numerous instances of cooperation. As that process neared completion, and the extra-liturgical aims of the Church were brought into line with those of the Government, it became evident that the Church might play, on a larger term basis, a significant role in extra-ecclesiastical affairs. Under certain circumstances, even religion as an ideological factor was welcomed. The era characterized by cooperation was therefore built upon, and followed the nationalization theory and process.

Conditions for Cooperation

The strategy of cooperation, even premature and isolated instances of cooperation, has been undertaken when three conditions prevailed. The first was when Communist governments had sufficient confidence in their own position as to be unafraid of ties to, or influence of non-Communist bodies.[3]

---

1. Premier Dimitrov of Bulgaria (*Chron.*, p. 356).
2. A notable example was during the great famine of 1921-22 (*Chron.*, p. 232).
3. The reference is to Communist governments, not to Communist parties. The Communist Party has frequently dressed up in a respectable "front" by linking up with other bodies, in order to gain power. The Comintern purist strategy which forbade such cooperation was rescinded in favor of the original Lenin strategy in 1935 after Dimitrov proved the value of the "front" approach.

(90)

The second necessary condition was when the Church was sufficiently "nationalized" as to accept, and to be accepted in the role of co-laborer. This was possible only in so far as the churches could demonstrate their solidarity with the same people with whom the government professed solidarity. In the U.S.S.R. this occurred on June 22, 1941, when Germany invaded the U.S.S.R. Metropolitan Sergius sent a letter to the Government proclaiming the solidarity of the Church with the Russian people and the people's Government. The Government thereupon no longer formally regarded the Church as its primary enemy, nor as a vestige of capitalism. The Church no longer regarded the Government as the principal enemy of the Church, but considered the two together to be the defenders of the people and their faith.

The third condition existed when factors external to the Church-State relationship itself demanded or permitted cooperation for mutually desirable ends, as when famine or military defeat threatened the Russian people, or when Communist governments recognized that Communism alone was not adequate to achieve the ends sought.

Development of a Cooperative Relationship

There is little evidence that Communist leaders had a calculated plan for realizing the "cooperative era," to be implemented as soon as the churches were nationalized. Rather they have accepted it as a necessity arising from their own inadequacy. For a period of ten years in Russia (1930-1941) while cautious Communist leaders warned that the churches should be concerned only with worship, more daring Government leaders were quietly feeling for a new relationship with the churches, and considering possible uses of the churches in the State program. The potential of the churches in time of crisis, likely concessions the Government would have to make for a cooperative relationship, possible ideological corruption—these were some of the unknown factors in their groping. One cannot, therefore, draw a sharp line between the "nationalization" process and the cooperative relationship—even in the U.S.S.R.— much less in other states where cooperation had to be effected as soon as the smallest element in the churches could be considered nationalized.

The first bid for official cooperation was made by the Soviet Government in 1930. The U.S.S.R. was facing crop failure from over-collectivization, and certain famine if diplomatic recognition by Western nations were, as seemed likely, withheld or withdrawn. The first overture was therefore to grant the churches a number of concessions and particularly to curtail the Communist excesses which would prevent a cooperative relationship. Stalin warned Government and Party officials against too hasty "de-Christianization" of the Soviet Union.[4] A law to close churches in one republic was rejected as being against the will of the people.[5] Even Yaroslavsky, who some years earlier had initiated and directed the anti-religious program, spoke out against the very program he had initiated.[6] The Government, or the Orthodox Church, or probably both went so far as to address an appeal to communities of Russian Orthodox refugees outside the U.S.S.R. to be loyal to their motherland and Mother Church.[7] The Government's efforts resulted in limited cooperation in local situations, but the era of cooperation was not yet achieved. The Church was not yet sufficiently "nationalized" to be entirely trusted by the Government.

Again, from 1934 to 1936, a bid was made for closer church relationships, perhaps based primarily on the Government's recognition that if Communism was to win the world, it must make some more adequate place for the Church and religion. Anti-religious education was curtailed, divorce and marriage laws improved, anti-religious demonstrations at Christmas and Easter-time were restricted, voting rights were restored to the clergy and priest's children were permitted to re-enter school.[8] These preparations toward cooperation suffered a temporary setback during the shift from international Communism to national socialism, 1937-1938.[9]

The next tide of cooperative endeavor came immediately after the 1937-38 purges, perhaps calculated in part to assuage the people's bitterness against the Government following these purges. More precisely, however, it was probably intended to mold the Church, so long as it existed, to fit the new nationalistic pattern and so serve it. Orthodox Christianity was declared officially a Russian phenomenon—reliable, loyal, historically Russian.[10] Anti-religious education was again discontinued. The seven-day week, with Sunday as a rest day, was restored. That tide ebbed in 1940 and 1941 with the alliance between Nazi Germany and Russia, and the consequent assumption that religion was not needed to ensure Soviet security.

Cooperation then, in the sense of a more prolonged era, was not really established until the Nazi attack on the U.S.S.R. in 1941. At that time the Church was desperately needed. Anti-religious programs were immediately suspended. Publications of the League

---

4. Anderson, *People, Church and State in Modern Russia*, p. 81 (*Chron.*, p. 239).

5. Timasheff, *Religion in Soviet Russia*, p. 45 (*Chron.*, p. 239).

6. *Ibid.*, p. 45 (*Chron.*, p. 239).

7. Anderson, *op. cit.*, p. 130 (*Chron.*, p. 239).

8. *Chronicle*, pp. 240-242, *passim*.

9. The 14th Congress of the Communist Party first decided to shift its aims from world-wide revolution to creation of a completely socialist nation in 1925. The 1937 purge comprised a radical implementation of that decision.

10. Statement of Oleschuk, Vice-President of the League of Militant Atheists, in *Antireligioznik*, Timasheff, *op. cit.*, pp. 115, 118 (*Chron.*, p. 346).

of Militant Atheists were discontinued "in order to conserve paper" and Yaroslavsky, leader of the League, was ousted for "incompetence."[11] Moscow radio accused the Nazi regime of menacing the very existence of Christianity and seeking the overthrow of Christ the King.[12] The Soviet Government and the Red Army were acclaimed by many churchmen as the "defenders of religion" against the Nazis. A Patriarch of the Orthodox Church was elected (Sept. 1943) and church commissions were established by the Government.

Reasons for Cooperation

Why has the Church been needed by Communist governments? Or rather, what have Communist governments thought the churches able to contribute or accomplish, which Communist governments alone could not accomplish?

In the U.S.S.R. several consequences of church-cooperation were anticipated. In the first place the churches could boost morale in time of crisis. This was particularly evident when Germany attacked Russia, or even earlier, when famine swept the land. In such a crisis, religion as an ideological force was therefore tolerated along with the institutional Church.

Secondly, the churches could encourage or provide material support for the national economy. The churches, particularly the Orthodox Church in the U.S.S.R., contributed funds for the purchase of tanks, guns and other assistance to the war effort.[13] While material support in such limited amounts may have been of secondary value from the Government's point of view, to a hard-pressed nation it was not unimportant. Later in Hungary churches were told by the President of the State Office for Church Affairs that "the church does her best (in the struggle for peace) when she explains to church members that the individual's best contribution . . . is to do his work as conscientiously as possible. This is what the State expects from the Church . . ."[14]

Further, the churches could help encourage a sense of national purpose. Historians have frequently emphasized the deep sense of mission or of messianic nationalism among the Russian people. This historic sense was not absent in Soviet Communism. On the other hand, if the new U.S.S.R. under a Communist administration was to be a new Rome, new Jerusalem, or new Byzantium, its acceptability as such even by the Russian people would be in direct proportion to the evidence of some religious concept at its

11. *ICPIS*, No. 35, Oct. 1941, and *N. Y. Times*, Oct. 1 and 7, 1941 (*Chron.*, p. 253).

12. Timasheff, *op. cit.*, p. 137 (*Chron.*, p. 252).

13. *ICPIS*, No. 6, Feb., 1943 (*Chron.*, pp. 255-256).

14. *EPS*, No. 17, April 25, 1952.

core. Orthodoxy appeared to be willing to provide that quality and was considered an admirable teammate. Since it was also a meeting ground between "Protestant anarchism" and "Roman Catholic despotic" extremes,[15] Moscow could conceivably become the center of world enlightenment, religiously as well as politically and economically. Cooperation between the Soviet Government and the Orthodox Church therefore appeared to be a requisite to the role of world leadership.[16] When the policy on religion and anti-religion in the Soviet Union was revised in 1937, the target of the remnant anti-religious organization became anti-Roman Catholicism.[17] The indigenous Orthodox Church was regarded as a useful collaborator in the Communist struggle against the Catholic Church and other non-Soviet or anti-Soviet religious forces. The Russian Church's denunciation of the Pope's decree of excommunication (July, 1949) carried more weight than anything the Government might have said concerning the Pope's decree, for the Church was able to call the Pope's decree a religious heresy, not only a political strategy, adding that loyalty to the Church and to the Soviet Union were not in conflict.[18] Any pronouncement from the Church in the U.S.S.R. concerning the World Council of Churches or Protestant groups would, it seemed, also carry more weight than statements by the Soviet regime, both within the U.S.S.R. and abroad. The Church's questions concerning the religious and theological bases of such movements would have a hearing.

Another expected value of primary importance was the way in which church cooperation could enhance Soviet international relationships. Shortly after Nazi Germany attacked Russia, Russia appealed to America for assistance in the form of financial support, munitions and other war materiel. America refused to provide such support until assurance was given that Russian churches enjoyed religious freedom.[19] Whether through this experience or others, the Kremlin must have learned that the churches could serve effectively as a front-line diplomatic corps in international understanding and "defensive expansionism."

Following the re-establishment of the Orthodox Holy Synod and Patriarchate in 1943, church delegations were sent to Jerusalem, Antioch, Alexandria, Egypt, Syria, Bulgaria, Rumania, Yugoslavia, Albania, Britain and the U. S. A.[20] Many small Orthodox

15. *Patriarch Sergius and His Spiritual Legacy*, Moscow Patriarchate, as quoted by *EPS*, No. 33, Sept. 1947 (*Chron.*, p. 264).

16. Later developments seem to indicate that by this time the failure of international Communism prior to 1939 was regarded as due in considerable measure to its lack of a suitable religious component (Chapter V).

17. *Bezboznik*, No. 12, 1938 (*Chron.*, p. 245).

18. *New York Times*, Aug. 7, 1949 (*Chron.*, p. 269).

19. *ICPIS*, No. 42, Nov., 1941; *N. Y. Times*, Oct. 5, 1941 (*Chron.*, p. 253).

20. *Chronicle*, pp. 256, 260-267, *passim*.

groups have been united or re-united to the Patriarchate of Moscow: among them the "Living Church" and others in the U.S.S.R., the Sub-Carpathian Orthodox Church, scattered groups in West Europe, Orthodox in Estonia, Czechoslovakia, a group of Finnish monks, Uniates in the Ukraine, Hungarian Orthodox, Polish Orthodox and certain Syrian Orthodox of India.[21] Conferences were held at one time with the Rumanian Orthodox Church concerning the possible union of all Orthodox Churches in the Balkans to the Moscow Patriarchate.[22] Overtures were made to the Serbian Church in the absence of Patriarch Gavrilo,[23] and to Russian Orthodox communities in America in an attempt to get them to join the Moscow Patriarchate.[24] Eventually, Russian chapels were installed in the respective capital cities of Rumania and Bulgaria. Representatives of the Moscow Patriarchate were installed not only in these newer "re-united" churches and chapels, but also in Jerusalem, and in Abyssinia and other places.[25] A missionary council for the Moscow Patriarchate was established[26] and at least one Chinese bishop was consecrated.[27] Attempts were also made to send a bishop to Japan but without success.[28] All of this international activity culminated in the Orthodox conference called by the Patriarchate in Moscow in 1948.[29] Delegates were informed that the Western capitalist *bloc* was seeking control of the World Council of Churches as a religious tool to be used against the East, and subsequently expressed a desire to set up a counterpart religious force for the Soviet *bloc*.

Further advantages of cooperation were anticipated in relation to the Cominform peace offensive. Church participation could give Cominform countries an enormous moral advantage in persuading popular feeling. Meetings held in Stockholm, Slovakia, Warsaw, Paris, Vienna, Budapest and other cities have been either set up or attended by church leaders. Statements have been prepared by churchmen and every attempt made to identify the peace offensive of the Communist State with ultimate purposes of the Church.[30]

---

21. *Chronicle*, p. 267.
22. *N. Y. Times*, March 27, 1948 (*Chron.*, p. 266), and Feb. 16, 1949 (*Chron.*, p. 332).
23. *ICPIS*, No. 47, 1945 (*Chron.*, pp. 261, 355).
24. *Chronicle*, pp. 239, 261.
25. *Chronicle*, pp. 267, 438.
26. *Chronicle*, p. 264.
27. *Religion in Russia*, no. 1, 1951, p. 7 (*Chron.*, p. 273).
28. *EPS*, No. 12, 1947.
29. *Chronicle*, p. 267.
30. The Moscow Patriarchate has published a 125-page book, *Die Russische Rechtglaubige Kirche in Kampf um den Frieden*, for distribution to Western churchmen. It contains resolutions, sermons, exhortations and prayers for peace.

Participation of the churches in programs of domestic reform has not been included in this list as it has been dealt with in earlier chapters. However, two other aspects of cooperation should be added which have been apparent in Central European Communist countries.

Communism despises that religion which prevents the oppressed from rising up and overthrowing the oppressor—so long as the oppressor is not a Communist regime. But Communist forces have been glad enough to have the cooperation of an "opiate" which would take some of the sting out of their own reforms, or lack of them, and make them more palatable to the masses.[31] In this sense they recognized that as an "opiate," religion could well serve whatever regime was in power, and not necessarily bourgeois or capitalist. Said East German Communist leader Hauschild to a meeting of Party leaders in Thuringia,[32] "Time-conditioned aspects demand that . . . with diplomatic cunning . . . we . . . protect religion."

Finally, Communist strategists were not beyond using the Church ultimately as an effective means of its own destruction. For, if by cooperation with the churches that kind of church could be maintained which appeared corrupt within, socially irresponsible, "superstitious" and unscientific, caring only for pomp and personal gain, and not for the needs of the people, then in that kind of church the Communist regime would have an excellent ally for the Church's own destruction. The incensed people themselves could hardly tolerate the existence of such an institution and leadership, claiming virtues which were no longer there.

In conclusion, cooperation is a phase in church-state developments originally accepted by Communist governments because they faced external conditions over which they did not have full control. Having tried cooperation and tasted its considerable advantages, it seems likely that Communist governments will want to continue this relationship to serve their own ultimate aims even in circumstances and conditions over which they do, as they see it, have control. "The Church is an institution with permanent usefulness in the life of the people. It is part of the State itself keeping pace with the spirit of the times."[33]

It is also more. Whereas the Communist State may regard the nationalized church as an integral part of its own structure, cooperation as it is presently practiced constitutes a *de facto* recognition of an *esse* of the Church which is still separate and independent.

---

31. U.S.S.R., *Agitators' Guide*, May, 1937 (*Chron.*, p. 296); Esthonia, *Chron.*, p. 313.

32. *The Church Herald*, March 10, 1950 (*Chron.*, p. 542).

33. New Year's greeting of Prime Minister Petru Groza to Patriarch Nicodim, Rumania, January, 1948. *EPS*, No. 3, January, 1948 (*Chron.*, p. 324).

"It is not religion that creates man, but man who creates religion . . ."[1]

Chapter V

COMMUNISTS CREATE A NEW RELIGION

Previous chapters have dealt with the purposes and the approaches of Communist states towards the *churches*. This chapter is concerned with Communist attempts to cope with *religion* itself.

Communist governments have treated "religion" and "churches" separately, with resulting dualism in policies, methods and time schedules. At one point, for example, the Soviet Government could collaborate officially with the Church, while permitting aggressive warfare against religion. In other circumstances it tolerated the cause of religion while castigating the churches. Anti-religious campaigns have been frequently carried on simultaneously with programs of close cooperation with the churches. Or, as during the purges of 1937-38, the Government professed its constitutional guarantees of "freedom of religion," while effectively incapacitating the churches by "prosecuting" their leaders for alleged criminal acts.

Two facts may account for this seeming paradox: strategically, to make simultaneous attacks on religion and the Church was more than the people would stand, and would result in political suicide. Preferred strategy, therefore, called for relaxing on one while pressing the other.

Secondly, in spite of the fact that many of the same people were involved, it was generally the Government which dealt with the churches at the level of institutional life, and the Communist Party and its related agencies[2] which dealt with religion as an idea. By this arrangement the Government was able to maintain some facade of neutrality in the conflict between anti-religious and religious interests. Theoretically it had no policy regarding religion and anti-religion except to guarantee their "freedom." It did have a policy regarding churches. In spite of evidences to the contrary, such as the preferential position given to "anti-religious *propaganda*" as opposed to "religious *confession*" in the 1929 Constitution,[3] Governmental forces generally have been a restraining

---

1. Karl Marx, *Critique of Hegel's Philosophy of Law.*
2. The Communist Party did not associate itself officially with the anti-religious program until April, 1926 (*Chron.*, p. 236).
3. Article V, Constitution of the U.S.S.R. (*Chron.*, p. 238).

influence on the anti-religious activities of Communist fanatics and even Party agencies. Indeed, where there has been, and if there is now some rapprochement between religion and Soviet purposes, the moderating influence of the Government may be largely responsible.[4]

Before considering any "New Religion" which has evolved in East Europe, consideration should be given to the circumstances and experimentation out of which it came.

Anti-Religion in the U.S.S.R. was tried and found inadequate.

During the few months immediately following the Revolution, when the Communist Party and Government were bent on destroying the Church, apparently it was assumed that when the Church was gone, religion would collapse. When it proved strategic to shift from a direct "obliteration" program to oblique "nationalization" in dealing with the churches, the direct thrust was shifted towards religion itself, it being then assumed that when religion was overcome, the churches would disappear. But, it was soon obvious that the roots of religion would not be pulled up overnight by "casual decrees and administrative coercion," that "the liberation of the workers from religious superstition" would require an intensive, and long educational process.[5]

Therefore, the Communists reasoned, a comprehensive program of anti-religious propaganda must be launched. Such a program was expected by Stalin not only to overcome religious "superstition," but in so doing, eventually to bring about the dissolution of the clergy and the demise of the churches. The Government therefore would seek to mollify and adjust the churches to their surroundings insofar as possible while the anti-religious propaganda program dissolved their *raison d'etre*,[6] and "conscious and deliberate planning of all the social and economic activities of the masses"[7] created the perfect Society in which no new "opiate" or "superstition" would be necessary. Apparently it did not occur to the Communist Party before 1937[8] that the more the Govern-

---

4. This is almost a complete reversal of the respective positions of Communist theorists and Communist politicians of the pre-1918 era. At that time the ideologists (along with more moderate socialists) maintained that religion would wither away when economic and social structures were reformed; while Lenin and other Communist "administrators" desired a more aggressive program.

5. Statement of the Central Committee of Trade Unions, 1923, Timasheff, *Religion in Soviet Russia*, p. 95 (*Chron.*, p. 234).

6. The "contradictory" roles of Government and Party are evident at many points: e.g., in Nov., 1922, an anti-religious seminary was opened in Moscow; in April, 1923, churches were permitted to hold elections and re-organize; and in June Patriarch Tikhon was released from prison.

7. Program of the All-Soviet Communist Party, Article 13, 1932, Anderson, *op. cit.*, p. 50 (*Chron.*, p. 293).

8. *The Agitators' Guide*, No. 23 (*Chron.*, p. 243).

ment could do to foster the development of a corrupt, superstitious and immoral rather than a reformed church, the more it would help undermine the religious foundation of the churches.

Techniques to be used in the anti-religious program were set forth in 1925 when the "Friends of the Godless" organization and its publication were established. They were (a) to demonstrate that religion was the enemy of the workers, (b) to teach that science explains all mysteries, and (c) to indoctrinate youth with the idea that religious belief was a form of disloyalty to the State (as in early Roman times).[9]

In 1937, the (anti-religious) *Agitators' Guide* reiterated these three methods, adding a fourth which has been discussed in a previous chapter, namely, "to show the vile moral image of the priests."[10]

Between its inception in 1922 and its dissolution in 1942, the organized anti-religious program was expanded from a diminutive bureau of an atheistic fanatic to a propaganda empire reaching around the world.[11] Offices had been established in every town of any consequence in the Soviet Union. Atheistic publications, before their suppression (for "lack of paper") in October, 1941, could boast distribution of 1700 books in several million copies and 43,000,000 copies of anti-religious journals. In the early thirties, at the peak of the anti-religious program, there were twenty-six workers' anti-religious universities, one Red Army anti-religious university, six anti-religious schools of higher education, one anti-religious correspondence institute, and thousands of local groups and trained personnel giving anti-religious instruction to 150,000 anti-religious leaders. The League of Militant Atheists claimed five million active members, and in its 1929 "five year plan" was seeking to raise that to 17,000,000. A special school to train "missionaries of atheism" for the Central Ukraine was opened in 1936. In public school rooms, the League had succeeded in getting teachers with a religious point of view ousted, and anti-religious text books introduced. Anti-religious carnivals, processions ridiculing and mocking religious ideas, miracles and "superstition" were presented before the public, particularly at festive religious occasions. Religious doubts, cynicism and superstition were given particular attention in the press, the class-room, public debates and lectures.

To all external appearances the Militant Atheists had an effective crusading program. However, no one was more aware

---

9. Timasheff, *op. cit.*, p. 35 (*Chron.*, p. 235).

10. *Agitator's Guide*, No. 23, as quoted by Anderson, *People, Church and State in Modern Russia*, p. 118 (*Chron.*, p. 243).

11. *ICPIS*, No. 25, June, 1941; Anderson, *op. cit.*, p. 90 (*Chron.*, pp. 240, 252.

than their leaders that long before the Government suppressed their work at the outbreak of war in 1941, the anti-religious program had practically disintegrated. There were many reasons, which became obvious from the Soviet's own assessment of developments.

Already in 1934 the anti-religious program in the public schools was proving so harmful to Communism that it was severely restricted. It was arousing too much "unhealthy curiosity!"[12] And at the adult level the anti-religious program was proving itself intellectually unsatisfying.[13] The following year, anti-religious Christmas and Easter demonstrations were banned.[14] One can guess that these, too, were creating interest among the youth, encouraging religious determination among adults. During the same year, *Pravda* reported that courts were facing difficulties in prosecuting Communists accused of continuing their religious activities because Communist members of the prosecution were also participating in religious rites.[15] This was during the peak of the anti-religious program!

In 1936 and 1937 an anti-religious opera which satirized the conversion of Russia to Christianity was suppressed by the Soviet Central Arts Committee.[16] The making of anti-religious films was discontinued. A special investigating committee reported that anti-religious activities in many villages had ceased, that local bureaus could not be located, that anti-religious museums were closed, and clubs which had been erected at great cost were unused.[17] In Stalingrad, members of the (Communist) Stakhanov movement were promised that they could have their (Orthodox Christian) Easter meats and cakes blessed by the priest before those of ordinary Christians as a special award for hard work.[18]

When investigations were made as to why so many youth were becoming Christian, it was revealed that they were attracted to the kindness and sympathy of religious people as against the dictatorial attitude of Communist youth leaders.[19] Members of Communist youth organizations were accused by their leaders of mis-

---

12. *N. Y. Times*, April 29, 1934, and *Anti-religioznik*, No. 7, 1940, as reported by *ICPIS*, No. 2, Jan., 1941 (*Chron.*, pp. 240, 250).

13. *Anti-religioznik*, Feb. 1941; *ICPIS*, No. 4, 1941 (*Chron.*, p. 251). The reason is evident from the techniques used; e.g., Holy Communion was attacked because it "spreads infection and encourages drunkenness"; an aviator was quoted as an authority on atheism because he had been up in the sky and found no God there (Pares, *Russia, Its Past and Present*, p. 109).

14. Timasheff, *Religion in Soviet Russia*, p. 46 (*Chron.*, p. 241).

15. *New York Times*, June 5, 1935 (*Chron.*, p. 240).

16. *Ibid.*, Nov. 10, 1936 (*Chron.*, p. 241).

17. *Izvestia*, March, 1937, as reported by *N. Y. Times*, March 11, 1937 (*Chron.*, 242).

18. *Comsomol Truth*, as reported by Timasheff, *op. cit.*, p. 88 (*Chron.*, p. 243).

19. *Ibid.*, p. 90 (*Chron.*, p. 242).

interpreting "freedom of religion" to mean freedom to abstain from anti-religious work.[20]

Between 1929 and 1936 membership in the League of Militant Atheists, according to the League's own figures, dropped from a high of five million to two million—about one per cent of the population, while Christians numbered between fifty and seventy percent.[21] The one remaining training center (of thirty-four in 1933) for anti-religious leaders was having difficulty in getting students in spite of its generous accommodations and scholarships.[22] The Red Army newspaper demanded that the League provide a new militant program of anti-religious education;[23] the League reported that the reason its program was not more successful was that local organizations were enrolling incompetent "scoundrels" as their leaders.[24] The League further complained that publishers—officially appointed publishers—were refusing even to consider anti-religious materials.[25]

Linked with general apathy towards the anti-religious program, the rising interest in religion and the spread of superstition among atheists was cause for no little alarm. At the same time, the political and military situation was rapidly deteriorating. A new tack on the religious question, among others, must obviously be considered.

Possibilities of a syncretized Christian-Communism were explored and abandoned.

Dark days were ahead. The Soviet Government could not do battle simultaneously on ideological, as well as military and political fronts. Thus the reason for urgency in resolving the dilemma of religion. It was a difficult dilemma. From the failure of the anti-religious program it had become evident that some form of religion was necessary. Anti-religion or even neutral agnosticism had proved inadequate to the people's intellectual, spiritual, mystical, emotional and artistic needs.[26] Anti-religion had aroused rather than dissipated religious interest. It provided no motiva-

---

20. *Pravda* report, as noted by Timasheff, *op. cit.*, p. 71 (*Chron.*, p. 243).

21. *Pravda* report from *N. Y. Times*, March 3, 1937 (*Chron.*, p. 242).

22. Timasheff, *op. cit.*, p. 105 (*Chron.*, p. 244).

23. As reported by *N. Y. Times*, July 23, 1938 (*Chron.*, p. 244).

24. Timasheff, *op. cit.*, p. 122 (*Chron.*, p. 243).

25. *Antireligioznik*, as reported by Timasheff, *op. cit.*, p. 106 (*Chron.*, p. 244).

26. A young Marxist engineer explained that Marxism did not provide satisfactory solutions for problems related to sickness and death, but that the solutions sought "had nothing in common with what we regarded as the only expression of religious feeling, namely church going. We were more inclined to seek the answer in mysticism, theosophy, and spiritualism, which were indeed prohibited too, but impressed us because of their scientific appearance" (*Church Chronicle* of Slovakia, No. 2, 1943; *ICPIS*, No. 18, May, 1943).

tion for human action. It offered no kindness, sympathy or love
for youth.

The people apparently must have a "religion" which would
cope with these matters. The Soviet Government, if it was to be
all it hoped to be, perhaps even if it was to survive, must have
some ideological base.

This, however, did not mean that the Government and the
Party would do an immediate about-face by espousing religions.
They sought to create an atmosphere, free from past suspicion
and hate, in which courtship between religion/church on the one
hand, and Communism/government on the other was possible.

This courtship, short-lived though it was, is highly illuminating in relation to possible future developments. The rapidity with
which conversations progressed is striking. First, Christianity
was re-interpreted as the basis for the Communist Society. In
the middle of December, 1938, after three joint sessions, the Central Committee of the League of Militant Atheists and the Historical Institute of the Academy of Sciences, obviously under instructions from higher up, endorsed a new statement of policy on the
meaning of Christianity.[27] The statement first declared previous
Communist policy in error in holding that Christianity was a religion of exploiters and an escapism. The elements of Christianity
which had made it successful were commended, namely it was a
new movement; it forbade racial and national discrimination; it
anticipated new forms of marriage; it recognized the dignity of
"abstract man," and proclaimed the equality of individuals; it
caused revolt against the existing social order; it was democratic
and revolutionary; it preserved its ideals of human dignity and
universalism; it introduced new ideas which provided bases for
building up a new society. It seems apparent that the authors
were thinking in terms of and spelling out a potential common denominator as between Christianity and Communism which might
allow either for a shift from one to the other, or for a syncretizing
of the two.

Secondly, "anti-religion" was re-interpreted as being against
the religious foes of Orthodox Christianity, not against religion
per se. This came in a statement from the anti-religious publication *Bezboznik* in 1938. "There is no reason to be afraid of objectively showing the role of the Church in Russian history. Anti-
religious propaganda is permissible . . . however, it must be directed not against the Orthodox clergy, but against Catholic
monks and the Roman Pope."[28] This was obviously a bid to keep
the few remaining anti-religious crusaders on the Communist

---

27. Timasheff, *op. cit.*, pp. 114, 115 (*Chron.*, pp. 244, 245).
28. *Bezboznik*, No. 12, 1938, as quoted by Timasheff, *op. cit.*, pp. 116, 117
(*Chron.*, p. 245).

bandwagon, while at the same time making a tentative place for Orthodox religion.

Then came a period of self-denunciation by the anti-religious forces. In January, 1939, *Anti-religioznik* declared that it was not and had not been fighting against religion.[29] Again in May, Oleschuk, Vice-President of the League, denounced his organization's former allegations "that the Christianization of U.S.S.R. was a reactionary step, as unfortunately, has been asserted by our anti-religious activity."[30]

In April all attempts to liquidate religion were out-lawed by Governmental decree.

At the same time Marxist doctrine was re-interpreted in terms of idealism. President Kalinin of the U.S.S.R. Supreme Soviet stated[31] that Marxism should no longer be taught as a doctrine, but as the inculcation of love for the Socialist Fatherland, friendship, comradeship, humanism, honesty and cooperation in work, respect for the Soviet Government and love for Comrade Stalin. Were the Government leaders trying to raise Communist practice to the level attributed by them to Christianity as summarized[32] by the Central Committee of the League of Militant Atheists and the Historical Institute?

Following this re-interpretation of Marxism in terms of idealism, the Christian religion was re-interpreted as a "cult of the abstract man" (which) emphasizes his ideal properties.[33] In its circular of instructions to propagandists, the League dissociated Christianity from other religions, and in defining it as a cult of the abstract man, suggested a possible relationship to their own "cult" which concerned itself with the "abstract man."

Thereupon the League's task was re-interpreted; whereas theretofore the League existed for no other purpose than the ultimate extinction of all religions, the League in April, 1939, became officially responsible for seeing that religion (presumably Orthodox Christian religion of the abstract man) was not suppressed by any administrative measures.[34]

The program of the Communist Party was re-interpreted. In its May, 1939 issue, *Anti-religioznik* declared that the Communist Party had always opposed both those who considered religion a

29. *Anti-religioznik*, No. 1, 1939, as quoted by Timasheff, *op. cit.*, p. 118 (*Chron.*, p. 245).

30. *Anti-religioznik*, as quoted by Timasheff, *op. cit.*, p. 115 (*Chron.*, p. 246).

31. In a speech at a conference of teachers; Timasheff, *op. cit.*, p. 124 (*Chron.*, p. 245).

32. Page 102.

33. *Circular to Anti-religious Propagandists*, League of Militant Atheists, as quoted by Timasheff, *op. cit.*, p. 115 (*Chron.*, p. 245).

34. Timasheff, *op. cit.*, p. 122 (*Chron.*, p. 245).

private affair of citizens, and those who demanded its immediate extermination by administrative measures.[35] Could this mean anything but that religion was now considered a public matter, not only not to be exterminated, but to be adapted by, for and according to government purposes?[36]

Then Marxist atheism and Christianity in the U.S.S.R. were further linked together and re-interpreted as being different from "bourgeois atheism" and non-Russian Christianity. Vice-President Oleschuk of the League of Militant Atheists accused Marxist atheists of being bourgeois atheists insofar as they denied Christianity in general without considering the special circumstances of Russian Christianity.[37]

Russian Communism denied responsibility for previous malfeasance toward churches. The 1937-38 "persecution" of Christians was attributed to non-Soviet Communist sources. *Antireligioznik* reported that all past activities against the churches and their leaders was carried out by Trotskyites, etc., to increase the people's hostility to the Communist Government.[38] Almost immediately, the trials and condemnation of "vandals" (including Communists) who had attacked churches was given wide publicity in the U.S.S.R.[39]

By this time, scarcely six months after the new policy was declared, adequate evidence of change had been given for a leading churchman to re-interpret Communism. The Orthodox Patriarch of Georgia said to a special representative sent by *Bezboznik* (The Godless journal) that he expected a revived religion to fuse with Communism in the future, since there was no conflict of doctrine. The editor added that this opinion was widespread among the clergy and the people.[40]

If this was accurate reporting, then in six-months' time a near miraculous feat had been accomplished: Russian Communism recognized that it had a religion, and that that religion was related somehow to Christianity!

Then came a new turn. President Kalinin stated that religion should not be destroyed, but apparently not swallowed *in toto* either. It should be replaced by something else. "We cannot root

---

35. *Anti-religioznik*, May, 1939, as reported by Timasheff, *op. cit.*, p. 118 (*Chron.*, p. 246).

36. Some time later (May 27, 1948), Minister of Justice Cepicka of Czechoslovakia stated: "Religion has its function in society during a certain stage in the development of human society . . . That is why we do not consider religion a private matter, but a public affair . . ." *N. Y. Times*, May 28, 1948 (*Chron.*, p. 494).

37. *Anti-religioznik*, as reported by Timasheff, *op. cit.*, p. 119 (*Chron.*, p. 246).

38. *Ibid.*, p. 97 (*Chron.*, p. 246).

39. *Ibid.*, p. 123 (*Chron.*, p. 246).

40. *Ibid.*, p. 113 (*Chron.*, p. 246).

out religion until we provide another religion." He then referred to Lenin's concept of the theater as the religion of the future society.[41] Shortly after Kalinin's statement (August, 1939), as though making excuses for another about-face, *Bezboznik* explained that it was the duty of every Marxist to evaluate the particular situation at any given time and place.[42] A few days later, *Pravda* urged that the war on religious belief be intensified,[43] and less than a year after the announcement of the Christian-Communism policy, Russian journals were attacking the religious celebration of Christmas.[44] The official review *Soviet Culture*, in its first issue of 1940, declared categorically "that socialism and religion have nothing in common." And the Commissariat of Education instructed teachers to improve their anti-religious programs for children as well as for parents.[45] In its fourth issue of 1940, *Anti-religioznik* confirmed that there had been an attempt "to fuse" Christianity and Communism, but that this was impossible since Communism and Christianity "are irreconcilably hostile to each other."[46] Similarly, Vice-President Oleschuk of the League of Militant Atheists, who wrote in *Anti-religioznik* in May, 1939, "It is especially wrong to think that the Christianization of Russia was a reactionary step, as, unfortunately, has been asserted by our anti-religious activity . . .,"[47] declared in October, 1940, that it was incorrect to ascribe progressive tendencies to Christianity as such, that it had played a progressive role only in specific epochs. Religion, he added, now hindered rather than enhanced progress and culture . . . Any attempt to find a compromise between Christianity and Communism was counter-revolutionary.[48]

Why the sudden change? Perhaps the syncretists or zealous but inexperienced Communists had gone too far before there was adequate discussion among Communists on a world-wide scale. This may have been one factor. The principal reason, however, is probably to be found at the military and political level. At the end of 1938, the Soviet Union needed every religious support it could muster in the face of almost certain invasion and defeat. By the end of 1939 it felt secure in its new-found atheistic ally, Nazi Germany.

For the next year and a half, anti-religious forces in the U.S.S.R. went at their work with much loud noise, but little ap-

---

41. Timasheff, *op. cit.*, p. 124 (*Chron.*, p. 246).
42. *Ibid.*, p. 120 (*Chron.*, p. 247).
43. *Pravda*, Aug. 20, 21, as reported in *N. Y. Times*, Aug. 21, 1939 (*Chron.*, p. 247).
44. As reported by *N. Y. Times*, Jan. 12, 1940 (*Chron.*, p. 248).
45. Timasheff, *op. cit.*, p. 129 (*Chron.*, p. 248).
46. *Anti-religioznik*, No. 4, 1940, as quoted by *ICPIS*, No. 47, Dec., 1940 (*Chron.*, p. 249).
47. Timasheff, *op. cit.*, p. 115 (*Chron.*, p. 246).
48. *Ibid.*, p. 131 (*Chron.*, pp. 250-251).

parent vengeance or enthusiasm. The League of Militant Atheists reported increases in numbers of participants and publications, and prepared new programs of anti-religious education, training of leaders, etc. Some attempts to undo previous syncretistic propaganda were made by the anti-religious magazines in warning that a refined, active (and apparently pro-Communist) religion was more dangerous than anti-Communist primitive religions.[49]

On the other hand, Communist leaders, except in newly acquired territories,[50] were not quite ready to revert to the radical anti-religious practices and policy of the pre-1938 era. Mikhailov, head of the Communist youth movement, Comsomol, was careful to leave out Orthodox Russian Christianity in his nomination of religious enemies of Communism and Nazism.[51] *Pravda* reported that neither the Communist Party nor Comsomol were supporting the League, hence the wane in anti-religious propaganda.[52] And even in the midst of making elaborate plans for intensifying their anti-religious programs, Yaroslavsky, leader of the League noted that there was some sentiment within the Communist Party for the dissolution of the League.[53]

That something had been learned by the Communists in their few months of courtship with religion is evident from their new strategy of anti-religion. The program outlined at the 1941 Con-

---

49. *Bolshevik*, Dec., 1940, as reported by *ICPIS*, No. 5, Feb., 1941 (*Chron.*, p. 251).

50. As new territories were taken over, they were subjected to the same techniques as in the early untried days of anti-religion in post-Revolutionary U.S.S.R. In Estonia, for example, a pamphlet entitled "The Ten Commandments of Communism" was published by the Central Committee of the Comsomol. It stated (according to *Lithuanian Bulletin*, Jan.-March, 1949):
(1) "Never forget that the clergy are the greatest enemies of the Communist state.
(2) Try to convert your friends to Communism. Remember that Stalin, who has given a new Constitution to the Russian people, is the leader of the godless, not only in the U.S.S.R. but in the whole world.
(3) Advise your friends to avoid clergymen and Christians.
(4) Beware of spies! Denounce saboteurs!
(5) Distribute atheistic literature among the population.
(6) A good Comsomol youth is a fighter for the cause of atheism. He must know how to use his weapons and harden himself in the art of war.
(7) Fight in the religious element wherever you can and prevent its influence on your comrade.
(8) A good godless youth must also be a good policeman. It is the duty of every godless youth to defend the security of his country.
(9) The godless movement grows also by means of monetary contributions which are indispensable for foreign propaganda, and which, owing to present conditions, can only work underground.
(10) If you are not a convinced adherent of the godless movement, you cannot be a good Communist and Soviet citizen. Atheism is inseparable from Communism. Both these ideals form the foundation of Soviet power."
51. Timasheff, *op. cit.*, p. 133 (*Chron.*, p. 249).
52. Timasheff, *op. cit.*, p. 101 (*Chron.*, p. 250).
53. *Bezboznik*, as reported in *ICPIS*, No. 33, Sept., 1940 (*Chron.*, p. 250).

gress of the Central Council of the League of Militant Atheists was on the basis "win the individual believer for atheism." Atheist missionaries were to show "loving understanding" for believers' problems, refraining from entering into fellowship or polemics (lest they themselves be converted to Christianity).[54] Godlessness was to be lifted to "an intellectually satisfying level."[55]

Then came the attack of Nazi Germany on the U.S.S.R. in 1941. Whereas her former ally had been atheistic, Russia's new allies were religiously inclined. Thereupon conversations on religious affairs within the Soviet Union could be picked up almost where they left off in the summer of 1939: "Is it possible to have an official Communist-Christian religion of the abstract man based on the foundations Christianity has laid?"

In the succeeding six war-years, the religious question was essentially as untouched as though it did not exist. It is true that anti-religion was outlawed, anti-religious publications ceased for "lack of paper," anti-religious leaders were ousted for "incompetence," and school manuals were revised, with religion treated less unfavorably. But the only suggestion of an encounter between religious and anti-religious points of view was when a Russian university dean praised Christianity for its historic contributions in promoting art, the "noble principle of love, equality, brotherhood" and general reform, then pointed out that society had now progressed beyond this stage to the advanced era of materialism.[56]

Where things did happen during the war-years was at the government-church level. As indicated in earlier chapters, the co-operative relationship between Church and State was consummated in such a way as to have remained practically unaltered ever since. But by 1947, after "cooperation" had proved its worth at the institutional level, church leaders were able again to refer to the ideological problem with hopes of developing a "Christian-Communism."

The Evolvement of a New "Scientific Religion"

What position should Communists take?

Unchecked Christianity, as they had known it in Czarist times, had been worse than a failure. Anti-religion (1917-1937) had also proved inadequate, both as a scourge of Christianity and as a new creative idea. "Christian-Communism" was written-off after the 1938-39 experiment as an impossible contradiction and a denial of Marxism. Co-existence (1941-46) with religion was regarded as

54. *ICPIS*, No. 15, April, 1941 (*Chron.*, p. 251).
55. *Anti-religioznik*, as reported in *ICPIS*, No. 16, April, 1941 (*Chron.*, p. 251).
56. *ICPIS*, No. 11, March, 1945 (*Chron.*, p. 260).

equally unacceptable—a step backward—so long as religion was "anti-scientific, reactionary—a hindrance to Communism."[57]

Yet, after thirty years' trial, the possibilities of creating a new Communist order completely void of attributes generally associated with religion seemed exceedingly limited.[58] How then? Hangers-on of the earlier anti-religious program called for a program "to step up scientific propaganda, inculcate the materialist world outlook, wage unremitting struggle against idealism (i.e., 'unrealism'), mysticism and any kind of obscurantism and expose the instigators of a new war . . ."[59]

Particular emphasis of the old-line "Militant Atheists" was on the last two points, namely, a renewed program of anti-religious education, but intellectually more satisfying and psychologically less offensive. "Skilfully and calmly, tactfully and persistently, the Soviet teacher must expose and overcome religious prejudices . . . and educate the younger generation in the spirit of Marxist-Leninist Science, in the spirit of a materialist and truly scientific world outlook."[60] This they have attempted to do in alternating waves of enthusiasm and apathy, but generally with little success. Some of the reasons, as earlier, lie in the disinterest of youth, the neutral or agnostic point of view of teachers, the presence of religious believers in the Party itself, and the fact that many influential leaders and most of the people considered that the Russian Orthodox Church was loyal, "fully Soviet,"[61] and working for the good of the people, that therefore they had no quarrel with religion.

On the part of the Government, and perhaps the new genera-

---

57. *Science and Life*, article by Oleschuk, as quoted by *Church Times*, London, Feb. 24, 1950 (*Chron.*, p. 301).

58. If the Communists did not want a religion, it was no less evident to them that irresistible forces over which they had no absolute control would create a "religion." In an article, "The Soviet Union, Land of True Freedom and Conscience," J. Ibrahimov indicated what Communists were recognizing as deeper sources of social change. Similarities, he said, between Russian Orthodox Church convictions and the Soviet Government's policy reflected that both sprang from "trends and feelings current among the same people. All efforts to ignore these trends have, as experience has shown, ended badly for traitors to the cause of the people . . ." (*EPS*, No. 39, Nov., 1949, *Chron.*, p. 270. See also footnote 26, p. 101. At about this time (Dec., 1950) *Bolshevik* reminded Communists that Lenin had suggested the technique of "leading" such fundamental forces in *The Significance of Militant Atheism*: "The advance guard fulfills (its) purpose . . . only when it does not separate itself from the masses it is leading . . . Without an alliance with non-Communists in the various fields of activity, any constructive Communist work is out of the question" (*Religion in Russia*, No. II, p. 2, *Chron.*, p. 274).

59. Article by S. Kovalev in *Bolshevik*, No. 19, Oct., 1950, as quoted by *Curren Digest of the Soviet Press*, Vol. II, No. 44 (*Chron.*, p. 274).

60. *Uchitelskaya Gazeta*, article by Oleschuk, as quoted by Barron and Waddams, *Communism and the Churches*, p. 32 (*Chron.*, p. 270).

61. F. N. Oleschuk, article in *Science and Life*, as quoted by *Church Times*, *op. cit.* (*Chron.*, pp. 270, 301-302).

tion of Communists,[62] the emphasis was on scientific education conducted in an affirmative "religious" manner. (On religious questions the Government still claimed to be agnostic and neutral.)[63]

The basic principle of the present (1951) phase is then that of the Government: a positive presentation of scientific materialism as the means and the end of the perfect order. The change from the former negative techniques and the Government's part in that change was signalized in the re-constitution of the former "League of Militant Atheists" as the "All Soviet Society for the Dissemination of Political and Scientific Knowledge" at the end of 1947. This new, positive approach could also make a place in its scheme of things for the church as a social institution. Indeed, facing realities in a somewhat more frank way than the anti-religionists, it has gone considerably further and recognized the necessity to deal with human beings as they are, not as "abstract man." It has attempted to clothe its "positive socialist materialism" in whatever robe is necessary to make materialism acceptable and meaningful to the real man. An attempt has therefore been made to deal precisely with those issues on which the anti-religious program had failed, or where Christianity was considered to have been successful, i.e., intellectually acceptable,[64] "loving understanding" in human relationships, morally strengthening,[65] spiritually and emotionally satisfying, positively motivating, and historically related in a way comprehensible to the people.

In contrast, then, to an earlier period (described on page 98) in which the Government was to re-do the churches, the Party was to un-do religion, and the anticipated Utopia was to provide a society in which there was no need for religion, in the present phase the Communist Government, insofar as possible together with the Church, seeks to provide a positive education, and the anti-religious forces seek to supplant religion with some "dynamic ideas." The result, whether intended or not, has been an atmosphere and structure which can be described only as religious.

---

62. *Pravda* in the spring of 1949 reprimanded the Communist youth movement for being neutral towards religious influences and challenged it to "uphold that doctrine of scientific progress to which all religions stood in direct contradiction." Another journal denounced a teacher for his reference to "religious science." *EPS*, No. 21, May, 1949 (*Chron.*, p. 269).

63. Statement of a Soviet university dean as reported in *ICPIS*, No. 11, March, 1945 (*Chron.*, p. 260).

64. P. 107.

65. "The reproach against the Atheists is that they have not been able to offer the people moral standards for their life. Religion answered moral questions in its way." Yaroslavsky in *Bezboznik*, No. 9, 1940 (*Chron.*, pp. 250, 252).

Content of Communist Religion

A summary comparison of the developing "religion" of Communism with the Christian religion will indicate the religious character of their situation.

Both Christianity and Communism hold that there is an ultimate purpose in history, that final fulfillment of that purpose is inevitable, that man may participate in the working out of that purpose and in that victory, even that all things, insofar as they move history toward that irresistible end, "work together for good." This is the Communist's fundamental faith.

But the Communists' "God," in the sense of the creating, sustaining and ordering process, is represented by Tension—or the Dialectic—between all extant forces, ideas, etc., in the universe. It therefore "sees" all, "knows" all and is in all.

When man fully comprehends this process, he will be his own and the universe's "God," and capable of freely creating, ordering and sustaining within the Dialectic framework. This ultimate, perfect scientific man is *ipso facto* an incarnation of Tension, but also a master of it. He is abstract science, or natural law *en homo, ergo* "Christ." He is the perfect Communist man.

The Party represents the "Presence" of the absolute law/tension complex in the workings of man. It alone is competent to consider all operative factors in the universe, to understand and to interpret.

Thus the abstract "trinity." For those Communists whose intellectual limitations make abstract conceptions difficult, there are concrete forms: Tension is represented by Revolution; Stalin or some type of successor is the "Christ," and the Party is still the "Presence," to be awed, feared, and obeyed. There is also an "ecclesiastical hierarchy."

"Prophets" are described as the seers who have the most nearly perfect understanding ("revelation") of natural law and therefore of cause and effect. Foreseeing "effects" they are therefore able to prescribe "causal" programs in relation to economics and politics. Among them have been included Marx, the Bolsheviks, the Communist Party, Lenin and Stalin. There is an "infallible" man or group of men at the top—a "Pope." He is authority; he, the true interpreter in a succession of revolution-anointed interpreters. To him and his "college of cardinals"—the political leaders, police, military, teachers and technicians—belong the prerogative of reinterpretation, definition of truth, adding of new dogmas, etc.

There are still other parallels. Those revered, indeed worshipped, for past leadership and self-sacrifice include not only ("Saints") Marx and Lenin, but secondary figures, such as Dimitrov in Bulgaria, and some lesser figures who have died in valorous activity or at least before openly becoming heretics. Special rites, processions and eulogies are conducted regularly at shrines erected to their honor. Among the "heretics" must be included the Mensheviks, Trotskyists, irredentists, Chauvinists, Titoists—in short, any who within the Communist sphere of concern diverge from the sacred canons. The trials, excommunications, and ultimate end reserved for heretics have already been described.

The concept of evil is not one of morality. It is related to man's weakness and ignorance. These forces of "darkness" which have periodically sought to overpower the children of "light" include feudalism (Kulaks), religion, capitalist imperialism, idealism, and, probably some day, socialism and communism.

There is an elaborately worked out dogma, condensed into popular slogans (creeds), and blind and passionate faith in authoritative "encyclicals." The "scriptures" of Marx, Lenin and Stalin are regarded as "sacred" writings, suitable for study, exegesis and the rule of life. Should some later revelation conflict with the older testaments, "biblical" scholars and textual critics can always find ways of explaining inconsistencies. There are, of course, many "apocryphal" writings which have not made the "canon" and not a small number of authors anathematized.

"Sacred shrines" have already been mentioned. No self-respecting Communist "prophet" or "saint" would think of being buried under a simple headstone. (A pilgrimage to a head-stone would be somewhat disappointing, and there are pilgrimages—whether to do honors or to get honors.) Centers of meditation (worship) in public places, especially schools, and even in homes include Communist flags, wreaths, "scriptures," etc., grouped around pictures (ikons) or statues of Communist "saints." Public parades with brightly colored banners, costumes and chants supply part of life's desire for pageantry and sense of victory. Group "worship" may be conducted in the theater, or on the village square or at any other public gatherings. Public "liturgies" include antiphonal slogans, cheers, and "hymns." There is a Communist "Christmas," and other "holy" days.

New converts have their form of repentance, renunciation of their former life and beginning a new life. One is not considered a convert from Christianity until "he has publicly repudiated his (former) faith."[66] One must wholly "surrender his life for the Communist order of society."[67] After initiatory rites, he must learn the Communist "catechism." Regular confession is expected in the local cell group, where a kind of "group counseling" helps

---

66. *Anti-religioznik*, March, 1941, as reported in *ICPIS*, No. 16, April, 1941.
67. *Anti-religioznik*, No. 7, 1940, as reported in *ICPIS*, No. 2, Jan., 1941.

him improve his Communist stature. If he has no sins to confess, he can, and many do readily fabricate some colorful ones.

Every means of mass communication is used to proclaim the new "gospel" for "it is necessary to reform the mind of the believer by persuasion . . ."[68] All over East Europe from 1945-48 the writer saw cafes, church and other buildings converted to book stalls. Nearly one out of three shops was selling Communist literature at near give-away prices. By radio, press, Potemkin-size photography, cinema and colportage their "gospel" is preached. And hardly any village is too small to have a public address system blaring out new doctrines over the village and countryside. Exponents of the "win the individual believer for atheism" school of evangelism are carefully trained in the methods, hazards and purposes of individual evangelism.[69] There is a sense of mission comprehensible to the simplest peasant when described in terms of liberating the oppressed, healing the sick, bringing justice, equality, peace and plenty to all mankind. At one stage it has evoked enthusiastic and sacrificial response from idealistic youth.

The Communist Utopia has some similarities to Christianity's "Kingdom on earth": education, opportunity, security, creative labor, abundant life for all. When all people are converted to the Communist idea, free from "Capitalist instincts, mystical ideas and religious superstitions," the Communist "Utopia" will have arrived. Then there is hope for the underprivileged, for dependent colonials, the down-trodden and oppressed. This is carried almost to the point of presuming that there will then no longer be natural catastrophies, disease, or accidents. Labor will then be only a pleasure, a channel of self-expression. In the meantime, people who pray about their dire situation should be taught "that their conditions are satisfactory."[70] Although Communism theoretically promises its Utopia for this life, there is a strong apocalyptic element in the Communist concept of future fulfillment. Their triumph is not expected until their foes disintegrate—from internal contradictions. Final victory, therefore, may not come for several generations. In the present it is necessary to sacrifice, to struggle, and to hold fast.

Marx held that "the final value belongs to collectivity; it alone is confident of immortality." This is something less than the Christian "company of angels" or "fellowship of the Saints," but

68. Oleschuk, "Statement on Anti-Religious Tactics," *Church Times*, London, Feb. 24, 1950 (*Chron.*, p. 301-302).
69. *Anti-religioznik*, March, 1941, as reported in *ICPIS*, No. 16, April, 1941.
70. *Pravda*, as quoted by Timasheff, *op. cit.*, p. 124 (*Chron.*, p. 248). Earlier Communists had damned the churches for propounding a similar idea and had urged the people to revolt against their dire situation.

not void of ultimate meaning for life. "Future" is generally an inter-related past and present:

"... In reality the future of human life is a scientific question, which has practical significance for the individual and society, for political planning and the class conflict. Without knowledge of the future man cannot live. His creative imagination enables him to know the course of events, provided he has a thorough knowledge of natural laws, of the materialistic forces which determine development. Nobody on earth before Marx and Engels knew the real mechanism of evolution; and so no man before them could prophesy the future.

"... For the future can be foretold only by one who knows the last word of science, dialectical and historical materialism, and who represents the interests of the most progressive class of men, the proletariat, to whom the future belongs,—a future which promises no terrible end.

"... All prophecy of the future is important for Marxism because it confronts it with concrete practical aims. To it belongs the final victory."[71]

In the meantime scientific materialism incarnate in post-Revolutionary Russia is called to save the world. This "Messiah" is regarded as having saved the world from Fascism during the Second World War, and again later from destruction by virtue of its representatives in the United Nations.[72] This focus on Russia as the Messianic instrument is an ancient Russian sentiment which has rather been taken over, than rooted out by Communism.

Man has been and is being formed by dialectic tensions in the universe. At present hindered by ignorance, superstition, fears and other limitations, he is expected some day, when he comprehends all, to create perfect man in the test tube.[73] Then "prehistory" will end and the real history of man begin. In the meantime, an effective program of Communist education takes account of his limitations and environmental formation and becomes "all things to all men" in order to achieve its ultimate goal, sacrificing the actual man of today if need be in order to have the "ideal" man of the future.

---

71. *Anti-religioznik*, No. 7, 1940, as quoted by *ICPIS*, No. 2, Jan., 1941.

72. Article by Fr. Levitsky in *Periodical of the Moscow Patriarchate*, Vol. II, 1948, *EPS*, No. 13, 1949 (*Chron.*, p. 268).

73. In 1950 the "All-Soviet Society for the Dissemination of Political and Scientific Knowledge" distributed 75,000 copies of a brochure refuting the religious "idealistic" concept of the origin of life as "fiction" and asserting that "life is nothing else than a particular form of the existence of matter . . ." which scientists might soon reproduce synthetically. *Religion in Russia*, No. II, 1951, pp. 8, 9 (*Chron.*, p. 274).

Communist morality like Christian morality now includes concepts of unselfishness, self-discipline, self-sacrifice, family honor, loyalty. But "Right" for the Communist is determined by the inter-play of forces (tensions) which propel history forward. "Truth" is not therefore an absolute, but a changing concept. Consequently, justice also must be determined from day to day. Ultimate natural law will not sit in judgment on Communist judges, since what is just today, may not be so tomorrow, but it is no less just today. These concepts—justice, right and wrong—are therefore determined by the Party which alone is competent to understand all factors in present tension.

Freedom is known only by those who understand the framework prescribed by "dialectic" tensions, and are able to act creatively within that framework. Once they understand and accept that framework, they have "freedom" to work within it. Similarly, a Christian is a slave and so labeled by Communists,[74] albeit a "slave of Christ." But within the framework prescribed by love, the Christian finds himself entirely liberated.

Finally, the Christian Gospel itself has its dialectics, its "peace" in war, its believing doubts, its faith at work, its saving of life by losing it, which foster movement, change, indeed life itself and faith. For such reasons Archbishop Temple called Communism a "Christian heresy," and Berdyaev took considerable pains to "show the affinities between the Christian conception and that inspiring Communism which began by denying Christianity but could not really detach itself from the profoundly religious and humanistic ideal of the Russian people."[75]

Thus the religious character of Communism is developing, to some extent shaped by Communist planning, to some extent shaping Communist ideas. Whatever it may be called—a leading Bulgarian Communist has called it "Marxist religion"[76]—it is no less a religion-type phenomenon which is taking place in much of East Europe. It is most evident in the U.S.S.R. But there are beginnings in other countries as attention can be shifted from the church-nationalization process.

The new "religion" factor poses some new problems for Communists and Christians alike.[77] One provocative question (already intimated on page 189) is whether, or to what extent Communism will be able to establish on foundations laid by Christianity its ide-

74. *Science and Life*, Sept., 1950, as reported by *Current Digest of Soviet Press*, Vol. II, No. 44, 1950 (*Chron.*, p. 273).
75. Widdrington, "Future of the Russian Church," *Christendom*, Vol. 14, No. 57, March, 1945.
76. Beltcho Nicolov, speech before the Bulgarian Communist Congress, Dec., 1948; *Free Independent Bulgaria*, July 27, 1948 (*Chron.*, pp. 370-371).
77. *Chronicle*, pp. 243, 250, 251, 296.

ological religious superstructure, as well as an institutional super-structure. Is this why an attempt is made to dissociate the Ortho-dox Church in the U.S.S.R. both from all churches abroad not obe-dient to it, and from other churches in the U.S.S.R.?[78] Is this why there is a re-shaping of theology in the U.S.S.R. orbit around the Orthodox Church?[79] Will Communists eventually transform the "vestiges of Christianity" into their new religion or continue to struggle against those "vestiges" until they disappear?

There is some evidence that they intend to do both. Tradi-tional religion is equated with its "harmful" elements—"fostering national antagonisms, violating the Communist concepts of nobil-ity of labor by encouraging monks, holy men, and other idlers and parasites,"[80] "teaching man to bear without demur .. poverty, hun-ger and persecution,"[81] hindering the development of science and enlightenment through ignorance, belief in a supernatural world, and primitive fear survivals,[82] encouraging the "ideology of sla-very, impotence, self-abasement and self-contempt."[83]

But desirable elements of religion now common to Commun-ism (p. 103) are identified as Communist phenomena or as ful-filled in Communism. Thereby elements of religion and presum-ably adherents of religion are assimilated. For these the conven-tional religious label may eventually be dropped. Presumably Russian Orthodoxy may be largely considered, in contrast with the rest of the Christian world, such a desirable element.

In East Germany a document called "The Meissen Theses" suggests that an attempt is being made there to integrate Chris-tian and Communist viewpoints. These "Twenty-Two Theses of Christian Realism" were prepared by the (Roman Catholic) Chris-tian Democratic Union of East Germany in October, 1951. The authors included a number of nominal Catholics whose chief con-cern was politics, and probably some Communists. This clear at-tempt at a harmonizing of Christian and Communist points of view may have little more than temporary political signifciance. But it may also signalize a serious attempt on the part of East German Communists and Christians to blend an old religion into the new, so that a popular shift can be made with the least possible disturbance. The frequency with which such statements recur at

---

78. *Chronicle*, pp. 265-267, 272.
79. Appeal of Bp. Hermogen, Rector of Orthodox Theological Seminary of Moscow, *Patriarchal Journal*, No. 12, 1948 (*Chron.*, p. 268).
80. Statement of an educator in Byelo-Russia, *N. Y. Times*, Sept. 28, 1948 (*Chron.*, p. 267).
81. Radio talk of Plitetsky as quoted by Barron and Waddams, *op. cit.*, p. 29 (*Chron.*, p. 270).
82. National Cultural Publishing House, *The Origin of Religion*, as report-ed by *Current Digest of Soviet Press*, Vol. II, No. 44, 1950 (*Chron.*, p. 273).
83. *Science and Life*, Sept., 1950, as reported by *Current Digest of Soviet Press*, Vol. II, No. 44, 1950 (*Chron.*, p. 273).

other times and places will indicate how seriously they are to be taken.[84]

Whether Christianity can absorb creative elements of Communism, once Communists are in power, is yet another matter. It seems likely that as Communists recognize the religious nature of their present situation, they will take special care to see that it is they who absorb some elements of historic Christianity, and not the churches which absorb the religious instincts and reforming elements of Communism. They can be expected, therefore, to be, as they have been in the past, doubly suspicious of any conciliatory move at the ideological level initiating with the churches, and may be required to denounce those very attributes of a resurgent Chris-

---

84. Some excerpts—
(1) "Christian Realism is the way of life by which Christians, following their faith, both in judgment and action, face all problems of life and the world. The content of Christian Realism is determined by the teaching and example of Christ and the example of the most resolute and faithful Christians of all times and all nations. The theoretical basis of the Christian Democratic Union is Christian Realism.

(4) "The Christian sees man as under the mark of sin, as a creature who is certainly destined for the highest and who is capable of the highest, but who remains tied to the lower and can become guilty of the most fearful degeneration and crime. The Christian sees man involved in a tension between the commission to subject the earth and the peril of being overcome by the burdens of the material, by the strength of the very techniques he himself has created. He sees man involved in the field of tension between dying and rising ideas . . .

(10) ". . . Jesus warned of the danger of riches, opposed the exploitation of the helpless by the ruling strata. He drove the traders and the money-changers out of the temple with a whip. He warned the ruling strata of his people that their course must end in a terrible judgment of God, in a catastrophe. It was the hatred of this ruling group that nailed Christ to the cross.

(17) "The great philosophical schools of the 19th century, idealism and materialism, marked themselves off from Christianity: Idealism, since it lost its picture of God in the idea of an absolute spirit, since further it saw men as perfect beings, as the measure of all things, and deified the State as itself a 'thing of reason'; Materialism, in its decisive form of dialectical materialism, since it declared the idea of God as outdated and marked religion as an over-rated thing which would be ended by changing the economical basis.

(18 ". . . Without being an adherent of dialectical materialism the Christian must see the correctness of the basic economic analysis of Marxism-Leninism . . .

(19) "The Christian Democratic Union recognizes the social renewal of community as a Christian responsibility. The struggle for a new and better community along the lines of Karl Marx, and the resulting struggle in the Soviet Union, is an effective example. This fact must determine us to go on working politically with the supporters of Marxism-Leninism on the basis of the joint bloc we now have, for the welfare of our people . . .

(21) "The fight for the national interests of his own people is, for the Christian, the fulfilling of the commission that the Creator has laid upon him by the fact that he has suffered him to come into the world among that people and at that time. The securing of the existence of the German people through its unification, and peace, is a duty which is compelled by decisions based on principles . . .

(22) "The fight for peace is the central task of the present moment . . . There can . . . be no true Christian who does not fight for peace in the conviction that peace will be secured and strengthened if the peoples will take their fate into their own hands."

tianity—love, humility, charity, patience, faith—while at the same time trying to inculcate them in Communism.

Another intriguing hypothesis should be at least mentioned. Communists have recognized that Christianity made a historic contribution in the transition of primitive society from paganism to monotheism. They maintain that society is now in the transition from monotheism to materialism, that Christianity in that process is outmoded, and that the Communist religion is the agent of that transition.[85] But the question arises: if society should continue to evolve beyond materialism, would Communists contend that the Communist religion in its turn will also be displaced?

In an article on the science of language,[86] Premier J. Stalin suggested another possibility. Heretofore the Marxist view maintained that the mind was dependent upon environmental factors, i.e., on the position of human beings in the system of production. In describing the relation between the economic basis of society and its ideological superstructure Mr. Stalin suggested that certain cultural factors, such as language, can be independent of, and influential upon the economic base of society. He added that these factors, language and culture, may develop directly from their origins in ancient times to the classless society without revolutionary changes—i.e., above the operations of the dialectic process. Whatever this may mean about the place of religious fact in Communist theory, it clearly indicates a recognition by Stalin that there are forces in history which shape the course of history and which Communist theorists had not previously recognized.[87]

The most startling conclusion one can draw from recent evidence is that Communists, having been forced to recognize another determinative "urge" in Tension which they had preferred to disregard or to regard as effect, not cause, have lost something of their absolute certainty that theirs is the *only* solution to the hu-

---

85. Statement of Soviet university dean as reported in *ICPIS*, No. 11, March, 1945 (*Chron.*, p. 260).

86. J. Stalin, "Der Marxismus und die Fragen der Sprachwissenschaft," an article which appeared in an East German paper in 1951.

87. That they were beginning to do so is also evident in a revised edition of a one-volume *Dictionary of the Russian Language*, containing 51,533 words, which was published in Moscow in 1952.

The compilers of the dictionary added to their definitions special classifications such as "obsolete," "archaic," "colloquial," etc. Religion and religious observance are very much in evidence, and here the presence or absence of the classification "obsolete" or 'archaic" presents considerable interest.

"Glory be to God," meaning "Fine, excellent!" is given as colloquial. Another word which is described as colloquial is "bezboshnik," "godless one," a word which before the war was very official indeed, being the one used in the title of the Union of Militant Godless (League of Militant Atheists). Now it is described as—"colloquial: person who denies the existence of God, struggles against religious narcotic." The adjective derived from it is given quite another meaning: "inadmissible, dishonest. Illustrations: a godless liar. To make a godless mess of it." *EPS*, No. 40, October, 1953.

man problem. If that "faith" has been shaken, anything is possible in the future. If Communists, even subconsciously, begin to doubt their absolute, to quicken in their own mental processes some aptitude to discriminate and judge, to grope for a more comprehensive concept of Tension, then Communism's absolute is broken, its "inevitable" or "beyond," which had "no Gods above it" must succumb to intellectual uncertainty and relativism. When the religion that Communist man has created has failed him, where might he turn next for assurance and faith?

"Our Church would cease to be a Church should she flee from this point of tension."[1]

B. INNER STRUGGLES OF THE CHURCH

Chapter VI

INTRODUCTION

In the preceding section and in the *Chronicle* consideration has been given to specific purposes and acts of Communist governments directed at churches and religion. Some instances in which Christians have deflected Communist tactics by specific acts of response have been cited. This section is principally concerned with internal factors in the life of the churches. It will deal with factors which conditioned the churches to respond as they have, with the way the responses of the churches have affected the churches themselves, with some later problems which confront the churches, and with apparent trends in the theology and patterns of church life.

The Church in East Europe has had more than scientific materialism to wrestle with. The Church was divided. There were not only conventional divisions between the historic confessions. In Slovakia, Hungarian Reformed churches opposed Slovak Reformed. In the Soviet Union, lower Orthodox clergy opposed the Orthodox hierarchy. In Hungary, Christian leaders with liberal views banded together across confessional lines to oppose conservative Christian leaders.

Past attachments of churches and church leaders to corrupt political parties, methods and motives involved in the churches' management of vast areas of land and the peasants who tilled it, the perpetuation in the name of religion of practices (indulgences, superstition, magic) little different from those of the pre-Christian era—for these, many churchmen had to struggle with a bad conscience simultaneously with their more tangible adversary.

Church statesmanship was diminished. Many of the Church's ablest warriors had been killed or had spent their energies in opposition to the Nazis.

The Church was materially vulnerable. Beyond what had already been lost in battle, when the sources of material support

---

1. Reformed Bishop Albert Bereczky, p. 136.

on which churches had come to depend were threatened, there was no alternative support to fall back on. With the exception of the small, "free" churches, believers had not developed the habit of direct voluntary support, and possibilities of subvention from abroad were quickly suppressed.

And though the Church had much tradition, and even discipline and formal theology, it had no clearly thought-out, vital theology adequate for such a demanding situation.[2]

The Church must wrestle, then, not only with Communism, but with internal problems of division, of material support, of leadership, of a sense of judgment and theological inadequacy. These were hardly conditions conducive to the preparation of a "strategy" in the face of Communism's challenge—even had there been time. And there was no time. Radical reforms were pressing in on the churches. The initiative lay in other hands, and the churches found themselves identified with the society and culture to be purged and remodelled. They, too, were on the defensive— "attacked" and "judged." Neutrality was impossible; flight was unthinkable. The churches must respond.

The question was, how? The churches developed no preconceived strategy of response, partly for reasons already suggested, but also because it was impossible to prepare a plan for an unknown future. Different things were expected by different churches. And not even the Communists could foresee the ultimate end.

The primary response has therefore been a pragmatic and dynamic one, rather than abstract or logical. The complex of the churches' whole experience and life was stimulated to respond daily by evolving measures of Communists. This response, often in forms unexpected by Communism,[3] provoked the Communists to new measures, and these new measures in turn prodded the churches to still other responses. The "response" has therefore been unbelievably complex, varieties of responses running through every confession and nation.

For the purpose of this study we shall deliberately focus our comments around three major groups of response which could not be foreseen, but which evolved, namely, the *resistance* (overthrow the Government), the *modus vivendi* (make a deal in order to ex-

---

2. Had there been such a theology, one may conjecture that it would have been so manifest prior to the venue of Communism as to have precluded the real possibility of the development of Communism on a broad scale.

3. When the Hungarian Government decreed that only those children whose parents made special application could receive religious instruction, nearly 100% of the parents made such application. The Government then attacked the applicants (*Die Protestantischen Kirchen in Ungarn, 1939-50*, Encl. 69; *Chron.*, pp. 451-452, 478).

ist), and the *reformist* (purify the Church) groups.[4] The resistance and *modus vivendi* points of view reflect a concept of the Church and of Communism in their political and institutional expressions. Religious reformation is more a response to the idea and spirit of Communism, but may have a more far-reaching effect on church institutions than either of the other positions. All three reflect certain presuppositions and a general frame of mind on the part of the Christians involved which require careful consideration.

Delineation must be made at this point between the leadership of the Church and the laity. Practicing believers in general, whether Baptist, Lutheran, Orthodox, Catholic or Reformed, resisted the initial changes of religious life effected by Communism. From a sense of general resentment and dissatisfaction, some believers entered the active opposition of the Underground. Others endeavored to adapt themselves and their religious life to the new situation. But among the latter no clear line can be drawn between those whose religious practices were re-formed because of governmental directives, and therefore related to the "modus vivendi" leadership, and those whose adaptations were considered re-formed of God, and therefore related to the "re-formation" leadership. They might in fact be related to both. Leaders of both sought a mode of living in the new social framework and at the same time both found their religious life very considerably changed. In this study, the categories, "resistance," "modus vivendi" and "re-formation" are therefore used with particular (but not exclusive) reference to church leadership, and the essen-

---

4. This is not to belittle a significant response at another level. As one thinks of many aspects of the churches' responses, the most thrilling and lasting is that of the courage and fidelity of individual Christians. It is also the most humbling: the faithful who do not conceal their regularity of worship, when worship may result in discrimination; the father who risks his job and the welfare of his family by refusing to sign denunciations of pastor or friend; the young mother who talks to Communist colporteurs of their former faith, of love and eternal law; the pastor who could easily flee west to comfort and safety, but stays to provide shelter in a converted hen-house for wandering orphans; the preacher who could have an important post in his nation's diplomatic corps if he would renounce his faith, but instead, rotting of TB in solitary confinement, has converted his jailor; the clergymen who could have higher salaries and favored postions as State employees, but prefer to identify themselves voluntarily with the workers and peasants whose level of life has been lowered; the church which is invited to acknowledge the supremacy of the State and receive preferential treatment, but prefers not to establish such barriers between itself and Western churches while at the same time being fully aware of barriers caused by the political associations and aspirations of Western churches.

There are stories of Christian heroism not unlike those of the second century in Rome. Some day they must be told. But this is not the time and place, nor is it our purpose here.

tial distinction between "modus vivendi" and "re-formation," perhaps an arbitrary one, is whether they conceived of their immediate directives for changing the patterns of church life as coming
from governments, or from God.

*"Turn the church altars into a tribune for Christian resistance against Communist Godlessness."** *

Chapter VII

RESISTANCE, AN IMMEDIATE RESPONSE

By "Resistance" is meant deliberate, organized opposition to Communist governments, their programs, personnel and actual existence. We are concerned here with steps towards, reasons for, and some results of this resistance.

Religious groups had no pre-conceived strategy of resistance. While their background may have given the churches a natural inclination to defend the *status quo* and oppose radical reform,[1] and although individual religious leaders may have been absolutely opposed to Communism, organized resistance with a religious connection did not appear until after Communist governments had had a chance to prove themselves. Aggressive resistance was not therefore the first inclination of the churches. They wanted peace—if possible. As their relatively simple attempts to cope with Communism day by day were frustrated, succeeding action by religious leaders led inevitably, but without prior intent, toward a crusading resistance, and eventually the Underground.

This process began with attempts at *consultation and negotiation* between churches and governments soon after Communist governments came into power. Discussions, often long and heated, but none-the-less seriously expected by churchmen to provide solutions, were undertaken on measures of reform: land, economic and education. Where Catholic Churches were involved (especially Hungary, Poland, Czechoslovakia, Rumania) negotiations centered around proposed concordats. Where others were involved, consultation was on church-state relations as reflected in proposed laws, or on state recognition of, and agreements with churches.

As the tempo and manner of government control over society increased, churches expressed *disapproval* of political methods and educational policy. In 1945, Hungarian Archbishop Mindszenty,

---

* Broadcasts of the Bulgarian Underground as reported in *RNS*, p. 3, April 12, 1954.

1. To the writer's knowledge, there has been no large communion in East Europe which at official levels has not, when first confronted by the Communist Order, resisted that Order, whether silently or overtly. Exceptions were the schismatic groups from larger denominations or minority groups previously presecuted by them.

after attempts at negotiation seemed unsuccessful, in order "to clarify wherein the government was democratic and where not," called public attention to various Governmental excesses and to his disapproval of them.[2]

Disapproval brought little improvement and churches began to protest against the police state, against methods of violence, infringement on human rights and curtailment of the free exercise of religion. Cardinal Mindszenty in December of 1945 protested against the disestablishment of the monarchial system. Protestants, much later and on issues more central to their religious work, protested against the censorship of radio and press, the monopolization by the Government of school books, the control of foreign church contacts, the increasing pressure on Christians to join political organizations. In this phase, the churches resorted to their most effective weapon of protest: the pulpit and the pastoral letter.

Next came *denunciation*. Here the way divided. Either the Church could refrain from denunciation and come to terms with the Government, a position often labeled "collaboration" and "compromise," or it could denounce the Government, in which case it was on the inevitable way towards active resistance. Few may have realized as they denounced Communist governments, rejected communications from those governments and advised believers to refrain from supporting Communist governments that there was no road back. However, once denunciation and, in the case of the Roman Catholic Church, excommunication was clearly indicated, Communist governments regarded and condemned such churchmen as "reactionaries and traitors."

From the churchmen's point of view, negotiation, disapproval, protest and denunciation had failed. Those who had pursued that course could thereupon hardly conclude that there was any effective way of coping with Communist governments except *active resistance*. Those who openly continued this course were displaced. The rest went underground.

These four steps may be further illustrated from other countries. In the Soviet Union, the Orthodox Church attempted a settlement with the pre-Communist reformers, prior to November 1917. After the Revolution, the Church expressed general disapproval of the Communist *coup*, in the expectation that the Communist administration was not final. When in January, 1918, the new Government decreed the separation of Church and State, with ensuing reforms, the Church denounced the Government and called on believers to resist or be excommunicated. Churchmen chal-

---

2. *Four Years' Struggle of the Church in Hungary*, Mindszenty, p. 26 ff. (*Chron.*, p. 434).

lenged Soviet powers to engage in open battle. Such resisting churchmen were not immediately forced underground, and there were some later attempts (March, 1918) to negotiate with the Government, but the general pattern was set.[3]

In Poland the process was more complicated. Negotiations between the State and the Catholic Church began shortly after the Government abrogated the pre-war Concordat in December, 1945, and continued through 1950. Apparently, Catholic leaders felt that the "agreement" proceedings were intended principally to stall Church criticism of Government measures, and that they would come to nothing. Nevertheless, churchmen did not wish to be held responsible for breaking off negotiations. In the meantime, they frequently and openly condemned various actions and leaders of the Government,[4] but until 1951 had not officially denounced the Government in the sense of calling for its overthrow. During the same period an active, though unofficial resistance was forming underground to which, said the Communists, Catholic leaders were giving sympathetic support.[5] The step from official church disapproval to active resistance was not therefore a long one, and while the Church itself could not officially take it, many individuals could and did.

One must ask what suppositions underlay the resistance point of view and method of many Christians. It will be noted immediately that active resistance was not aimed at the ideology called Communism. Many churches, except for certain vestiges of medieval inquisition, would have been willing for the Communist ideology to try to make its case in the market place by the democratic process. Militant resistance springs from, and aims at a different level. The following presuppositions, evident in East Europe, have provided bases for active resistance.

Fear of Reform

Reforms which disrupt the normal patterns of life are generally resisted by those responsible for such patterns. Leaders of churches which had participated in the creation and sustenance of the pre-Communist *status quo* in East Europe[6] were no exception. They were in a large measure in power, and rather well satisfied with the *status quo*. Many could hardly conceive of the Church as capable of existing apart from its control over governments, its prestige, its manipulation and administration of thousands of acres of land and millions of tenants, of hundreds of buildings and

---

3. *Chronicle*, pp. 229-230.
4. This was done both indirectly, e.g., via the Pope (*Chron.*, pp. 394, 395) and directly (*Chron.*, pp. 389, 390, 393, 397, 400.
5. *Chronicle*, pp. 387-389, 392, 400.
6. In most cases this would exclude minority religious groups.

of profit-bearing industries, and its dictation of social and political *mores*. For them any reform, whether agrarian, educational, political or economic, not of their own making, meant loss of the Church's power. And loss of power meant loss of the Church. For these churchmen this was a battle between two empires over a common domain. Co-existence was impossible. If the Church lost, as its former political allies had lost, it meant annihilation, or relegation to a second-rate position, a kind of impotent institution they could neither imagine nor accept. To those who conceived of the Church as depending on power for its existence, the Church must obviously engage its opponent in mortal combat.

Distrust of Communist Intentions

Even those who welcomed basic social reforms must still face up to ultimate, perhaps ulterior intentions of the Communists *vis-a-vis* the churches. On this point, Lenin had been very clear; and what had already happened in Russia was anything but re-assuring. Were these experiences to be repeated in every other country? Would the regime first interfere, then control the churches? As soon as churchmen saw the first evidence of similarity, many foresaw the worst possible eventualities: persecution, injustice and terror. Related to this distrust was the conviction that Communism represented a foreign power bent on destroying the freedom, indeed the very being of their own nations.

Many therefore joined up quickly with the Underground to try to overthrow Communist regimes in their infancy.

Total Support or Total Resistance

Many churchmen who recognized the totalitarian aspect of the new regimes concluded that any possibility of supporting projects of common concern in the Communist program while opposing other elements of that program was ruled out. There would be no picking and choosing. The Church would either be for the total program, or against it. To resist at one point made the Church a resister against all points. Under those circumstances, the only solution many could see was to attack, not the program, but those who created it. *Ergo,* the Communist regime must be overthrown.

Righteous Indignation

Millions of Christians found their own lives circumscribed, their standard of truth and justice mocked, and their noblest aspirations thwarted. Further, as they observed the disappearance, imprisonment and trials of innocent compatriots, believers concluded that there was no possibility of justice triumphing through governmental offices. In that situation there was no neutral or passive position. If the government was persecuting and destroying innocent victims, including church leaders, to stand idly by was to assent to their destruction. On the other hand, to destroy Communists apparently meant to save Christians. What was the Christian to do? If he is faced with the alternatives of destroying Communists or Christians, will he long debate over which he should do? For many the answer was clear and compelling. Slovakian peasants took up their pitchforks and attacked the persecutors of their priests.[7]

Christian Duty

Christians believed they had had laid on them by their Creator certain definite responsibilities. Among these were some, such as the religious training of youth or, for Catholics, unity of the Catholic Church under the Vatican, which were being restricted by an atheistic regime. The Church, at its legitimate, divinely-ordered business, was being molested. What, then, was the Christian's responsibility? The Communist regime was atheistic, it was regarded as evil, often called the "anti-Christ." Any crusade against that evil, though it involved deceit, black marketing or murder, was considered less evil than acquiesence to the regime. Indeed, for some it became a sacred duty to thwart and slay these "powers worse than Satan' 'at every opportunity. If necessary, they would also "make an alliance with Satan. . . ."—to defeat Communist regimes.

Once having entered on resistance, there was no turning back. Any change of mind, any attempt at reconciliation with government forces invited immediate execution both by fellow-resisters and by the regime.

Once "underground," the climate in which religious groups have learned to live is conditioned by an awareness of an unremitting enemy which encompasses a "false" or "collaborating" church, an organized underground "government" with a rigid discipline and ethic, an expectation of early victory, or of deliverance by friendly political powers, a compelling sense of secrecy, urgency and self-abandon, and a crusading spirit—almost of messianic purpose.

In that context the resisting church takes on less the character of a church than of a mystic, patriotic counter-revolution. It is passionately nationalistic,[8] fiercely militant, boldly authoritarian.

---

7. Trnva, Slovakia, July 1949 (*Chron.*, p. 500).
8. In pre-Easter broadcasts the Bulgarian Underground Radio Goryanin (Man of the Forest) declared: "Let us make Easter a demonstration of national unity against Communist oppression, of nation-wide Christian resistance against Communist atheism. Let us demonstrate by mass attendance at Easter

Clergy and believers alike may be armed and engage in every sort of violence. Young men are secretly trained in guerrilla warfare along with their theology. The underground church-army-government-nation, is a fusion into one compelling religion—*resistér!*

The Resistance, even of religious groups, is not to be confused with the "catacomb" churches or the "ravine worshippers." These latter comprised believers whose daily life might be pursued in the regular patterns of Communist society without any particular view to overthrowing the government of that society, but who withdrew to a secret place only for their group religious ministrations. The Resistance, on the other hand, comprised those whose aim it was to overthrow Communist powers whether through clandestine life or not. But the two might worship together in the same "ravine." That the resistance groups were affecting the attitudes of otherwise useful citizens through such contacts in catacomb churches was undoubtedly a major factor which led the Communists in Russia to encourage the reestablishment of the Church at an "above-ground" level.[9]

Perhaps one can conclude therefore that resistance groups have benefited the Church indirectly because of such concessions which governments have proferred less fanatical groups, in order to diminish the Resistance.[10] But if one can assess the direct effect of the religious Resistance on Communist governments, it has not been so salutary. Reprisals, secret police in churches, severing of foreign contacts, trials and persecution of leaders were all part of the Communists' attempt to protect themselves from the underground resistance. Within the Church itself, the resistance position has posed very difficult problems. A major one, that of relationships, will be examined later.

The personal religious problem has also been an acute one. There have undoubtedly been those in the Resistance whose consciences were untroubled by moral dilemmas and uncertainty. Others have voiced the terrible conflict of spirit and conscience which tore at their thoughts and energies. Involved in forgery, destruction, violence, terror, murder—could one in these acts bear witness to Christ. Some found solace from the *rationale* that Communists were inhuman creatures, or from the ministrations

---

services our silent contempt of Communist oppression and our firm belief in the triumph of justice and truth. Easter is not only a holiday of faith in the immortality of the Savior, it is also a holiday of victory over oppression." Bulgarian priests were called on to "turn the church altars into a tribune for Christian resistance against Communist godlessness." RNS, p. 3, April 12, 1954.

9. This has been dealt with in greater detail in Section A.

10. It is even conceivable that had there been no such secret religious life and resistance, Communist powers would have succeeded in suppressing the Church and religion, and there would be no recognized Church in East Europe today.

of clergy in the Resistance, or from appeals of the Pope to resist, or from moral preachments and exhortations of Western powers. The implication often was that this was a holy crusade, that allowance was made in the Divine scheme of things for illegal and immoral acts committed against evil.

But many Eastern Christians who have resisted record that for them there was no possibility of righteousness, no position at which they could have a clear conscience. To do nothing was clearly wrong. Whatever they did, they recognized they were doing wrong, relatively less wrong than any other way, but hoping they were accomplishing right, and hoping more fervently for guidance and mercy.

*"If the legislation . . . takes . . . from us, we bow
before it. The boundary line (of martyrdom) is not yet."*[1]

Chapter VIII

MODUS VIVENDI—A DELAYED RESPONSE

The "People's Democratic Churches" are often regarded as "compromising" or "collaboration" churches. To the Western observer they seem to bow to the dictates of government leaders, to exchange support of governmental programs for certain privileges and position in the political arena. To them, it is true, have gone the use of church buildings, seminaries, publications and such other ecclesiastical properties as are officially permitted. Leaders of these groups have often been described in the West as cowardly, ambitious and lacking any moral character or church statesmanship.

But the instances when churchmen have taken the initiative in creating a "compromise" or "collaborationist" situation have been exceedingly rare. There have been some cases. In every such case known to the writer, the individual or group concerned has been driven to offer himself to government offices by motives not absent among churchmen in other parts of the world. Generally, however, it has been the governments which have approached individual churchmen, frequently already compromised, and used them as nuclei around which to build "nationalized" churches.[2]

But the factors which led many churchmen to welcome a *modus vivendi* with their new governments were not the most publicized: not weakness, nor fear for personal safety, nor delusion with Communist propaganda.

Political Realists

As monarchies and multi-party republics were replaced by Communist governments, and it became evident that these governments would not quickly disappear, many churchmen, whether for reasons of theological conviction or political realism, accepted the new regimes as their *de facto* governments.[3] This

---

1. Hungarian Lutheran Bp. Veöreös, *Uj Harangszo; Die Protestantischen Kirchen;* 1939-1950, Enc. 42 (*Chron.*, p. 442).
2. Described in Chapter III, p. 72 ff.
3. Russian Orthodox Patriarch Tikhon, after his release from prison in 1923, stated, "The Soviet Power is indeed the power of the people, the workers and peasants. Therefore, it is stable and unshakable." Beginning from this presupposition the Church developed a new set of relations with the new Govern-

(130)

did not mean they heartily agreed with all actions of such governments, or would not have welcomed another had such a possibility been likely.[4] This was the government in power and change was unlikely. They sought therefore for the Church to continue in its actual situation, not in some world of fantasy.

Concept of the Church

The basic concept of the Church held by those seeking a *modus vivendi* seems little different from that of the resisters and, in fact, most early leaders of the *modus vivendi* group had been at one time near or in the resistance camp. Their change from one to the other may have had less to do with a changed concept of the Church, than with their acceptance of the fact that Communist governments were here to stay. Both thought of the Church in terms of institution, of prestige and power. The one held that these were possible within the framework of the new State, the other did not. More will be said on this point in Chapters X and XI.

Spiritual Fatigue

This has been mentioned briefly. Many outstanding leaders had been killed. Physical weariness sapped the spiritual resources and surrendered the sense of determination and moral indignation of many others. Any crusading, aggressive witness was further undermined among those who retained their physical strength by an acute sense of guilt over past injustices such as Nazi-royalist or anti-Communist collaboration, and anti-semitism. Still others were weakened by their confusion over the complexities of the new situation, and by lack of conviction of their own rightness and infallibility.

Moral Relativism

Many churchmen could find no clear line at which the Church should take an absolute stand, no martyr-point at which the Church must issue a categorical "no!"[5] The Church itself had been too deeply involved in past injustices to take on the

---

ment, and went on with its work (The Moscow Patriarchate, *The Truth About Religion in Russia*, p. 28; *Chron.*, p. 234).

4. Said one East European churchman: "Many prefer democracy, after the Anglo-Saxon model, but, to be sincere, democracy with us can have no other form than Communism. Our middle class is incapable of thinking democratically, incapable of altruism. . . ."

5. In Hungary, Lutheran Bishop Veöreös wrote that while the Lutheran Church did not wish to give up its schools, "if the legislation . . . takes them from us, we bow before it . . . The boundary line (of martyrdom) is not the school question." (*Die Protestantischen Kirchen*, 1939-1950, Enc. 42; *Chron.*, p. 442. Many agreed with his conclusion. The difficulty was in trying to find where that boundary line was.

role of martyr now, even if Communist governments were so foolish as to force it to that position. Consequently, as, bit by bit, Christians gave in on minor issues which were not adequate cause for spiritual battle, they were eventually to find that they had no adequate ground left for a *cause celebre*, and no will to resist on major issues. Absolute principles and moral sensibilities had been worn through on the little, and often non-religious issues.

Yet, in the changing situation, the Church could not be neutral. It must either demonstrate to Communists that it did not support reactionary elements, or else it would be incriminated by its silence for supporting them. The possibility of a third alternative would never occur to many churchmen, particularly those who assumed that if the Church continued, it must do so as an institutional entity. If, then, the only alternatives were to be "reactionary," or to "support the government's reform program"; if the Church were invited to pray for the welfare of the people and the government, or by not praying seem to oppose the people's welfare; if it might support agricultural and economic reform, or be lumped with feudal tyrants—what was the Church to do?

Here, the doctrinaire attitude of Western churches did not make it any easier for Eastern Christians. For, if, apprising their situation, East European churches supported some aspect of their government's program, Western churches, following the lead of the Resistance, labelled them "Communist churches" and scarcely any longer fellow-Christians. Or, if they sought to maintain fellowship with Christians in the West on terms comprehensible by the West, the absolutist nature of their domestic situation implicated them as being in opposition to their government's total program, and they could therefore make only an opposition witness at home.

A great number of church leaders, well aware of the risks involved, have seen the alternative of governmental cooperation the lesser of evils. They have sought to temporize at a crucial time. In the very difficult and chaotic post-war situation, they needed to re-group their forces, re-assess the weakness and strength of a bombed and mutilated church. During that period many leaders sought to avoid brutal and total disruption of the remaining church structure. In choosing that position, in going along with Communism on issues where the Church had a common interest, some undoubtedly hoped it might be possible to temper, if not transform Communism's worst aspects. As has been evident from the events, they have done so, not without frequent protests, long negotiation and much intervention. One cannot easily say they have not had some success, even measured by human standards, and they have maintained the churches' presence and ministry.

However, it has since become evident that ultimately every official church leader must become a "nationalized" churchman—a "collaborator," in the vocabulary of the totalitarian anti-Communist. What does this comprise? His role has already been described on page 54 and following. His government is different, but in principle his position is not unlike that of any churchman in a state-church set-up. The government supports him; he supports the government. His religious work is assured.

But it would be false to imply that all church leaders in positions of responsibility in East Europe are government stooges. Most are not. Even some of those most enthusiastic in their apparent praise of Communist governments have expressed fundamental reservations concerning their church-government relationship. Churchmen in high positions of leadership, under some government pressure to make pronouncements on various issues, frequently come out with thinly-veiled "tongue in cheek" statements, or with deliberate over-statements which satirize the whole affair, or with total silence when much loud noise would be expected. With such touches of humor they reveal some spiritual integrity and independence in a situation where overwhelming odds are against them. A message of congratulation from an Orthodox Church to Stalin on his seventieth birthday is a good example:

> "It was thanks to your political acumen that the Russian Orthodox Church came into being, and rose, as was its due, to be the highest authority in the Communist resistance of pernicious influence from the West."

In several countries discourses frequently begin with such words as, "Freedom of religion, as proclaimed and guaranteed by the Constitution of the People's Republic, is the basis of our religious life today!"

There is a "Peoples Democratic Church," or "nationalized" church, a church which has reached a *modus vivendi*, in every Communist situation. Seen from one point of view, someone must represent the Church *vis-a-vis* the incumbent government. But that "Church" may prove to be little more than an official shell thrown up to shelter the deeper life of the Christian community.

"It is either we who become the obedient instruments of Jesus Christ, or it is Him that we try to make our instrument in serving our own designs and ideals. . . . (Any other) possibility would only mean open atheism. But let us be satisfied with the double possibility of either faith or hypocrisy."[1]

Chapter IX

RENEWAL AND RE-FORMATION—A SPIRITUAL OFFENSIVE

Where there has been a third alternative to the "modus vivendi" and "resistant" church positions, it has been based on a different concept of the Church and a different atttiude toward the State.

Concept of the Church

"Resistance" and "modus vivendi" church leaders were concerned with the Church as an institution whose destiny seemed dependent upon its relationships with the world about it. In this chapter we must consider the practical consequences of those who conceived of the Church as a spirit and a community whose power was neither given nor controlled by secular authorities. The former were concerned with survival (perhaps combined with obedience); the latter with obedience.

One induces the reformers' concept of the Church and its calling by their effect upon the life of the Church (p. 137 ff.) and by a few statements from principal leaders (esp. Bishop Bereczky, Professor Hromadka).

The re-formation position began with an acute sense of judgment: the Revolution and Communism were manifestations of the chastising hand of God. In Czechoslovakia, Protestant theologian J. Hromadka called the *coup d'etat* an indigenous revolution springing from legitimate demands for justice and integrity. Protestants in Hungary had long been convinced of the inevitability of a radical change in ecclesiastical and political orders. Many others in East Europe who recognized that the churches had failed in their "day of grace," that is, to correct social injustices while they were in a position to do so, turned first to themselves and their churches to see what corrective message the revolution might

---

1. Statement of the Ecumenical Study Commission of the Hungarian Reformed and Lutheran Churches, *Hungarian Church Press*, Aug. 15, 1953, p. 28.

embody for them, before taking up the battle against that movement which now boldly proclaimed justice.

They concluded that God had penetrated history and their immediate lives with judgment. If so, then that act in a specific historical situation should have primary authority over hierarchy, councils, or church. Whatever the consequences to church structure, polity or program, God's judgment as revealed in that historical situation should be heeded. *Deus vult.*

As those sensing judgment observed the turbulent situation about them, they saw old patterns of church life disintegrating. At the same time new patterns were already evident, formed as they were more by circumstances than man's design (p. 137 ff.). There were remarkable similarities to early apostolic forms and practices. Christians concluded that God not only judges and wills in the actual situation, but confirms and guides with acts of Grace.

This gave a new set of values. Institutional patterns, whether church or otherwise, were neither absolute nor sacrosanct. Primary values were in the historical situation, in seeing judgment fulfilled. And whether they wished to be or not, the re-formers, because they were a minority bucking established church patterns, were often regarded as being as much in rebellion against the churches as against the new "historical fact" of Communism. They were perhaps an *ecclesiola*, but not necessarily *in ecclesia*, and those who did maintain a relationship to established church patterns, did not speak for official churches. They spoke for the historical situation—or God in it.

It was perfectly natural, then, that the re-formers, who had not sought reform for reform's sake or even for the churches' sake, should have to conclude that the Church must also have its revolution. It was evident to them that "what really mattered was not the priest, but the power he served"; not the icon or religious custom, but their hidden meaning. They rejoiced that institutional importance was giving way to kindness, love and solidarity; ecclesiastical titles and prestige to simplicity. At conferences in East Germany pastors spoke of their vocation not in terms of defending the traditions of the Church, or even extending its influence, but rather in making the Lordship of Christ visibly real.

It became evident that Christians could and must carry out their mission in a situation where many facilities—Bible Schools, church clubs, youth groups, recreation halls, orphanages, endowments, estates, publications and so on—were severely limited.

"The Hungarian Protestants are not preoccupied with all the undecided questions of East versus West, nor with the memory of Russian horrors, nor with the question of the justice or injustice of their present government; they are concentrating on their own positive task as a Church. They are trying to formulate the Word of God in fresh terms. And they are endeavoring to carry that message to the members of the Reformed Church themselves, first and foremost, as the first step towards all future work and towards determining their future attitude."[2]

Hungarian churchmen called on the Church to break from worldly ties and material comforts originating in Constantine and to become a missionary movement, a pilgrim people of God. Some went so far as to suggest that the Church should voluntarily relinquish all properties, facilities and coventional forms in order to free itself for its spiritual tasks.

Concept of the State

This concept of the Church and its calling could not be dissociated from a new attitude toward the State. In general it can be characterized as one of critical acceptance, or perhaps aloofness. Christian leaders might not, and many did not like the Communist regime, but it provided a framework in which they could still witness, teach and preach effectively. Said Reformed Bishop Bereczky in Hungary:

"Our Church, by the judgment and grace of God, lives on that spot of the world where, between two struggling giants, there is not the slightest doubt as to which is the sphere of power in which we live. We belong to the Hungarian Reformed Church which, in her earthly life and service, shares the destiny of the Hungarian people. Our task is to be Christ's Church in this part of the world, to stand here in the tension of prophetic service. No selfish longing for salvation may justify our escaping from here to a God whom we try to expropriate for our use or to a disobedient people. We must stay on the critical spot where the Church of the apostles and prophets discharges her double task: to proclaim God's Gospel and law and to intercede, in repentance, in the sight of our forgiving and gracious God, for our people. Our Church would cease to be a Church should she flee from this point of tension. She must recognize her situation, here and now, in order to be able to discharge her God-given functions. Our Church is not between East and West: our Church is in the East. She must serve here, and she must accept from God's gracious hands all struggles, travails and positive

2. Karl Barth, comment concerning the Hungarian Reformed Churches *E.P.S.*, May 7, 1948.

achievements of the great transition in which we live, as opportunities to serve. . . ."

Those Christians who saw elements of judgment in their situation and who conceived of the Church as an apostolic movement believed it to be possible to approve of some measures of their governments and to disapprove of others. They assumed that negotiation was the proper method for resolving differences, rather than reproof from the pulpit, or rebellion. However, they did not peg their Christian vocation to idealistic hopes that their governments would be facilely redeemed. Whatever would happen to their governments, they maintained that they had a continuing Christian responsibility.

Principal characteristics of groups springing from, or contributing toward the formation of the reformist position can be briefly described:

Church Structure

A visitor to East Europe reported that

"Under Hitler, the German Protestant resistance used to speak frequently about a return to the system of the primitive Church, without central administration, without organizational ties between the congregations or 'cells.' Such an evolution may take place in countries of East Europe."

For one part of the Church during a prolonged period of time this is precisely what happened. Much of Christian life revolved around small cells of individuals.[3] Much of the life of the Church, its home missions, laymen's training, religious education, family and pastoral care during the most critical and chaotic post-war period was able to continue through this type of smaller, local Christian family group. These were frequently tied together by some roving Pauline-type tentmaker. Some in turn, were related to an official church administration which dealt with government offices. In general, however, the central administration of the "re-forming" group as a missionary movement became an extremely nebulous affair. There simply was not the machinery, nor the desire to give major attention to administrative matters. This did not mean that their religious life was not effective, or that the contact between worshipping groups was not very real. The occasional visit of a "presbyter" who brought news of Christian communities in far places had a significance scarcely paralleled except in apostolic times.

---

3. Later referred to as "Closed groups of spiritual fellowship" by Bp. John Peter, Lutheran Church of Hungary, *H.C.P.*, May 15, 1953, p. 88, 89.

Church Property and Support

A basic assumption of the reformist groups seems to have been that the Church in the new State could have no property or stabilized material support. Little matter. The Church as a missionary movement had no inherent desire to amass property.[4] Christian communities insofar as they had an organized life might use facilities made available by the State, but they were not dependent on such facilities for their Christian life.

Pastor Janos Victor of the Reformed Church of Hungary stated:

"The same theological scrutiny which has helped us to discover the sin in our close intertwining with the life of the world, has also had to make clear to us: the Church is, in this world, an absolute unique cause of God, which *should contain in herself all* resources necessary for her maintenance, including the material resources."[5]

Russian Evangelical Churches also reported that

"The simplicity of the early days of Christianity is our ideal, and we strive for it in all our life and work . . . Most of our blessings we received not in luxurious and costly houses of prayer but in simple rooms of the type of the Jerusalem chamber. . . . We pray unceasingly that our Russian Evangelical Churches may not deviate from the simplicity of early Christianity. It is our principle to carry on God's work in our country with our own means. The observance of this rule has developed in our Russian churches the spirit of selfless physical service. Our brothers and sisters have learned to sacrifice not only everything within their power, but even beyond their power. In this respect our churches resemble the Macedonian Churches. The generosity of our believers finds expression in large offerings which cover all the needs of the work of God in our country.[6]

While in the theoretical socialist state individuals may not hold property, in the factual situation Christians did have some property, and such as they had, in the spirit of the apostolic Christian movement, they "held in common." This was a kind of spiritual collectivism which proved to be both a judgment on Commun-

---

4. In Transylvania Protestant Churches voluntarily gave up their estates when it became clear that ownership was hindering the spiritual work of the church.

5. Janos Victor, *Five Years of Hungarian Protestantism*, p. 36.

6. *I.C.P.I.S.* No. 17, May, 1947.

ism and later, a hope for those disillusioned with strictly materialistic collectivism.

Worship

In the disrupted situation following Communist accession to power those who continued to worship publicly did so not from any expectation of social or political and religious advantage—indeed, they often lost advantages—but of conviction and need. In addition to officially approved liturgical services, there was more "private" worship. In the most difficult days of the anti-religious purges Christians in Russia established "hidden houses of prayer." Government officials referred to those participating as "ravine worshippers." In other countries "communities of prayer" and "churches in the home," in which a family or group of families came together for prayer, for worship, Bible study and mutual encouragement sprang up. The following report of a midnight meeting of a group in Russia is not unlike that of a small group meeting two thousand years ago at a town called Troas—except that one boy went to sleep at Troas!:

> " 'In Stavnoye, a little town situated in the Upper Carpathians, the meeting began at 11 p. m. In spite of the lateness of the hour, nobody went to sleep, although they all had a hard day's work behind them. They listened with gleaming eyes to the preaching of their infrequent visitors, which was to come as a strengthening of their immortal souls.' After the service they wanted to know more about 'the work of the Kingdom of God in Kiev, in the Ukraine, in Moscow, and in the whole of the U.S.S.R.' At two in the morning they broke up 'without being a bit tired.' At other places it was the same. There, too, it was always, 'don't bother about us being tired; we'd like to go on listening to you all night!' "[7]

The essential truths which were discovered in such critical times were a continuing part of the re-formers' experience; namely, that the place and time and paraphernalia of worship are not the essential factors of worship. The fact of God's presence and of a corporate offering and listening are.

The Ministry

In the nationalized church situation most clergymen have been officially appointed to their positions by Communist governments. Because they received government support, these "officials" were often distrusted by their parishioners. Other clergymen have been

---

7. *E.P.S.*, No. 49, Dec. 10, 1948.

accepted, but not entirely trusted by their governments for pastoral posts. They have been consequently shifted from parish to parish. Under these circumstances, and partly as a result of the "obliteration" era, a new type of minister has appeared. These pastors and bishops have lived, not in luxurious palaces or monasteries, but in simple, oft-times bare apartments or barracks with their people. Many, like Paul, have secured their livelihood as travelling cobblers, tailors, knife-grinders, veterinarians, or accountants. In Latvia, clergymen took up work as day laborers when they were classified as "non-workers" and lost the right to professional employment.[8]

In the U.S.S.R. Archbishop Luka of Tambov became consultant surgeon to military hospitals and eventually was decorated with the Stalin award for new surgical methods which he developed.[9] At the funeral of another well-known and beloved scientist, laymen were startled to see the corpse dressed in the full regalia of an Orthodox archbishop. Groups of monks, organized as an agricultural workers' union have traveled about the country in civilian clothing to do "migrant" harvesting. They found the "fields white unto harvest" in more ways than one. Thousands of deaconesses who had to forego life in the cloisters scattered into the villages where they made gloves and stockings, or performed other "essential" tasks while continuing to teach religion and to assist in administering sacraments in the homes.

A fundamental result of this transformation has been the breaking down of barriers between clergy and laity. The clergy, in adopting a simple life, have identified themselves with the people. And the laity, facing up to the demands of their time, have had to become responsible shepherds of their flocks, pastors, educators and missionaries.

The Laity

"The priesthood of all believers" has again become a common expression among Christians in East Europe. In their crisis situation many Christians had to forego the idea that a professional clergy was necessary to the life of the Church. Many parishes have been led by "presbyters" who continued their labors as farmers or industrial workers, and ministered to the congregations in their homes whenever opportunity afforded. A small number of roving missionaries occasionally visited the parishes to maintain a bond of fellowship and a sense of spiritual solidarity.

In one country women memorized simple liturgies and the New Testament, then went from home to home doing missionary

---

8. *Chron.*, p. 305.
9. *ICPIS*, No. 12, 1946, p. 61 (*Chron.*, p. 262).

work. Some of them baptized children, instructed the faithful and administered communion. Others, frequently called deaconesses or "readers" or "mothers," did a more lay-type social work and counselling. In another country laymen served communion, administered the sacraments and cared for the congregations. They did not necessarily desire the official sanction of their church authorities, for their action as they saw it was an imperative laid on them by God. They visited the sick, the families with children, giving religious instruction, counsel and encouragement. Many pledged themselves to bring at least ten other neighbors into their laymen's Bible study groups.

In East Germany "home visitation conferences" were organized to train leaders on four critical issues: (1) the Christian faith as related to work, to political authority, to peace and freedom; (2) the meaning of the Church, its structure and functions; (3) the Church and the world, secular ideologies, etc.; and (4) home conversation and pastoral help.

In several countries lay movements of reform and renewal, with an effective program at the level of prayer, worship, Bible study, moral reform and Christian solidarity, pre-dated Communism. In one country where specialized training was given for leaders of laymen and laywomen, youth and Sunday Schools, special attention was given to the "official ideology of today" so leaders could render a better spiritual ministry.

While it could be said by 1950 that there was less preaching than a few years earlier, it has also been said that more people were being confronted with the solid Gospel than in several generations.

Official and responsible church leaders pointed out that there was grave danger of these lay movements becoming individualistic and sectarian; but younger Christians eagerly participated in them. Many students, disillusioned with the possibility of being effective pastors in nationalized churches, preferred to be lay missionaries. Thereupon, rather than prepare themselves with theological degrees, they sought degrees in secular sciences and, after some study in "unofficial" seminaries or through private tutoring, went out as lay-pastor-missionaries.

Evangelism

In the crisis situation a carefully organized evangelistic program after Western patterns was hardly feasible. But there, where the contrast between secular hopes, hatred, deceit and corruption on the one hand, and the good news of God's love on the other, was so vivid, the communication of that good news from person to person became real evangelism. A word of encouragement from one laborer to another, a word of comfort to a doubting

mother, a small group of men meeting near their factory for mutual counsel and Bible study—this has been the climate of their
evangelism. Hungarians spoke of the "invisible evangelism"
which took place among those who gathered in homes to share
their experiences, to counsel and study together. In Poland Bible
study groups frequently met daily. And in the U.S.S.R. reports
indicated that Christians had penetrated atheistic associations,
youth groups, the army and other bodies to do missionary work.
Said the Protestant Christians of one country,

> "We do not strive for numbers, although we take joy in
> the conversion of every sinner. Figures interest us very
> little and we are not especially concerned with statistics
> of our members . . ."

In that situation they have not organized campaigns for half-con-
vinced Christians to tell the world about their half-convictions.
Individuals simply professed their faith at every opportunity, and
very often most potently in silence.

Religious Education

With the banning of religious instruction from the public
schools

> "responsibility (falls) now on the parents, godparents
> and teachers . . . who must become missionaries and shep-
> herds of children and youth."[10]

In many countries laymen and women received special training for work among children. Parents met together to prepare
themselves for such responsibility. Religious instruction might
then take place within the church, in the home, or out of doors.
In one country religious training has been given in a travelling
circus van.

While religious instruction has not been as systematic as in
pre-Communist times, the quality and spirit of that given in the
homes, in the immediate family circle, in neighborhood Bible study
groups, during pastoral visits, and through the intensity of witness of those children who dared be seen worshipping in the sanctuary, may somewhat compensate for any losses in system and
quantity.

Where organized church youth work became no longer possible, churches faced one of their greatest problems. Efforts to
establish youth organizations, such as the CHRISTOMOL (patterned after the Communist youth organization COMSOMOL),
have been shortlived. The only specialized effort churches have

---

10. Statement of a Hungarian church leader in 1949.

carried out for young people with any marked success has been the organization of religious choirs.

Social Message and Action

The social witness of the "re-former" groups has been made in at least four ways: (1) in their message to governments; (2) in their message to the Church; (3) in their relationship to the masses; and (4) in the nature of the reformed *Koinonia* itself.

Christian groups and individuals who identified themselves with their indigenous situation and demonstrated their loyalty and concern for the ultimate good of the people have been able to speak out courageously on social issues. These voices are not to be confused with those which simply echoed the statements of their governments. The "prophets" who have spoken fearlessly have had a tremendous domestic impact—they were either heard and heeded or else destroyed.

Immediately after the Communist *coup d'etat* in Czechoslovakia, Protestant leaders called on Communists to fulfill the responsibilities which fell upon them. This could hardly have been possible had not those leaders, prior to the revolution, been active in seeking social justice and reform. Where the prophets have spoken in a spirit of creative love, they have had a salutary effect. Untried Communist leaders have been counselled. Confused populations have often found new purpose and possibilities of action.

As to the Church, the re-formers have appealed to Christians, whether anti-government or pro-government, to fulfill their non-political spiritual mission of proclaiming God's message of truth, justice, love and mercy, "the standards by which all is to be estimated." They have urged fellow-Christians not to be resentful about the loss of bourgeois comforts, nor to withdraw into pietistic solitude, but to bring the most creative force of their faith into the situation in order to save the noblest aspirations of the new order from materialistic corruption, to assist in the elimination of class privileges and social and economic injustices, at all times reserving their right of criticism.

Czech Brethren, for example, called on Christians in hope and love and intercessory prayer to help

> "in the building up of juster social institutions . . .
> Though this is being done on a basis differing from the
> ultimate truths of our faith, we should for the sake of
> that very faith, set its true value on the positive side of
> this effort. We must return to the beginnings of the
> church, to apostolic times. . . . We don't know what will
> happen tomorrow."[11]

---

11. *E.P.S.*, March 10 and October 13, 1950.

With regard to the masses, re-formers have recognized that the one class which the proletarianization of society was expected to produce would come about, if a tall, very often through legalistic and oppressive measures. Such Christians sought in advance to identify themselves with other human beings across existing "class" barriers of distrust and hostility, confident that in fulfilling this law of Christ much oppression and suffering would be avoided.

Where the Christian community has dealt most effectively with social problems, and made its most significant social witness, has been in the nature and function of the community itself. For in East Europe, effective social witness does not come from legislation or political pressure, nor from idealistic resolutions, but from the interdependent relationship of Christian to Christian, the sense of solidarity and of responsibility one with another.

If the official Church has had to forego its social welfare agencies and program, it has not surrendered the normal processes of Christian sharing between individuals and groups. Thus in country after country former programs carried out by agencies have been replaced by the personalized services of congregations and individuals to those in need. When catastrophe hit one member of the community, when a bread-winner was imprisoned or injured, the whole community would take responsibility for the family. And that sense of interdependence and solidarity extended beyond any narrowly defined Christian community into areas where refugees sought housing, the unemployed sought a crust of bread, and the hunted sought refuge and comfort. In many cases it has been more effective materially—and certainly spiritually—than when these responsibilities were pushed off on professional associations or institutions.

Church Universal

In this situation lines of division among Christians could no longer be drawn strictly on the basis of confessional adherence. Home worship groups might include former members of several confessions, and a chapel might house the altars of two, three or even four communions in different corners. Sacraments administered by one denomination could be more readily received by members of another. Small groups, families and individuals might be isolated, but there was still an abiding sense of their participation in the Church Universal.

Reformist groups, *ecclesiola,* or prophets sprang up in the midst of chaos when former patterns were disrupted and new patterns must be found. They did not set out to restore old patterns or to invent something new. They sought first to be obedient to the One Whom they felt had shaken the foundations, Who had made Himself known among them, and in Whose ultimate victory they were assured. They were often individualistic, eclectic; their greatest peril was their own sectarianism. Yet they did experience a new kind of community—the family of Christ—which could scarcely escape developing certain patterns of life and taking on more permanent forms.

As the situation in which they existed became normalized, it was inevitable that they should have to face up to the question of their relationship to the officially organized, institutional churches.[12] This is the point at which the Communists also had a particular interest. In the same way that socialism is regarded by Communists as their worst political enemy, Communists recognized that a revived and reformed religion was a more serious threat to Communism than either the "resistance" or the "modus vivendi" church. In its issue of December, 1940 *Bolshevik* magazine stated:

> "On the basis of the work of Lenin and Stalin and the experience of the Bolshevik Party in its struggle against the 'builders of the city of God' and the 'God seekers,' we must continually lay bare the attempts of the clergy to renew, purify, adapt religion to the new conditions. It must be demonstrated to the workers that all religion, whatever its camouflage, is hostile in principle to Communism."[13]

Recent attacks on Protestant Christianity in the U.S.S.R. indicate that there is a real desire on the part of some Communists to root out this "refined religion" which is not of their own making. That they cannot do so by administrative measures, Communists have conceded. Whether they can do so by substituting their own, or an impure, "unrefined" religion is another question.

---

12. Discussed more fully in Chapter XI.
13. *ICPIS*, No. 5, February, 1941.

"Individuals . . . speak as servants of the whole Church . . ."

Chapter X

THE CONDITIONING INFLUENCE OF CONFESSION AND TRADITION

In the three preceding chapters the three major responses to Communism have been dealt with as they developed among individuals, principally among Christian leaders. It was indicated that all confessions were represented in all three groups and that therefore no position, "resistance," "collaboration" or "reformation," could be precisely identified with any confession. However, this is only partly true.

The response of the body of believers has been of a different sort from that of individual leaders, and an important factor in the total response of the Church. Believers did not confront Communism in the abstract. Few were concerned or able to draw up a "position" based on careful research and analysis, which should be applied logically wherever Communist practices challenged the Church. When the average believer was challenged by Communism he acted. His action sprang primarily and often subconsciously from the deposit of centuries of church life and thought and practices in his own framework of thought and temperament.

One believer did not therefore act in isolation. People with a common experience of the history, theology and habits of one tradition formed a body of response. Those of a different tradition formed, or tended to form another. Differing traditions have therefore resulted in some variance in the corporate actions of their respective adherents. Such actions, or bodies of response have, in turn, affected, if not shaped the official positions of churches.

At the highest administrative level, common experience, traditions and historic policies, plus the existence of a body of response among believers, predetermined that there should be near-official policies on a confession-wide basis. The Orthodox churches after their conference in Moscow, July, 1948, had what could be called an official position. Roman Catholics, following the excommunication decree of the Vatican in July, 1949, had no doubt

---

* Paraphrase of a message to the churches of Saxony, (*E.P.S.*, No. 16, 1953).

as to the official position of the Roman Catholic Church. Protestants had no centralized authority. They therefore had no fixed political position, but they did have a body of response and that in itself amounted to a position of empiricism.

The following comparative summary suggests that the tendency among the Orthodox Christians was toward a *modus vivendi* position, among Roman Catholics toward opposition, and among Protestants toward an attitude of critical acceptance and independence of secular authority—perhaps re-formation.

Protestants

In general, the response of Protestants has been determined by three principal factors: (1) their concept of the Church as the gathered community, the pilgrim people of God; (2) their concept and practice of the priesthood of all believers; and (3) concepts and experiences of Protestants in relation to the State and the Catholic Church. The last is the most obvious and perhaps most determinative. It involves the human factor: the social and political status of the Protestant community and whether Protestants had become accustomed to a place of influence in the affairs of State.

Where Protestants were small in number and where they lived already in a social or political ghetto, they not only did not resist, but to a certain extent welcomed Communist governments as giving some promise of liberation from, or equality with their larger "ancient foe" of Roman Catholicism or state churches.[1] But if they did not resist, neither did many collaborate. They were prepared to see the re-forming of the Church, but they no more intended to become vassals of the Communist State than of previous states.

Where Protestants were of such proportions as to have a measure of political power (Hungary, Czechoslovakia, East Germany), their practical response to the Communist State depended very much on their recent relations to Nazi powers. Where they had collaborated with the former power, they did not maintain firm resistance to the new. It was a day of judgment, not of shifting loyalties, and repentance and reformation were more widespread than was collaboration. Those who had resisted Nazism, also resisted Communism. But it was not a blind, nor underground resistance. They maintained that a witness must be made among people in the existential situation and therefore, even while protesting and resisting, they were prepared to make provisional

---

1. This was true in Poland, Bulgaria, Rumania (except Transylvania), and Bohemia.

adaptations in church life and structure in order to witness in their real world.

Protestants have held diverse concepts of the State which need not be examined here. This point is relevant and has been rather widely accepted: that while the State has no right to determine the shape of the Church, if it attempts to do so, the Church can still work and witness. The Church does not require a patron State in order to do its work.

Secondly, Protestant experience and theology did not require a specialized priestly order for its continued existence. Generations of proclaiming the priesthood of all believers suggested an immediate alternative to Protestants when the priesthood of the official clergy was restricted. So long as there were Christians there were priests.

The third factor shaping a Protestant response has been their concept of the Church as the gathered community of God. If it is that, then Protestants were clear that so long as there were scattered individual believers, there was a church. They could adjust or be adjusted to the political framework in which God had set them and still be His people. In many places prior to the Communist order, small Protestant groups living under the oppression of church-state regimes had formed themselves into "home churches." Lay responsibility and voluntary church support was a common practice. It had been done. It could be done again. "Let the church be the church" in its preaching, healing, and prophecy, became the Protestant slogan for the new day.

While many exceptions can be found to these broad generalizations, there is still sufficient evidence to indicate where one genius of Protestantism lies, namely, in its freedom from inflexible traditions and its openness to purification and re-formation.

Orthodoxy

Several factors which influenced Orthodox Christians in their response to Communism were common also to Roman Catholics. For example, the majority of Orthodox and Catholic believers were peasants whose natural tendency was to see the political religious struggle in terms of black and white. They would therefore see no alternative to absolutist responses: either resist, or support the regime. In Russia, the Orthodox Church began by resisting; the Catholic Church tried to negotiate some settlement with the Communist Government.[2] As will be indicated in Chapter XI the underlying question was, can the Church exist? When Orthodox

---

2. R. C. Bp. Cepliak declared in 1923 that the Catholic population had always been loyally Soviet, that the Revolution had freed the Catholics and that the idea of counter-revolution had never occurred to them (Timasheff, *Religion in Soviet Russia*, p. 53; *Chron.*, p. 234).

Church leaders realized that the Church could not have its "minimal" existence by resisting, it was ready for any overtures toward a *modus vivendi*. When the Catholic Church realized it could not have the existence it required by mutual agreement, it began fighting back. The fundamental question was the same.

However, certain factors have helped incline Orthodox believers toward the *modus vivendi* position both in the U.S.S.R. and later in other lands. First is the fact that there was a principal center of Orthodoxy in the Communist orbit, i.e., Moscow. Had the headquarters of such a significant Church been beyond the reach of the Communist machine, its position would undoubtedly have been very different.

Secondly, the Orthodox Church historically has never had, nor claimed the secular freedom of churches in the West. Since the time of the Byzantine empire Orthodoxy has had a definite relationship, and has often known subjection to secular authority. It has existed victoriously in spite of tyranny and tragedy. What import, therefore, one secular tyrant more? The State could be regarded as a necessary evil, a consequence of sin, to be endured rather than transformed or countered and still an entity of which one must take cognizance.[3]

Further, Orthodoxy in its theology is Christ-centered. The focus of religious experience is beyond this life. Human existence is not expected to provide ease and comfort. Through centuries of tragedy and death Orthodoxy had come to realize that the dividing line between life and death was not sharp and not of primary importance. Orthodox faith was therefore inclined to make more allowance for this world's tragedies and to esteem death as neither final nor the worst possible alternative.

Finally, Orthodox Christians held that history was not measured in terms of a year or a decade, or even a century, that God's ultimate triumph was assured in spite of all temporal reverses.

Given these underlying concepts, it was not unnatural that Orthodox Christians should, like Protestants, accept many reforms,[4] but unlike Protestants who were not ultimately concerned about recognition by secular powers, should eventually seek a mode of living with whatever regime was in power while at the same time protesting the disparity between the Christian faith and Communism.[5]

---

3. Paradoxically, Orthodox Christians in Russia felt that the Russian people were an instrument of Divine purpose in history and possibly that Divine purpose must be expressed through whatever body-politic existed.

4. In *The Truth About Religion in Russia*, pp. 36, 37, reference is made to the return of the Church to "Apostolic times" (*Chron.*, p. 297).

5. Message of Metropolitan Sergius on the recognition of the Orthodox Church, June 10, 1927; P. Anderson, *People, Church and State in Modern Russia*, p. 74 (*Chron.*, p. 288).

Roman Catholicism

The characteristic Catholic response has not sprung, as in the case of Orthodoxy and Protestantism, from the past, through the body of believers, to common action and eventually to some form of policy. The Catholic response has proceeded from official policy to the action of Catholic groups. The latter have had little to do with its formulation. So long as they remained in the Church, Catholic faithful were expected to obey and implement official policy, or be silent, or be excommunicated.

In determining policy, however, Roman Catholic officialdom was scarcely at liberty to choose from among several alternatives. The Catholic Church could not choose to continue its customary friendly relationship with state powers. The Communist powers determined that. Concordats were abrogated, diplomatic missions were recalled, and neither was replaced. Co-existence was not a live alternative.

The main reason on the part of the Communists was that they did not trust, or if they trusted, did not accept Catholic intentions. Their immediate experience of Roman Catholicism led them to believe that Catholicism was essentially imperialistic, that it would be satisfied with nothing less than a position of political primacy in East European affairs. This they could not allow.

There was considerable evidence to support their conclusion. They were undoubtedly aware that in 1939 the Vatican rejected a proposal from Britain for the Roman Catholic Church to participate in an anti-Communist *bloc*. At that time Roman Catholicism had no major stake in the battle between Communist and non-Communist forces. The only Roman Catholics affected directly by Communism were a few believers in the U.S.S.R., and they had apparently effected some *modus operandi* with the Soviet Government.

Two years later, when the Axis forces invaded the U.S.S.R., Roman Catholic voices were heard calling for Catholic missionaries to follow Italian Fascist occupation armies into southern Russian territory. At the same time, Catholicism in Germany was supporting the Nazi German invasion of Russia from the West. And in America, when the U.S.S.R. was pleading for war materiel in order to repel the Nazi invaders, Roman Catholics in America effectively vetoed any such assistance until assurances were given that the Churches in the U.S.S.R., would be given free reign.

The Vatican's excommunication decree of July, 1949, simply uncovered and confirmed to Communists the absolutist demands of a political nature of Roman Catholicism.[6] Communists were not unaware that the final break which the excommunication decree signaled might have been avoided, as well as excommunication itself. Although all the great Italian statesmen of the last hundred years had been excommunicated,[7] Mussolini had not been. But the Communists were not prepared to accept the Catholic Church in the role which that kind of deal involved. Nor were former Catholics and members of other confessions. On this point they were scarcely less determined than government officials.

If the co-existence of Catholicism and Communist authority was improbable, a *modus vivendi* position for the Church as an ultimate solution was impossible, for this would require a pattern of church life, and a status of church existence which Roman Catholicism could not accept. This came out very clearly in the concordat negotiations in Hungary, Poland and Czechoslovakia. For the Catholic churchman, Christ is the King above all kings, the President presiding over all presidents. As Christ's vicar on earth, the Pope, his nuncios, the Church, have authority above secular powers. The State should therefore respect and obey the voice of the Church. To the mind of Catholic authorities, the acceptance of a *modus vivendi* under Communist governments was tacit recognition of their superior authority. This, the Catholic Church could not accept beyond a very temporary basis.

For similar reasons, the Catholic Church could not take the re-formist position described in the preceding chapter. The Catholic Church does not re-form its pattern and structure because of a shifting external situation. The current situation, once a church pattern is set, is expected to conform to the Church's less transitory pattern. If the Church cannot have its forms under a given government then the government must change.

---

6. The excommunication decree had very particular reference to the authority of the hierarchy over the lower clergy. Another point at which Catholic absolutism became evident was on the education question. When Communist governments began nationalizing educational systems, Catholics complained of tyranny in education. The conflict was not over ownership of schools. In Hungary the Roman Catholic Church had owned nearly twice as many schools as did the State, and in Poland practically none. Poland was so completely a Catholic nation that it was not necessary for the Church to maintain separate Catholic schools; all schools were Catholic schools, and Catholic teachers were appointed, and priests were admitted to a share in the teaching, as a matter of course ("The Pattern of Persecution," *The Tablet*, April 8, 1950). In both cases, in Poland and Hungary, the Church was relatively satisfied with historic property arrangements. But, in both places, and in other parts of the world where Catholicism is in power, its insistence on authoritarian method and doctrinaire content of education, its attempts to control staff and textbooks, its imposition of Catholic dogma on non-Catholic children suggested to Communists that its ultimate concern was not freedom of thought and the processes of liberal education. Catholicism was rather a rival for control of the minds of the next generation.

7. Among those excommunicated: Mazzini, Garibaldi, General Cadorus, Prince Umberto, D'Szeglio (article by Mario Rossi, *The Nation*, Sept. 10, 1949).

There was also another reason; the attitude of non-Catholics would scarcely allow the Catholic Church to adapt or purify itself, and still go by the Catholic label. As they saw it, Roman Catholicism had had its great opportunity to reform, and to change society, and had not done so. Until Communism came into power, Roman Catholicism, particularly in Poland, Hungary, and parts of Czechoslovakia, either had determinative influence, or was in political control for several generations. The Hapsburg Empire apart from Roman Catholicism was practically impossible. So also, as a competent East European has reminded us, Dollfuss in Austria, Pilsudski in Poland, revisionism in Hungary and autonomism in Croatia, without their respective Roman archbishops and political clericalism, are unthinkable. These intimate relationships of the Roman Catholic Church to medieval feudalism, to inquisitions and economic injustice during more than two hundred years when the Church might have reformed society, have convinced many that Roman Catholicism was not basically concerned with alleviating man's existence, and any pretensions in that direction would run against strong suspicion and opposition. Catholic policy in countries where Roman Catholicism is presently in a position of influence, in Spain and several countries of Latin and South America, has not allayed these suspicions. The basic attitude toward man involved therein has been a far heavier indictment of Roman Catholicism in East Europe than its bad war record in France, Yugoslavia, Hungary or other areas of East Europe.[8]

This is not to suggest, however, that Roman Catholicism has not championed the rights of man lately restricted by Communist Governments. In Poland, Czechoslovakia and Hungary, Catholic churchmen have courageously charged their governments with specific violations of human rights, and pledged themselves to defend those rights.[9] Where the authors had taken a similar line in previous circumstances, their protests would obviously have some considerable popular, and therefore official hearing. But in Rumania, when, in 1947, Catholic bishops protested to Premier Groza that the arrest of conservative politicians and Catholic Church leaders was an infringement on human rights, Groza silenced them by asking why they had not similarly protested when Communists and liberals were being arrested by the preceding quasi-religious conservative government.[10] Under such circumstances, Commu-

---

8. Though many Roman Catholic leaders were personally staunch anti-Fascists, *Izvestia* accused the Vatican of supporting Hitler's and Mussolini's campaigns and cited considerable evidence (*Chron.*, p. 257).

9. Letter of Polish Cardinal Sapieha to the President of Poland (*Chron.*, p. 420); pastoral letter of Hungarian Card. Mindszenty on government abuses (*Chron.*, p. 472); statement of the Czechoslovakian R. C. clergy against the Law of Oct. 14, 1949 (*Chron.*, p. 522).

10. *Chronicle*, p. 324.

nists and some other East Europeans questioned whether Catholicisms' protests were based on transgressions of truth, or on the infringement of Catholic prerogatives.

For such reasons as this, pronouncements and protests alone have not convinced non-Catholics in East Europe of Catholicism's sincerity or purity of motive, nor of its desire or possibility to reform.

The Pope's message, "Menti Nostrae," of 1950, a definition of Catholicism's opposition to secular materialism, whether capitalistic or communistic, and an appeal to follow Catholicism's new, religious way, was apparently scarcely noticed in East Europe. Catholicism to non-Catholics there meant politics, not religion. And evidences of the "new" way in the Catholic Church's treatment of worker-priests in France, the establishment of Catholic political parties in Germany, Austria, Belgium and Italy suggested that if the "new" way in East Europe was intended to mean religion, in West Europe, the actual way apparently still meant politics.

Catholicism's possibilities of reforming, or of getting popular support for some new position or program were as unlikely, then, as its desires to reform. That part of the Catholic Church which has changed its form has also changed its name: "National Catholics," or Orthodox (former Uniates), Protestants, or Communists, but not modified Roman Catholics.

If Catholicism could not reform and would not accept a secondary status by mutual agreement with Communist governments, and Communist governments would not accept Catholic superiority, then the only alternative for Catholicism was to try to change the governments, and the alternative for Communist governments was to try to overcome (nationalize) Catholicism. Such have been their respective actions.

What has been the effect of Catholic resistance? In the West the Roman Catholic Church is presented as the innocent victim of Communism's savage onslaught in East Europe, the holy martyr of the faith, God's lonely crusader for righteousness and truth. Emphasis is placed on the sufferings of Catholic leaders, the losses of charitable and educational institutions, the deprivation of basic human rights, and restrictions on the Church's performance of its religious tasks. Roman Catholic spokesmen intimate that suffering is inflicted on the Catholic Church because it champions and defends the dignity and liberty of the individual and insists on performing its religious calling.

While in the East Communists have concluded that they are dealing with a political power, not a religion, that its ultimate concern over man is not *how* he is treated, but *who* is treating him and for what purpose, that political Catholicism's purpose is to re-establish its own empire, that the Vatican is "the center of the oldest imperialist tradition," that it represents the exploitation of ignorance and superstition at its worst and most powerful, that Catholic believers, following the excommunication decree, are ultimately responsible to a foreign authority and therefore nationally untrustworthy.[11]

Insofar as the Roman Catholic Church maintains that its historic political aspirations were correct, continues its opposition on non-religious issues, and conceives of, or demonstrates its vocation in terms of political power, Communism has a prop to lean its case against, relying on the people's memories of Roman Catholicism's past mistakes and injustices and their fear of Catholicism's future ambitions. Douglas Hyde[12] states that

> "when I was in the Communist Party we took the view that most of the anti-Communist campaigns helped no one but the Communists themselves. And this (he said after renouncing Communism) was very largely true."

Similarly, an American ambassador in a Communist country where the Roman Catholic Church is not yet wholly nationalized reported to the writer that in that country, by its tyrannical practices in the religious realm, and its excessive and unenlightened abuses of Communism, Roman Catholicism was converting more people to Communism than were the Communists. One may well ask whether Catholicism, by its negative political opposition, rather than buttressing the Church, is not buttressing Communism. This is a matter of very deep concern to many devoutly religious Roman Catholics.

In an earlier chapter it was suggested that within a given body of response to Communism there is fellowship across confessional lines. But, as was suggested in Chapter III (p. 68 ff.), where these bodies of response harden into official policy the unity of the Church Universal is terribly strained. It is not our purpose here to imply that one church is opposed to another. They know in East Europe that Communism is not a war simply against Roman Catholicism. On the other hand, it is clear that any alliance with one totalitarian power, regardless of its name, to oppose another totalitarian power is to lose the Church and the ultimate hopes it espouses. There are Roman Catholics who desire to see the Church as the Holy Church. The real question in relationships between confessions in East Europe is whether Christians of diverse political groups can help one another regain their first, religious calling and effect together a creative, affirmative witness.

---

11. *Chronicle, passim.*
12. Douglas Hyde, *The Answer to Communism*, p. 55.

"We have to learn to live according to faith ..."[1]

Chapter XI

SOME LATER THEOLOGICAL DEVELOPMENTS AND TRENDS IN CHURCH PATTERNS

The last two chapters have pointed toward some basic theological issues. Not all can be considered here, but one fundamental issue should be considered. It has been posed to Eastern churchmen in the form of a simple question: Shall the Church exist? Or shall it be obedient?

This question probes deeper than church practice and policy, deeper than concepts of the Church, the ministry, the traditions or the Scriptures (though these are all ultimately involved). It seeks answering at the level of one's concept of Divine penetration and revelation in history, indeed of God Himself—and not only one's concept of God, but one's personal knowledge of God.

This question will be considered in relation to three situations:[2] Orthodox Christians in the Soviet Union; Reformed Christians in Hungary; and Lutheran Christians in East Germany. Except for one brief comment it need not be considered further in relation to Roman Catholicism; it is not a live question for Roman Catholics. For the Catholic Church, to be obedient requires that the Church be maintained, in a particular form. God has revealed His truth to the Church in *past* history, and the Church is charged as trustee to safeguard and transmit that truth from person to person and generation to generation. The Church at any point in history is one link in a continuing chain from Beginning to End. But if one link disappears, then the whole chain is lost. The visible Church must therefore secure its existence by whatever means because of a charge laid on it by God. It has no choice in the matter. Its principal concern is to secure *its* existence.

Theological Trends as Reflected Among Orthodox Christians in the Soviet Union

For this study we can take as our point of departure some resolutions of the Conference of Orthodox Clergy and Laymen, held in June, 1917. The Conference was held on the eve of popu-

---

1. Unpublished documents from East Germany.
2. While something might be said concerning smaller Protestant groups and Orthodox Churches in other countries these three describe principal positions and developments involved.

lar uprisings against the royal Government and in some respects against the Church. It was already evident that drastic reforms affecting the Church were likely to follow.

The concept of the nature and vocation and method of the Church prevalent among Orthodox leaders is indicated in resolutions from the Conference. The Church not only did not expect its shape to be determined in any sense by its environment, but did in fact expect, by virtue of its own social and political status, to determine something of the shape of society.

> "In the Russian State the Orthodox Church must hold, among other religious confessions, a place of priority, most favored in government and in public rights, as is fitting to her as the supreme sacred object of the people, of exceptional historic and cultural value, and also as the religion of the majority of the population . . ." (Further), "the Orthodox Church in Russia, in matters concerning its structure, legislation and teaching of faith and morality, services of worship, internal church discipline and external relationships with other churches is independent of governmental authority."[3]

Six months later Patriarch Tikhon protested in a pastoral letter that the Church (now called "the Holy Church of Christ" rather than the traditional "Russian Orthodox Church") was being persecuted by those "endeavoring to destroy the work of Christ." After appealing to the Communists to "come to yourselves, ye idiots, cease your bloody deeds," the Patriarch excommunicated all those involved aggressively in persecution and went on to appeal to "beloved brethren, archbishops, bishops and priests" to come "to the defense of the down-trodden rights of the Orthodox Church . . . to enter the ranks of voluntary spiritual fighters . . . that the enemies of the Church of Christ will be shamed and scattered . . ."[4] A month later (February, 1918) the Holy Synod of the Orthodox Church issued instructions to the scattered parishes indicating how they should defend the churches against Government acts and how they should establish underground churches in order to continue their existence.[5] The Church, as it was, must be defended. This would be a holy service in obedience to Christ.

An incidental point of view which has considerable relevance was expressed in a message of the "Sobor" of the splinter "Living Church" (of Archpriest Vvendensky) of August, 1922. The mes-

---

3. Paul Anderson, *People Church and State in Modern Russia*, p. 41 (*Chron.*, p. 278).

4. Paul Anderson, *op. cit.*, pp. 53-55 (*Chron.*, pp. 279-280).

5. *Ibid.*, pp. 55-57 (*Chron.*, pp. 282-283).

sage was in effect a precursor of the position to be taken later by the official Church.

"The Holy Sobor urges all churchmen to abandon all attempts to use the Church for temporal political schemes, for the Church belongs to God and must serve Him only . . . Churchmen must not see in the Soviet authority the anti-Christ; on the contrary, the Sobor calls attention to the fact that the Soviet authority is the only one throughout the world which will realize, by governmental methods, the ideals of the Kingdom of God. Therefore, every faithful churchman must not only be an honorable citizen but also fight with all his might together with the Soviet authorities for the realization of the Kingdom of God upon earth."[6]

The "ideals of the Kingdom of God" were then defined as a standard of material and social life. The Church affects these ideals or standards only through the cooperative action of individual Christians supporting their (now-to-be) recognized governments. The Kingdom of God was evidently conceived of as something different from "ideals of the Kingdom," and the role of the Church was to prepare the people for that eternal Kingdom.

After his release from prison the following summer, Patriarch Tikhon indicated a new position on the part of Orthodox Church leaders radically different from that of June, 1917.

"With a calm conscience . . . submit to the Soviet power, not for fear but for conscience's sake, remembering the words of the Apostles, 'let every soul be subject to the higher powers. For there is no power but God; the powers that be are ordained of God.' "[7]

Having suggested that churchmen should "submit to the Soviet power" (he had learned from his own prison experience that in relation to his physical being there was no alternative), he went ahead to say that they should not submit their *consciences* to the Soviet power. "There is no power on earth that could bind our conscience as a hierarch and our patriarchal word."[8]

The Church, then, was not to fight for its material existence by aggressive acts of resistance, but, "in all things material submitting to the powers that be," was to maintain its independent conscience and spiritual ministry. Both immediately prior to, and following this statement of the Patriarch, local parishes as well as the higher administrative structure of the Church underwent radi-

---

6. *Ibid.*, pp. 63-64 (*Chron.*, p. 284).
7. The Moscow Patriarchate, *The Truth About Religion in Russia*, p. 28.
8. *Ibid.*

cal transformations. The creation of catacomb churches and secret theological training schools, the meetings of "ravine worshippers," the semi-clandestine work of bishops, monks, nuns and
others who maintained labour status and in their laboring professions performed their religious ministry were a part of this transformation. The significant fact is that at this stage the highest
Orthodox leader accepted the possibility of radical reforms in
church life while at the same time maintaining that the Church
could and must be obedient in its conscience only to its Lord.

That the Church might exist *and* be obedient in a hostile State
was spelled out in considerably more detail in the well-known
"Solovetsk document" of May, 1927. In summary, the document,
addressed as to the Government, specified that the Church desired
neither to direct the Government nor to submit to it, but rather
to co-exist with it on the basis of a mutually agreeable truce. The
basic conflict between State and Church, which was clearly recognized by the document as being between the religious teaching of
the Church and the materialistic teaching of the Communist
Party, was to be resolved by this simple formula: political and
economic life is the domain of the State. The Church would
keep out of that domain and was prepared to be loyal to whatever government ruled over that domain. The moral and spiritual
realm, however, is the domain of the Church. The document
requested that the Government recognize the Church's responsibility in that domain, and keep out of the Church's domain. The
Church was prepared to "render unto Caesar" if the Government
was prepared to "render unto God."[9]

The co-existent arrangement for which the Solovetsk document appealed materialized in June, 1927. A message of Metropolitan Sergius[10] indicated that at the level of its "existence" the
Church was prepared to accept the reforms in material and struc-
tural patterns which were demanded by the new situation (though
it was later to seek the alleviation of those patterns by calling on
the Government to live up to its own ideals).[11] However, in its own
sphere the Church would be obedient only to God and considered
the "whole aim of our existence (to be) in confessions of faith in
God." The Church, then, was prepared to accept reforms in order
to exist, but only insofar as that existence allowed for confession
of faith in God.

By 1942 there had been little change in basic theological presuppositions. In a book issued by the Moscow Patriarchate, *The*

---

9. Paul Anderson, *op. cit.*, pp. 70-74 (*Chron.*, pp. 285-287).
10. Paul Anderson, *op. cit.*, p. 74 (*Chron.*, p. 288).
11. Letter of Metropolitan Sergius on Controlling Abuses against the
Church, Feb. 19, 1930, as quoted by Anderson, *op. cit.*, pp. 82-84 (*Chron.*, pp. 291-
293).

Truth About Religion in Russia, there were clear indications that the "existence" of the Church at an austere level was not only accepted as possible but was considered a virtue. One of the authors compared the status of the Church to that of "the apostolic times, when the Church and the ministers followed exactly along their true paths to which they had been called by Christ . . ." The writer then indicated the realm of the churches' "obedience": "when they looked upon their ministry not as a profession among other worldly professions, providing them the means of livelihood, but as the following of Christ's calling." This, in fact, amounted to "confessing this faith, thanking the Lord that he in the new conditions of our life helps us to become true followers of Christ. . . . to receive . . . spiritual food . . . in the worship services and sacred rites. . . ."[12]

On January 31, 1945, the Sobor of the Russian Orthodox Church accepted a detailed statute regulating Orthodox Church organization.[13] With the acceptance of that statute the Church achieved a fundamental understanding with the Government and its "existence" from that point on was to be on the basis of that understanding. The content of the State-Church relationship was not the same as it had been prior to 1917, but the fundamental concept underlying it so far as the Church was concerned was relatively the same. The Church now had a mode of existence on a predetermined basis. It should follow that prescribed code or pattern. It could not thereafter as flexibly confront changing situations with changing church patterns. At the same time the reformist element which stood apart from the Church during the more difficult periods of persecution was now brought fully within the orderly, responsible structure of the recognized Church.

If the existence of the Church was now relatively assured, the question it faced was whether in its obedience it would now be acutely sensitive to the possible penetration by God of the existential situation with fresh "revelations," or whether Divine guidance must come solely through the historic structure and traditions of the Church.

Several documents from this period (1946-48) indicate that churchmen did not entirely rule out the former, but held that such "revelations" were subordinate to the latter.[14] In its introduction

---

12. *The Truth About Religion in Russia* as quoted by Anderson, *op. cit.*, pp. 36-37 (*Chron.*, p 297).

13. *Dokumente Zur Ordnung der Kirche,* July, 1951 (unpublished).

14. In Bulgaria, when reformist tendencies developed within the Orthodox Church, a more categorical answer was given. At the Pan-Orthodox Conference in Moscow in 1948, Archpriest Schpiller referred to "the undermining of a feeling of the consciousness of the Church as the one thing necessary for salvation . . . ., a certain worldliness on the part of the Church in the direction of adaptation . . . ., a breaking loose from the traditions of the Holy Fathers, both in theology and in life, (and a shaking of) faithfulness to liturgical tradition (*The Proceedings of the Conference of the Heads of the Autocephalous Ortho-*

to a book entitled *Patriarch Sergius* (died 1944) *and His Spiritual Legacy*,[15] the Moscow Patriarchate seems to justify the changes in its own life and structure on the basis of God's special working (or "revelations") in the contemporary scene. "Elements of genuine ecclesiasticism in the Orthodox Church have outlived the period of dependence on the State . . ." The fact that genuine elements of ecclesiasticism could be changed at all suggests a less than rigid concept of the existential church-God relationship. It is further recognized in the book that this process was "facilitated by conditions under the Soviet regime." Being "separated from the State,"[16] "but not aloof from it . . ." the Church is in a position "to carry out the Commandments of our Lord Jesus Christ in practical life." Among these commandments two were noted which seem particularly involved in contemporary "inspiration": one, that the Church should "cultivate and uplift the particular gifts and characteristics of the people," and the other, that "the light of Christianity shining from the East (should very soon) light up the West." Does this mean that a special revelation in history is to be made through the medium of Russian Orthodoxy?

There were "many new ideas (which) came to birth" when the 1945 Sobor met, "which throw fresh light on the meaning of world events today." "Fresh ideas" outside the Church, or Sobor, were normally very suspect,[17] but apparently were considered legitimately of God if passed by the Church (Sobor).[18] In the final analysis ideas, according to this document, are controlled by the soul, but the "religious conscience (of the soul) belongs to the Church." The Church therefore must determine the religious validity of ideas.

The Church in its *sobornost* (or wholeness) is "der eigentliche Trager der unfehlbaren Wahrheit und der unfehlbaren

---

dox Churches, p. 230)." Reflecting on these developments in 1948, the Archpriest condemned them as being unOrthodox, untheological, originating in the ecumenical movement and contributing toward heretical schismatic groups in the Church. By 1948 it again became evident that once it was possible for the church "to exist" in traditional patterns, it was practically heresy to make adaptations in those practices. Such reforms were not true to tradition; they were not, therefore, true to the Church. They were not, therefore, "in obedience."

15. Excerpts from *EPS*, No. 33, 1947.

16. The document adds, "the State which loves justice more than any other in the world."

17. For example, the Orthodox Church "opposes the individualistic principle of the West with the principle of (its own) close unity" through its example.

18. The difficulties of overcoming provincialism and relativism are immediately evident from the Patriarch's justification of various contemporary Church activities, such as its peace efforts, the incorporation of Uniate Churches into the Orthodox Church, etc.

Kirchlichen Vernunft. . . . Nicht die eigene Vernunft findet die Wahrheit, sondern die Kirchliche Vernunft teilt sie mit."[19]

The question remains, whether, in its "discerning," the Orthodox Church is the wholeness of the Church and could therefore consider its discernment absolute, or whether it, too, is not in its existential manifestation subject to provincial limitations. Rose continues:

"Das lumen naturale rationis leuchtet zwar, jedoch zu ungenügend, um vor Irrtümern bewahrt zu sein. Dies bezieht sich auch auf das kollektive Denken (kraft dessen die Wahrheit—was auch haüfig vorkommt—auf der Seite einer nichtigen Minderheit stehen kann). Überhaupt kann unsere Vernunft nur dann den Anspruch auf Unfehlbarkeit erheben, wenn sie zur kirchlichen Vernunft, zur Vernunft der Kirche wird. Selbstverständlich bezieht sich der Begriff der "kirchlichen Vernunft" auf die Kirche als den gottmenschlichen Organismus, auf die Kirche, die durch den heiligen Geist lebt, kraft dessen das kirchliche "Kollektiv" eben zum "Leib Christi" verklärt wird. Deshalb lesen wir in der klassischen Formel, die schon auf dem ersten Konzil in Jerusalem festgelegt wurde: "Den es gefällt dem heiligen Geist und uns" (Acts 15:28). Die Heiligung der "Versammlung" zu einem "Konzil" (Sobor), in dem die Kirche nicht mehr als menschliches Kollektiv, sondern als Gottmenschlicher Organismus erscheint, tritt nicht einfach dort ein, wo gläubige Menschen versammelt sind, sondern wo "es dem heiligen Geist gefällt." Nach der orthodoxen Lehre wird die Wahrheit auf den Konzilien nich durch ihre kanonische Richtigkeit gewährleistet, sondern nur durch die gnadenreiche Wirkung des Heiligen Geistes, was die Kirche durch die Rezeption der Entscheidungen des Konzils erkennt. Überhaupt garantieren uns weder Inspirationen noch gar Genialität der individuellen Vernunft die Wahrheit,—in unserem Orthodoxen Bewüsstsein ist der individuellen Vernunft zwar die volle Freiheit

---

19. The whole church is the true bearer of the infallible truth and the infallible discernment of the Church. Truth is not found through one's personal discerning, we receive it through the discerning of the Church. Karl Rose, *Predigt der Russisch-Orthodoxen Kirche*, p. 19. In the same book, pp. 164-168, Rose quotes a sermon of Mtr. Nikolai, delivered in Moscow, 1946: "We are the children of the Orthodox Church. She teaches the child what is good and wrong and she prepares the child to meet the unavoidable needs of life."

gegeben, die Wahrheit jedoch nur der kirchlichen Vernunft."[20]

In this case the contemporary situation is a very potent factor in the determination of Truth. Almost any change might be justified on grounds of the work of the Holy Spirit—if such change were acceptable in the existential situation.

A bit later, in 1948, at the Pan-Orthodox Conference in Moscow, the nature and vocation of the Church was spelled out in more detail in terms of keeping the tradition. In what appears to be a carefully prepared statement, Orthodox Archbishop Seraphim[21] described the Church and its function in relation to revelation and the work of the Holy Spirit:

> "The Church is called holy because she is the distributer of the grace of the Holy Spirit, which she imparts to the faithful in the sacrament of Chrismation when baptism is administered. . . . In this sacrament the Holy Spirit is bestowed on us with all his gifts, which help us to grow and strengthen us in a spiritual holy life. . . . But the Protestants cannot possess this blessing (and presumably neither can any not in the exact prescribed tradition) . . . for they have no sacrament of Chrismation."

The Archbishop added:

> "The grace of the Holy Spirit expresses itself in two forms: as the grace of a general external providence which anticipates and prepares people to receive the true faith, and as an inner grace which quickens, saves and acts *only in the Orthodox Church.*"

---

20. Basillius Zenkowsky, *Das Bild vom Menschen in der Ostkirche*, Stuttgart 1951, S 36.f. (Summary translation follows). The "lumen naturale rationis" burns, but it is inadequate to protect us from errors . . . Only then can our discerning claim infallibility when it becomes a "churchly discerning," that is the judgment of the Church . . . The definition of "churchly judgment" refers to the Church as the God-Man organism, the Church which lives through its Holy Spirit, through which the church "collective" is transfigurated into the "Body of Christ." Therefore we read in the classical formulation already put down at the first Council of Jerusalem: "For it seemed good to the Holy Ghost" (Acts 15:28). The sacrificing of the "gathering" for a "council" (Sobor), in which the Church no longer appears as a human collective but as God-man collective, does not come about just where there is a gathering of pious people but "where it seems good to the Holy Ghost." According to the Orthodox teaching the truthfulness of the councils is not guaranteed by their correctness of the canon but only through the merciful effect of the Holy Ghost, which the Church recognizes through the receptivity of decisions of the councils.

21. Archbp. Seraphim was a Russian Orthodox churchman under Moscow jurisdiction, but resided in Bulgaria. It is evident from the proceedings of the Conference that, probably largely due to his residence in Bulgaria, he was one of the most keenly interested in, and informed about the Ecumenical Movement.

While presumably this might allow for some concept of a Divine penetration in the events of history, such a penetration could be explained only in terms of established Orthodox tradition.

> "The interpretation given to the attribute of the Church and to her other attributes by Orthodox ecumenists (those who allow that God may manifest His Will and His Presence to those outside Orthodoxy and in special ways in History) is not merely erroneous. This error is in its essence an overthrowing of our Orthodox *faith in the church*."[22]

Archpriest Razumovsky of Moscow, an outspoken critic of the Ecumenical Movement, in the ensuing discussion concerning participation in the Ecumenical Movement first asked:

> "Is it enough to say that our entire faith consists only in the recognition of Jesus Christ as our Lord, God and Savior?"[23]

He then answered,

> "Of course, 'the spirit bloweth where it listeth' but we have the Church as the unit of salvation and we are obliged to submit to this Church."

These Orthodox spokesmen would clearly not describe the Church as simply the gathered people of God whose manifest forms are determined in some measure by the external circumstances in which the individual member Christians exist; but rather that the Church is the gathering instrument of God which, with certain prescribed patterns, is necessary to the fulfillment of God's purposes in any contemporary situation.

Following this line of thought, if to receive the gift of the Holy Spirit it is necessary to participate in certain practices of the Church or preserved traditions, and if those traditions or sacraments require the existence of the Church, if the people must have "faith in the Church," then the Church in a recognizable form must first exist. The primary task of the Church, therefore, would be, not to know the meaning of God in the contemporary historical situation, but to "safeguard the ancient Universal Apostolic Orthodoxy . . ."[24]

---

22. *Proceedings of the Moscow Conference*, pp. 211-212.
23. A reference to the Basis of Membership statement of the World Council of Churches.
24. Introductory statement to the Conference at Moscow by Assistant Professor N. I. Mouraviev, Dozent of the Moscow Theol. Academy, *Proceedings of the Moscow Conference*, p. 15.

The problem of church and state authority and vocation is resolved in a simple manner. Said Archpriest Razumovsky,

"There is secular authority and there is also the Church
. . . The Lord God has left it to the State to be concerned
with social economic questions . . . While the role of the
Church is to lead the flock . . . toward the Kingdom of
God . . . The truth of God would be fulfilled by those . . .
who say: I am entitled to something according to the
Law, but I have no authority to demand it, if God sends
it, glory be to God! In this case we have the truth of God
toward which the Church should strive."

Razumovsky then added (and Orthodox representatives from
the West took exception to him) that there is no connection between the struggle of society and the State for justice, and the
struggle of the Church toward "the Truth of God."[25]

In its "resolution" on the question of the Ecumenical Movement and the Orthodox Church the Conference alleged that all
Protestantism (i.e., "church reformism") was essentially an attempt to overthrow the apostolic rules and the traditions of the
past, that toward this end Protestantism had engaged in a conflict
with Rome and presently sought collaboration with Orthodoxy "to
acquire for itself a significance of an influential international
force." The Conference recognized the great temptation of Orthodoxy under such circumstances to evade the search for the
Kingdom of God and (to enter) into a political realm which is so
alien to it.[26] The Conference then proceeded to define how, in its
own terms and for the purposes of the kind of Church it conceived,
it would resist Roman Catholicism by its own "international force."

Much time was spent at the Conference defining how the
Orthodox Churches and their representatives should maintain and
preserve the purity of the faith, not so much from their political
environment as from revisionist influences within and without
Orthodoxy. Orthodox leaders who participated in the work of the
Ecumenical Movement were singled out particularly for criticism
as very dangerous threats to the purity of the Orthodox faith
(especially Professors Zankow, Zonevsky, Bulgakow and Zenkov-
sky).[27] If it was essential that the Church exist, then it was essential that it exist in its pure faith, conceived of in terms of an
established dogma. The Church "must preserve without distortion and innovation that faith passed on to us by witnesses who
had themselves apprehended it, and by ministers of the word, the

---

25. *Proceedings of the Moscow Conference*, pp. 223, 224.
26. *Ibid.*, p. 240.
27. *Proceedings of the Moscow Conference*, pp. 207-209, 214, 219, 237, 238.

divinely ordained apostles."[28] "Our dogma, and the teaching of the Eastern Church have already in ancient times been correctly investigated and piously defined and confirmed by the Holy General Councils; to add to them anything or to subtract from them anything, is not permissable."[29] The religious experience of those in the past line of tradition was then of primary importance. Any change, any additions or subtractions were considered "a purely human invention," and were condemned as being opposed to the purposes and nature of the Church and its calling. Even participation in the prayers, speeches, material benefits or hymns of non-Orthodox groups was considered a dangerous threat to the purity of the Church.

While in another situation the conciliar test of truth or revelation might take precedence over the traditional, in the contemporary situation Orthodox leaders have concluded that the Church must exist, full revelation has been given as to how it must exist and any suggestion of a change as coming from God in a contemporary situation has been ruled out.

There is little evidence of any change in these fundamental precepts since the Moscow Conference. Russian Orthodox Metropolitan Nicolai, visiting in Hungary in January, 1954, declared that the Church could not consider "an armed defense of Christianity." He added that it is "not our attachment to any earthly system but our loyalty to Christ" which should determine the Churches' action in the cause of peace.[30] In such circumstances his suggestion that the Church must be involved in a specific plan for peace implies that the Church's concern for its existence is not entirely unaffected by its present circumstance, but an attempt is made to maintain a purity of tradition at all points possible.

In an article in the January, 1954, issue of the *Journal of the Moscow Patriarchate*, the Patriarch indicated his concern to maintain the ancient forms of the Church without such adaptations as electric lighting and other modern conveniences which alter the function of the Church in relating people to the saints and traditions of the past.[31]

Commenting on the Universal Week of Prayer observance in the West and the general practice of repentance and petitions for purifications, A. Wedernikof, in the third issue of the *Journal of the Moscow Patriarchate*, 1954, asserted that such prayers for repentance and purification are not necessary for the Orthodox

---

28. First rule of the Six General Councils, quoted by the final resolution of the Moscow Conference dealing with the Vatican and the Orthodox Church.
29. Epistle of the Patriarchs of the Eastern Catholic Church on the Orthodox faith as quoted in the same resolution.
30. *E.P.S.* No. 7, Feb. 19, 1954.
31. *E.P.S.*, No. Feb. 26, 1954.

Church. Its doctrine and practice have presumably been kept pure.[32]

Another commentary on the relationship between Christ and the Church was indicated in the August issue of the *Journal of the Moscow Patriarchate* in another article by Prof. Wedernikof on the subject of the Evanston Assembly of the World Council of Churches. In a comment on "hope" Prof. Wedernikof identified Christ as "this unique hope . . . whose present purpose is to illuminate the way which leads to the Church." Whereas Russian Orthodoxy had previously denounced the Ecumenical Movement as being politically slanted, Prof. Wedernikof took considerable encouragement from the fact that it was now interested in theology, that it was concerned with the hope which led to the Church.[33]

In Russian Orthodoxy, then, there has theoretically been no theological change or renewal apart from tradition. No judgment has been hurled by God in these times at the Church—the Church is holy. True, some practices of the institutional life of the Church have been altered, but these are not of the essence of the Church. The Holy Spirit, operating through the Church, not through the exigencies of the contemporary scene, may renew and inspire individuals toward the Church. But there is no new Church, the continuity of the Church in history has neither been broken nor altered. The traditions of the Church have been preserved and the Church must still defend its existence in order to maintain the continuity of those traditions and the body of faithful. Since this may require some definitive relationship with the State, the Church is prepared to establish that relationship. And whereas details of that relationship may not be the same today as before the Revolution, the fact of the relationship and the Church's acceptance of it has not changed. The Church, through tradition, has its body of dogma and has its instructions; to be obedient it must exist.

Theological Trends as Reflected Among Reformed Protestants in Hungary

Quite a different picture is given by Reformed Protestants in Hungary. Many Protestant churchmen, probably most, did not conceive of the Church as having or being certain forms, practices and dogmas which *they* must preserve. When Communist forces rolled into Hungary in 1944-45, Reformed theologians did not prepare to defend the Church. They repented.

The Church Under Judgment. That there were some whose "repentance" was a theological rationalization for a political neces-

---

32. *E.P.S.*, No. 17, April 30, 1954.
33. *E.P.S.*, No. 42, October 8, 1954.

sity is quite possible. That some directed their penitence toward their new over-lords and prepared to adjust their personal lives and church patterns according to Communist wishes is also likely, as is evidenced by the opposition of other churchmen to "proclamations of guilt"[34] and exaggerated statements about the virtues of Communism.[35] Still others, at a different level, were not above repenting in order to be renewed.[36]

But the most significant fact was that large numbers of churchmen were convinced that God was acting afresh in history. And they saw His activity, in the first instance, in judgment:

> "(with) anguish of heart . . . as the debacle ending the war was approaching . . . (churchmen) were awaiting the Divine judgment so well deserved by so much sinful omission; and how many had taken it for granted that all possibilities of our future activities would be lost to us owing to our unworthiness."[37]

Protestant Christians had been involved in Nazi crimes, in the persecution of Jews, in "proud anti-Romanism," in politically motivated educational activities. So also had their Church; they were the Church. The Church was neither pure, nor infallible, nor absolute, and Communism was seen as a scourge in the hand of God, an instrument of judgment directed at the Church. That Christians and the Church should continue to exist at all was not at all certain. What they sensed was certain, was that the Church would not and should not be allowed to exist, whether by God or by God through the Communists, in the same way as in the past.

Grace and Obedience. God's acting in the immediate situation was next seen in the evidence of Grace. Churches expected—"deserved"—destruction and dispersion.[38] That they found themselves much better treated than expected was "as a resurrection" from the dead.[39] While there may have been some tendency to confuse the Communist strategy of "generosity" towards the churches with the grace of God,[40] the fact rests that churchmen

---

34. *Die Protestantischen Kirchen*, 1939-1950, p. 12 (*Chron.*, p. 433).

35. Declaration of the Council of the Synod, April 30, 1948, *Die Protestantischen Kirchen*, Encl. 30 (*Chron.*, pp. 465-468).

36. "The greatest task of the clergy is to call the people to penitence in order that a renewal might be made possible." Clergymen's Statement of Guideposts to Christians, Item 4 (*Chron.*, p. 432). (Incidentally, one senses a greater integrity among those who believed that in order to be obedient the church must secure its existence, than among those who would use obedience in the deliberate hope of ensuring existence.)

37. A. Bereczky, radio speech, January 1, 1949 (*Chron.*, p. 432).

38. Report of Prof. Thurneysen and Rev. Luthi as quoted in *Hungarian Church Press*, No. 12, Oct. 4, 1949 (*Chron.*, p. 458), and ref. A. Bereczky above.

39. *Ibid.*, also refs. *Chron.*, pp. 433, 459, 461, 462 ff.

40. A later question was, is grace universal or individual, and to what extent does Communism contribute to its operation?

were thinking of God alone as the Absolute, not the Church: "Christ, not the Church, is the hope of the world."[41]

In its existential situation the Church should be obedient to the living Christ. But obedience informed by what, or whom? This was the question confronting Hungarian Protestants. How was the meaning of God acting in history to be sorted out from the complex details, counter forces and reverses in history? If the Church was as severely judged as these Reformed churchmen maintained, then it lacked the integrity, the objectivity and the continuity necessary for discerning God's acts in history and His Will in the contemporary scene. If it was so judged, then not only was it not normative, but it could not even serve as a relatively tried comparative. Were the only alternatives for discerning God's meaning then either the historic churches, corrupt as they were, or the individual's personal experience of "God" in some direct revelation?

Eventually[42] Hungarian Reformed leaders were to combine several factors into a working standard of judgment, but not until after some years of experimentation. In the process provisional answers to the problem of revelation and obedience, when applied to church forms, resulted in a variety of church patterns and life, some opposing others, some combining with others, to create new forms.

Ecclesiastical Patterns. Major ecclesiastical patterns have been described in some detail in Chapter IX. Consideration is therefore given here only to the development of patterns among Hungarian Protestants as related to changing concepts of revelation and obedience.

The first major departure from traditional patterns has been described by a Hungarian in terms of "closed groups of spiritual fellowship."[43] Their origin involves in part a pietistic concept of direct personal revelation and in part a "radical reaction against former liberal theology and conservative churchism."[44] Even prior to World War II this "radical reaction" had produced a kind of "association Christianity." These associations

> "drew their adherents into their independent organizations instead of integrating them with the congregations. Hence they could produce, in most cases, only Christian

41. Further elaborated in "The Second Statement of the Hungarian Ecumenical Study Commission on the Main Theme of the Second Assembly," *"Hungarian Church Press,* Aug. 15, 1953, p. 161.

42. In order to give a not-too-distorted picture of Hungarian Reformed churchmen some developments since 1951 must be considered in this chapter.

43. "Ecumenical Perspective," by John Peter, *Hungarian Church Press,* May 15, 1953, p. 89.

44. Private comment of a Reformed theologian.

individuals who had no firm roots in the life of the congregation. The theological pattern in terms of which the worldly vocation of the members was viewed was generally the idea that these men must be supplied with the subjective experience of a pietistic Christianity . . ."[45]

After World War II, and the accession of the Communist Government, the churches moved to integrate all such independent associations and activities into the life of the congregations. Some were integrated. Others felt "called" to reform and redeem the Church. Their method and purpose they described as evangelistic.

"A group of villages is intensely evangelized through a team of evangelists. After this concentrated attack on the 'statistical' church the follow-up work is done by 'Congregation-builders,' who try to gather the 'awakened' in dynamic, evangelizing groups. It is generally held that these groups will be the units of Christian life in the church of tomorrow, when the official church will be an instrument of the State. These cells are formed all over the country already (house congregations, Bible circles, etc.) and they function (as in the future they will have to) without clergy—'We cannot sleep further on the soft cushions of the institutional church, but have to change our church radically into a missionary and evangelistic force. Our device should be: the 'missionary-transqualification of the church must begin with me and through me.' "[46]

Later, commenting on this period in their church life, some who had participated in such activities joined in writing that

". . . mostly under the influence of 'lay' leaders (they) began establishing independent preaching stations in their own groups, then later moved under the cover of the congregations' life, forming closed and very exclusive groups within the congregations. These separatistic and closed groups soon developed two characteristic features. The first was that the group itself began to decide who can be accepted as believing and converted persons and to exclude those who were declared infidels and unconverted. The second trait was reflected in the idea that the world,

---

45. Statement of the Hungarian Ecumenical Study Commission on the Sixth Subsidiary Theme, *Hungarian Church Press*, August 15, 1953, p. 201.
46. From an unpublished document.

and the work in the world are considered to be rather a punishment."[47]

Lutheran Bishop Ladislas Dezséry later referred to "the so-called 'general evangelical' patterns" as having sectarian tendencies.[48] Whatever they were called, Christian action, to these groups, meant obedience to the revelations of God, and the revelations of God meant primarily the individual's experience of Him in the contemporary situation.

While the trend towards an intensive, individualistic religious life at the periphery of the churches was at its height (1947-1949), official church leaders were seeking to salvage whatever was possible of the churches' situation in relation to the new Government. This was not simply a matter of institutional status for status' sake. Stated theologically, the Church must have administrative independence from the dictates of an atheistic government if it was to obey the dictates of God, however His Will was to be revealed. The general sentiment among responsible church officials was for separation of church and state (but without loss of church properties) ; or, if a more specific agreement was necessary, for one which would allow the churches to exercise what they considered their minimum obligation under God.[49] The question was, what was the minimum framework necessary for the minimum fulfillment of that obligation? Lutheran Bishop Ordass pointed out that even under Nazi occupation the Church had guarded her administrative independence, but added that the churches would be willing to discuss relations with the Government on equal terms.[50]

By mid-1948 Government-prescribed boundaries for church life were imposed. For Lutherans this framework was particularly difficult to accept because it restricted their traditional institutional method of performing their "obedience," e.g., religious instruction in the schools. At this point, a distinction can be seen between Lutheran and Reformed positions. For Lutherans the problem was not whether there was direct revelation from God in the existential situation, but whether the community to which God's Will was revealed did not also receive from Him inalienable rights to perform acts of obedience. Theologically they would not maintain that such "rights" were absolute requisites to a life of

---

47. Statement of the Hungarian Ecumenical Study Commission, *op. cit.*, pp. 201-202.
48. *Hungarian Church Press*, May 15, 1953, p. 94.
49. *Die Protestantischen Kirchen, op. cit.*, Encl. 36 (*Chron.*, p. 439).
50. Unpublished documents.

obedience.[51] However Lutherans were sufficiently resentful that they could not perform their calling in accustomed ways as to respond, in general, in defiant resignation: "We must stand by the forces of reconstruction, work, peace, because it is God's Will that we lead a quiet, still life in worshipping Him."[52]

While several Reformed churchmen had already come to a similar position, and others would eventually, at this stage official emphasis was on knowing the Will of God in their situation, rather than insisting on what framework was necessary to implement it. Institutional forms and practices were not considered so central to Christian obedience as to preclude the acceptance of new patterns of church life. Indeed, Reformed churchmen were able to take the initiative in suggesting a new pattern of relationships with the Government with consequent changes in church life.[53] (Whether they were primarily motivated by a desire for a "protective" agreement as of the pre-war era, or by the conviction that such an agreement was inevitable and they would do well not to wait, or by a sense of imperative springing from a sense of obedience to the Will of God were questions observers raised. Whatever the reason, or reasons, the result was to provide a frame of mind on the part of Christian leaders, and a relationship with Government leaders which gave expanded possibilities of creative witness.) When a pattern of relationships and of church life was finally decided upon by the Government,[54] the Reformed Church accepted it somewhat less grudgingly as "the sign of God's mercy on us, and we seek for guidance in His Word for what is to be done by us."[55]

By this time (Aug., 1949), interest in the Bible as primary source of authority and revelation was growing stronger, both in the congregational life and in the "separatist" cells. An attempt had been made by the Reformed Church a year earlier to contain this element of Biblical renewal, together with the more radical pietistic groups, through "missionary work groups"[56] and organized Bible study groups.

"At this time the plan was conceived to give these 'laymen,' who had now come of age, a theological instruction

---

51. Lutheran Bishop Veöreös said of the nationalization of Lutheran schools, that while the Lutheran Church did not wish to give up its schools, "if the legislation . . . takes them from us, we bow before it. . . . The boundary line [of martyrdom] is not the school question." *Die Protestantischen Kirchen, op. cit.*, Encl. 42 (*Chron.*, p. 442).

52. *Ibid.*, Encl. 82 (*Chron.*, p. 450).

53. Proposal of the Reformed Church Synodical Council, *Die Protestantischen Kirchen, op. cit.*, Encl. 40 (*Chron.*, p. 440).

54. As outlined in the Constitution of August, 1949.

55. *Five Years of Hungarian Protestantism*, 1945-1950, p. 26 (*Chron.*, p. 451). *Declaration of the Council of the Synod*, April, 1948, Item 6, expressed the same position (*Chron.*, p. 467).

56. *Chronicle*, p. 444.

in order that they may independently find their way in the world of their daily work and also to take a more active part in the life of the congregations. In the Reformed Church, Bible Schools were organized for this purpose, enrolling men and women of the most different professional backgrounds and ages. Alas, these efforts did not lead to the desired ends, for the graduates generally refused to undertake anything but the service of preaching and teaching, and so, abandoning their former work in the world, wished to live henceforth as professional church workers, as the pastors, yet without the more thorough theological training of the latter. We thank God that He reminded us, in our repentance, that we cannot take in the Church the line of least resistance, that is, in our case, the way of 'universal pastorhood' instead of the 'universal priesthood' of the believers. The narrow way on which God leads us makes us realize that the renewal of our churches can only take place by the renewal of the congregations. We confess that God has judged our attempt at solving the problem of the 'laity,' that is, the problem of our Church members engaged in their work in the world, as though this problem could and should be solved independently of the other tasks of our church."[57]

This evaluation seems to indicate three things: (1) that by 1949-1950 Reformed Church leadership, among which were some who had been in the radical reformist groups, recognized that the Church could and should exist as an organized body in the new Hungarian society; (2) that the radical renewal movement at the periphery of the Church was clearly recognized as having gone too far toward sectarianism in its "direct revelation" theology and in its reaction against liberal theology and organized church life, and (3) that, to be obedient, the Church must have some responsible form which must depend on more than the religious experience of a few individuals or a literalistic reading of the Bible for its discerning of God's Will, but should nevertheless embody both. The result was the adding of another criteria for the discerning or "testing" of revelation:

"It has been the study of the Scriptures, amid our constant prayers for the light of the Holy Spirit, the guidance of our confessions of faith as well as the witness of great theologians—old and living—that has liberated us,

---

57. Statement of the Hungarian Ecumenical Study Commission, *Hungarian Church Press*, Aug. 15, 1953, p. 202.

step by step, from the sectarian understanding and practice of spiritual fellowship. As a result, our attention
and activity has been turned off from the so-called 'closed
groups of spiritual fellowship' toward those forms of fellowship that make claim upon the entirety of the Church.
But we did not stop here. If we had stopped here, we
would have bogged in the temptation of making *the
church itself* (Peter's italics), instead of isolated groups
only, a 'closed group,' in the sense of sectarian interpretation and practice; that is, we would have turned the
church itself into a sect. We have in this way arrived at
the fuller and more obedient understanding of the Koinonia realizing that the koinonia is not a fraction, neither
a corporation, neither an organization, neither an organism, but a function, the life function of the Church in the
exercise of which the Church partakes of the fruits of the
Lord Jesus Christ's sacrifice. . . ."[58]

Reference is then made to the function of the *koinonia,* defined as
"the entire communion of saints," in the redemption of the universe.

If, in 1947-1948, Reformed Protestant leaders in Hungary
were determining the "ought" of their action on the basis of historic church patterns on the one hand, or some individual experience of God's revelation on the other, by 1953 many leaders were
thinking of God's Will as being revealed and tested through a complex of factors including the spiritual life of the individual, the
Scriptures,[59] the contemporary situation, history,[60] the "koinonia
of the (local) ecclesia,"[61] and the Church Universal.

Many recent statements concerning God's acts in history and
the special revelation of God in the events of history are not unlike those of the radical reformers of the 1947-1948 period. But
the difference is that they are now coming from out of the Church,
rather than being directed at the Church from outside the Church.[62]
The assumption that God reveals Himself freshly in history still
stands. But revelation is never received as complete or final,

"hence they take care not to make their confessions absolute, and are open to receive a better, fuller and deeper

---

58. Bp. John Peter's report on "Ecumenical Perspective," *Hungarian
Church Press,* May 15, 1953, p. 89.
59. Statements of the Ecumenical Study Commission of the Reformed
and Lutheran Churches on the Subsidiary Themes, *Hungarian Church Press,*
Aug. 15, 1953, p. 174.
60. *Ibid., pp.* 163, 164, 165, 175.
61. *Ibid.,* pp. 175, 177, 178.
62. The fact that the statements are similar is due in part to the fact that
it is the same people who have made them.

understanding of the supreme Standard from whatever quarter this better instruction may come . . ."[63]

To be obedient, they say, the Church must serve and witness in its actual historical situation with whatever means are at its power, guided by such revelations. The Church may accept the limitations of the secular order, though not approving them, in order to proclaim in them and on them God's penetration of their situation. Such a theology, because of the difficulty of applying its several criteria to every "ought," may understandably involve its adherents in strange alliances, in support of political "peace" movements, government programs, etc. At the same time, it may allow, not only an individual, but a whole church to demonstrate strong elements of the prophetic. That the Reformed churches of Hungary have undergone a deep spiritual renewal under such theological testing it is not necessary to argue.

Theological Trends as Reflected Among Lutherans in East Germany[64]

Lutherans in East Germany affirm that the Church is not dependent on its institutional manifestations, on the clergy, or on the State for its existence. Said Bishop Dibelius to the Synod of Berlin-Brandenburg in May, 1954, "The day of the State-Church is finished long ago. Today we may say that the day of the clerical Church is finished too."[65]

---

63. Statements of the Ecumenical Study Commission, *op. cit.*, p. 174.

64. Lutherans in "East" Germany and Lutherans in "West" Germany are part of the same Church. Their diverse experiences and positions are interrelated in the deliberations and decisions of their common supreme church councils. But West and East churches also affect the life and witness of each separately. It would be too much, therefore, to claim that what follows, though based largely on documentation about East Germany, represents a "pure" position of East German Lutherans unaffected by the positions of West Germans or the temptations their existence affords East Germans. In addition, the problem of discerning the actual mind of East Germans from reports by West Germans, or from East-West Church councils which must speak for both, is no easy matter. When, for example, Bishop Hanns Lilje of Hannover (West Germany) claims that the East German Government abruptly halted its antichurch campaign in 1953 because "the Church demonstrated its strength (Religious News Service, June 22, 1953), one must know that "strength" to East German churches means something quite different from "strength" in the West. And when the Council of the Evangelical Church in Germany asks Christians in East Germany to "have no fear" (Message of May 11, 1953, *E.P.S.*, No. 21, 1953) one cannot on this evidence alone assume that Christians in East Germany are afraid, or share in a major way in drafting such messages. We cannot pursue these matters here, but only suggest some lines of development, mostly since 1951, in contradistinction to those among Orthodox Russians and Reformed Hungarians. A more comprehensive study of East Germany is being carried out by another colleague.

65. Report of Bishop Dibelius to the Synod of Berlin-Brandenburg, May, 1954, *E.P.S.*, No. 21, 1954.

But the Church exists. "The Church of Christ, renewed through suffering, cannot be destroyed. Thanks be to God, which giveth us the victory through our Lord Jesus Christ."[66]

If the existence of the Church is God's prerogative, then it is not necessary for Christians to defend the Church, but to witness.[67] This poses the questions, in what consists *the Church which is*, and how shall it determine its witness or its obedience? While there are exceptions (this is a very live issue currently in East Germany), present evidence from East Germany suggests a trend somewhat as follows.

If the Church is not the State church, nor the clerical church, neither is it now regarded as the *Volkskirche*, in the sense of encompassing the whole people. The Church rather comprises believing persons acting in obedience. To some extent this reflects the Barthian influence (a Church is formed when believers confess Jesus Christ in word and deed), but in large measure it springs from the realities of their own situation:

"We have to learn . . . to live according to faith, and this has meaning only if it has meaning in individuals. . . . The second and real lesson (is) . . . that God's protection and power manifests itself in the smallest things and in the greatest occurrences by obedience to His Word. . . . And the fear of Him, Who has loved us in giving us His Son, is for us the only possibility of living . . ."[68]

This and similar statements suggest that for Lutherans in East Germany the Church is built up on the religious life and faith of *individuals* and their obedient witness, that so long as there are living persons obedient to God, there will be a living Church in East Germany.

At the same time the political situation, "the massification" of society, tends to usurp from the individual any sense of responsibility or faculty for making decisions.[69] Great emphasis is there-

---

66. Message from the Council of the Evangelical Church in Germany (hereafter EKiD), May, 1953, *E.P.S.*, No. 21, 1953.

67. In a statement on "The Christian Between East and West" (*Evangelische Theologie*, Oct., 1950, Kaiser Verlag, Munchen), Prof. Helmut Gollwitzer summarized what appears to be the position of many Lutherans in East Germany: "Non-Christians may regard the Christianity of the West as one of the higher values of its civilization, which they will defend with arms; but Christians must know that Christianity is not a possession that can be defended; it is something which must be *lived*. That is why the Christianity of the West (and presumably the East) cannot be defended at all; it is rather something which can only be witnessed through unselfish sacrifice. 'Videant Christiani. . . .' "

68. Unpublished document from East Germany.

69. Pastors have pointed out however that, in contrast to the Hitler attack on religion by attacking the pastors, the present regime's strategy is to force the individual believer to make a flat rejection or acceptance of the regime (*Chron.*, p. 554).

fore placed by Christian leaders on developing the individual's personal faith and faculties for making independent personal decisions in the framework of a living relationship and obedience to
God—a feat rendered no less difficult through some generations
of dependence on clerical authority.

The obedience of the Church, then, is not unrelated to the obedience of individuals. How is the individual believer to determine
his obedience? Helmut Gollwitzer,[70] after stating that the Christian should not confuse obedience with "the realization of some
idea . . . (e.g.) a Christian conception of the state," adds that "in
practical obedience . . . the Christian in the East receives different
commands from our common Lord; his political responsibility
takes an entirely different form in practice from that of the Christian in the West"—and perhaps of fellow Christians in the East.
This seems to represent the experience of many East German
Christians: God does reveal His Presence to the individual, He
does "command" and guide.

But the individual believer in East Germany has not been totally isolated nor felt that his "commands" were to be interpreted
in isolation. He is bound together with other believers in a solidarity of obedience. He does not determine his obedience alone. A
statement prepared by the theological faculties in East Germany
in answer to charges that their only authority was the hierarchy
indicates something of the process of knowing, testing and applying Truth in relation to obedience:[71] "Eternally valid truth has
continually to be sought after and reformulated." In that process
one should be ready to use scientific methods, but should also be
open to all "living forces of the present day," should depend on
the Word of God and "be at one with the Church of Christ." And
finally, together with the hierarchy, one should be "subordinated
to the Congregatio Sanctorium," in discerning "valid truth." For
the Christian, the "real sphere of life is still the Church of
Christ."[72] He should "draw strength from the Word of God, and
stand fast by the Lord's Table . . ."[73] Pastors and church workers
should ask "the advice of . . . fellow-pastors and the leaders of the
Church" . . . in important decisions.[74]

This series of focii, individual experience, Bible, fellow Christians, Congregatio Sanctorium, has remarkable similarities to that
which evolved in Hungary. Given the human difficulty of discerning objective "commands" of God from subjective imagination, the

70. *Op. cit.*
71. *E.P.S.*, No. 11, 1953.
72. Gollwitzer, *op. cit.*
73. Letter of Bishop Mitzenheim to the youth of Thuringen, *E.P.S.* No. 20, 1953.
74. Resolution of the Synod of Berlin-Brandenburg, May, 1954, *E.P.S.*, No. 21, 1954.

question arises, why has this individual, experience-centered religion not led to radical individualistic extremes, to sectarianism and atomization of the Church as it did somewhat earlier among Reformed Christians in Hungary? Church practices and forms have been altered, but not in such provincialized and radical ways as in Hungary.

The most likely reason[75] is that Lutherans of East Germany, both laity and leadership, were more deeply rooted in their confessional heritage and their devotion to the Church, whatever its weaknesses. The renewal of their faith under "persecution" was accepted not so much as revealing new truths which stood out in opposition to the Church, as in illuminating truths already given. Hence there has been less of reaction against the Church, a greater readiness to test individual experience by that of the whole Church and a greater sense of historic continuity within the Church than in Hungary (continuity not so much dependent on a body of dogma, or on institutional manifestations as on the continuing life and witness of the obedient people of God).

Further, not only the nature of the Church and the sense of continuity, but the divisive strategies of the Government made a close solidarity of faith and witness imperative.[76] When Pastor Erich Schumann of Zwickau was sentenced for "incitation to boycott democratic institutions," the Lutheran Church of Saxony declared that "whereas the sentence states that Pastor Schumann was responsible solely as an *individual*, we declare that he spoke *as a servant of the Church* on the basis of the Word of God. Thus the sentence touches the whole Church . . ."[77] If, in his obedience, the individual had a responsibility to know and exercise his obedience in the total community of the obedient and to carry the "sin of the Church,"[78] so also did that community have its responsibilities for the individual, to protect,[79] to warn,[80] to advise and serve.

This concept of the Church, as the continuing people who witness in obedience to God alone, must inevitably affect the relation of the Church to the State and may qualify Luther's statement on obedience to governments. The fundamental concept being given

---

75. A comprehensive consideration of underlying differences would need to take into account, in addition to theological differences, differences of temperament, of experiences under the Nazi regime, of political ambitions of churchmen and their relative strength in the two churches, of the shift in church leadership in Hungary which has not been paralleled in East Germany, of the fact that East Germany is not quite so completely in the East, and other factors.

76. *E.P.S.*, March 13, 1953.

77. Message to the parishes of Saxony, *E.P.S.* No. 16, 1953.

78. But he regards the sins of the Church as his sins, to be borne, not to be cast on others or "the Church" apart from himself. Gollwitzer, *op. cit.*

79. Gollwitzer, *op. cit.*

80. Message of the Synod of Berlin-Brandenburg, *E.P.S.* No. 21, 1954.

fresh emphasis is in that the Church is not regarded as a law unto itself, nor an end in itself. "The Church is not, and cannot be primarily concerned with itself . . ."[81] It is not a "power" *bloc,* and does not achieve its "ends" through stubborn strength.[82] Its strength is in being steadfast. It speaks to the State on the basis of truth, whether its speech will achieve some "end" or not. It speaks of justice:[83] "the State, too, is subject to the law and not above it."[84] It speaks of property because of Truth, not because the Church depends on property for its existence.[85] It defends its witness at every point, and its members—"not because the Church expects to win the case . . . but to remind the State of its proper function as upholder of the law . . . It is this opportunity to witness to God's rule in Christ, in every kind of difficulty and against every kind of pressure, which is the opportunity and the glory of the Church in East Germany . . ."[86]

The Church must be obedient, not in order to exist—obedience may mean extinction—but simply because it is what it is and because it *does* exist.

---

81. Unpublished documents.
82.Though in the past it has tried, and as the situation normalizes and institutional expansion is again conceivable, it will presumably be tempted to do so again.
83. Statement of the Synod of the EKiD on "What Can the Church Do for Peace," *E.P.S.* No. 18, 1950.
84. Report of Bishop Dibelius to the Synod of EKiD, *Religious News Service,* March 18, 1954.
85. *E.P.S.,* No. 18, 1953.
86. Unpublished documents.

"We, though many, are one body in Christ, and individually members one of another."[1]

Chapter XII

C. THE CHURCH UNIVERSAL

INTRODUCTION

Christians in East and West recognize the imperative for maintaining their solidarity: they are members one of another, and apart from each other none is made perfect.[2] This has become increasingly clear to those who would discern the meaning of God in their situation. It is sensed in the feeling of incompleteness which goes with estrangement. It is increasingly recognized as of the nature of the Christian's being, of the *esse* of the Church.

No part of the Church may rejoice but that all of it rejoices, and none suffer but that all suffer. The witness the Church has to make, it can make only as whole. The judgment it has to receive is a judgment on every part of it. The hope and renewal of one part may become the hope and renewal of all.

To recognize these facts is one thing. To realize them is another. Responsible Christians in East and West recognize the difficulties involved, the irrelevance of facile "solutions." One does not "organize" Christian solidarity.

On the other hand, it is clear that there is meaning in the situation under study which is for the whole Church, and which has not yet been adequately probed. The author's intent is that this study may contribute something in that direction. In the following chapters, therefore, consideration will be given to some hindrances and helps in "being" together and in discerning together the deeper issues (and perhaps God's meaning) underlying the present conflict, in applying provisional findings in the several situations in which the Church finds itself, and in manifesting in the Church itself the fundamental nature of the Church as illuminated by the present situation. Some conclusions are posed as questions to the churches, some as suggestions.[3]

---

1. Romans 12:5.

2. Cf. Hebrew 11:40; John 17:23.

3. For these reasons what follows is more hortatory than descriptive or apologetic in style.

"The question arises whether our inability to understand each other is due to differences in our attitude to Christ or whether it is due to different interpretations of the present historical situation."[1]

Chapter XIII

ECUMENICAL FELLOWSHIP TESTED

Can Christians maintain their solidarity in the face of formidable historic and political barriers and new tensions among Christians themselves?

External and Ancient Barriers

The conduct of Christians in East or West often has an immediate adverse or beneficial effect on the life of the other for reasons external to the churches' life. Reference has been made to the severing of relations between churches of East Europe and the Vatican or Western Protestant and World Council of Churches' headquarters. It is entirely possible that Eastern European churches would have been able to re-establish these relations sooner and more intimately had Western churches not seemed so deeply involved in a political-centered anti-Communist crusade. The reason for this lies partly in the factual situation in the West and partly in a misinterpretation of that situation in the East. The converse is equally true.[2]

Pronouncements of Western churches concerning the situation in East Europe have often called on East European Christians to oppose their regimes, or have condemned them for not doing so. It is as though the West expected them to live in their situation by the same standards as Western Christians in the Western situation.

Because of the close associations between Western churches and anti-Communist politics,[3] any friend of Western churches in

---

1. Prof. J. Hromadka, address to Hungarian Ecumenical Study Committee, Feb., 1954, *Hungarian Church Press*, Feb. 15, 1954.
2. A bishop from one country of East Europe pointed out that he had been in office six months, had dedicated two new churches and initiated significant programs. There was no word in the Western press about it. "But," he said, "as soon as there is something negative to advertise, then there are numerous articles about it" (Private documents).
3. To many East Europeans the Roman Catholic Church is the voice of churches in the West. So far as they can see, the several committees for "Free Europe" in the West are controlled by a predominantly Catholic point of view. It is probably true that in the United States much of the information concern-

the East is *ipso facto* suspect, and inter-church aid programs from Western to Eastern churches appear to imply that a common politic is being waged. It is not surprising therefore that East European churches have often been forced to refuse offers of aid from Western churches.

Another complicating factor is that Western Christians, whether in fact or only in appearance, through their ministry to homeless refugees seem to identify themselves with political refugees from East Europe to the exclusion[4] of Christians remaining in East Europe.

The net result is described in the East in clear terms:

"Communists fear that the Church in Western countries is committing itself to a world crusade against Communism.[5] Communist governments are still suspicious of the churchmen in their own countries; and the slightest indication that those churchmen are in fellowship with those who have expressed their determination to destroy Communism will bring upon the Church (in East Europe) a fierce persecution. For this reason any withdrawal (by churches of East Europe) from the World Council of Churches and the world councils of the various denominations must not be taken simply as obedience to a Government order but as the expression of their own desire to disassociate themselves from 'the enemies of the new order.' There is a deep Christian desire to maintain fellowship with all Christians, but they feel that there is a point at which they may have to choose between freedom for their own Church and fellowship in a world body which has taken the wrong road."[6]

The current position in which Hungarian Protestants find themselves in relation to their World Council participation further indicates how the churches are caught in an external political situation which tends to set them against one another:

"Our church leaders have come to the recognition that, after Toronto and Rolle (meetings of the Central Committee which passed resolutions condemning North Ko-

---

ing East Europe, and the propaganda about East Europe, on which public opinion and to a considerable extent State policy are formulated, has been introduced through Roman Catholic channels.

4. Albeit circumstantially enforced exclusion.

5. The parallel fear among conservative politicians in Western countries concerning East European churchmen, or even some of their own, has recently resulted in action approaching that taken by Communist governments in East Europe.

6. Private documents.

rean aggression) the World Council of Churches has been threatened by the fatal danger that it ceases to be the council of the churches . . . and becomes the exponent of a certain block of political powers. Should this ever happen, it would of course, make it impossible for Christians in States outside this power block or lined up against this block to feel themselves at one with the council and to identify themselves with its aims."[7]

Allegedly political barriers between East and West go deeper than contemporary politics. Their foundation was laid long before 1945—or even 1917. And, even if East-West political tensions should cease tomorrow, it cannot be assumed that the curtain between East and West would disappear, though it might shift slightly, in some places westward, in others eastward.

There is a language difference: one is Cyrillic, the other Latin. There are ethnic differences: one is Anglo-Saxon-Latin, the other Slav and Mongol. There are vocational differences: the East being principally agricultural, the West industrial. And there is the fundamental religious difference, the East being largely Orthodox, the West Roman Catholic or Protestant.

Orthodoxy has been regarded as "mystical," "superstitious," "other worldly" on one side; Renaissance Protestantism and Roman Catholicism have been seen as "activist," "this worldly," "untheological" on the other. Christians of the West, Catholics and Protestants alike, have seldom regarded Orthodox believers as Christians, and have repeatedly undertaken missionary endeavors to remake them in the Western image.

New Tensions Among Christians

Added to a long history of distrust, misunderstanding and fear are new tensions created since the Communist Revolution, many within the life of the churches themselves.

A Puritan or a Purified Church? There is an element of self-righteousness which almost imperceptibly creeps into the thinking of Christians in East and West alike. Where there has been revolution, one may think "we have suffered, we have been judged, we are purged, we are clean. Our austere life is *the* Christian (martyr) life." And where there has not been revolution, one may think "we have checked the tide, we have held off the force of atheism, we have maintained Christian civilization, we are the uncontaminated church."

Christians in one situation tend to assume that the preachments, actions and political conversations of Christians in the

---

7. Ecumenical Conference of Hungarian, Czechoslovak, and Polish Protestant leaders, *Hungarian Church Press*, June 15, 1954, pp. 87, 88.

other must be addressed in familiar words to a situation with which they are familiar, that pronouncements can be measured by the same moral values, and their effect gauged in terms of one's own situation. It is almost inconceivable to many Christians in the West that within his framework an East European pastor may be fully as capable of speaking an effective, prophetic word, though in radically different terms, as is a pastor in Madison, Wisconsin, or Athens, Greece.[8]

Christians of the West have criticized their Eastern brethren for participating in Communist elections. Christians in East Germany remind them that it was Western politicians who, contending that no one would take the elections seriously anyway,[9] encouraged them to vote Communist in the 1951 elections counter to their own moral principles. What are Eastern Christians to make of Western duplicity or misinformed conclusions, and what of Western condemnation of them or their compatriots for very similar "collaboration" a few years previously under the Nazis?

Austere or Comfortable Kingdom? There is a subtle drifting away from each other in meaning and manner of living. East German Christians recently addressed a letter to their West German brothers. Among other things, they wrote:

> "Christians of the East Zone, at best, may listen in on the wireless to the final declaration (of a mass church meeting in the West), and for this modest participation have to allow ourselves to be accused (by Eastern governments) of lending our ears to war-mongering voices! Now we have really become 'poor-relations.' A dangerous development, accepted too naively and uncritically by us: *there* (in the West)—Freedom, the rule of law, a prospering economy, a benign government, money and official protection for the churches; us—slavery, arbitrary judicature, planned disorder, and an attitude towards the churches which, according to tactical demands, contains any possibilities and which nowadays, with the separation of the two German would-be or half states from each other, has become only too inimical. If all the signs are not misleading, the threads between the brethren over there and over here are now becoming so thin that the possibilities of talks of an outward as well as of an inward nature become very few indeed (how much have we not both omitted in these seven merciful years!) and the mutual picture we have of each other becomes still vaguer, more unclear and ambiguous than it already is.

---

8. Cf. statement of Gollwitzer on p. 176.
9. *Chronicle*, p. 540.

Yes, the false picture which now already we have of each other will sow new trouble and drive each of us further apart to satisfy the demands of the day. The false picture which we now already have of each other: for you people are not those which in the longing and despairing imagination of the East Zone inhabitants you should be! Nor such as you are depicted in our newspapers! Neither are we such as seems certain to you from letters you receive, from your newspapers, from what refugees relate. And that is our burning fear, that you shall let yourselves be deluded by newspapers, the wireless, politicians who mislead you for reasons of their own, and last, but not least, *by a desire for comfort . . .*"[10]

Ministers from West Germany have visited East Germany with a view to taking up pastoral work there. Few stayed. Those who returned to the West were sufficient to convince East German Christians that their brethren in the West were more concerned with conventional comforts than with the ministry of hope in an austere situation. This is but one example.

Pervading the East-West relationship there is a subconscious movement toward identification of austerity as Christian vocation on the one hand, and of comforts and luxuries of the West (for those who have them) as the Kingdom of God on the other. These two factors of "self-righteous proletarianism" and "self-righteous bourgeoisism" are perhaps the most difficult to recognize, and being mutually radicalizing, are a most serious threat to ongoing conversations and understanding among Christians.

Institutions or Eschatology? Contrasts in the sense of God's immanence and of eschatology align themselves also along the East-West barrier. American Christians react strongly to theological opinion in West Europe. But the difference between West Europe and East Europe seems far more marked. Interpretations and manifestations of the nature and mission of the Church have moved in opposite directions.[11] Brethren from the East, speaking the same language, members and pastors of the same church, attend church gatherings in the West and are aghast to find Western churchmen toying with constitutional or architectural or other formal trivia. "The world's afire, and you bother about this foolishness!" On the other hand, when Western churchmen hear them speak in almost apocalyptic language of the sense of urgency, of

---

10. Private documents. Italics mine.
11. In East Europe laymen have led their churches in a deep theological, Biblical renewal. How *can* there be any serious basis of understanding between them and the civic-club mentality of many laymen's groups in the West? The latter might well seem to have more in common with East European non-religious (Communist) men's fellowships.

God's presence, of pentecostal communities in the East, the Westerner wonders at their fanaticism: "why are they so worked up of a sudden!"

When they say in the East—

"There is no light in the foreseeable future, no earthly hope on the horizon. There are times and places, and this seems to be one of them, when human beings are called to live directly in the light of their own death, and the death of the things they value and love"—

Western Christians can scarcely, indeed almost fear to understand them.

Mutual Judgment? Prof. Hromadka of Prague, addressing the Hungarian Ecumenical Study Commission in Budapest, Feb., 1954, stated:

"The question arises whether our inability to understand each other is due to differences in our attitude to Christ or . . . to different interpretations of the present historical situation."[12]

A critical point in question is judgment.

If, as has been suggested, Communism as an idea is breaking or has broken up in East Europe, then it has done so before its role as an instrument of judgment was fulfilled. Western Society has not fully realized the profound meaning of judgment contained therein. Few are they who will say with Jacques Maritain, French Catholic philosopher:

"What is the cause of this (atheism of Communism?) . . . It originates chiefly through the fault of a Christian world unfaithful to its own principles, in a profound sense of resentment not only against the Christian world, but . . . against Christianity itself . . ."[13]

It may fall to Eastern churches in their responsibility for a revelation they have received, and their responsibility to the whole body of the Church, to see to the continuation of that judging process on Western society in and through Western churches. That is not an easy situation for any part of the universal Church. Christians in the West or East do not like to face up to the fact that judgment is a common one, in spite of reminders of the Spirit, of the Church and of an uneasy conscience that all are involved in

---

12. Cf. *Hungarian Church Press*, Feb. 15, 1954, address of Prof. Hromadka.
13. Jacques Maritain, *True Humanism*, Charles Scribner's Sons, New York, 1938, p. 33.

it. It does not make it any easier to have Christian brethren remind them of the fact. This kind of exhortation from the East, necessary as it may be, does not endear Eastern and Western churches to one another:

> "I hope and pray that the churches in Great Britain will be spared the ordeal of totalitarianism, but if they have to face one day the assault of the modern godless powers and find themselves ill-equipped and disunited for this struggle, they have themselves to blame, for they have witnessed the fate of other Christians and have had ample time to learn from their experience. The East is not so far removed from the West as some people (in the West) still think, and the things that were first tried have been copied and reproduced in other parts of the world. It is time for us to realize that we who are Christians are all members of the same body and that we face everywhere the same problems and dangers. We need the help of one another for God has given to us different gifts and it is His will that we share them with the other members of His Church."[14]

Great patience, humility and Christian identity in love must obviously be exercised if Christians are to exhort one another under such circumstances.

Isolation and Fragmentation. Isolation contributes toward a partial and eventually an impure witness to the fullness of Truth in West as in East. The limiting of the broader world fellowship means the limiting of the Christian's comprehension of God—result: differing, if not contradictory interpretations of God's revelation in East and West.[15] Snatches of sermons, of letters or articles carried through secular channels may exaggerate the contrast and further increase tensions. Statements or resolutions, or lack of them, by Christians in East or West may need to be denounced in the other area, according to the same Gospel, but as seen in that area. Christians come to wonder seriously whether Christians of so divergent opinions can be said to constitute legitimate churches.[16] Who can deny that there are churches in the West which are "handmaids of the ruling classes?" But who may say that all are? Barth and others may accuse Reformed Hun-

---

14. Nicolas Zernov, *Journal of the Fellowship of St. Alban and St. Sergius,* *I.C.P.I.S.* No. 4, 1943.

15. While some churches in the West accuse churchmen of East Europe of "withdrawing into a theological fortress," the latter may regard statements of Western churchmen as "without real theological foundation." (*Hungarian Church Press*, Aug. 15, 1953, p. 187).

16. The Lutheran Church of Hungary is not presently (1953) regarded as a legitimate Lutheran Church by the Lutheran World Federation.

garians of theological instability in their consistent sanction of whatever regime is in power.[17] Church may denounce[18] or oust sister-churches; Christians may disown fellow-Christians. What else are Methodists in East Europe to do when Methodists in America advertise in their leading publication that "Methodist dollars fight Communism in China?" Or others, when Christians in West or East make anti-Communism or pro-Communism their Gospel?

Once there is any feeling of isolation or abandonment, then there is fertile ground for propagandists, deliberately or unconsciously, to plant seeds of doubt in any broader Christian fellowship. People, and Christians among them, become "distrustful, reserved and used to giving evasive answers."[19] One of the most painful experiences the writer has had has been to sit in informal conference with Christian brethren in East Europe but to have no spiritual relationship, only a cool, official business contact. They did not know whom they could trust; or if they did, they did not feel free to demonstrate it. The effect of propaganda in the East as in the West has been to convince many Christians that their religious brethren across the Curtain and their associates at home have resigned themselves to blind participation in their respective governments' political struggles.[20]

Sudden changes in theology, ecclesiology, church structure, the ministry, evangelism and social action—some of necessity, some of preference—result in contrasts as great as between several centuries. Understanding is not easily reached between Christians of the same confession, of the same era, of the same culture and tradition. How, then, reach understanding between two different worlds and two epochs?

A New Rift?

Is the ecumenical fellowship drifting towards a clear rift? Is it destined to come to two separate "world" councils of churches, plus the Vatican? This is a possibility; it may, at various times, even seem likely. It does not, however, seem likely at the moment.

In the first place, the political powers in the Eastern block do not want to see a too intimate relationship of a religious nature develop among churches in their sphere, independent of government control. It is too risky. They prefer to deal with isolated units

---

17. Karl Barth, letter to Hungarian Bishop Bereczky, *Christian Century*, July 30, 1952.
18. E.g., a recent denunciation of Protestant leaders in America by the Evangelical Augsburgian Church of Poland for allegedly supporting revision of Poland's frontiers and preparing for war (*RNS*, Feb. 16, 1954).
19. *EPS*, No. 18, 1943, p. 93.
20. The attitude of many Americans towards delegates from East Europe at the Second Assembly of the World Council of Churches is a case in point.

of Christian believers than to have churches strengthening, exhorting, counselling and purifying one another.

Secondly, at the level of local congregational life, there is an abiding sense of fellowship and participation in the world Christian community. This stands in spite of pressures and tensions to the contrary.

It is at the level of ecclesiastical *haute politique* that indications of a rift have been most evident. Ostensible reasons have been a combination of pseudo-confessional (e.g., Orthodox versus Protestant) and political factors. Orthodox churches in the Soviet sphere have alleged that the rise of the Ecumenical Movement coincidentally with the transition of capitalism to its "imperialistic phase" is evidence that the movement was created as another tool of capitalist imperialism.[21] Few Orthodox individuals themselves seem seriously convinced of that allegation, and, since the Second Assembly (August, 1954) the Russian Orthodox Church has indicated an open interest in the World Council.[22]

Orthodox churches have further alleged that the Ecumenical Movement is Western and Protestant in character. Unfortunately, there is much truth in that statement. But if the Movement is that, it is precisely because the Eastern Orthodox have not been at the center of the Movement since its inception. And if the "councils of churches" of East Europe are strictly Eastern in character, it is because they have not brought Western churches into their counsels. This is not their responsibility. They sense the tragedy of it, as does any discerning spirit in the West. They are in a political situation in which there is no other possibility. They desire ecumenical contacts, but "for the moment find it impractical."[23]

This does not mean that churches in East Europe are intent on establishing a rival council of churches to the World Council of Churches. They have legitimate reason and right to hold meetings according to realistic possibilities. Nor does it mean that they are, or will be entirely ready, in whatever political circumstances, to accept a predominantly Western interpretation and manifestation of the ecumenical movement as presently represented in the World Council of Churches.

The present emphasis among Orthodox in East Europe on Jerusalem as the mother of the Church and the legitimate center

---

21. This accusation may also be taken to reveal something of recent relationships between, and intentions of the Russian Church and the Soviet State.

22. ..*Journal of the Patriarchate of Moscow*, No. 1, Jan., 1954 (*EPS*, April 30, 1954).

23. Private documents, 1951. More recently, however, churchmen from the West have been invited (as they were previously) and have succeeded in participating in conferences in several East European countries.

of ecumenicity[24] may be a very significant attempt to overcome present political, theological and ecclesiological barriers to an inclusive ecumenical movement. Jerusalem is in several ways neutral territory. It is a suggestion which needs serious consideration.

Toward Deeper Fellowship

Information about East Europe is poor. Such as has come until now has been largely from the biased sources of the dispossessed aristocracy, or from a church which is losing a world of power and fears it may not be regained, or from people in the West who fear their economic bubble is about to be punctured. Christians in the West hear too little from Christians in East Europe, and hardly enough even from governments. If fellowship is to be maintained, then it will be done only by Christians exercising their utmost in imagination, in patience, in humility and in prayer. In East and West Christians may strengthen their brethren by maintaining spiritual fellowship, by pursuing such opportunities for conversation as arise, and by looking to their own renewal. But as possibilities of greater contact arise,[25] Western churches cannot and must not rush in as though they had all the answers.[26]

Ecumenically-minded leaders of East European churches are often young, and international experience is new to them. It can be expected that they will approach international contacts cautiously; they have a government to reassure. In academic or abstract theological conversation they may feel unsure of themselves, whereas their religious experience may give them unparalleled confidence and depth. On political issues they can be expected to have blind spots, just as any churchman or politician from the West will have blind spots in that broader *milieu*.

---

24. On the 1500th anniversary of the re-establishment of the Jerusalem Patriarchate, the Orthodox Church of Rumania declared: "Only now in the perspective of so many centuries and after the disappearance of the political, economical or some other glory of the old Patriarchates, one begins to concede to the Jerusalem Patriarchate its unique position in the whole of Christendom, the position by which it is in the eyes of every true Christian raised far above all others" (*Bulletin of Rumanian Orthodoxy*, April/May, 1952, p. 250).

25. Churches in East Europe which have established their independence from Western authority may increasingly converse with Western churches, particularly those which have given evidence of their independence from control or domination by anti-Communist politics, or by any remnants of former regimes seeking to re-establish themselves in East Europe.

26. The presumption of certain Western churches that they should train leaders (mostly East European refugees) for East Europe's churches for the day when East Europe is "liberated" is no help toward understanding. In the first place, the political possibilities of such a return seem most unlikely. But if Western-trained leaders could return, it is unlikely that East Europeans would be disposed to accept them as leaders, and it is unlikely that any training in the West could qualify them for such leadership.

But one thing is sure, the desire for re-establishing spiritually-based ecumenical relationships is there, and the hurdles to be overcome at the political level are not insurmountable.

A Common Language. Partly from religious changes already listed, partly from the linguistic evolution which accompanies any thorough social revolution, Christians in East and West have no common language. That they think they have, when in fact they haven't, makes understanding more difficult. A good illustration is in the fact that the so-called "common language" of Britons and Americans, or of East Germans and West Germans, has in fact made it more difficult for those groups to get on with each other than with groups radically different. They expect too much of each other simply because of a "common" tongue. Because they are of a common religion, Christians in East and West can no longer assume that they have a common language, even a religious language. There has never been a great deal of common ground between East and West, and there is extremely little on which to begin now. A fundamental reacquaintance experience is a requisite to future understanding.

Diversities of Gifts. Christians presently must recognize that they are in different situations fraught with different limitations and opportunities which may require different forms, manner of life and Christian witness.[27] The Apostle Paul lived a quite different life among the Gentiles from that of Peter among the Jews. It could not be said, then or now, that one life was more legitimate than the other. "If one thinks he is of Christ, the other is Christ's also" (II Cor. 10:7). But Christians, as then, have a responsibility to study and know the Christian values, the complexities and restrictions in their apposites' *milieux*.

"Forbear one another in love." At times this may mean to criticize, at other times to listen and to be silent. Christians have a responsibility to exhort one another in the spirit of love. It is one way of exercising their mutual responsibility, of developing and fulfilling a whole Christian witness. This excludes any spirit of accusation, of demand for another's repentance, or of considering one another to be a "mission field" to be converted to one's own point of view. Where conflict arises, it must be seen as an evident sign

---

27. "The Christian in the East receives different commands from our common Lord; his political responsibility takes on entirely different form in practice from that of Christians in the West" (Helmut Gollwitzer, *op. cit.*, p. 176 of this document).

"that the church is under God's judgment and it behooves the church to seek, in repentance and humility, the cause of such judgment."[28]

This requires that the churches hear one another, that each "listens to the Word of the entire church, the Communion of saints . . ."[29] while exhorting one another.

If gestures of affection and attempts at understanding are rebuffed, inter-church aid for example, it must be recognized that there are serious, and often unrevealable reasons, and go right on in love and in mutual trust. While not universally evident, the restraint of Christians in the East is cause for encouragement.

"Our love towards churches living in conditions different from ours has often kept us back, in the interests of fraternal understanding, from publicly defending ourselves against untenable charges, when we felt that our self-defense would only intensify the tension, whereas we believe that the task of the churches is rather to lessen the tension. We have often obeyed to the Word, 'Forebear one another in love,' and, instead of going to law, we preferred to 'take the wrong.' "[30]

One of the most significant gestures Western churches could make toward deeper fellowship would be to set their own houses in order. Racial segregation in America, class discrimination in West Europe, deportations of Asians from Australia: these mockeries of human rights and spiritual truths strike at the bonds of spiritual kinship in religious as well as political ways. And if churches of the West have human weakness, it is no less true of churches under the Communist system. There is room for humility and confession of guilt, and intercession, but also for serious action and a sense of corporate responsibility for an unredeemed society in both places.

"One another's burdens." Eastern Christians sense acutely that there is no position they can take which frees them from guilt. If they are silent, they are guilty; if they acquiesce, they are guilty; if they simply oppose social changes, they are guilty. From this burden they are liberated only partly, and then by the knowledge of the Grace of God. In that situation Christians in East Europe count on the moral and spiritual support of the whole household of faith.

---

28. Letter of Hungarian Reformed and Lutheran churches to Central Committee of World Council of Churches, Feb. 1, 1951.

29. Comment of the Hungarian Ecumenical Study Commission concerning Hungarian Protestantism, *Hungarian Church Press*, Aug. 15, 1953, p. 189.

30. *Ibid.*, p. 193.

They are not so much interested in pronouncements, study documents and abstract counsel as they are in a simple sharing in the life and experiences of other Christians around the world.

"We ask more comprehension, patience, love and trust of our . . . brethren who, lacking an adequate knowledge of our history and present-day conditions, frequently regard us with prejudice and judge us with bias. We ask them to feel more responsibility for us and pray more for us."[31]

Beyond this, East European churchmen, as Prof. Pap declared of the Hungarian Reformed and Lutheran churches,[32] "have realized that (they) have a serious responsibility for the World Council of Churches," and have expressed it in many ways:[33] in meetings of the Council, in studies of and comments on documents of the Council, in a broad program of interpretation within Hungary. Similarly, in Czechoslovakia, Rumania, Bulgaria, Poland and the Soviet Union a determined effort has been made by leading churchmen to fam"iarize themselves and their contemporaries with the ecumenical movement and to speak to it. They would welcome every similar and imaginative effort undertaken by Christians in the West. And some of the heavy burdens which the West also has it might well share with Christians in the East.

"We are One in Christ with you all, even if one must be sometimes elastic because of the situation. Most hearty greetings in Christ's Name."[34]

---

31. Letter of Hungarian Lutherans to Lutheran World Federation, *News Bulletin of L. W. F.*, p. 2, April 1, 1950.

32. Introductory Remarks to the Bratislava Ecumenical Conference, *Hungarian Church Press*, June 15, 1954, p. 87.

33. E.g., "the task of the World Council of Churches is to perform its service with the spirit of making peoples and societies know each other, love each other, and of deepening the mutual confidence among them . . ." (Statements of the Ecumenical Study Commission of the Hungarian Reformed and Lutheran churches, *Hungarian Church Press*, Aug. 15, 1953, p. 186).

34. Private documents from East Europe.

Shall Christians "obey God rather than men," or "be subject to governing authorities . . . as instituted by God?"[1]

Chapter XIV

WHERE IS THE CHURCH UNIVERSAL TO TAKE A STAND?

Christians in East Europe, confronted by Communist encroachments on conventional aspects of church life, have had to decide whether and where the churches should take a stand, whether it was possible to establish an absolute line beyond which the churches could not go. And in the whole body of the Church Universal, earnest Christians, whether from a sense of impending judgment, or of historic revolution, or for fear of Communist occupation, have found it to be their problem: at what point must the Church boldly and categorically pronounce a resounding "No?"

Informed Christians in East and West, concerned with the ills out of which Communism springs and equally aware of the ills it breeds, claim no absolute position at either extreme, pro-Communist or anti-Communist. Where, then, is the Church to stand?

In East Europe the churches once owned nearly fifteen million acres of land and hundreds of profitable buildings, enterprises and investments. In losing them, the churches lost power they had held for hundreds of years. In the West where churches are rapidly accumulating fortunes and properties, are they to draw the battle-line between those church properties and creeping governmental control? Whether the government in question is Communist or non-Communist is of little import, the churches could raise considerable noise and support for their position. Ought they? In East Europe, churches which fought against long-overdue reforms only further alienated their tenants and debtors. Once severed from their economic empires, those churches found their relationship to oppressed peoples transformed from intimidation and fear to identification and devotion. The churches' work and strength was based on believers, not on bricks, banks and business. Opposition to property reforms has not proved a suitable place for a church stand.

But Communism has effected changes more central to the life of the Church: its works of mercy, for example. Is the Church to demand the right to organize charitable endeavors? Does it

---

1. Acts 5:29, Romans 13:1.

necessarily abrogate its Lord's injunction to heal, comfort and feed the needy if it cannot so organize?

Should the Church balk when confronted with secularized education and the loss of religious education? Religious education where?—in the schools? Or by whom and how? In East Europe special activities are organized by government-related agencies to occupy children at the hours of worship. Is the Church to make its stand with demands for a specific place and method of worship and religious education? Then what of Sunday football games, picnics, excursions and parades in the West?

Is the Church to give unremitting opposition to limitations on its pronouncements concerning political and social justice? Or are there other ways of preaching "justice" quite as effective in a difficult situation, and perhaps universally, as public pronouncements and demonstrations?

Is the Church to take its stand when governments seek control of ecclesiastical organizations, of pastors, teachers, appointments, constitutions, finances? Are these requisites to the ongoing life of the Church?

Shall the Church expend itself against restrictions on worship? What is worship that can be restricted? But if one assumes that it cannot ultimately be restricted, what is the Christian to do when obliged to sing hymns of praise and prayer to Communist leaders?

Where is the Church to stand when family life is disrupted, children taught to deceive, parents to deny responsibility for the moral and physical well-being of their off-spring? Can it find there a martyr-stand? Does it, in the West?

What shall the Church do when apparently confronted by no other alternative but persecution and martyrdom? Stephen was stoned; was that persecution or a Christian witnessing to a victorious faith through suffering? Can the real Church indeed be persecuted? From the perspective of the "persecutor," perhaps it can, but from the perspective of the Christian, what is "persecution" more than being forced to make a dramatic witness to his faith?

In East Europe, churches, one after another, have attempted "stands" at various points along a retreating way. One has fought nationalization of institutions; another, secularized education; another, nationalized church administration. What they fought for they lost. As a strategy one can say that the 'bulldog' stand of the churches has failed. But win or lose, there can be no recourse from battle—the witness of the convinced—for ultimate Truth. Here, however, they were not permitted the privilege of losing as martyrs for Truth or religion. They were overcome issue after issue as "political reactionaries," "traitors of the people," "feudalists," etc. Nor has appeasement and bargaining brought more than a few days' respite.

Where is the Church to take its stand? To ask that question is to confuse the techniques of the Church with those of a political or military power. It assumes that the purpose of the Church is to "defend" certain values, including her own self-preservation, and that the Church has the kind of power necessary so to do. It suggests that a certain pattern of church life, generally Nineteenth Century Western European church life, is indispensable to her perpetuation. It thereby identifies the Church with a fixed time and place in history. It conditions the life and message of the Church more towards negations of this world, rather than by the affirmations God has given her, turns her into a pseudo-political or military power far removed from her primary vocation and unites her in an unnatural and unholy alliance foreign to her nature.

Here is the central danger to the churches of being mislead by the militant resistance, by political Catholicism, or fearful capitalism—namely, that the churches become enjoined in a power struggle on some "stand" which may involve deep spiritual and religious consequences, but which prostitutes the Church until she can no longer be the Church—to either party—blinded to the need for reform and reconciliation, heedless and speechless of God's revelations.

If, as John Bennett suggests,[2] the fundamental quarrel between Christians and Communists is not over an economic system, or social goals, or materialism, or moral relativism, or violent revolution, or even atheism, but rather the tendency of Communism to absolutize its system to the point of practical idolatry, then Christians are of little help if they, too, "stand" on idolatry, albeit an ecclesiasticized idolatry.

The first requisite in the Church's stand is to recognize that it has no "stand" as this world reckons. It has no "rights," and ought never to have assumed that it had. It has responsibility. Incidentally, governments also ultimately share this status of having no rights—but responsibility—though few ever recognize it. But governments do have power, power to alter, transfer or otherwise affect all things material, including the churches' things. The Church has no such earthly power or position to take a "stand" on. Its only "power" is spiritual, its only "right" is to claim Christ— and love, mercy, grace, hope and prayer, and victory.

But the alternative to power, for the Church, is not appeasement. Appeasement is as misleading as, and more foolish than engagement in an anti-Communist crusade. Attempts at "appease-

2. "The Christian Answer to Communism," *Social Progress*, Jan., 1951, pp. 6, 7.

ment" have demonstrated how the weakness of the churches lies precisely in their false estimation of power, "things" and privileges as commodities to be desired and bartered. Does submission to Communist powers, sanction of Communist acts, participation in Communist victories, and "peace" rallies, or any other government's powers, acts, or rallies, spring from a concern for the Truth inherent therein, or from a desire on the part of churches to enhance their own worldly position? In negation at that level the churches can only lose, for these are a-spiritual matters controlled by governments, not by churches. The Church's treasure and her courage consist of Truth and the Spirit. To scheme and appease is to lose both the worldly "powers" or the status desired, as well as the essential and external *charisma* which belong to the Church. In this regard, East European churchmen have been no less distraught over Western churchmen's attempts to "appease" or flatter East European Communist governments into desired responses than over their absolute opposition to those governments. In either case the Church is further separated from that mind and spirit in which she receives her own kind of power and works her victory.

No offensive of the secular world can corner the Church at some "stand," or fixed place, or absolute line as defined by the materialistic world. That is a cardinal principle.

The second principle is its corollary: the Church has and is essentially an affirmation independent of (but not unrelated to) its secular environ. If the Church does not receive its essential "rights" or "freedom" or responsibilities from governments, neither can governments control their continued reception, and indeed their operation. Governments can suppress or destroy Christians, they cannot destroy the essentials of Christian faith.

What are those fundamentals which can exist, and have existed in any conceivable situation? These three are primary: (1) the believer's inner relationship to his Lord and his consequent conviction of the victory of God's will; (2) the believer's spiritual relationship to other believers; and (3) the believer's attitude, his possibility of identity with, responsibility and forgiveness for the world about him.

This is the dimension of the spirit and of prayer. This is the fortress—sometimes surrendered, but never conquered by worldly powers—from which the Christian sallies forth to minister and to witness. This is the rock bottom on which the whole structure of the churches' witness must be built. Take away church property, sanctuaries, publications, organizations, pastors, teachers, sacraments, public worship, community—this still can remain. This, then, is where the Church stands. It is an unfortunate church which assumes it cannot exist with so little; and an equally unfortunate government which makes provision for no more.

The third principle relates to the superstructure. We have spoken of fundamentals, of the essence of faith. At that level the believer "must obey God rather than men" (Acts 5:29). We come now to the tools and methods which the believer, in community with others, creates and employs to manifest the fundamental affirmation given him. At this level, he is "in subjection to the higher powers" as ordained of God (Romans 13:1). If at the deeper level, his purposes are determined by God, at this level his acts are circumscribed by his social and political environment. This existential framework, with its limitations, restrictions and opportunities is determined by governments, often on the basis of physical strength, not by the Church. To act and to witness in it, the Church must accept the fact of government, and indeed recognize the responsibility of a specific government. But the use which is made of opportunities in that framework is determined by the Church, which neither demands nor accepts such opportunities as being granted by governments, and therefore with obligations, but as from God.[3] The Church, therefore, simply and quickly, must claim every real opportunity for preaching, teaching and witnessing within its existential situation. At this level of overt witness, flexibility, adaptation and opportunity are the Christian's watchwords. This is the third principle.

So long as, and in whatever ways the Christian can make public witness, he must do so. He has a responsibility to pronounce judgment which he has no power to implement, to proclaim eternal principles which he has no power to enforce. Nevertheless, he must warn, counsel, evaluate and point to those principles and basic human aspirations without which every government and every society is bound to fall.[4] He proclaims spiritual and moral requisites for individual fulfillment as well as for responsible society. The broader his opportunities of method, the greater is his responsibility to proclaim. But if his mouth be sealed, he does not regard his situation as void of religion, nor is he consumed with bitterness. He has still his foundation. What is essential is that

---

3. Said I. Veöreös, a leading Hungarian pastor during the negotiations over the nationalization of church schools: ". . . the State should understand that we cannot give up our schools which we received from God as a holy possibility to serve church and nation in the course of history, and cannot give up any of our rights to maintain schools. If the legislation of the Hungarian republic takes them from us, we bow before it and accept it as being just and the beginning of a new task from God's hand. We also know that where God closes a door, He opens another one" (*Uj Harangszo,* June 6, 1948).

4. "The Church of Christ has the task . . . of criticizing everything that is evil and unjust. To do that in a way that will be understood, with complete frankness and honesty, is very difficult today." (Prof. Hromadka, Conference on Mission of the Church, *E.P.S.,* Oct. 13, 1950).

the truth be witnessed to where it can and in ways it can, rather than that the powers of darkness be cursed where it cannot.

This means that Christians, in their diverse situations, have diverse ministries and emphases of witness. What constitutes those diversities in relation to Communism? We shall have to consider four phases of Communism.

Post-Communist[5] Society

In the post-Communist situation the predominant mood can be described as anarchy. The aspirations and enthusiasm of idealistic youth have been frustrated. The hopes of the oppressed have been largely unrealized (whether in objective fact or in their subjective assessment of their situation). People who for years have been subjected to regimentation, to "collectives," "cooperatives" or organized "community responsibility," do not take kindly to disciplines, whether of society, government or conscience. In that situation the Church cannot simply plead for "Christian solidarity" and "corporate responsibility."[6] It must manifest, and often has manifested an organized, responsible society in its own being. Widespread disillusionment and vengefulness call for an emphasis on a hope and vision which give meaning and purpose in a spiritual-material context, and for reconciliation, forgiveness and trust. The Christian is challenged to hold before his contemporaries the hard realities which many (including avowed Communists) seek to escape in some world of fantasy and superstition.[7] Moral dualism and negativism require a bold integrity and critical affirmations for their antidote. And the Church may do much to ensure that Communism, though containing much evil in itself, not go down in history as a passing tragedy of negation, but that in an

---

5. "Post-Communist" is intended to mean that situation in which ideological Communism has been subordinated to the expediencies of political authority and responsibility of Communist regimes. Communism arose in several countries as the champion of the rights and aspirations of the oppressed. So long as it was a minority, and often a persecuted minority, and could maintain its identity with the downtrodden, it was in the ascendancy. It was aggressive, flexible, positive, evangelistic. But when Communism—via military occupation, *coups d'etat*, etc.—came into power and was responsible for the conduct and welfare of a nation, it must of necessity shift from an aggressive minority position to the defensive. It then becomes no longer a crusading ideology, but an institution which must defend its position and must find excuses for its failures. True, Communist governments are in power, but they are now implicated, and must now speak and act, within their real situation, not in some abstract Utopia.

6. In an unpublished document a competent observer wrote of East Germany: ". . . due to the impact of the two eras of collectivization (men) shy away even from the corporate and collective expressions of the 'Christian faith.' "

7. A young Communist leader in one East European country confided to the writer that he was a convinced astrologist, but dared not let his colleagues know.

eternal perspective the lessons learned from it and through it be communicated to future generations. It must strive to set that deeper, nobler, historic revolution, as the yearning of man for justice and harmony, (which has in many respects been set back by Communism) again on the road to fulfillment.[8]

Communist Society

In the Communist society, where the atmosphere is charged with fear, negation and reprisal, where untried governments cast about, often recklessly, for certainty and finality, Christians readily acknowledge that they have often confused church essentials with tools and techniques, even to the point of identifying the Church's destiny with the material on-going of anti-Communist interests.

Accepting Communist governments as *de facto* governments, Christians in Communist-controlled societies must pronounce judgment on their new social order with whatever voice is left to them, holding up before governments eternal laws, and exhorting Communists to responsible stewardship, at times advising, at others warning on proposed actions. Their method is not by ultimatum which they have no power to carry out. Their strength lies only in the truth of that which they speak. Human "rights" must be set forth without implying that they are Christian "musts." But they are political "musts" for any government which hopes to continue.

Religious encounter with Communists is not impossible, and may occur on an unexpectedly frank basis with Christians who give evidence of boldness and honesty. It is not uncommon for Communists who have been enveloped in a dungeon of fear and guilt and lack of forgiveness to seek out recognized Christians for spiritual guidance.

From negative reaction, the people must be called to creative action. Fear must be displaced by hope, and any facile idolatry or materialistic idealism with a new appreciation of life as spiritual, eternal and purposeful. The Christian community must stand out as a clear alternative to Communist massification and bourgeois conformism, in economic as well as social and spiritual terms. These are tasks which the Church alone can do. It is her responsibility.

---

8. Widdrington, in *"Future of the Russian Church,"* quotes Serge Bulgakoff, the late dean of the Russian Academy, Paris, himself a Russian emigre: "Communism has arisen on the basis of a search for the truth of life, for the Kingdom of God on earth, with an apocalyptic tenseness of faith in the future, and a sincere desire to realize it, and we may hope that this will for the future is not displeasing to God, and will not be turned to shame . . ."

Pre-Communist Society

America is probably the classic example of a pre-Communist society in which the churches have an enormous responsibility. Here where political and social decisions, indeed even religious preachments, are determined as much by fears of Communism as by ultimate truth, the Church has a particularly difficult role. In the first place, the churches can only by the most agonizing reformation dis-entangle themselves from a too-close identity with one economy or politic or ideology, and be the Church. If they have no external restraining forces, the churches must curb their own ambitions which exceed their spiritual calling, and see that governments carry their own proper responsibilities beyond that point. Only such churches can keep from becoming empires of a socio-political nature, and only thus can the churches maintain a clear position between the extremes involved in a church-state or an anti-religious state. This is the churches' first task, to be the Church.[9] Then their concern is not their own preservation. The destiny of *the* Church is assured. It does not ask for special privileges, and does not depend upon State support. Then its concern for society—at a new dimension—stems not from fear that (Western) civilization is endangered by external materialistic forces (as though that civilization were presently free from materialism!), but from a Divine imperative that society must be judged, refined and redeemed. Then, and then only can the Churches confront Communism, and minister to people confronting Communism with courage and conviction. For only that church more profoundly comprehending, and more actively engaged in the fundamental historic revolution than is Communism can understand Communism, apprize it and surpass it. It is for that Church to seek justice where there is injustice, enlightenment where there is fear, affirmation where there is negation, responsible society where there is "civilization," spiritual renewal where there is religious formalism and Western materialism.

Western Churches must surely recognize that in Western society the fact that people who become Communists are the bored intellectuals, frustrated idealists and unchallenged humanitarians says something very special to the Church concerning its message and method.

There are also pre-Communist societies which would welcome Communism as a hopeful step towards a more abundant life. Here, frequently, Christians with a deep social concern will be found associated with Communism. One thinks particularly of present or former colonies and of oppressed minorities or smaller nations.

---

9. See next chapter.

Here the Church must be quick to point out on the basis of facts that while anti-Communism is no guarantee of spiritual fulfillment or historic continuity, Communism certainly is no less an idolatry of materialism, and has proved an equally hazardous political adventure. The whole Church can and must confront such peoples with the totality of the Communist picture, as well as with some positive alternatives. Here, again, the Church must acknowledge the profound depths from which the demands for revolution spring, and counsel, judge and encourage the working out of reforms on the basis of eternal and spiritual principles.

The Church in the pre-Communist situation must prepare for the time when it can be rejoined more closely to fellow-Christians in the Communist orbit. This means the practice of trust, patience, charity and prayer. The last thing it means, if ever, is that the West should prepare leaders, political or ecclesiastical, who might one day return to the East to set things right. The practical possibilities of such an arrangement (assuming that the West would do the "liberating"!) are about as unthinkable as the possibility of Americans accepting the Communist American G.I.s in Korea as their leaders if America were some day "liberated" by Soviet forces. This does not mean there should be no thinking about such an eventuality, but such thinking must recognize that major responsibilities in such circumstances will have to be carried by those who have endured *en situe,* and that the Westerner's major responsibility will likely be related to where he now stands.

Secluded Society

It is conceivable that there are eddies of society so far removed from the stream of current revolution that there is not only no desire for the Communist Order, but no awareness or fear of it. But the Church in such a place is not in a world apart. Neither the nature of the Church itself, nor the present revolution can allow such an "aristocracy," be it of wealth, culture or values for which all men yearn. The Church must enquire as to why that society is detached, exhorting the people to become identified with fellow man. It must preach of judgment and humility and grace. It must remind them of God's involvement as an innocent Son in the evils of man, that man could know again a relationship with God and with fellow man.

Finally, the fundamental "stand" of the Church is the same universally. There are particulars of witness in particular situations, but the fullness of the Church's witness is dependent upon the Church's wholeness. In the West, churches may have opportunities to exercise in more demonstrable ways the fundamental faith of the whole Church; while in East Europe, Christians—not all of them—are finding and demonstrating a simplified, positive witness day by day, step by step. They do not assume that their regime is the best, and may in fact be in favor of quite another political pattern. But if it is their *de facto* government, their question is: can we give a Christian witness in that framework? It is a question the Church must ask in whatever situation it finds itself. Many in East Europe feel that they have a special witness which they can give and are giving in a "totalitarian" society. It is often a witness of silence, of grace and prayer, and of community. It is decidedly a different form of social witness from that seen in Western society. But if they are not identical, they are complementary. Without either, the other is not made whole. The voice of the Christian in a "free" society must speak for the Christians muted in dungeons, and those silenced and hidden must strengthen the spiritual foundations of those on the house tops. In the present world, or "worlds," the Church has not a stand, but it has "stands"—witnesses to the same truth but taking many forms. This is of the essence of its unity.

"The Church is not embarrassed by the developments of history . . ."[1]

Chapter XV

THE WHOLENESS OF THE CHURCH AND RENEWAL IN ITS SEVERAL PARTS

What are the implications of what has happened in East Europe for the inner life of the Church Universal, and more precisely for churches of the West? Is there any particular meaning for the practices and structure and ecclesiological presuppositions of Western churches?

The Form of the Church

Western Christians may take heart from the signs of renewal among Christians in East Europe. But there are subtle dangers at this point in that Western churches may be tempted to seek a *formula* for their own renewal in East Europe.[2]

The most obvious and least consequential danger is that Western Christians might hope to find the source of church renewal in East Europe and ultimately their own renewal, in some simple form or pattern of life.[3] That they will not find such a form lessens the danger. For there are many forms and a variety of practices in East Europe. And no single pattern, nor all together, can adequately explain what God has wrought there. Western Christians may, nonetheless, have to seek such a form to find that it does not exist, indeed that the dependence upon any form for the churches' revival or preservation has been proven

---

1. From the Statement of the Hungarian Ecumenical Study Commission, *op. cit.*, August 15, 1953, p. 178: "The Church interpreting the Gospel herself and the world in Christ, is not embarrassed by the development of history, but is ready to accept the great historical events from the hand of God the Father, the supreme Ruler of history, and seeks in these events the new opportunities of service, recognizing and doing what is timely and proper, what God has prepared beforehand that in discharging her service, she may become fit and authentic to give an account of the hope that is in her."

2. Mention has already been made (p. 185) of the opposite tendency, to reject any intimation from East Europe that churches in the West *ought* to revise their ways.

3. This temptation is the more insistent because of similarities between patterns in East Europe and those of the apostolic churches.

dramatically invalid since the time of the churches' too-close identity with, and copying of feudal patterns.

But if Western churches, in discovering the variety of forms in East Europe, are stimulated to confront one another in a vital conversation, and not simply to go each his own way, unaware of and unaffected by one another, the end result may be salutary.

There is another danger more subtle and grave, with three facets: one, that Western Christians might seek to use the experiences of Eastern Christians for their own purposes; two, that they thereby violate the integrity of the historical situation itself, and miss the deeper significance of the Communist-Christian encounter as well as the involvement of God in it, and preclude the possibility of those developments speaking for themselves, or of God speaking through them; and, three, that they regard their vocation as their own preservation or renewal, and in their pre-occupation with ensuring their own life do in fact lose that life which is given to those who sense God's concern for the world and who lose themselves in ministering to it.

If the renewal of the life of the Church is not to be found in a specific form, nor in many forms, neither is it to be found in an intense seeking after renewal. The reality underlying the vital life of the Church is God, and God only. But before He is known, simply and with power, the eyes of the great and the comfortable may need to be stripped of the scales of security and strength and ambitious pride. Perhaps such scales are falling. If Western Christians look to the East for new forms, it is already an encouraging sign that they recognize the inadequacy, and perhaps judgment of their own forms. More encouraging still is the fact that discerning spirits are finding in the East, not in the first place forms, but judgment and grace—their judgment and God's grace for them.

The Common Judgment of the Churches

During the most trying days of Communism's ascent, Communist reforms and Communist propaganda constantly reminded the churches of their involvement in past injustices, their need for repentance and reformation. This nurtured an excessively *acute sense of guilt* which eroded the prophetic quality of Christian statesmanship. Communists may have preferred not to "offend religious sensibilities." But Christians, sensitive of their guilt, expecting severe judgment, were hardly in a position to be "offended." The Communists could therefore push their program to considerable extremes. A *repenting* church had little to say. On

---

4. In the Middle Ages, churches of Central Europe adjusted their practices and life to feudal patterns in order to be more effective, only to find their own existence threatened when feudalism gave way to other forms.

the other hand, an unrepentant church was in no position to speak out boldly on matters of justice and judgment. A large part of the problem of Christians lay in a confusion of the media of judgment (was it the churches or the Revolution?) with the Divine Judge. To whom were they repenting? This is still a real problem.[5]

But few Eastern church leaders would presently maintain that because Communism has been an instrument of holy judgment on an unholy society it is thereby due some particular respect and penitence as something holy. God, not Communism is the Lord and Judge of history. And while the delicate balance between the sense of being judged of Him via Communism (or the Revolution) and the sense of being called of Him to pronounce judgment over the whole of society including Communism has not been easy to achieve, some East Europeans have demonstrated that it is not impossible.

In this connection the problem in East European churches has moved beyond judgment-penitence, and in some measure beyond reform and renewal. Their immediate problem has to do with ways and means of "prophesying" God's judgment over society.

In a general way, it might be said that the central problem of churches in the West is the same problem. The difference is that in the West there is no fundamental sense of present judgment, no deep sense of identity with and responsibility for what has happened in East Europe, no urgent conviction that reform is necessary, and renewal a gift of grace.

It is at this point that the Church Universal is a most difficult and imperative reality. It speaks to the West and the East. A civilization which, along with its good seed, sowed corruption, injustice, oppression and greed should scarcely have expected to reap no weeds. Neither that civilization nor its component institutions, in violating eternal principles, could escape judgment. But if, in the contemporary revolution, society has been judged, not the whole of society has recognized it. And until society recognizes its judgment, society would appear to have little chance of redirection and renewal.

---

5. Churchmen quick to repent for sins committed in association with ancient regimes have not necessarily applied the same measure of repentance to similar sins committed in league with present Communist regimes. (Karl Barth, in his famous letter to Bishop Bereczky of Sept. 16, 1951, poses the central question, and perhaps assumes more than anyone should: "Must Reformed Hungary always be 100% in agreement with whatever regime happens to be in power?") Such action would not have been easy under any circumstances. In Hungary it was said that the church "has no right to accuse the present time or judgment on it . . . It is our duty to intervene, give a helping hand and to serve . . . The Party . . . is working in strict self-criticism and discipline, it uproots all recognized mistakes, and gives us an example and a warning how to do this in our own ranks" (Makkai, *Hungarian Church News*, Feb. 15, 1950).

Further, apart from the presence and ministry of judged and renewed churches, the "judging" (travail) of society holds little meaning. It is merely revolution, not judgment. It is death without resurrection. And apart from the judgment and renewal of the whole Christian community, those Christian communities which have been refined as by fire can neither reveal any fullness of Divine judgment in revolution nor give an adequate prophetic lead to the society in the throes of revolution. Here renewal, or perhaps better "renewing" communities are both dependent upon and inhibited by the Christian communities which live still in an atmosphere of pre-judgment. The burden of the universality of judgment therefore lies heavily both on churches which have not yet acknowledged judgment[6] nor been renewed, and on those which have in some measure experienced judgment and must communicate the reality of that experience to the whole Church.

The question arises, however, is judgment a requisite of renewal and is suffering a requisite of judgment? Should churches of East Europe hope for persecution as a purifying process to engulf the whole of the Church? Should they pray for refining fires of such intensity as will burn from the whole visible church all dross and corruption, and of such duration as will consume every temptation to apostasy once the travail of revolution is done?

Christians in East Europe know the price of judgment, the millions of people who have lost faith, the hundreds of thousands killed, the institutions and *mores* shattered. And still the Church in East Europe is not wholly pure, nor are all people wholly Christian. For every man who has found a deepened faith, several have been bestialized.

East Europeans know, too, that no amount of persecution-judgment has lasting effects. There is no guarantee that the judgment of this generation will have meaning for the next.[7]

---

6. The Oxford Conference Official Report, pp. 85-86, stated: "The churches must not regard an attack directed against themselves as an attack directed against God. They must acknowledge that God has spoken to their conscience through these movements by revealing through them the real situation of millions of their members." But this is not necessarily acknowledgment of judgment on the churches which demands their penitence.

7. It remains to be seen whether the *bekennende* spirit forged in fires of suffering will persist in more normalized times. In West Europe it has been noted that persecution-inspired church renewal has given way to static conventional religious life, that some of the gaunt prophets and judges persecuted by the Nazis today sink contentedly into the plush comforts of institutional churchism. Churchmen in East Germany have noted that "clergy who have taken refuge in Western Germany have managed to establish themselves under better conditions than others of their brethren. They are now tempted to keep their distance from their companions in misfortune who are yet not benefiting by such alleviations, and whose special distress should be to them above all others a matter of burning concern. We can see from this how desperately bourgeois we have already become again. We can see how we are gradually starting once more to dally with that thought of the old Adam, 'Am I my

Indeed, it should be clear from the experience of East Europe that involuntary subjection to the violent purging of persecution or revolution is not only not a guarantee of judgment (suffering is not inevitably followed by redemption) but immediate involvement in physical revolution is not even a requisite for judgment, for refining and renewal. Revolution, suffering, complete social turmoil only provide an atmosphere in which judgment can take place. In itself it is not judgment.

Judgment, in the positive sense of repentance and resurrection, lies not in circumstance, violent as it may be, but in the one judged, and his relationship to his Judge. Judgment, theoretically, can take place under non-violent circumstances as well as violent. The basic question for the churches, whether they be involved directly in violent change or not, is whether they can recognize and appropriate the ever-present judgment which encompasses them. The fact of judgment is inevitable. Whether the be-calmed churches *can* appropriate its spiritual reality through identification with those who endure or have endured suffering vicariously, or must themselves experience physical purgation depends on the churches.

Here, surely, lies a more portentous judgment for churches of the West than of the East: lacking the external compulsions to reform, we have not the inner courage and the spirit so to do. The high price of spiritual re-generation we may recognize, intellectually, but are reluctant to pay until forced to. The possibilities of being re-generated while holding fast our bourgeois comforts and mien-securities are too tempting.[8] Who will renounce them until catastrophe strikes? And who, though acknowledging the inevitability of judgment, whether in a voluntary or a catastrophic context, will still appropriate it voluntarily? This is the tragedy of America, that lacking a sense of spiritual involvement in world

---

brother's keeper?' We can see how we are even getting back to being given over to good works, instead of ourselves taking over our fellow-man's suffering . . . !" The essential question is whether the reformation gains made in turbulent times will be lost in the flesh pots of an established church in more tranquil times, whether in the West today, or in a more comfortable Communistic climate of tomorrow in East Europe, or in some post-Communist bourgeois society.

8. The Hungarian Protestant churches, in answer to A Letter to Member Churches of the World Council of Churches from the Executive Committee (Bievres, Feb. 1, 1951), after noting the possibility that there might be those in the West who questioned the legitimacy of the Hungarian churches asked: "Why is it the Church feels herself at home in the capitalistic system? Does she really obey the will of the Lord in a world based upon this system? If she abhors a change, is it because it would endanger her life as a church or because it would radically change the environment in which she lives comfortably? The scrutinizing question, whether the Church lives and acts really as the Church, should be addressed with the same emphasis towards the Churches of the West as it is being directed in anxious doubts towards our Churches."

tragedy, she invites eventual cataclysm on America and finds herself with no faculty to apprehend its meaning and potential.

Theoretically at least, man-made catastrophe can be avoided; judgment, at least in some part, can be appropriated. (This is a significant part of the meaning of the Cross.) Churches can bare themselves to expurgation and regeneration by the hand of God. Will they? Or will they push off on Communism or some other form of revolution the task of forcing the churches to their reformation and redemption? Must even God's revelations in fact, if not in theory, wait on catastrophe to penetrate a callous Western consciousness?

Where churches have waited until revolution forced them to act—on issues such as education and land reform—they lost for a time the initiative of moral authority. And those who should have been posing the questions and affirmations of God and judgment on society were actually having judgment pronounced on them by society.[9] There is no reason except human weakness why Western churches should wait for that eventuality. But that may be a near-insuperable reason.

To enter voluntarily and penitently into judgment through identification with those who suffer vicariously our common judgment—to the point of sharing the burdens of their suffering— therein lies the promise of sharing also a common hope, renewal and re-creation as the Body of Christ.

Signs of Grace and Renewal

If renewal is not *achieved*, it has been nevertheless *received*. Where there has been renewal of churches in East Europe, three things have been evident: one, the rediscovery of the fundament of the Church as God's Presence; two, the manifestation of the Church as *koinonia;* and three, the method of the Church as *kerygma.* While these basic characteristics may allow for a variety of forms and practices in different situations, it is clear that church structure and life is largely determined by attitudes at these three points.

God's Presence. East European Christians at "rock bottom" have known afresh God's presence. When the normal structure of society, together with established patterns of thinking, ethical norms, customs and property ownership were swept away, any sense of security in things external to one's own person, including

---

9. Their discerning of judgment was further complicated in that God's judgment was mixed with human savagery. Liberation of the spirit, but also despair often accompanied loss of simple comforts. With new spiritual freedom came new and inescapable responsibilities, but often with limited possibilities to make determinative decisions. These are some of the complexities which Western churches do not face in the same way in relation to judgment.

friends and family, was shattered. And even within one's own being there could be no confidence in the future. In that crisis situation many found themselves in the presence of God, the Lord of
history, a real Person—not an abstract idea, nor an ethnic, nor a
body of truths. It was this re-discovery, rather God's self-disclosure to those suddenly wrenched out of pre-occupation with trivial
things, and the realization that He had always been near which
has kindled a new spirit within the Christian community and led
to its renewal.

Others in East Europe who have not concluded that aspects of
the present situation point towards God's presence, have nonetheless had to consider whether God *is* present and how His Person is
manifested. Orthodox churches have emphasized His direct presence nineteen hundred years ago, and thereafter His presence
through the continuity of His Church, acting under the Holy
Spirit. Hungarian Reformed Christians have emphasized His
eternal "contemporariness" freshly and personally revealed to individuals under judgment. Others have emphasized His self-disclosure through the contemporary revolution within the sweep of
a meaningful history. But whether in one manner or another,
Christians universally maintain that God reveals Himself.

This diversity, however, points up the historic ecumenical
problem, and may suggest a likely place for its resolution. It has
to do with the relationship between revelation and authority, but
also judgment, and the Christian's responsibility for the fulfillment of revelation in a dynamic revelation-judging process. The
problem begins with supposed revelation. An individual or a group
has a vivid knowledge of God in some particular place or way, and
concludes that this represents the whole of God, or the most suitable way for God to reveal Himself. The problem is not in the
knowledge mediated, but in the fact that the recipient group does
not recognize the possible partialness of it, nor the probability that
God reveals Himself to other personalities in other circumstances
in other ways. Consequently, one group fixes its norm or authority
or *raison d'etre* on the Scriptures, another on tradition, another on
a particular "order" of mediation, another on a simplified (called
"apostolic") structure, another on a defined doctrine, another on
some future hope, another on a personal experience, and so on.

East European experience has posed the question, is any one
of these to be taken *ipso facto* as entirely of God, and, if so, does
that exclude all others. The deeper problem is evident: how is
man to determine whether any specific "revelation" is of God, or
whether it springs from an overworked imagination combined
with much wishful thinking. The experience of Hungarian Reformed Christians in relation to individual and personal confrontation of God indicates that the supposed revealing of God in one

particular way does not supercede or annul the Christian's responsibility to examine and confirm that "revelation" by other known or supposed media of God's revelation. Indeed, an experience which *may*, but also *may not* involve God's self-disclosure requires all the more careful and bold scrutiny. For if one starts off at a tangent here, and, as has often happened, absolutizes his "revelation," he departs very quickly from the potential corrective of fellow Christians with variant "revelations," and, indeed, from openness to further enlightenment from the supposed Originator of his supposed revelation.

What are likely norms or places for the cross-examination and illumination of any supposed revelation? Presumably, these ought to be no less than the total complex of media through each of which God may reveal aspects of Himself: His Presence in prayer and the Spirit, the Scriptures, the whole Christian community through all time, the course of history.

Any "revelation" from any one of these media should be submitted to the others for testing and confirming. This presupposes that an actual revelation from God is not intended to be put "under a basket," but is to be affirmed to the whole household for its enlightenment. Whoever has a potential revelation therefore cannot have fulfilled his responsibility even to that "revelation" until he has submitted it for testing by, and witness to other "revelations."

Some "revelations" so tested will be considered valid, some partially valid and subsequently further illumined, perhaps some invalid. Such conclusions, however, can never be regarded in history as absolute. History is not finished, nor is the Christian community, and neither can therefore give its final judgment. This should mean that if one is convinced that his oracle is of God, he should not necessarily regard it as invalid simply because the contemporary Christian community considers him deluded. The prophets were judged by the community of their day as fools. Later communities of God's people have vindicated their position, not that of the majority. Only provisional decisions can be found on such matters. They are sufficiently authoritative for those in God to proceed in confidence, but in openness to Him. Such is the dynamic of this unfinished revealing-judging process.

In the contemporary situation churches with differing traditions, Scriptural interpretations, dogmas, practices and orders, with variations of criteria for authority or media of revelation are increasingly submitting their "unique" emphases or positions or "revelations" to the scrutiny of one another, of the Scriptures, of tradition and history. This is the most likely place and way for judgment to begin. But the point of least scrutiny is probably the most crucial, namely, in personal confrontation with God. While supposed revealings *of* God may need careful examination by revelations *from* God, "revelations" *from* God can certainly have meaning and be fulfilled only when confirmed in the presence *of* God. Thus must formal dogmas, canons and practices be tested, in the corporate act of worship of the whole Church. It is at this point that Eastern Orthodoxy speaks to the whole ecumenical conversation, at least in theory: that councils of the whole community of believers through all time and illumined by the Scriptures and history have validity only if the community is *under the Holy Spirit.* Their testimony is more than confirmed by others in East Europe who have re-discovered that God's personal presence is the beginning of the Church's life and its constant point of focus.

Churches which accept a common judgment, enter jointly into their crises, and there, in the presence of the Spirit, confront one another with their peculiar revelations may find the structure of the Church to be less of a plan to be designed than a given fact in their present inter-relationship. They may also find, however, that some major revolution is entailed in applying and perhaps redeeming static institutional life at the dimension of dynamic relationships.

The Church as koinonia. The revolution in East Europe forced upon Christians these questions: "What are you? Why do you exist?" Those who did not answer with open resistance formed an answer they could themselves hardly have expected. Gathered together in His Name, and He in their midst, they were impelled to share the good news of His abiding Presence with others near by. They were the Church. It existed in their being what they were and doing what they were doing, and not as a causal entity created *in order to* achieve quite another.

If the nature of the Christian community is identification or oneness in God's love, and the function of the Church is to manifest His love and His Will in the context of time, then its structure is no more than the means expedient to that nature and function. Its continuity in some form is as sure as His Will to redeem.

The place where the Church, the *koinonia,* is rooted then, is where people live or where they work, that is, where they manifest God's love. Where the Church has been under fire it has been blessed in its re-organization on that basis. It exists in relation to normal units of fellowship. According to a competent authority, one of the best things that ever happened to the Dutch Reformed Church was the Nazi decree which forbade meetings of more than fifteen or twenty persons in one place. Broken up into such small groups which met in the homes of believers the Dutch Church recovered its own soul as a church.

If in its nature the Church is oneness in God's love proclaiming that love, then the Church essentially may have little in common with buildings, lands, publications, clubs, roll books, stewardship canvasses and evangelistic campaigns. Certainly it should not be *identified* with these external things, useful as they may seem in modern religious life. The family of early Christians, like many Christian communities today, had no such paraphernalia. But the fact that they had no such "tools" did not hinder their functioning.[10] They could leave these worries to the scribes and pharisees, and get on with telling their neighbors in the synagogue and on the highways of God's Love. It was not of primary importance to wait the pleasure of world powers, seeking endowments, tax concessions, farm lands, parochial schools, publication facilities, or building rights as requisites to the preaching of the Gospel. The job they had to do could be done, and had to be done first in the informal encounter of a handful of like-minded people, met in prayer and mutual service in the home, at work, in the arena. This was where life and God's message were significant.

What significance has this for churches of the present era in the West? Surely it does not mean that they should dampen their great zeal or glibly renounce their enormous facilities for the Gospel. But zeal for what, and facilities for what? At a deeper level the question points up certain dangers related to the origin and content of that gospel.

Christians in the West readily acknowledge that the specific structure and techniques of Christian witness consume an enormous amount of time and energy of the Christian community. Indeed, there is a very real danger that they are displacing the essential nature of that community. This is the locus of the problem. It is not to imply that the tools of Christian witness are in themselves evil. They are evil if they replace Christ, if the structure of the Church becomes an end in itself—its nature and Divine function lost in a wilderness of committees, constitutions, campaigns, buildings and high finances,[11] if the "church" becomes big business.

---

10. This very fact, incidentally, makes Christian living somewhat less hazardous, in that there is less temptation to confuse the "things" of the fellowship with the spirit and purpose of the fellowship.

11. "The introversion of the churches, in which we have been put to shame, came to pass because the so-called "inner concerns" of the Church have monopolized our attention. We were churches caring primarily for ourselves. Our zealous enterprises, which we were wont to call evangelism, were in fact such attempts at soul-saving, that is, essentially, church-saving and congregation-building exertions. And so these efforts yielded mostly fruits of self-seeking men, escaping into closed groups and devoid of missionary responsibility. Now God is cleansing us by making us realize that God's main concern is not the "church," but man; that He did not send His Son into the "church," but into the World. The outcome of the Messianic service of Jesus Christ, and of His Kingdom is not a church that is an end in herself, but the new heaven and the new earth, for this is the end of His ways, even when working through the Church." (Statement of the Hungarian Ecumenical Study Commission, *op. cit.*, Aug. 15, 1953, p. 178.)

The problem becomes acutely evident in the relationship between membership and evangelism. Where "membership" in the church is equated with participation in the liturgical, cultural and other actviities of a socio-religious group, or where it is equated with the names listed in a "membership roll book," "evangelism" has come to mean "membership drives," very often with goals set for the numbers of persons to be added in a given time; and the theology of evangelism has been replaced by the psychology and salesmanship techniques of the civic club. "Churches" with such a veiwpoint vie with one another to "get" more members, and their "evangelism" tends to draw sharper lines of separation between communities of Christians, even at times of the same confession.

The background and present situation of churches in East Europe speaks helpfully to the West at this point. There, where identity with the community of Christians has no social or economic advantage—indeed, the contrary—"putting on Christ" and putting on His cares for the world is not a matter to be taken lightly. People are not encouraged to identify themselves as part of His Body until they are spiritually ready. The fundamental spiritual facts involved here are, and ought to be seen as, just as true in a society which pampers Christians as in one which persecutes them. And it is now clear in both places that numbers alone have little meaning.

At a deeper level, however, Christians do not add members to the Church. If the Church is the redeeming activity of God, Christians engaged with Him in that activity *are* part of Christ's Body, of the Church. In their proclaiming Him, He may add others to them as they come to know Him. Those added to their number any other way are added to something other than the Church.

If the Church exists only as the activity-being of persons in God, then the place of its existence is where those persons are and where they act with Him, that is, where Christ is proclaimed and where those hearing are led by the Spirit to know God. This may be in a factory, or in a sanctuary or in a home. East European experience suggests that a fundamental locus of the Church is the home. Here is where, if there is to be reality at all in the God-penetrated community, sacrifices must be made, prayers held in intimate fellowship, the Bible studied and God's love received. Christians in the East who have re-learned this the hard way may well ask Western churches whether their intensively "church-centered" programs are disrupting or strengthening and encouraging this fundamental unit of the Church.

With regard to religious education, the Church in East Europe became vulnerable. Generations ago, when the churches took responsibility for providing organized programs of religious instruction in the schools, most parents forthwith foresook their responsibility. The Church in the West is no less vulnerable, unless religious education can become a major concern of the home. And the primary purpose of Sunday Schools should be to supplement, to train and to encourage parents to provide adequate religious training in the home (as some are now doing) rather than to usurp their responsibility.

One further word must be said concerning the *koinonia*. The Church is not simply an agglomeration of individuals unilaterally attached to God. It may well result from their identity in God, but they are nontheless members, one of another. The *koinonia*, with its solidarity, sharing, and sense of common destiny, as evidenced, for example, among small groups in East Europe, is therefore the most natural and inevitable consequence of man's personal relationship to God. One must therefore ask whether existing congregations, some numbering into thousands of members, actually provide for this kind of relationship, or, rather, whether they are a manifestation of it. If the congregation should be so intimate that the spiritual elders may really be shepherds of the flock and every member part of a team of witnesses, what of such enormous congregations? In every congregation is there the kind of trust and love which sees that one in need is helped, one in sorrow comforted? Some careful re-study of the nature and formation of the Church in relation to present institutional realities would appear to be imperative.

Church Method as Kerygma. The Church exists because believers exist, and in their existence manifest God's love, not by intimidation, nor assault, nor coercion, but by proclaiming. But the goodness of what has happened to them is such that it *must* find its venting. It cannot wait for political censors to give permission for some specific form of proclaiming, nor can it wait for professionals to organize special "campaigns" or "revival meetings." God's love is so full that it cannot be contained. Christians manifest it, whether in offices, factories, farms or dungeons. It is here that Christians in East Europe are a judgment but also a real encouragement to the West: the Good News can be, and *is* articulated in some way at all times and in all places. This is evangelism. It is not a device to increase church membership. It is an urgent necessity for that Church which has no end in itself. That Church stands of God in the world, and its task and its joy is to tell the world of God. That is evangelism.

The West may well ask: what, then, of the tools of proclaiming? the church properties, radio stations, publications, financial resources, and so forth? One reason churches in East Europe were so vulnerable was that they had come to depend on governments and on properties to sustain the work of the churches. This not only affected *how* the churches' message was proclaimed, but *what* was proclaimed. Churches in the West are in no better position, politically or spiritually, in so far as they come to regard as their effective source of power, and to depend upon investments, endowments, securities, special privileges, lands, and identification with social custom and national purpose—which distinguish them only a degree from *Volkskirchen.*

The business of the Church is not business. And in the transition from one civilization to another no church can lay up treasures which it can carry through that transition. It will either rust and corrupt with the treasures, or it may leave them behind and enter new life. It cannot do both. A heavy price has been paid in East Europe for the whole Church to learn that. At this point a searching review of the Western churches' relations to their respective states and societies is in order.

If the Church's securities lie only in her relationship to God, and in her ensuring that all things over which God has given her stewardship are dedicated to Him, that stewardship means that such goods are not to be used by the Church for its own glory. However, this does not allow for irresponsibility with regard to the material world. Christians will have, and will hold property as stewards. And the whole household of faith has a common responsibility to succor the Christian proprietor in his stewardship. The inter-dependence of Christians in the East and in the West is a problem, but also a help at this point. If in the West the magnitude of the Christian enterprise is a temptation to pre-occupation with resources and self-perpetuation, among many Christians in East Europe simplicity has become a necessity and the Christian witness has benefited thereby. Is that desirable in the West? Here is a spirit which "constrains us." If the churches of means do identify themselves with those in distress, the result will be simplicity in both places, but a profound solidarity of witness.

Christians together in crisis may also replace in their proper sequence the motivation and the implementation of social "reform." The impulse for social reform stems not from fear of Communism or any other power. Nor is it a matter of condescension or sentimentalism. It comes alone from an affirmation of God. "Charity" is an expression of spiritual concern and solidarity which God Himself has first manifested and not an instrument of religious, political or any other persuasion. Emphasis therefore must lie, not on transactions of foods, clothing and money, but on the relationship between two or more human beings, at least one of whom knows the Presence of God. And their relationship is characterized by identity, love of neighbor, comfort, encouragement, mutual counsel. Social action is not therefore a "forced" activity. It is the normal result of Christian community.

In its social message the Church proclaims clearly that while it is in the world it is not of it and its message is not determined by any fears concerning this world. This message is not simply one of advice, but of revelation from that other world which lies beyond time and is not adversely affected by contemporary catastrophe. Its message is hope and its delivery bold.

One further point; what is the ministry in relation to the *koinonia* and the *kerygma?* Does it consist of professional priests, pharisees, writers, shepherds who are to shape the community and do the witnessing? Christians in East Europe, particularly Protestants, have intimated that God's love knows no distinction among professions. And any distinction between layman and pastor is not one of quality in relation to His love—nor of quantity, nor is it in relation to the pastoral responsibility of one for another. All are responsible; all are in His love. The basis for any distinction among the "many members" or diverse professions among Christians is solely one of functional gifts. But every person in the Christian fellowship must be evangelist, pastor and layman. All should be fervent in proclaiming, responsible one for another and diligent in labor.

Finally, it is not the paraphernalia or functions of the Christian community—the buildings, the activities, the services, the leaders, nor even the forms, whether associations or movements, or state churches, or foundations, or democratic churches—which make the community God's community in either East or West. It is rather God Himself and whether the people have received Him and become His people. If they are of Him, they proclaim Him with whatever tools are available to them. How many tools, and what color or size or form is not of primary importance.

Indeed, whether the Church will even go on in its present form, it is irrelevant to ask. Whether Christians are *in Him* engaged in His activity is the question before us. The redemptive activity of God is sure.

A French Communist paper[12] recently carried the following statement:

"The Gospel is a much more powerful weapon for the renewal of society than is our Marxist philosophy. All the same it is we who will finally beat you. We are only a handful and you Christians are numbered by the millions. But if you remember the story of Gideon and his 300 companions you will understand why I am right. We Communists do not play with words. We are realists, and seeing that we are determined to achieve our object, we know how to obtain the means. Of our salaries and wages we keep only what is strictly necessary and we give up the rest for propaganda purposes. To this propaganda we also consecrate 'all our free time and part of our holidays.' You, however, give only a little time and hardly any money for the spreading of the Gospel of Christ. How can anyone believe in the supreme power of the Gospel if you do not practise it? If you do not spread it? And if you sacrifice neither time nor money for it? Believe me, it is we who will win, for we believe in the Communist message and we are ready to sacrifice everything, even our life, in order that social justice may triumph. But you people are afraid to soil your hands."

This may be a romanticized version of Communism, but one could hardly state more pointedly that the real struggle of Christians is not simply with Communists, but also with ourselves.

It is no less clear from what has happened in East Europe that that struggle is not hopeless. Men can be renewed with a vitality of faith and action and prophecy exceeding human expectations—when in their encounter with one another they encounter also their Lord.

---

12. "The Gospel of Christ and The Communist Manifesto," *Pax et Liberte*, as quoted by the *National Christian Council Review*, p. 290, Aug. 1955, Nagpur, India.

COMMUNIST—CHRISTIAN ENCOUNTER

in

EAST EUROPE

PART II

Chronicle of Events

UNION OF SOVIET SOCIALIST REPUBLICS

Introduction

Rus   For centuries the flat plains and rivers of the land now called Russia provided a principal travel route between the North Sea and the Black Sea and beyond. Scattered tribes along this route were often at the mercy of the more powerful and technically advanced foreign traders passing through.

988   Prince Vladimir of Kiev, convinced that the people of Rus could not remain free unless united, and could not be united except by a common religion and culture, persuaded the people of Kiev and the surrounding tribes to be baptized in the Christian (Byzantine) faith. Missionaries were sent out from Constantinople to assist in establishing a church.

1223   The Metropolitans of "all Russia" resided at Kiev until the Tartar invasion, when provincial princes and churchmen retreated northward to Novgorod and Suzdal. During the Tartar occupation, religious tolerance was granted. The Orthodox Church became a symbol of national unity, and the only institution embracing the majority of Russians. Church leaders became less preoccupied with ecclesiasticism and identified themselves with the people.

Ukraine

As the Tartars withdrew from the Moscow area and Ivan III of Moscow consolidated the forces of neighboring tribes and provinces, the King of Poland sent military forces to help the Cossacks drive the Tartars out of Kiev. Concurrent with Polish military assistance Roman Catholicism was introduced.

For three centuries the Cossacks and the Slav natives of Kiev (Rus) resisted the land-grabbing of the Polish nobility and the Romanizing of their church. The Polish King, whom they recognized also as their king, joined with them in resisting the landed Polish nobility, but permitted the forced conversion of Orthodox believers to
1595   Roman Catholicism (Uniate). Pleas for religious freedom were made
1607   from time to time by the Orthodox believers, but without success. However, in 1633 Peter Mogila was consecrated Orthodox Metropoli-
1633   tan of Kiev by the Patriarchs of Jerusalem and Constantinople, and the Orthodox faith again became dominant in the Western Ukraine.

1649-   In the middle of the 17th Century, the Ukrainians sought the help
1686   of the Tsar of Moscow to liberate them from the Poles. When this was accomplished, their church became part of the Russian Orthodox
1920   Church and remained so, except in Poland, until the Polish occupation of the Ukraine following the First World War. Under Polish occupation many Ukrainian churches again came under Roman Catholic jurisdiction. Following the Treaty of Riga (1921) an autonomous national Ukrainian church was established for Ukrainians within the U.S.S.R.,

recognized by the "Living Church," but not by Patriarch Tikhon of the historic Russian Orthodox Church.

Russia

1453
In 1453, with the defeat of the Byzantine Empire by the Turks, the "Mother-Church" of Constantinople could no longer extend guidance and succor to Russian Orthodoxy. Russia began to think of itself as carrying on the cultural and spiritual mission of Byzantium: "Moscow—the third and final Rome."

By the early part of the 16th Century two conflicting schools of thought had developed around the meaning and the mission of the Russian church. The "Possessors" or "Josephites," led by Abbot Joseph of the wealthy monastry of Volotzk, held that the church must have power and wealth if it was to attract the intelligentia, that secular as well as ecclesiastical authority was of God and should be obeyed. that the Tsar should be heard and obeyed as a father by his children, and that the Sovereign should take a leading role in church government.

The "Non-Possessors" or "Trans-Volga-Elders," led by Nil of Sorsk, maintained that the church's business was essentially spiritual, that it should give up its material possessions in order to achieve spiritual strength and independence, that the church should stand aloof from and should not hesitate to criticize the state, that "heretics" should not be persecuted for "disobedience." The State tried to contain both
1522
factions. It desired the lands which the "Non-Possessors" would give up, and the obedience which the "Possessors" would give. However, when Tsar Basil III desired to remarry and Metropolitan Varlaam, a "Non-Possessor," refused on spiritual grounds to sanction the marriage, the "Non-Possessors" were suppressed, a "Possessor" was installed as Metropolitan, and church and state fell into the hands of a single power-conscious autocratic party. Thus was linked together a power-conscious, materially ambitious, obedient church, and a self-deified, powerful, and cunning state.

Ivan the Terrible was the child of that union; ruthless slaughter and persecution, forced reform and assassination of religious dissidents followed.

1589
Patriarchate Established—In 1589 the office of the Orthodox Metropolitan was elevated to that of Patriarch by the combined efforts of the Tsar, Russian church leaders and the Patriarch of Constantinople, all of whom were ambitious for the Russian church to be the religious embodiment of the "New Rome."

1598-
1613
State-Church—In the 17th Century, after the Polish occupiers were expelled from Russia, Michael, son of Patriarch Philaret, was chosen Tsar. The Patriarch, a Conservative, actually directed affairs of state. In the provinces, a basic spiritual revival was developing.

1653
When Alexis, son of Michael, was Tsar, he succeeded in having Nikhom elected Patriarch. Orthodox Christians of other lands turned for help to the Tsar and the Patriarchate of Moscow as the successors of their Byzantine counterparts. Tsar Alexis instituted a number of reforms, particularly liturgical, in hopes that Russian Orthodoxy would be generally regarded as pure Orthodoxy and would result in

uniformity among various Orthodox peoples abroad. He was opposed by a minority who maintained that the Russian church was already superior and required no reforms. Patriarch Nikhom supported Alexis until he was deposed by a church council which had become enraged by his political ambitions and by the persecution of dissenters by Alexis. One result was an open split in the church between the "Old Ritualists" and the reformers. The State outlawed the "Old Ritualists," the patriarchal office became even more subject to the Tsar.

1722   *State Reforms of the Church*—Tsar Peter, influenced by his own Western sympathies and by Prokopovich, introduced various anti-clerical reforms. A Synod was established to replace the Patriarch, with a state-appointed "Procurator" at its head. In effect this was a "ministry of religion" controlled by the all-powerful Emperor, but resisted by the majority of church leaders. The official church for the next two centuries was controlled by the State.

1762-
1796   During the rule of Catherine II, the peasants organized a revolution for their own liberation from foreign (Germanized Dynasty of Peter) autocratic leadership. Most church estates were re-distributed and the church was provided with subsidies by the Government. 496 monasteries were closed.

1905   *Religious Revival and Political Revolt*—By the beginning of the 20th Century, as a result of the "Old-Ritualist"-Reformer schism, 200 years of state control of church administration, the rapid rise of sects, the loss of priests, and the secularization of the intelligentsia, the official church was in a very weak position. Spiritual life among the peasants, however, flourished. A spirit of rebellion was linked to a revival of religious interest. It was a priest who led the "Bloody Sunday" petitioners who were fired on by palace guards in January of 1905. The revolution was subdued, but religious equality and freedom of conscience were introduced—*for* religious beliefs as well as *from* religious beliefs. This did not, however, resolve basic conflicts as to the nature of the church, its relationship to the state, and the relationship of the whole to the people. The church Synod condemned the Revolution, and many leading churchmen participated in the Government and other secular organizations opposing long-awaited reforms.

"Russian prophets. . . . were sure that they were living on the eve of one of the fiercest religious conflicts ever known in human history. They described the choice which had to be made . . . as a choice between the tyrannic, self-deified, totalitarian (Tsarist) state and the challenging freedom of a Christian community."[1]

1914   Russia was thrown into the First World War and the March Peoples' Rebellion and the October Revolution with this background. The Russian people could hardly dissociate their idea of the West from past invasions of Swedes, Germans, French, Poles; from forced-conversions to Catholicism; from the tyranny of the St. Petersburg monarchy; from the forcing of religious reforms alien to their nature. Protestants in Russia were looked upon as Germanizers, hardly to be trusted in spite of their little strength. Roman Catholics represented would-be foreign conquerors; the Swedish and German Crusaders of

---

1. Zernov, *The Russians and Their Church*, p. 142.

the 13th Century and the Polish invaders of the 17th Century had been blessed by the Pope, and their mark left in the forced conversion of countless Orthodox believers to Catholicism. Orthodoxy, on the other hand, was regarded by the people as the people. They had been betrayed and they had been saved in time of crisis by the Orthodox Church—but it was their church. 100,000,000 of the total population of 142,000,000 were considered members.

1917 *People's Church*—In rural areas, where religious life was strong, the "church" was not identified indiscriminantly with the "clergy." To these people, the church was not a matter of the State nor of the upper classes. The church was the liturgy and the community of the faithful. Services were well attended, pilgrimages to holy places were frequent. Christian literature was being developed. Parish activities were relatively limited. Charitable work was done by monasteries or special institutions.

Religious Education—Religious instruction in public schools was obligatory for Orthodox children. There were no Orthodox Sunday Schools and the Orthodox Church had no confirmation classes. Protestants, Roman Catholics and others had opportunity for their own religious education programs.

Theological Training—Owing to the poverty of the priests, most children of clergy took advantage of the free education offered in the Orthodox Church's theological seminaries. As a result, a self-perpetuating priestly class seemed to be developing. Many students sought a liberal education and, when that desire was suppressed, rebelled against the church and the Tsar or drowned their boredom in drunkenness.[2]

2. Anderson, *People, Church and State in Modern Russia*, p. 34.

Priests—Except for occasional grants from their superiors, priests supported themselves by assessing believers for performing religious rites, and by farming or other labor. Very often they lacked authority, were exploited by local petty officials of church and government, and were scorned by the intelligentia. Much of their time was taken up in performing the clerical functions of state officials: recording marriages, births, deaths and other vital statistics.

Hierarchy—Candidates for high church offices were generally selected from monastic orders, a fact resented by the lower clergy. Though few bishops were wealthy, and government "privileges" were available to a few only, the paternalistic, autocratic manner in which bishops ruled over their clergy and flocks further widened the rift between hierarchy and clergy.

Monasteries—By 1917 most monasteries had lost their wealth, and existed principally by the labors of the monks. Still there were 2,000,000 acres of monastery lands, 1,000 church farms, 2,000 (non-religious) church buildings.

Church Government—The Orthodox church was administered by the Holy Synod, consisting largely of government-selected bishops, and directed by the government-appointed Procurator. No aspect of church life was free from state control.

	Population		
	1917	1941-45	1950
Total Population	142,000,000		190,000,000
Total Christians	130,000,000	80,000,000	130,000,000
Orthodox Believers			
(Patriarchal)	100,000,000	60,000,000	110,000,000*
Churches and Chapels	71,457	9,225	20,000
Priests	50,960	5,665	7,000*
Monasteries	1,026	38 (1941)	90
Seminaries	58	0 (1941)	10
Theological academies	4	0 (1941)	3
Hospitals and Institutions	1,450	0	0
Other Orthodox (Non-Conformist)			
Believers	25,000,000	10,000,000*	7,000,000
Roman and Uniate Catholic			
(Russia and Ukraine)			
Believers	Less than 6,000,000	6,000,000*	Less than 1,000,000*
Baptist, Evangelical-			
Christian, Pentecostal			
Believers	Less than 1,000,000*	4,000,000	4-5,000,000
Churches	500	2,000	3,000

League of Militant Atheists
(Organized 1925)

	1926	1928	1932	1937	1941	1945	1950
Members	465,438	123,000	5,500,000	2,000,000	3,450,000	Dissolved	0

* Writer's estimate, based on figures of S. Bolshakoff, *Russian Non-Conformity*, and others.

Other figures from *Bezboznik*, Jan., 1935; *Soviet War News*, as quoted by Paul Anderson, *People, Church and State in Modern Russia* (p. 120); MacEoin, *The Communist War on Religion*, and other sources.

Chronicle of Events

January, 1917—

Orthodox Metropolitan Makarii of Moscow appealed to the people to "Fear God and honor the Tsar. Honor the Tsar as the Anointed of God. . . . Let us unite around our mighty Orthodox Tsar! Let us stand in defense of the divinely established authorities appointed by the Tsar!" (*Moskovskiia Tserkovnyia Vedomosti*, No. 3-4, 1917, as quoted by Curtiss, *The Russian Church and The Soviet State*, p. 10.)

Metropolitan Vladimir of Kiev stated to the press: "We are Orthodox Christians, members of a monarchial state, to the bottom of our souls loving our Tsars. . . . The waves of party strife must not undermine love and respect for the ruling house." (*Golos Tserkvi*, No. 4-5, 1917, as quoted by Curtiss, *op. cit.*, p. 10.) Clergymen in the diocese of Kiev urged the dissolution of the Duma as a requisite for overcoming the threat of revolution.

February 25, 1917

The official journal of the Orthodox Church published an address by a bishop "condemning the dangerous tendencies then manifest and calling on all to 'hasten . . . to the aid of the local representatives of the Autocrat . . . Now . . . let the cathedral bell call all Russians together under the one great and holy banner . . . For Father Tsar and fatherland!'" (*Tserkovnyia Vedomosti*, Feb. 25, 1917, Gregorian Calendar, as quoted by Curtiss, *ibid.*, p. 10).

February 25-27, 1917—

Popular revolt and overthrow of the Royal government.

February 27, 1917—

The Orthodox Holy Synod rejected a proposal by the Over-Procurator to condemn the revolutionary movement (*Ibid.*, p. 11). Bishops and clergy were generally cautious and non-commital, although some continued to include the name of the Tsar in the liturgy. Priests in several cities refused to read the Tsar's message of abdication.

March 3, 1917—

A provisional government was formed pending the holding of a constitutional assembly.

March 4, 1917—

The Over-Procurator of the Holy Synod was replaced by Prince Vladimir L'vov, opponent of Rasputin. At the suggestion of the new Over-Procurator, the Holy Synod appealed to the people to "put aside all quarrels and dissensions, unite in fraternal love for the good of Russia, trust the Provisional Government . . ." The revolution was referred to as "the will of God," and prayers for "the divinely protected Russian Power and its true-believing (Orthodox) Provisional Government" replaced prayers for the Tsar in the liturgy (Curtiss, *The Russian Church and The Soviet State*, p. 12).

March 7, 1917—

The Petrograd League of Democratic Clergy and Laymen, lead by Deans Popov, Egorov and Vvedenskii, took a strong stand against the monarchy, capitalism and the rule of the church by the hierarchy. The League supported the republican form of government, land reforms, profit sharing by workers, and democratic reforms in church government. Some leaders of the League had been active in the 1902-1905 reform movement. Speaking of Marxism, Vvedenskii stated: "We have a similar principle—equal distribution of worldly goods—but a different method: moral action." Other groups of liberal clergy expressed similar convictions and aspirations. Several bishops were ousted by the lower clergy (*Ibid.*, pp. 13, 14, 16).

March 11, 1917—

Rech, journal of the moderate "Kadet" party, expressed the hope that the clergy would not follow reactionary leaders (*Ibid.*, p. 12).

After conflicts with Rasputin-supported bishops on issues such as divorce, responsibility for church publications, and general church reform, L'vov replaced conservative bishops in the Holy Synod with more liberal-minded bishops.

April 12 1917—

Rech expressed regret that so few clergy had taken a liberal attitude towards the Provisional Government. Other reports indicated that many clergy were opposing the Government, and stirring up reaction among the people. Many clergy turned against the reform movement and the Provisional Government for fear of losing parochial schools and their special church concessions, or for fear of ecclesiastical reforms affecting lower clergy as well as high. Popular feeling towards the conservative trend among the clergy was apathetic, or even hostile. As demands of the people grew more radical, influence of the Church diminished (*Ibid.*, pp. 12, 21).

April 28, 1917—

The Holy Synod proclaimed that "with the change of regime, the Established Church could not preserve the old order, which had outlived its time" (Anderson, *People, Church and State in Modern Russia*, p. 39).

May 8, 1917—

At the request of Over-Procurator L'vov the Orthodox Synod issued a call for a Pre-Sobor Council to consider church issues (*Tserkovnyia Vedomosti*, May 20, 1917, as quoted by Curtiss, *The Russian Church and the Soviet State*, p. 26).

May 9, 1917—

At the request of the Russian Commander-in-Chief, Orthodox Deans Vvedenskii, Egorov and Boiarskii of the League of Progressive Democratic Clergy toured the Russian front lines (against Germany) to raise morale and warn against the Bolsheviks (Curtiss, *The Russian Church and The Soviet State*, p. 18).

June, 1917—

An all-Russian Conference of Clergy and Laymen was called to discuss church reform. 1200 delegates attended. The Conference called for wide-sweeping social and land reforms, and a popular democratic form of church government. On the assumption that the government to be established would be friendly towards the Orthodox Church, the Conference approved resolutions calling for complete church independence in ecclesiastical affairs, recognition of the Orthodox Church by the government, preference given to the Orthodox Church over other faiths in state functions, state support of the Orthodox Church (Appendix I; Anderson, *People, Church and State in Modern Russia*, pp. 39-41).

June 12, 1917—

In its final session, the Conference opposed the projected separation of Church and State as an act of "persecution," condemned the seizure of church and private lands, and urged factory laborers to work harder in order to save the country (Curtiss, *The Russian Church and The Soviet State*, p. 21).

June 20, 1917—

Parochial schools were taken over by the Ministry of Education. Religious education was to continue on a compulsory basis. The Orthodox Church had some 37,000 schools. Russian teachers, including many parochial school teachers, had urged the nationalization of the school system. The Orthodox Conference of Clergy and Laymen protested the ministry's action and appealed to the Government to rescind the order (*Ibid.*, p. 19; on p. 31 the date given by Curtiss is July 20).

June/July, 1917—

A conservative priests' "League of Church Unification" appeared and opposed measures of educational and land reform, urging that liberal and leftist clergy be excommunicated (*Ibid.*, p. 22).

July 13, 1917—

A commission preparing for the Orthodox Sobor to be held later in the year adopted resolutions calling for autonomy of the church in internal affairs, church courts, records, laws, holy days, for recognition of special status by the Government, for the continuing of parochial schools, and for religious education to be obligatory for Orthodox children in all schools (*Ibid.*, p. 14).

July 14, 1917—

The Provisional Government enacted a law providing for freedom of religious profession, freedom to change religions and freedom to profess no religion (*Ibid.*, p. 14).

July 26 (?), 1917—

With the establishment of a new government, L'vov was replaced as Over-Procurator by Kartashev (*Ibid.*, p. 13).

August 5, 1917—

The office of the Over-Procurator (Kartashev) was changed to "Minister of Confessions" (*Ibid.*, p. 13). Kartashev advised the Holy Synod that he regarded the Synod as an autonomous body.

August 11, 1917—

"The Provisional government (has) adopted the following resolution . . .
(1) to authorize the National Sobor of the All-Russian Church, convening on August 15, in Moscow to elaborate and present for the approval of the Provisional Government, legislation covering the new order of free self-administration of the Russian Church;
(2) to retain, pending the acceptance by the Government of the new order of supreme church administration, all matters concerning the internal administration of the Church, under the direction of the Holy Governing Synod and the organs related thereto" (Declaration presented to the Sobor by Kartashev for the Ministry of Religion. Anderson, *People, Church and State in Modern Russia*, p. 39).

August 12, 1917—

The Orthodox Pre-Sobor Council, after listing a series of problems to be considered by the Sobor, added: "only the voice of the Mother Church could bring people to their senses. . . . The work of bringing the Russian land to society, so necessary at present, is possible only on a religious basis . . . (A. I. Vvedenskii, Tserkov'i Gosudarstvo, pp. 66-72; Curtiss, *op. cit.*, p. 26).

August 15, 1917—
(Curtiss gives date as August 16)

A Great Council (Sobor) of the Russian Orthodox Church (first since 1696) voted (141 to 112) to restore the Patriarchate with a Synod of bishops as the supreme administrative body. Many delegates considered the revival of the Patriarchate as a new tyranny. When, during the discussion, a lay member charged that the Sobor was concerned only with ecclesiastical matters, Bishop Arseny replied that the Church was equally interested in retaining the rights of the private land-owners—"the landlords and the Church stand together" (Anderson, *op. cit.*, p. 43).

During the summer peasants and soldiers on leave from the front had been frantically grabbing up bits of former estates, and increasing numbers of churchmen considered that the revolution had gone too far. Strong appeals were made at the Sobor for the unity of Russian peoples and the cessation of internal strife in the face of their common enemy. On August 24 the Sobor issued a message to the "All-Russian Christ-loving troops and fleets," appealing for loyalty and return to patriotic service. "German spies and hirelings and our betrayers and traitors from the rear have poisoned the mind of the Army . . ." (*Tserkovnia Vedomosti*, Sept. 20, 1917; Curtiss, *op. cit.*, p. 29). Liberal or reform-minded churchmen were denounced as Bolsheviks, at least 17 of whom quit the Sobor, thus leaving it more firmly in the hands of the conservatives.

October, 1917—

A delegation was sent by the Orthodox Church to discuss with the Kerenskii Provisional Government the reintroduction of compulsory religious education in public schools and the return of parochial schools to the Church. They reported an unsympathetic reception: "The Russian State is breaking the ties with the Church of Christ" (Curtiss, *The Russian Church and The Soviet State*, p. 32).

October 20, 1917—

Church demonstrations and special speeches organized by the Orthodox Church, including a procession of the Sobor, were interpreted as directed against the radicalism of the Bolsheviks.

November 5, 1917 (Nov. 19?)*

Metropolitan Tikhon was elected Patriarch of the Russian Orthodox Church. His first act was to try to stop the slaughter between revolutionaries, monarchists and Bolsheviks in the Kremlin (Pares, *Russia, Its Past and Present*, p. 71).

---

* It has been difficult to be entirely accurate as to dates, owing to the two calendars used in Russia during this period and by subsequent writers.

November 7, 1917 (October 24, 1917—
Petrograd*) Communist Revolution.

After a meeting of the Social-demo-
cratic Soviet, the Bolsheviks seized
control of the Provisional Government. Landless peasants, under the
revolutionary slogan, "land, bread,
and peace," had already begun to
seize large estates and monastic lands,
or to prevent the monks from farming. The monks were disliked, not
only for their land holdings, but for
their spiritual tyranny over the people and village priests. Without land
and support the monasteries were immediately impotent (Anderson, *Peo-*
ple, Church and State in Modern Rus-
sia, p. 43).

November 17, 1917—

The Orthodox Sobor prepared recommendations for the forthcoming
Constituent Assembly: the Orthodox
Church was to be free from State control, was to have special prerogatives
and State support, its property should
be tax free, its schools retained, compulsory religious education re-introduced in public schools, and church
marriage and divorce recognized by
the State (Curtiss, *The Russian*
Church and the Soviet State, p. 42)

November 21, 1917—

The Orthodox Patriarch was installed in the Uspenskii Cathedral in the
Kremlin (*Ibid.*, p. 42).

December 4, 1917—

Banks, factories, and buildings were
nationalized. Schools soon followed.

December 18, 1917—

By Government decree, church marriages were no longer to be recognized as valid. "Birth itself shall be the
basis of the family. No differentia-
tion whatsoever shall be made between relationships by birth, whether
in or out of wedlock" (Pares, *Russia,*
Its Past and Present, p. 210).

January 19, 1918—

In a pastoral letter, the Patriarch
announced that people and churches
were being oppressed, persecuted, and
murdered, that the sacraments of bap-

tism and marriage had been declared
unnecessary, that church buildings
had been blown up or looted, monks
and nuns seized, schools and other
church property confiscated. He called on believing Christians to resist or
be excommunicated (Appendix II).

January 23, 1918—

The Soviet Government decreed the
separation of the Church from the
State and of education from the
Church. Religion might be taught
privately. Church property was declared national property. Local congregations could be accorded use of
places of worship by contractual
agreement between the Government
and twenty believers. No provision
was made for a nation-wide Church
administration. Civil records were to
be kept by the State. The religious
oath was abolished. Citizens should
have equal rights whether they professed any or no religion (*"Religion*
in Russia," No. X, 1950, p. 3; Appendix III).

Kolossow explained the separation
of State and Church as follows: "In
the first place the separation of
Church and State makes it impossible
for the Church to interfere in any
way in political matters of the State.
The Soviets maintain . . . that the
task of the Church lies merely in worship. Any kind of moralizing or educational activity beyond the scope of
a certain religious community is forbidden the Church. By the separation
of school and Church the State has
liquidated a condition which was
averse to the interests of the Soviet
nation, i.e., the fact that religious
dogmatics—which are incompatible
with the principles of a materialistic
ideology—were forced upon the students by religious instructions" (*The-*
ologische Literaturzeitung, 1950, No.
8, pp. 502-3).

A court interpretation of the regulation permitting private religious instruction stated that the maximum
number of children which could be
considered "private" would be three.
Subsequently, large numbers of religious education units comprising three
children were organized.

As religious literature became scarce,
lending libraries were established;
books and publications were copied by

---

* It has been difficult to be entirely accurate as to dates, owing to the two
calendars used in Russia during this period and by subsequent writers.

hand and circulated. Church choirs organized community singing fests, and priests organized athletic activities. All institutional and social welfare activities were banned. Some monasteries organized themselves for a time into "Labor Communes," but were later dissolved by governmental action.

February 28, 1918—

The Patriarch and Synod issued instructions to the Church, (a) advising local congregations to set up lay holding societies which would hold title to property and prevent its confiscation; (b) calling on believers to resist any changes in the system of education or vital statistics; and (c) excommunicating any believers who disobeyed the instructions (Appendix IV).

Subsequently, numerous processions and speeches were planned which appeared to be open challenges to the Communist Soviet authorities to engage the Church in battle.

March 15, 1918—

A delegation of 7 churchmen (4 from the Sobor) conferred with Government officials, and concluded that while the Government intended to go through with its political and economic reforms, the Government was benevolent towards religion, and conflict between Church and State was not inevitable (Curtiss, *The Russian Church and the Soviet State*, p. 58).

April 6, 1918—

The Orthodox Sobor decreed that all churchmen who disobeyed their superiors in turning to civil authorities hostile to the Church were in danger of unfrocking and excommunication (*Ibid.*, p. 59).

July 10, 1918—

A new constitution was adopted by the Government. Article 13 stated:
"To the end of assuring actual freedom of conscience in behalf of the toilers, the Church is separated from the State, and the school from the Church, but freedom of religion and anti-religious propaganda is conceded in behalf of all citizens" (Barron and Waddams, *Communism and the Churches*, p. 16).

Article 69* stated that:
"Ministers of religion of all beliefs and doctrines actually following their profession, and monks" are non-workers and servants of the bourgeoisie and are deprived of the right to vote and to be elected (*Ibid.*, p. 21).

In the debate over Article 13, moderate Socialists who believed that religion would crumble away with the loss of political and economic support proposed the formula "religion is a private affair of the citizens." Lenin, however, insisted on the adopted formulation (Timasheff, *Religion in Soviet Russia*, p. 22).

August 24, 1918—

The People's Commissariat of Justice issued instructions for the implementing of the laws of January 23 and of the Constitution with regard to the churches. Nationalization was expected to be completed in two months (Curtiss, *The Russian Church and the Soviet State*, p. 62).

August 30, 1918—

The Orthodox Sobor declared that Church property was holy, and its confiscation a "blasphemous seizure and an act of violence to be countered by every Christian." Those helping in the confiscation of church property were threatened with excommunication (*Ibid.*, p. 63).

October 13, 1918—

Following the dissolution of the Sobor in August many churchmen turned to the Orthodox Patriarch for protection. In a message to the Council of People's Commissars, he accused the Councilors of encouraging murder, plunder, arrests and other crimes, and called on them to celebrate the first year of their rule by releasing prisoners, stopping bloodshed and providing a just Government (*Ibid.*, p. 65).

December, 1918—

Msgr. Budkiewiecz of Petrograd, in an "Instruction to the Clergy," advised Roman Catholic clergy:
(a) To ignore the form of the Government's contract dealing with the use of church buildings. The signature of the parishioners who were to receive from the Government the use

---

* According to Timasheff, *Religion in Soviet Russia*, this was Article 65.

of the church and of articles of worship was contrary to canon law; the representatives of the parishioners were to point out that the Church cannot be deprived of her independence; and to demand that the Government of Russia be satisfied with the presentation of the Protocol, according to which the property of the Church passes to the care of the parishioners;

(b) If the "department of protection" does not consent to this, then to propose immediately to introduce into the text of the contract, corrections in conformity with the spirit of the Church;

(c) If the authorities will not consent to corrections, the parishioners may sign the contract, but they must declare that they have yielded to force in signing, with the explanation, however, in the spirit of the corrections indicated above, where the contract is considered as a legal fiction;

(d) Not to surrender Church property of their own accord, but to await the demand of the authorities. In the meantime, to make every effort to save such property from confiscation (in general to adopt the policy of delay);

Moreover the priests are to keep a copy of the registers of the parish outside the church and to send another to the Consistory. When the authorities demand the registers, the reply is to be made that they have been sent to the Consistory . . .

"The fundamental principle on which the Metropolitan based his decree that one might sign the so-called agreements and contracts regarding the churches and ecclesiastical property, with reserves, was that the present Government will be of short duration and that consequently the results of the signing will not have time to appear" (Anderson, *People, Church and State in Modern Russia*, pp. 57-58).

March 3, 1919—

A circular from the Commissariat of Education stated:

"Teaching religious doctrine to persons younger than 18 years is not permitted." However, special lessons and readings might be conducted for older persons to prepare them for the priesthood (Curtiss, *The Russian Church and the Soviet State*, p. 77).

March 18-23, 1919—

The eighth congress of the Communist Party declared:

"The aim of the Party is finally to destroy the ties between the exploiting classes and the organization of religious propaganda, at the same time helping the toiling masses actually to liberate their minds from religious superstitions and organizing on a wide scale scientific-educational and anti-religious propaganda.

"It is, however, necessary to avoid offending the religious sensibilities of believers which leads only to the strengthening of religious fanaticism" (*Notes on Soviet Affairs*, No. 138, June 23, 1952).

Spring, 1919—

Several rulings were issued by the Central Government to the effect that excessive acts of violence or hostility by government authorities towards religious leaders were discouraged.

September 12, 1919—

Roman Catholic Archbishop Cepliak, in a circular letter, declared that Church properties had been given exclusively to the Church, that only the Church could negotiate concerning their disposal, that the Church had protested against nationalization of Church property, and that no congregations or persons could enter into any contracts regarding Church property without permission of ecclesiastical authorities (Anderson, *People, Church and State in Modern Russia*, p. 58).

November 7, 1920—

Orthodox Patriarch Tikhon, in a circular letter, advised bishops, if they should lose contact with the central administration of the Church, to set up regional combines, to appoint bishops and ensure the continuing of the church (Curtiss, *op. cit.*, p. 94).

Outside Bolshevik-controlled Russia, Russian Orthodox churchmen took a leading role in the battle against the Bolsheviks.

May 1, 1921—

When Labor Day celebrations coincided with Easter, the government of Petrograd planned Labor demonstrations on May 1, approved Easter demonstrations on May 8. Few people participated in the former; nearly 200,000 in the latter (Timasheff, *Russia, Its Past and Present*, p. 60).

August, 1921—

Orthodox Patriarch Tikhon appealed to churches abroad to aid Russians facing famine. Though the Government at first distrusted the Church's involvement in national disaster, on December 9 instructions were given to government relief agencies to cooperate with the churches (Curtiss, *The Russian Church and the Soviet State*, p. 107).

February, 1922—

A "non-party publishing company" called "The Atheist" was formed (Timasheff, *Religion in Soviet Russia*, p. 34).

February 23, 1922—

The Government ordered the confiscation of all church valuables not of religious significance in order to provide food for the famine-stricken Volga area. Already in 1921 Patriarch Tikhon had offered to collect unconsecrated movables of the Church in order to secure a foreign loan and buy food for the famine victims. After initial agreement the Government declined on grounds that church property had been nationalized and therefore the Church had no property to offer, and secondly that the Church should conduct worship, and not relief. When the Government demanded the surrender of movable articles, the Patriarch agreed only to the surrender of unconsecrated objects. Thereupon the Government issued the decree.

The Patriarch called on faithful believers to resist and to hide church valuables from the "robbers" (Anderson, *People, Church, and State in Modern Russia*, p. 60).

March 28, 1922—

A number of liberal church leaders supported the Government in its relief concerns, and Kalinin invited Bishop Antonin to join the Relief Commission as representative of the Church (Curtiss, *The Russian Church and the Soviet State*, p. 116).

March, 1922—

Conservative church leaders were arrested, convicted and executed or deported, or escaped. One thousand, four hundred fourteen "bloody conflicts" with parishioners were reported in the Soviet press (A. A. Valentinov describes early "persecution" in *The Assault of Heaven*). The common indictment against the clergymen was: "By proclaiming the church valuables inviolable, the defendants incited the masses of the people to engage in civil war" (Timasheff, *Religion in Soviet Russia*, p. 29).

April, 1922—

"At the meeting of the Council of People's Commissars . . . it was decided that the policy towards the Church should assume an aggressive character, while . . . the confiscation of valuables should serve to sunder the crumbling body of the former State Church" (Miliujoff, "Russian Culture"; Anderson, *People, Church and State in Modern Russia*, p. 61).

April 11, 1922—

Orthodox Patriarch Tikhon reportedly sent a circular letter to all bishops urging them to dissuade the faithful from resorting to violence when church property was confiscated (Curtiss, *The Russian Church and the Soviet State*, p. 212).

April 22, 1922—

By Patriarchal decree, the emigree "Ecclesiastical Administration of the Russian Church Abroad" (Karlovci) was declared dissolved. Six weeks earlier the emigrees had gone on record as supporting the restoration of the Romanov house to the throne, and had called on the rest of the world not to recognize the Bolshevik government. The famine was referred to by the Karlovci meeting as the result of Bolshevik disorder. The Government thereupon demanded excommunication of the Karlovci participants (Bolshakoff, *Russian Non-Conformity*, p. 166).

May, 1922—

Patriarch Tikhon was soon placed under house arrest. When called as a witness at the trial of other Church leaders, he declared that in accordance with canon law he must condemn the confiscation of sacred vessels, and that whenever civil and canon law conflicted, it was his duty to obey canon law. The court ordered him tried at once (Timasheff, *Religion in Soviet Russia*, p. 30).

May 12, 1922—

A radical wing, led by Archpriest Vvedenskii, opponent to the Patriarchal form of Church government and leader of the "All-Russian Union of Democratic Orthodox Clergy and Laymen" which was organized shortly after the Tsar's abdication, met and declared Patriarch Tikhon unfit for his office, and sent a delegation to Patriarch Tikhon to accuse him of being personally responsible for the execution of thirteen churchmen in Moscow (Anderson, *People, Church and State in Modern Russia*, p. 62). A new ecclesiastical body, "The Living Church," was organized, plans made for reforms to surpass those of Luther, and the hope expressed that early agreement would be reached with the Government (Timasheff, *Religion in Soviet Russia*, p. 31).

May 14, 1922—

Izvestia published a declaration that Patriarch Tikhon had been responsible for the condemnation of many churchmen, and called for his abdication (*Ibid.*). He was charged with maintaining contacts with the emigree Russian clergy and seeking to exploit the famine to overthrow the Government (Curtiss, *The Russian Church and the Soviet State*, p. 120).

Patriarch Tikhon began steps to turn over the Patriarchal office to Metropolitan Agathangel as Locum Tenens.

May 18, 1922—

Another delegation from the Vvedenskii ("Living Church") group visited Patriarch Tikhon, advised him that the Church suffered from his absence under arrest, and asked permission to take over and re-open the Chancery until the Patriarch's substitute should arrive, depending on bishops currently in Moscow to assist them until that time. The Patriarch gave permission to the delegation to re-open the Chancery and to make preparations for turning it over to Agathangel.

The Vvedenskii group took over the Chancery, but instead of turning it over to Agathangel, who was deported to Siberia after refusing to cooperate with them (Bolshakoff, *Russian Non-Conformity*, p. 160), set up a Provisional Supreme Church Administration to replace the Patriarch and Holy Synod (Anderson, *People, Church and State in Modern Russia*, pp. 61-63).

July, 1922—

Metropolitans Benjamin of Petrograd and Vladimir of Kiev, and Roman Catholic Msgr. Budkiewiecz, along with others, were condemned to death (Barron and Waddams, *Communism and the Churches*, p. 11).

Vvedenskii was one of the principal witnesses against Metropolitan Benjamin, his diocesan bishop (Anderson, *People, Church and State in Modern Russia*, p. 61).

August 3, 1922—

The Government's Central Executive Committee decreed that all non-profit societies (principally churches) must register with the Government. All others would be considered illegal and their members subject to trial as counter-revolutionaries.

August, 1922—

Vvedenskii's "Provisional Supreme Church Administration" convened a Sobor which took strong action against the monastic element in Church leadership, and replaced the Patriarchal form of Church government with a Supreme Church Administration of presbyterian form.

The Sobor issued a statement calling on churchmen to abandon attempts to use the Church for political purposes and for counter-revolution, praising the Soviet Government for providing a framework in which the Kingdom of God could be realized, and appealing to Christians to work with the revolutionaries for a better social order (Appendix V).

Until the wane of the "Living Church" and recognition of the Patriarchal administration in 1927, Soviet authorities supported Vvedenskii by making buildings available, by placing "Living Church" leaders as bishops, deans and rectors, at times removing and exiling those who would not accept the new Church order. The "Living Church" had many "leaders," few followers (Anderson, *People, Church and State in Modern Russia*, p. 64). Laymen showed open opposition to its leaders.

November, 1922—

An anti-religious seminary was opened in Moscow (Timasheff, *Religion in Soviet Russia*, p. 34).

December, 1922—

The first anti-Christmas carnival was celebrated with mock processions, parodies of miracles, the Immaculate Conception, etc. (Timasheff, *Religion in Soviet Russia*, p. 35).

December 26, 1922—

A Governmental decree required clergymen to submit their sermons to Government censors. In the preamble, religion was declared "a brutalization of the people . . . Education was to be so directed as to efface from the people's mind this humiliation and idiocy" (*Ibid.*, p. 37).

January, 1923—

Roman Catholic Bishop Cepliak wrote to the British representatives in Petrograd: "Both the priests and the Catholic population have always been loyal to the Soviet Government." When he was later brought to trial he declared that the Revolution had freed the Catholics, and that the idea of counter-revolution had not entered their minds (Timasheff, *Religion in Soviet Russia*, p. 53).

April 27, 1923—

By special decree of the Commissariats of Justice and Interior, religious organizations might apply for special permission to convene provincial or central conventions to conduct elections, etc. The "Living Church" immediately called a nation-wide Sobor (Timasheff, *Religion in Soviet Russia*, p. 31).

April 29-May 9, 1923—

At the second Sobor of the Vvedenskii administration, Patriarch Tikhon was deposed and defrocked, his excommunication of Bolsheviks repealed.

Three schismatic groups stemming out of the 1922 change in church government and leadership, the Living Church, Ancient Apostolic Church, and Regenerated Church were reunited in a single Holy Synod.

June 9, 1923—

The Central Committee of the Trade Unions declared:

"The final liberation of workers from religious superstition may take place only as the result of durable educational activity directed towards inculcating the principles of materialism in the masses at large; the struggle against religion will not be terminated by casual decrees and administrative coercion, but by persistent and systematic propaganda for Marxism" (*Ibid.*, p. 95).

June 19, 1923—

A Governmental decree forbade local authorities to support certain religious groups against others. Church buildings were to be re-distributed to existing groups according to the numbers of believers.

June 27, 1923—

After confessing in a petition to the Government (June 16) that as a Monarchist he had opposed the Soviet regime in the past, and declaring that he would no longer do so, that he had severed connections with foreign and domestic Monarchists and counter-revolutionary activities, Patriarch Tikhon was released (Appendix VI, Anderson, *People, Church and State in Modern Russia*, p. 66).

His spiritual authority and popularity were immediately recognized by the main body of the Church. Metropolitan Sergius, later to become Patriarch, and others quit the Vvedenskii group and allied themselves with Tikhon. Certain elements, however, expecting the Soviet soon to crumble, accused Tikhon of betraying the Church. Others, (including the Karlovci refugee Synod abroad) claimed that the confession was signed by the Patriarch under duress, or not at all (*Ibid.*, p. 67) and that since the Mother Church had no freedom, they must maintain a forced autonomos status abroad.

"A testament made public at the Patriarch's death disclosed his attitude and action following his release from prison:

'The Soviet Power is indeed the power of the people, the workers and peasants. Therefore it is stable and unshakable . . .'

"He appointed a special commission to investigate the activities of the hierarchs and priests opposing the regime at home or abroad. With regard to charges of the Karlovci refugee 'Synod' that he had not been free in making his 'confession' he stated:

'We declare that there is no power on earth that could bind our conscience as a hierarch and our patriarchal word . . .

'Calling down on hierarchs, priests and our faithful children the blessing of God, we pray you with a calm conscience . . . to submit to the Soviet Power, not for fear, but for conscience's sake, remembering the words of the apostle, Let every soul be subject to the higher powers. For there is no power but God; the powers that be are ordained of God'" (The Moscow Patriarchate, *The Truth About Religion in Russia*, p. 28).

The "Regenerated" or "Renovated" wing of the Living Church sought reconciliation to the Patriarchal Administration, but was refused since its establishment was not considered as conforming to canonical procedure.

December, 1923—

The Government decided that insurance adjustments on burned church property should be paid to the State, although the congregations were responsible for paying insurance premiums (Timasheff, *Religion in Soviet Russia*, p. 37).

1924—

The Thirteenth Congress of the Communist Party stated:

"It is necessary to liquidate all attempts to uproot religion by administrative measures, such as the closing of churches. Anti-religious propaganda in the countryside must be limited to the materialistic explanation of those natural and social phenomena which frequently recur in the peasants' life. It is especially important to avoid anything which could jar the religious sentiments of the believers; such sentiments can be extirpated only by patient work in the course of decades" (*Ibid.*, p. 86).

July 16, 1924—

A new decree forbade the teaching of religion in churches (*Ibid.*, p. 37).

Autumn, 1924—

At a meeting of the Central Committee of the Communist Party of Georgia, a member stated:

"Today there is no intelligent Party member who would not agree that our anti-religious activity has been overdone. All talks that peasants do not want their churches and voluntarily close them are self-delusion. We must make up for our mistake and give the peasants back the keys of their churches, granting them full liberty to pray as they like. However, at this point we shall meet resistance on the part of our local comrades" (*Ibid.*, p. 96).

February 7, 1925—

The "Friends of the Godless" organization (eventually "League of Militant Atheists") was created by a small journal, *Bezboznik* ("The Godless") for purposes of organizing "anti-religious propaganda." Three techniques were to be employed:

a. demonstration that religion was the enemy of the workers;

b. education, that science explains all mysteries;

c. indoctrination, that religious belief was a form of disloyalty to the Socialist State.

The Comsomol (Communist Youth Movement) increased its publications and activities.

Simultaneously with Christmas Eve and Holy Saturday religious services, special anti-religious demonstrations were to be organized by the League (Timasheff, *Religion in Soviet Russia*, p. 35).

April 7, 1925—

Patriarch Tikhon died, after having appointed three Locum Tenens to succeed him, Metropolitan Peter of Krutitskii was proclaimed acting church leader by 60 bishops.

May 11, 1925—

The revised Constitution of the Russian Soviet Federative Socialist Republic left the article on religion in the 1918 Constitution un-changed.

October, 1925—

In 29 out of 87 provinces, 1003 Orthodox Churches, 27 mosques, 27 Old Ritualist Churches and 29 other religious houses had been sequestered since 1917. Three hundred of the Orthodox Churches were vacant, six destroyed and the remainder used for schools, clubs, dwellings, etc. (Anderson, *People, Church and State in Modern Russia*, p. 70).

October 25, 1925—

When the Sobor of the Orthodox "Revolutionists" (Vvedenskii) was poorly attended owing to Metropolitan Peter's opposition to it, the Revolutionists accused Peter of seeking to restore the monarchy. In December Peter was arrested and later exiled to Siberia. He named Metropolitan Nishni Novgorod as Deputy Locum Tenens.

December, 1925—

At the Fourteenth Communist Party Congress, on the proposal of Stalin, it was decided to create a completely socialist (and industrial) Soviet Nation rather than to seek simultaneous world-wide revolution. Special emphasis would be placed on total domestic planning, less on foreign trade (*Ibid.*, p. 77).

1926—

Evangelical and Baptist Churches printed 25,000 copies of the Bible on State presses with the help of the British and Foreign Bible Society (ICPIS, No. 7, Feb., 1947).

April 27-30, 1926—

The Central Committee of the Communist Party called a special conference to consider ways and means of furthering anti-religious propaganda (Barron and Waddams, *Communism and the Churches*, p. 11).
The Congress concluded that
a. a varied program of anti-religious propaganda was necessary;
b. the Communist Party should cooperate with Godless groups;
c. more anti-religious agitators should be trained in schools and universities (Curtiss, *The Russian Church and the Soviet State*, p. 267).
Publication of religious literature was further restricted (Anderson, *People, Church and State in Modern Russia*, p. 68).

May 28, 1926—

Orthodox Metropolitan Sergius addressed an appeal to Orthodox Christians stating that "he had taken upon himself to assure the Soviet Government of their sincere willingness to become law-abiding citizens, resolved to keep aloof from political parties and activities" (Barron and Waddams, *Communism and the Churches*, p. 22).

December, 1926—

Metropolitan Sergius was arrested, and not released until April, 1927 (*Ibid.*, p. 184).

May, 1927—

A long document was presented to the Government, reportedly prepared by bishops in exile in the Solovetsky Monastery on the White Sea, asserting that the Orthodox Church had no quarrel with the Government except at the basic level of religious vs. materialistic philosophy. The document called on the Government to carry out the law separating Church from State in order that the Orthodox Church might again take up its religious work, and explained at length that the uncanonical "Living Church" did not and could not function for the large body of Orthodoxy (Appendix VII).

May 18-31, 1927—

Soviet authorities approved the registration of the Patriarchal Church. As Vice-Locum-Tenens, Metropolitan Sergius became acting Patriarch. Locum Tenens Metropolitan Peter was in exile in Siberia (Barron and Waddams, *Communism and the Churches*, p. 22). Until this time the Church had been in a weak position with no central administration for the exchange of information, or for advising churches regarding legal and other matters. During this period of five years the Living Church, with government favor, held three Sobors, took over cathedrals, placed bishops, maintained two theological seminaries, had 17,000 parishes registered and was officially recognized by the Patriarchs of Constantinople, Jerusalem and Antioch (Anderson, *People Church and State in Modern Russia*, p. 75).
Metropolitan Sergius' request for permission to call a Sobor, elect a Patriarch, and establish church schools (for persons over 18 years of age) was refused.
An official bulletin, *Journal of the Moscow Patriarchate*, re-appeared. Circulation was limited to church officials (*Ibid.*, p. 75).

June 10, 1927—

Metropolitan Sergius and members of the Synod issued a statement clarifying the differences between Communism and the Church, asserting that the Church should remain above politics, and calling on Christians to be good citizens:

"We must prove by acts, as well as by words that not only those indifferent or hostile towards Orthodoxy can be loyal citizens of the Soviet Union, but also . . . (faithful Orthodox Christians). We desire to be Orthodox and at the same time to feel the Soviet Union as our homeland, its joys and successes as our joys and successes, and its failures as our failure. Remaining Orthodox, we bear in mind our duty as citizens, not only through fear, but by conscience" (Appendix VIII).

1927—

According to J. Zhidkov, chairman of the Baptist and Evangelical Union, Baptist Churches were able to print 10,000 copies of the Bible on State presses (ICPIS, No. 7, Feb., 1947).

September, 1927—

In a speech to a delegation of American laborers Joseph Stalin stated:

"Communism will agitate against both Catholicism and Protestantism and against Orthodoxy in order to bring about the triumph of the Socialistic world outlook. The Party cannot be neutral toward religion and does conduct anti-religious propaganda against all and every prejudice. . . . The Party cannot be neutral toward the bearer of religious prejudices, toward the reactionary clergy who poison the minds of the toiling masses. Have we suppressed the reactionary clergy? Yes, we have. The unfortunate thing is that it has not been completely liquidated. Anti-religious propaganda is a means by which the complete liquidation of the reactionary clergy must be brought about. Cases occur when certain members of the Party hamper the development of anti-religious propaganda. If such members are expelled, it is a good thing because there is no room for such 'Communists' in the ranks of our Party" (Reproduced in the *Worker's Voice*, March 1, 1933, under the title, "Communists and Religion" and in Stalin's *Leninism*, Vol. I, Cooperative Publishing Society of Foreign Workers in the U.S.S.R., 1934 edition, also *New York Times*, Jan. 24, 1937; Anderson, *People, Church and State in Modern Russia*, p. 78).

July 28, 1928—

Orthodox Bishop Eugen of Murom outlined a program for Christian youth including: special preparation of children for first confession; special sermons for children; talks with parents concerning the Christian education of children; organization of lectures, excursions for children and athletic teams for children; material aid to needy children; organization of teams of adult believers to care for children while parents were at work.

In some provinces the movement was called Christomol (Christian Youth Movement) in contra-distinction to the Comsomol or Communist Youth Movement (Timasheff, *Religion in Soviet Russia*, p. 91).

March, 1929—

The Minister of Education, Mr. Lunacharsky, in a published article, stated that "a believing teacher in a Soviet school is an awkward contradiction . . . The departments of popular education are bound to use every opportunity to replace such teachers with new ones, of anti-religious sentiment" (*Ibid.*, p. 44).

April 8, 1929—

The All-Russian Central Executive Committee and the Council of People's Commissars approved an omnibus law combining a vast number of existing and new decrees and court decisions regulating religions and religious associations (Giduluanov, *Separation of Church from State in the USSR: a Complete Collection* (1600 pages) *of Decrees, Instructions and Court Decisions*). Religious groups must be registered before they could function. All functions excepting worship were prohibited. Accomodations for worship were the property of the State. Religious associations could collect funds from their members to support their clergy and executives or keep up the place of worship, but could not establish mutual aid funds, special groups of any sort, or perform any other activity not necessary for services of worship and prayer. Special meetings could be held only after receipt of a special permit. The Minister of Education announced that anti-religious propaganda was to become a function of the State schools. Monastic life was forbidden (Appendix IX).

May 18, 1929—

The Fourteenth Soviet Assembly declared that "by May, 1937, no church (building) is to be left in the Soviet Union" (By the end of the year, 1440 churches had been closed, Timasheff, *Religion in Soviet Russia*, p. 38). "God will be expelled as a medieval relic . . . The hidden corners of religion and idolatry are to be transformed into light-houses of the future civilization" (*The Australian Christian*, June 3, 1952). A number of institutions were planned as training centers for anti-religious leaders (Anderson, *People, Church and State in Modern Russia*, p. 89).

May 22, 1929—

Article V of the Constitution was changed from "Freedom of religion and anti-religion is granted to everyone" to read, "There is freedom for religious confession and anti-religious propaganda." The anti-religious magazine, *Bezboznik*, declared that churches and believers could no longer conduct any activities except religious services. "Religious propaganda is not permitted. Confession, but not propaganda" (Anderson, *People, Church and State in Modern Russia*, p. 80). Religious associations could not extend membership to residents outside their own community or township. No association should have more than one building at its disposal (Timasheff, *Religion in Soviet Russia*, p. 42).

At Kimri, the Orthodox priest was sentenced to death after some women of the congregation resisted Government confiscation of the church building for a maternity hospital. Others were sentenced for "opposing the collectivization of the farms." Local authorities often taxed clergymen or sentenced them beyond the limit of the law. In some instances of severe sentence, the Government heard and gave favorable decisions to local appeals (Anderson, *People, Church and State in Modern Russia*, pp. 52 and 81).

Clergymen were again classified as non-productive members of society, thereby losing their civil rights, bread ration cards, residence rights in communal houses, and educational facilities for their children.

Many bishops and clergymen were arrested and exiled or executed. Religion, sorcery, drunkenness, theft, ownership of private property were "crimes" lumped together for eradication as remnants of Capitalism (*Ibid.*, p. 81).

June 10-13, 1929—

At a conference of the "Godless Society" (League of Militant Atheists) the Comsomol representatives introduced a motion to compel trade union members to withdraw from membership in religious associations. The motion was defeated when the Commissioner of Education explained that this would only intensify religious feeling. Shortly thereafter, however, printers' unions refused to print religious publications, transport workers would not carry religious equipment, and postal workers would not deal with communications for the clergy (Timasheff, *Religion in Soviet Russia*, p. 43).

The Society announced its anti-religious "five-year plan" to enlist 17,-000,000 members, 1,750,000 subscribers to *Bezboznik* ("Godless Magazine") and *Anti-religioznik* (Anti-Religious Magazine) (Anderson, *People, Church and State in Modern Russia*, p. 86).

September 24, 1929—

The six-day week was introduced. Public worship became difficult on Sunday except when Sunday fell on the sixth or rest day (Timasheff, *Religion in Soviet Russia*, p. 40).

Summer, 1929—

The Orthodox Church applied to the Government for permission to open an academy for theological training in Leningrad (Anderson, *People, Church and State in Modern Russia*, p. 84).

January 5, 1930—

The People's Commissariat of Finance decreed that property of individual believers could not be confiscated to cover debts or taxes of the Church.

February 19, 1930—

Metropolitan Sergius, in a memorandum to M. Smidovitch of the Commission on Religious Affairs, requested the Government to assist and protect the Orthodox Church: by preventing excesses in insurance and other forms of taxation; by guaranteeing normal legal protection; by preventing excesses on the part of local civil administrators; by registering ministers as "free professionals" and not non-workers or Kulaks; by permitting children of priests to study in schools; by permitting the opening of a higher theological academy; by permitting the publication of a monthly bulletin for the whole Church; and other points (Appendix X).

February, 1930—

In an interview with foreign correspondents, Metropolitan Sergius denied that there was persecution of religion in Russia, but admitted that many religious leaders were being prosecuted as counter-revolutionaries, etc. (Timasheff, *Religion in Soviet Russia*, p. 23).

March, 1930—

The Central Committee of the Communist Party published an article by Stalin, "Dizziness with Success," in which he warned against too rapid socialization, including overcoming of religion (Anderson, *People, Church and State in Modern Russia*, p. 81).

March 15, 1930—

The Government decreed that the closing of churches by local authorities was against the will of the people and should be stopped (Timasheff, *Religion in Soviet Russia*, p. 45).

1930—

Russian Orthodox (refugee) bishops and priests outside Russia received communications allegedly from Metropolitan Sergius demanding their pledges of loyalty to the Mother Church and to the Soviet Government (Anderson, *People, Church and State in Modern Russia*, p. 130).

September, 1930—

E. Yaroslavsky, leader of the League of Militant Atheists, in an article in *Bezboznik*, No. 17-18, criticized those who demonstrated against religious activities, or organized other activities to divert people from religious activities (Timasheff, *Religion in Soviet Russia*, p. 45).

1932—

The All-Soviet Communist Party, in a definition of its program, described its approach towards religion (Article 13):

"Conscious and deliberate planning of all the social and economic activities of the masses will cause religious prejudices to die out."

Churches were to be separated from "the exploiting classes" and scientific educational and anti-religious propaganda was to be organized among youth. Religious sentiments of believers were not to be offended, lest fanaticism be strengthened (Appendix XI).

A large volume, *Fifteen Years of Atheism in USSR*, listed the achievements of the "Godless Society," including the sale of 820,000 copies of the 370-page manual, *Anti-Religious Textbook* (Anderson, *People, Church and State in Modern Russia*, p. 88).

July, 1932—

In answering a question from a group of American teachers, Emil Yaroslavsky, President of the Godless Society, stated:

"We are not conducting an anti-religious campaign at present . . . We are carrying on systematic, day-by-day anti-religious propaganda . . ."

He estimated that if 100,000,000 (of a total 160 million) adults were believers, less than half of the children were believers (Anderson, *People, Church and State in Modern Russia*, p. 88).

Autumn, 1932—

The *Journal of the Moscow Patriarchate*, No. 11-12, carried the message:

"At present the Patriarchal Holy Synod, with the Vicar of the Patriarchal Locum Tenens at its head, is filled with the hope that, with the all-powerful help of God, Church life in the future may flow along the accepted course and that, in spite of the difficulties which have always existed and will always exist in the earthly conditions of the existence of Christ's Church, she, this Church, will be a faithful haven for believers, where they may replenish their spiritual strength for struggle with sin and with the temptations of the world for the sake of salvation to Life Eternal" (As quoted in Anderson, *People, Church and State in Modern Russia*, p. 86).

November 20, 1932—

A law was enacted which would make absence from work for a single working day grounds for dismissal, or for losing the governmental allowance of food and living quarters. Since, with the six-day week, Sunday was seldom a "rest-day", workers could seldom attend regular religious services (Timasheff, *Religion in Soviet Russia*, p. 40).

December 4, 1932—

In some areas food supplies were moved from stores to factories to ensure that people would continue work (Pares, *Russia, Its Past and Present*, p. 115).

December 27, 1932—

A special decree required all citizens to carry identity cards, and prohibited "non-workers", the category given priests, from residing in larger cities.

June 15-18, 1933—

The Executive of the League of Militant Atheists heard reports that twenty-six Workers' Anti-Religious Universities, one Red Army University, six anti-religious institutions of higher education, the Anti-Religious Correspondence Institute, and many local groups were giving anti-religious instruction to more than 150,000 anti-religious leaders. Outstanding students received scholarships; awards were given for special competitions (Anderson, *People, Church and State in Modern Russia*, p. 90).

1934—

Bezboznik reported after a survey of rural villages that religion still flourished:
". . . Icons have been removed from the walls, but are hidden in chests . . . Sometimes one of the corners of a peasant's room is decorated with icons, and another with pictures of Party leaders" (Timasheff, *Religion in Soviet Russia*, p. 88).

April 19, 1934—

Metropolitan Sergius was installed as "Most Holy Metropolitan of Moscow and Kolomna" (The Moscow Patriarchate, *The Truth About Religion in Russia*, p. 31).

April 24, 1934—

Following a resolution of the Central Committee of the Communist Party indicating that the teaching of Marx-Lenin doctrines in public schools was proving harmful to Communism, the anti-religious propaganda program was restricted (*New York Times*, April 29:1:2).

Easter, 1934—

Traveling priests were reported to be performing baptism and other rites and giving religious instruction.

Summer, 1934—

The Government discouraged frequent divorce and marriage as "a petty bourgeois deviation from Communist ideals", increased fees and required registration of marriages and divorces on passports so that "silly girls would think it over twice before marrying a man with twenty or thirty marriage records", and abolished the "postcard divorce" which allowed for the annulment of a marriage by either party simply by writing a letter to that effect (Timasheff, *Religion in Soviet Russia*, p. 48).

June 3, 1935—

The Supreme Court ruled that persons teaching religion or religious rites to children without the consent of their parents would be subject to imprisonment and confiscation of their property (*New York Times*, June 3:1:2).

June 5, 1935—

Pravda urged renewed activities to stamp out religious beliefs, after reporting that prosecution of Communists who had engaged in religious activities had been impossible because Communist members of the prosecution had also participated in religious rites (*New York Times*, 5:5:4).

July 1, 1935—

The Czechoslovakian Minister of Foreign Affairs, M. Benes, on returning from Russia, indicated that he believed Russian leaders would like to drop their anti-religious program.

December, 1935—

A governmental decree abolished discrimination against children of non-workers in school enrollment (Barron and Waddams, *Communism and the Churches*, p. 23).

Children of clergy thereupon could enrol in all classes. This made training of religious leaders less difficult.

Christmas (January), 1936—

The lighting of Christmas trees was permitted for the first time in several years.

Anti-religious Christmas demonstrations in Sverdlovsk and Vologda were officially censored. It was reported that instructions had been given by high authorites that anti-religious demonstrations at Christmas and Easter time were to cease (Timasheff, *Religion in Soviet Russia*, p. 46).

February 6, 1936—

The League of Militant Atheists charged that Orthodox priests were posing as revolutionaries in order to lure peasants into the Church (*New York Times*, Feb. 6:15:6).

February 8, 1936—

In announcing its plans for increased opposition to the churches, the League of Militant Atheists noted that churches were continuing their religious activities in more than 40,000 villages (*New York Times*, 8:7:3).

April 9, 1936—

The League of Militant Atheists opened the first school to train missionaries of atheism for the Central Ukraine (*New York Times*, April, 9:11:2).

April 12, 1936—

In spite of pressure from the League of Militant Atheists, the Government refused to interfere with Easter celebrations of the churches (*New York Times*, April 12:1:2). ..

Religious equipment for the services was available in markets and State stores (Barron and Waddams, *Communism and the Churches*, p. 23).

April 22, 1936—

Pravda reported on the Tenth Congress of the Comsomol as follows:

"Regarding religious prejudices. The left-overs of bourgeois ideology have their reflection in religious superstitions and prejudices. Of course the roots of religion in our country have been fundamentally destroyed, and the greater part of our youth, of our children, are growing up free from any religious influence. Yet it would be wrong to think that the struggle with religious prejudices, even among youth, has been finished.

"In the initial draft of our Program we wrote: The Comsomol decisively, mercilessly, struggles against religious prejudices. But Comrade Stalin pointed out to us: 'Why write 'decisively, mercilessly'; that is not the point. It is necessary patiently to explain to youth the harm of religious prejudices, to conduct among youth prapaganda for a materialist world view, the only scientific world view' " (As quoted in Anderson, *People, Church and State in Modern Russia*, p. 110).

May 28, 1936—

Pravda declared:

"So-called free love and loose sexual life are altogether bourgeois and have nothing in common either with Socialist principles or ethics . . . Marriage is the most serious affair in life. . . ." (Pares, *Russia, Its Past and Present*, p. 120).

August 29, 1936—

Patriarchal Locum Tenens Peter of Krutitskii died in exile in Siberia (Anderson, *People, Church and State in Modern Russia*, p. 74).

September 22, 1936—

E. Yaroslavsky (League of Militant Atheists) indicated his approval of a proposal to grant voting rights to the clergy on the grounds that religion was dying. He admitted however, that there were still millions of believers (*New York Times*, September, 22:17:2).

November, 1936—

The Central Arts Committee suppressed an anti-religious opera which satirized the conversion of Russia to Christianity in a baptism scene depicted as a drunken farce. The Committee labeled the production as anti-Marxist, "a frivolous attitude towards history and a cheapening of the history of our people" (*New York Times*, November 10, 1936).

November 25, 1936—

The Revised U.S.S.R. "Socialist" Constitution modified the Article on Religion of the 1918 and 1925 Constitutions to state (Article 124):

"In order to ensure to citizens freedom of conscience, the Church in the U.S.S.R. is separated from the State, and the school from the Church. Freedom of religious worship and freedom of anti-religious propaganda is recognized for all citizens" (This sentence previously read: "freedom for religious and anti-religious propaganda").

A court ruled that sermons were permitted so long as they did not take on the form of a series of lectures. Article 135 restored the franchise to the clergy (Appendix XII). In introducing the Article, Stalin said:

"Some say that there is danger that there may creep into the supreme organs of the country elements hostile to the Soviet power, perhaps some of the former white guards, kulaks, priests, etc. . But what is there actually to fear? Those who fear wolves should not enter the forest. In the first place, not all former kulaks, white guards or priests are hostile to the Soviet power. In the second place, if the people here and there should elect hostile persons, that will only mean that our agitation (propaganda work) is badly handled, and we fully deserve such shame; but if our agitation work is carried on in Bolshevik manner, then the people will not let hostile persons get into their supreme organs. This means we must work and not whimper. We must work and not simply expect that everything will be provided ready-made by administrative order" (As quoted in Anderson, *People, Church and State in Modern Russia*, p. 106).

The question arose in many localities as to whether the Church should not be regarded as a "society of the working people" and therefore able to nominate candidates for election to the Supreme Soviet. There is no evidence that the Patriarchate considered the possibility of participating in elections. Article 126 (Relations between the Communist Party and the Government) stated:

". . . the most active and politically conscious citizens from the ranks of the working class and other strata of the working people unite in the All-Union Communist Party (of Bolsheviks), which is the vanguard of the working people in their struggle to strengthen and develop the socialist system, and which represents the leading nucleus of all organizations of the working people, both social and state" (As quoted in Anderson, *People, Church and State in Modern Russia*, p. 49).

1936—

A question concerning belief in God was included in the census to be taken at the turn of the year (*New York Times*, 21:15:5).

March 3, 1937—

Following the announcement of census figures, *Pravda* expressed alarm at the mushroom growth of religion, particularly of religious sects with reactionary ("Trotskyist") political possibilities in some provinces. According to census figures, 98% of the people were non-Christian. However, observers estimated that 70% were Christian, and the leaders of the League of Militant Atheists estimated that at least 50% were Christian (one-third of town people; two-thirds of country people) while membership in the League had fallen from five million to two million or less than 1%. *Izvestia* (March 11) accused the League of being responsible for the religious revival and deplored the fact that anti-religious activities had ceased in many villages; that local bureaus often could not be located by an investigating committee; that the Commissariat on Education was closing the anti-religious museums (*New York Times*, March 3:5:2; 11:16:6).

March 11, 1937—

Comsomol Truth reported that when investigations were made to discover why so many youth were becoming Christian, it was found that youth were attracted by the kindness and sympathy of religious people in contradistinction to the dictatorial attitude of Communist youth leaders (Timasheff, *Religion in Soivet Russia*, p. 90).

April, 1937—

A mass campaign to close churches in Vologda was forbidden by the provincial committee of the League of Militant Atheists, on grounds that it would only embitter the believers (*Ibid.*, p. 46).

April 15, 1937—

Pravda reported that the leader of the Comsomol, Kossarev, had found many members misinterpreting freedom of religion to mean that they were free to abstain from anti-religious work (*Ibid.*, p. 71).

He also accused religious leaders of seeking to reconcile religion with the State in order to let God penetrate into the framework of socialism (*Ibid.*, p. 88).

April 23, 1937—

The *Comsomol Truth* reported that in Stalingrad members of the Stakhanov movement would have their Easter meats and cakes blessed before those of other people (Timasheff, *Religion in Soviet Russia*, p. 88).

May 2, 1937—

Throughout Russia, the anti-religious campaign was revived to counteract the renewed activity of priests and nuns who had been assured of religious freedom under the new Constitution (*New York Times*, May 2: 32:1).

May 9, 1937—

The Commissariat of Education instructed teachers to train children to be active atheists. The Communist Party, in the *Agitator's Guide*, No. 8, decreed that religion should not be persecuted, but that anti-religious propaganda must be intensified (*New York Times*, May 9:28:1; Appendix XIII).

"Every religion brings harm to the workers . . . Lenin taught that the more refined the religion, the more harmful it became, because the more difficult for believing workers to comprehend its reactionary role . . . No matter how churchmen and sectarians greet and praise the Soviet power, no matter how they try to 'adjust' their 'gods' to Communism, the essence of religious activity is profoundly reactionary and at its root inimical to socialism" (Paragraph 12 from the *Agitator's Guide* as quoted in Anderson, *People, Church and State in Modern Russia*, p. 105).

May 30, 1937—

The Soviet journal *Orlovskaia* published the account of a trial of thirty churchmen. Among other things, they were charged with: joining a counter-revolutionary Fascist organization of churchmen; seeking to strengthen the Church as an anti-Soviet center; working with youth in an anti-Soviet spirit; derogating the Constitution; opposing the All-Union census; preaching counter-revolutionary sermons; attracting youth to church and baptizing children.

One churchman "confessed" to being a non-believer, while acting as a priest only for financial reasons (*Ibid.*, p. 115).

August 2, 1937—

Forty churchmen, including nine bishops, nuns and others were arrested and sentenced for "counter-revolutionary activities, sabotage and espionage" (*New York Times*, August 2:1:4; November 23:13:2).

Similar charges were brought against the old guard (internationalists) of the Communist Party.

November, 1937—

The *Agitator's Guide*, No. 23, instructed anti-religious workers to "help the believers to release themselves from religious opiate and from the influence of priests and sectarians." They should show the anti-scientific character of religion; help laborers form a materialistic world view; illustrate from actual events the reactionary, counter-revolutionary role of religion and the clergy; "show again by facts, from past and present life the vile moral image of ministers of religious cults."

The article then accused Metropolitan Sergius of having "saved up more than 300,000 rubles . . . often has drunken parties." Other leading churchmen were accused of becoming rich "magnates in the church" and of committing acts of immorality (Anderson, *op. cit.*, p. 118).

November 29, 1937—

When the Communist Party officials of Smolensk invited people at electoral meetings to sign petitions for the closing of churches, *Pravda* declared this to be provocation, and demanded punishment of the officials (Timasheff, *Religion in Soviet Russia*, p. 122).

February, 1938—

The League of Militant Atheists declared that the reason the anti-religious program was not more successful was because "local organizations have enrolled scoundrels, individuals with a dark past" or those who were incompetent for any other task (*Ibid.*, p. 101).

March 2, 1938—

The League of Militant Atheists' publications were revived (*New York Times*, March 2, 9:2).

April 2, 1938—

Dr. Platonoff, Metropolitan of the Orthodox Church of Leningrad (Living Church) was converted to Sovietism, and denounced the clergy (*New York Times*, April 2, 1:2).

April 21, 1938—

Children were told to disobey parents who attempted to force them to celebrate Easter (*New York Times*, April 21, 20:2).

April 25, 1938—

At Easter time, the announcement was made that great numbers of religious leaders had been arrested on charges of espionage, arson, establishing a "miracle factory," instructing believers to organize secret "home" churches, collaborating with foreign Fascist organizations, giving assistance to traveling "espionage" priests, stealing church property, etc.

July 23, 1938—

The Army newspaper demanded more active anti-religious propaganda (*New York Times*, July 23, 3:3).

August 8, 1938—

The last Lutheran Church in Moscow was closed (*New York Times*, August 8, 4:3). *Bezboznik* reported the existence of unregistered religious groups, "ravine worshippers," a "League for the Revival of the Church," and other "catacomb-type religious activities" (Timasheff, *Religion in Soviet Russia*, p. 79).

October 24, 1938—

The Education Commissariat publication called for a new anti-religious drive among children (*New York Times*, October 24, 1:6).

November, 1938—

Anti-religious film-making was discontinued. The one remaining training center for anti-religious education was having difficulty in getting students (Timasheff, *Religion in Soviet Russia*, p. 105).

December, 1938—

Many anti-religious clubs, erected at great expense usually near churches, were reported unused, while churches were full (*Ibid.*, p. 107).

Anti-religioznik charged that many official publishers were refusing even to consider publication of anti-religious materials (*Ibid.*, p. 106).

Christmas-(January) 1939—

Oleschuk, assistant to E. Yaroslavsky, reported that during the Christmas season, collective farmers ceased work for three days (Timasheff, *Religion in Soviet Russia*, p. 73).

December, 1938—

The Historical Institute of the Academy of Sciences and the Central Committee of the League of Militant Atheists, after three joint sessions (December 12, 16, 22) endorsed a new statement of policy on the meaning of Christianity, as prepared by Prof. Ranovich:

"The Communist Party has been in error about the origin of Christianity. Two theories had prevailed: Professor Wipper's, to whom Christianity had been from the beginning a religion of exploiters, and Kautsky's, to whom Christianity was an escape from misery, primarily a religion of slaves and freedmen. Actually, Christianity is an opiate for the people, as every religion is; but it must be explained why it has proved to be the most successful. The answer is that Christianity was a substantially new religious movement. It did not allow racial or national discrimination. It anticipated new forms of marriage. It recognized the dignity of the "abstract man" and proclaimed the equality of men independently of their social status. Among early Christians, revolt against the existing social order was the rule. Early communities were democratic, and their spirit was revolutionary. Later on, Christianity was subjected to many changes, but still preserved its ideals of human dignity and universalism. The progressive role Christianity has played in comparison with other religions, is undeniable: it introduced new ideas, a basis on which a new society could be built" (As quoted in Timasheff, *Religion in Soviet Russia*, pp. 114 and 115).

Bezboznik stated, No. 12, 1938, "In the film 'Alexander Nevsky' the clergy is almost altogether absent. There is, however, no reason to be afraid of objectively showing the role of the Church in Russian history. Anti-religious propaganda is permissible in films of this kind; however, it must be directed not against the Orthodox clergy, but against Catholic monks and the Roman Pope" (As quoted, *Ibid.*, pp. 116-117).

January 2, 1939—

E. Yaroslavsky, in an article in the League of Militant Atheists' publication, urged children to defy their parents if their parents showed any interest in religion (*New York Times*, 2:5:2).

With the dismissal of Yezhoff, Minister of Interior, and his replacement by Beria, outright trials of religious leaders, etc., ceased abruptly (Timasheff, *Religion in Soviet Russia*, p. 53).

Anti-religioznik, No. 1, 1939, stated: "We frequently hear that believers and non-believers are two hostile camps which necessarily must struggle against one another. This is an insidious lie, discrediting to the anti-religions movement. We cannot stop the struggle against religion for we have never fought it" (*Ibid.*, p. 118).

February 1, 1939—

An evangelist, Rev. Yesipenko, was sentenced to ten years' imprisonment for "counter-revolutionary activities" (*New York Times*, February 1:5:2).

Bezboznik stated that: "The Christianization of Russia by Prince Vladimir certainly was a progressive act. Christianity struggled against slavery and blood feuds; it condemned the sale of Christians into slavery and fostered the replacement of slavery by the milder institution of serfdom; Christianity favored the advance of culture and laid the foundation of Russian art and literature" (Timasheff, *Religion in Soviet Russia*, p. 116).

Soviet agencies were directed to stop all attempts to liquidate religion (*Ibid.*, p. 122).

April, 1939—

Bezboznik reported the decree forbidding all attempts to combat religion by administrative measures. Atheists were to avoid offending believers' religious feelings, and Christian children in the schools were not to be ridiculed (*Ibid.*, p. 122).

April 10, 1939—

Churches were reported filled for Easter services (*New York Times*, 10:10:1).

Bezboznik reported that icon painters and restorers were permitted to resume their work. Oil for icon lamps was sold in State stores (Timasheff, *Religion in Soviet Russia*, p. 124).

Attempts at disturbing worship by over-zealous Communists were denounced for increasing anti-Soviet feeling and not decreasing religious prejudice (*Ibid.*, p. 123).

President Kalinin of the Supreme Soviet of the U.S.S.R., at a teachers' conference, said that the teaching of Marxism should no longer be the teaching of Marxist doctrine, but the inculcation of love for the Socialist Fatherland, friendship, comradeship, humanism, honesty and cooperation in work, respect for the Soviet Government and love for Comrade Stalin (*Ibid.*, p. 124).

April, 1939—

The League of Militant Atheists distributed a circular to anti-religious propagandists, introducing the Ranovich (December, 1938) statement with: "Christianity should not be identified with capitalism. Early Christians were not rich, and they did not pay much attention to wealth. Christianity should not be identified with other religions: for it is a cult of the 'abstract man' and emphasizes his ideal properties. The beneficial role Christianity played in the development of family relations should not be denied, for it helped to establish monogamy. Christianity has contributed to the improvement of folkways and customs; it has eliminated bloody and orgiastic rites; it insisted on the abolition of harmful customs such as fights between gladiators and the coursing of men by beasts in the circus (As quoted in Timasheff, *Religion in Soviet Russia*, p. 115).

The League of Militant Atheists was to be responsible for seeing that no agencies should attempt to suppress religion by administrative measures (*Ibid.*, p. 122).

At the same time *Anti-religioznik* demanded "that the Soviet State conduct anti-religious propaganda. Certainly not by administrative measures but by ideological means, speeches, press, school, theater, club, radio" (Timasheff, *Religion in Soviet Russia*, p. 129).

May, 1939—

Oleschuk, Vice-President of the League of Militant Atheists, reported that in the whole U.S.S.R. no more than ten anti-religious clubs had effective propaganda programs. In *Anti-religioznik* he wrote:

"It would be wrong to think that everything connected with religion is necessarily reactionary because religion in itself is reactionary. It is especially wrong to think that the Christianization of Russia was a reactionary step, as, unfortunately, has been asserted by our anti-religious activity . . ." (*Ibid.*, p. 115).

In the same issue was the statement:

"The Communist Party has always struggled on two fronts: first against those who considered that religion was a private affair of the citizens, and second, against those who exaggerated its importance and demanded its immediate extermination by administrative measures" (*Ibid.*, p. 118).

It was also stated that

"It was wrong to put on the black list events and personalities only because they were in some manner connected with the Church . . ." e.g., St. Nevsky, who had protected Russia from Swedish and German invasions.

"The Church canonized him in consideration of the love of the people; the League of Militant Atheists has failed to pursue an equally wise policy" (Timasheff, *Religion in Soviet Russia*, p. 116).

June, 1939—

Anti-religioznik reported that

"During the previous years (1937-39) a number of priests and religionists were declared counter-revolutionaries and many more churches were closed; but it now appears that in many cases this was carried out by the enemies of the people (i.e., the purged followers of Bukharin and Trotsky) in order to increase the hostility to the Soviet Government" (*Ibid.*, p. 97).

Oleschuk wrote:

"Our League has committed many blunders in regard to Christianity. Marxist atheists have assumed the policy of bourgeois atheists. They denied Christianity in general without taking into consideration special circumstances. Marxist atheists must exercise a concrete approach and must realize that the Church has not always been a harmful influence" (*Ibid.*, p. 119).

July 1, 1939—

Pravda reported the trial and sentencing of Yaroslavl Party members who had organized an Easter "raid" on a village church.

"The trial . . . proved that in U.S.S.R. there is freedom of worship. But the trial produced also detrimental effects: rumors were spread that the atheists had been tried because the Communist Government needed the support of religion" (As quoted in Timasheff, *Religion in Soviet Russia*, p. 123).

July 2, 1939—

Bezboznik, journal of the League of Militant Atheists, cited as proof of religious freedom in the U.S.S.R. the fact that three drunkards had been imprisoned for raiding a church near Moscow. The journal added that religion must be fought with propaganda, not illegal acts (*New York Times*, 2:8:2).

Bezboznik reported an interview of its representative with the Orthodox Patriarch of Georgia. The representative told the Patriarch that overt disturbances of religious services was strongly condemned by the League. The Patriarch conjectured that in the future a revived religion would fuse with Communism, since there was no conflict with Christian doctrine. The editor added that this opinion was widespread among the clergy and people (Timasheff, *Religion in Soviet Russia*, p. 113).

July 12, 1939—

Several priests were arrested as "foes of collective farms."

Supreme Soviet President Kalinin stated that it was not enough to destroy religion; it must be replaced by something else and that Lenin had called the theater the religion of the future society (*Ibid.*, p. 124).

August, 1939—

The removal of icons from a room against the will of the head of the family was declared a violation of the Constitutional guarantee of freedom of religion (*Ibid.*, p. 125).

Bezboznik reported that religious interest was growing.

"Icons are reappearing in the homes of the members of collective farms, and of members of the Comsomol . . . Similar habits are re-appearing among Soviet teachers . . . Members of the Party and of the Comsomol as well as Stakhanovists display absolute indifference to the restoration of religious practices in their families, such as the baptism of children, church weddings, celebration of church holidays, special divine services" (As quoted in Timasheff, *Religion in Soviet Russia,* p. 75).

The magazine, in discussing the functions of the League, explained that it was the duty of every Marxist to evaluate the particular situation at any given time and place (*Ibid.*, p. 120).

August 20, 1939—

Pravda reported that "many still retain belief in the power of charms and sorcery and in the interpretation of dreams." Other indications were that superstition among "atheists" was growing (*Ibid.*, p. 109).

August 21, 1939—

Pravda urged that the war on religious belief be intensified (*New York Times*, August 21:6:7).

September, 1939—

Orthodox Msgr. Vissarion, Metropolitan of recently annexed Bucovina, in a letter addressed to Stalin, stated that the revolution had been necessary even in the life of the Church in order to accomplish long-awaited reforms, but that the time had come for friendly relationships between Church and State. The Church, he suggested could be helpful to the State in securing the sympathy and support of the people, both at home and abroad (*ICPIS*, No. 29, July, 1940).

November, 1939—

The *Patriinoye Stroitelstvo* of the Communist Party's Central Committee declared that

"It is much more difficult to uproot religion from the consciousness of the workers than to liberate them from the exploitation of capitalists" (As quoted in Timasheff, *Religion in Soviet Russia*, p. 98).

December, 1939—

A Christian who was released from prison and escaped to West Europe reported (apparently on the situation prior to 1939) that many parents had been arrested because their children had denounced them; that teachers instructed children not to obey their parents; that many children ran away from home. Permission to baptize must be secured both from parents and their employers. Baptism without such permission was a crime, both for the priest and the parents. Similarly for weddings and funerals. Nonetheless, these sacraments continued, often clandestinely. Women missionaries traveled the country, baptizing, administering the Lord's Supper, counseling and teaching. Churches which were open were overflowing, though services were observed by government agents. Clergy were supported often by secret contributions from the congregations. Most church workers wore civilian clothes and clergy usually must live outside the towns. Church buildings must be restored or were confiscated. After congregational efforts to restore them, many had been taken for warehouses or other governmental purposes. Private worship was discouraged, icons and candles could be made and used only secretly (*ICPIS*, No. 7, February, 1940).

January, 1940—

Russian prisoners of war in Finland reported that there remained very few churches in Russia, that the number of priests was exceedingly small, but that nearly all children were being baptized and given some kind of Christian instruction by older generations. The excesses of the antireligious drive (1937-1938) was causing great hostility towards the Communist Party, but a certain success had been achieved in making religion seem ridiculous, or at least socially undesirable (*ICPIS*, No. 9, March, 1940).

Many people crossed themselves at meals, openly claimed to be Christian and non-Communist, but they had not been active in church functions because of a high religious tax (*ICPIS*, January, 1940).

January 1, 1940—

Russian journals carried articles against the celebration of Christmas in a religious manner (*New York Times*, 1:12:1).

The official review, *Soviet Culture*, in its first issue of 1940, stated:

"It is obvious that socialism and religion have nothing in common, since they are two things quite opposite to each other. Religion obscures the minds and dupes the people. It cannot be tolerated in the country of the proletariat dictatorship that anti-socialist, reactionary and ignorant ideas are allowed to spread freely. The Soviet state which protects the interests of the people, does not permit free propagation of religious ideas, since this intoxicates the workers' consciousness."

February, 1940—

Izvestia reported "counter-revolutionary rumors of the coming religious persecution in Western White Russia and Western Ukraine." Party leaders were instructed to deny the rumors. Yaroslavsky declared that no League units would be organized in the areas recently annexed to U.S.S.R. in the common war with Nazi Germany (Timasheff, *Religion in Soviet Russia*, p. 133).

February 27, 1940—

The Commissariat of Education issued instructions for the improvement of anti-religious work in the schools, including special reading, visits to anti-religious museums, organization of anti-religious circles for parents (*Ibid.*, p. 129).

March, 1940—

The journal, *Anti-religioznik*, No. 3, 1940, denounced Western churches and church leaders as "agents of munition factories," "exploiters," "aggressors," and "supporters of the capitalist system and imperialistic wars." The chaplaincy work of the Church in the West was cited as one example of the Church's warring spirit (*ICPIS* No. 34, September, 1940).

March 19, 1940—

The League of Militant Atheists celebrated its fifteenth anniversary. In a report on the work of the League, leader Yaroslavsky stated:

"The atheistic question is of particular interest to the workers in Western Europe today and especially to those who are under the influence of religious organizations.

"The Communist Party . . . will always make propaganda against these religious prejudices, more especially because this propaganda constitutes one of the best ways of undermining the influence of the reactionary clergy . . . Does there exist such a thing as a clergy which is not reactionary? No, such a thing does not exist, for all the religious organizations of our day are in themselves reactionary . . . Religious prejudices are not only the heritage of the capitalist system but they are a reversion to a pre-capitalist past" (*ICPIS*, No. 23, June, 1940).

Yaroslavsky reported that membership in the League had fallen from five million in 1937 to less than three million, and that the Godless Movement had not yet learned how to carry on anti-religious propaganda among believers (*ICPIS*, No. 19, May, 1940).

March 20, 1940—

Pravda accused the League of Militant Atheists of making the mistake of bourgeois atheists in basing its anti-religious program on the assumption that religious strength rested on proletarian ignorance and the betrayal of the masses by the priests, whereas Lenin and Stalin taught that religion was rooted in social conditions (Timasheff, *Religion in Soviet Russia*, p. 119).

"The fact that many people still pray is evidence that they are dissatisfied with their material and moral situation. The League should explain to them that their conditions are satisfactory" (*Ibid.*, p. 124).

April, 1940—

In order to help convince the Soviet peoples of the validity of a close alliance with Germany, the Soviet Government released a report, stating, *inter alia*:

"2. Germany and the Soviet Union are fighting together against the capitalism of Europe and the U. S. A., against the Church, and for a new social life;

"3. the German nation and the nations of the Soviet are godless and socialistic;

"4. the Germano-Soviet agreement has hindered the military campaign of the Church against atheism;

"5. Stalin and Hitler are enemies of capitalism and adherents of atheism;

. . . .

"8. the Soviet-Russian Godless will soon have an opportunity to get to know the German Godless;

"9. through cooperation with Germany, the forward march of communism and atheism to other countries is secured;

"10. Stalin has remained faithful to communism, world revolution, and atheism" (*ICPIS*, No. 17, April, 1940).

Mikhailov, head of the Comsomol, said (1940-41) that both the Soviet and the Nazi States were opposed to the Christian ideology and had common enemies, chief of whom were the Catholic clergy, that the two governments must exchange information and act together (Timasheff, *Religion in Soviet Russia*, p. 133).

The atheists' magazine, *Bezboznik*, Nos. 10 and 11, scoffed at British weakness in "Using religious prejudices for their military propaganda . . . that the war against Germany is a Holy War" (*ICPIS*, No. 17, April, 1940).

April 26, 1940—

Pravda reported that Yaroslavsky had complained at the meeting of the Presidium of the League of Militant Atheists about the lack of an aggressive anti-religious education program on the part of the departments of public education (Timasheff, *Religion in Soviet Russia*, pp. 105, 129).

A special committee for work among children was created.

April 28, 1940—

The League of Militant Atheists was reported to have asked Molotov to try to persuade the Soviets' ally, Nazi Germany, to cease supporting churches in Germany (*New York Times*, 28:19:4).

April 29, 1940—

Pravda reported that special pre-Easter anti-religious lectures were being given to industrial workers, farmers and others on the topic, "Origin and Class Nature of the Easter Holidays" (*New York Times*, April 29:3: 6).

The *Anti-Religious Magazine*, in its No. 4 issue, criticized those who try to fuse Christianity and Communism or Socialism, and declared categorically that Communism and religion "are irreconcilably hostile to each other." Reasons why religion still existed in Communist U.S.S.R. were listed: (a) "Man's conceptions (sentiments) lag behind his economic transformations . . ."; (b) "Individual exploitations exist . . . (in) badly organized kolkhoses. . . ."; (c) "Socialist society has not yet entirely mastered the forces of nature . . ."; (d) "Capitalist surroundings . . . favor the survival of religion" (*ICPIS*, No. 47, December, 1940).

May, 1940—

An OGPU leader instructed frontier police to send to Siberia all Polish priests and ministers being returned by Germany from German-occupied Poland to Soviet-occupied Poland (*ICPIS*, No. 20, May, 1940).

The magazine *Bezboznik* accused Western religious leaders of trying to drive people into a war when the people sought peace (*ICPIS*, May, 1940; No. 34, September, 1940).

May 9, 1940—

Pravda indicated its support of a campaign to put more anti-religious training into the schools, (*New York Times*, 10:3:2) and to establish more schools to train anti-religious propagandists. It complained that anti-religious work in many schools took place only at Easter and Christmas time.

June 21, 1940—

The *Godless Magazine* (*Bezboznik*) reproached schools and teachers for not making full use of their opportunities to inculcate the anti-religious philosophy, and called for an intensified program within the schools and in extra-curricular activities (*ICPIS*, No. 27, July, 1940).

Metropolitan Alexius of (formerly) Poland visited Metropolitan Sergius of the Orthodox Church of Russia, was absolved of the sin of heresy for his temporary detachment from Russian Church jurisdiction as leader of a Polish Orthodox Church. Metropolitan Sergius urged that all priests be faithful to their apostolic mission, trusting that God would open the Soviet Union to Christian work (*ICPIS*, November, No. 45, 1940).

July, 1940—

The monthly periodical, *Anti-religioznik*, reported that numbers of women ministers were conducting liturgy, funerals, prayers and other church services. Noting that the women's sermons "often make a greater impression than those conducted by priests," the journal accused the Church of using this "trick" to mislead people into thinking services had become more "democratic" and called upon "Godless women" to mobilize for the struggle against believing women" (*ICPIS*, No. 29, July, 1940).

Another article (Issue No. 7) in the magazine denied that there are "prophetic" elements in religion, illustrated how Biblical prophesies had not been fulfilled, but asserted that Marx, Stalin, *et al* could fortell the future because they were pure scientists. The magazine charged that anti-religious ideas were not being taught properly in the schools among children who are "especially susceptible to the influence of the clergy," and warned that caution must be taken lest in teaching anti-religion, an "unhealthy curiosity" in religion is aroused (*ICPIS*, No. 2, January, 1941).

July 22, 1940—

A former church deacon, teacher in rural schools, was tried and sentenced "for spreading religious fables" (*New York Times*, 22:8:6).

July 25, 1940—

Training for anti-religious instruction was to be introduced into high schools and universities (*New York Times*, 25:4:8).

August, 1940—

In an article in *Bezboznik*, Yaroslavsky stated:

"The reproach which might be made against the Atheists is that they have not been able to offer the people moral standards for their life. Religion answered moral questions in its way."

Yaroslavsky maintained that the the first step in overcoming religion in newly-Sovietized areas (Baltics) was to demonstrate the harmful character of religion. Religious organizations were still permitted in the USSR not because the Government respected the Church, but because some citizens had not yet learned of the Church's harmful character. He noted that there was some sentiment within the Communist Party for the dissolution of the League of Militant Atheists, but asserted that such a special organization was indispensable (*ICPIS*, No. 13, September, 1940).

September 22, 1940—

Pravda reported that the Central Committee of the League of Militant Atheists at a special conference had acknowledged that anti-religious propaganda was on the wane, principally because of the lack of cooperation of the Comsomol and the Communist Party (Timasheff, *Religion in Soviet Russia*, p. 101).

September 24, 1940—

Pravda heralded the release of a new *Anti-religious Textbook* by the State publishing house as particularly beneficial in awakening the masses "from their religious slumber."

"Anti-religious propaganda is and must remain an inalienable element in Communist propaganda. A realization of Communism is possible, as Lenin emphasized, only if the anti-religious fighting program is carried out. The theory that religion dies away by itself through a natural process of decay is false and dangerous, because it weakens the militant ardour for Communism. . . . This book . . . is of eminent political significance for the future . . . because from the altars and pulpits of the Christian churches and chapels . . . a dark, dirty flood of calumny pours forth . . ." (*ICPIS*, No. 38, October, 1940).

October 10, 1940—

F. Oleschuk, Vice-President of the League of Militant Atheists, declared that it was incorrect to ascribe progressive tendencies to Christianity as such, that it had played a progressive role only in specific epochs. Religion now hindered rather than enhanced progress and culture as it had done in early Christianity and early Russian history when it brought unity, education and culture to Russia. Any attempt to find a compromise between Christianity and Communism was counter-revolutionary (Timasheff, *Religion in Soviet Russia*, p. 131).

December, 1940—

Prayers in Orthodox Churches were to be said for the forgiveness of persecutors and the salvation of those estranged from the Church (*EPS*, December, 1940).

Anti-religioznik (No. 12, 1940) in an article entitled "The Defense of the USSR and Religion," stated that the defense of the USSR included "the fight against the adversary of the Soviet Union all over the world . . . For this reason the fight against religion is an indispensable instrument in national defense for the final victory of socialistic humanism. The Christian religion, with its proclamation of love of neighbor, is especially dangerous for this humanism. The only worthy attitude of the Soviet citizen in his fight for Communism is therefore hate, for this hate creates the basis for the true love of mankind of the future, which is given not by religion, but only by the Communist Party" (*ICPIS*, No. 5, 1941).

The journal *Bolshevik* (December issue) stated that the Bolshevik Party must lay bare all attempts of the clergy "to renew, purify, adapt religion to new conditions . . . It is the task . . . of . . . every citizen to struggle for the complete elimination of religious concepts."

In this connection the Scientific Academy of the USSR expanded its section "History, Religion and Atheism," and the Philosophic Institute of Moscow and the Anti-religious Museum in Leningrad increased their staffs (*ICPIS*, No. 5, February, 1941).

Bolshevik, No. 24, in answering the question, "Who were the God-seekers?" pointed to the social philosophers who "sought to link up the religious stirrings of the early 20th Century with the Marxist social movement" (Anderson, *People, Church and State in Modern Russia*, p. 12).

January, 1941—

With the re-establishment of the seven-day week, Sunday became the day of rest (*The Tablet*, February 15, 1941).

January, 1941—

At a congress of the Central Council of the League of Militant Atheists, plans were outlined for a "Win the individual believer for atheism" program as the basic technique in the struggle against religion. Atheist missionaries were advised to show "loving understanding" for the believers' deepest concerns, and to point out that their religious attitude was prejudicial to the country. It was noted that most believers considered themselves faithful citizens, that only three believers had been "won" in Moscow in 1940. Respected people should therefore do the missionary work, but should not enter into Christian fellowship, nor participate in any polemics with Christians (*ICPIS*, No. 16, April, 1941).

February, 1941—

Anti-religioznik reported that whereas the external life of the Church, the crosses, prayers, church attendance and priests, had disappeared, everyone knew about Jesus Christ and even the smallest people knew the Bible story. Family icons and religious festivals were still honored. The magazine concluded that "in view of this inconquerable vitality . . . it is necessary to lift Godlessness to an intellectually more satisfying level" (*ICPIS*, No. 16, April, 1941).

April, 1941—

An anonymous USSR Government official visiting West Europe took part incognito in Orthodox services. He reported that in Russia great festivals of the Church were still celebrated. Many priests wore civilian clothes and lived in caves, but were cared for by the faithful (*ICPIS*, No. 17, May, 1941).

Life magazine (USA) reported that priests traveling as cobblers, tailors, knife grinders, and groups of monks traveling as agricultural workers' unions were able to continue their Christian ministry. Some Christian leaders had penetrated the League of Militant Atheists and were carrying out missionary work among its members.

Hidden houses of prayer had been established where churches had been destroyed, and secret theological seminaries established to train priests and leaders. While the number of priests had diminished, their influence had increased (*ICPIS*, No. 37, October, 1941).

May, 1941—

In a general survey of the status and work of the League of Militant Atheists, leader Yaroslavsky reported in *Anti-religioznik* (May issue) that membership had increased by 500,000 since 1939 (still 1,500,000 below 1937 —5,000,000), but that "the influence of the Church has been weakened less than is often thought," as was evident from the way church buildings were cared for—an indication "of the joy of believers in making sacrifices . . ." (*ICPIS*, No. 25, June, 1941).

June 22, 1941—

GERMANY OPENED WAR ON RUSSIA.

June 22/26, 1941—

A pastoral letter bearing the signature of Metropolitan Sergius of Moscow was read in Orthodox Churches. After comparing the Nazi attack to earlier invasions by Tartars, Teutons, Swedes and French, when the Church blessed the people, the letter called pastors and laity to defend the nation at all costs and ended: "Our Orthodox Church has always shared the fate of the people. Together with the people she has borne their suffering and been comforted by their victories. She will not leave the people even now. She blesses with heavenly blessing even the present effort of the people . . . The Church of Christ blesses all the Orthodox who defend the holy frontiers of the country" (*ICPIS*, No. 45/46, December, 1941; Anderson, *People, Church and State in Modern Russia*, p. 23). More than 12,000 worshippers were said to have participated in the service in Moscow Cathedral.

July, 1941—

Special prayers were offered in Orthodox Churches for victory over the Axis invaders. Anti-religious signs and posters disappeared "because of the lack of paper," said Lozovsky, President of the Soviet Bureau of Information (*ICPIS*, July, 1941).

August 12, 1941—

Metropolitan Sergius, apparently in reply to criticism of some Christians for his support of the war effort, called on Christians to pray for all those killed in battle and added that per-haps in the instant of death Christ appeared even to those who did not believe in prayer nor wish to be prayed for (Anderson, *People, Church and State in Modern Russia*, p. 23).

August 21, 1941—

Moscow radio appealed to "all Godloving inhabitants of the occupied countries" to defend their religious freedom. It accused the Nazi regime of menacing "the very existence of Christianity and seeking the overthrow of Christ the King to install instead the myth of the 20th Century of Alfred Rosenberg" (Timasheff, *Religion in Soviet Russia*, p. 137).

(Note: Information that Hitler had restored the Orthodox Churches of Berlin and nineteen other German cities and intended to be the "defender of Christianity" to the "liberated" Russian people preceded the march of Nazi troops Eastward.)

August 22, 1941—

The Press Department of the Soviet Embassy in London released a statement on the life of "Religious Communities in the Soviet Union":

"Believers freely practise their religious worship, baptize their children, marry, perform funeral ceremonies, celebrate religious festivals and fasts, attend Church ceremonies, keep icons in their homes, elect leaders of religious communities, and so on.

"The Soviet Government provides buildings for religious purposes, free of charge and exempt from taxes. The Soviet Government ensures that no one disturbs the rights of believers, offends their feelings or jeers at their belief. Soviet courts severely punish those who try in any way to infringe on the rights of believers.

"The clergy in the U.S.S.R. enjoy equal rights with all other citizens. The most important right of citizens of the U.S.S.R.—to elect and be elected members of the supreme organs of the Soviet Government—is fully guaranteed to preachers, priests, mullah, rabbis, etc." (Quoted by Stanley Evans in *Churches in the U.S.S.R.*).

September 3, 1941—

Mr. Maisky speaking in London, said:

"The Soviet Union recognizes that the internal order in each State is its own concern. The Soviet Union also considers that religion is a private matter for each citizen . . . In spite of what is thought by so many, religion in my country is not persecuted and every citizen has the right to believe or not to believe, according to his or her own conscience . . .

"In general there is a considerable variety in the religious life of the Soviet Union, and no obstacles are put in the way of their activities, so long as they remain in their natural sphere of their human conscience and faith" (As quoted in Barron and Waddams, *Communism and the Churches*, p. 24).

September 9, 1941—

The Milan Roman Catholic journal, *L'Italia*, reported that Italian occupation forces in south USSR were finding great religious interest on the part of the people and called on Italians to provide religious leaders, materials and money for Christian work in USSR (*ICPIS*, No. 32, September, 1941).

In German-occupied areas of Russia, cathedrals, some lately anti-religious museums, were reopened and the liturgy celebrated in some cases for the first time in twenty-five years. People were still able to sing the liturgy and say prayers. Russian prisoners of war in Germany showed great interest in religious services and the sacraments (*ICPIS*, No. 34, October, 1941).

The anti-religious publications, *Bezboznik*, and *Anti-religioznik*, weekly and monthly of the League of Militant Atheists were discontinued "in order to conserve paper" (*New York Times*, October 1 and 7, 1941).

October, 1941—

The Anglican Bishop of Fulham claimed that the Russian Army had Orthodox priests "who exercise an unofficial ministry to the troops." The Polish Army constituted in the USSR had a chaplain for each regiment.

The Berlin Russian Orthodox weekly advised that in German-occupied Russia, the Russian people must be permitted to re-constitute their own religious life naturally and not along super-imposed (German) patterns (*ICPIS*, October, 1941).

October 5, 1941—

S. A. Lozovsky, of the Soviet Bureau of Information, in reply to Western accusations and President Roosevelt's expressed hope of October 4 that there should be full freedom of religion in USSR before American citizens could support their war effort, re-affirmed that there was such freedom, guaranteed by the Constitution of 1936.

"The Soviet Union provides not only the right to adhere to this or that religion, but also . . . not to belong to any church and to conduct anti-religious propaganda. Soviet law does not consider it possible to force citizens to worship this or that religion . . . Freedom of worship . . . assumes that religion, church or congregation will not be utilized for overthrow of the existing regime" (*New York Times*, October, 5:1:6).

October, 1941—

Russian and Finnish radio announced that Yaroslavsky had been suspended as leader of the "League of Militant Atheists" for "incompetence." Sunday was restored as a national day of rest (*ICPIS*, No. 35, October, 1941).

October 6-7, 1941—

U. S. Representative Fish reported that 90% of American Roman Catholic clergy would oppose American aid to the USSR. German Roman Catholic clergy supported the German war against the USSR (*New York Times*, October 6:8:5 and November 10:1:6).

November, 1941—

At a special dinner in the Kremlin, Stalin offered a prayer-toast to President Roosevelt with the words, "May God help him in his task" (*New York Times*, November 19:6:3).

1942—

Rev. P. Widdrington (British) reported that a number of concessions had been made by the Government in favor of the churches since June, 1941, including:

The restoration of civil rights to the clergy;

Suppression of blasphemous plays and films;

Abolition of the test for the Army and Civil Service which penalized members of the Church;

Revision of the manuals used in schools and the excision of scurrilous and offensive attacks on religion;

Studied moderation in the treatment accorded to the Uniate and Orthodox Churches in the Western Ukraine, formerly Poland;

Legalization of the manufacture and sale of objects connected with religion (e.g., icons);

Relaxation of the Labour Disciplinary laws to enable the faithful in the country districts to keep the great festivals;

Restoration of the seven-day week with Sunday as the universal Rest Day, in place of the week of six days with a rotating free day;

Re-opening of the shrine of the Iberian Virgin in Moscow (the shrine had been closed since 1929 when the icon was removed and a plaque, with Marx's words, "religion is the opium of the people" placed outside the building);

Removal of the atheist Dimitrov from the staff of broadcasters;

Permission to the Polish regiments to have the services of Roman Catholic chaplains, and the release of 150 Roman priests, Soviet citizens, from prison;

Tacit understanding that no objection would be raised to Orthodox clergy, serving as soldiers, ministering to their fellow Orthodox at the front;

Appointment of a number of teachers from the seminaries of the Western Ukraine to professorships in Soviet universities;

Suspension of the vast publishing undertaking of the Godless Union (in ten years they published 1700 books and brochures and their papers, including *Bezboznik*, had a sale of 43,-000,000 copies) (*Christendom*, March, 1942; *ICPIS*, No. 19, May, 1942).

January, 1942—

Russian papers complained that German Armies, retreating before the Red Army, left churches looted and burned (*New York Times*, January 5, 1952).

Orthodox Metropolitan Sergius addressed an epistle to Orthodox believers in German-occupied territory, calling on them to remain faithful Russians, even if captured (The Moscow Patriarchate, *The Truth About Religion in Russia*, p. 34).

January 20, 1942—

Churches of German-occupied USSR were reported crowded by people seeking to pray. In some areas services were difficult owing to the lack of trained leaders. There was reluctance to participate openly owing to fears that the Communists might return and seek revenge (*ICPIS*, No. 6, February, 1942). Twenty-five of 454 former Orthodox Churches in Moscow were open for worship. Reported *Pravda*—"Yaroslavsky (deposed leader of the League of Militant Atheists) weeps today over the ruin of the Russian churches and sanctuaries" (*ICPIS*).

February 5, 1942—

Metropolitan Sergius of Moscow severely criticized Orthodox Metropolitan Dionysius of German-occupied Poland for his cooperation with the Nazis, stripped Bishop Polycarp Sikorski of any authority for declaring himself head of an autocephalous church, and urged people to remain faithful to their Mother Church in Moscow (*New York Times*, February, 22:12:3).

In reply, Bishop Polycarp accused Metropolitan Sergius of having obtained the office of Acting Patriarch by illegal means (The Moscow Patriarchate, *The Truth About Religion in Russia*, p. 64).

March 28, 1942—

The Council of Russian Hierarchs confirmed Acting Patriarch Sergius' warning to Bishop Polycarp that he would be dismissed from holy orders unless cleared by an ecclesiastical court. He was particularly criticized for his political ambitions "to attain the national (Ukranian) ideal"—a united and independent National Ukranian Church (*Ibid.*, pp. 65-69).

April, 1942—

Metropolitan Sergius denounced the Germans for their part in trying to split the Ukrainians and sever their religious connection with the Orthodox jurisdiction of Moscow (*New York Times*, April 12:24:5).

May, 1942—

German occupation authorities gave the Orthodox Monastery of Riga permission to send a mission into occupied Russia to open churches, consecrate priests and open factories for religious equipment.

Russian prisoners in Rumania received religious instruction, relief and literature from Rumanian and German authorities (*ICPIS*, No. 20, May, 1942).

August-September, 1942—

The Orthodox Church published 50,-000 copies of a book entitled *The Truth About Religion in Russia*. In the foreword, Acting Patriarch Metropolitan Sergius stated that the Orthodox Christians do not seek "liberation" by Fascists from their own Soviet authorities;

That many instances cited abroad as persecution never occurred;

That the situation of the Russian Church should not be compared with the persecutions of the Graeco-Roman period, but that the Church in coming back to its true calling has similarities to the apostolic churches;

That there was unbelievable chaos in the Church because of the liberty for each individualist to act as he pleased;

That the Church has suffered plundering and destruction at the hands of Fascist invaders;

That the Church had lost many members, but had gained in spirit and strength (The Moscow Patriarchate, *The Truth about Religion in Russia*, p. 5).

"It is true, as is well known, that anti-religious propaganda is being carried on in Russia, the freedom of which is guaranteed by the Constitution. It is equally well known that anti-religious ideology is the ideology of the Communist Party. But at the same time, it must be stated quite objectively that the Constitution, which guarantees full freedom for the celebration of religious services, in no way impedes the religious life of the faithful and the life of the Church in general."

The editors added that early Soviet repressions of the clergy were because of activities of the clergy against the Soviet regime, and not because of their religious activities (*Ibid.*, pp. 20-21) (Appendix XIV).

September, 1942—

The Slovakian *Pravoslavnaya Russ* published an article by P. Perov describing the religious transformation in Russia during Communist rule. Religious attitudes are basically three: (1) the great mass of people who have retained their faith and under-

gone an inner renewal and deepening during persecution; (2) great numbers of apathetic; and (3) a small group of convinced atheists, or at least anti-church workers (*ICPIS*, No. 35, October, 1942).

September, 1942—

The Orthodox Metropolitan of Kiev, Nicolai, was appointed to the Soviet War Crimes Commission (*ICPIS*, No. 40, November, 1942).

October, 1942—

The Archbishop of Canterbury and Metropolitan Sergius exchanged fraternal greetings on the accession of Dr. Temple to the office of Archbishop and mentioned the unity of their peoples in the common battle against Fascist paganism (*ICPIS*, No. 41, November, 1942).

November, 1942—

A reliable observer reported that in Rumanian-occupied Russia, the Communists had some years previously encouraged the division of the Church into the old "Tyckon Church," the "Living Church," the "Revival Church" and the "Church of the Self-Consecrated." He noted that these groups had proved useful to the Government in dealing with the traditional Orthodox Church.

November 7, 1942—

Pravda published the following telegram from Metropolitan Sergius to Stalin:

"On the day of the twenty-fifth anniversary of the Soviet Republic, in the name of the clergy and believers of the Russian Orthodox Church, faithful sons of our country, I heartily and with prayer greet you personally as the leader appointed by God of our military and cultural forces. . . . Let God bless with success, and with glory your great deeds for the sake of our country" (Lauterbach, *These Are the Russians*, p. 272).

January, 1943—

In a letter to Stalin, Metropolitan Sergius stated the Church's intentions to collect funds for the "Dimitry of the Don" tank fund. On receipt of the church gifts for the Soviet Army, Stalin sent an appreciative message: the Orthodox Church was doing much to "stimulate patriotic feeling . . . and aid the effort against the common enemy." A total exceeding 300,-000,000 rubles was collected by the Church during the war (*Religion in Russia*, No. X, 1950, p. 5). Litanies were celebrated in Moscow for the liberation of Stalingrad. Churches were to participate in forthcoming holiday celebrations of the Red Army. (*New York Times*, January 5:7:2 and *ICPIS*, No. 6, February, 1943).

April, 1943—

The Roman Catholic-directed "Congregation for the Eastern Church" printed a liturgy, prayers and religious calendar in Russian corresponding to similar Orthodox publications, but omitting the names of certain Orthodox saints and substituting "Pope" for the "Holy Synod" in the prayers.

May 15, 1943—

The Communist Internationale was dissolved.

July, 1943—

A number of high church leaders faced expulsion for their pro-Axis sympathies (*New York Times*, July 2:7:4).

September 4, 1943—

Stalin received Metropolitan Sergius, who had just returned to Moscow from evacuation, with Metropolitan Alexei (Leningrad) and Archbishop Nicolai (Kiev and Galicia) (*ICPIS*, No. 31, September, 1943).

"Metropolitan Sergius informed (Stalin) that the authoritative circles of the Orthodox Church had the intention of convening in the near future a conclave of bishops for the election of a Patriarch of Moscow and of all Russia, for the establishment of a Holy Synod . . . Stalin then stated that on the part of the Government there would be no objection to this proposal" (*The Times*, September 6, 1943).

September 12, 1943—

Metropolitan Sergius, elected by the Holy Synod on September 9, was enthroned as Patriarch of Moscow and all Russia. International politicians interpreted the Government's sympathetic attitude as an indication of a turning from the defensive to offensive expansion in relation to international politics (*ICPIS*, No. 32, September, 1943). The Holy Synod was reestablished with five bishops and the Patriarch. It would not have a government-appointed chairman as in former times (*ICPIS*, No. 45, December, 1943). Russian emigrees declared the election invalid. Churches of Britain and other lands sent greetings and assurances of solidarity with the Christian people of the Soviet Union (*ICPIS*, Nos. 35, 36, 37, October, 1943). The Russian Orthodox Church appealed to all Christians of Allied lands "to unite in the Name of Christ for victory" (*New York Times*, September, 18:9:5).

On his return from Russia, the Archbishop of York, the first official church visitor since 1917, reported that churches were crowded, there was a growing spirit of tolerance, anti-religious propaganda had ceased, the Communist Party-favored "Living Church" had become a "dying church"; and that in view of the great need for young leaders, plans were being discussed for a theological training center. The *Patriarchal Journal* had resumed publication (*ICPIS*, No. 44, December and No. 37, October, 1943).

September 19, 1943—

The Council of Orthodox Bishops voted to excommunicate priests and laymen who aided the enemies (*New York Times*, September 19:45:4, 1943).

October 8, 1943—

The Council of People's Commissars decreed the formation of a committee to "see that the laws and regulations of the Government which concern the Orthodox Church are complied with." M. Karpoff was named chairman (*Dokumente zur Ordnung der Kirche*, unpublished).

October 30, 1943—

Plans of the Orthodox Church to send a delegation to Jerusalem, Antioch and Alexandria were seen by Western politicians as a Soviet move to widen its area of influence towards the Middle East (*New York Times*, October 30, 1943 3:1).

November, 1943—

Patriarch Sergius and other churchmen sent congratulatory messages to Stalin on the anniversary of the establishment of the Soviet State and pledged their support through the war and reconstruction periods (*IC-PIS*, No. 5, February, 1944).

December, 1943—

Yaroslavsky, deposed leader of the League of Militant Atheists and editor of its two publications, died. *Pravda* published an obituary stating, *inter alia*, that he "had devoted his whole life to the cause of the people" (*ICPIS*, No. 45, December, 1943).

January 8, 1944—

Orthodox plans for the eventual establishment of Orthodox theological seminaries were approved by the Holy Synod. Students, eighteen years of age or older, would be admitted on completion of regular studies. The curriculum would include social and political as well as theological studies. Rural priests would study two years in diocesan seminaries, city priests three years in an Orthodox theological institute in Moscow. Tuition would be provided by the Church (*New York Times*, January 8, 1944: 2:5).

February 2, 1944—

Izvestia accused the Vatican of pursuing a pro-Fascist policy since the conclusion of the Lateran Treaty (1929) and cited the report of the Foreign Policy Association (New York) on the Vatican's support of "Hitler's and Mussolini's Spanish adventures" and the African campaign (*New York Times*, February 2, 1944: 1:6).

April 5, 1944—

Orthodox clergy and laity gave another sum to the Red Army for the production of planes and other war materiel (*New York Times*, April 5, 1944:3:1).

Baptist and Evangelical churches formed a provisional union, to be finalized when circumstances would permit a general convention.

April 8, 1944—

Patriarch Sergius, in an article in the *Patriarchal Journal*, challenged the Pope's claim to be "Christ's vicar" on the grounds that no spiritual mediator was needed between Christ and His Church (*New York Times*, April 8:5:3).

May 13, 1944—

An American Roman Catholic priest, Rev. Orlemanski, after an interview with Stalin, reported that Stalin would not exclude the possibility of friendly relationships with the Vatican in order to combat the coercion and persecution of the churches by the Nazis. The next day Orlemanski was suspended by his superiors (*New York Times*, May 13:4: 3; 14:34:2; 15:6:4).

However, shortly thereafter, Polish children in Russia were permitted to have Roman Catholic religious education by Roman Catholic priests; Bibles and prayer books were printed at government expense; Catholic chaplains were attached to (Russian) Berling's Polish Army Corps (Lauterbach, *These Are the Russians*, p. 277).

May 15, 1944—

Orthodox Patriarch Sergius died of apoplexy, aged 78 (*ICPIS*, No. 2, May, 1944). He had asked that Alexei, war-decorated Metropolitan of Leningrad, carry the responsibilities of his office until another election could be held (*New York Times*, May 16:21:3).

May 20, 1944—

Metropolitan Alexei was appointed by the Holy Synod as Acting Patriarch. He accepted the appointment. In an open letter to Stalin (*New York Times*, 21:31:1) he stated his determination to follow the policies of the late Patriarch Sergius, and to cooperate loyally with the State. He presented his suburban villa near Leningrad to the Red Army for orphans of army men. In a message to the clergy he wrote:

"Our Orthodox Church has ever shared her people's destiny . . . She will not desert her people today. She blesses with a heaven-sent blessing the forthcoming exploit of the whole people . . . and (her) blessings gave victorious force to the Red Army" (*Broadsheet*, August, 1944).

Russian Orthodox monks and nuns in Jerusalem indicated their readiness to submit to the authority of the Moscow Patriarchate (*New York Times*, May 19:8:2).

June, 1944—

Metropolitan Alexei conducted special services on the third anniversary of the war.

July 1, 1944—

The Government established a "Commission on Religious Affairs" to deal with Roman Catholic, Uniate, Lutheran, "Old Believers," Armenian Gregorian, United Evangelical/Baptist, Seven-day Adventists, Moslem, Jewish and Buddhist groups. Mr. Polyanski was named chairman of Evangelical groups. Only the Lutheran churches were represented in the Commission. The purpose of the Council was to receive requests from the churches which required government attention and to assist with maintenance and construction of churches, training of religious leaders, and contributions of the churches to the war effort. Twenty-five to thirty field representatives had been appointed, to be raised to one hundred, to deal with religious councils in the different soviets (*ICPIS*, No. 35, October, 1944).

July, 1944—

The Pope denounced a newly-formed "Communist-Catholic" movement in the Soviet Union.

July 8, 1944—

By government decree,
"All children born after July 8, 1944, outside of a registered marriage have no succession rights to the father's property and may not claim the father's name, and . . . he is not even liable for their support."
Divorce was to be granted only for reasons held by the courts to be serious (Pares, *Russia, Its Past and Present*, p. 210).

August, 1944—

M. Karpoff, Chairman of the Commission on Orthodox Religious Affairs, defined the functions of the Commission and the status and rights of the Orthodox Church. "Our purpose is threefold: (1) contact between Church and State; (2) preparation of laws and regulations *re.* Church problems, and (3) supervision to insure that all laws relating to the churches are faithfully carried out."
The Commission was to handle petitions for new churches. "We place absolutely no barriers to church expansion." Petitions were to be received regardless of the size of a "church." They were rarely refused, and then either because there was no building available, or too many churches already in the area, or too few people to maintain a church. Its work also included negotiating with the Church for the establishment of theological training centers, intervening on behalf of priests *re.* compulsory military service, and conferring with churches *re.* repairs and taxation of church property.
Regarding church status and rights, Karpoff stated that Orthodox priests were permitted to carry out religious propaganda in and out of churches.
"Priests may go to their parishioners and may engage in proselytizing work either in the Church or outside without any restriction except those placed upon any orderly citizen of USSR. They may go about church business wherever they wish . . . They may officiate in private homes if they so desire, may perform baptismal, marriage and funeral services in or outside churches.
"The Orthodox Church, being a private non-profit society, has all the rights possessed by every private society."
When asked about the Church's role in post-war reconstruction, he replied,
"At present we are mainly concerned with the role of the Church in achieving victory. The other question seems somewhat distant" (*New York Times*, August, 12:13:3; 18:6:6).

September, 1944—

In reply to a Religious News Service query, Karpoff stated:
"Under our laws, each person may or may not teach his children religion. However, religion may not be taught in schools. Parents may educate their children themselves in their homes or may send their children to the priests. Children may also gather or be gathered in groups to receive religious instruction."
He declared that there was no ban against printing and distributing religious propaganda.
"In fact we have given explicit permission for the Church to order any quantity of Testaments, prayer books and liturgy books, and are ready to facilitate this step in every way, even to the extent of making representations to the paper rationing authorities" (*New York Times*, September 15:5:2).

The Orthodox Theological Training Seminary at Monastery Novo Devichi near Moscow was re-opened (*ICPIS*, No. 31, September, 1944).

Russian education authorities expressed their dissatisfaction over the "all too great tolerance shown to reviving religious life in the Soviet Union. No one should be persecuted for his religious beliefs . . . but religious belief is an error which can be rectified by an enlightened form of education" (*ICPIS*, No. 39, November, 1944).

October, 1944—

Evangelical Christians, Baptists and Pentecostals formed an alliance to further their common interest and to deal with the Government's Commission on Religious Affairs. M. Polyanski, Chairman of the Government's Commission, stated that Roman Catholic churches have the same rights as all other churches and may communicate with the Vatican so long as they deal only with purely religious matters. Religious instruction could not be given inside a church as "this would be against our established laws, which maintain that the church is given to the congregation for prayer purposes and no other." He added that there were sufficient Russian Roman Catholic priests and no foreign priests were needed (*New York Times*, October 3:12:5; 4:8:7).

October 7, 1944—

With the submission of "Metropolitan" Vvedenskii, the *Patriarchal Journal* announced that the leaders of the "Living Church" had openly repented and been re-admitted "to their former rank of priests in the Orthodox Church" (*ICPIS*, No. 36, October 1944; Bolshakoff, *Russian Nonconformity*, p. 161). The "Living Church" disappeared.

October 10, 1944—

Orthodox church officials in Moscow and Tula were awarded USSR medals for their part in the defense of Moscow (*New York Times*, October 10:8:3).

November, 1944—

Thirty-nine Orthodox bishops met and agreed to convoke a council for the election of a new Patriarch in January, 1945. Patriarchs and delegates from other Orthodox Churches were to be invited (*ICPIS*, No. 1, January, 1945).

The Soviet Government sent representatives to the funeral of Msgr. Szepticki, head of the (Roman Catholic) Uniate Church, Lwow. Szepticki had once appealed to Orthodox Churches of the Ukraine to break with Moscow and unite with the Uniates (*ICPIS*, No. 41, November, 1944).

December, 1944—

Twenty-three priests of "Sub-Carpathian Russia," once under the Ecumenical Patriarch and later the Serbian Patriarch, petitioned the Moscow Patriarchate to come under its jurisdiction. A delegate sent to Moscow was received by the Government's Commission on Affairs of the Russian Orthodox Church and by Acting Patriarch Alexei and the Holy Synod (ICPIS).

February 1-5, 1945—

The Council of Orthodox Bishops elected Metropolitan Alexei Patriarch of Moscow and all Russia. Archbishop Germanos of Thyateira and representatives of other Orthodox Churches abroad were present. The President of the Religious Affairs Council praised the great role of the Russian Orthodox Church in the history of Russia, and promised "liberty of conscience" as guaranteed in the Constitution. The enthronement was radioed to all Russia, and the liturgy conducted in Greek and Russian. Ten thousand attended. A message was sent to the Government:

"We send our first greetings to the Government and to the highly-honored J. Stalin and our thanks to the Government for its aid to the Church . . . The Church prays for the speediest victory of the USSR . . . over the enemy and for the successes of the Red Army which is led and inspired by the great leader, Marshall Stalin" (*Christian Century*, September 6, 1950, p. 1046).

The Articles of Church Organization were approved and published. They indicated

(1) that separation of State and Church was an accepted fact,

(2) that no Sobor or Council may meet without Government permission,

(3) that the churches have self-administration and election in the dioceses, with Government assent,

(4) that congregations must have a minimum of twenty members,

(5) that the Government provides churches with religious equipment.

(6) that churches may receive voluntary contributions for support,

(7) that embezzlements must be reported by bishops to the Council (Appendix XV).

By two special decrees, the central Government had assisted in restoring ancient shrines and some churches. One-half the Church property confiscated in 1932 was returned by the Government to the Orthodox Church, including 300 churches.

Two dioceses near Moscow organized theological training seminaries. Similar requests "will be received with sympathy" by the Soviet Council for Orthodox Church Affairs (*ICPIS*, No. 2, January, 1945; 23, June, 1945).

Izvestia published a pastoral letter of Patriarch Alexei. The letter deplored the spreading of "Godlessness" and called for the restoring of church traditions, customs, wedding, baptism and confession; it noted the corruption of certain clergy, the renewal of religious interest during the war, the reunion of most non-conformist groups with the Orthodox Church.

The Orthodox Church Council simultaneously published a message to Christians all over the world condemning those pleading for mercy and pardon for Fascists "who dare call themselves Christians" (*ICPIS*, No. 7, February, 1945).

February, 1945—

Patriarch Alexei hailed the Yalta Conference as an assurance of peace (*ICPIS*, No. 8, February 1945).

Permission was given to the Armenian Church to call an assembly for the election of the Senior Catholicos, an office vacant since 1938. Representatives were to be invited from various parts of the world (*ICPIS*, No. 8, February, 1945).

An Orthodox delegation visited Orthodox communities in Egypt, Syria, and other Mid-Eastern countries (*ICPIS*).

February-March, 1945—

The Roman Catholic publication *Action* accused Stalin of planning to use the Orthodox Church as an instrument for political expansion. In reply, Ilyin criticized the Roman Catholic Church for its political meddling. The Vatican which had had no diplomatic relations with USSR since 1917 was said to be seeking the right to deal with religious matters in USSR-occupied territory in East Central Europe (*New York Times*, Feb. 13-11:1; March 11:28:6; 22:16: 6).

March, 1945—

A Russian university dean praised the neutrality and openness of the Soviet educational system on matters of religion and faith. Christianity was studied in relation to its services in promoting art, "the noble principle of love, equality and brotherhood" and Reformation advances. Materialism, however, was presented as another step forward just as monotheism once was. The existence of God was not denied, but rather the policy was to be agnostic and let students decide for themselves. Owing to the shortage of public buildings, the dean said, one-third of the buildings formerly belonging to the Church were held by the State, one-third by the Church, and one-third by atheistic societies—all with equal rights. The Government permitted no propagation of beliefs in neutral public buildings, in general publications or among youth groups (*ICPIS*, No. 11, March 1945, App. XVI).

April, 1945—

Stalin received the temporary leader of the Armenian Church (*ICPIS*, No. 23, June, 1945).

April 7, 1945—

In reply to a request from Russian (emigree) Orthodox leaders in America, Canada and Alaska that they be given authority to establish an autonomous church, Patriarch Alexei stated that this could be done only on condition that they abstain from criticism of the Soviet Union's political activities (*New York Times*, April 8:25:4).

April 11, 1945—

Patriarch Alexei conferred with Stalin on Church affairs (*New York Times*, April 12:4:1).

May 5, 1945—

The USSR Government released a film on the election and coronation of Patriarch Alexei (*New York Times*, May 5, 1945, 7:6).

May 13, 1945—

Patriarch Alexei called on Orthodox churches to support the Soviet Government in its efforts for peace (*New York Times*, 13:15:8).

The Patriarch sent a church delegation to visit Orthodox churches in Bulgaria, Rumania, Yugoslavia, Albania and Syria (*ICPIS*, No. 34, September, 1945).

July, 1945—

An Orthodox Church delegation to Britain reported that no inter-church aid would be needed in the Soviet Union since the churches would have the assistance of the Soviet Government (*ICPIS*, No. 26, June; 27, July, 1945).

August 15, 1945—

By special Governmental decree, Orthodox churches would be permitted to build, buy or rent buildings with Government consent, and to own, manufacture and transport articles of worship. Permission was given to ring church bells again.

August 3, 1945—

Pravda severely criticized the Vatican for its anti-USSR campaign (*New York Times*, August 3, 1945:2:6).

September, 1945—

The Holy Synod named Metropolitan Eulogi, Paris, as Exarch of the Patriarchal (Moscow) Church in West Europe. Bishop Seraphim was confirmed as bishop (formerly from the Karlovci emigree anti-Moscow synod) and submitted to the authority of the Moscow Patriarchate. He condemned Orthodox schismatics and hoped for the day when all Russian Orthodoxy would be reunited under the Moscow Patriarchate.

Patriarch Alexei sent a "last appeal" to Bishop Anastasi, leader of the anti-Moscow emigree group to recant of his heresy and sins and rejoin the Patriarchal Church (*ICPIS*, Nos. 32, 33, 36, September, October, 1945).

Patriarch Alexei invited anti-Communist Bishop Dionysius of the Serbian Orthodox Church in America to come to Russia for a personal interview to discuss certain religious questions *re.* the Serbian Church. In his reply, Bishop Dionysius criticized Alexei for decorating priests in the Serbian Church via the political regime rather than through appropriate church channels, and accused him of interfering and seeking the subjection of the Serbian Church (*ICPIS*, No. 47, December, 1945).

November, 1945—

The Government placed a printing press at the disposal of the Orthodox Church for printing Bible and theological literature.

Ten seminaries were functioning; two Orthodox academies were to open. The Orthodox Church had 30,000 parishes, 89 dioceses, 87 convents (according to the Metropolitan of Kiev).

The Religious Affairs Commission published a denunciation of Nazi destruction of churches as "mocking the religious sentiments of men."

The Government announced that the clergy might vote in the February elections and might hold office in the Supreme Soviet.

Uniates of the Ukraine addressed a plea to the Government to release their bishops and priests, and to permit self-government instead of government by an Orthodox "Committee for the Union of Uniates to Orthodoxy." They requested the right to practice constitutional freedoms. Uniate bishops of former Polish and Czech territory had been deported eastward.

Archbishop Alexei of Rostov, sent by the Patriarch to confer with Russian Orthodox in America, reported that there was complete church freedom in the Soviet Union (*New York Times*, November 28:25:2).

American (Russian) Orthodox decided to postpone until 1947 a decision on the Moscow Patriarchate's request that they become subordinate to the Patriarchate (*ICPIS*, No. 7, February, 1946, and others).

December, 1945—

The autocephalous Orthodox churches of Estonia confessed their "guilt" of schism in separating from Moscow under German occupation and were accepted again under the jurisdiction of the Moscow Patriarchate (*Journal of Moscow Patriarchate*, No. 4, 1945; *ICPIS*, No. 12, 1946).

January 1946—

A delegation from the Orthodox churches in Czechoslovakia visited

Moscow and sought acceptance under the jurisdiction of the Moscow Patriarchate (*ICPIS*, No. 3, January, 1946).

Roman Catholics, Protestants and other religious groups related to the Government's Commission on Non-Orthodox Religious Affairs reported enlargement of their publication and training facilities. The Government was showing "benevolent tolerance" towards religion, two-thirds of the population were declared "believers" (*ICPIS*, No. 4, January, 1946).

In the first two issues of 1946 of their joint monthly publication, *Bratskij Vestnik*, the Council of United Baptists, Evangelical Christians and Pentecostal Churches reported that the federation of the three churches achieved in October, 1944, had "proved historically right, that God has blessed it . . ." Fifty elders were nominated as "trustees" and traveled about the Soviet Union organizing churches and ministering to the people. About 2000 churches existed in the Soviet Union as compared with 500 before 1917. The Government made building materials available for new churches.

Visitors to the Soviet Union reported that churches were full, with a majority of women, some soldiers and youth, many children. In rural areas about two-thirds of the people attended church. Pastors and priests could give private religious instruction to children if so requested by the parents (*ICPIS*, No. 17, April, 1946).

Roman Catholic churches were publishing literature in the Baltic republics (*ICPIS*, No. 4, January, 1946).

A new type of priest and bishop was seen in the person of Archbishop Luka of Tambov, who was not only a church statesman, but also a medical professor and consultant surgeon to military hospitals in the Tambov area. He received the Stalin award for developing new surgical methods (*ICPIS*, No. 12, March, 1946).

February, 1946—

The meeting of the General Council of the Armenian Church was filmed by the Government. The Chairman of the Commission on Religious Affairs brought greetings from the Government to the Council.

The Russian Soviet Republic exempted church monasteries from taxes on buildings and lands. Other republics were expected to grant similar exemption. Eighty-nine monasteries and convents were reported operating (*New York Times*, February 23:7:6).

March, 1946—

Orthodox monks in Finland confessed themselves guilty of schism in separating from the Moscow Patriarchate, and were admitted again under Moscow jurisdiction (*ICPIS*, No. 11, March, 1946).

March 1, 1946—

Pravda accused the Vatican of following a pro-Fascist, pro-Nazi policy during the war. The Catholic Church had cooperated with Fascist regimes in Africa, Greece, Albania, Croatia, Spain, France, and Hungary. The Vatican denied *Pravda's* charges, and denounced the USSR for its pact with Germany in 1939 (*New York Times*, March 1:11:2; 5:4:6; 2:2:1; 7:11:3).

March 8, 1946—

The General Council of the Uniate Church (about five million people in Western Ukraine, Ruthenia) meeting at Lwow denounced the Vatican and requested admission into the Orthodox Church under the Moscow Patriarchal jurisdiction. A letter was addressed to Stalin thanking him for the re-union of the Ukrainian people. The Council had been called by three Government-appointed priests who served as temporary head of the Church during the absence of its imprisoned bishops. The Uniates were brought under Vatican administration from the Orthodox faith in 1596 (*ICPIS*, No. 12, 13, March, 1946).

April, 1946—

An all-time high was reported in attendance of believers at Easter celebrations (*ICPIS*, No. 19, May, 1946).

May, 1946—

Patriarch Alexei was visited by Patriarch Nicodim of Rumania. Alexei returned the visit and went on to Bulgaria (*ICPIS*, Nos. 20, 25, June, 1946).

June, 1946—

Russian Orthodox in America announced that they would decide on the question of subordination to the Moscow Patriarchate at a meeting in November, 1946 (*ICPIS*, No. 26, June, 1946).

August, 1946—

Orthodox Bishop Seraphim (Russian) was appointed by Patriarch Alexei to succeed the late Metropolitan Eulogius as Russian Exarch of West Europe. Vladimir and other allegiants to the Patriarchate of Constantinople refused to acknowledge his appointment. The Patriarchate of Constantinople appointed Vladimir to succeed Eulogius. The Patriarchate of Moscow advised the Patriarchate of Constantinople of the appointment, and of the return of Russian Orthodox in West Europe to the Moscow jurisdiction and therefore of the cessation of Constantinople's authority and responsibility.

Bishop Seraphim appealed to Western Orthodox believers to return to the jurisdiction of the Moscow Patriarchate.

A delegate was sent to France by the Moscow Patriarchate. He described Russian piety in terms of separate areas of life, one of which is obedience to the Church, the other to the State. He added that all Russian Orthodox should be obedient to the Moscow Patriarch, the spiritual leader of the Russian people.

Chairman M. Karpoff of the Orthodox Religious Affairs Commission visited Orthodox churches in Prague.

September, 1946—

British visitors returning from the Soviet Union reported that the Government did not subsidize churches. Church support was provided by collections, donations and the sale of candles. The Government helped the churches by making building and worship materials available at State (minimal) prices.

Eight hundred thirty-seven church buildings formerly used for other purposes had been made available for Orthodox Church purposes since 1944.

Roman Catholics did not have direct relations with the Pope since, according to M. Polyanski, Chairman of the Council for Affairs of Religious Bodies, the Soviet Government did not have diplomatic relations with the Vatican State.

Anti-Soviet clergy had largely left USSR with the retreating Nazi forces. (*ICPIS*, No. 34, September, 1946).

October, 1946—

Evangelical churches made regular monthly collections for war orphans.

Orthodox churches collected for the blind.

Among Evangelicals, printing of their Protestant journal, the Bible, the New Testament, and hymn books continued. Thirty thousand converts were baptized in the first half of 1946 (*ICPIS*, No. 17, May, 1947).

Orthodox theological academies were opened in Moscow, Leningrad and Kiev (Of eighty new applicants to the Leningrad Academy and Seminary, fifty-two were accepted). The Moscow Orthodox Seminary celebrated its second year's work with eighteen graduates from thirty-six who had begun together. The Moscow Academy and Seminary had 161 students. At Leningrad, the students were exhorted "to announce the faith and be Christian patriotic citizens"; and at Moscow to give less room to human reasoning except in obedience to faith.

Patriarch Alexei denounced (Constantinople-appointed) Bishop Vladimir of West Europe and warned against plans to hold a separatist Russian Orthodox diocesan meeting in Paris. However, the meeting (of Anti-Moscow Russian Orthodox) was held and Vladimir was elected Exarch. The Patriarch of Constantinople was asked to give his blessing. The idea of subordination to Moscow was emphatically renounced. The Patriarch of Moscow announced that a delegation would be sent to Constantinople to settle the dispute.

Armenian Christians opened twenty additional churches. The Government erected a palace for the recently elected Catholicos. Thirty thousand Armenians were resettled in the Soviet Union from the Balkans and the Middle East (*ICPIS*, No. 40, November, 1946).

November, 1946—

The All-American Russian Orthodox Council acknowledged the Moscow Patriarchate as its spiritual head, but declared itself administratively independent from both the anti-Moscow Karlovci Synod and from Moscow (*ICPIS*, No. 46, December, 1946).

January, 1947—

Patriarch Alexei agreed to the American Russian Orthodox proposal to acknowledge the Moscow Patriarchate as its spiritual head and lifted the Patriarchal decree of suspension. A delegation was sent to America to draft an agreement to define the degree of administrative autonomy sought by the American churches (*EPS*, No. 7, February, No. 15, April, 1947).

Baptist churches were given permission to create new Baptist seminaries, to re-open a previously-established theological school and to print Bibles (*EPS*, No. 7, February, 1947).

March, 1947—

The Patriarch of Constantinople confirmed the appointment of Vladimir as Exarch for Russian Orthodox Christians in West Europe (*EPS*, No. 12, March, 1947).

An Orthodox Missionary Council attached to the Moscow Patriarchate was established to promote the expansion of Orthodox Christianity in the Soviet Union and the Far East and to deal with growing communities of Orthodox Christians in Hungary, Czechoslovakia, and other areas (*EPS*, No. 12, March, 1947).

April, 1947—

Patriarch Alexei received 105,000 gift Bibles and New Testaments from the American Bible Society (*EPS*, Nos. 13, 14, April, 1947).

American Orthodox leaders denied Roman Catholic Rev. Sheen's accusation that they were bound politically to Moscow. They stated that their connection with Moscow was no different from that of American Catholics to Rome (*EPS*, No. 15, April, 1947).

May, 1947—

A small group of Russian Orthodox in America broke away from those affiliating with the Moscow Patriarchate and joined the anti-Moscow Karlovci (Anastasi) Synod.

In France, Bishop Vladimir and his colleagues were denied clerical rights and orders under the Moscow Patriarchate because of their rejection of Moscow's authority and their subsequent affiliation with the Patriarchate of Constantinople (*EPS*, No. 25, June, 1947).

June, 1947—

In a new book, *Patriarch Sergius and His Spiritual Legacy*, the Moscow Patriarchate praised the separation of

Church and State as the only system which could ensure independent development for the Church, characterized Sergius' attitude towards the Soviet revolution as "standing for what is reasonable in the new, for the sake of justice." Russian Orthodoxy was seen as the new center of world enlightenment, being neither at the Protestant anarchic nor the Roman Catholic despotic extremes. The hour was not far off, said the book, "when the light of Christianity shining from the Orthodox East will light up the West." In the tradition of Patriarch Sergius the Church "wants to cultivate and uplift the particular gifts and characteristics of the people . . ." and the Government and people were sympathetic to the Church for that reason.

Fascism was called "an outgrowth of Protestant subjectivism." The Patriarchal Church would "oppose the individualistic principle with the principle of close unity" (*EPS*, No. 33, September, 1947).

Orthodox leaders were optimistic about the Government's attitude, considered conditions favorable for a Christian-Communism, and declared that the Church was regaining its influence on youth (*ICPIS*, No. 23, June, 1947).

Patriarch Alexei proposed holding a pan-Orthodox conference in September to discuss relations with the Vatican, the Orthodox attitude to the Ecumenical Movement, recognition of Anglican orders, relations with Armenian Gregorians, Syrian Jacobites, Ethiopian and Syrian Chaldean churches, canonical affairs, church calendar, etc. (*EPS*, No. 25, June, 1947).

September, 1947—

The proposed Pan-Orthodox Conference was postponed to the Summer of 1948. When other Orthodox churches objected to the Moscow Patriarchate calling such a conference, Patriarch Alexei replied that any autocephalous Patriarch had such a privilege and that Moscow was the only place at this time where freedom from political pressure for such a conference was assured by law (*EPS*, No. 33, October, 1947).

An Orthodox leader from Hungary, visiting Moscow, was named by Patriarch Alexei Administrator of Orthodox Churches in Hungary (*EPS*, No. 42, November, 1947).

Seminaries and academies established scholarship accounts and solicited contributions from the dioceses (*EPS*, No. 39, November, 1947).

October, 1947—

Following Stalin's authorization to transfer the remains of Moscow's patron saint to the Patriarchal Cathedral, Patriarch Alexei offered special prayers for Stalin, "our great and wise leader who is firmly piloting our country along the ancient holy road of power, greatness and glory" (J. Newman, Editorial, *New York Herald Tribune*, November 12, 1949).

The Communist Party's publication, *The Bolshevik*, identified the Roman Catholic Church as the bulwark of reaction, and a tool of capitalists who used the Church to form reactionary political parties with a religious label. Protestant churches were not used for political purposes because they were not centralized or authoritarian (*EPS*, No. 38, October, 1947).

When the *Bolshevik Youth* publication criticized a Comsomol meeting for forbidding members to attend Church services, to believe in God, or to observe religious rituals, the Comsomol publication, *Comsomol Pravda* replied that "a young person cannot be a member of Comsomol if he is not free from religious convictions . . ." The Central Committee of the Comsomol decreed that Communists may not go to church and reprimanded the *Bolshevik Youth*, whose position was "nothing less than an attempt to prove the possibility of compromising materialism with priestism and idealism. That necessarily means leaving Marxism" (*New York Times*, October 19:54:2).

November, 1947—

In his inaugural address as Rector of the Orthodox Theological Academy in Moscow, Bishop Hermogen characterized Western theology:

Roman Catholicism—a purely earthly, political organization interested in economic monopolies;

Protestantism — confusion resulting from arbitrary interpretation of the Scriptures;

Anglicanism—"vague theological conceptions, seeking to bridge Orthodoxy and Protestantism, (and) compromising both."

"Only the Russian Orthodox Church could show Christendom the way to authentic ecumenical Orthodoxy" (*EPS*, No. 7, February 20, 1948).

December, 1947—

The December issue of the *Bolshevik Youth* summed up the Kremlin attitude to religion:

"With the triumph of socialism in our country, the social roots of religion have been eliminated, but religious convictions exist in the form of survivals from the past in the consciousness of the backward and as a rule still inadequately educated and cultured persons.

"Although these remainders are withering away they will not disappear by themselves because within the country church leaders are trying to strengthen their religious influence over the backward part of our people and especially over the politically immature youths, taking advantage of any weakness in the training work of the Comsomol as well as other social and cultural organizations.

"The movement of our society forward to Communism requires a constant increase in the socialist awareness of the Soviet people and demands an intensified struggle against all survivals of bourgeois ideology and morals, including religious superstitions and prejudices" (*New York Times*, April 2:8:1).

The All-Soviet Society for Dissemination of Political and Scientific Knowledge was created as the successor to the League of Militant Atheists, dissolved in 1942 (*EPS*, No. 29, July, 1949).

Archbishop Makari, representative of the Moscow Patriarchate sent to America to confer with American Russians about their relationship to the Patriarchate, was opposed by the Americans on the issue of church subordination, namely, Moscow's insistence that the Americans could not call councils and elect bishops without the consent of the Patriarchate (*EPS*, No. 41, November, 1947).

1948—

Andrei Vyshinsky, in a book, *The Laws of the Soviet State*, summarized the current legal position of the Church law of April 8, 1929 and added:

"The State does not intrude in the internal affairs of organizations of

church folk. . . . Local soviets supervise the activity of religious organizations. Closing churches is appropriate only if the toilers themselves have
passed a directive concerning it"
(Barron and Waddams, *Communism
and the Churches*, p. 21).

1947-1948—

The *Great Soviet Encyclopedia* (Moscow, 1947, 100,000 copies) carried an
8000 word article describing "Religion
and the Church in the USSR." The
Russian Orthodox Church (prior to
the Revolution) was identified as the
tool of the Tsar, persecuting all other
faiths. Immediately after the Revolution of 1917, the "Reactionary elements" had to be suppressed for their
political activities and attempts to re-
establish the monarchy through international intervention. When church
leaders, according to the article, saw
that the masses were fully supporting
the Government, the leaders also came
to support the Government. The separation of the Church from the State
and of the school from the Church is
presented as the basic principle of
the Government towards the Church.
The All-Union Communist Party maintains its position to overcome religion
by "complete destruction of the connection between the exploiting class
and the organizers of religious propaganda, by promoting the effective liberation of the working masses from
religious prejudices and by organizing
scientific, educative and anti-religious
propaganda. Offending the feelings of
the faithful, however, should be carefully avoided as this would only strengthen religious fanaticism.
"Until religion dies out . . ." the
Soviet State not only guarantees
"freedom of worship," but assists religious communities with the necessary
facilities for worship. "The Soviet
State proceeds from the principle . . .
that the only concern of the Church is
worship. All propagandist, moralizing
and educative activities . . . should
not belong to the church . . ."
The article included a list of pre-
scriptions *re.* church organization and
functions, of the functions of the Council on Religious Affairs, and a description of churches in the Soviet Union
(*Religion in Russia*, No. X, YMCA
Press, Paris, 1950).

January, 1948—

Patriarch Alexei addressed an open
summons to American Russian Metro-

politan Theophilus and four other
American Orthodox leaders to appear
for trial before the Russian Orthodox
Council of Bishops for their canonical
insubordination and for breaking relationships with their Mother Church.
He appealed to Orthodox believers in
America to submit to his representative in America. Archbishop Makari,
the Patriarch's delegate to America,
stated that if the American Russian
Orthodox churches would submit to
the jurisdiction of the Moscow Patriarchate, they would be subject only to
orders not conflicting with U. S. civil
laws. The American Orthodox, however, who had agreed in 1946 to Moscow's "spiritual" authority, refused,
on the grounds that "submission" was
equivalent to allegiance to the Soviet
Union. Russian Orthodox in America
joined in establishing an independent
seminary (*EPS*, No. 3, January, 1948,
New York Times, January 11:29:3;
21:12:8).
The Vatican radio accused the
Soviet Government of persecuting
Catholics in former Polish territory
to force them to join the Russian
Orthodox Church (*New York Times*,
January 29:13:1).

March, 1948—

In an interview with a representative of Tass (Soviet News Agency)
Metropolitan Nicolai of Krutitsky
stated that the Russian Orthodox
Church had no desire to assume control over any aspects of the life of
sister Orthodox churches, neither the
Ecumenical Patriarchate, nor the Serbian, nor any other church (*EPS*, No.
9, March 5, 1948).

March 27, 1948—

Representatives of the Rumanian
Orthodox Church went to Moscow reportedly to confer with the Patriarch
concerning plans for the unification
of the Rumanian, Bulgarian and Yugoslavian Orthodox churches (*New
York Times*, March, 27:6:5).

April, 1948—

Orthodox Archbishop Luka of Crimea appealed to British and American Christians to thwart "the bloody
plans of their militarists" and warned them of the fate of conquerors under Hitler, Napoleon, and Biblical
war-lords (*EPS*, No. 16, April 23,
1948).

The lower clergy of the Orthodox Church were reported to be under pressure because of opposition to the higher clergy and the Government (*New York Times*, April 2:8:1).

May, 1948—

Patriarch Alexei, in an interview with a Western journalist, stated that the Church had the benevolent support of the Soviet Government and of Stalin, and that religious freedom was guaranteed by the Constitution (*EPS*, No. 21, May 28, 1948).

June 28, 1948—

Citing the statements of Marx, Lenin and Stalin, a *Pravda* article called for increased scientific education against religious faith (*EPS*, No. 29m July 23, 1948).

The Polish Government ordered the Orthodox Church in Poland to submit to the Moscow Patriarchate. A delegation was sent to Moscow and (in August, according to *New York Times*, June 11:12:3) an agreement was worked out, giving the Polish Church an "independent" status within the Moscow jurisdiction (*Religious Life in Poland*, p. 23).

July, 1948—

Leaders of Bulgarian, Yugoslavian, Rumanian, Georgian, Albanian, Czechoslovakian, and other Orthodox Churches, assembled for an All-Orthodox Congress on various ecumenical and international concerns, (a) denounced the Vatican, the "center of international intrigues against the people especially of the Slav nations," for seeking to "incite a new war," (b) dissociated themselves from the Amsterdam Assembly of the World Council of Churches, (c) characterized the World Council of Churches as "political, anti-democratic and non-theological," (d) appealed to Christians around the world to fight for peace and against war-mongers, and (e) agreed to a closer union among Orthodox churches, recognizing the leadership role of the Moscow Patriarch in achieving it.

Some outstanding delegates whose signatures appeared on resolutions of the Congress had neither signed nor given their assent to the contents thereof (*Proceedings of the Conference of the Heads of the Autocephalous Orthodox Churches*, YMCA Press, Paris).

According to the *Journal of the Moscow Patriarchate*, the Syrian Church (Jacobite Syrian Church of Malabar) of India applied to the Moscow Patriarchate and was accepted under its jurisdiction (*EPS*, No. 31, August, 1948).

August, 1948—

In an article in the *Red Star*, Prof. Tokarev demanded that the religious revival in USSR be stamped out (*New York Times*, August 19:13:3).

August 22, 1948—

Metropolitan Dionysius of the Polish Autonomous Church, "aware of the temporariness and canonic deficiency of the autonomy granted by the Patriarch of Constantinople in 1924," appealed to Patriarch Alexei for the blessing of the "Russian Mother Church" on the autocephalous status of the Polish Church (*Religion in Russia*, No. I, 1951, p. 4). Eighteen months later, the Patriarchs of Russia and Constantinople exchanged sharp words over this matter.

September, 1948—

An educator in Byelo-Russia called religion harmful to the Communist Party because it "fertilizes the soil" for hostile, anti-Soviet elements. "Why is it necessary to wage an increasing struggle with religious prejudices? We must do our utmost to emphasize that religious survivals in our country play a reactionary, harmful role . . . foster national antagonisms, violate the Communist conception of nobility of labor by encouraging monks, holy men, and other idlers and parasites" (*New York Times*, September 28:9:4).

A Bulgarian Orthodox church and religious center was established in Moscow as a gift of Patriarch Alexei "as an expression of considerable attention towards the Bulgarian Church" (*Tserkoven Vestnic*, September 21; *EPS*, No. 48, December, 1948).

The Moscow Patriarchate established a new religious periodical to present theological issues and works of the Russian Church.

In Vol. I, the Patriarch cited the solidarity of the Church with the Government during the war, and after victory . . . The Church "helps the Government and does its bidding." In all pastoral letters, the Church "exhorts (the people) to fulfill their duties as citizens . . . (interceding) for the God-protected and powerful Russian State, headed by its wise leader, whom Divine Providence has appointed to guide our country on the path of glory and well-being" (*EPS*, No. 22, June, 1949 and *EPS*, No. 41, October, 1948).

The Uniate Bishop of Lemberg, one-time advocate of union with the Moscow Patriarchate, was murdered. The Patriarchate fixed blame on an "agent of the Vatican" (*EPS*, No. 41, October, 1948).

October 15, 1948—

Bishop Hermogen, rector of the Theological Academy in Moscow, stated in his convocation address that the crisis in Christian thought arose from the new socialist order in Russia, and that two world wars and U. S. preparation for a third war called for a re-shaping of theology around the Orthodox Church. He denounced the Ecumenical Movement as fundamentally and politically unacceptable (*Patriarchal Journal*, No. 12, 1948; *EPS*, No. 17, April, 1949).

November, 1948—

The Russian Orthodox Church in Bucarest was re-opened with special services with Government officials participating.

A representative of the Russian Orthodox Church was installed in Jerusalem (*EPS*, No. 51, December, 1948).

The *Journal of the Patriarchate* carried a half page appeal to Russian Orthodox in the West, to prisoners of war and others to return to the Soviet Union, where jobs and shelter were assured . . . "the whole of the future now belongs to our powerful country . . . Do not believe the false propaganda with which you are fed."

The U. N. Assembly Commission included religious freedom in an International Bill of Human Rights. Article 16 stated:

"Everyone has the right to freedom of thought, conscience and religion; this right includes the freedom to change his religion, or belief, and freedom, either alone or in community with others and in public or private, to manifest his religion or belief in teaching, practice, worship and observances."

Soviet delegate Pavlov proposed that "religion" be deleted and provision made for religious services to be subject to the "laws of the country concerned and the requirements of public morality." He finally voted for the article because it "denoted a progressive approach, although inferior to the articles on religion of the Soviet Constitution" (*New York Times*, November 10:5:1).

November, 1948—

In the *Periodical of the Moscow Patriarchate*, Vol. II, 1948, Priest Levitsky praised Russia for saving the world during the war, and for presently saving the world through her representatives in the U.N. He attributed the attraction of sister Orthodox churches to Moscow as resulting from the brilliance of Christian light which draws "those of a progressive, democratic and Christian mind" (*EPS*, No. 13, April, 1949).

Roman Catholic Jesuit Szekalla, after a secret trip to the Soviet Union, reported that churches (Roman Catholic) were worshipping in caves, and that millions of Orthodox Christians were opposed to the official leadership of the Orthodox Church (*New York Times*, November 30:4:6).

January, 1949—

The Moscow Patriarchate dissolved its Exarchate of Central Europe. Archbishop Sergius was transferred from the former Viennese Exarchate to the Berlin Archbishopric. Austrian parishes were transferred to the West Europe Exarchate under Exarch Seraphim, Paris (*EPS*, No. 1, January, 1949).

Films of the 500th Anniversary of the founding of Moscow, of the Pan-Orthodox Congress (July, 1948) and of the transfer of allegiance of the Uniates in Soviet territory to the Orthodox Church were shown in the Soviet Union and the Balkans (*EPS*, No. 4, January, 1949).

The *Patriarchal Journal* charged that the Russian Orthodox priest, Dr. Kostelnik (formerly Uniate) had been assassinated by an agent of the Vatican (*New York Times*, January 9: 24:5). The Vatican denied the charges (*EPS*, No. 5, February, 1949).

The Vatican radio was jammed in Soviet territories (*New York Times*, February 6:40:6).

March, 1949—

The Union of Evangelical Christians (Baptists, Evangelical Christian, Pentecostalists) worked out a detailed constitution for their federation. Former "communities of prayer" became "churches." Three "types" of church were described by the Union:
(1) the universal, invisible, eternal congregation of the redeemed;
(2) the visible church, comprising many local churches, and commissioned to establish the Kingdom on earth;
(3) the "church in the home" (*EPS*, No. 4, January, 1949; *EPS*, No. 9, March, 1949).

Patriarch Alexei, on the occasion of a leftist "Peace" meeting in New York, appealed to all Christians to stop the war-mongers and "the spectre of a new war" (*EPS*, No. 14, April, 1949).

Pravda reprimanded the Communist youth movement, Comsomol, for its neutrality toward churchmen extending their influence among youth, and challenged the organization to uphold the doctrine of scientific progress "to which all religions stand in direct contradiction" and to improve its propaganda program. Another journal denounced a teacher for his reference to "religious science," quoting Stalin: that "the Party cannot maintain a neutral attitude as regards religion" (*EPS*, No. 21, May, 1949).

The Moscow Patriarch sent a delegation and its blessings to the World Congress of Partisans for Peace (Paris). The Russian Orthodox delegate's speech was said to have received a "thunderous applause" (*EPS*, No. 16, April, 1949).

May, 1949—

Soviet Baptists declined an invitation to send a youth delegation to the World Congress of Baptist Youth in Stockholm on the grounds that, as in the early Christian Church, they did "not distinguish between believers by age groups" (*EPS*, No. 19, May, 1949).

Orthodox Archpriest Rasumowsky (Moscow), in the *Patriarchal Journal*, No. 5, denounced the World Council of Churches as the "third Rome . . . feverishly trying to build up an organization so as to become a political power . . ." while Russian Orthodox Christians devote themselves to the "way of God's Kingdom" (*EPS*, No. 35, October, 1949).

In the *Moscow Patriarchal Journal*, No. 6, Mr. D. Krasheniunikov identified the Russian Orthodox Church with the great moral drive for peace, and accused Western Protestant and Catholic churches with meddling in non-spiritual affairs (*EPS*, No. 40, November, 1949).

The Stalinabad Communist publication called for a new drive against religion (*New York Times*, June 13: 2:3).

Government officials took over the Roman Catholic Church in Moscow which served Russians and members of the diplomatic corps (*New York Times*, June 3, 1949; *New York Herald Tribune*, November 12, 1949).

July 13, 1949—

The Vatican excommunicated Communists and any others aiding the Communists (*New York Times*, July 14:1:4).

July 22, 1949—

The *Soviet Monitor* condemned the Vatican as seeking through its excommunication decree to split the united front of people fighting for peace while at the same time supporting Western war-mongers (*Soviet Monitor*, July 22, 1949).

August 6, 1949—

Patriarch Alexei, in a statement in *Izvestia*, called the Pope's excommunication decree contrary to faith and declared that in the Soviet Union loyalty to the Church and to the Soviet Union were not in conflict (*New York Times*, August 7:19:1).

Roman Catholic Bishop Buchko declared that the Church had been liquidated in the Ukraine (*New York Times*, August 5:18:7).

October, 1949—

The *Patriarchal Journal* urged all Christians to unite for peace, and called on governments to solve their disputes through the U. N. (*New York Times*, October 7:5:1).

The Government published "selected works" of the 19th Century Christian educator Ushinsky with sympathetic comments and distributed copies to educators with a note that some points were not wholly in line with the present educational philosophy (*EPS*, No. 37, October, 1949).

November, 1949—

The Berne Legation of the USSR circulated copies of an article by J. Ibrahimov, "The Soviet Union, Land of True Freedom of Conscience." The author called churches in bourgeois states "handmaids of the ruling classes," whereas in the Soviet Union the majority of people rejected religion as a hindrance to development of their lives. Though the Government desired to liberate people from their medieval prejudices, it enabled religious organizations to exist in peace and guaranteed them facilities for defending their convictions publicly and for observing their customs. The similarities of Russian Orthodox Church convictions and the Soviet Government's policy simply reflected that both sprang from "trends and feelings current among the same people. All efforts to ignore these trends have, as experience has shown, ended badly for traitors to the cause of the people; they are driven forth from their midst by the faithful themselves." The Government asked of the Church only that it "not meddle in social and political activities." The Church is a private society with limited functions concerned solely with performing acts of worship . . . "All other undertakings, particularly in the social and political field, are plainly unsuited to the Church as a whole, and must therefore not be allowed" (*EPS*, No. 39, November, 1949).

November 15, 1949—

In a radio talk on "Science and Religion on the Origins of Man," Plitetsky stated:
"There will always be 'poor on the earth' teaches the Bible. Quoting the Holy Scriptures, the bourgeoisie is in a position to assert that class society is inexhorable and permanent, that the violation of the laws of a capitalist State is tantamount to the violation of the Holy Testament . . . The New Testament teaches man to bear without demur the misfortunes and burdens of his earthly existence—poverty, hunger, and persecution" (As quoted in Barron and Waddams, *Communism and the Churches*, p. 29).

November, 1949—

F. N. Oleschuk, of the Department for Agitation and Propaganda in the Communist Party Central Committee, formerly Vice-President of the League of Militant Atheists, in an article in *Science and Life*, called religion an anti-scientific, reactionary ideology and a hindrance on the path to Communism. He urged the All-Union Society for the Dissemination of Scientific Knowledge to conduct propaganda for atheism systematically and ceaselessly . . . toward convincing the masses, without adopting compulsion or prohibitions. "Capitalist encirclement," said Oleschuk, was continually trying to export religion into Russia, and many Russians were compromising the materialistic ideology justifying "their attitude by saying that the Church is fully loyal, fully Soviet." Others stated that the Government had changed its attitude. He called for a return to true Communism (Appendix XVI).

November 26, 1949—

In the *Uchitelskaya Gazeta*, Oleschuk wrote:
". . . The outstanding Soviet teacher, entrusted by the Party with the education of youth, cannot and must not be neutral to religion or assume a policy of non-interference, the position of a detached observer, in circumstances in which believers sometimes try to infect children with the poison of religious dope. A Soviet teacher must be guided by the principle of the Party spirit of science; he is obliged not only to be an unbeliever himself, but also to be an active propagandist of Godlessness among others, to be the bearer of ideas of militant proletarian atheism. Skillfully and calmly, tactfully and persistently, the Soviet teacher must expose and overcome religious prejudices in the course of his activity in school and outside school, day in and day out. The problem of the teacher is to educate the young generation in the spirit of Marxist-Leninist science, in the spirit of a materialist and truly scientific world outlook, which is incompatible with any religion" (As quoted in Barron and Waddams, *Communism and the Churches*, p. 32).

December 21, 1949—

On the occasion of Stalin's seventieth birthday, Orthodox leaders thanked him for "unrestricted freedom of worship and preaching" and for his "favorable consideration and cooperation" toward the Church (*Christian Century*, September 6, 1950, p. 1046).

A brochure, *The Origin of Religion*, was printed and distributed by the National Cultural Publishing House. In it, religion is identified as a hindrance in the development of science and enlightenment, involving principally ignorance, belief in a supernatural world, and primitive fear survivals in the forms of "charms, prophesies of sorcerers, fortune-tellers and other quacks . . . Advanced science has unveiled the nonsense of religious dogmas and rites—a savage inheritance."

"God is a phantom, born out of imagination of men subdued by natural forces and class oppressors. There is no God in a universe where everything is subject to unchangeable natural laws. In the hands of priests, god (small "g") is an empty vessel which they fill with any content they like, a variegated, many-faced puppet which they turn from one side to the other, according to their purposes . . . The whole history of humanity at every moment confirms the anti-popular and reactionary role of religion . . . as alcohol and opium . . . religion surreptitiously but surely intoxicates the mind of the popular masses, diverting them from the struggle for a real liberation, weakening their resistance against oppressors and exploiters, breaking their will to victory . . ." (*Religion in Russia*, No. II, 1951, p. 5).

January, 1950—

A new American Roman Catholic chaplain to the diplomatic corps was not permitted to conduct mass for Catholic foreigners in Moscow.

February, 1950—

Bolshevik published an article by Bagrov of the Communist Party accusing the Vatican of waging cold war against the governments of Czechoslovakia and Poland, and citing the Mindszenty case as the kind of spying and reactionary attitudes involved (*New York Herald Tribune*, February 7, 1950).

In the same publication (No. 3, 1950), in an article entitled "The Sacred Rights and Duties of Soviet Citizens," K. Molichev asserted that the Soviet Constitution not only proclaimed democratic liberties, "but assured

them . . . by certain material means . . . Freedom of conscience is assured by the fact that the Church is separated from the State and is recognized for all citizens" (*Religion in Russia*, No. X, April, 1950).

Orthodox Metropolitan Nikolai, President of the Patriarch's Office of Foreign Relations, during a visit to Slovakia reported that the Orthodox Church in USSR comprised 20,000 congregations, 70 dioceses and 90 monasteries (*EPS*, March 3, 1950). He stated that the Orthodox and Baptist churches "are endeavoring to surpass each other in mutual respect and love . . . (and) to find the most effective ways to help each other" (*EPS*, March 17, 1950).

March, 1950—

The Moscow *Literaturnaja Gazeta* denounced the World Council of Churches as a world center of religion set up by American imperialism to defend world reaction. The Bangkok Conference of the International Missionary Council and the World Council of Churches was denounced as an attempt by the American imperialists to restrain the liberation of Asian peoples via the churches (*EPS*, March 31, 1950).

A Comsomol (Communist youth) member, in reply to an enquiry as to whether he might marry his Christian fiancee in a religious ceremony, was told that such conduct would be an open violation of the (Comsomol) charter, opposed to Communist morals and that he should set an example to other youth who continue their religious prejudices and activities by converting his fiancee to Communism (*EPS*, May 26, 1950).

After subscribing to the resolutions of the Stockholm Congress of the Peace Partisans, Patriarch Alexei appealed to the heads of all Orthodox churches to be more active in the Church's fight for world peace. He proposed that Orthodox leaders meet to plan a program for peace work (*EPS*, April 7, 1950; *EPS*, April 21, 1950).

April, 1950—

In his Easter message, Patriarch Alexei stated:

"Beyond the boundaries of our homeland, which heads the movement for peace, extensive preparations for war are being conducted. . . . However, alongside the actions and utterances hostile to peace, the international struggle for peace is growing . . . and more and more millions of people are joining this holy struggle which, we believe, will end in victory" (*The Christian Century*, September 6, 1950, p. 1046).

April, 1950—

Easter services in Orthodox churches were well-attended. U. S. Roman Catholic Chaplain Brassard was unable to hold services for diplomatic personnel (*New York Times*, April 9:7:1).

May, 1950—

German technicians brought to the Soviet Union were able to arrange religious services in special chapels. Bibles, hymn books and other religious supplies were imported from Germany. Most services were conducted by lay preachers (*EPS*, June 9, 1950).

May, 1950—

Patriarch Alexei called the attention of the new Bishop of Tallinn (Esthonia) to "two phenomena in church life which are distressing bishops and doing notable damage to the Church:
"the tendency of numerous laity to assume power which does not belong to them in the Church" and "efforts of individuals to set themselves up, quite unrequested, as judges of their own pastoral shepherds." The bishop, "who cannot tolerate such monstrosities in the Church, has the duty to expel from the temple these crafty elements which have transferred their intrigues to the realm of the Church because they could not satisfy their vanity in the sphere of the State" (*EPS*, October 13, 1950).

June, 1950—

Rev. M. J. Deary asserted that the Soviet Government was training Communist agents in Roman Catholic rituals thus enabling them to gain the trust of the Catholic populace in Communist lands while posing as priests (*New York Times*, June 12:25:5).
In an interview with a Bulgarian Press Agency correspondent, Metropolitan Nikolai of Krutitsky stated that the Orthodox Patriarch of Constantinople was trying to revive the idea of papism in suggesting in an encyclical

to "all members of the Orthodox Church" that the Church of Constantinople was the Mother Church of all Orthodox churches and expected "obedience and loyalty of her children. . ." He named Jerusalem as the Mother Church, and minimized the title "ecumenical" formerly applied to the Constantinople Patriarchate (*Religion in Russia*, No. I, 1951, p. 2).

July, 1950—

Bolshevik published an article with the following statement:
". . . after the October Revolution the enemies of our homeland, the rapacious imperialists, with the utmost fury, used and are still using every means of struggle, among others, religion . . .; the warmongers, the Anglo-American imperialists, the Pope, the instigators of a new war, the American monopolists—pretenders to world domination—are quite prepared to use any means for attaining their aim, and among them Christianity as well as Islam . . .; the massive spy activity and the plots which have involved clergymen, disclosed at recent trials in the countries of popular democracy; is this not further proof that the clergy were, and still are, used as spies and subversive agents" (*Religion in Russia*, No. II, 1951, p. 3)?

July, 1950—

In an article entitled "Sin against the Mother Church," a *Patriarchal Journal* contributor warned Russian Orthodox in America that they would fall into "spiritual improverishment" and "sectarian isolation" separated from the Mother Church, and urged them to re-unite with the Mother Church, from which position they might become the nucleus for establishing an All-American Orthodox Church (*Religion in Russia*, No. I, 1951, p. 4).

July 2, 1950—

At a peace meeting of clergy in Czechoslovakia, Metropolitan Nikolai denounced the aggressive war preparations of the West and of the Vatican, and called on Christians to come "to overcome the evil of war. This, if we are not united, will cause us to be justly condemned by the non-Christian people . . ." (*Religion in Russia*, No. I, 1951, p. 13).

July 27, 1950—

A delegation sent by the Patriarch of Moscow to Damascus presented the Orthodox Patriarch of Antioch with gifts, the diploma Doctor of Theology *honoris causa*, and diploma of "Honorary Member of the Moscow Theological Academy" (*Ibid.*, p. 7).

July 27, 1950—

The Moscow Patriarchate consecrated a part-Russian Chinese as Bishop of Tien-Tsin (*Ibid.*, p. 7).

August 5, 1950—

Orthodox Patriarch Alexei, the Patriarch Catholicos of the Georgian Church, and the Patriarch Catholicos of the Armenian Church met and issued an appeal to Christians of the world regarding peace. The enemies of peace were identified as "seeking to camouflage their intentions by helping other nations on a large scale, to represent their treacherous purposes of aggression as measures of a united effort for defense."

The three Patriarchs called on the World Council of Churches as representative of the Protestant world and on the Anglican Church to give substance to their peace intentions by supporting the Stockholm Peace Manifesto (outlawing the atomic bomb; *EPS*, September 1, 1950).

Leaders of the Orthodox Church protested to the Security Council of the United Nations against "American aggression" in Korea and called for a cessation of war and withdrawal of foreign troops (*EPS*, September 8, 1950).

Science and Life, publication of the All-Soviet Society for Dissemination of Political and Scientific Knowledge (successor to the Godless Society which was dissolved in 1942) published an article asserting that religion would not die away of itself but that a "systematic, scientific atheist propaganda is the basic means of struggle against religious prejudices."

The struggle should be renewed, but "without sudden attacks and dictatorial measures, and without offending the feelings of religious persons" (*Current Digest of the Soviet Press*, Vol. II, No. 40, 1950).

Leningrad radio added that a large number of propagandists would be sent to all Soviet Republics with anti-religious films and that 29,000,000 pamphlets would be distributed. "The struggle against the Gospel and Christian legend must be conducted ruthlessly and with all the means at the disposal of Communism," said the Chairman of the Society (*New York Times*, August 29:19:6).

September 13, 1950—

The Archbishop of Canterbury (Britain) urged Christian churches to unite in the fight against Communism (*New York Times*, September 13:15:3).

September, 1950—

In its September issue, *Science and Life* denounced the Baptists, Evangelical Christians, Seventh-day Adventists and other "sects" as Western innovations, dominated by the bourgeoisie, and essentially anti-scientific and anti-social in spite of their casting off the religious "savagery" of ikons, worship of relics, etc. In the past the sects fought against industrialization, collectivization of agriculture, cultural advance and Communist education, but lately tried to reconcile Communism and Christianity, claiming Communism was a product of Christianity. *Science and Life* called such propaganda merely attempts to mask the reactionary substance of sect precepts and morality. The preaching of "love for all people" was lulling the vigil of the Soviet people. The "ideology of slavery, impotence, self-abasement and self-contempt was condemned, and the publication called for persistent, patient, and well-argued propaganda, inoffensive to believers, to overcome the "anti-scientific" reactionary ideology of the sects" (*Current Digest of Soviet Press*, Vol. II, No. 44, 1950).

The Pope urged all Catholic clergy to fight the evils of both Communism and Capitalism (*New York Times*, September 26:25:3).

October, 1950—

In an article in the *Bolshevik*, No. 19, October, 1950, S. Kovalev stated: ". . . Among the widespread survivals of the old capitalism which the educational work of the Party is aimed at overcoming is the survival of religion. The majority of Soviet people are free of religious prejudices. But these prejudices still cling. Moreover, in some instances in which appropriate educational work is not being carried on, these prejudices are becoming stronger. The U. S. S. R. Constitution guarantees freedom of conscience and freedom of anti-religious propaganda. The task of our propaganda and cultural enlightenment institutions is to step up scientific propaganda, inculcate the materialist world outlook, wage unremitting struggle against idealism, mysticism and any kind of obscurantism and expose the instigators of a new war, who likewise employ religion in their propaganda . . ." (*The Current Digest of the Soviet Press*, Vol. II, No. 44).

October 30, 1950—

Moscow radio reported that Baptist churches in the Soviet Union appealed to Baptists all over the world, and other Protestants, to protest American "aggression" in Korea and to support the Stockholm Peace Manifesto (*EPS*, November 17, 1950).

Rev. Zhidkov, head of the Baptist-Evangelical Council, expressed his indignation "that among the most rabid supporters of war" was Baptist Harry Truman, President of the United States (*Ecumenical Courier*, New York, November-December, 1950).

October, 1950—

The Orthodox Church published a volume entitled *The Russian Orthodox Church and its Part in the Struggle for Peace*, including numerous resolutions and speeches of church leaders. Patriarch Alexei is quoted:

"The Russian Orthodox Church, as bearer of the message of peace handed down to us from Christ Jesus, looks with grief upon the anti-Christian deeds of people who call themselves Christians, and are in reality filled with enmity for those who defend the cause of peace in faithfulness to the injunctions of Christ" (*EPS*, February 9, 1951).

November, 1950—

The Russian Orthodox (Karlovci) Synod outside the Soviet Union declared that the "Government-controlled" Church was not the real Russian Church and pointed to the persecuted Church of the underground as the "real" Church (*New York Times*, November 30, 9:6).

The Moscow Patriarchate's Exarch for West Europe sent a message of greeting to Russian and "Western Orthodox Christians" speaking other than Russian (*EPS*, December 1, 1950).

December, 1950—

The *Bolshevik* published extracts from Lenin's works including this statement from *The Significance of Militant Materialism*:

"The advance guard fulfills (its) purpose . . . only when it does not separate itself from the masses it is leading, but really leads this whole mass ahead. Without an alliance with non-Communists in the various fields of activity, any constructive Communist work is out of the question" (*Religion in Russia*, No. II, 1951, p. 2).

The "All-Soviet Society for the Dissemination of Political and Scientific Knowledge" distributed a brochure (75,000 copies) refuting the religious, "idealistic" idea of the origin of life as "fiction," and asserting that "life is nothing else than a particular form of the existence of matter . . ." which scientists might soon be able to reproduce synthetically (*Religion in Russia*, No. II, pp. 8, 9).

Summary of Religious Situation, 1951

Principal Christian Communions:

1. Russian Orthodox—headed by Patriarch Alexei and the Holy Synod.
2. Old Believers (Orthodox)
   Three branches:
   a. Bielokrinitsa (Priestist) Synod—Archbishop Irinarch.
   b. "Priestless."
   c. "Runaway Priests"—Archbishop John.
3. Georgian Orthodox Church—Patriarch Catholicos Calistratos.
4. Armenian Gregorian Church—Patriarch Catholicos George VI.
5. Evangelical-Baptist-Pentecostal—federated in the All-Union Council—President J. I. Zhidkov.
6. Lutheran Church—Augsburg Confession.
7. Small groups—Seventh-day Adventists, Methodists, Reformed.
8. Roman Catholic—Metropolitan Antony Springovitch, one archbishop, two bishops.

The "Living Church" no longer exists, nor does the "Josephite" or "Possessor" group. It is said that there is considerable mistrust, particularly among smaller groups, not so much on confessional as on political attitudes. There are apparently anti-regime as well as pro-regime extremes in each church. There is little exchange, theological or otherwise, between the confessional groupings, except on such matters as "Peace."

Ecumenical Relations:

The churches' possibilities of contact with churches abroad have depended very much on their ability to prove their loyalty at home. Roman Catholic churches have virtually no contact. Indeed, their allegiance has been so seriously suspect as practically to secure their liquidation. Protestants have occasional contacts with foreign visitors to the USSR. The Orthodox and Armenian churches have had relatively close relations with their own constituency and their sister churches abroad, particularly within the Soviet orbit. The Orthodox Church now has authority over dioceses, or church bodies in Czechoslovakia, Finland (monastery), West Europe, North America, Hungary, Jerusalem (Monastery), Ethiopia, Syria, and recently consecrated a bishop for China. There have been exchanges of delegations, literature, messages and planning. Other churches outside the Soviet orbit, whether Anglican, Lutheran or Quaker, are officially considered to be under the influence and control of "Western imperialists," and theologically illiterate. The World Council of Churches is looked upon as the agent of Western "Protestant" churches and therefore the agent of their political overlords—"friendly to the idea of war." The World Council's support of churches of the Russian emigration is strongly resented.

Church and State:

Separation of Church and State is an accepted principle. It is understood that the churches should not interfere in politics; the Government should not interfere with worship. Local soviets are permitted to help local churches.

The churches are expected to participate loyally in "Peace" appeals, both domestically and internationally. "Separation" has already, therefore, been interpreted in a liberal manner. Civil rights have been restored to the clergy; some hold political offices. Sunday is again a day of rest, and Christian feast days can be observed without too great difficulties. Materials for worship can be manufactured and sold on local markets. The Government's Commission on Religious Affairs helps the churches in relation to their material needs and their negotiations with civil authorities. Statistical records—marriage, birth and death—are kept by the State.

Church Buildings:

Pre-1917 church buildings are administered by the State. Roughly one-third are used for religious purposes, one-third for Government purposes, and one-third for cultural, anti-religious or social purposes. Buildings are made available to local congregations on the basis of a petition signed by twenty members, and the payment of rent and insurance premiums. The fact that local congregations are receiving Government help in securing building materials for church construction seems to indicate either that newly-built structures belong to the congregations or else that they have no objection to State ownership. Some 20,000 church buildings and chapels are being used by 30,000 Orthodox congregations, and 4,000 Evangelical communities have 3,000 churches.

Church Lands and Monasteries:

Orthodox monastic life, which was suppressed* and forbidden in 1929, has again been tacitly legalized. Ninety monasteries are in operation, and have been exempted from taxes on lands and buildings since 1946. Monks who had continued their vocation in secret can openly profess their vows. Many continue their itinerant life of service and evangelism as laborers, medics, repairmen. Nuns are openly assisting with family life, worship services and pastoral care. The Government has returned to the Orthodox Church one-half of the smaller properties confiscated in 1932.

Church Support:

Voluntary contributions and gifts for performing the sacraments are almost the sole support of the Church. People apparently are ready to give.

Theological Education:

Three Orthodox higher theological academies (Moscow, Kiev and Leningrad) and ten provincial seminaries are functioning relatively normally under church administration. Applicants are rather carefully screened by Church authorities, and a considerable number turned away. Students come with a real sense of Christian calling, and not for political or economic reasons. Baptist churches received approval for re-opening the former Baptist Seminary in 1947.

Church Leaders:

Among Orthodox, priests are often in civil dress. Higher clergy and bishops generally maintain their religious habit, although during recent years

---

* When the Semeonovsky Monastery of Moscow was blown up, cinemas recorded the event for showing throughout the country.

many have taken up lay professional work as well. The average age level of the (approximate) 5500 experienced priests is probably above sixty, with less than 1500 newly-ordained from the theological schools, or tutored privately by a bishop—a total of some 7000 as against a need seven times that great.

Among Protetsants, lay elders are ordained as pastors and missionaries, many combining official travels in connection with their professions with contacting isolated parishes and organizing congregations.

Youth:

Youth in general have been curious about superstitions, charms, and other metaphysical phenomena. Many are attracted to Christianity for its obvious morality, idealism and fellowship of love. Christian youth are assimilated in the congregations. Special activities probably do not go beyond choirs and an occasional service project. The "Christomol" (Orthodox youth), "Bapsomol" (Baptist youth), and student work in organized movements have been short-lived, recurring from time to time and from place to place, depending on local conditions.

Religious Education:

There are no parochial schools. Religious education may not be taught in schools or other public places, including churches. Where parental approval is given, religious instruction can be given privately by the clergy. Most effective instruction, however, is probably that given by parents or grandparents of children in the home, or in small, private groups in the atmosphere of the church.

Publications:

The Orthodox Patriarchate has its *Patriarchal Journal*, the monthly *Theological Messenger*, and annual religious calendars and occasional prayer leaflets. Local congregations occasionally publish small bulletins.

The Evangelical Union (Baptist, Pentecostal and Evangelical Christians) publishes its monthly *Bratskij Vestnik* (Brotherly Herald). In principle, the Bible can be published.

With the dissolution of the League of Militant Atheists and the creation of the All-Soviet Society for the Dissemination of Political and Scientific Knowledge, the emphasis on anti-religious propaganda has changed from anti-religion to pro-science. Two major distributions of brochures on science and religion have been made, the monthly *Science and Life* carries frequent articles on religion, as do also *Bolshevik, Comsomol* and other official publications. "Scientific" films and missionaries have been sent to many areas.

Evangelism:

Traveling monks and nuns, lay missionaries, priests and youth carry the Gospel to remote provinces as well as industrial centers. Singing has become an effective evangelistic medium. Small groups gather together in private homes or "houses of prayer," for worship, mutual encouragement, Bible study and the sacraments. More striking even than the way in which Christians make their witness, is the seeking and openness of non-Christians.

Since the war the Orthodox Church has established a missionary council and a department of foreign relations, but except for official visits of delegations to Orthodox communities abroad, there is too little evidence of its work for any comment.

Worship:

Worship has been and is the center of Russian religious life. Services, especially in rural areas, are well-attended. People desire the sacraments, and in remote villages gather quickly around transient clergymen. In the cities, there is a noticeable absence of early middle-aged and younger couples, especially young men, but school children, mothers and older people attend faithfully.

Family worship and use of icons in the home have increased. As under earlier Tsarist regimes, preachers are not free to criticize the State publicly. It is the more astonishing therefore that preaching of the Gospel is now a normal part of the worship service.

Through the years of struggle and reform, the Church—the State-Church, the powerful, possessing Church—has come again to the position of the "Non-Possessors" of the 16th Century. Yet in doing so, Christian people of Russia have not forsaken their heritage as a national entity, nor their sense of Divine Mission. It is the concept of the role of the Church in that mission which has become more sharply defined in relation to the (worldly) powerful Soviet State. The

"essence and purpose of life is re-discovered as the praising of God and trusting in His love . . . With wealth, prestige, earthly authority, even the teaching function removed, the Church not only survives but grows in power and influence. Stripped to the only elements permitted by law—conscience and celebration of the sacraments—the Russian Church makes bold to say that this is sufficient; the knowledge of God has been kept alive, and the power and love of God have been made manifest even to those who do not believe" (Anderson, *People, Church and State in Modern Russia*, pp. 35-36).

Appendix I

RESOLUTIONS OF THE CONFERENCE OF ORTHODOX CLERGY AND LAYMEN

June, 1917

In the Russian State, the Orthodox Church must hold, among other religious confessions, a place of priority, most favored in government and in public rights, as is fitting to her as the supreme sacred object of the people, of exceptional historic and cultural value, and also as the religion of the majority of the population. In harmony with the recognition, by the new governmental regime of Russia, of freedom of religious conscience and of confessions, the Orthodox Church must hold such freedom in all its fullness. These fundamental considerations should be expressed in the following principles: (1) The Orthodox Church in Russia, in matters concerning its structure, legislation, administration, courts, teaching of faith and morality, services of worship, internal Church discipline, and external relationships with other Churches—is independent of Government authority (autonomous). (2) Resolutions issued for itself by the Orthodox Church in accordance with order established by herself, will be recognized by the Government as the norms of law having, from the moment of their publication by the Church, obligatory meaning for all persons and institutions belonging to the Orthodox Russian Church, whether in Russia or abroad. (3) The actions of organs of the Orthodox Church are subject to supervision by the Government only in regard to their corresponding to the laws of the State: furthermore, these organs are responsible to the Government only through court procedure. . . . (10) The twelve Great Holidays, Sundays and the days especially honoured by the Orthodox Church are recognized by the Government as holidays. (11) The head of the Russian State and the Minister of Confessions must be Orthodox. (12) In all moments of State life where the Government turns to religion, the Orthodox Church shall be preferred . . . (17) The Orthodox Church shall receive from the State Treasury annual subventions in the amount of its actual needs, under condition of accounting for amounts received in due course.

(As quoted in Anderson, *People, Church and State in Modern Russia*, p. 41)

Appendix II

PASTORAL LETTER OF PATRIARCH TIKHON

January 19, 1918

"May the Lord deliver us from the evil spirit of the times."

The Holy Church of Christ in Russia is at present passing through a time of trouble. Persecution has been set up against the Christian Truth and the confessed and secret enemies of this Truth are endeavoring to destroy the work of Christ and are everywhere sowing the seeds of anger, hatred and destructive accusations instead of brotherly love.

The forgotten and downtrodden sermons of Christ on the love to our neighbour: We daily receive news of the terrible and beast-like murders of perfectly innocent and bedridden people, guilty only in having performed their duty towards their country honestly, and that they only applied their strength to the service of their country's welfare. And all of this is carried out not only under cover of the night, but in daylight, with heretofore unheard-of impudence and unmerciful severity, without any legal hearing and with abrogation of all rights and law—all of this is being practiced during our time in almost all of the cities and throughout all of our land in the capitals and in the far distant districts (Petrograd, Moscow, Irkutsk, Sebastopol, etc.).

All of this fills our heart with deep sorrow and forces us to turn to such outcasts of the human race with threatening words of accusation according to St. Timothy I. 5-20: convict him who is guilty before all that the people may take warning.

Come to yourselves, ye idiots, cease your bloody deeds. Your deeds are not only cruel—these acts are in reality the work of Satan, for which you are subject to everlasting fire in the life to come after death and the terrible curse of posterity in the present life on earth. By authority given us by God, we forbid you to approach the holiness of Christ, we excommunicate you if you still bear the name of Christian, and in accordance with your birth belong to the Orthodox Church. We exhort you all true believers in the Christian Orthodox Church not to enter into communication with such outcasts of the human race (1 Cor. V. 9-13).

The severest persecution has been against the holy Christian Church. The blessed sacrament illuminating the birth of man into the world or blessing the marriage ties of the Christian family—these are openly declared unnecessary, useless; the holy edifices are subject to destruction by gunfire (Cathedrals, Moscow Kremlin) or are subject to loot and scoffing or degradation (Chapel of the Saviour in Petrograd). The holy residents of the cloisters, honoured by the believers, are seized by the ungodly dark powers of this age (Alexander Nevsky and Pochaevskaya Cloisters). The schools supported by the means of the Orthodox Church for the education of priests of the Church and teachers of the Faith are declared unnecessary and are turned into schools of non-believers or into institutions of immorality.

The property of monasteries and churches is confiscated under the pretext that it forms national property, but without any process of law, and even without the wish to consider the legal right of the people, and finally this power having promised to establish Law and Justice in Russia, to secure freedom and order, manifests only everywhere its uncurbed will and complete violence over all, and in particular over the Orthodox Church. Where are the limits to this blasphemy against the Christian Church? How and by what means can this attack against the Church by her furious enemies be stopped?

We call all of you believers and true sons of the Church; place yourselves for the defense of our insulted and oppressed Holy Mother. The enemies of the Church seize the power over her and her property by force of deadly weapons, but you revolt against them by the power of your faith and the strength of your voices as a nation which will stop the madmen and will show them that they have no right to call themselves defenders of the national welfare, builders of the new life by authority of the public understanding, as they act directly against the public conscience.

Even if it should be necessary for the cause of Christ, we call you, beloved children of the Church, we call you to these sufferings with ourselves in the words of the holy apostle (Romans VIII. 35). And you, beloved brethren, Archbishops, Bishops and priests, not losing an hour or a minute in spiritual labours, with strong faith, call your children to the defense of the downtrodden rights of the Orthodox Church, without loss of time arrange spiritual unions, call them to your aid not by compulsion but of free will to enter the ranks of voluntary spiritual fighters, who will place against the inner powers the strength of their own spiritual forces, and we are firmly convinced that the enemies of the Church of Christ will be shamed and scattered by the force of the cross of Christ, as it is inevitable to avoid the promises of the godly crossbearer (Matthew XVI. 18).

Tikhon, Patriarch of Moscow and all the Russias.

(As quoted in Anderson, *People, Church and State in Modern Russia*, pp. 53-55)

Appendix III

DECREE DEFINING CHURCH AND STATE RELATIONS—1918

1. The Church is separated from the State.

2. Within the Republic it is forbidden to issue any kind of local laws or resolutions which would restrict freedom of conscience, or to grant privileges or advantages of any kind which are based on the religious confession of the people.

3. Every citizen has the right to profess any or no religion. All legal favours or discrimination connected with any kind of faith, or non-faith, are herewith cancelled.

Note: All reference to any kind of membership of a citizen to a religious community, or of his non-membership, will be omitted from all official documents.

4. All acts of the state or similar official acts may not be accompanied by religious rites or ceremonies.

5. The unhindered practice of religion is permitted so long as it does not interfere with the general order or encroach upon the rights of citizens of the Soviet Republic. Local authorities have the right in such cases to take all necessary measures in order to ensure the public order and safety.

6. Nobody may refuse on the basis of his religious conviction to fulfill his national duties. Local People's Courts may make exceptions if in place of one national duty another one is fulfilled.

7. All religious vows and oaths are abolished.

(Later addition: If necessary merely a solemn promise may be given.)

8. Civil documents may only be issued by civil authorities, viz., by the authorities for the registration of marriage and births.

9. The school is separated from the Church.

Religious instruction in state, public schools, or private institutions where general instruction is given, is not permitted. Soviet citizens may give and also attend religious instruction privately.

10. All church and religious groups are subject to the general rules for private groups and organizations and are not allowed to accept any kind of privileges or assistance either from the State or from local autonomous or independent institutions.

11. Collection by force of fees and taxes by the church or religious communities is not permitted.

12. No church or religious association has the right to possess any kind of property.

(Later addition: Such communities do not have the rights of a juridical person.)

13. The entire property of the churches and religious associations in Russia is herewith declared to be the property of the people. The buildings and worship materials are lent to the religious groups free of charge by the local or central state authorities.

(Later addition: and do not have to pay contributions.)

Note: This law was first only applied to the Greater Russian Republic, but soon was accepted by all other Soviet Republics: in the Ukraine on January 22, 1919; in "White" Russia on February 4, 1919; in Georgia on April 15, 1921; in Armenia on November 26, 1922. In the smaller Republics no separate laws were issued, the Great Russian Law was applied everywhere.

(O. Fjodorow, *Die Religion in der USSR*)

Appendix IV

INSTRUCTIONS TO THE ORTHODOX CHURCH AGAINST GOVERNMENT ACTS

February 28, 1918

The new conditions of Church life demand of Church workers, especially local ones, extraordinary care and unusual efforts, in order that requisite spiritual work may be carried on with good success, regardless of the obstacles to be met and even persecution. The Holy Assembly and Holy Patriarch direct the general method to be followed at the present time by the spiritual pastors; inviting them to independent action under the present difficult conditions and cautioning against possible erroneous action on their part, propose the following instructions:

Call to the Priests:

1. Priests are invited to be strictly on guard in protecting the Holy Church in the heavy years of persecution, to encourage, strengthen and unite the believers, for the defence against attacks on the freedom of the Orthodox Faith and to strengthen the prayers for the enlightenment of the doubting.

2. The priests should encourage the good intentions of the believers directed towards the defence of the Church.

Organizations of the Church:

3. Parishioners and worshippers of all parish and other churches should be organized into united societies whose duty it shall be to defend all the sacred things and other church property against violation.

4. These organizations must have an educational and charitable character as also a name, and can be presided over by a layman or priest; but should not be called either church or religious societies, as all church and religious societies are by virtue of a new decree deprived of all legal rights.

5. In extreme cases these societies can declare themselves the owners of church property, in order to save them from seizure at the hands of the non-Orthodox or even those of another faith. Let the Church and church property remain in the hands of the Orthodox believing in God and devoted to the Church.

6. The Superiors, sister superiors and brothers of monasteries, hermitages and resting-houses to be appointed by similar united societies from among local residents and regular worshippers of the parish and all loyal parishioners.

7. The principals and teachers in church educational institutions shall establish relations with the parents of the pupils and the employees of the united societies for the protection of educational societies from seizure and guarantee of their future activity for the benefit of the Church as also the well-being of the Orthodox people.

8. These societies must firmly demand and endeavor by all means to ensure that the situation in the educational institutions should remain strictly intact until further orders of the church authorities.

9. Teachers of religion in the non-ecclesiastical educational institutions should by all means in their power extend their influence over the councils of educators and parents so that they may firmly defend the instruction of religion in educational institutions and co-operate with every new effort of the same for the benefit of religious training and education.

10. The removal by force of the clergy and members of the parish or monks from the monasteries should under no circumstances be permitted. In case of forceful removal, by the congregation or other persons, of the clergy from the posts occupied by them, the diocesan authority does not fill their places and demands the reappointment of those removed to their former posts, as also the re-establishing of their rights. Every interference with a priest or member of the parish should be reported to the Church authorities, which alone have the authority, after investigating the matter, to remove priests, church employees from the parish congregation.

11. If it should be established that the forceful removal was due to the request of any member of the clergy, the guilty person is subject to an episcopal tribunal and strict punishment, denied the right of clerical duties and is expelled from the clergy.

12. Church vessels and other appurtenances of the church service should be protected by all possible means against desecration and destruction, and for this reason should not be removed from safe depositories, and the latter should be constructed in such a manner that they could not be easily opened by robbers.

13. In case of attempted seizure of church vessels, appurtenances of the church service, church registers and other church property, the same should not be surrendered voluntarily, inasmuch as (a) church vessels and other appurtenances of church service are blessed for church use and the congregation should not even touch them, (b) church registers are indispensable for church uses, and the secular authorities, if in need of same, should see to the preparation of them themselves, (c) church property belongs to the Holy Church, and the clergy and all Orthodox people are merely their guardians.

14. In cases of attack by despoilers or graspers of church property, the church people should be called to the defence of the church, sound the alarm and send out runners, etc.

15. Should the seizure nevertheless take place, it is absolutely necessary to make a report thereof, signed by witnesses with an accurate description of the articles seized, indicating by name those guilty of the seizure, and forthwith to report thereon to the diocese.

. . . .

(Articles 16-27 deal with excommunication of guilty persons; Articles 28-31 with Church marriages.)

32. Until further notice of the Church authorities, it is obligatory to enter promptly in the books of record the births, certificates of baptism, marriages and deaths in the usual manner.

33. The collecting by the clergy of statistical data and the forwarding of the same to the civil authorities is not compulsory on the clergy. However, the representatives of the civil authorities must have access to the church records for the copying of information required by them under the supervision of members of the diocese.

(Anderson, *People, Church and State in Modern Russia*, pp. 55-57)

Appendix V

MESSAGE OF THE LIVING CHURCH "SOBOR" OF AUGUST 6, 1922

The Holy Sobor urges all churchmen to abandon all attempts to use the Church for temporal political schemes, for the Church belongs to God and must serve Him only. There must be no place in the Church for counter-revolution. The Soviet Government is not a persecutor of the Church. In accordance with the constitution of the Soviet Government all citizens are granted genuine religious freedom of conscience. The decree regarding the separation of the Church from the State guarantees such freedom. The freedom of religious, equally with anti-religious propaganda affords the believers an opportunity to defend by argument the merits of their purely religious convictions. Hence churchmen must not see in the Soviet authority the antichrist; on the contrary, the Sobor calls attention to the fact that the Soviet authority is the only one throughout the world which will realize, by governmental methods, the ideals of the Kingdom of God. Therefore every faithful churchman must not only be an honorable citizen, but also fight with all his might, together with the Soviet authority, for the realization of the Kingdom of God upon earth.

(Quoted in Anderson, *People, Church and State in Modern Russia*, pp. 63-64)

Appendix VI

PATRIARCH TIKHON'S "CONFESSION"

Published on June 27, 1923

Appealing with the present declaration to the Supreme Court of the Russian Soviet Federation of Socialist Republics, I regard it as my duty, dictated by my pastoral conscience, to declare the following:

Having been nurtured in a monarchist society, and until my arrest having been under the influence of anti-Soviet individuals, I was filled with hostility against the Soviet authorities, and at times my hostility passed from passivity to active measures, as in the instance of the proclamation on the occasion of the Brest-Litovsk peace in 1918, the anathematizing of the authorities in that same year, and finally, the appeal against the decree regarding the removal of church treasures in 1922. All my anti-Soviet acts, with the exception of a few inexactitudes, were stated in the act of accusation drawnup by the Supreme Court. Acknowledging the correctness of the accusations of the Supreme Court and its sentence as conforming to the clauses of the criminal code, I repent of all my actions directed against the Government and petition the Supreme Court to change its sentence and to set me free.

I declare hereby to the Soviet authorities that henceforth I am no more an enemy to the Soviet Government, and that I have completely and resolutely severed all connections with the foreign and domestic monarchists and the counter-revolutionary activity of the White Guards.

(Quoted by Anderson in *People, Church and State in Modern Russia*, p. 66)

Appendix VII

THE "SOLOVETSK DOCUMENT" OF THE ORTHODOX CHURCH

May, 1927

Notwithstanding the fact that the fundamental laws of the Soviet Constitution declare full liberty of conscience, of religious gatherings, and of preaching, the activity and the religious life of the Russian Orthodox Church is still subjected to very considerable limitations. The Russian Orthodox Church is forbidden to have a regularly organized central and diocesan administration; it cannot concentrate its activity in Moscow—its historical centre—the bishops are either altogether forbidden to reside in their diocese, or else are deprived of the right to perform the most essential duties of their service; preaching from the pulpit or visiting the parishes which are subjected to their authority; sometimes they are even deprived of the right of ordaining new priests. The Locum Tenens of the Patriarchal See and about half of the Orthodox bishops are imprisoned, exiled or condemned to hard labor. The State organs do not deny these facts, but they explain their necessity by political reasons. They charge the Orthodox bishops and the clergy with counter-revolutionary activity, with plots directed towards the overthrow of the Soviet authority and the restoration of the old order. The Orthodox Church has tried many times to dissolve this atmosphere of suspicion. First Patriarch Tikhon, and then his Locum Tenens have written officially to the Soviet Government regarding this point. These efforts have been in vain, but the sincere desire to put an end to the distressing misunderstandings between the Church and the Soviet authority (misunderstandings which weigh so heavily on the Church and which complicate the task of the State) induces the leading organ of the Russian Orthodox Church to make one more effort and to state quite openly and justly before the Government the principles by which it is guided in relation to the State.

Those who have signed the present statement are fully aware of the difficulty of establishing mutual friendly relations between the State and the Church under present actual conditions. They cannot be silent regarding this. It would not be true, it would be beneath the dignity of the Church, and besides it would be quite useless and unconvincing to assert that there were no points of discord between the Orthodox Church and the State authority of the Soviet Republic. But these points of discord lie not at all in the matters designated by the political distrust of the State; it is not at all points ascribed by the calumny of the foes of the Church. The Church stands aloof from the new repartition of wealth, the nationalization of property; this has always been considered by it as the domain of the State, for the conduct of which it is not responsible. The Church also stands aloof from the political organization of authority, for it is loyal to the Government of all the countries within the limits of which it has its members. It lives at peace with all the different types of State organization, beginning with such despots as were formerly in Turkey and ending with such Republics as the North American United States. The discord lies in the irreconcilability of the religious teaching of the Church with the materialism and the official philosophy of the Communistic Party and of the government of the Soviet Republics directed by that Party.

The Church recognizes the existence of the spiritual principle; Communism denies it. The Church believes in the living God, Creator of the world, Guider of its life and fate; Communism does not admit His existence, believes that the world was self-organized and that no reasonable principles or purposes govern its history. The Church sees the aim of man's life in the heavenly calling of the spirit, and never ceases reminding her children of their heavenly fatherland. She does this even when the conditions of outward culture and material well-being are at their height. Communism desires to know no other aim for man except his welfare upon earth. And this difference of ideology and philosophical viewpoint which exists between the Church and the State manifests itself also in the realm of practical everyday life, and in that of morality. The Church believes in the steadfast principles of morality, justice and law. Communism looks upon them as the conditional results of class-struggle, and values moral questions only from the standpoint of their usefulness. The Church instils the feeling of that humility which elevates man's soul. Communism abases man through his pride. The Church protects purity and the sacredness of childbirth. Communism sees but the satisfying of instincts in the marriage tie. For the Church religion is not only the living force enabling man to attain his heavenly destiny, but also the source of all that is greatest in human relations, which is the foundation of earthly welfare, happiness and the health of nations. For Communism religion is the opium that drugs the nations, that weakens their energy; that is the source of their poverty and misfortunes. The Church wants religion to flourish. Communism wants it to perish. With such deep difference in fundamental principles separating the Church and the State, it becomes impossible that an inner nearness or reconciliation could exist between them. There can be no reconciliation between assertion and negation, between yes and no. For the very soul of the Church, the circumstances of its existence and the reason for its being, is just that which is categorically denied by Communism.

By no compromise or concession, by no partial changes in its teaching, by no explanation of it in a communistic spirit can the Church attain such a reconciliation. Pitiful attempts have been made in this direction by the "Regenerated" in the Church; some of them have tried to instil into the souls of the faithful the idea that Christianity and Communism are really similar in all important points; that a communistic State is striving to attain the same objectives as the Gospels, only by different means, i.e. not by religious persuasion, but by force. Others again have recommended reviewing Christian dogmatics in such a way as to present the teaching of the relations of God to the world in a manner that should not resemble the relation of a sovereign to his people, but should stand more in accordance with republican ideas. Others again have insisted that all saints of bourgeois origin should be excluded from the calendar and deprived of the veneration shown to them by the Church. All such attempts are not sincere and they have called forth the deep indignation of the faithful.

The Orthodox Church will never stand on this unworthy path. It will never deny either the whole or part of that teaching which has come down to it from all that has been holy in the past centuries, in order to accommodate ever-shifting popular opinions. When the ideological difference of opinion between the Church and the State is so deep, it is unavoidable that it should be reflected in the everyday life of both these organisms. A conflict in the activity of both can be avoided only by the strict carrying out of the law regarding the separation of the Church from the State. According to this law the Church must in no way mix itself in the activity of the civil Government, which has to take care of the material welfare of the people. Neither must the State hinder the Church in its religious and moral activity.

Such a law was among the first issued by the revolutionary Government; it has been incorporated into the constitution of the U.S.S.R., and might have, up to a certain point, satisfied both sides, now that the political system has been so much modified. There are no religious motives preventing the Church from accepting it. Our Lord Jesus Christ has ordered us to give unto Caesar what belongs to Caesar, i.e. the material welfare of the people is the realm of the Government. He left no commandments to His followers to seek to alter the forms of government or to guide its activity. According to the teaching and traditions of the Orthodox Church it has always stood aloof from politics, and has remained obedient to the State in all that did not concern its faith. That is the reason why it was able to remain loyal to the civil Government, both in former Turkey and the ancient Roman Empire, even when it was quite alien to the Government spiritually. A contemporary State can demand no more of it. A contemporary State, in opposition to former political theories, does not find it necessary that the political union of its citizens should be strengthened by an inner religious unity. It does not consider this of importance, and openly declares that it does not need the aid of the Church to attain the aims set before it, and that it allows its citizens complete religious liberty.

As things stand at present the Church only desires a systematic and complete carrying out in actual life of the law which separated the Church from the State.

* * *

(As quoted in Anderson, *People, Church and State in Modern Russia*, pp. 70-74).

(The document goes into great length in explaining the nature of the difference between the Patriarchal Church and the Renovated "Living" Church. On the basis of this difference as well as the uncanonical standing of the Renovated, the Orthodox claimed that they were not represented by the Renovated Church administration, and consequently had need of their own restored administration.)

Appendix VIII

MESSAGE OF METROPOLITAN SERGIUS ON THE RECOGNITION OF THE ORTHODOX CHURCH

June 10, 1927

Thus receiving the right to legal existence (official registration May 18-31, 1927), we clearly take account of the fact that with rights we also take on obligations with reference to the authorities who give us these rights—and thus I have taken upon myself, in the name of the whole of our Orthodox old-church (Tikhon) hierarchy and flock, to register before the Soviet authorities our sincere readiness to be fully law-abiding citizens of the Soviet Union, loyal to its Government, and definitely to hold ourselves aloof from all political parties or enterprises seeking to harm the Union.

But let us be sincere to the end. We cannot be silent about the contradiction which exists between us Orthodox and the Communist Bolsheviks, who govern our Union. They set as their purpose struggle with God and His power in the hearts of the people. We on our part see the whole sense and whole aim of our existence in confession of faith in God and strengthening of the faith in the hearts of the people. They recognize only the materialistic interpretation of history, and we believe in the providence of God.

In spite of all this, we are convinced that the Orthodox Church, sacredly observing this faith and living according to its precepts, for this very reason will be, always and everywhere, a desirable and exemplary citizen of any State, including that of the Soviets, in whatever area of life he is called upon to work; in the factory, in village or city, in the army or mine, etc. Should the State demand rejection of property, should it be necessary to lay down his life for the common good, should it be to show an example of temperance, honesty, earnestness in serving society—all this indeed the Christian is taught by his faith. In any case, since not only Communists but people of religious faith are citizens of the Union, in the leading ranks of these citizens must be found every Orthodox Christian, especially as the vast majority of the population is Orthodox.

(As quoted in Anderson, *People, Church and State in Modern Russia*, p. 74)

Appendix IX

BASIC DECREE ON RELIGIONS AND RELIGIOUS ASSOCIATIONS

April 8, 1929

Article 2:

A religious association of believers of any cult shall be registered as a religious society or group of believers . . .

Article 3:

A religious society is a local association of believers having attained the age of 18 years, of one and the same cult, belief, conviction and doctrine, and numbering not less than 20 persons, who have combined for the purpose of making provision for their requirements in the matter of religion. Those believers who, owing to lack of numbers, are unable to form a religious society, may form a group of believers. Religious societies and groups have no juridical rights.

Article 4:

A religious society or group of believers may only carry on its activities after registration. . . .

Article 10:

Believers belonging to a religious society with the object of making provision for their requirements in the matter of religion may lease under contract, free of charge from the Sub-district . . . special buildings for the purpose of worship and objects intended exclusively for the purposes of their cult.

Furthermore, believers . . . may use for religious meetings other buildings which have been placed at their disposal by private persons or by local Soviets and Executive Committees. . . .

Article 17:

Religious associations may not

(a) create mutual credit societies, co-operatives or commercial undertakings, or in general use the property at their disposal for other than religious purposes;

(b) give material assistance to their members;

(c) organize for children, young people or women special prayer or other meetings, or generally, meetings, groups, circles or departments for biblical or literary study, sewing, working or the teaching of religion, etc., or organize excursions, children's play-grounds, public libraries or reading rooms, or organize sanatoria or medical assistance.

Only books necessary for the purposes of the cult may be kept in the buildings and premises used for worship.

Article 18:

The teaching of any form of religious belief in State, public or private teaching and educational establishments is prohibited. Such teaching is permitted exclusively at special theological courses organized by citizens of the U.S.S.R. by special permission of the Commissariat of Internal Affairs of the R.S.F.S.R. and in the territories of the autonomous Republics. . . .

Article 19:

The work of ministers of religion, religious teachers, and instructors, etc., shall be restricted to the area in which the members of their religious associations reside, and to the place where the premises used for worship are situated.

Article 20:

Religious societies and groups of believers may organize local, All-Russian and All-Union religious congresses and conferences, but they must obtain permission on each occasion.

Article 22:

Religious congresses and executive bodies elected by them do not possess the rights of a juridical person and, in addition, may not

(a) form any kind of central fund for the collection of voluntary gifts from believers;

(b) make any form of enforced collection;

(c) own religious property, receive the same on contract, obtain the same by purchase or hire premises for religious meetings;

(d) conclude any form of contract or deal.

Article 25:

Property necessary for the observance of the cult, whether handed over under contract to the believers forming the religious society or newly acquired by them or given to them for the purposes of the cult, is nationalized and shall be borne on the charge of the competent Town Soviet. . . .

Article 40:

Upon the liquidation of a place of worship, religious property shall be disposed of as follows:

(a) All articles of platinum, gold or silver, or cloth of gold or silver, and precious stones shall be placed to the credit of the funds of the State and shall be handed over to the local financial or administrative body of the People's Commissariat for Education, if those articles are on their list, for disposal at their discretion.

(b) Articles of historical, artistic or museum value shall be handed over to the administrative body of the Commissariat of Education.

(c) Other articles (ikons, robes, banners, covers, etc.) having a special significance in the observance of the cult shall be handed over to the believers for transfer to another place of worship of the same cult. . . .

(d) Articles in general use (bells, furniture, carpets, chandeliers, etc.) shall be placed to the credit of the funds of the State and handed over to the local financial body or administrative body of the educational authorities, if these articles are on their list, for their disposal at their discretion.

(e) Cash and consumable property such as incense, candles, oil, wine, wax, wood and coal, which are necessary for the execution of the contract or for performance of religious services, shall not, if the society continues to exist after the liquidation of the place of worship, be subject to expropriation.

Article 45:

The construction of new places of worship may take place at the desire of religious societies. . . .

Article 54:

Members of groups of believers and religious societies may raise subscriptions among themselves and collect voluntary offerings, both in the place of worship itself and outside it, but only amongst the members of the religious associations concerned and only for purposes connected with the upkeep of the place of worship and the religious property, for the engagement of ministers of religion and for the expenses of the executive body.

Any form of forced contribution in aid of religious associations is punishable under the Criminal Code of the R.S.F.S.R.

Article 58:

No religious service or ceremony may take place in any State, public, cooperative or private institution, nor any religious object be placed within such institution.

This prohibition shall not apply to the performance, at the request of a person who is dying or seriously ill in a hospital or prison, of a religious service in a place apart or to the performance of religious services at cemeteries or crematoria.

Article 59:

Religious processions or religious services may only take place in the open if a special permit is obtained for each occasion. . . .

(As quoted by Barron and Waddams in *Communism and the Churches*, pp. 17-20)

Appendix X

LETTER OF METROPOLITAN SERGIUS ON CONTROLLING ABUSES AGAINST THE CHURCH

February 19, 1930

1. The insurance assessment of the churches, especially in villages, is sometimes so exorbitant that it deprives the community of the possibility of using the church buildings. It is essential that the valuation of the church buildings should be lowered (it must not stand on a par with buildings that bring in revenue), as well as the rate for insurance assessment.

2. Collections of the authors' honorarium in favour of the Drama Union must be carried out within legal limits, i.e., the collection may be made only for the performance in church of such musical works as have been nationalized or the rights of which belong to a certain individual, and not simply because singing took place in church, and especially during divine service; the ministers of religion, when performing divine service, must not be looked upon as artists performing musical pieces, and therefore the churches must not be required to pay 5 per cent of all the revenue received by the clergy, i.e., the revenue received for all ecclesiastical services performed in church or outside.

3. It is essential to discontinue the collection of premiums for the insurance of the choristers, which was cancelled in 1929, but is collected from the churches for all the years it had not been paid in (sometimes since 1922), and which together with the accrued interest reached considerable amounts (e.g., over 4,000 rubles).

4. It is essential to suppress the assessment of the churches for various agricultural products (e.g., bread, grain, wool, etc.); also special obligatory agricultural collections; e.g., for tractors, for industrialization, for floating Government loans, etc. As the churches have no land of their own, these as-

sessments of course fall on the members of religious communities; therefore it becomes a new form of taxation for faith, which the faithful have to pay over and above all the other taxes they pay, together with all other citizens.

5. The Instructions of the NKF (People's Commissariat of Finance) of January 5th, 1930, N. 195, according to which fines or confiscations for non-payment of taxes by the Church should not be applied to the property of the individual members of the church council, must be applied to the insurance assessments, to authors' honorariums, etc.

6. It is essential to explain that members of parish councils, church-wardens, church guardians, and other persons ministering to the needs of the local church, should not for this reason be rated as kulaki and, therefore, should not be burdened by heavier taxation.

7. It is essential to explain that local representatives of justice, when Orthodox communities or the clergy send in their complaints, should not refuse them lawful protection of their rights, when the latter have been infringed by local administrative authorities or by some organizations.

8. It must be accepted as a rule that before closing a church the decisive factor should not be the desire of the unbelieving part of the population, but the existence of believers who desire and are able to use the given building; that an Orthodox church, if given up by one community (congregation), be transferred only to another Orthodox community; and that if a church is closed (whatever the reasons for this step), the members of the Orthodox community retain the right to invite their priest to perform all manner of family rites in their own homes.

9. It is necessary to give explanations regarding the going into effect of the decree of the SNK (Soviet of the People's Commissaries) of the 8th April, 1929, concerning religious unions, and also the reference to the instructions (October 1st, 1929) and other orders concerning this same question, for the reason that sometimes local authorities do not accept petitions for registrations of communities (congregations) and even forbid their taking any steps towards registration (whereas the law clearly gives the final date for registration—1st May, 1930—for all communities which desire to continue their existence).

10. Desires of the clergy. The ministers of religion, as persons not employing hired labor, should be registered, as hitherto, as persons belonging to free professions, and not as non-working elements of the population, or still less as kulaki.

11. That income should not be fixed in an arbitrary manner, sometimes quite surpassing all possibility of payment (for instance, in Ijevsk, Bishop Sinezii Zarubin was taxed 10,300 rubles, with an additional 7,000 rubles as an advance for the following year), and that taxation be fixed on a par with other persons of liberal professions.

12. That local village authorities should receive clear instructions fixing the limits and terms of local taxation and assessments for ministers of religion, as non-kulak elements.

13. That ministers of religion not employing themselves with agriculture, cattle breeding, hunting, etc., should not be taxed in kind in such products as bread, grain, wool, butter, game, etc. Sometimes these taxes are demanded without delay, in the course of twenty-four hours.

14. That in cases when the property is being requisitioned for non-payment of taxes a lawful minimum of furniture, clothing and boots should not be taken away.

15. When forced services are being fixed, they should be reasonable in fixing the amount of service. For instance, in the village Liuk, of the Votski district, the priest was demanded to fell, saw into timber, and cart away 200 cubic sajen of wood. Also that the age and state of health should be taken into consideration.

16. That the ministers of religion should not be deprived of the right of having their home within their own parish and near their church, even in villages transformed into collective farms; and that those who rent them rooms should not be more severely taxed on this account.

17. That the children of the clergy should be allowed to study in the first and second grade schools, and that those of them, who by autumn 1929 were registered as students of the VUZY, should not be expelled simply because of their origin; also that those who have already been expelled should be permitted to finish their education.

18. It is desirable that professional or voluntary singers who are members of the "Rabis" union (Art Workers) or other trade unions, and who take part in church choirs as a means of earning money on the side, should not, because of this, be excluded from the "Rabis" or other unions.

19. In the summer of 1929 the question was raised of opening in Leningrad higher theological courses of the Orthodox Patriarchal Church. It is very desirable that this petition be granted, if only to equalize our section of the Church with that of the Renovated, which has its own academy.

20. For a long time the patriarchate has felt the need of having some sort of periodical publication, if only a monthly bulletin in which the decisions, pastoral letters, etc., of the central church authorities could be published, as being of interest for the whole Church.

21. In view of newspaper articles demanding that the constitution of the U.S.S.R. should be revised to forbid all religious propaganda and to restrict further the activity of the Church, we request protection and retention for the Orthodox Church of the rights granted to it by the existing legislation of the U.S.S.R.

(As quoted by Anderson in *People, Church and State in Modern Russia*, pp. 82-84)

Appendix XI

PROGRAM OF THE ALL-SOVIET COMMUNIST PARTY, 1932

Article 13—Religion:

With regard to religion, the Communist Party of the Soviet Union does not confine itself to the already decreed separation of Church and State and of school and church, i.e. measures advocated in the programmes of bourgeois democracy, which the latter has nowhere consistently carried out to the end owing to the diverse and actual ties which bind capital with religious propaganda. The Communist Party of the Soviet Union is guided by the conviction that only conscious and deliberate planning of all the social and economic activities of the masses will cause religious prejudices to die out. The Party strives for the complete dissolution of the ties between the exploiting classes and the organizations of religious propaganda, facilitates the real emancipation of the working masses from religious prejudices and organizes the widest possible scientific educational and anti-religious propaganda. At the same time it is necessary carefully to avoid giving offence to the religious sentiments of believers, which only leads to the strengthening of religious fanaticism.

(As quoted by Anderson in *People, Church and State in Modern Russia*, p. 50)

Appendix XII

CONSTITUTION (FUNDAMENTAL LAW) OF THE UNION OF SOVIET SOCIALIST REPUBLICS* of December 5, 1936, as amended by the Supreme Soviet of the USSR on February 25, 1947, on the recommendations of the Drafting Commission

Chapter X

FUNDAMENTAL RIGHTS AND DUTIES OF CITIZENS

Article 124:

In order to ensure to citizens freedom of conscience, the church in the USSR is separated from the State, and the school from the church. Freedom of religious worship and freedom of anti-religious propaganda is recognized for all citizens.

Article 125:

In conformity with the interests of the working people, and in order to strengthen the socialist system, the citizens of the USSR are guaranteed by law:
(a) Freedom of speech;
(b) Freedom of the press;
(c) Freedom of assembly, including the holding of mass meetings;
(d) Freedom of street processions and demonstrations.

These civil rights are ensured by placing at the disposal of the working people and their organizations printing presses, stocks of paper, public buildings, the streets, communications facilities and other material requisites for the exercise of these rights.

---

* *Constitution (Fundamental Law) of the Union of Soviet Socialist Republics* English text published by Foreign Languages Publishing House, Moscow, 1947, and transmitted through the courtesy of Mr. Alexander P. Morozov, Acting Representative of the USSR to the Economic and Social Council of the United Nations. Text of the amended articles arranged for comparison. Translation of the former text published by Ogiz, State Publishing House of Political Literature, Moscow, 1938; *Yearbook of Human Rights*, 1947.

Article 126:

In conformity with the interests of the working people, and in order to develop the organizational initiative and political activity of the masses of the people, citizens of the USSR are guaranteed the right to unite in public organizations: trade unions, co-operative societies, youth organizations, sport and defence organizations, cultural, technical and scientific societies; and the most active and politically-conscious citizens in the ranks of the working class and other sections of the working people unite in the Communist Party of the Soviet Union (Bolsheviks), which is the vanguard of the working people in their struggle to strengthen and develop the socialist system and is the leading core of all organizations of the working people, both public and State.

Article 127:

Citizens of the USSR are guaranteed inviolability of their person. No person may be placed under arrest except by decision of a court or with the sanction of a procurator.

Article 128:

The inviolability of the home of citizens and privacy of correspondence are protected by law.

. . . .
Chapter XI

THE ELECTORAL SYSTEM

Article 135:

Every citizen of the USSR who has reached the age of 23 is eligible for election to the Supreme Soviet of the USSR, irrespective of race or nationality, sex, religion, education, domicile, social origin, property status or past activities. (*Yearbook of Human Rights, 1947*)

(Note: Paul Anderson has quoted Article 135 as follows: Elections of deputies are universal: all citizens of the USSR who have reached the age of eighteen, irrespective of race or nationality, religion, educational and residential qualifications, social origin, property status or past activities, have the right to vote in the election of deputies and to be elected, with the exception of insane persons and persons who have been convicted by a court of law and whose sentences include deprivation of electoral rights. Anderson, *People, Church and State in Modern Russia*, p. 106.)

Appendix XIII

THE *AGITATOR'S GUIDE*, ON OVERCOMING RELIGIOUS VESTIGES

May, 1937

1. "All religion is contradictory to science" (Stalin). Science gives man a correct understanding of the world and the laws of nature. Equipped with knowledge, man in the process of working actively transforms nature, adjusting it to his needs. Science arms the workers in the struggle for the recon-

struction of social life, for the destruction of exploitation and oppression. The workers of our country, mastering science, are successfully building communism under the leadership of the Party of Lenin and Stalin.

2. Religion at its very roots is inimical to science. It teaches man to have blind faith and not to study, not to carry on research. Religion gives the believer a wrong, distorted conception of reality. The origin of the universe, of life on earth, of man, of mind—all this is wrongly, anti-scientifically, primitively explained in religious books. Religion holds man in darkness and ignorance.

3. Religion teaches the would-be existence of a special unearthly, supernatural world, unsubordinated to any natural laws: god, devils, hell, paradise, life beyond the grave, and so on. All that happens on earth depends, according to religious teaching, on "the will of God" . . . Religion thereby inculcates the idea of the complete passivity of man, the idea of predestination from above of the whole pathway of life of a man, the idea of his uncomplaining subordination to his "destiny," "fate."

5. Religion teaches that true human happiness is not on earth but "in heaven," that earthly life is simply a stage to the attainment of happiness after death. In order to procure "eternal bliss" after death, believing workers, according to religious teaching, must uncomplainingly carry their "cross" on earth. Patience, humility, love of enemies—these are the rules of conduct recommended to workers by religious "morality."

6. "Religion is the opium of the people" (Marx). Poisoning the mind of the workers, it turns believing workers and peasants into submissive slaves, simplifies the mastery of exploiters in class society. Religion is a weapon in the hands of the exploiters, by means of which they restrain the workers from revolutionary struggle against their enslavers.

7. Religion spreads national jealousy, arousing enmity between people of various faiths.

8. By pacifistic preaching of peace, calling for love and universal forgiveness, religion and religious organizations seek to modify in capitalistic countries the alertness of workers and to disarm them before the face of wars now in preparation by the imperialists.

9. In our beautiful country, the land of triumphant socialism, religion is a vestige of capitalism in the minds of part of the workers. Religion favours the strengthening in actual life, in the habits and minds of the believing workers, of a whole range of harmful, reactionary, capitalistic vestiges.

10. Religious customs (especially religious holidays) bring vast material loss to socialistic economy, and put a brake on the rise of culture in the masses.

11. Religious vestiges still resting in the minds of a not unimportant part of the workers favour reactionary activity of anti-Soviet elements.

12. Every religion brings harm to the workers . . . Lenin taught that the more refined the religion, the more harmful it became, because the more difficult for believing workers to comprehend its reactionary role. . . . No matter how churchmen and sectarians greet and praise the Soviet power, no matter how they try to "adjust" their "gods" to Communism, the essence of religious activity is profoundly reactionary and at its root inimical to socialism.

13. The Communist Party always has considered and considers anti-religious propaganda one of its most important tasks. "Our propaganda must

include the propaganda of atheism," taught Lenin. "We conduct propaganda and shall conduct propaganda against religious prejudices," teaches Stalin. The struggle against religious poison is a struggle for the new man, for the mastery of science and technics, for the dawn of culture and of the whole human process, for Communism. The overcoming of religious vestiges is one of the most important political tasks.

(As quoted by Anderson in *People, Church and State in Modern Russia*, pp. 104-105)

Appendix XIV

ORTHODOX CHURCH ON "THE TRUTH ABOUT RELIGION IN RUSSIA"

(1942)

We continue, in our country, from day to day, and from year to year, freely to pray in the Orthodox churches and to celebrate all the sacraments and rites of our faith; to christen children, to serve Te Deums, requiems for the dead, etc. No one hinders our freely confessing our faith in the Lord Jesus Christ, who came in the flesh, and will come again in glory to judge the living and the dead. And we, confessing this faith, thank the Lord that He in the new conditions of our life helps us to become true followers of Christ . . . The Russian believing people continue . . . to receive their spiritual food in the Orthodox Church—in her worship services, at sacred rites, on holy days, etc. . . .

Another priest writes:

The Soviet Government has regulated its relations with the Church by special legislation, and in strict conformity therewith it has placed the Church under conditions favouring her perfection, in the spirit of the first Christians, and thereby achieving Christian salvation. In the Orthodox churches we freely pray to God, celebrate the sacraments, and satisfy our high spiritual, religious needs.

Church bourgeoisie sees persecution chiefly in the rejection by the Government of Russia of its age-old union with the Church, as a result of which the Church, or more exactly the Church institutions, such as monasteries, and the clergy, as a social class or a profession, were deprived of certain rights: the ownership of land and commercial enterprises, various class privileges as compared with the "common people," etc.

As a matter of fact, the common Orthodox people, hearing in the Gospel the commandments of Christ to the Apostles, reading the epistles of the Apostle Paul or the life of some hero of Christianity like Saint John Chrysostom, are inclined to see in the changes that have taken place not persecution but a return to the Apostolic times, when the Church and the ministers followed exactly along their true paths, to which they had been called by Christ, when they looked upon their ministry not as a profession among other worldly professions, providing them the means of livelihood, but as the following of Christ's calling.

Along this path, quickened by the people's ideals, sanctified by the highest traditions of the Orthodox Church, and at the same time the spiritually more fruitful path of ministering unto the salvation of men, our Orthodox Church endeavours to move, and to this path she calls her ministers.

(From *The Truth about Religion in Russia*, as quoted by Anderson in *People, Church and State in Modern Russia*, pp. 36-37.)

Appendix XV

STATUTE ON ORTHODOX CHURCH ORGANIZATION

(Accepted by the Sobor of the Russian Orthodox Church on January 31, 1945)

In the Russian Orthodox Church the highest authority regarding dogmatics, church leadership and church law—legislative, administrative and jurisdictional—rests with the Sobor, which meets periodically and consists of bishops, clergy and laymen.

I. The Patriarch

1. In accordance with article 34 of the apostolic canon, the head of the Russian Orthodox Church is the Most Holy Patriarch of Moscow and all Russia and the Holy Synod.

2. The name of the Patriarch will be said in all sanctuaries of the Russian Orthodox Church in the S. U. as well as abroad in the following way: "For our Most Holy Father (name), the Patriarch of Moscow and all Russia."

3. The Patriarch has the right to send pastoral letters to the whole Russian Orthodox Church concerning religious questions.

4. On behalf of the Russian Orthodox Church the Patriarch has contact with the leaders of other autocephalous Orthodox Churches in church matters.

5. If necessary, the Patriarch gives advice and directives to the bishops concerning their duties and the leadership of their church area.

6. The Patriarch has the right to reward the Most Holy Bishops with certain honorary titles and highest church honors.

7. With the permission of the Government and for the purpose of deciding important matters relating to the Church, the Patriarch may call the Council of the Bishops and preside over it. If, however, it is necessary also to hear the voices of the clergy and laity, and he has the technical possibility of calling such a meeting, the Patriarch may call an All-Soviet Sobor and preside over it.

8. The Patriarch is the Eparchial Bishop of the Moscow Eparchy (Diocese).

9. The Patriarch is assisted by the patriarchal representative with the title "Metropolitan of Krutizi (Krutitsky)."

10. The Theological Institute, the highest religious educational institution which trains the future priests of the Church and professors for the theological subjects, is subordinated to the Patriarch of Moscow.

11. In questions requiring the decision of the Government of the Soviet Union, the Patriarch contacts the Soviet Council for the Affairs of the Russian Orthodox Church in the Council of the People's Commissars of the S. U.

12. In case of the death of the Patriarch or if for any other reason he is not able to carry on his office, the eldest member of the constant members of the Holy Synod will carry on his work.

13. During a patriarchal vacancy
    (a) the leadership of the Russian Orthodox Church is in the hands of the patriarchal representative together with the Holy Synod;
    (b) the name of the patriarchal representative is mentioned in the worship services in all Russian churches;
    (c) all letters to the whole Russian Church and also the letters to the leaders of the other autocephalous churches, are sent out under the signature of the patriarchal representative;
    (d) Metropolitan of Krutizi takes over the leadership of the Moscow diocese.

14. If the place of the Patriarch becomes vacant, the Holy Synod under the presidency of the patriarchal representative, discusses the calling of a meeting of the Sobor for electing a new Patriarch, and sets the date of the meeting which may not be later than six months after the Patriarch's place has become vacant.

15. The Sobor, called together for electing the new Patriarch, is presided over by the patriarchal representative.

16. The Patriarchate has seals and stamps which are duly registered by the local civil authority.

II. *The Holy Synod*

17. The Holy Synod consists of six members, the eparchial bishops, and is presided over by the Patriarch.

18. Three members of the Holy Synod are constant members, three only temporary.

19. The constant members of the Holy Synod are the Metropolitans of Kiev, Leningrad and Krutizi.

20. The temporary members of the Synod are elected for the period of one meeting, in accordance with the list of bishops and according to their rank.

21. The synodal year comprises two meeting periods: a summer period, March-August; and a winter period, September-February.

22. Six departments may be established within the Holy Synod, including educational department, publication department, economics department.

III. *The Dioceses*

23. The Russian Orthodox Church is divided up into dioceses confined by the respective civil boundaries of the areas and republics.

24. At the head of the diocese is the diocesan bishop. He is nominated by the Most Holy Patriarch and is titled according to his cathedral town.

25. If necessary, vicar-bishops assist the diocesan bishops.

26. The bishop of the diocese is responsible for his diocese. Either he leads it personally according to local conditions or cooperatively with a diocesan council. He uses stamps and seals which are registered by the local authorities.

27. Such a diocesan council, if such is formed by the bishop, consists of 3 to 5 persons in the rank of presbyter. Their task is to prepare matters for the decision of the bishop.

28. The bishop of the diocese has the right to send letters within the diocese.

29. The bishop of the diocese nominates several provosts.

30. The provosts watch the activity of the clergy of the community and visit the communities at least twice a year. They explain to the church personnel the regulations of the bishop of the diocese. They also take care of the religious requirements in communities which temporarily have no clergy. They discuss with the bishop the reward for those who have deserved it and at the end of every six months they give a full report to the bishop of the dioceses on their activities and the situation of the various areas. However, on extremely important issues they report immediately. They also supervise the correctness of the budget of the community.

31. The bishop of the diocese gives the Patriarch annual reports on his diocese.

32. Where it is possible in the dioceses, and with the permission of the local authorities, theological priests' courses are arranged for preparing candidates according to directives issued by the Patriarch.

33. In order to provide the sanctuary with the items necessary for worship services—candles, incense, etc.—a candle shop may be established within the dioceses, with the permission of the local authorities, and also wreaths, crosses, prayer pamphlets and similar articles may be made.

34. The monasteries in a diocese are directed along lines indicated by the Patriarch.

IV. *The Communities*

35. At the head of every community of believers there is the church leader elected by the bishop of the diocese.

36. The church leader is responsible to the bishop of the diocese for the correct holding of worship services in accordance with the church order. The church leaders are responsible that the life in the community does not interfere with their public duties, for example in rural areas, worship services may not be held at a time when there is agricultural work to do.

37. The community may be built up by the believers after registering with the local authorities.

38. The loan of a church building to the religious community (at least twenty persons) is effected on the basis of an application of the community to the local authorities in accordance with the bishop of the diocese.

39. The Orthodox community in the form of a group of believers (less than twenty persons) is permitted by the local authorities to use the church building and the worship materials free of charge, and property thus lent is in charge of three persons and the church leader. These people are responsible to the local authorities for the safekeeping of the property.

40. The head of the church is a constant member of the community and president of its executive body (church council) which consists of four members: the president, the church elder, his assistant and the accountant.

41. The executive body of the community under the direct leadership and supervision of the head of the church is responsible to the local civil authorities for the maintenance of the building and the church property; it makes the budget and supervises the maintenance, heating, lighting ant repairs of the building and the provision of the necessary worship equipment, such as incense, wreaths, crosses, etc. For obtaining the equipment it sends the required amount of money through the bishop of the diocese to the Patriarchate. It is responsible for the distribution of the funds of the community. It supervises

the accounts. It takes from the funds the payments required for the Patriarchate and for paying the personnel if according to contract the church personnel is paid for its work by the church. It makes the necessary payments for the support of the bishop of the diocese, his administration, the theological priests' courses in the diocese, and also the general church requirements, for the leadership of the Patriarchate and for the support of the theological institutions.

42. The general conference of the community elects a revision commission of three persons. The Revision Commission must constantly supervise the state of the church property and the use of the church funds. Every three months they revise the books and control the correctness of expenditures. Misuse or incompleteness of church property is referred to the local Soviet authority.

43. Church funds are composed of: voluntary contributions of the community at collections during the worship service, contributions for candles, etc., and of general sacrifices for the local churches.

44. Church funds are in keeping of a bank (deposited in the name of the church) and may be disposed of by checks signed by the church leader and accountant of the community.

45. Each year the head of the church submits to the bishop of the diocese a statement of receipts and expenditures of church funds.

46. Any incorrectnesses must be reported to the bishop of the diocese by the head of the church and the bishop has to make an investigation, reporting to the Soviet authorities.

47. In case of the death of the head of the church or if he should go to another local church, the executive body must draw up an inventory on the church property, and according to this inventory the new head of the church takes over the administration of the church property.

48. The head of the church has seals, and stamps which are registered by the local civil authorities.

(*Dokumente zur Ordnung der Kirche*, July, 1951)

Appendix XVI

OLESCHUK ON ANTI-RELIGIOUS TACTICS, 1949

Communism and religion are incompatible and irreconcilable. It is particularly important to appreciate this, because a desire to justify religion—to whitewash it—is not infrequent. Some people adopt a conciliatory, non-Marxist, non-party attitude and try to justify it by saying that Churchmen are not only loyal now but fully Soviet in their outlook. Others say that the Soviet regime itself has changed its attitude.

Yet in fact all these arguments have nothing whatever to do with Marxism or Communism. It is impossible to accept the argument that the Soviet State's attitude has changed. It is, of course, true that throughout its existence the Soviet State has based its attitude on disestablishing the Church from the State, separating the schools from the Church, and on freedom of conscience. The Soviet regime never meant to "liquidate" the Church, or to persecute the clergy, or even to forbid believers to practice their cults. And naturally the Church welcomed the chance to restore the Patriarchate, revive the Synod, publish journals and call its councils. But that is no evidence of a change in principle. Religion in our society remains an anti-scientific reactionary ideology . . .

It would be a mistake to think that religion is already extinct in our country. Religious prejudices continue to exist. Now a few of our people still believe in God and are the prisoners of religious superstitions and prejudices. Even among the youth there are religious survivals. There are instances of young men and women going to church and performing religious rites. . . .

The Bolshevik Party and the Soviet Government have never embarked on the path of banning religious beliefs or the exercise of religious ceremonies, nor that of an administrative struggle against religion. This path is organically alien to the Marxist-Leninist conception of the way to defeat religion. It is necessary to reform the mind of the believer. This cannot be achieved by a mere ban. The minds of the masses must be reformed by persuasion, not by compulsion. . . .

Anti-religious propaganda must be carried on skilfully. The lecturer must have the appropriate knowledge, must possess a certain tact in his ap-approach to the audience, and must know the mood and requirements of religious people. . . . There can be no pattern in this. Propaganda for atheism in the Soviet East, in the regions and republics where the main mass of the believers is Moslem, is one thing, and it is another in the Western regions, where there are many Catholics and where the influence of the reactionary clergy is still considerable. The struggle against religion will have little effect if the audience consists, for example, of Protestants and the lecturer attacks Orthodoxy or Catholicism.

(*Church Times*, London, 24/2/1950)

THREE BALTIC STATES

Introduction

The small Baltic states became independent republics at the end of World War I. Their rich and varied heritage included their origins as early Indo-Aryan (Lithuanian) and Mongolian (Finno-Ugrian Estonian) settlers in Europe, a Christian tradition dating from the Middle Ages, a strong national spirit and folklore, a deep-seated respect for the rights of others, and a strong desire for their own independence. Their experience has included two hundred years of Russian domination.

During their twenty years of independence between the two world wars their achievements in government, education, and general social life surpassed that of many nations which had scarcely known foreign occupation and suppression.

LATVIA

Population (1939)	2,000,000
Lutherans	1,095,000
Roman Catholics	475,000
Russian Orthodox and Old Believers	275,000
Others	3,700

The Constitution of the Latvian Republic (1918) guaranteed religious freedom. A Department of Cults in the Ministry of Interior acted on behalf of the Government in relation to religious affairs. A council of representatives of the religious bodies functioned parallel to the Department. Registered congregations (minimum, fifty believers) could conduct religious services publicly, receive voluntary donations from individuals or organizations, establish their own churches, schools, cemeteries, and give religious instruction. The churches had juristic status and unrestricted property rights. The Roman Catholic and Lutheran churches maintained theological faculties in the University of Latvia, subsidized by the State. There was an active Christian youth program. The Lutheran Church operated a publishing house and carried on mission work abroad. The Catholic Church secured a concordat with the Government in 1922 which provided certain other concessions, e.g., tax exemptions. Catholic orders, some of which operated underground during the Tsarist occupation, worked freely, establishing schools, publications, youth and student groups, social welfare institutions and churches. Bishop J. Camanis and Auxiliary Bishop J. Rancabs played an active role in public life as Assistant Minister of Education and Vice-President of Parliament, respectively.

(303)

Chronicle of Events

August 23, 1939—*

According to a secret pact between Hitler and Stalin, 70,000 Soviet troops were to occupy the independent Baltic States.

* The major outline of events in all three Baltic States from August, 1939 to August, 1940 is practically identical. Information from these three states has been meager and it has therefore been difficult to fix precise dates.

September 1-17, 1939—

The Baltic States and the USSR exchanged notes pledging military neutrality in the event of war.

October 5, 1939—

Mutual assistance pacts between the Baltics and the USSR provided for the USSR to have ports and air bases in the Baltics and to supply Baltic armies with USSR weapons.

June, 1940—

Baltic governments were advised that "friends of the Soviets" should be put in power, after charges had been made that the Balts had violated their mutual assistance pacts with the USSR by signing mutual help treaties among themselves. Organizations created before June 20 were considered a "jeopardy to public security."

June, 1940—

Following the invasion of Latvia by Russian troops, the Latvian Government was requested to suppress religious activities by dismissing pastors, forbidding religious instruction in the schools and by transforming churches into clubs or anti-religious museums. The Church of Our Saviour in Riga became an army warehouse, the church in Ludza a cinema, and the parsonages in Lubana and Liezere became machine and tractor stations (C'Uibe, *The Lutheran Church of Latvia Behind the Iron Curtain*, p. 7).

A special manifesto subjected all organizations to State control, and proclaimed "freedom of anti-religious propaganda."

Public demonstrations for incorporation into the Soviet Union frequently took place near church buildings during services of worship.

July, 1940—

The respective parliaments were dissolved as "not representing the will of the people," and new elections called. The new parliaments voted to request incorporation as republics in the Soviet Union. Demonstrations were organized to stir up enthusiasm for incorporation.

July 23, 1940—

A "Nationalization Law" stipulated that all church buildings and lands would become State property, that churches would have the status of voluntary associations rather than "juristic persons," that all church records should be turned over to the State. Government support for the churches and clergy ceased. Four Lutheran Churches, 40 chapels, 15 parish houses, 150 cemeteries and 240 parsonages were assigned to non-religious purposes. Buildings were assigned to congregations for their use on the basis of approved petitions and payment of rent by the congregations. In Vecpiehalga a congregation of 3000 members was assessed an annual rent of 18,000 rubles ($4000); (C'Uibe, *op. cit.*, p. 7).

Ousted pastors had difficulty finding lodging, as many people feared reprisals if they rented accommodations to the clergy.

Religious publications ceased.

The Student Christian Movement, founded in 1918, was dissolved on orders of the Russian authorities.

August 5, 1940—

Latvia was incorporated into the Soviet Union and the USSR Church Law of April, 1929, became applicable in Latvia.

August 5, 1940—

The Baltic Socialist Republics adopted constitutions patterned after that of Russia.

In discussing the religious situation in the Baltics, E. Yaroslavsky, head of the USSR League of Militant Atheists, stated:

"Since 22 years have not been enough to liquidate the Church in the USSR, we shall have many difficulties in extirpating the remains of religious prejudices in the Baltic countries. One of the reasons is that many people consider anti-religious propaganda no longer necessary. This opinion is false. Anti-religious propaganda is one of the essential aspects of Communist propaganda and must be carried out by a special organization. The reproach which might be made against the atheists is that they have not been able to offer the people moral standards for their life. Religion answered moral questions in its way" (Timasheff, *Religion in Soviet Russia*, p. 130).

The Lutheran Faculty of theology was closed and its property confiscated.

Religious services were restricted to assigned church buildings except by special permission from local Russian officers or Government officials. Religious rites for Communist Party members were forbidden. Worship services were observed by special governmental representatives.

The Commissar of Agriculture refused to consult with the Lutheran Archbishop regarding procedures in the nationalization of church lands.

Following the arrest of several members, the Lutheran Supreme Church Board disbanded. Any new board was to include only clergymen.

Elections of congregational administrative bodies was prohibited. Communications between churches and between pastors and the Church hierarchy were restricted. A network of contact men was established by the Lutheran Church to maintain contact between the central Church administration and the pastors. Connections with foreign churches were prohibited. The work of the Lutheran Society of Foreign Missions was suspended when correspondence and foreign money transfers were prohibited.

The Lutheran Institute of Theology for church officials as well as its Grammar School were closed.

September, 1940—

Following an order restricting the Church from social welfare work, the Lutheran Church Society of Domestic (Inner) Mission was dissolved.

Regular church (voluntary) taxes were suspended. Special committees for securing support for the churches were forbidden.

January, 1941—

The State Publishing Office destroyed 18,000 copies of the *Psalm Book*.

A mutual aid fund was organized among Lutherans to provide for families of deceased, imprisoned, or exiled pastors and churchmen.

The *Anti-religioznik* (USSR) of January stated that the Reformation had been introduced into Latvia to assist the ruling class exploit the people (*ICPIS*, No. 5, February, 1941).

February, 1941—

The State Printing Board rejected the Lutheran Church's application for permission to publish an ecclesiastical bulletin or a new translation of the New Testament.

A printer in Limbazi was fined and threatened for printing an order of service for a congregation.

According to Rev. Leous C'Uibe (*The Lutheran Church of Latvia Behind the Iron Curtain*), by June, 1941, when the Russian occupiers fled before the advancing Germans, the following additional measures had been taken:

Church functionaries were classified as "not working" citizens. This excluded them from employment in State-related enterprises, including schools. Professors of the closed theological faculty had been dismissed and denied the right to receive pensions. Theological students were not permitted to re-enter the University in other faculties.

The USSR *Anti-religioznik*, No. 12, 1940, reported that the frequent requests of the clergy to be enrolled as peasants were rejected by the Government "because the peasants are too happy to have got rid of the influence of the clergy and have received with joy the decree for the partition of church land" (*ICPIS*, No. 7, February, 1941). A number of clergymen took up work as day laborers in order to support their families.

Church leaders' identity documents restricted them to travel in a very limited area. The press described church leaders as "reactionaries," "saboteurs," and "fascists." Clergymen were carefully watched by Government agents. Several were arrested, and 41 were deported to Russia or killed, some after long periods of torture.

Of 280 Lutheran pastors at their posts in 1940, only 166 remained in June, 1941.

There were no church schools.

Religious education in the schools, church history, the catechism, etc. were replaced by studies of Yaroslavsky's works (head of the USSR League of Militant Atheists).

Teachers were asked to check on children's attendance at religious services. Pupils might not attend confirmation courses, and during confirmation services were often required to attend specially scheduled school functions.

All youth work was in the hands of the Comsomol.

Anti-religious propaganda units had been established in State institutions, schools and military centers.

Religious radio broadcasts were prohibited.

Thirty Lutheran congregations were dissolved from lack of pastors or deportation of believers. Thirty thousand Christians were deported to USSR.*

State employees and soldiers who maintained their religious affiliations were threatened with punishment and discharge. Members of the Communist Party and trade unions were forbidden to participate in religious activities.

Christmas and other Church holidays were suppressed. It was forbidden to observe religious festivals on work days. Wayside crosses and other religious symbols in public places were destroyed or replaced with political symbols.

It was reported that although Latvian Christians were cut off from the Christian world, they continued in fellowship in silence.

"Some people wipe off all connections with the Church and religion for fear of men. But services are better attended, the number of communicants has risen, collections are larger and devotion is deeper."

1941-1944—

During the German occupation (July, 1941 - October, 1944) Protestant churches were able to regain most of the legal rights, property, and administrative structure which had been lost during the Russian occupation period. A persistent struggle was carried out against Nazi deportation of Jews and others, against Nazi indoctrination, compulsory labor, obstruction to free religious life and other measures of an anti-Christian nature. The final conclusion was that German occupation was not preferable to Russian.

Catholics reported that the only concession accorded them by the Germans was freedom for religious instruction.

In October, as the Germans retreated, nearly 170,000 Latvians were taken with them, many as forced laborers, some as refugees from the advancing Russians. Included among them were Lutheran Archbishop Grinbergs, Roman Catholic Bishop Rancans and other Orthodox, Roman Catholic, and Protestant leaders.

As Soviet troops advanced, churches and church leaders were not spared. Of 96 Lutheran pastors remaining, ten were deported, four imprisoned, ten died and six were missing. Of the original 280 in 1940, only 66 were left. The Lutheran Deputy Archbishop was replaced by G. Turss, a pastor who had earlier been removed from office by the Church for immoral conduct.

All laws relating to church property and administration, effective when the Russians had fled, were re-introduced.

1947—

"Latvian schools have been given the task of training 'fighters for Com-

---

* According to MacEoin (*The Communist War on Religion*, p. 179) a secret order had been issued in 1939 by Serov, Soviet Vice-Commissar of Public Security, to displace the Baltic peoples and resettle their lands with Russians. Members of the Russian Orthodox Church in Latvia were mostly descendants of Russians who had been resettled in Latvia during Tsarist occupation. Before the German invasion a young bishop arrived from Moscow demanding the submission of the Orthodox Church of Latvia to the Moscow Patriarchate. When Orthodox Metropolitan Augustinus refused, he was dismissed and prosecuted. Many Russian Orthodox believers were deported to Russia, some fled and others submitted. During the German occupation, Metropolitan Augustinus fled to West Europe (*ICPIS*, No. 46, December, 1940).

munism', . . . and school holidays are fixed so that they should not coinside with Christian holidays. . . .

Anti-religious broadcasts . . . openly defiled (religion) as 'a superstition propagated by the bourgeois elements in order to fool the working people' . . . pastors are called 'lackeys of the exploiting classes—servants of the bourgeois reaction' " (C'Uibe, *The Lutheran Church of Latvia behind the Iron Curtain,* p. 25).

1947—

Permits for celebrating Christmas were refused. Special services were held in many churches to celebrate the victories of the Soviet Army, the October Revolution, etc.

No religious instruction of any kind was permitted and children under eighteen were not permitted to go to church.

The Roman Cotholic Church was permitted to establish a private (and the only) theological seminary.

March 14, 1948—

Two thousand, two hundred lay delegates of the Lutheran Church came together under the leadership of "Acting Archbishop" Turss and elected Turss Archbishop. Said Dean A. Vitols, "a Church servant is also a defender of the laws of the Soviet State."

A Committee of Religion and Worship was established within the Ministerial Cabinet to deal with religious affairs.

July, 1948—

The Riga radio broadcast an appeal to Communist Party members and youth to destroy the last remnants of religious "prejudices" and to overcome the pastors and defenders of religion. All persons sympathetic to, or not actively opposed to religion were to be expelled from the Communist Party.

Three Lutheran pastors who had voted against a Government-sponsored candidate for the office of Dean of the Riga District were "punished (deported to the USSR), not for their religious activities, but for their anti-Soviet political activities" (C'Uibe, *The Lutheran Church of Latvia behind the Iron Curtain,* p. 29).

Remaining clergy, freely or forcibly, participated in programs for the economic and cultural development of the country as part of the USSR.

1950-1951—

Laiks, a Latvian journal published in New York, reported that churchgoers must obtain special permits before attending church services. The permit cost $2.00. Many people feared that the permits "may prove to be tickets for Siberia."

New regulations required that Sunday worship services be held only very early in order "not to interfere with more important meetings."

Volunteers were forbidden to rebuild or repair church buildings as "this might interfere with rebuilding of the State (*The Christian Advocate,* April 12, 1951, p. 11).

LITHUANIA

Population (1940)	3,032.863
Roman Catholics	80%
Protestants	9.5%
Orthodox	2.5%
Other Christians	.09%
Jews	7%

The Constitution of the Republic of Lithuania (1922, 1928, 1938) guaranteed religious freedom and equality. Religious education in the public schools was compulsory. Exception was made if parents objected. Special provision was made for teaching children according to the confessional adherence of their parents. Churches could establish private schools and received State subsidies if the schools measured up to normal educational requirements.

Recognized communions were free to build and administer churches, schools, welfare institutions, commercial buildings and monasteries. The State provided building materials at reduced rates, or free. Non-profit buildings were tax-free. State subsidies provided for salaries of church functionaries and other administrative expenses. The churches kept birth, marriage, and death records. The churches organized evangelistic and mission work, published journals and books, and conducted active youth and student programs. Roman Catholic lay organizations, with some 800,000 members, operated orphanages, hospitals, old people's homes, asylums, schools, libraries, lecture halls, theaters and service centers. The (Catholic) Christian Democratic Party was the strongest political party. The extensive Agrarian Reform of independent Lithuania was prepared by a Catholic priest who was Minister of Agriculture. Religious holy-days were recognized as official holidays.

Chronicle of Events

July, 1940—

Following the Russian occupation, an order was issued to separate Church and State; discontinue all State support of churches, their pastors, and institutions; expropriate the land of churches and monasteries.

Church social and cultural organizations were supressed on grounds of endangering the safety of the State.

Churches were to serve only believers. In the property reform, the clergy were allowed to retain only their private homes and furniture.

Monasteries were converted to museums and cultural or medical centers.

The Concordat between the previous Government and the Roman Catholic Church was rescinded.

The four Roman Catholic theological seminaries and one theological faculty were closed or occupied by Russian troops, their property taken by the State. One was subsequently re-opened. Religious books were destroyed.

The Roman Catholic periodical, *The 20th Century*, was replaced by *Antireligioznik* and *Bezboznik* (The Godless). An early issue declared:

"The struggle against religion must be pursued prudently, so as not to deepen still further the discontent of the population. The people are to be shown that the new regime does not wish to impose anything upon them. However, the Militant Godless Movement has obtained the assurance of the Government that in the constitution of the new Soviet republics there will be a clause authorizing the Godless to organize all kinds of antireligious manifestations freely" (*Maunis Kovänuen* (Finland), October 3, 1940).

August 21, 1940—

An agrarian reform decree provided for three hectares (eight acres) of land for every parish priest. Those who already owned land could, as could the peasants, keep a maximum of thirty hectares (Timasheff, *Religion in Soviet Russia*, p. 134).

August, 1940—

The Constitution of LSSR was adopted August 25, 1940. Article 96 (as amended, April 7, 1948) read: "In order to ensure to citizens freedom of conscience, the Church in the Lithuania SSR is separated from the State, and the school from the Church. Freedom of religious worship and freedom of anti-religious propaganda are recognized for all citizens" (As of Article 127 of the Constitution of the Russian Soviet Federated Socialist Republic—*Yearbook of Human Rights*, 1948, p. 205).

The building of the former Roman Catholic Seminary of Vilnahas was handed over to the Atheistic Movement for its headquarters (*ICPIS*, No. 46, December, 1940).

October, 1940—

Soviet Deputy Minister of Interior Gladkov gave instructions to the police that the Roman Catholic Church in Lithuania was anti-Soviet, that priests should be brought under "formal control" and that a dossier should be prepared on every priest. Secret agents were to be recruited locally to report on the priests. Monks were considered particularly suitable for such employ because of their economic impoverishment (MacEoin, *The Communist War on Religion*, p. 177).

November, 1940—

Deportation order No. 0054, paragraph 5, included for deportation "every person, who, by his political or social position, his chauvinistic national spirit, his religious convictions, his political or moral instability, is opposed to the socialist regime and is susceptible to be used to anti-Soviet purposes . . ., the ministers of religious communities, sympathizers and active members."

December, 1940—

Although Christmas cards, trees, and family religious festivals were forbidden, churches were crowded on Christmas Day. Students were hopeful for the future and talked of evangelizing among Russian soldiers.

January, 1941—

Teachers and students in the one remaining Roman Catholic seminary refused to vote in the national elections. The school buildings were thereupon requisitioned. When an appeal proved unsuccessful the school was reopened in the suburbs, where students and professors were housed by the people, their lectures held in chapels and larger residences.

February, 1941—

The Soviet *Anti-religioznik* attributed Lithuania's social and economic evils of the past to church preferentialism, which must be overcome (*ICPIS*).

April, 1941—

Clergymen were forbidden to give religious instruction to children, and were required to sign notices acknowledging receipt of the restraining order:

"I, ———, sign the attached as evidence that I was informed on April —, 1941, that I am strictly enjoined not to give religious instruction to school children . . . in churches . . . or in the homes of children or in my own apartment or elsewhere. Thus I have no right to talk to them about religious matters . . ." (*News Behind the Iron Curtain*, February, 1953, Vol. 2, No. 2, p. 27).

Priests under forty were ordered to serve in the Soviet Army. Roman Catholic sources reported that bishops had to "take up residence in the Crimea and the Caucasus (deportation)." In an exchange arrangement with Germany, the clergy were offered the possibility of emigration to Germany. Some accepted. Twelve Roman Catholic priests were deported to USSR; fifteen were killed. Their houses and those of ejected clergy were taken over by the Red Army. Of Lutheran and Reformed pastors, only three and five, respectively, remained.

May, 1941—

The one remaining Roman Catholic seminary was ordered closed after Roman Catholic bishops protested that earlier action taken by the Government in requisitioning its buildings was unconstitutional. Before the school could be closed, the Communist leaders and Russian occupiers had to flee before advancing Germans.

Other measures taken during the Russian occupation, in summary, included suppression of religious orders, nationalization of all church buildings and conversion of many buildings into museums, cinemas, clubs, recreation centers and military billets. Youth work and charitable enterprises had been taken over by the State. Missionary work and religious publications were suspended.

1942-1944—Nazi Occupation

As the Soviet forces withdrew, the Lithuanians proclaimed their independence, set up a new Government, and prepared to re-establish religious life as it was prior to the Russian occupation.

As the Germans retreated from Lithuania in 1944, they took with them nearly all the Protestants and a considerable number of Roman Catholics.

1944-1950—Second Russian Occupation

With the return of the USSR occupation forces, Lithuania was again declared a Soviet Republic and the government, laws and measures of 1941 were re-established. To these were added other measures, and some adaptations.

One Roman Catholic seminary continued on a private basis, meeting in homes and churches, until the winter of 1947-48, when it was closed.

In 1947, an unsuccessful attempt was made to establish a "national Catholic Church," independent of Rome. Priests were subjected to tempting offers as leaders, or were threatened, tried, replaced, or deported.

Clergymen and members of religious communities were included along with spies, former professional soldiers, and others practicing liberal professions who were to be removed "either by evacuation or annihilation, in the event of . . . imperilment by hostile forces, mutiny, sabotage, etc., or in the interests of the security of the armed forces" (*Current News on the Lithuanian Situation*, April, May, 1949 as quoted by MacEoin, *The Communist War on Religion*, p. 185).

After a decree was published which would put all "cultural monuments," including church buildings, under Government supervision, congregations were required to establish committees of twenty as trustees of churches assigned to them for purposes of worship. The congregations through the committees were to be responsible for repairs, insurance, employment of clergy, etc. . . . The people generally resisted or found ways of effecting the decree without breaking church ties and regulations. Rental on church buildings used by congregations ran from $10,000 to $40,000 per year. In January, 1949, the "Commission for Religious Affairs" issued a decree forbidding the operation of more than one church within a seven-mile radius. In larger cities, e.g., Kaunas, if the decree were adhered to, it would mean one church for 150,000 inhabitants. Actually two are functioning.

State employees (i.e., all people classified as workers) were warned that attendance at church "witchcraft sessions" would be considered as a "demonstration of disloyalty to the existing order." Teachers who attended religious services were dismissed. Parents of children who entered churches were warned that their children would be subject to expulsion from school.

Religious objects, ikons, and crucifixes in homes were frequently destroyed by searching parties.

Summary, 1951

Nevertheless, preaching continues, in spite of Government auditors and intimidation. Church services are well attended, particularly by women and peasants. Religious processions are not banned but are discouraged by church leaders as unnecessary exposure. Marriages may be blessed in the church. The sacraments are performed without difficulty. Church collections are prohibited. Parents, clergy and laymen provide religious instruction to children in the homes or clandestinely.

Inter-confessional relations are difficult, if not impossible. The Orthodox are looked upon by non-Orthodox as Russian spies, agents of the secret Russian police. Protestants are regarded by the strongly nationalistic Catholics and Government alike as untrustworthy occidentals. The Catholics are considered by the Government to be politically disloyal for their obedience to Rome, and temperamentally incorrigible owing to their strong nationalism and religious devotion.

Except for the Orthodox of late Russian origin, the Christians in general regard their present regime and leadership as a foreign occupation, mixing their religious convictions with their political aspirations in resistng the invaders.

The following statistics* give some picture of the changes which have taken place since 1940:

Roman Catholic	*1940*	*1948*
Believers	2,776,422	possibly 2,000,000
Churches	1,202	ca. 600
Clergy	1,646	400
Archbishops and Bishops	14	1**
Theological schools	5	0
Publications	52	0
Lutheran and Reformed		
Believers	300,000	Very few
Churches	63	Less than 10
Pastors	25	3-8

* *Lithuanian Bulletin*, No. 1-3, January-March, 1949, p. 4, and other sources.
** Since this report, the last Roman Catholic bishop is said to have been driven underground (*New York Times*, July 5:13:2, 1949).

ESTONIA

Population (1939)	1,250,000
Lutherans	900,000
Orthodox (Russian)	215,000
Roman Catholic	2,000

Following her liberation from Russian domination at the end of World War I, Estonia, like her Baltic neighbors, quickly developed her own democratic Government, constitution and general social framework for unhampered religious life.

Church and State enjoyed cordial relationships, the Church was subsidized by the State, and every other reasonable facility put at the disposal of the Church for the development of charitable works, evangelization and education.

Three months after the arrival of Soviet troops in eastern Estonia in 1939, the President of the Republic confirmed in office the newly-elected Lutheran Bishop, Professor Kopp. There was a general revival of interest in Bible study and religious activities.

Chronicle of Events

June, 1940—

Russia occupied the rest of Estonia to "forestall military attack on the USSR." The Estonian Government accepted Russian conditions of occupation. There was no resistance.

On the sixth day of occupation, Russian authorities announced that an investigation was to be made concerning the continuance of religious education in schools.

Religious radio was prohibited (H. Perlitz, *The Fate of Religion and Church under Soviet Rule in 1940/ 1941*).

Lutheran Bishop Kopp exhorted the people to go on quietly and fearlessly with Christian works. Some church properties were sold where Russians established military and naval bases (*ICPIS*, No. 27, July, 1940).

July, 1940—

Bible camps for first communicants and other gatherings of a religious character were prohibited.

The Salvation Army and Christian youth organizations were dissolved (H. Perlitz, *The Fate of Religion and Church under Soviet Rule in 1940/ 1941*).

August, 1940—

After Estonia was admitted to the Soviet Union as a republic, and a new constitution patterned after the Russian Constitution was adopted, Bishop Kopp stated that the Church desired to continue as a National Church in a new situation, "so that the Nation may grow and flourish, and become stronger spiritually . . ." Statesmen assumed that there would be no hindrance to church life and work.

Church registers must be surrendered to the State.

Religious education was removed from schools. Morning prayers and ceremonies in the schools were prohibited.

The Lutheran Theological Faculty at the University of Tartu was closed (*ICPIS*, No. 34, September, 1940).

Bishop Kopp exhorted parents to teach their children as Christians, and to pray.

August 9, 1940—

"The Church loses the support of the State and all privileges. . . ." (*Kommunist*, August 9, 1940; as quoted by H. Perlitz, *The Fate of Religion and Church under Soviet Rule in 1940/1941*). Clergy must pay taxes for

(312)

schooling, utilities, rents — above charges to productive labor, *e.g.* electricity rates for clergy were fourteen times those for laborers (*Official Journal USSR*, No. 22, February 26, 1941).

August 11, 1940—

A systematic anti-religious campaign began in the press:

"The new socialist school will sweep-away religion, a merely bygone means for deceiving the people" (*Kommunist*, official Party Organ, August 11, 1940, quoted by H. Perlitz, *The Fate of Religion and Church under Soviet Rule in 1940/1941*).

August 17, 1940—

"The clergymen must be unmasked as exploiters or their henchmen . . . acting secretly, enlisting agents for the intelligence service of the Capitalist countries . . . deceiving and deluding the masses of people . . . selling them out to the plutocrats and warmongers" (*Kommunist*, August 17, 1940).

August 22, 1940—

The Chief of Internal Security ordered the confiscation of religious literature "aiming at political ends." Religious periodicals were discontinued (H. Perlitz, *The Fate of Religion and Church under Soviet Rule in 1940/1941*).

September 4, 1940—

"Since religious teaching is forbidden in schools, religious activity among children and youth outside schools is forbidden . . . confirmation classes, Sunday Schools, church choirs and all other devices for obscuring the minds of children at houses of prayer and at Bible lessons in the homes are to be stopped" (*Kommunist*, September 4, 1940).

Religious teaching and confirmation were listed as crimes punishable under Section 122 and 123 of the Criminal Code of USSR (H. Perlitz, *The Fate of Religion and Church under Soviet Rule in 1940/1941*).

September, 1940—

The periodical *Människovännen* (Finland), published the following information from Soviet sources (October 3, 1940):

"The Baltic countries occupied by USSR must be de-christianized. But the old methods of twenty years ago must not be applied in these new Soviet republics. Thus, executions of 'priests, monks and other religious fanatics' are rare, but other means are used to undermine religious life and give prerogatives to the Godless. In a country parish in Estonia, the minister, who had made a 'political sermon' and criticized the new regime, was condemned either to pay a fine of a hundred crowns or to go to prison for a fortnight. The congregation collected the sum needed to pay the fine" (*ICPIS*, No. 39, October, 1940).

October 2, 1940—

The Government ordered the "nationalization of all church property, e.g., funds, cars, homes, lands," without compensation. Many pastors were ousted from parsonages. People providing them refuge were arrested and deported (H. Perlitz, *The Fate of Religion and Church under Soviet Rule in 1940/1941*).

October 9, 1940—

"Religion is a reactionary social factor. During hundreds of years religion has served the purposes of exploiters and defended the capitalist society based on class-divisions. It will defend this society in future too. Religion is an obstacle in the way of the working people, preventing them from becoming masters of their destiny. The Communist party fights against every kind of religion. Making use of the freedom of anti-religious propaganda, we must develop all propaganda embracing a scientific anti-religious form" (From *Kommunist*, October 9, 1940, as quoted in *ICPIS*).

"In social conditions based on exploitation real freedom of conscience cannot be realized, since in such conditions religion is deeply rooted in economic life. In capitalist countries working people cannot possess any freedom of speech, press and conscience. Lenin writes about this: 'Freedom of conscience in a bourgeois democracy is freedom used by the capital to buy or bribe whole clerical organizations for intoxicating masses with the opium of religion'" (*Ibid.*).

October 14, 1940—

"One ought to avoid offending religious feelings, as this might

. . . strengthen religious fanaticism" (*Rahva Hääl*).

The "League of Anti-Religious Fighters" was organized for developing a systematic anti-religious campaign in schools, radio, cinema, press.

October 15, 1940—

By Government decree, children of pastors were excluded from the category "child of working intelligentia" for free school fees. Pastors were to take up "socially useful work (as) honest members of the Soviet community." Sermons were taken down verbatim. No reference in sermons to "actual events" was permitted as this consisted of "political activity." Pastors were required to report on congregations.

October 31, 1940—On Reformation Day

Rahva Hääl and other journals attacked Luther as the "lackey of oppressors and exploiters, whose following fought a bloody battle against the peasants, seeking to make the new church the same instrument of oppression and exploitation as all other churches" (As quoted by H. Perlitz, *The Fate of Religion and Church under Soviet Rule in 1940/1941*).

December 19, 1940—

Människovännen (Finland), December 19, 1940, stated that it was forbidden to send Christmas cards, Christmas not being a legal holiday in the Soviet Union. New Year's Day, on the contrary, was an official holiday. New Year trees—instead of Christmas trees—were to be sold on that occasion. The population was hopeful that an early start in the sale of these trees might enable them to get trees in time for the Christmas holiday. The Soviet authorities condemned family festivals as being contrary to the Bolshevist doctrine.

December 25th and 26th were declared working days by order of the Government. The order was rescinded three days prior to the 25th. The churches were crowded on Christmas Day.

Journals attacked Christmas as "spiritual rubbish of religion" (*Kommunist*, December 25, 1940).

February, 1941—

The USSR *Anti-religioznik* recommended the utilization of Godless propaganda as an effective means for the "spiritual defence and cultural development of the Estonian Soviet Republic." Over against the "inner enemy," i.e., the Church, which sought to maintain contact with the external enemies of the Soviet Union, the nation must "hold itself constantly ready to fight." The Godless Association therefore "has the great responsible task" of bringing the "unlimited freedom" of a progressive religionless development to the Estonian people, who under the bourgeois regime of the free State of Estonia were exposed to "all kinds of persecution and bondage."

The Estonian Church, continued the article, had for twenty years, "under the hypocritical mask" of a cultural institution, simply pursued the aim of its own enrichment and aggrandisement. The formal separation of Church and State was the "democratic disguise" of a system of social and political oppression, which was encouraged by the "grey barons" of Estonian nationality with the help of the Churches and religious associations connected with the "Christian National Party." In the free State of Estonia, which described itself as a "bulwark of European culture in the East," the Church, with the help of the reactionary Government, gradually got back the property which to some extent had been taken from it in the "partial revolution of 1919." The "nationalistic" spirit of the Church, at first concealed, was later openly encouraged by its leaders, said the report. In schools, the teachers were selected on "nationalistic and religious" principles, and freedom of conscience was prevented by the preference shown to "believers." The religious press lowered the general cultural level of Estonia and delivered the people over to social distress and a gloomy hopelessness.

The progressively-minded groups, continued the article, were deliberately persecuted, especially in the Russian frontier area, where "the Lutheran and Orthodox clergy together directly encouraged the provocative proceedings of the police towards the classes of the population who were friendly to the Soviet Union" (e.g., drunkards, encouraged to do so by ministers and priests, disturbed classes at school).

An increased effort of Godless propaganda in Estonia, the article concluded, was justified, not only in view of this attitude of the Church in the recent past, but also because these legally-favoured conditions offered an excellent example of the way in which "the principle of separation of Church and State is administered in practice in the other bourgeois countries of the world today" (*ICPIS*, No. 13, April, 1941).

March 7, 1941—

"The great and long experiences which have been gathered on the antireligious background in Russia during more than twenty years must be taken advantage of in Estonia, too" (*Kommunist*, March 7, 1941).

The official paper, *Rahva Hääl*, 7th of March, 1941, published an article entitled, "Anti-religious Propaganda Is to be Conducted with Knowledge and Dexterity":

"All religions are hostile to Communism. Religion is the adversary of every kind of progress and science. Religion will not by itself vanish from human consciousness. On the contrary, to overcome religion, patient and hard educational work must be carried out among the masses. It will take a long time to liquidate it from the human mind. It is our duty to explain systematically every day the perniciousness of religion and to help the working people to get rid of the fetters of religious ideas. It is necessary to create all over the country an all-embracing net of the League of Anti-Religious Fighters. The Communist party, trade unions and organizations of Communistic youth must in every way assist the League of Anti-Religious Fighters."

Special training courses were organized for anti-religious propagandists by the People's Commissariat of Education. Teaching in an international and anti-religious spirit was prescribed for children of three to seven years.

People did not attend anti-religious meetings. Some spoke out openly against them (H. Perlitz, *The Fate of Religion and Church under Soviet Rule in 1940/1941*).

April, 1941—

The Swedish paper *Kyrkor under Korset* (Church under the Cross) reported as follows:

"The ministers of religion in Estonia, Latvia and Lithuania have been allowed to become Soviet citizens, but not to have the right to vote. A number of clergymen, including Metropolitan Alexander of the Estonian Orthodox Church, are being prosecuted. Pastors and priests are being banished; and special concentration camps are said to have been established for them, because they are not to be allowed to come in contact with their fellow prisoners.

"One of the first things to be transformed is the school system and education in general. There is no longer any such thing as a Christian school. Hundreds of school teachers have been dismissed; in their place students are being appointed after a course of instruction in Communism. At the University of Riga 'Communism and Leninism' has been introduced as a special subject with a staff of seven teachers. A Protestant and a Catholic professor were both given the choice either to be deported to Siberia or to undertake the scientific development of Godless propaganda. They chose the former. Molotov has guaranteed the promotion of the anti-religious struggle in these republics.

Estonia: "The number of people attending church is larger today than it was before the country was attached to USSR. The church attendance of the younger generation is now very considerable. The churches are as a rule packed full on Sundays. The ministers marry, baptize, and bury people unhindered as they used to do. State officials have been ordered to stay away from church and not to ask the ministers for any official services. Most of the theological students at Dorpat have changed over to the medical faculty. Bishop Kopp of the Lutheran Church of Estonia lives in Dorpat, where he used to be a professor, and maintains contacts with the clergy from there.

"The situation of the Orthodox Church is generally similar to that of Lutheranism. The priests were still at work up to the last few months, but their economic situation is growing more and more difficult.

"The Roman Catholic priests continue to wear their official dress. Many of them, like the clergy of the other confessions, have learned a craft so as to maintain themselves more easily.

"Methodists and Baptists have suffered severe material losses. Their places of worship were mostly in business houses which have been seized by the authorities. It is thus particularly difficult for them to hold services.

"Anti-religious posters are not yet anywhere to be seen. Members of the Communist youth groups are obliged to declare themselves to be atheists. Atheistic propaganda which is still in its preliminary stages, is for the time being chiefly confined to the schools.

"The President of the Godless League, Yaroslavsky-Gubelmann, is personally directing the 'de-Christianization' of the Baltic Soviet republics. In his 'collected works' which are now being used in schools instead of Bible, catechism and hymn books, this irreconcilable enemy of God declares: 'The only Kingdom of Heaven that exists is the one which we are making for ourselves today under the leadership of Comrade Stalin; and the only real hell is to be found in the capitalistic countries, where the workers are being sucked dry and plagued to death'" (As quoted in *ICPIS*, No. 21, May, 1941).

June, 1941—

Perlitz, Vice-rector of the University of Tartu, reported that twenty-nine pastors and elders of the Lutheran Church had been murdered (apart from those who were killed during war operations). One hundred sixty-three active members of leading Church courts, and thousands of Church members, were deported to Soviet Russia, including the former Bishop H. Rahamägi, K. Saarse of Tallinn, Dean H. Kubu. The Vice-President of the Consistory, Kristian Kaarna, was kept in prison for a long time before he disappeared into Soviet Russia. Seven Lutheran pastors were mobilized for military service in the Soviet Army. The churches were not closed on a large scale, but fifty-two (about one-third) were destroyed or damaged (some were transformed into clubs, cinemas, theatres, etc.).

The Lutheran Church and the tiny Roman Catholic Church (0.2% of the total population) were particularly persecuted. "On the contrary," states the document, "the Orthodox Church, to which belong 19% of the population, suffered nearly no persecution at all" (*ICPIS*, No. 16, April, 1943).

Orthodox churches were frequently referred to as "instruments of Russification."

Under a Russo-German agreement, people of German ethnic origin were permitted to emigrate to Germany. Many clergy fled to Germany. Homes belonging to other clergymen were confiscated by the Soviet Army. The clergy sold their furniture, and had difficulty finding any accommodations.

Leaders of the Christian Youth Movement were replaced by members of the Communist Party (*ICPIS*, No. 23, June, 1941).

1941-1944—Nazi Occupation.

Again, as in Latvia and Lithuania, between the retreat of the Soviet forces and the Nazi oocupation, Estonia declared herself an independent republic and proceeded with the re-establishment of her own political and ecclesiastical patterns.

Her experiences under the Nazis were similar to those in Latvia. As the Germans once again retreated many Lutherans fled or were forcibly deported with them.

1944-1950—Second Soviet Occupation.

Estonia's experiences under the second Soviet occupation were little different from those of her neighbors. In 1950 a Ukrainian, V. Moskalouko, was appointed Minister of State Security. Shortly after his arrival "luxury" taxes were levied on church buildings, church weddings, christenings and confirmations, the latter ranging from $250 to $375. These funds were applied to the expenses of the anti-religious propaganda program (Mac Eoin, *The Communist War on Religion*, p. 186).

Christian holidays were suppressed. Churches, particularly the Baptist and Evangelical Christians, meet as "prayer groups." Special home courses are held for lay preachers and elders including pastoral theology, Bible study, and the Soviet Constitution. Pentecostalists are forbidden to speak in "tongues" in public meetings. A number of damaged church buildings are reported by the Baptists to have been rebuilt.

Summary of Religious Situation, January, 1951

The Baltice peoples had twenty-two years of free development as independent republics. Now it has been eleven years since their assimilation into the Soviet Union began. For the past three years, very little information has come out concerning religious life in the Baltics. Based on past history and the fact of their Protestant and Roman Catholic rather than Orthodox majorities, one could elaborate a long list of probable differences between the present situation there and in other republics of the Soviet Union. Lacking facts, however, the writer must leave the reader to draw his own conclusions from the foregoing information and from the "Summary of the Situation in the USSR," pages 275 to 278.

RUMANIA

Introduction

The conversion of Rumanians to Christianity began in the fourth century. Since shortly after that date the churches have played an important role in the national, cultural and political life of Rumania. Local nationalities or ethnic groups have been largely identified with particular churches. "Orthodox," for example, became almost synonymous with "Rumanian," and "Catholic" with "Swabian." Up to the middle of the 19th century education was exclusively confessional; since that time the State has taken increasing responsibility.

Orthodox in History—The history of the Rumanian people is closely interwoven with that of the Orthodox Church. The Orthodox Church was the preserver of national unity during centuries of Turkish domination in Moldavia and Wallachia and of Hungarian domination in Transylvania. The Metropolita (Primate Archbishop) has been, *ex officio*, president of the Prince's Council, his chief adviser, and Regent of the country during the Prince's minority or a vacancy of the throne. This tradition was followed during the minority of the presently exiled King Michael I, when Patriarch Miron was one of the three Regents of the Kingdom. The same Patriarch Miron was called upon to preside over a national Cabinet in 1938, during an acute political crisis. Priests could be and were elected to Parliament.

The churches' greatest contribution in the life of the nation is characterized by a competent Rumanian as "defender of the national culture. During the dark Middle Ages, as well as under foreign yoke, the monasteries and convents were the real schools of the people, the depository of historical and literary treasures and traditions. Monks kept the chronicles of events, translated the Old and New Testament into the national language, established the first printing press. There would have been no Rumanian history, no Rumanian literature, no Rumanian literary tongue if the old convents hidden in the mountains had not unflinchingly kindled the flame of national culture through all the period of deadly dangers which menaced the existence of the race."

Roman Catholicism—From the 13th to the 16th centuries, leaders of Rumania (Moldavians and Wallachians) were frequently tempted by marriage or court privilege, or other interests, to ally themselves with Rome, but on the whole remained Orthodox. However, in 1698, after the annexation of Transylvania to the Austrian Empire, the Metropolitan of Alba-Julia, Athenasius, summoned 1,617 clergy, and united Orthodox communities of Transylvania to Rome in a "Uniate" Church. Since that time the Vatican has had, in both Uniate and Roman Catholic churches, an important stake in Rumanian politics and religious life, and has improved its position on various occasions. When a small Rumanian army under Stephan the Great withheld an invading Red Army, Pope Gregory VII called him "the Defender of Christianity and the Athlete of Christ."

On May 10, 1927, a Concordat between the Vatican and the Rumanian Government was signed. The agreement included regulations concerning the organization and function of the Catholic Church (Articles 1-10), dispositions concerning confessional teaching (Article 19), administration of seminaries

(Article 16), and resolutions concerning administrations and conduct of welfare orgaizations, foundations, hospitals, convents, etc., under the Roman Catholic Church (Article 14). In general, the Church was to have freedom of action, initiative and leadership (*Persecution of Religion in Rumania*, Rumanian National Committee [in exile] hereafter "RNC," p. 14).

Church-State Regulations—Pre-1940—The position of the Churches in Rumania at the outbreak of World War II as compared with 1948 was as follows:

	1940	1948*	National origin
Total population	18,000,000	16,000,000	
Rumanian Orthodox	72.6 %	72 %	Rumanian
Uniate (Catholic)	7.9 %	10 %	Rumanian
Roman Catholic	6.8 %	7 %	Hungarian, German
Calvinist (Reformed)	3.9 %	4.6%	Hungarian
Lutheran	2.12%	1.6%	German
Unitarian	0.4 %	0.4%	Hungarian
Baptist		0.7%	Rumanian
Others—Armenians, Adventists, Lipovans		0.5%	

The predominant position of the Orthodox Church was emphasized in the Rumanian constitution. Its special privileges, though not numerous, included required allegiance of the King and his descendants to it. The two "Rumanian" Churches—Orthodox and Uniate—enjoyed a political advantage over the others in that all their bishops sat, *ex officio*, in the Senate, while only the heads of the other denominations, small in number, enjoyed that privilege, and then only if their congregations numbered at least 200,000 adherents.

The Constitution guaranteed liberty of conscience, and equal freedom and protection for all cults consistent with public order and morals. The position of the minority churches was defined in detail by the Law of Cults of 1928, which repeated these guarantees. The Baptist churches, however, were not formally recognized until April, 1940. Religious belief could not exempt any person from the obligations imposed upon him by law, and political organizations could not be formed on purely confessional bases, nor could political questions be debated within ecclesiastical corporations or institutions. A Church could not be subordinated to any authority or ecclesiastical organization outside the country, except in so far as its dogmatic or canonical principles required. The heads of the Churches had to be approved by the Crown and take an oath of loyalty to the King and obedience to the constitution and the law.

---

* *News Behind the Iron Curtain*, p. 30.

Chronicle of Events

Period of German Occupation

June, 1940—

Bessarabia and North Bukovina were ceded to the USSR; this was accompanied by suppression, disorder, rioting, burning of the Cathedral at Cervanti. Two Orthodox seminaries were located in the ceded territory. Priests were attacked; some fled to the south and west; others were deported to Siberia. Many Lutherans migrated toward Transylvania (*ICPIS*, No. 27, July, 1940).

September, 1940—

The new Antonescu Rumanian (Axis) Government announced its intention to purge the Orthodox Church.
Free churches were suppressed (*ICPIS*, No. 34, September, 1940).

October, 1940—

Church and State were separated in Russian-occupied territory. Attacks on religion and the church were made by Soviet officers through police, educational, military, and press facilities. All church property was expropriated.

October, 1940—

After Antonescu's announcement concerning his intention to re-organize the Orthodox churches, Patriarch Nikodim suggested that candidates for priesthood must give evidence of the necessary spiritual equipment and must spend a minimum of one year in a monastery before ordination. Nikodim expressed his willingness for Church and Government cooperation, with State representatives participating in higher church governing bodies and the State controlling church finance. Antonescu replied that since Rumania was a Christian State, the Church could fulfil its mission. He announced that he would place a church reorganization plan before the church council (*ICPIS*, Nos. 41, 43, November, 1940).

November 17, 1940—

The Pope received General Antonescu in Rome.

December, 1940—

The Iron Guard (Antonescu Nazi element) pressed for the replacement of older bishops with Nazi-selected priests, for the reorganization of theological education and for the intensification of home missions and social activity.

December 4, 1940—
The Orthodox Holy Synod pledged its loyalty to the Iron Guard State (*ICPIS*, No. 11, March, 1941).

December, 1940—

In USSR-occupied Bessarabia, Godless propaganda was resisted by the people. The Godless propaganda slogan was "Religion makes the people stupid." A revival of religious life was seen in the attendance of Red soldiers at liturgy and sacraments. All church property was in the hands of the occupying powers. The Cathedral of Kishinev was transformed into a community house (*ICPIS*, No. 37, October, 1941).

April, 1941—
Lutheran Bishop Glondys of Transylvania was replaced by Staedel of the National Socialist renewal movement (*ICPIS*, Nos. 15 and 19, April and May, 1941).

January, 1942—

In Rumanian re-occupied Bessarabia the Orthodox churches restored their monasteries and colleges. Special missionary work was organized in Rumanian-occupied Russia. Orthodox missionary work was labelled by the Russians "Rumanization" along with official Rumanian Government activities (*ICPIS*, No. 3, January, 1942; No. 21, 23, June, 1942).

January, 1942—

Rumanian journals called for the deportation of all Slavs to Siberia. The Bulgarian Orthodox Church opposed the deportation, stating that the war was not against the Russian people; it quoted Rumanian journalists: "The Government was exclusively concerned to save the Orthodox faith from barbarous suppression by Godless Communists" (*Ibid.*).

May, 1942—

Orthodox Metropolitan Balan of Transylvania provided liturgy, religious training, service books and relief for Red prisoners of Rumanian (Axis) forces. The Rumanian people gave food and clothing (*ICPIS*, No. 20, May, 1942).

June, 1942—

The Orthodox Church sent 100 priests to Odessa to preach and re-open the Russian Orthodox seminary. The priests were welcomed by the population (*ICPIS*, No. 21, June, 1942).

October, 1942—

Nikodim retired as Orthodox Patriarch. Metropolitan Balan of Transylvania presided over the provisional commission (ICPIS, Nos. 37, 38, November and October, 1942).

November, 1942—

Balan resigned as provisional president of the Holy Synod (*ICPIS*, No. 39, November, 1942).

January, 1943—

The Antonescu Government confiscated all property of the "sects" as "foreign and hostile to the State." A large number of Baptists and Adventists were arrested and sentenced to long imprisonment (*ICPIS*, No. 2, January, 1943).

July, 1943—

The Orthodox mission in occupied Russia failed to establish a seminary because of German objections (*ICPIS*, No. 28, July, 1943).

January, 1944—

Metropolitan Balan established churches and a spiritual ministry for 1,000 prisoners of war in the Vulcan mines. The prisoners built their own Russian churches, requested religious facilities (*ICPIS*, No. 2, January, 1944).

Between April 1942 and the liberation of Rumania (from Axis forces) in 1944, the Evangelical churches were subjected to measures similar to those used in Germany by the Nazis: The National Consistory of the German Lutheran Church under Staedel condemned the Old Testament as a Jewish stumbling block to Germans who would follow Jesus. It discontinued the use of the Old Testament and sought to purge the churches of all Jewish heritage. However, the Evangelical churches opposed Staedel, who, they alleged, sought to curtail freedom of religious confession and preaching, to subject the church to the new German social order, to transfer the educational (parochial) system to national supervision, to dissolve church and religious associations, to hand over the procuring of support for church work to the German *Volksgruppe*. A number of the members of the national consistory resigned.

Period of Uncertainty under the Allied Control Commission

August 23, 1944—

The military alliance with Germany was broken off; an armistice was signed in Moscow. A special department was created in the Soviet Legation, Bucarest, to deal with religious affairs in the Balkans. The "Vishinsky Plan," outlined for advancing Soviet forces in Southeast Europe, included provisions for—

(1) control of clergy and religious leaders by controlling or providing their stipends;

(2) compromising of clergy and church leaders;

(3) liquidation of undesirable leaders and planting of Soviet-trained religious leaders in key positions;

(4) forbidding any church or religious activity except worship and the liturgy (i.e., within church walls);

(5) creation of a loyal Orthodox front against Western churches under the leadership of the Moscow Patriarchate.

This was initiated with an order from the Soviet high command of the Southeast European front that the clergy should keep their services going and their churches open, that they should collaborate in all social activity, especially the relief of the poor, and that they should not boycott the regime; Soviet troops were ordered to return all confiscated church property.

Autumn 1944—

The Government began bi-monthly secret investigations of church leaders.

September, 1944—

The "Patriotic Defense" organized a form of social assistance, requiring clergy to register and participate in all sessions of the "Patriotic Defense"; to make collections in the churches for the "Patriotic Defense"; to prohibit Christian welfare activity outside the "Patriotic Defense."

First adherents were largely those compromised clergy who had been in the "Iron Guard" or on trial before ecclesiastical courts and were assured by the "Patriotic Defense" of livelihood and rehabilitation.

End of 1944—

The "Patriotic Defense" executive bodies were instructed to overcome clerical resistance by conciliation, exempting parish houses from requisition, restoring land taken from rural churches by local Soviets, granting churches funds to repair war damages.

January, 1945—

Religious education in the public schools was replaced in some places by "civic duty" courses. However, the confessional schools of Transylvania continued freely (*ICPIS*, No. 9, March 1945).

January, 1945—

Twenty-six "Saxon" Lutheran pastors were deported to Russia, along with hundreds of laymen, for labor.

January, 1945—

A number of Uniate priests were charged with opposition to Russian annexation of Carpathian Rumania and were deported to Russia (*Ch. Cent.*, March 16, 1949).

February 11, 1945—

Papal Nuncio Mgr. Cassulo was permitted to send messages to the Vatican, but not in code (*N. Y. T.* 11:5:8).

Period of the "Popular Front"

March 6, 1945—

A predominantly Communist government was established behind a coalition "Popular Front." A former Iron Guard priest, Burducea, was named as Minister of Cults. He sought to organize a "Union of Democratic Clergy."

The Patriarch exhorted the people to forget their divisions and the past, and to support the new Government of Prime Minister Groza in setting up a legal and just administration (*ICPIS*, No. 12, March, 1945).

January 14, 1946—

The Minister of Cults called a conference of all religious leaders to discuss their part in the restoration of civil liberties (*N. Y. T.* 14, 3:2:5).

May, 1946—

Orthodox Patriarch Nicodim visited the Moscow Patriarchate. The Government stressed the fact that Groza was the son of an Orthodox priest and a professing Orthodox; that the Minister of Education was an Orthodox priest; the Minister of Propaganda a theological professor (*ICPIS*, No. 21, May, 1946).

May 25, 1946—

The Rumanian Legate to the Holy See denied a report that the Government requested the withdrawal of the Apostolic Nuncio from Bucharest (*N. Y. T.* 25, 8:1). However, Nuncio Cassulo was shortly recalled and replaced by Bishop O'Hara of the U. S. A.

May, 1946—

The Bucharest Theological Faculty planned a pan-Orthodox theological conference (*ICPIS*, No. 21, May, 1946).

September, 1946—

An Orthodox publication heralded the World Council plans and the ecumenical fellowship as a work toward "international friendship," and expressed eagerness for the world assembly of churches. It announced the second international congress of Orthodox theological professors. The Rumanian "Association for Orthodox Theology" was formed to promote theological studies, ecumenical work and cooperation among lecturers (*ICPIS*, No. 39, November, 1946).

Late Summer, 1946—

Religious publications were restricted by censorship of the Ministry of Cults and the Ministry of Information and Propaganda, and by the allocation of paper for political purposes by the Government. All religious meetings were to be cleared through the Ministry of the Interior.

The Government granted subsidies to priests and pastors on certification of allegiance; Groza promised better salaries if the church leaders would give stronger support to the Government. The Ministry of Cults began censorship of all mail to and from the Patriarchate.

Late Summer, 1946—

Saxon Evangelicals were persecuted as "Germanic sympathizers." Saxon confessional schools were placed "under supervision." The use of the Russian flag and the national anthem in some churches brought criticism from others.

The Parliament proposed outlawing all foreign support for the churches.

October, 1946—

Patriarch Nicodim was received by the Government and Groza before visiting Moscow "to consolidate Russian-Rumanian good relations." Vasca, Director of the Ministry of Education and President of the "Democratic Priests' Union" accompanied Nicodim; he sought Russian aid for the Orthodox churches (*ICPIS*, No. 42, November, 1946).

November, 1946—

Nicodim expressed his personal desire for ecumenical contacts, but found them impracticable at this time. Vasca stated that although Rumanian Orthodox were autonomous, they would be guided in World Council relationships by Moscow's lead (*ICPIS*, No. 42, November, 1946).

December, 1946—

The Minister of Cults, addressing the Orthodox Synod, requested the neutrality of the Church in the coming political changes. The Synod urged the Ministry of Education to increase religious instruction in the schools.

The churches planned to expand their publications (*EPS*, No. 4, January, 1947).

March, 1947—

The Minister of Cults, Radu Rosculetz, a member of the liberal dissident group under Tatarescu, made known his decision to submit to Parliament two draft laws, the first concerning pensioning of priests; the second aimed at a redistribution of Sees and establishing new rules for episcopal assemblies. The first became a law (No. 166/1947) immediately. It provided an age limit of seventy years for all clergy. Exceptions might be made, upon advice from the Minister of Cults, in favor of such prelates as "have an exceptional activity." One Orthodox metropolitan and three bishops were retired almost immediately. The Orthodox Metropolitan of Jassy was thereby retired; he had been in line for election to the office of Patriarch.

March, 1947—

Nicodim appealed for international aid against the famine (*EPS*, No. 16, April, 1947).

April 5, 1947—

Premier Groza accepted the Catholic Welfare Conference's (US) offer to distribute supplies; he pledged freedom of action. The Roman Catholic bishops attended a conference, in Bucharest, on means of distribution (*N. Y. T.* 5, 6:6).

June 15, 1947—

The first Church World Service shipment of relief goods was reported distributed with the sanction of the Government (*N. Y. T.* 15, 63:3).

June, 1947—

Patriarch Alexei, of Moscow, visited Rumania. He declared the necessity of an all-powerful pan-Orthodox front (*EPS*).

Summer, 1947—

The International Red Cross was expelled. All subsequent relief was to be distributed via the Rumanian Red Cross.

Some Roman Catholic church hospitals, etc., were reported to have been taken over by government agencies.

August, 1947—

Some Evangelical leaders were arrested and charged with receiving money from the World Council of Churches to organize a resistance movement.

The Government attempted to force confessions that the World Council was in political services.

Free Church leaders were charged with being "Imperialist agents."

October, 1947—

The Roman Catholic Seminary in Timisoara was requisitioned for a school of medicine (*Tablet*, Feb. 25, 1950). (Later, some parts of the building were vacated for the Seminary.)

November, 1947—

Rev. Justinian, later to be Patriarch, was made Metropolitan of Moldavia.

November, 1947—

The second draft law of the Minister of Cults (March 1947) was put into effect. Until then, episcopal assemblies had been elected by the faithful, who delegated their members for a three years' period. In the terms of the new law, these assemblies were to be made up with a *de jure* majority comprising members of Parliament, ministers of State, and State under-secretaries belonging to the diocese. The significance of the episcopal elections was underlined by the Communist press. *Universul* of August 28, 1948, stated:

"The guidance of the country's destinies having been taken up by the hands of the working class and of democratic organizations, special attention is being given to the renewal of the high cadres of the church. This was evidenced by the elections which took place in November, 1947, when three hierarchs of the people entered the synod. This concern of the working class for the destinies of the church culminated on May 24, 1948, when the new Patriarch of the Rumanian People's Republic was elected in the person of His Holiness Justinian."

November 21, 1947—

Minister of Finance Luca in a public address praised the freedom of religious worship in Rumania, stating that the churches were being favored by the exemption of church farm lands from agricultural reform. He stated that the imperialists seek to use the church in inciting a new war against the people.

"The altar must remain the altar and not become a reactionary political club. There can be no state within a state . . . There can be no turning back. The democratic Rumanian State cannot be asked to permit confessional schools to preach anti-democratic policy."

December 3, 1947—

Premier Groza's conferences with Roman Catholic bishops were reviewed by Minister Luca. When the Roman Catholic bishops protested to Groza regarding political arrests, Groza silenced them by asking if they had protested when Communists and Leftists were arrested by Rightists some years earlier. Groza condemned the churches' role in politics (*N.Y.T.*, December 3, 12:3).

Period of the Present Regime in Complete Authority

December 30, 1947—

The People's Republic of Rumania was proclaimed.

January, 1948—

"The Presidium of the Rumanian People's Republic—the Council of five set up after King Michael's abdiction—accompanied by Premier Groza and Minister of Cults Stanciu Stoian paid a visit to Patriarch Nicodim, head of the Rumanian Orthodox Church. After expressing New Year's greetings to the Patriarch Mr. Groza said: 'The Church is an institution with permanent usefulness in the life of the people. It is part of the State itself keeping pace with the spirit of the times. The Orthodox Christian Church, having always understood this, will surely understand it this time'" (*EPS*, No. 3, January 30, 1949).

"Representatives of the Orthodox, Roman Catholic, Greek Catholic, Baptist and other Protestant Churches gathered in Bucharest to take an oath of allegiance to the new Republic. They took the oath in the presence of the Minister of Cults, the formula of allegiance being the same as that used by the State employees. In some cases, religious leaders added additional assurances of fidelity to the new Government" (*EPS*, No. 4, January 30, 1948).

January, 1948—

The liquidation or assimilation of Christian youth associations was reported. Buildings, libraries and equipment were taken over.

February 28, 1948—

Patriarch Nicodim died.

February 29, 1948—

Metropolitan Justinian of Moldavia automatically became Locum Tenens of the office of Patriarch.

February 29, 1948—

Pastor Wurmbrandt, of the Norwegian Jewish Mission, Bucharest, disappeared en route to church. The Government stated officially that he had not been arrested, but had crossed the frontier clandestinely, and had been seen in Denmark and Norway. Information later revealed that he was in solitary confinement in a dark cellar-cell, and was not being allowed to speak to anyone, or to read. He was offered release if he would enter the special services of the Government, but he refused.

March 14, 1948—

Metropolitan Justinian of Moldavia and acting Patriarch praised the draft constitution of the Rumanian Government in a pastoral letter (*RNC*, p. 32).

March 31, 9148—

Certain Catholic Priests were listed as undesirable by the Government's *Official Monitor* and dismissed (*RNC*, p. 13).

April 11, 1948—

On the occasion of the ratification of the new Constitution (Appendix I—Rumania) Gherghiu-Dej spoke before the National Assembly:
"The Pope will undoubtedly find occasion to assail our constitution because it does not tally with the Vatican's tendencies, which are to interfere in the internal concerns of various countries under the pretext of evangelizing the Catholic faithful. Who knows whether the Vatican will not consider anathematizing us on the pretext that our constitution does not provide for the submission of our fellow countrymen of Catholic persuasion to the political directives of the Vati-

can, or because we do not allow ourselves to be tempted by America's golden calf, at the feet of which the Vatican would bring its faithful" (*RNC*, p. 12).

April, 1948—

Religious publications were limited and the name "Jesus Christ" was reported not to be permitted in any publications. The single Orthodox publication was the *Journal of the Holy Synod*. The one Roman Catholic publication still functioning was *The Children's Paradise;* it was also suppressed at the end of May, 1948 (*RNC*, p. 13).

May 15, 1948—

At the centennial of the liberation of Rumania (when Orthodox Bishop Saguna and Uniate Bishop Leweny demanded national rights for the Rumanian people) an appeal was addressed to the Uniates to join the Orthodox Church:
"Today, when the Rumanian Popular Republic guarantees equal rights, political, cultural, and religious, to all, no matter what their creed or race might be, to persist in the spiritual disunity which stemmed from the grave jeopardy in which the Rumanians of Transylvania found themselves in 1700, means to desert the united front of the new destinies that our working people are creating for themselves in the dawn of the future."

May 24, 1948—

Justinian, Metropolitan of Moldavia, was elected Patriarch after necessary changes were made in the church statutes so that he could qualify. According to reports, he was elected after insistence from Moscow that no other leader was acceptable. *Universul* quoted Justinian as desiring a new church constitution in keeping with social changes in the new government.

May 24, 1948—

On the occasion of Justinian's election Rev. Stoian, Minister of Cults, stated:
"There are two religious institutions of which world reaction is trying to make special use: The Roman Catholic Church and the so-called Ecumenical Movement. The Roman Catholic Church, in Italy and throughout the

world, is joining its tendency to domination with that of Yankee imperialism, while the Oecumenical Movement, created and supported by the Church of England, is obviously under the influence of hard-pressed British imperialism.

"We must make ourselves clear. We do not mean Roman Catholics or members of the Church of England. We do not even mean their religions, as such. For these we can only feel the respect due to any religion. What we mean is the guilty interference of those who wish to turn these religious institutions into weapons for struggle and domination, against the peace and liberty-loving peoples . . ." (Barron and Waddams, *Communism and the Churches*, pp. 74, 75).

". . . What Catholicism is driving at is clear to everyone, especially after what happened in Italy. The Vatican's action cannot leave us indifferent when it attempts to interfere with and to pass judgment upon our democratic regime" (*RNC*, p. 12).

"It is not a matter of indifference to us that the so-called Oecumenical Movement wishes to attach Orthodoxy to the chariot of Western Anglo-American imperialism . . ." (Barron and Waddams, *Communism and the Churches*, p. 75).

"The Orthodox Church refuses to become victim of the Oecumenical imperialist movement."

June 6, 1948—

Justinian was enthroned as Patriarch in the presence of the President of the Presidium and the diplomatic representatives of the Soviet Union, Bulgaria, Yugoslavia, Czechoslovakia and other governments. In his inaugural speech he stated:

"The priests of our Church, who work in the midst of our people, have been trained in the mentality and atmosphere of the past. This being so, they are an obstacle in the new social activity of the Church. Our people must be guided, orientated and convinced of the social apostleship required by men of the new times. For this work a well thought-out programme and a body of well-trained guides are necessary. It is necessary, therefore, to select and promote those elements which have proved themselves capable of the new mission and to eliminate those who no longer correspond to their evangelical mission.

"Secondly, the Rumanian Orthodox Church must reform its monasteries in accordance with canonical and monastic law, and reorganize them on a new basis in order that they may respond to the ideals and aspirations of our people.

"Thirdly, the weapons of our priests must be reviewed and they must be armed with the weapons of the new spirit, so that they can assist the new man in his aspirations . . . To this end the preaching of the Gospel, both by word and written letter, must be organized in the new light . . .

"At this moment, our thoughts turn to our Greek Catholic brothers, who until 250 years ago, were part of our flock . . . The grievous spiritual agitations which made the life of Transylvanian Rumanians a great tragedy began with the feudal rule of the Hapsburg dynasty . . . In these conditions part of the Orthodox flock in Transylvania, threatened with death, joined the flock of the tyrannical wolves and they have not yet had the courage to return to the Mother Church. . . .

"But all evils come to an end. The last pillar of the Caesarian Papacy and of imperialism in this part of the world, the last Hohenzollern, has abdicated. We know all about the latest attempts to maintain the schism between brothers and to use the Greek Catholic clergy—their only hope—as an instrument to serve the dominating aims in our country . . ." (Barron and Waddams, *Communism and the Churches*).

He also stated regarding the Roman Catholic Concordat that it was

"Imposed upon our people by the Pope of Rome with the connivance of the former regimes, whereby the Popish See was awarded greater rights than our own Church" (*RNC*, p. 12).

Regarding Uniates he stated:

"What separates us at this time? Nothing but the faithful submission you still give to Rome. Give back this loyalty to the Church of our nation, the Church of our forefathers and of yours. The energies we have all spent up till now in defending the national and religious identity of our nation let us henceforth spend—under the paternal protection of the Rumanian state, of the Popular Republic of Rumania—only in consolidating the sovereignty and the national independence of our democratic state. The widest prospects open before us and before our future activity, once we no longer work in isolation, abandonment, and persecution as we have in the past . . ." (*RNC*, p. 23).

"Be true Rumanians, like your forefathers . . . return to the ancestral Church, the Church of your and our forefathers . . ." (Barron and Waddams, *Communism and the Churches*, p. 74).

Semnalul commented as follows:

"The higher clergy of the Uniate Church would do well to examine their conscience regarding their people and their faith in good time, before their faithful do this for them, by declaring down to the last man that they care nothing for Rome, the Pope or Catholicism, and by abandoning their false position as Catholics, by returning to the Mother Church beside their other Russian and Orthodox brothers . . . The Orthodox Church, prelates, priests, and faithful will do its best to facilitate the return home of our Orthodox-Uniate brothers" (*Semnalul, Press Review*, No. 129-3, p. 74.

June 21, 1948—

Bishop Antal in the publication, *Semnalul*, referred to the return of some Uniates of Galicia to Orthodoxy in April, 1946:

"Will our people too know this joy? It is our conviction that it will, even though we may have to wait until October 7, 1948, when the 250th anniversary of the Act of Union of Alba-Julia will be celebrated . . ." (*RNC*, p. 23).

July, 1948—

Patriarch Justinian commissioned select priests to start a movement against Anglican, Catholic and ecumenical sympathies, and against American missions in the Far East, and to propagandize for incorporation of the Rumanian Orthodox Church into the Russian Church. Some objectors were imprisoned.

July 17, 1948—

The Concordat with the Vatican (entered into in 1927 and ratified in 1929) was severed by a Government Communique from the Council of Ministers, without the required six months' notice prescribed in Article 23:

"In order to accomplish the constitutional provisions relating to the un-trammeled liberty of religion, the Council approves the abrogation of the law of June 12, 1929, concerning the approval of the Concordat with the Vatican; the denunciation of that Concordat; and the cessation of the application of the provisions contained in that Concordat, as of the date of its denunciation" (*RNC*, p. 13).

The Concordat had ensured freedom of worship for Catholics, and freedom to organize religious teaching and social welfare, to organize and administer property and to have diplomatic privileges in all its communications with the Vatican. Following the repudiation of the Concordat, the Government was to take control of the Roman Catholic institutions and implement a compulsory law for Catholic priests to take an oath of allegiance, for the Government to nominate priests, for the Archbishoprics to be reduced to three. A number of priests joined the Orthodox Church, allegedly under pressure to receive government stipends. Objectors reportedly were imprisoned along with Evangelical pastors and teachers (*N. Y. T.*, July 19, 3:7).

July, 1948—

The Communist publication *Scanteia* caricatured the Pope with the American flag in his tiara, bowing down and kissing the hand of American Secretary of State Marshall (*RNC*, p. 14).

August, 1948—

Patriarch Justinian, upon his return from Moscow, attacked Roman Catholicism:

"The Vatican is the center of the oldest imperialist tradition, which has not hesitated in the least to use every means of the capitalist system to commercialize holy things, with the help of the 'Bank of the Holy See' and of other enterprises that have common interests with Anglo-American financial circles. To that end, Pope Pius II does not hesitate to use any means whatsoever, even though it be contrary to the letter and spirit of Holy Writ" (*Informations Roumaines*, Bulletin of Rumanian Legation in Paris, August 26, 1949).

He also stated that

"The political interests pursued by the Vatican are alien to the very spirit of our Christian faith. Hence the patriarchs and representatives of all

Orthodox churches hailed with joy the Rumanian Government's decision to eliminate completely the possibility of the Vatican's interference in the internal concerns of the Rumanian People's Republic" (*The Tablet*, Feb. 26, 1950; *RNC*, p. 14).

August 3, 1948—

Church educational institutions were included in a decree of the Government (Article 35) stipulating that "All private and confessional schools and all private schools belonging to the Roman Catholic religious community become state institutions" (Appendix II).

According to a report of the Minister of Public Instruction, the new educational law was designed and elaborated "Upon instructions from the central committee of the Workers' Party" (*RNC*, p. 15).

August 4, 1948—

By a decree issued by the Presidium of the National Assembly, steps were to be taken immediately to effect some parts of the proposed new law of cults (Appendix III, *Monitorul Official*, No. 178).

A summary of the worst elements of the decree as seen by some Rumanian churchmen follows:

"All religious symbols must be approved by the Government.

"All ministers and priests must take an oath of allegiance to the Government, pledging themselves 'to secrecy on all matters connected with service to the State.'

"Pastors must be citizens in good standing, i.e., no convictions by law.

"All church budgets, properties and membership lists shall be controlled by the Government. Salary subsidies will be granted to 'democratic' leaders. Religious communities, who by 75% vote to transfer to different faiths, may transfer church property with them.

"Foreign contacts shall be only through the Ministries of Religion and Foreign Affairs. No Church may be supported from abroad. No foreign religious leader may exercise jurisdiction or religious leadership in Rumania. Committees responsible to Government authorities must oversee parish life.

"Churches may have no social welfare institutions.

"Number of church seminaries prescribed by law and placed under supervision of Government ministries. All others confiscated.

"Military chaplaincy abolished.

"Clerical insurance, pensions and cultural associations reorganized into a clerical union under the auspices of the General Confederation of Labor. To receive benefits, clergy must be approved by the Confederation."

All Churches except the Orthodox were ordered to reorganize and apply for recognition.

"In order to function on the territory of the Rumanian People's Republic every cult must be recognized by an order given by the Presidium of the Great National Assembly" (Art. 13).

August 11, 1948—

The Mother Superior of a nationalized Catholic school in Bucharest was investigated for the destruction of school archives (*RNC*, p. 15).

September 8, 1948—

Two Roman priests of Timisoara were indicted for "anti-democratic attitudes" (*RNC*, p. 15).

September, 1948—

The Hungarian Lutheran Church in Siebenburgen introduced a voluntary church tax and the General Convent voted to provide subsidies for religious institutions (*Protestant Churches in Hungary, 1939-1950*, p. 30).

September 16, 1948—

According to the Government's *Official Monitor*, Mgr. Scheffler, the Apostolic Administrator of Oradea and Satu-Mare, was suspended from office for his "clearly anti-democratic attitude" (*RNC*, p. 17).

September 18, 1948—

Decree No. 244, published by the *Official Monitor*, implemented Article 22 of the laws regulating cults (text, Rumania, Appendix II), whereby two Orthodox bishoprics were abolished (*RNC*, p. 32).

By the same decree Catholic dioceses were limited from six to two, and two bishops were retired. Uniate dioceses were limited to two, and three bishops were retired (*RNC*, p. 17; *N. Y. T.*, Sept. 21, 10:5).

October 1, 1948—

At a meeting called in Cluj to prepare for "the return of the Greek Catholic Church to the Orthodox Church" (*RNC*, p. 24) thirty-eight Uniate delegates of Transylvania and Banat voted to re-join the Rumanian Church (*N. Y. T.*, Oct. 3, 67:3). The Government had allegedly selected delegates and secured their "election" as area representatives (*RNC*, p. 24). The request for reunion was signed by the thirty-eight delegates, plus the attached names of 423 Uniate priests. Uncooperative priests and laymen were jailed or held incommunicado (*RNC*, p. 25).

October 2, 1948—

The Apostolic Nuncio protested in a note to the Ministry of Foreign Affairs that the representatives to the Cluj meeting were forced to attend: "The priests were in many instances brought by force to the local prefectures. In the offices of the Sigurantza (security police) they were intimidated, threatened with imprisonment, with separation from their families, with deportation, and even with death. Those who resisted the initial acts of violence were thrown in underground cells, ill-treated, subjected to exhausting questioning, and finally set free only when, broken by the inhuman treatment of their jailors, they accepted to sign. . . . These offenses, knowledge of which soon spread throughout the country . . . were confirmed by officials of the Bucharest Patriarchate and by members of the so-called 'Congress for Union with the Orthodox Church' of Cluj. Some of the latter themselves displayed visible marks of the duress they had suffered" (*RNC*, p. 25).

Uniate Bishop Hossu of Cluj was confined to his house from September 30 to October 4, the period during which the above decision was taken. Thirty priests and laymen who sought to see him were jailed (*RNC*, p. 25).

The Apostolic Nuncio further described the Cluj meeting as a "Carefully prepared action, cleverly coordinated . . . against the Catholic Church of Greek rite."

After mentioning the international obligations undertaken by Rumania in Article 3, Section 1 of the Peace Treaty, and the guarantees set forth by the Government of the Rumanian

People's Republic in Article 27 of the Constitution, and Articles 1 and 2 of the Law on Cults, he referred to "Action undertaken, not merely by certain irresponsible elements, but by the civil authorities themselves."

He went on to state that, "Faced with this unqualifiable attitude of Government organs, on behalf of the Holy See and in the name of the entire Christian world (I) protest with all the energy demanded by the circumstances against such procedures, unworthy of a civilized state."

October 2, 1948—

A delegation from the Cluj council of Uniates was received in Bucharest by representatives of the Orthodox Patriarchate (*RNC*, p. 26).

October 3, 1948—

The Cluj Uniate delegation presented to the Orthodox Synod a resolution requesting re-entry into the Orthodox Church; by special act of Synod, the proclamation of "return" was accepted, setting forth the re-establishment of unity of faith, and the reception into the Orthodox Church of all who desired to break with Rome (*RNC*, p. 26; *N. Y. T.*, Oct. 4, 7:1).

October 7, 1948—

In a memorandum to Petru Groza, Uniate Bishops protested that the Government blocked Uniate attempts to retain the loyalty of their members, at a time when Orthodox leaders were free to proselytize: "The Government censor's office refused approval for the printing of the pastoral (letter), although it had not the least polemic and still less political character," and the Government interfered in purely religious affairs, replacing the Church's personnel with "members belonging to parties of the Government bloc, and eliminating our priests from the administration of the Church's parish properties." With regard to the Cluj meeting, "the immediate agents of this campaign . . . did not scruple to confess that this is an action by the Government for the abolishment of the Rumanian Uniate Church—something that might not be believable, had they themselves, deputies, inspectors of security, etc., not amply proven it by the coercive measures resorted to, and the impunity this wave of illegalities clearly enjoys, in pursuit of an obvious goal. . . . We are firmly determined to remain the pastors and sons of the Church of Jesus Christ, undivided from Catholic unity. . . ." (*RNC*, pp. 23, 24, 27).

October 18, 1948—

Because of clerical and lay opposition to the "conversion" of Uniates to Orthodox churches, the Ministry of Cults decided to deal only with heads of families, and count them as for entire families (*RNC*, p. 29). Government agents were reported to have gone from house to house to get signatures testifying to their new allegiance to the Orthodox Church (Markham, p. 68). When, according to the Law of Cults, 75% of Uniate members had become Orthodox, church properties were transferred to the Orthodox Church.

October 21, 1948—

Orthodox Patriarch Justinian set October 21 as a special feast-day to celebrate "the re-integration of the Rumanian Church in Transylvania." A motion was voted declaring "We break forever our ties of all nature with the Vatican and with Papal Rome . . ." The Orthodox Cathedral of Alba-Julia was consecrated as "the Cathedral of Reintegration of the Rumanian Church of Transylvania."

October 21, 1948—

In reply to the October 2 protest of the Apostolic Nuncio, the Ministry described the protest as "an interference in the domestic affairs of the Rumanian Popular Republic and an attempt to attack freedom of religion," and "rejects the manifest calumnies contained in this note . . . These defamatory assertions are a new proof of the antagonistic attitude systematically adopted by the Apostolic Nunciature toward the Popular Republic of Rumania and toward its reforms and realizations in democracy" (*RNC*, p. 27).

"The Rumanian Government denounced at the same time the attempt of blackmail contained in the threat that the alleged violation of religious liberty in Rumania 'will soon alarm the world public opinion'; this blackmail is in keeping with the campaign waged by imperialist circles and by their agents against the democratic

achievents of the Rumanian People's Republic (Waddams, p. 83). . . . the Government rejects . . . this Note . . . considering it to constitute an act of provocation against the Rumanian State and people" (*RNC*, p. 27).

October 27, 28, 1948—

Because of stubborn resistance of Uniate clergy to unite with the Orthodox, all Uniate bishops, many priests, and (by the end of November) at least 600 churchmen were reported under arrest (RNC, p. 28).

October 27, 1948—

In accordance with Article 14 (Rumania, Appendix II), Roman Catholic Bishop Marton submitted a draft statute of the organization, conduct, and functions of the Roman Catholic Church for "examination and approval."

October, 1948—

Lutheran, Reformed and Unitarian Churches were required to establish a joint seminary at Cluj. The professors were employed by the Government; the seminary was later to become a state institution. The professors were approved by the State, were supported by the Church and State.

November 2, 1948—

The Government *Official Monitor* of November 3 published a decree for the nationalization of private health institutions whereby clinics, hospitals and sanatoria "pass into the property of the state as common possessions of the entire people, free of all encumbrances and charges, under the administration of the Ministry of Public Health" (*Tablet*, Feb. 25, 1950; *RNC*, p. 18).

November 3, 1948—

Ministry of Cults letter no. 41622, 1948, requested Catholic Bishop Marton to instruct responsible Catholic orders, etc., for the "timely" execution of the nationalization of institutions decree (*RNC*, p. 19).

November 8, 1948—

Official Monitor published a decision of the Council of Ministers to end the mission of Bishop Iuliu Hossu, the last of four Uniate bishops still in office.

November 29, 1948—

Roman Catholic Bishop Marton, in reply to the Minister of Cults' letter of November 3, concerning nationalization of institutions, called the decree contradictory to the constitution of the Rumanian People's Republic, and all other governments (*RNC*, p. 19).

November, 1948—

The Russian Orthodox Church in Bucharest was re-opened, with USSR Government officials, church leaders and Ministry of Cults officials officiating.

November, 1948—

The "Army of the Lord," an Orthodox lay movement, was allegedly persecuted. Leaders of Christian lay movements were imprisoned. Orthodox welfare societies were replaced by lay committees who were responsible to the Government.

The Government summoned Protestant representatives to form a federation for official Government liaison. On the acceptance by the Government of the constitution, the Ministry of Education secured the signatures of the leaders to statements that they had religious freedom, and were grateful that the Rumanian People's Republic Government accepted their constitutions and paid the salaries of ministers. Religious instruction was permitted in church buildings in Transylvania, but parochial schools were taken over by the Government.

The Bible Society was closed.

The people's interest in the Bible and worship was increasing. There was increased attendance at worship, usually no sermon.

Many delegates to the Cluj Uniate "re-union" meeting of October 1, upon release from prison, repudiated their declarations and resolutions. By the end of November, over 600 priests and laymen were reported imprisoned (*RNC*, p. 28).

December 1, 1948—

The Presidium of the Grand Assembly issued decree No. 358 declaring null and void all Uniate dioceses, chapters, and religious communities, as well as institutions. All properties (Art. 2) were to pass immediately to the State, excepting parish buildings and chapels which went to the

Orthodox Church. The decree was based on Article 13 of the Law of Cults (Text, Appendix IV; *N. Y. T.*, Dec. 4, 3:4; *RNC*, p. 29).

December 5, 1948—

At the inauguration of the Orthodox Theological Institute of Cluj, Stanciu Stoian, Minister of Cults, asserted that the Rumanian people were responsible for the re-union of Uniates with the Orthodox Church: "the people itself desired its own spiritual reintegration; the people alone freed itself from the oppression of the act of 1700."

December, 1948—

The Government reminded Evangelical Churches that all clergy were employees of the State; that nationalized church property was lent to the communities; that there was to be no (central) church control over parish meetings; that those who wished to belong to churches must register; that church contributions must cease; that religious instruction would be voluntary (*Die Protestantischen Kirchen in Ungarn, 1939-1950*, p. 29).

January 12, 1949—

The Government replied by letter to Bishop Marton's draft constitution for the Catholic Church, submitted for "approval" on October 27. The Government stated that nine statutes must be suppressed, others modified, including the statements re. the general dogmatic position of the Roman Catholic Church, the Papal dogma and the Canonical attributes of the Pope, the norms applicable to the Uniate Church, which "church has ceased officially to exist in Rumania," and the right to give religious instructions in all schools (*RNC*, p. 18).

Bishop Marton replied that he could not alter theological and dogmatic positions (*Tablet*, Feb. 25, 1950).

January 30, 1949—

The Orthodox University Theological Institute was opened in Bucharest. Special "missionary courses" were established for priests to guide them "in the service of the people and of peace." Communist publication *Universul* stated (Feb. 26):

"The need for these courses had been felt lately, in the first place, because a new and proper orientation of the clergy had become necessary in all directions in which popular democracy seeks to raise the masses of the people."

An examination was to be given at the end of courses "to qualify and evaluate . . ., calling some to higher posts, reducing others to lower places . . . Today the social order is different, and the outcasts of yesterday are now at the head of public affairs. We must not expect their compassion . . . It is entirely on ourselves to remain in the responsible jobs we have" (*RNC*, p. 34).

February 5, 1949—

The *Official Monitor* published decree No. 37* for the organization and function of the Ministry of Cults: "The Ministry of Cults is the public service through which the State exercises its right of surveillance and control guaranteeing the use and exercise of freedom of conscience and of religion. To this effect—

"It supervises and controls all religious cults and their institutions, communities, associations, orders, congregations, and foundations of a religious nature, whatever their kind may be;

"It supervises and controls special religious education for training personnel of all religious dominations;

"It approves the founding of new religious communities, parishes, and administrative units, the creation of new personnel posts, and the appointments, whether they are paid by the state or not, in the services of the various denominations;

"It supervises and controls all funds and possessions, whatever their origin and nature may be, of the religious cults;

"It assures the task of watching over the relations and correspondence between the cults of the country and those abroad;

"It has various other tasks in connection with religious cults."

February 5, 1949—

A decree of the Ministry of Cults set forth detailed bases for the "economic-administrative organization of the Orthodox Cult," limited dioceses to 14 (in place of 18), established

careful control measures over priests, bishops, and professors (*RNC*, p. 32).

February 18, 1949—

The Government removed fifteen Orthodox priests from office (*N. Y. T.*, Feb. 18, 13:7). Refugee priests Galdau and Bazil reported that Patriarch Justinian sought incorporation of the Rumanian Church into the Russian Church (*N. Y. T.*, February 16, 18:5).

February 22, 1949—

Scanteia, in an article entitled "In the Matter of Religious Liberties," set forth the official position of the Rumanian People's Republic on religious freedom:

"Our clergy has before it the example of the Orthodox clergy of the Soviet Union . . . The Church is the place where the faithful pray . . ."

The author separated education entirely from the idea of religion and the church. The "sects" were labelled as subversive elements and imperialistic tools (Text, Rumania—Appendix V).

February 24, 1949—

In reply to the Government's letter of January 12 demanding changes in the Catholic Church constitution and organization, Bishop Marton expressed his "deepest sorrow to find that the Greek Catholic (Uniate) bishops are prevented from expressing their opinions" re. the draft statute, refused to compromise on points dealing with the primacy of Papal jurisdiction, with the exclusive right of the Pope to appoint bishops and establish the number of dioceses, and with the freedom of relations with Rome (*RNC*, pp. 18, 19).

February 27, 1949—

In a pastoral letter, Patriarch Justinian quoted the *Scanteia* article, "In the Matter of Religious Liberties," expressing his approval. He also referred to the "religious thirst of the people" (*RNC*, p. 34).

Patriarch Justinian called to Bucharest some 500 priests, addressed them: "The regime of popular democracy in our country . . . assures us full freedom of organization and ac-

---

* If the number of the decree may be taken as evidence, apparently this decree was established prior to June, 1947.

tion, without interfering in the least in religious concerns of the Church." He exhorted them to abstain from "hampering the activity of the State" (*RNC*, p. 34).

February 27, 1949—

Universul published an Orthodox priest's statement that the Vatican and the World Council of Churches supported the "capitalistic world and the imperialists in preparation for a third world war."

March 4, 1949—

The Government liquidated the Protestant women's organizations in Sibiu (*N. Y. T.*, 4, 6:2, 3).

March, 1949—

The Ministry of Education issued a decree for the control of religious communities:

"The purpose of this control is to check whether freedom of conscience and freedom of religion are being fully observed. The Education Ministry will consequently control all the denominations, their organs, the religious orders, associations and other groupings. Only the Education Ministry can authorize the establishment of new parish churches" (As quoted by MacEoin, p. 97).

March, 1949—

All land holdings in excess of 50 acres were nationalized.

April, 1949—

The *Moscow Patriarchal Journal*, Issue IV, described the position of the Rumanian Church (Text, Rumania—Appendix VII) as not separated from the State, but separated from the schools,

"An association of believers . . . subject to the civil power, and as having a positive contribution in maintaining peace, defending the independence of the people, combating superstitions, exposing the intrigues of the Vatican, etc." (*EPS*, Sept. 8, 1950).

May 17, 1949—

The Rumanian Government reported that 120 priests enrolled for "orientation" courses in an institute held at Cluj, presumably intended principally for former Uniate priests (*N. Y.*

T., 17, 14:2). In Bucharest, the Orthodox Theological Institute was opened with a ceremony "attended by Patriarch Justinian and the Bishops of Buzau, Suceava, Oradea and Constanza. In his speech the Rector of the Orthodox Theological Institute, Deacon Nikolaiescu, said that 'To carry out their social apostolate, and to enable them to free themselves from the prejudices and mental confusions of the dark past, the priests must receive guidance. The professors must cleanse the minds and souls of the priests of all the filth of political, social and theological prejudices which have led them astray from the path of the Church and the Holy Gospel. The Scriptures must be rightly interpreted; it is the duty of the professors to develop social consciousness in the priests. Without this consciousness they cannot see the face of God. Christ in his nine beatitudes said that the peacemakers will be blessed. The magnificat of the Blessed Virgin Mary also shows that the happenings of today are in accordance with the prophesies of the Bible. There is no contradiction between the will of the working people and the Holy Scriptures. The Rumanian Orthodox Church must support the struggle for social justice and peace. It cannot associate itself with the imperialist papal Church, nor with the different sects which exist in Rumania. There are agents of the Anglo-American imperialists, who aim at undermining the achievements of the working class.'

". . . In his concluding remarks Patriarch Justinian said that these guidance courses would permit the mass of the priests to profit from the 'pastoral experience' of professors who had reached a high degree of political development. Many priests were not 'on the level of the present situation,' therefore their shortcomings had to be condemned. All guilty priests would be suspended and excluded from the Orthodox Church" (*East Europe*, Vol. V, No. 223, May 26, 1949).

May 29, 1949—

By decision of the Ministry of Cults Bishop Aron Marton and Anton Durcovici, 3 canons, 132 priests and administrative officials of the Roman Catholic Church were excluded from financial support of the Government, retroactive to February 1, for "anti-democratic attitudes" . . . "the regime of popular democracy cannot and does not tolerate the enemies from within the country to take advantage of any of our democratic liberties to mask their actions directed against public authority, against peace, independence, and liberty, against the united struggle for socialism carried on by the working people" (*Scanteia*, May 29). *Scanteia* further charged that Apostolic Nuncio O'Hara had urged the clergy to oppose the State (*New York Times*, May 30:2:6).

June 20 and 26, 1949—

The remaining Roman Catholic-Uniate Bishops Marton and Durcovici were arrested (*RNC*, p. 19). According to Roman Catholic sources, Marton was accused as an agent of imperialism, a spy of the Vatican, of having illegal connections with Mindszenty (*Tablet*, Feb. 25, 1950).

June 23, 1949—

"The heads, or their representatives, of the following Rumanian religious bodies met in Bucharest: the Orthodox, Reformed, Lutheran-Evangelical (Augsburg), Lutheran-Evangelical S. P., and Armenian-Gregorian Churches, the Old Rite Christians (Lipovenians), the Jews and the Moslems. The Conference was presided over by the Patriarch Justinian" (Barron and Waddams, *op. cit.*, p. 85).

A number of resolutions were passed (Text, Rumania—Appendix VI) praising the religious equality, liberty of worship and education and cooperation of the Government in religious matters in the changed situation in Rumania; condemning the Roman Catholic Church which "in the past enjoyed considerable privileges at the expense of the other churches and engaged in an activity injurious to the sovereignty of the state" (*Tablet*, February 25, 1950).

July 10, 1949—

The Vatican reported that Roman Catholic Archbishop Cisa was under house arrest (*New York Times*, July 10:11:1).

July 29, 1949—

Roman Catholic sources reported clashes between organized groups of Catholics and Communists in Transylvania (*New York Times*, July 29:6:6).

August 1, 1949—

By order of the Council of Ministers (Rumania—Appendix VII) fifteen Roman Catholic welfare and educational organizations and any others engaged in similar activities were banned. Monks and nuns were to proceed to one of five stipulated monasteries or register with the Ministry of Labor as unemployed. Foreigners were to report to the police in ten days (*Tablet*, Feb. 25, 1950; Waddams, p. 87).

October 22, 1949—

The Government took steps to dissolve the Y. M. C. A. and confiscate its holdings (*New York Times*, October 22:7:1).

End of 1949—

At an Evangelical pastors' conference on evangelism, Government representatives spoke on the pastors' role in the "One Year Economic Plan." The Minister of Education addressed the pastors, stressing the importance of their cooperation, as contrary to the Roman Catholics'. He secured a resolution from the pastors stating that they had learned very much at the conference and would continue studying new social theories, that they would aid with the reconstruction of the country and strengthening the spiritual life of the people. Prof. Bela Bende (Professor of Unitarian Theology at Cluj) addressed the group:

"We Communists have to try (to help fellow-man) in our own manner, and you pastors in yours. We don't want you to preach class-struggle from your pulpits, but we want you to do everything with your methods and opportunities to aid the people in a very difficult situation."

Lutheran pastors pledged one another to take care of each others' families under all circumstances if anything unexpected should happen to one.

The Synod reported a shortage of pastors and diminishing numbers of theological students.

Land and property caused so much trouble that they decided to turn over all land to the State except one hectare each for pastors' gardens.

January 12, 1950—

According to the "Law of January 12," "all clergy is subject to state jurisdiction" (*Buletnal*, March/April, 1950, p. 15).

February 27, 1950—

"Charges that the Vatican and the World Council of Churches are supporting 'the capitalistic world and the imperialists' in preparation for a third world war were made in articles published by *Universul*" (Rumanian Government paper).

"(In one article) Father V. Agura (Orthodox priest) declared that although the Vatican refuses to recognize or support the World Council of Churches, both organizations are united in a common 'international political strategy.' (He) chided 'scattered Orthodox groups' which have affiliated themselves with the World Council, branding them as 'traitors to the cause of world peace.'" (*RNS*, 27:2).

March 2, 1950—

"Patriarch Justinian, head of the Orthodox Church in Rumania, in a pastoral letter accused the Vatican and the World Council of Churches of being linked with western forces 'preparing for a new war.'

"He said his letter was intended as an appeal to all Orthodox and other Christians to 'unite their efforts in defense of world peace . . . The Holy Synod regrets that while Eastern Orthodox Christianity aligns itself alongside those fighting for peace, part of western Christendom, including the Vatican and the World Council of Churches, has placed itself in the ranks of those preparing for war . . . For these reasons, the Holy Synod, with fraternal love, appeals not only to Orthodox but all faithful Christians in Rumania to consolidate their ranks in defense of peace and humanity.'

"Patriarch Justinian ordered the letter be read in all Orthodox churches throughout the country on Sunday, March 5, and that special 'peace sermons' be preached on that occasion" (*RNS*, 2:3:50).

April 27, 1950—

In cooperation with the Government, Rev. Don Andrea Agotha and other Roman Catholic priests held a conference in Targul Mures at which a resolution was approved to establish a "Catholic Action Committee," for the purpose of resolving the "un-

suitable relations which presently exist between the Church and the Government of our Fatherland." The Roman Catholic Church should "integrate itself as soon as possible in the spirit of the Constitution and in the framework of the laws of the Republic" (*Notes on Soviet Affairs*, no. 138, Washington, June 23, 1952). Priests were also urged to sign the Stockholm Manifesto against use of the atomic bomb and to condemn "the warmongers and those who have placed themselves in their service." Vatican sources interpreted the conference as a step on the way to a "democratic Rumanian Catholic Church," excommunicated Agotha (May 3), denounced the Government for "bribing" the delegates (*New York Times*, July 10:13:1).

May 18, 1950—

Roman Catholic Msgr. Glaser, assistant to the Roman Catholic Bishop of Iassy, ordered all priests to read a declaration from their pulpits denouncing the Targul-Mures Congress as a Communist Front. Adherence to the Congress and signing of the Stockholm Peace Manifesto were also forbidden.

May 24, 1950—

Roman Catholic Archpriest Agotha made a proposal to the Rumanian Government concerning the creation of a commission for the control of church property and the payment of Roman Catholic priests' and officials' salaries.

May 25, 1950—

Roman Catholic Msgr. Glaser was arrested and "died of heart failure."

June 7, 1950—

The Vatican reported that the Roman Catholic Church lacked any leadership since the arrest of Msgr. Boga and the death of Msgr. Glaser: it charged that the Government was seeking to force mass conversion to the Rumanian Orthodox Church (*New York Times*, June 7:7:4).

June 28, 1950—

Papal Nuncio Bishop O'Hara (American) and other Roman Catholic leaders were linked in the indictment of seven Rumanians on trial on charges of plotting to overthrow the Government, of gathering and sending abroad military information on the U.S.S.R. and Rumanian troop movements, military and civil airfields, radios, oil production, opinions of the Communist Party. O'Hara was named as the leader of the underground espionage plot (*New York Times*, June 29:21:4).

July 4, 1950—

One hour after the conviction of the above seven, Bishop O'Hara was summoned to the Foreign Office and told to leave Rumania in three days, with his staff. He stated, "I am accused of supplying British and U. S. Legations and the Turkish Embassy with vital military, political, and economic information" (*New York Times*, Sept. 7:34:3).

July 4, 1950—

A statute was issued giving the Pope "supreme ecclesiastical authority on questions of faith, morals, dogmas and spiritual jurisdiction," but all other clerical rights were made subject to Rumanian law. Creation and modification of ecclesiastical constitutions, nomination of bishops, organization of religious congregations, meetings between clergy and bishops, direction of seminaries, administration of church properties, all required specific approval of the Government. Bishops were to have no relations with the Vatican except through the Ministry of Cults and the Ministry of Foreign Affairs (*News Behind the Iron Curtain*, p. 32).

August 8, 1950—

The Government decreed that all movable and immovable property of the Roman Catholic Church should be taken over by the Catholic Action Committee under Priest Agotha (McEoin, p. 99).

September 6, 1950—

At a congress in Transylvania presided over by Archpriest Agotha of "Catholic Action Committee," "peace-loving priests and laymen" approved a resolution to create a "National (Catholic) Church without any connections with the Holy See" (*News Behind the Iron Curtain*, p. 32).

November, 1950—

The Orthodox Holy Synod decided to rearrange the Orthodox eparchies in accordance with the new administrative divisions of the Rumanian People's Republic. It further approved of the collectivization of life in the monasteries, and authorized priests to participate in the kolkhozes, "accepting the obligation of executing such manual labor as should be assigned to them."

December 19, 1950—

Patriarch Justinian convoked the leaders of all denominations to discuss the launching of a new program for peace. After a statement by Metropolitan S. Rusan (who represented the churches of Rumania at Warsaw) on the work of the Warsaw Congress, the assembly adopted an appeal for peace to be addressed to all believers. Patriarch Justinian thereupon sent a circular letter to all parish leaders inviting them to give assistance to the 17,000 local "Committees for Peace." In the parishes, Orthodox priests were to publish or present from their pulpits the resolutions of the Warsaw Congress and the speech of Metropolitan S. Rusan of Moldavia at the Congress. A number of Orthodox priests, 60 in Bucharest, were reported arrested for refusal to cooperate (*La Natione Roumaine*, Jan. 1, 1951).

December 19, 1950—

The "Catholic Action Committee" in a letter to the National Committee for the Defense of the Peace, pledged its full support to the Warsaw Congress decisions, and indicated its intentions to call on all Catholic priests and believers to support the Peace Movement (*Ibid.*, Jan. 15, 1951).

December 25, 1950—

In another circular letter, Patriarch Justinian called the priests' attention to the regulations concerning the "winter celebrations" (replacing Christmas) issued the previous year, and advised that sermons on the occasion of the "winter celebrations" must be in keeping with the Government's position and propaganda in the struggle for peace. In his "winter celebrations" message, the Patriarch stated:

"The fighting between the pacific populations of the entire world and a handful of war instigators, cannot make the real Christian feel indifferent" (*La Natione Roumaine*, Jan. 1, 1951).

December, 1950—

The Presidium of the Rumanian People's Republic approved the statutes of organization and function of the Baptists, Adventists, Pentecostalists, and Gospel Christians. The leaders of the four churches declared that they would not maintain contacts with foreign countries which could be harmful to the existence of the State, or the interests of the people and their democratic advancement, and would take immediate stringent measures against any pastors who worked against the interests of the State (*La Natione Roumaine*, Jan. 1, 1951).

Summary of Situation—January 1, 1951

Religion and the State:

Religion is a department of the Government along with education and other departments and has a special function in the new order. As described by the Government, the purpose of religion, especially as organized in the Orthodox Church, is to maintain peace, "to defend the sovereignty and independence of the people, to combat superstitions and deleterious sects, to expose the intrigues of the Vatican, etc." Organized religious bodies which serve these purposes are supported by the Government through the Ministry of Religions (Cults). Leaders are approved by the Government, and dioceses or church administrative boundaries conform to provincial boundaries of the Government.

While "Peace," to all external appearances, has become a favorite subject for sermons, pastoral letters and resolutions of religious bodies, with the removal of opposition among the hieararchy, the lower clergy in considerable numbers now express opposition to the forced nature of the "Peace" emphasis, and the purposes of religion as defined by the Government.

The Churches and the State:

Worshipping communities are dealt with as "association(s) on equal footing with other associations." They may not engage in general educational activities or social welfare. Christmas has been replaced by "winter celebrations." There is no Bible Society. Religious publications are controlled by the Government, and limited in quantity, but appear to be taking on more of a spiritual and theological, and less of a political tone.

The Government supports the training of religious leaders. The Orthodox Church has two theological institutes and one theological faculty for the training of priests and choristers. The pastoral service of lay-priests is supervised by Church authorities. All priests must attend a two-month "missionary and social instruction course." The Roman Catholic Church has two monasteries and three cloisters for nuns. Monasteries have been organized into production corporations. Every monk and nun must learn a trade, and as members of the monastery corporation, contribute to the community work. The Uniate Church technically no longer exists.

Though the evangelical "sects" were recently described as "subversive elements and imperialistic tools," their statutes were approved by the Government at the end of 1950. The combined training center for Evangelical religious leaders is in Cluj. The number of candidates seeking training for professional religious leadership is decreasing. A home for theological students has been converted into a theological training institute. Special short training courses are being held for pastors. The Hungarian Lutheran Church (in Siebenburgen) now permits women to become pastors. Membership in the Lutheran Church has fallen from 350,000 in 1939 to 140,000, by reason of emigration, deportation or death.

The Faithful and the Church:

As stated publicly by church leaders, the church is "the place of worship of the faithful, the place where they exercise freely their religious belief." It is true that more people worship in the church today than ten, or even five years ago. It is equally true that a great movement of spiritual renewal is underway quite independent of official church leadership. It is primarily lay in character, with emphasis on prayer, worship, Bible study, morals and Christian solidarity. This is a movement which antedates the political revolution, and maintains a positive spiritual and evangelistic note. It may now be greatly enhanced by leaders in high circles who have become disillusioned with Government purposes and practices and seek an inner renewal of the life of the churches and the spiritual and moral integrity of their leaders. Vows of solidarity of certain leaders in any crisis, renunciation by some individuals and communities of materialistic pursuits may indicate a trend toward a more austere and more devoted life and witness.

Although there is less and less preaching, fewer theological students, and limited publications, there are more people being confronted with the Gospel than in generations. If there is no official church social welfare (formerly possible largely through tax support), there is far more of Christian sharing among believers. And there are contacts, and a real sense of Christian fellowship among religious groups within Rumania and with Christians abroad.

Formal religious education is forbidden. It is here in carrying on the effective religious training of their children that the churches, the Christian families and groups are least prepared. Fewer children have any religious training—it is done almost exclusively in the homes—but the quality may compensate somewhat the loss in numbers.

The pressures of the present regime, combined with the movements of renewal already active in the churches for several years are bringing about a grass-roots reformation in the structure and life of the Rumanian church congregations.

Appendix I

THE CONSTITUTION OF THE PEOPLE'S REPUBLIC OF RUMANIA

Ratified April 13, 1948

Article 16:

All citizens of the People's Republic of Rumania, irrespective of sex, nationality, race, religion or educational qualifications are equal before the law.

Article 27:

Freedom of conscience and freedom of worship are guaranteed by the State. Religious creeds are free to organize themselves and can freely function provided their ritual and practice are not contrary to the Constitution, public security or morality.

No religious denomination, congregation, or community can open or maintain institutions of general education, but may only run special schools for training personnel necessary to the cult under State control.

The Rumanian Orthodox Church has its own head and is unitary in its organization.

The way of organizing and functioning of the religious creeds will be established by law.

(*The Yearbook of Human Rights*, 1948, p. 178)

The Rumanian Orthodox Church is and remains independent of any foreign episcopate, while conserving its unity with other sections of the Orthodox Church in matters of dogma.

(Barron and Waddams, *Communism and the Churches*, p. 71)

Appendix II

EDUCATION REFORM ACT

August 3, 1948

Article 1:

In the People's Republic of Rumania public instruction is an equal right for all citizens of the People's Rumanian Republic, without distinction as to sex, nationality or religion. It is organized exclusively by the State on the principle of unification of structure and is based on democratic, popular and realist scientific principles.

Public education is secular.

Article 35:

All sectarian or private schools of whatever nature become State schools.

Article 36:

Members of the teaching staff of sectarian or private schools that have been transferred to the State shall be incorporated in the State educational structure according to the degrees that they hold and in accordance with the legislation in effect at the date of enactment of the present Act.

Article 37:

Any person who obstructs or attempts to obstruct by any means whatever the operation of Article 35 of the present Act shall be sentenced to hard labor for from five to ten years and confiscation of all his property.

(*Yearbook of Human Rights*, 1948, p. 180)

Appendix III

GENERAL REGIME OF RELIGION

Monitorul Official No. 178, 4th August, 1948

The Presidium of the Grand National Assembly of the Rumanian People's Republic by virtue of Article 44, Para. 2 and of Article 45 of the Constitution of the Rumanian People's Republic, in view of the Decision of the Council of Ministers No. 1, 180 of 1948, issue the following Decree No. 177, establishing the General Regime of Religion.

Chapter I

GENERAL PROVISIONS

Section I

RELIGIOUS FREEDOM

Art. 1.—The State guarantees freedom of conscience and of religion throughout the territory of the Rumanian People's Republic.

Anyone may belong to any religion or embrace any faith, if its exercise is not contrary to the Constitution, to security and public order, or to morality.

Art. 2.—Religious hatred manifested by acts which hinder the free exercise of recognized religions are offences and shall be punished by law.

Art. 3.—No one may be prosecuted for his religious faith or for lack of it.

Religious faith does not prevent anyone from acquiring and exercising political and civil rights and exempts no one from obligations imposed by law.

Art. 4—No one may be compelled to attend any kind of religious service.

Art. 5.—No one may be compelled by State administrative measures to contribute to the upkeep of any religion or to submit to the decisions of any ecclesiastical court.

Section II

FREEDOM TO ORGANIZE RELIGIOUS WORSHIP

Art. 6.—Religious bodies are free to organize and may function freely if their practice and rites are not contrary to the Constitution, security, public order or morality.

Art. 7.—Religious bodies shall be organized according to their own rulings, teachings, canons and traditions, being also allowed to set up institutions, associations, orders and congregations of their own.

Art. 8.—Recognized religions may have ecclesiastical courts of their own for maintaining discipline among their staff.

Disciplinary courts shall be organized by special regulations, in accordance with the canons and statutes of the respective religions. The regulations shall be drawn up by the courts of the respective religion and approved by decrees of the Presidium of the Grand National Assembly, at the proposal of the Ministry of Religion.

Art. 9.—The local component parts of recognized religions may have and maintain, alone or in association with others, cemeteries for their congregations.

Communes are obliged to set up common cemeteries, or to reserve sections in the grounds of the existing ones, for the burial of those who do not belong to religions having cemeteries.

Chapter II

RELATIONS BETWEEN THE STATE AND RELIGIOUS BODIES

Art. 10.—The faithful of all religions are obliged to obey the laws of the country, to take oaths when and how the law requires and to register births, deaths, marriages, etc., within the period stipulated by law.

Art. 11.—Offences against the common law and crimes committed by the heads or hierarchs of religions shall be heard by the law courts with right of appeal to the Supreme Court.

Art. 12.—Recognized religions shall have a central organization to represent them irrespective of the number of the faithful.

Art. 13.—In order to be able to organize and to function, religions must be recognized by decrees of the Presidium of the Grand National Assembly, issued on the proposal of the Government, following the recommendation of the Minister of Religion.

Recognition may be withdrawn in the same way for good and sufficient reasons.

Art. 14.—In order to obtain recognition, each religion shall forward, through the Ministry of Religion, for examination and approval, its statute, including the system of organization, management and administration used together with the articles of faith of the respective religion.

Art. 15.—The Rumanian Orthodox Church is independent and unitary in its organization.

Art. 16.—The organization of political parties on a religious basis is banned.

Art. 17.—Local component bodies of recognized religions such as communities, parishes, units, groups, shall be entered in a special register at the respective mayoralty giving the names of the leading and controlling officials and the size of the membership.

Art. 18.—Civilian foundations and associations whose aims and purposes are religious, totally or in part, must in order to be recognized as legal entities have the approval of the Government, through the Ministry of Religion, being subject to all obligations issuing from laws concerning their religious character.

Art. 19.—Inscriptions and symbolic signs, as well as the seals and stamps showing the denomination of the religion, must be approved by the Ministry of Religion before they are used.

Art. 20.—The heads of religions, hierarchs, and in general the entire personnel in the service of religion must be of Rumanian citizenship enjoying the full exercise of civic and political rights.

Art. 21.—The heads of religions and all metropolitans, archbishops, bishops, superintendents, apostolic administrators, administrative vicars, and others with like functions, elected or appointed in accordance with the charters of the respective religions, shall be able to function only after approval of the Presidium of the Grand National Assembly, given by decree, at the proposal of the Government, following the recommendation of the Minister of Religion.

Before taking up their duties, they shall be sworn in by the Minister of Religion.

The wording of the oath is as follows:

"As a servant of God, as a man and a citizen, I swear to be true to the People and to defend the Rumanian People's Republic against its enemies abroad and at home. I swear to respect that I shall not allow my subordinates to undertake or to take part, and that I myself shall not undertake or take part, in any action likely to affect public order and the integrity of the Rumanian People's Republic. So help me God."

This form of oath is compulsory also for the leaders of civilian associations of a religious character coming under Art. 18.

The other members of the clergy belonging to the various religions, as well as the presidents or leaders of local communities shall, before taking up their duties, be sworn in by their hierarchic chiefs with the following oath:

"As a servant of God, as a man and a citizen, I swear to be true to the people and to defend the Rumanian People's Republic against its enemies abroad or at home; I swear to respect the laws of the Rumanian People's Republic, and I pledge myself to secrecy with regard to all matters connected with the service of the State. So help me God."

All other employees of religious bodies shall be sworn in by the State authorities responsible, with the oath of allegiance provided by Art. 8 of Law No. 363 of 30th December, 1947, by which the Rumanian State became the Rumanian People's Republic.

Art. 22.—Religions with eparchial organizations may have a number of eparchs in proportion to the total number of the faithful.

For the establishment and functioning of eparchs (dioceses, superintendencies) an average of 750,000 faithful shall be reckoned for each eparchy. The areas of eparchies shall be established and the distribution of the faithful by eparchies shall be carried out by the statutory bodies of the respective religion, and shall be confirmed by a decree of the Presidium of the Grand National Assembly, on the proposal of the Minister of Religion.

Chapter III

ACTIVITY OF RELIGIOUS BODIES

Art. 23.—The activity of recognized religions shall be developed in accordance with their religious doctrines, and their approved charter and in accordance with the laws of the country and morality.

Art. 24.—Religious bodies may hold congresses or general assemblies with the approval of the Minister of Religion, and give lectures and hold local meetings (eparchial, diocesal) with the approval of the respective local authorities.

Art. 25.—The Ministry of Religion may suspend any decisions, instructions, or orders, as well as any orders of an ecclesiastical-administrative, educational, philanthropical or statutory nature, infringing in any way the charter of the respective religion, the provisions of the foundation deeds, or the deeds of associations, or affecting in any way the security, public order or morality of the country.

Pastoral letters and circulars of general interest shall be brought in due time to the notice of the Minister of Religion.

Art. 26.—In their activity religions may use the mother language of the faithful. Correspondence with the Ministry of Religion shall be carried on in the Rumanian language.

Art. 27.—When, as it is customary, the supreme authority in the State is mentioned at various religious services and in official celebrations, provided by laws and decisions, only formulas previously approved by the Ministry of Religion shall be used. Religions must also avoid in the prayer books the use of expressions, or formulas contrary to the law or to morality.

Chapter IV

PROPERTY OF RELIGIOUS BODIES

Art. 28.—Recognized religious bodies are bodies corporate. Their local organizations, if they have the membership provided by the body corporate law, are also bodies corporate; so are the institutions, associations, orders, and congregations provided by their charters, if the latter have been drawn up in accordance with the provisions of the body corporate law.

Art. 29.—The real and personal property of religious bodies, of their various organizations, institutions, associations, order and congregations, shall be inventoried by statutory agencies.

The central authorities of religious bodies shall forward all the data concerning these inventories to the Ministry of Religion, to enable it to exercise its right to verify and control.

Art. 30.—Religious bodies, their various organizations, institutions, associations, orders and congregations shall have their own budget, showing income and expenditure.

These budgets are subject to control by the Ministry of Religion.

The budget and financial management of the central agencies and institutions, of eparchial centres and their institutions shall be verified and approved by the Ministry of Religion.

Art. 31.—Expenditure for the maintenance of religious bodies may also be covered by subscriptions from the faithful.

Art. 32.—Subsidies granted by the State shall be accounted for and controlled in acordance with the Public Accountancy Law.

Art. 33.—Infringement of the laws concerning the democratic order in the Rumanian People's Republic may entail the withdrawal of State subsidies. Clerics with an anti-democratic attitude may be struck off State pay-rolls, temporary or for good.

Art. 34.—The salaries of the personnel of religious bodies shall be established in accordance with the laws in force.

Art. 35.—The institution of patronage, concerning property coming from private persons or institutions of any category, remains abolished.

Art. 36.—The property of religious bodies which no longer exist or from whom recognition has been withdrawn shall belong by right to the State.

Art. 37.—In the event of at least 10% of the number of faithful of the local community of a religion passing over to another religion, the local religious community of the religion given up shall lose by right a part of its property proportional to the number of those who have left it, and that proportionate share shall be transferred, also by right, to the assets of the local community of the new religion embraced.

Should those passing over from one religion to another form the majority, the church (place of prayer, house of prayer) as well as the attached buildings, shall belong by right to the local community of the newly adopted religion, the balance of the property being divided between the two local communities, in the ratio specified in the above paragraph.

Should those passing from one religion to another represent at least 75% of the number of faithful in the local community of the religion given up, all the property shall be transferred by right to the assets of the local community of the religion embraced; the community given up shall have a right to compensation proportional to the number of remaining faithful, without taking into account the church (place of prayer, house of prayer) and the attached buildings. This compensation is payable within three years from its establishment.

Cases provided in this article shall be tried and solved by the people's court of the locality.

Chapter V

RELATIONS BETWEEN RELIGIONS

Art. 38.—Anyone is free to pass to another or to give up a religion. The declaration of intention to give up a religion shall be forwarded to the local body of the religion given up, through the local communal authority. The respective communal authority is obliged to issue proof of that communication upon application for same.

Art. 39.—No religion may register new adherents if those applying for registration fail to prove that they have notified their former religious sect of the change.

Art. 40.—Relations of the religious bodies with foreign countries shall be only of a religious nature.

Religious bodies and representatives of any religion shall maintain contact with religious bodies, institutions or official persons abroad only with the approval of the Ministry of Religion, and through the inter-medium of the Ministry of Foreign Affairs.

Art. 41.—The jurisdiction of religious bodies in Rumania cannot be extended outside the territory of the Rumanian People's Republic, nor may any religious body abroad exercise its jurisdiction over faithful within the Rumanian State.

Art. 42.—Assistance and offerings received from foreign countries by religious bodies of this country, or sent to foreign countries by the latter, shall be under the control of the State.

Art. 43.—Ecclesiastical property abroad and religious interests of Rumanian citizens broad, may form the object of international agreements on a reciprocal basis.

Chapter VI

RELIGIOUS INSTRUCTION

Art. 44.—Religious bodies are free to organize schools for the training of clerical staff under State control.

The setting up of schools and drawing up of curricula shall be effected by the competent agencies of the respective religious bodies, and shall be submitted for approval to the Ministry of Religion.

Art. 45.—Teachers shall be appointed by the statutory bodies of the respective religions, in accordance with the statute and rules approved by the Ministry, with prior approval by the Ministry for those paid by the State, and with confirmation within 15 days from the date of the appointment for those paid by the religious body.

The Ministry of Religion may cancel appointments made, should this be required for reasons of public order or State security.

Art. 46.—Diplomas and certificates issued by schools for training ecclesiastical personnel are valid only within the respective religion.

The validation of foreign diplomas and certificates for religious training shall be made by special commissions recognized by the Ministry of Religion.

Art. 47.—Religious bodies are obliged to communicate to the Ministry of Religion all their data concerning the organization and functioning of the schools for training ecclesiastical personnel.

Art. 48.—Religious bodies may organize, with the approval of the Ministry, schools for church singers, and schools for training the clergy.

Schools for church singers shall admit only applicants who have attended unified medium schools or else seven elementary classes.

Schools for training the secular clergy or monks may be theological colleges whose students must have attended unified medium schools or seven elementary classes; theological institutes attended by secondary or pedagogic school graduates; or theological institutes with university standing whose students must have matriculated or graduated from pedagogic schools.

Each religious body shall select for the training of its clergy the kind of institution which it prefers.

Special colleges for training monks may be set up by religious bodies with the approval of the Ministry. Students attending such colleges must have attended unified medium schools or seven elementary classes.

Art. 49.—For the training of its clergy, the Orthodox Church may have two theological institutes with university standing.

The Roman-Catholic Church may have one theological institute of university standing with the necessary special sections.

The Protestant Churches may have one theological institute of university standing with the necessary special sections.

Art. 50.—Religious bodies may give board and lodging to the pupils or students attending the schools or institutes for the training of their clergy, but only to their own pupils or students, and only at the respective schools or institutes.

Art. 51.—Canonical jurisdiction and dogmatic teaching at schools for church singers, colleges and institutes shall be carried out by the respective religious bodies. Didactic and administrative control shall be carried out by the Ministry of Religion, irrespective of the kind and grade of the school or institute.

Art. 52.—The re-appointment of existing teachers shall be made by decree, at the proposal of the Ministry of Religion.

Chapter VII

FINAL AND TRANSITORY PROVISIONS

Art. 53.—Existing theological colleges, in which general subjects are also taught, are abolished. Teachers of lay subjects at such colleges, and the amounts allotted for their pay, shall pass from the Ministry of Religion to the Ministry of Public Education. Teachers belonging to these categories shall be re-appointed in accordance with possibilities, to teach the same subjects or similar ones.

Graduates of theological colleges who took their degrees before the publication of this law shall have the right to attend higher theological institutes, in the same way as students who have matriculated or graduated from pedagogical schools.

Art. 54.—The Bucharest Faculty of Theology shall become a Theological Institute with university standing. Its teachers and administrative staff, and the amounts allotted for their pay, shall pass from the Ministry of Public Educaion to the Ministry of Religion.

Art. 55.—All matters pertaining to the distribution of property among various local communities still pending shall be solved in accordance with the provisions set forth in art. 37 of this law.

Art. 56.—All religious bodies are obliged to forward their charters, drawn up in accordance with this law, within three months from its publication, to the Ministry of Religion, for approval.

Approval of charters shall be given by decrees of the Presidium of the Grand National Assembly, at the proposal of the government, through the Ministry of Religion.

Art. 57.—Subsequent amendments in the charters of religious bodies shall be made in the same way.

Art. 58.—The provisions of law No. 68 of 19th March, 1937, for the organization of the army clergy, are repealed.

The clergy of all religions are obliged to grant religious assistance to, and to officiate for service men whenever required. Refusal to fulfill this obligation is an infringement, subject to disciplinary penalties.

Art. 59.—Army churches and chapels, with their entire property, shall be included in the assets of the parishes of the same religion, in whose area they are situated.

The Alba-Julia Army Cathedral and its assets become the property of the Rumanian Orthodox Bishopric of Cluj, Vad and Felead.

Art. 60.—Army clergymen who, on publication of this law, have served the State for at least 20 years, may apply for pensioning off, by derogation to the provisions of the General Pension Law. A surplus of five years' pension shall be added to the time actually served.

Military clergymen not in a position to benefit from the provisions of the preceding paragraph shall be allotted posts as priests, on individual application, in the eparchies where they have worked or in other eparchies where there are vacancies.

The bishop of the Armed Forces shall keep his present personal title and rights. He shall remain at the disposal of the Holy Synod, which shall allot to him duties corresponding to his rank.

Art. 61.—The salaries of clerical staff taken over by the Ministry of Religion shall be paid out of an extraordinary budgetary credit, to be opened by the Ministry of Finance on behalf of the Ministry of Religion, and to be covered by striking off an equal amount from the budget of the Ministry of National Defense.

Art. 62.—Law No. 54 of 7th April 1928, for the general regime of religions, as well as other provisions contrary to this law, are repealed.

Bucharest, 3rd August, 1948
Minister of Religion
Stanciu Stoian
Minister of Education
G. Vasilichi

C. I. PARHON
POPA EMIL
Minister of National Defence
E. Bodnaras

Minister of Justice
A. Bunaciu

Appendix IV

DECREE ABOLISHING THE UNIATE CHURCH

Decree No. 358, issued on December 1, 1948:

Article 1:

As a result of the return of the local communities (parishes) of the Greek-Catholic (Uniate) cult to the Rumanian Orthodox cult, and in conformity with Art. 13 of the decree No. 177/1948, the central statutory organizations of this cult, e.g., the metropolitanate, the bishoprics, the chapters, the orders, the congregations, the archparishes, the monasteries, the foundations, the associations, as well as all other institutions and organizations under any other name cease to exist.

Article 2:

The entire property of any description belonging to the organizations and institutions shown as under Art. 1 above, with the express exception of the former parishes, accrues to the Rumanian State. The latter will take possession immediately.

An interdepartmental commission, composed of the delegates of the Ministries of Finance, Agriculture, Education and the Home Office, will decide upon the fate of this property, and may allocate part of it to the Rumanian Orthodox Church, or to its various component parts.

(Barron and Waddams, *Communism and the Churches*, p. 82)

Appendix V

OFFICIAL STATEMENT—"IN THE MATTER OF RELIGIOUS LIBERTIES"

Scanteia, February 22, 1949

In the eyes of the faithful, the Church has a clear mission. It is the place where the faithful pray, the place where they can give free rein to their religious belief. As to the school, in the eyes of the State and of the citizens it has the mission of providing youth with the necessary general and scientific knowledge, of raising the cultural level of the whole people, of supplying the country with specialists in every field of human activity, and of giving youth a spiritual education based on progressive ideas, of turning them into responsible, devoted and active citizens of the Rumanian People's Republic.

Anyone who has common sense and good faith knows that the school cannot and must not fulfil the mission belonging to the Church, while the Church cannot and must not fulfil the mission belonging to the school. . . .

Incitement to religious hatred among the citizens of the country belonging to different religious creeds was part of the policy of all reactionary governments. When the discontent of the oppressed working people became acute, the reactionary governments provoked anti-Semitic programs, organized hooligan action against citizens of other religions, and tried to drown in innocent blood the hatred of the workers for the exploiting classes. . . .

The return of the Greek Catholics (i.e., Uniates) to the Orthodox Church is an example of respect for religious freedom. The people's democracy, taking the view that this is a problem which each man has to solve according to the dictates of his own conscience, has allowed the citizens full freedom of decision. . . .

Obviously, there is a profound difference between the religious conception of the world and the scientific conception of dialectic and historic materialism of the origins of the world and of life, and of the causes of various natural and social phenomena. But the masses can learn the materialist dialectic conception only as the result of work for raising their level by widespread scientific knowledge, certainly not by restriction of the liberty of conscience and of religious freedom. . . .

This does not mean that the working class party can remain indifferent to various prejudices and mystical ideas with which the bourgeois—landowner regime has imbued those who work. The class enemy is trying to make use of these prejudices in order to disorganize the creative effort of the workers in our country, by encouraging fatalism, passivity, resignation in the face of difficulties, instead of the will to struggle to remove these difficulties, and to achieve a life of prosperity and culture.

(Barron and Waddams, *Communism and the Churches*, p. 83)

An especially harmful part is being played by the various religious sects, which, behind the screen of religious faith, hide their ties with diverse imperialist offices of reactionary propaganda and espionage (RNC, pp. 34, 36).

Appendix VI

RELIGIOUS LEADERS' RESOLUTIONS RE. CHURCH-STATE RELATIONS

Conference of religious leaders, June 23, 1949, including representatives of the Orthodox, Reformed, Lutheran-Evangelical (Augsburg), Lutheran-Evangelical S. P., and Armenian-Gregorian Churches, the Old Rite Christians (Lipovenians), the Jews and the Moslems.

2. The new organization adopted by the Churches in the Rumanian People's Republic, in conformity with the Constitution and with the law for the general regime of sects in the Rumanian People's Republic, has eliminated the former injustice which granted to certain sects and Churches special privileges. Today in the Rumanian People's Republic, in accordance with the legislation of popular democracy, there no longer exist dominating nations and dominated nations, but only nations dwelling together. In the same way, in the field of religion, equal rights are assured to all sects to organize themselves in adminitsrative units according to the number of their believers and the way in which they effectively place themselves in the service of the people.

One sect alone, which in the past obtained privileges hostile to other sects and to the very sovereignty of the State, is showing dissatisfaction. Only the representative of this sect is today missing from our midst, for which fact we believe the members of that sect are not responsible. . . .

3. The new legislation defines the position of the Churches in the Rumanian People's Republic in relation to the State and in relation to the other State institutions. In this order of ideas the missions of the school and of the Church have been established. As the official text states: "The school is the institution whose mission is to provide the rising generations with necessary knowledge of a general scientific nature; to provide the country with specialists in all fields of human activity; to educate conscious and devoted citizens of the Rumanian People's Republic. The Church is the place of worship of the faithful, the place where they exercise freely their religious belief."

4. Religious education of their members of all ages is assured to all sects in their Churches and places of worship.

Under the new legislation of the Rumanian People's Republic religious sects have acquired the right to organize their own schools of training for their staffs, clergy, choristers, organists, etc. Up to recently some sects, being unable to maintain such schools, had to send their future clergy abroad to study. For the first time in the history of the Church in this country, these sects are now able to organize theological training here in the country, with a teaching staff paid by the State.

6. Great changes, destined to abolish every kind of exploitation of man by man, have taken place in the Rumanian People's Republic.

These profound changes have not always been understood as they should be. Some clergy have allowed themselves to be influenced either by the mentality of the past, by reactionary propaganda in the country, or by that of imperialists abroad, in whose service they have placed themselves. The State of the people's democracy has taken measures against those guilty of such actions.

Not one of the faithful, not a single priest, has been punished in the Rumanian People's Republic for his religious belief or for being loyal to his faith. Only those who have placed themselves in the service of imperialist interests and have intrigued against the Republic, its independence and its sovereignty, have been punished.

We shall not cease to carry on the work of enlightenment of our clergy and our faithful, urging them to place themselves in the service of the people and of the regime of the people's democracy.

8. The sects which we represent here, covering about 94% of believers in this country, have decided to take their place in the social order created by the State of a people's democracy, which has assured to us by law and has created in fact concrete conditions for free organization and functioning.

On the basis of liberty of conscience and of religious freedom, the leading authorities of our religious bodies have drawn up organizational Statutes for our sects, and have forwarded them to the Ministry of Cults, in accordance with Art. 56 of Decree 177.

Appendix VII

DECREE ABOLISHING CATHOLIC SERVICE AND EDUCATIONAL ORDERS

Official Bulletin of the Ministry of Cults, August 1, 1949

Having regard to the fact that there still exists in the Rumanian People's Republic formations and organizations of Roman Catholic orders and congregations for the education of the young, care of the sick and social assistance, the Cabinet has decided under Art. 66 of the Constitution—

Articles 1.—Formations and organizations of the following Roman Catholic orders and congregations will cease to function throughout the Rumanian People's Republic which function as corporate bodies or as *de facto* associations.

(Then followed the names of fifteen orders and congregations, ending with the words "and any other Roman Catholic societies with like activities.")

Article 2.—(In summary) provided that men wishing to continue their monastic life must register in 20 days to join the cloister of the former Roman Catholic Archbishopric of Bucharest or of the Bishopric of Alba Julia. Women were given the choice of three convents. Inmates who are foreigners must report to the police within ten days. Others must register with the Ministry of Labor as unemployed.

(Barron and Waddams, *Communism and the Churches*, p. 87)

Appendix VIII

POSITION OF ORTHODOX CHURCH AND RUMANIAN STATE

Excerpts from the *Moscow Patriarchal Journal*, No. IV, 1949

The relations of Church and State in Rumania are characterized by "the liberation of religious consciousness among the Orthodox clergy from the injurious survivals of the old order of State and society," which has thus "brought to the mass of the believers freedom of religion and of conscience."

It is a characteristic of the Rumanian constitution that, while there is no decree on the separation of Church and State, a special ordinance has separated the school from the Church. The Orthodox Church can therefore only have theological colleges for the training of future priests.

The State regards the Church as "an association of believers on an equal footing with other associations whose rights before the law are recognized and whose activity is subject to the civil power." In this way, "there can be no question of religious persecution."

In an article by the head of the Rumanian Government, Dr. Peter Groza, "what the State asks of the Church" is described as follows: The State, "which seeks to co-ordinate all the democratic forces of the country, counts the Church also as a concrete phenomenon of life. If the new patterns of life do not force the Church out of its way, the Church has no right to impede the development of the people, but must keep pace with a genuine unfolding of life arising from objective reality." The basic prerequisite for good relations between Church and State is therefore "the co-ordination of freedom of belief and conscience with civic rights and duties."

The Patriarch of the Rumanian Orthodox Church, Metropolitan Justinian, would like to see "the freedom of the Church bound up with its responsibilities towards the new order in the State." The People's Democracy "guarantees the Church full freedom of organization and action, without interfering in its religious affairs . . ." For this reason, "under the guidance of the Church, servants of the altar are being trained in the clerical colleges who are conscious of their apostolic mission and at the same time of their civic obligations. We, the servants of Christ and His Church, hold aloof from the materialistic doctrine of life, but that does not prevent us from recognizing and being grateful for everything that is good in social justice and in what the Government does for us. Hence a priest will be the better fulfilling his apostolic mission today the more he serves the people and supports it in its struggle for a juster order of things . . ." The Patriarch holds that "the Church of Christ has never had such favourable opportunities for the putting into effect of the Gospel's injunctions as today under the democratic order."

The Rumanian workers have drawn up a series of resolutions concerning the activities of the clergy within the democratic People's State. The clergy must do its share in the maintaining of peace, "defend the sovereignty and national independence of the people, combat superstitions and deleterious sects, expose the intrigues of the Vatican and work against chauvinism, anti-Semitism, race hatred and so on. If it does this, the clergy will be serving its God and its people" (EPS, No. 33, Sept. 8, 1950).

BULGARIA

Introduction

In the year 815 Christians in Bulgaria were persecuted by Omortag because to him they represented imperial Byzantium. Fifty years later King Boris saw that Bulgaria would be much stronger in relation to Byzantium if allied with Rome. Forthwith he had himself and his subjects baptized and set about establishing a strong national church—a reasonable guarantee of continuing Roman interest and support. By the tenth century the church had been drawn fully into the royal courts through the old propertied Bulgars, who stood in opposition to the influx of the Slavs. In 1393, when Bulgaria lost its independence to the Turks, the Bulgarian Patriarchate, established under Greek influence, was suppressed, and Bulgarian Orthodoxy was placed under the Constantinople Patriarchate. Bulgarian nationalism became centered in, and resisted through the Orthodox Church. Until the end of Turkish domination in 1877 it was the Bulgarian Church which preserved the unity and language of the people, protected their literature and culture, and produced the leadership for independent Bulgaria.

In 1870 the Church sought and obtained from the Turkish sultan a decree permitting the establishment of an independent Bulgarian Orthodox Church. When in 1872 the Ecumenical Patriarch called a Synod meeting and declared the Bulgarian Church schismatic, the Bulgarians disregarded the decision. The Russian Orthodox Church concurred in the Synodical decision, but, though the Bulgarian Church was technically "schismatic," the Russian and other Orthodox Churches lived in communion with it. Bulgaria was liberated from the Turks in 1877 by an international combine to which early Protestant missionaries made a significant contribution. Since their arrival from 1857 onwards, they had called the situation to the attention of the West, and secured the intervention of Western powers and of Russia.

Bulgarian—Russian Relations: Bulgaria, as one progenitor of the Russian language, religion and culture has been looked upon sympathetically by Russian leaders since the early 19th century, and even in the intra-Balkan wars, when Russia disapproved of Bulgaria's excessive territorial claims, Russian-Bulgarian amity never waned. In the last war Bulgaria was careful not to fight Russia, and Russia subsequently "acquitted" the Bulgarians of Fascist collaboration by blaming their rulers. The Bulgarian Orthodox Church has shared this affinity in its relations to the Russian Orthodox Church, but since 1917 has persistently opposed any Russian Communizing influence.

Bulgarian—German Relations: At the beginning of World War II, the Bulgarian Churches did not openly take a strong stand against Germany. Many of their leaders had been trained in pre-Nazi Germany; they had great respect for her technical achievements, and had some appreciation for her cultural, educational and religious background. However, with the beginning of the persecution of the Jews and other oppressive measures, a number of Orthodox bishops took a strong anti-Nazi position, notably Metropolitan Stefan, leader of the Orthodox Church.

Bulgarian—Western Relations: Bulgarian-Western Church relations until the past decade could be described as almost identical with Bulgarian-Protestant relations. Toward the last half of the 19th century, missionary societies in America and Britain, and later in Germany, considered the Turkish province of Bulgaria as an important mission field. Missionaries were sent out by Methodist, Congregationalist, Baptist, Pentecostalist and Adventist Churches, which joined efforts with evangelical minded Bulgarians to establish scattered churches. Two schools were opened, the Bible translated into Bulgarian, a weekly newspaper established, and an active program of lay education, evangelism and service undertaken. From their origin, Bulgarian Evangelical Churches have had close ties with the Occident, have received assistance from sister churches in the West, have sent their leaders to the West to be trained, and have followed ecclesiastical and theological patterns of the West. "Protestant" and "American" to many Bulgarians in the past fifty years was almost synonymous.

Religious Composition:

Population	7,022,000
Orthodox	6,000,000
Muslim	900,000
Roman Catholic	53,000
Jewish	20,000
Armenian	23,000
Evangelical	15,000

Chronicle of Events

Period Immediately Prior to, and Including Nazi "Occupation"

May, 1940—

The proposal by a Yugoslav Church delegation for a rapprochement between the Bulgarian and Yugoslav Churches and peoples was warmly accepted in Bulgaria (*ICPIS*, No. 21, May, 1940).

July, 1940—

At its 25th annual assembly, the Association of Orthodox Priests urged the adoption of a religious "Five Year Plan" which would include religious education in the schools, and the development of youth groups in the parishes.

The Association approved a resolution supporting the "neutral" position of the Bulgarian royal government, protesting the unjust conditions of the treaties of Neuilly and Paris, and supporting the territorial and reparations claims of the Bulgarian Government (*ICPIS*, No. 28, July, 1940).

Spring, 1941—

In agreement with the German authorities, the Bulgarian Orthodox Church took over the administration of the Orthodox churches of Thrace from the Greek Orthodox Church (until 1944).

January, 1942—

The Bulgarian Orthodox Church collected icons, chalices and vestments for distribution to the Orthodox churches being re-opened in Rumanian-occupied Russia (*ICPIS*, No. 2, Jan., 1942).

The Bulgarian Orthodox Church rejected a Rumanian journal's demand that all Russians should ultimately be deported to Siberia, and pointed out that the war was not against the Russian people (*ICPIS*, No. 3, Jan., 1942).

June, 1942—

The Bulgarian Orthodox Church collected 300,000 levs to purchase prayer and liturgical books for shipment to Russia. Orthodox Church youth held meetings to study "love and peace" (*ICPIS*, No. 21, June, 1942).

January, 1943—

In a radio broadcast, Orthodox Metropolitan Paissy stated that "right and justice will win the final victory —the victors will be those who have God's blessing and help" (*ICPIS*, No. 7, Feb., 1943).

Autumn, 1943—

Pressure was brought on the Orthodox Holy Synod to denounce as a Communist manoeuvre the election of Sergius to the Patriarchate of Moscow. The Holy Synod refused, and instead interpreted his election as an indication of the end of religious persecution in Russia (*ICPIS*, No. 1, Jan., 1944).

January, 1944—

After the death of King Boris III, the Bulgarian Government elected a regent for the religious training of the Crown Prince. The Holy Synod, however, refused to confirm the appointment on the grounds that a very strong Orthodox regent was needed to counteract the Roman Catholic influence of the Prince's maternal relatives (*ICPIS*, No. 1, Jan., 1944).

July, 1944—

Though Bulgaria was still not entirely freed from Nazi occupation, the Bulgarian Orthodox churches spoke out openly against all forms of totalitarianism.

Period under Allied Control Commission and the "Fatherland Front," *1944-1947*

September 5, 1944—

The U.S.S.R. declared war on Bulgaria, and the following day occupied the country.

September 9, 1944—

The Bulgarian Resistance, with Allied (largely U.S.S.R.) support, defeated the Axis occupying forces. In a public address, Fr. Georgiev, President of the Union of Orthodox Clergy, welcomed the "revolution." Fr. Jonovsky, rector of the Russian Orthodox Parish in Sofia gave a public address on Russian-Bulgarian friendship.

Orthodox Archimandrite Iriney, assistant to the Bishop of Sofia, disappeared and was later reported killed. Archimandrite Paladiy, assistant Bishop of Vidin and religious instructor in a public school, disappeared and was reported cut to pieces alive; similarly, Archimandrite Naum, theological seminary professor in Sofia. Many other priests were arrested, and some were sentenced to death without trial. Bishops Cyrill of Plovdiv and Paissy of Vratza were imprisoned from October till March, 1945.

September 21, 1944—

The Bulgarian provisional government announced its hopes for the separation of Church and State, and for greater religious tolerance and freedom.

October 28, 1944—

An Armistice guaranteeing human rights and religious liberty was signed with Russia, the U.S.A., and Great Britain.

December, 1944—

The Holy Synod of the Orthodox Church voted to send one million levs to war charities in Russia, another million to Yugoslavia.

December, 1944—

Orthodox Metropolitan Stefan acclaimed the late conversion (war's end) of Bulgaria to friendship with its Slavic neighbors as an expression of Bulgaria's true spiritual character. He attributed the initiative for the conversion to the Fatherland Front. He appealed to the people for continued friendship towards U.S.S.R., and respect toward the people of the U.S. and the U.K. He spoke in favor of friendly relations between the Moscow Patriarch and Canterbury. On domestic affairs, he cautioned against a hasty separation of Church and State (*ICPIS*, No. 1, January, 1945).

January 19, 1945—

Metropolitan Stefan was elected to the office of Exarch of the Bulgarian Orthodox Church. He expressed the opinion that the Moscow Patriarch was predestined to become the leader of the Orthodox Churches, and requested the Patriarch to intercede at the Ecumenical Patriarchate at Constantinople to secure official recognition of his election to the Bulgarian Exarchate and to end the schism between the Orthodox Church in Bulgaria and the Patriarchate of Constantinople (*ICPIS*, No. 12, March, 1945).

February 22, 1945—

Moscow Patriarch Alexei agreed to the request of Exarch Stefan, and sent a delegation to Constantinople which secured recognition of Stefan's election and ended the schism. Patriarch Alexei then requested Stefan to prepare a report on the history of the schism (*ICPIS*, No. 34, September, 1945).

May, 1945—

A delegation from the Moscow Patriarchate visited Bulgaria. It had not succeeded in getting an invitation to visit Yugoslavia because of its alleged purpose to subordinate the Serbian Orthodox to Moscow.

June, 1945—

Exarch Stefan paid a return visit to Moscow where he was received by Church and Government leaders and enthusiastic crowds (*ICPIS*, No. 34, Sept. 1945).

June, 1945—

The Bulgarian YWCA, YMCA, and SCM, banned during the Nazi occupation, were forbidden to be re-established.

January, 1946—

The Ministry of Cults by official decree abolished religious education and prayers in public schools, and proclaimed dialectic materialism as the only sound educational philosophy. Parents might, however, engage religious instructors for private tutoring (*ICPIS*, No. 21, May, 1946). All religious life in the Army was considered abolished. Church activities were said to be limited largely to worship services which were observed by Government agents. Pastoral appointments were subject to the approval of the Ministry of Cults. The Orthodox

Churches published a protest against these measures.

A few weeks later, Premier Dimitrov advocated the separation of Church and State, but called for Church cooperation, "as in Russia, with the forces of progress, truth, justice, and nationalism" (*ICPIS*, No. 27, August, 1946).

April, 1946—

Some churches began Sunday Schools to replace public school religious education which had been forbidden. Paper for religious printing became more difficult to procure, and some church property was expropriated for Government purposes without compensation. Civil marriage became compulsory, but religious ceremonies could be held in addition.

May, 1946—

Patriarch Alexei of Moscow visited Bulgaria. On this occasion Premier Dimitrov attributed the preservation of the Bulgarian nation and its culture to the Bulgarian churches and monasteries (Text, Bulgaria, Appendix I). At a dinner party at Rila monastery, Dimitrov alluded to the Metropolitans of the Bulgarian Church as "old men with bony brains."

Suspicion of the World Council of Churches was increased when Patriarch Alexei stated that the World Council of Churches is primarily Anglo-Saxon and West European and does not truly reflect world Christianity.

June, 1946—

The Bulgarian Government called on the Evangelical Churches because of their Western contacts to help write a statement to be presented as a document of the Evangelical Churches to Western delegates at the Paris Peace Conference. The final statement, which the Evangelicals did not help write, hailed the religious liberties extended by the New Order in Bulgaria, and supported claims of Bulgaria to Thrace. Evangelical publications were curtailed, and informed that they must print only materials previously cleared with the Government. In conversation with an Evangelical leader, Premier Dimitrov stated:

"We will not persecute the churches, but we do not want to leave nests of reaction. Stick to your spiritual work."

June, 1946—

The League (Union) of Orthodox Clergy met and decided to call for an Orthodox Church General Council—

(1) to draft a "democratic" church constitution;

(2) to seek to introduce religious instruction in the public schools with priests as instructors;

(3) to stand behind the theological faculty in its status as part of the University of Sofia (it had been intimated that the theological faculty might be closed);

(4) to promote and expand church social work in order to counter-balance increased Government efforts to take over this work (the Government had taken over many orphanages, summer camps and welfare institutions); the priests stated that while the Church no longer depended on Government support, it insisted on the right to fulfill its God-given duties;

(5) to promote the unity of the Churches (*ICPIS*, No. 27, August, 1946).

December, 1946—

Orthodox Church publications protested against the Government's obstructionism toward newly opened Sunday Schools, and against anti-religious propaganda in the schools, e.g., public educator's labelling all religious belief as a mark of "ill-breeding," wretchedness and narrowness of intellect" (*EPS*, No. 9, March, 1947).

February, 1947—

Religious publications were further curtailed by rigid control of the limited paper supply, and by union restrictions. Church access to the radio was discontinued (*Ibid.*).

February, 1947—

The Orthodox Holy Synod addressed a memorandum to the Government protesting against the proposed separation of Church and State, and pointed out that the Church was the predominant historical factor in the preservation of the Bulgarian nation. The Church requested that, if it was not to receive State support, the Government should guarantee certain ties of loyalty and recognition of the Church as the institution safeguarding public rights. It demanded guarantees of freedom within its own constitution, freedom of worship, belief and instruction, and the right to carry out its Christian task of "love thy neighbor." The Synod requested that civil marriage be voluntary, that unbiased education be taught in the schools, and that religious instruction be optional (*EPS, ibid.*).

May, 1947—

Rev. G. B. Georgiev, leader of a small pro-Government block of priests, stated at the congress of the "Association (Union) of Orthodox Clergy": "Now we (pro-Government) are twenty, next year we shall be 200." A few months later Pavel Grozev, leader of the Association, was replaced by G. B. Georgiev. Priests were shortly required to spend 2 months as "volunteer laborers."

May 27, 1947—

In a report to the Ministry of Foreign Affairs, entitled "The Fatherland Front and the Evangelical Churches," Rev. V. Ziapkov, President of the Union of Evangelical Churches, expressed gratitude to the Government for granting Evangelical Churches equal rights, and for assisting with publications and rebuilding ("Religious Freedom in Bulgaria," *New Central European Observer*, No. 2).

June, 1947—

Orthodox publications included articles on "Primitive Man," "Science and Religion," "Traces of God in Nature" (*EPS*, No. 38, October, 1947).

September 16, 1947—

A peace treaty guaranteeing "human rights and religious liberty" was signed between Bulgaria and the Allied Powers (Text, Bulgaria, Appendix II).

November, 1947—

In a discussion on the proposed new constitution, the Minister of Cults declared that the Orthodox Church would continue to receive certain State subsidies even after the final separation of Church and State.

Period of Present Regime in Full Power

December 6, 1947—

The new constitution was adopted (Text, Bulgaria—Appendix II). It stipulated that the Church would be separated from the State and from education, but that a special law would regulate questions of material support and government of the churches. The constitution guaranteed freedom of conscience and religion, and the equality of religion. It forbade the "misuse of the Church and religions for political ends." The Government assured the Orthodox Church that it might continue its historic mission freely and creatively, and might continue to receive State subsidies. Exarch Stefan concluded that the article on religion (78) "contains constructive stipulations" (*EPS*, No. 1, January, 1948).

January 26, 1948—

In a circular letter to the parishes, the Orthodox Holy Synod called upon the people and churches to support "all useful undertakings" of the Government, such as charities, justice and economic and social progress ("Religious Freedom in Bulgaria," *New Central European Observer*, No. 2). In similar letters of Feb. 8, 12, and March 22, Evangelical, Catholic and Mohammedan leaders exhorted their people to support the Government and its program.

February, 1948—

"Secret orders" of the Fatherland Front to provincial committees connected the growing Evangelical Churches with the "imperialist West war activities." Pastors were labelled "spies" and saboteurs for destroying the people's confidence in their own strength (by preaching man's weakness and God's strength). The orders called for local groups to expose the pastors publicly as agents of reaction (Text, Bulgaria—Appendix IV).

February, 1948—

The Fatherland Front adopted a program including the guarantee of religious freedom, and equal rights to all minorities (Text, Bulgaria—Appendix V).

February, 1948—

A number of provincial pastors were arrested for "traveling without permits"; one was accused of being a traitor. When a protest was lodged with D. Illiev, Minister of Foreign Affairs and Cults, he explained that these were only local incidents which did not require special Government attention.

March-April, 1948—

In local parishes Orthodox priests extended Sunday School activities, and the "Orthodox Christian Brotherhood" extended its evangelistic, education and social welfare activities.

June 30, 1948—

The Orthodox journal, *Tserkoven Vestnic*, protested the Government's ousting of a school teacher for teaching religious music to a pupils' choir. Some "teachers were ordered not to teach forgiveness, love, kindness and humility, as these create sheep-mindedness, but to teach revenge and hatred." Some were dismissed with promises of re-instatement if they would renounce their religion. "For nothing in this world will we renounce our religion," was one teacher's reply.

June, 1948—

D. Illiev, of the Ministry of Foreign Affairs and Cults, addressed a circular letter of directives to all church leaders, stipulating that: they should not criticize the Government; they should support the nationalization of private industries and mines; they should acknowledge and preach that the State stands above the church; they should support fully all Government measures, and train theological students to fulfill their Government obligations; "Since every Bulgarian is expected to become a member of the Fatherland Front, all pastors and priests must join"; they should counteract anti-Communist and anti-Russian propaganda from the pulpit and the religious press; they should display portraits of Government leaders in the church and preach love for State leaders; they should prevent the polarization of opposition around the churches; they should acknowledge and support the official children's, youth and women's organizations as the only "people's democratic organizations."

At the meeting of the Fatherland Front which drafted the circular, two members of the Orthodox Holy Synod agreed to proposed clauses that the Church should keep out of politics, should not organize demonstrations or pilgrimages to monasteries, and should approve of and portray pictures of the leaders (including Stalin) and the program of the Government in the Churches. They objected to clauses restricting religious education.

July 4, 1948—

The Fatherland Front charged that the clergy were using their pulpits for anti-Government propaganda, and stated that the Holy Synod cannot bar the clergy from participation in the Fatherland Front (*N. Y. Times*, July 5, 1948, 8:1).

July 19, 1948—

The Holy Synod declared in its publication, *Tserkoven Vestnic*, that the letter of directives circulated by the Government (June, 1948) should "be considered as undelivered, un-received and invalid" (*Tserkoven Vestnic*, July 19, 1948). The Ministry of Foreign Affairs called the circular letter a private affair of Mr. Illiev.

July, 1948—

The Ministry of Cults instructed the editor of the Evangelical publication *Zornitza* and the leaders of the Union of Evangelical Churches as to what could be said and printed in church publications.

July-August, 1948—

Pastors and priests were contacted in their homes by Government representatives to secure their membership in the Fatherland Front. By the end of August, a score of Evangelical pastors were in prison on various charges.

August 3, 1948—

By an edict from the Presidium, all foreign schools were to be closed as of September 1. Diplomatic missions were permitted to operate, on a reciprocal basis, special schools for their own children under the control of the Ministry of Education (Bulgaria—Appendix VI).

August 12, 1948—

The Union of Democratic Clergy approved the decisions of the Orthodox Congress in Moscow against participation in the W.C.C. Amsterdam Assembly and denounced Protestantism, Catholicism and the Ecumenical Movement for being "under the influence of the imperialists" and for trying to draw the Orthodox Churches into a struggle to start a new war. They condemned inter-church aid from the West, and pledged their full support to the Fatherland Front, the Russian Orthodox Church, and the Russian people (*Otechestren Front*, September 1, 1948).

September 4, 1948—

Exarch Stefan resigned owing to "bad health . . . and certain important considerations of a purely church character." Metropolitan Michael remained as Deputy President of the Holy Synod (*Naroden Pastor*, 13-9-48). A reliable source of information stated that Stefan was forced to resign. Six weeks later, Minister of Cults D. Illiev stated "after the resignation of Exarch Stefan, the relations between the Government and the Church were soon improved. I have just received a statement from the Holy Synod (Oct. 20) that it has decided to stop religious education, group visits to Rila Monastery, and to encourage priests to cooperate with the Government's program . . . Priests should not now worry about their salaries; the Government will take care of the support of the Church."

September, 1948—

"As an expression of considerable attention . . ." Patriarch Alexei of Moscow presented the Bulgarian Orthodox Church with a chapel and parish center in Moscow. Archimandrite Methodius, secretary to ex-Exarch Stefan, was named rector (*Tzerkoven Vestnic*, Sept. 21, 1948).

October 7, 1948—

The Orthodox Church in its journal *Tzerkoven Vestnic* objected to numerous fiction writers presenting clergy as immoral and unlawful—"the black enemy" of the people—and to the official Government paper, *Fatherland Front*, carrying such stories (*Tzerkoven Vestnic*, October 7, 1948).

October 12-14, 1948—

At the 30th Congress of the Union of Orthodox Clergy, approval was given to the home and foreign policies of the Government as being in accordance with the basic Christian principles of peace, brotherhood and love. Article 79 of the Constitution, placing all education under State control, was considered as not directed against the Church, or against liberty of conscience and religious convictions. The plans of the Holy Synod to organize large scale clergy participation in the labor brigades were approved. Representatives of the Government and of Orthodox Churches in Russia, Poland, Yugoslavia, and Albania participated in the Congress (*Tzerkoven Vestnic*, Oct. 23, 1948).

October 20, 1948—

The Orthodox Church reported in its official journal that the Holy Synod, "under strong pressure from the Government, agreed to accept the demands which had been resisted for some time." These included granting permission for priests to participate in the Fatherland Front; relinquishing all religious training of youth and children; and cooperating with the State in social projects and in establishing national sovereignty (Text, Bulgaria—Appendix VII, *Tzerkoven Vestnic*, Oct. 23, 1948).

November 8, 1948—

Metropolitan Boris of Nevrokop, a staunch anti-Communist, was shot to death by a priest who had been defrocked by the Metropolitan for criminal acts. Prior to his death the Metropolitan had publicly criticized the Government for its policy towards the Church, whereupon the Communist Party organ *Rabotnichesko Delo*, attacked him in an article entitled "An Unworthy Clerical Servant." The assassin was sentenced to 6 years imprisonment and shortly released.

December, 1948—

Orthodox Metropolitan Michael, acting Exarch of the Orthodox Church, resigned. Metropolitan Paissy, onetime prisoner of the Communist Government, was elected in his place.

December, 1948—

The Orthodox theological faculty added courses in "Scientific (Marxist) Philosophy," Sociology, and the "Constitution of the People's Bulgarian Republic" to the theological curriculum (*EPS*, No. 4, Jan. 1949).

December, 1948—

In an address before the Communist Congress of Sofia, Beltcho Nicolov denounced religion as "the poison of the people" which must be broken with forever. He proposed that Communists who are sympathetic towards the Church should "be punished at once—be expelled from the Party and persecuted more intensely than any Fascist" (Text, Bulgaria—Appendix VIII; *Free Independent Bulgaria*, July 27, 1949, from Bulgarian Communist journal, *Rabotnitchesko Delo*).

December, 1948—

Between 30 and 40 Evangelical pastors were in prison, their wives and friends being "questioned" to make accusations and sign statements.

January, 1949—

Dimiter Illieff, Minister of Foreign Affairs and Cults, acknowledged that "some" Evangelical churchmen had been "detained" by the Government, not for their religious activities, but for their "infringement of other laws. Others . . . not involved (in law-breaking) carry on their religious services freely."

February 10, 1949—

Fifteen leading Evangelical pastors were indicted for espionage, assistance to the German Gestapo, spreading rumors against Russia, black marketing, immorality, treason, seeking to overthrow the Government, etc. American and British State and Church officials denied charges that they had assisted in activities or charges even vaguely resembling those named (Tobias, *Fifteen Bulgarian Pastors*, p. 27).

February 12, 1949—

Dimiter Illieff announced that a number of Protestant ministers (none of whom were listed as pastors in the 1948 report of the Evangelical Churches) were negotiating with the Government to form a new "loyal" Evangelical Church council to replace that directed by the imprisoned pastors. Three delegations had visited him to express appreciation that "no obstacle had been placed in the way of the Evangelical Churches" (Tobias, *Fifteen Bulgarian Pastors*, p. 55).

February 17-20, 1949—

The following Bulgarian religious communions in three days' time condemned the "traitorous activities" of the Evangelical pastors, and added their appreciation for the religious freedom enjoyed in Bulgaria:

The Plenary Session of the Holy Synod of the Bulgarian Orthodox Church: reservedly "condemns all subversive activity" of the faithful (Bulgaria—Appendix XI);

The Union of Orthodox Priests: ". . . disgust at the traitorous and criminal activity of the Protestant pastors . . . instruments of Anglo-Saxon imperialists . . ." (Bulgaria—Appendix XII);

The Catholic and Apostolic Exarchate: a reserved statement exhorting the priests to good works . . .;

Provisional Council of the Baptist Church: "look with disgust upon . . . the traitorous pastors . . . We knew nothing about such deeds";

The Administration of the First Evangelical (Congregational) Church: "surprised . . . profoundly moved . . . and condemn this traitorous activity";

The Council of the Methodist Church, Sofia: "has nothing to do with these pastors . . .";

Etc., from other Evangelical Churches, students of the Orthodox Theological Faculty, the Seminary of Plovdiv, the Turkish religious community, the Jewish community, the Armenian religious community.*

February 17, 1949—

Vassil Kolarov, Vice-President of the Council of Ministers, introduced a church law to the Grand National Assembly to "defend the canonical purity, and to ensure independence

---

* The uniformity of response indicated on three points, namely, (a) approval of the proposed new law on religions, (b) appreciation of religious liberties extended by the Government, (c) denunciation of the Evangelical pastors, implied a common source of these replies.

and church freedom for all Bulgarian churches, and to prevent churchmen from becoming agents of foreign political centers" (Bulgaria—Appendix X).

The law (Text Bulgaria—Appendix IX) would separate Church and State, but allow for State subsidies where evidently necessary; name the Orthodox Church as "the traditional religion of the Bulgarian people . . . a People's Democratic Church" (Articles 2, 3); provide for State control of support from and contacts with churches abroad, of all local conferences, assemblies, processions, publications, budgets and leaderships; of building, church constitutions, theological training (Articles 6, 7, 8, 13, 14, 15, 20, 22, 24); allow only ministers with full civil rights (i.e., not sentenced to loss of same in court) to serve as pastors (Article 10); turn over to the State all church hospitals and other institutions, youth activities, on the day the law becomes effective (Article 21); close all churches with headquarters abroad and the State take over the property (Article 23); terminate the office of the Apostolic Mission (Roman Catholic) in Bulgaria (Article 23); prosecute any religious pressure groups seeking to hinder any individuals from exercising their civic rights (Article 27).

Churches would be recognized when their statutes were approved by the Minister of Foreign Affairs and Cults.

February 18-20, 1949—

The various religious communities responded to the proposed law.

The Holy Synod of the Orthodox Church made a non-commital statement (Bulgaria—Appendix XI) that it had "always exhorted its clergy to regard themselves bearers of the Divine Word . . . and to keep aloof from all political influences hostile to the country and its people."

The Union of Orthodox Clergy pledged support to the common good, and to work for the advancement of socialism . . . to the glory of God" (Bulgaria—Appendix XII).

February 27, 1949—

The new law on religions (Bulgaria—Appendix IX) was adopted by the Grand National Assembly.

February 25-March 8, 1949—

The fifteen Protestant pastors plead guilty, and were sentenced to imprisonment and fines ranging up to life. The Government acknowledged that an additional forty pastors were either "detained" or forbidden from performing their religious functions (Tobias, *Fifteen Bulgarian Pastors*, pp. 59, 95, 96).

April 27, 1949—

In accordance with the new law on religions, the Methodist and Baptist Church assemblies severed ties with mother churches abroad and drafted new constitutions as indigenous Bulgarian Churches, electing new governing boards (*New Central European Obesrver*, Pamphlet No. 2).

April, 1949—

The Orthodox Churches joined with other organizations in a week's peace campaign, at which irritation was expressed that the question of religious liberty in Bulgaria had been placed before the United Nations; the assembly condemned the spending of such great wealth in the West for war purposes, and heralded the Soviet Union as the leader of the nations for peace (*N. Y. Times*, 27/27/5, *EPS*).

May, 1949—

Government representatives at the annual meeting of the Evangelical Churches assured delegates that they now have perfect freedom and nothing further to fear. When the representatives requested a standing vote of approval of telegrams to the United Nations stating that the Evangelical Churches had freedom and did not wish foreign interference, several members raised objections openly.

July, 1949—

Archimandrite Miron, leader of the Orthodox "Brotherhood" movement for church renewal, religious education, and welfare, was arrested. Interest in, and support of the movement had been growing since its nearliquidation in 1944.

1949—

Archimandrite Simeon, senior Secretary of the Holy Synod, was dismissed. The Government suggested the names of two men, allegedly Communists, for the position. The Government's third candidate, Archimandrite Ioana, was appointed over the protest of members of the Synod who considered his moral, intellectual and administrative faculties inadequate for the task.

January, 1950—

The Orthodox Holy Synod sent a cable to Stalin on his 70th birthday: "It was thanks to your political acumen that the Russian Orthodox Church came into being, and rose, as was its due, to be the highest authority in Orthodoxy's resistance of pernicious influences from the West" (*EPS*, January 25, 1950).

April 11, 1950—

A former Bulgarian Foreign Office Secretary stated that Orthodox Archimandrite Kalistrat, former Superior of the Rila Monastery, was serving a fifteen year sentence for "treason and espionage on behalf of the Americans" (*Religious News Service*, April 11, 1950). Rila was a popular mass pilgrimage center, and continued to be so after organized pilgrimages were banned in June, 1948. Archimandrite Kalistrat had asserted in 1946 that there was no conflict between Christianity and Communism, and that Christ was the first Communist.

July, 1950—

By Government order, the Orthodox theological faculty was separated from the University of Sofia, and became a theological academy of the Orthodox Church. Students were admitted on completion of their seminary courses, without registration or examination fees. The Church established a hostel to provide living accommodations for the students.

September, 1950—

The pre-faculty seminaries of Sofia and Plovdiv were united, and established in the Monastery at Cherepiche. The Priests' Theological Institute in the Cherepiche Monastery was closed. The Sofia Seminary building was taken over by the children's branch of the Communist youth movement. The Plovdiv Seminary buildings had been occupied by the Government since the end of the war, and the Seminary was situated in the Bachkovo Monastery until it burned in December 1947 (*Tzerkoven Vestnic*, Nos. 32 and 33; *EPS*, Nos. 33 and 47, 1950).

November, 1950—

A Government publication carried a message by Archbishop Cyrill of Plovdiv, member of the Holy Synod, in which he accused the Anglo-American imperialists of seeking to provoke a new war against the will of the people, while "at the head of the world movement for peace stands the Soviet Union . . . The Church proclaims peace . . . and opposes" all types of war. After quoting the resolution of the 1948 Orthodox Assembly in Moscow against the Vatican and American Protestantism, he added that the Bulgarian Orthodox Church had appealed to the people to proclaim peace, and to defend it. "The clergy has supported with all its power the Stockholm Appeal. Thus they would forestall the temptations to create a new war" (*La Bulgarie Nouvelle*, 23 November, 1950).

December, 1950—

Metropolitan Paissy resigned (or was dismissed) as acting Exarch of the Orthodox Church, and was replaced by Bishop Cyrill. Cyrill, formerly Bishop of Plovdiv, was imprisoned in 1944, and after his release made statements and wrote articles in favor of the Government.

December, 1950—

The secretary of the Orthodox Holy Synod, Archimandrite Ioana (Yona), in reporting on his attendance at the Warsaw Peace Congress, said: "We, the representatives of the various churches, had a private conference in the course of which we expressed our unshakable attachment to the program of the Congress and our conviction of a future of love and peace. Christian faith is inseparable with fighting for peace. Christendom must recover the forgotten message of the Gospel and join the ever growing army which is fighting for peace. To serve the cause for peace must be the primary task of all ecclesiastics and a moral obligation of each true Christian" (*La Bulgarie Nouvelle*, December 8, 1950).

December, 1950—

Negotiations were under way between the Orthodox Church and the Government to establish a new Church constitution which would be acceptable according to the new laws and regulations. The suggestion was made that the Orthodox Church should now elect a Patriarch. This met with wide popular approval, but was discouraged by responsible Orthodox leaders. The Church was expected to be financially self-supporting as of January 1, 1951. A "voluntary church tax" or stewardship plan prepared by the Church towards complete self-support was vetoed by the Government.

Summary of Situation—January 1, 1951

State—Church Relations (the following remarks concern particularly the Orthodox Church):

The Government has exclusive prerogatives in certain aspects of Bulgarian society, e.g., education, youth work, publications and information, social welfare, charities, economics and property, law and international affairs. In some of these areas it has initiated measures of positive value—the literacy program, free compulsory education, the reconstruction program, agricultural reform and mechanization.

The Church does not have primary responsibility in any of these areas, and although it is technically separated from the State, from the Government's point of view it still has a function and purpose in the social development of the people. It is a part of the life of the people; it is treated as a department of the Government. The "purposes" which the Church may serve are

(a) to support the Government in its program of peace, reconstruction and reform;

(b) to calm the restiveness of the people;

(c) to encourage friendly ties between the Russian and Bulgarian people on a religious basis;

(d) to serve as a whipping post in educating youth away from superstition and social complacency toward scientific materialism and revolution.

Any measures taken by the Church which serve these ends, including participation in labor brigades, various pronouncements on "peace," pastoral care, and the mysteries ("superstitions") of worship are welcomed.

That these purposes might be served more effectively (a) loyal exponents of the Government's program are situated in most local congregations, in regional church bodies, unions of clergy, etc.; (b) a "disloyal opposition" which is never wholly eliminated is periodically and publicly purged; (c) details of church administration, congregational life, treasuries and leadership are regulated in accordance with prescribed laws of the country and statues of the churches, without Government approval of which a church may not function.

At present the Government is careful to avoid measures which would encourage a "martyr" position in the churches, perhaps largely because of the growing loyalty of the people to their church.

Within the Church:

As seen from within, recent developments in Church-State relations have not been without their compensations. The churches are no longer involved formally in social welfare, institutional and charitable activities. But the personalized services and aid of brotherhoods, congregations and individuals to those in need is probably more extensive and more effective materially—and certainly spiritually—than when these responsibilities were pushed off on specialized church institutions and societies. Educational work and religious instruction are formally forbidden, but in the intimate family circle, in Bible study, in the pastoral visits of the clergy, in the small groups of children meeting in homes, in the intensity of witness of those children who have dared worship in the sanctuary, religious instruction may more profoundly affect future generations than it has in the past. Theological training was formerly linked to secular university life; today it is wholly the responsibility of the Church. There are more candidates than facilities, and more determination than can be contained. It is among youth that the losses can be measured in greatest numbers. Still there is a Christian youth work, and beginnings of a leaven of the Christian youth in brigades, schools and industries. Bible study, prayer and fellowship groups are not advertised, but are nonetheless not uncommon. There are religious publications issued with Government cooperation. But the Good News and most other news of relevance to the Christian communities is spread by word of mouth. Perhaps there is more communication among religious communities now than when there was a greater number of publications printed and read without restrictions—and therefore little read. Most church property and economic life involving capital and production, with great travail, have been transferred to Governmental departments. Once past the travail, regrets of many communities seem not to be too enduring because of compensations in their new-found freedom for religious work.

Among the people, there is less indifference. True, more are opposed to the Church than formerly; but a greater number stand staunchly in it. More people worship, more participate in various unoffocial Christian movements. Public processions, assemblies and demonstrations may be undertaken only by Government approval—so they are fewer. But there is more of devotion in the homes, of Bible studies where two or three families gather together, of caring for one another's needs, praying for each other. Where there are no ordained preachers, there are lay preachers; where there are no lay preachers, there are laywomen preachers. The fact that those churches to which Government-appointed clergy are sent are soon emptied, that the Communist Congress has had to take strong measures against Party members who persist in their religious life is not without significance.

The Church has been and continues to be the center of life for many, if not most people. The increased participation in public worship, taken alone, could indicate little more than a means of protest against the Government. However, the fact of the deepening of religious life in the homes, and in the relationships among the people indicates that the increased number in worship springs from a deeper motivation. If state subsidies for the Orthodox Church cease January 1, 1951, as expected, perhaps the Church will in a large measure be ready for it. Indeed, one cannot be entirely discomfited at the thought of suppression of the "organized" Church; it is rooted too deeply to be so superficially plucked out.

Church Leadership:

There is a very great struggle still going on in the Orthodox Church. There are a few who appear unreservedly pro-Government. There are a few who are willing to go along with the Government on most issues to gain time, some who are led near a pro-Government position by apologists for the Government in high church circles. But the majority have taken an oft-silent stand as church statesmen, seeking to maintain the Church as the Church, and a relative purity of witness and ministry. They do go with the Government on domestic, practical programs of reconstruction, modernization and "peace." On issues such as religious instruction, youth work, and religious publications they have been over-ridden only after a determined struggle. On such matters as church administration, clerical training and ordination, and episcopal authority, they remain adamant. The new Church constitution has not yet been ratified for just such reasons.

This struggle is rather clearly indicated in the contrasting tones and contents of various statements and resolutions from the different groups. The authorship of such resolutions should be deduced by these factors, rather than by the names attached as signatories; too many documents have been released without the signatory having seen or agreed to them, for the name to be taken seriously. Care must also be taken to read the meaning of silence, and of the nuances and subtleties of pronouncements, which in effect change the entire meaning, e.g., the Orthodox Church Synod's message to Premier Stalin on his 70th birthday.

There is, or was, still a fourth element in the leadership of the Church— that is, the open opposition. This element, however, whether because of relations with churches to the West (e.g., Evangelicals and Catholics) or because of outspoken criticism of the Government has been eliminated (e.g., Exarch Stefan "exiled," or Bishop Boris assassinated), or transformed (Methodist and Baptist Churches are now considered loyally Bulgarian after severing all contacts with the West; the Catholic Church is just entering its period of crisis because of its international attachment), or driven underground.

In the struggle between Church and State a large body of the Church appears to be taking on new forms, determined not so much by the dictates of a secular regime, as by a deepening sense of obedience to God .

Appendix I

PREMIER DIMITROV, ON THE ORTHODOX CHURCH

May, 1946

It is to the credit of the Bulgarian Orthodox Church that throughout its history it has preserved Bulgarian national sentiments and consciousness. In the struggle for the liberation of our people, the Bulgarian church has acted as a preserver and protector of the national spirit of the Bulgarian people during centuries of severe trial . . . It can be said, without fear of contradiction, that the new, democratic Bulgaria of the Fatherland Front would not be in existence if, during the grim, black period of the foreign yoke there had been no

Pastors to preserve the nation. . . . We, the Fatherland Front, and in particular, we Communists, express our gratitude and thanks to these patriots, the servants of the Bulgarian national Church. I would frankly stress that as a Bulgarian, I am proud of the Bulgarian Church ("Religious Freedom in Bulgaria," *New Central European Observer*, No. 2, p. 2).

Appendix II

THE BULGARIAN-ALLIED PEACE TREATY

September 15, 1947

Article 2:

Bulgaria shall take all measures necessary to secure to all persons under Bulgarian jurisdiction, without distinction as to race, sex, language or religion. the enjoyment of human rights and of the fundamental freedoms, including freedom of expression, of press and publication, of religious worship, of political opinion and of public meeting.

Article 3:

Bulgaria, which in accordance with the Armistice Agreement has taken measures to set free, irrespective of citizenship and nationality, all persons held in confinement on account of their activities in favour of, or because of their sympathies with, the United Nations or because of their racial origin, and to repeal discriminatory legislation and restrictions imposed thereunder, shall complete these measures and shall in future not take any measures or enact any laws which would be incompatible with the purposes set forth in this Article.

Article 35:

1. For a period not to exceed eighteen months from the coming into force of the present Treaty, the Heads of the Diplomatic Missions in Sofia of the Soviet Union, the United Kingdom and the United States of America, acting in concert, will represent the Allied and Associated Powers in dealing with the Bulgarian Government in all matters concerning the execution and interpretation of the present Treaty.

2. The Three Heads of Mission will give the Bulgarian Government such guidance, technical advice and clarification as may be necessary to ensure the rapid and efficient execution of the present Treaty both in letter and in spirit.

3. The Bulgarian Government shall afford the said Three Heads of Mission all necessary information and any assistance which they may require in the fulfillment of the tasks devolving on them under the present Treaty.

(*Yearbook on Human Rights for 1947*, Published by the United Nations, p. 390)

Appendix III

THE BULGARIAN CONSTITUTION

December 4, 1947

Article 71:

All citizens of the People's Republic of Bulgaria are equal before the law.

No privileges based on nationality, origin, religion and material situation are recognized.

Every preaching of racial, national or religious hatred is punishable by law.

Article 77:

The State takes special care of the social, cultural, labour, physical and health education of the youth.

Article 78:

Citizens are guaranteed freedom of conscience and religion, and of performing religious rites.

The Church is separate from the State.

A special law regulates the legal status, the questions of material support, and the right to self-government and organization of the various religious communities.

It is prohibited to misuse the church and religion for political ends or to form political organizations with a religious basis.

(*Yearbook on Human Rights for 1947*, Published by the United Nations, pp. 62, 63)

Appendix IV

COMMUNIST DIRECTIVES TO LOCAL COMMITTEES

February 2, 3, 1948

Directive for the Local Agitators of the Fatherland Front in Connection with the Second Historical Congress of the Fatherland Front:

In vain our enemies, within and without, waited for a disagreement between us. In the Congress (of the Fatherland Front) one could not distinguish between Communists, Agrarians, Socialists, Zvenoists, or non-party men. All spoke one language. One could read in the faces of all delegates, their great faith in tomorrow, their enthusiasm and their will to go forward under the banners of the Fatherland Front, in building the People's Republic of Bulgaria, in preserving our national independence and sovereignty, in preparing for the definite struggle against the provokers, sabotagers, and inciters of new wars.

Our Special Orders with Regard to the
Growing Strength of the Evangelical Church:

The growing activity of the Evangelical Church in our country lately is closely connected with the mad activity of the imperialists inciting a new war, and obstructing the progress of democracy and socialism.

The international reaction found before in Bulgaria adequate support among the opposition, through whom it spread and organized all types of provocations and sabotage, destroying the people's faith in tomorrow. Today the opposition is thoroughly un-masked and disavowed by the people. It can no longer serve reaction and the inciters of new wars. That is why reaction searches for new support. And through the help of its agents, the "Reverend Pastors" and the spies of the imperialists, reaction does its best to exploit the ignorance of the masses, and under the veil of various religious doctrines introduces the policies of foreign influence in our country, intending to capture the positions in Bulgaria necessary for reaction.

If we analyze carefully the sermons of these pastors, we shall see that in spite of their outward innocence and virtue, behind their words wrapped in mysticism and religious secrecy are hidden anti-national reactionary tendencies.

And certainly what other meaning can their words have concerning the deceitfulness of this world, their words prophesying the terrible hardships and final punishment in store for humanity?

By these words they intend to create among the Bulgarian people unconfidence in their own strength, just at the time when this confidence is most necessary in order that a new and prosperous society be built. These pastors intend to demoralize the people and to divert them from their only path to salvation, the path of democracy and socialism.

We must take a definite and resolute stand concerning this question. We are not against the religious convictions of people, but when, under the veil of religion, they indulge in a policy of undermining the foundations of the people's power, we can no longer remain indifferent.

It is our duty to lead a broad explanatory campaign among the people, exposing these evangelical preachers as the agents of international reaction, and accusing them publicly of working for the creation of positions necessary for reaction in Bulgaria.

It is our obligation to go to their meetings in churches, and to ask them the following questions:

1. What is your attitude toward the building of our State and the power of the Fatherland Front?

2. If you have a positive attitude, how do you express it practically?

3. From where do you obtain the financial backing for your church and pastor?

4. What is your attitude toward the policy of the Anglo-Americans' aiming to kindle a new war and to enslave foreign peoples?

5. Why do you not speak out against inciters of war?

(Churches' Commission on International Affairs, London)

Appendix V

FATHERLAND FRONT PROGRAM ON RELIGIOUS FREEDOM

February 3, 1948

(g) Guarantee Freedom of Religion. Institute the Separation of the Church from the State. Disseminate scientific knowledge among the people on the evolution of nature and society.

(h) Guarantee equal rights to all minorities before the law, and freedom to speak their mother tongue. To fight every attempt at implanting hatred and discrimination against the minorities.

("Religious Freedom in Bulgaria," *New Central European Obesrver*, No. 2, p. 1)

Appendix VI

DECREE ON EDUCATION

August 3, 1948

Presidium of the Grand National Assembly

(a) As from September 1, 1948, all foreign schools, colleges and courses in Bulgaria, opened and maintained by Governments of foreign States, religious missions, etc., are to be closed.

(b) The French schools may continue to exist for nine months after the denunciation of the Schools (Convention of 1936 between Bulgaria and France). But after September 1, 1948, no children of Bulgarian citizens may attend these schools.

(c) Diplomatic missions may, under mutual agreement, open and maintain schools for children and citizens of their country living in Bulgaria, but permission for such schools may be given only by law, and no Bulgarians may attend.

(d) In the foreign schools permitted, it is obligatory that the Bulgarian language as well as the history, geography and constitution of the People's Republic of Bulgaria be studied. Such schools are to be under the control of the Minister of Education.

(e) Ex-students of foreign schools will be transferred without examination to the corresponding Bulgarian State schools.

(Barron and Waddams, *Communism and the Churches*, pp. 37, 38)

Appendix VII

THE ORTHODOX HOLY SYNOD CIRCULAR ON STATE-CHURCH
RELATIONS—L. No. 5253

October 20, 1948

From now on all priests are allowed to take an active part in the united
political organization, called Fatherland Front. (In order to understand the
consequences of this very grave decision one must be acquainted with the social
and political structure of the country today.) At the same time it is understood that they must not undertake obligations incompatible with the teaching of the Christian faith and the dignity of the priesthood.

Because of the demands of the Fatherland Front that the Church should
not carry out any religious propaganda among children, and that no religious
organizations should be allowed for them, the Holy Synod announces that the
Church is not undertaking any such propaganda, and that for some time there
have been no organizations of a church character for the children.

In the future, only the religious and ethical truths of the Eastern Orthodox Church will be expounded from the Church pulpit and, on no account, will
the pulpit be used for political propaganda.

Referring to the subject of mutual relations between Church and State the
Holy Synod declares that it lawfully fulfills the constitution by paying due respect to the leaders of the People's Republic and all lawful authorities and that
it will continue to cooperate with the State in achieving its social projects and
establishing its freedom, independence and sovereignty.

(*Tzerkoven Vestnic*, October 23, 1948)

Appendix VIII

COMMUNIST CONGRESS ADDRESS ON RELIGION

December, 1948

Speech of Beltcho Nicolov before the Communist Congress, Sofia, December,
1948, as it appeared in the organ of the Communist Party, *Rabotnitchesko Delo*:

The time has come to break with religion forever, which for centuries has
poisoned and continues to poison the souls of our people. Religion is nothing
else but hearth of the black fascist past, under whose cover the work toward
new enslavement of the Bulgarian people goes on. It is a shame and disgrace
there are some among us communists, who have taken communism to heart,
who are weak on the subject of religion. For instance, in the city of Varna
comrades X.Y., P.H., A.K. . . . attend services regularly, light candles, kneel,
pray to God, give money and, instead of being ashamed to be seen, they leave
the church elated as if for them religion were something more than Marxism-
Leninism. These comrades hit themselves on the chest and proclaim that they
are old communists, but for me and for the Party they are lost and are more
dangerous than all the rest of our enemies.

Others, occupying prominent posts in the Party, are married and baptize their children in the church, while the son of an active communist is even a church cantor.

I propose that everyone who attends church services or protects the church be punished at once—be expelled from the Party and persecuted more intensely than any other fascist.

For the present time, while the road is lighted by the brilliant and great doctrine of Marxism-Leninism and Dimitrov's regime, religious people are abnormal. The fight against these enemies must be persistent and unmerciful. Only empty and befuddled heads feel the need for attending church services, but not we communists who are the pride and honor of the people. The doctrine Leninism-Stalinism repudiates religion.

There has not been, there is not and there will not be in the future a greater and more sacred religion than Marxism. Every communist is an enemy of religion—it is in the last days of its existence. Therefore, I appeal to all to fight religion to the point of its destruction. Forward without God and Church. Forward with our glorious Communist Party under the wise leadership of comrade Dimitrov.

(*Free Independent Bulgaria*, Wednesday, July 27, 1949)

Appendix IX

LAW ON THE CHURCHES

February 24, 1949

Voted by the Grand National Assembly

Article 1:

Freedom of conscience and belief is guaranteed to all citizens of the People's Republic of Bulgaria.

Article 2:

The churches, as religious communities, are separated from the State. They can perform their religious rites freely within the framework of the Constitution and the laws of the country.

Article 3:

The Bulgarian Orthodox Church is the traditional church of the Bulgarian people and being inseparable from their history, is in form, substance and spirit a People's Democratic Church.

Article 4:

Nobody can be persecuted or have his civil or political rights restricted, nor be exempted from the fulfillment of the duties incumbent on him according to the laws of the country, on the ground that he belongs to one or another of the churches or that he belongs to no church at all.

This provision applies equally to the ministers of religion.

Article 5:

In their organization, in their rites and services, the various churches follow their own canons, dogmas and statutes, provided that these are not contrary to the law, public order or public morality.

Article 6:

From the moment that the statutes of a church are officially ratified by the Minister of Foreign Affairs, it is recognized as a legal personality. The same applies to all local bodies of the same church.

When the activities of a church transgress the laws of the country, public order or public morality, the Minister for Foreign Affairs withdraws recognition of this church, stating the grounds for his action.

Article 7:

The churches can build and open up places of worship as well as publicly perform their religious rites and hold services in them.

Open-air religious services and processions must conform to the general laws and administrative regulations.

Article 8:

The churches may convene national or local congresses, conferences, meetings, etc., which conform to the laws and administrative regulations.

Article 9:

Each church has a leadership which represents it responsibly before the State. The statutes of each church must determine its executive and representative organs and regulate the way in which they are elected or appointed.

The ministers of churches which maintain canonical relations with churches abroad cannot take up office before being recognized by the Minister for Foreign Affairs.

Article 10:

Only Bulgarian subjects, honest citizens of good reputation who have not been deprived of rights by a sentence in a court of law, may be ministers, or hold office in any church.

Article 11:

The churches may, in accordance with their canons and dogmas, set up disciplinary councils for their ministers and for the other officials of their churches. Their organization is defined in the statutes of the church.

The disciplinary punishments imposed by them are considered null and void if they are contrary to the law, to public order or to public morality.

Article 12:

Ministers, as well as all other officials of the churches, who break the law, offend against public order or public morality, or who work against the democratic institutions of the State, may, at the proposal of the Minister of Foreign Affairs, be temporarily suspended from office or dismissed, apart from any other liabilities. The temporary suspension or the dismissal is effected immediately by the leadership of the church as soon as notice is received of this proposal of the Minister for Foreign Affairs.

If the minister is not suspended by the leadership of the church concerned, he is suspended by administrative order.

Article 13:

The churches collect revenues and make expenditures according to their budgets prepared in accordance with their statutes. In cases of need, the State may subsidize their maintenance.

The churches send their budgets to the Ministry of Foreign Affairs for information.

The finances of the churches are liable to supervision by the financial organs of the State, in the same way as those of all public organizations in the country.

Article 14:

Each church may open, with the permission of the Minister for Foreign Affairs, secondary or higher theological schools for the training of ministers.

The organization and programmes of these educational institutions are drawn up according to special regulations approved by the Minister of Foreign Affairs.

Young people may be sent to study in theological schools abroad only with the permission of the Minister for Foreign Affairs.

Article 15:

All organs of the churches are required to send all circular letters, epistles and publications of a public character published by them to the Ministry for Foreign Affairs, for information.

The Minister for Foreign Affairs may ban the circulation and putting into effect of such epistles, circular letters or other publications of a public character which are contrary to the law, public order and to public morality.

Article 16:

The central leading organs of the various churches are required to register with the Ministry for Foreign Affairs, and the leaders of their local bodies to register with the local People's Councils by giving the full names of all members who constitute the executive of those bodies.

Article 17:

Bulgarian is the official language used in any communication between the churches and the organs of the State, or the Government, of the State, as well as in the business transactions of the different churches. In their intercourse with believers, or in the performance of their ceremonies and services, they may use another language.

Article 18:

The mentioning of the Supreme State Authority, or of its organs, during religious services and ceremonies, or on solemn occasions, is done only in terms previously approved by the Ministry for Foreign Affairs.

Article 19:

The churches notify the Ministry for Foreign Affairs of the various names, symbols, signs and seals which they use.

Article 20:

The formation of societies and organizations for religious-moral purposes, as well as the issuing of publications for religious education, conform with the existing laws and regulations.

The education of children and young people and the establishment of youth organizations is under the special care of the State, and is outside the scope of activity of the churches and their ministers.

Article 21:

The churches may not open hospitals, orphanages or similar institutions.

Such institutions already in existence at the time when this law comes into force, are taken over by the Ministry of Public Health or the Ministry of Labour and Social Service. Their real estate and equipment become the property of the State.

The owners of this property are given just compensation which is fixed by a committee appointed by the Minister for Foreign Affairs, consisting of a representative of the Ministry for Foreign Affairs, a representative of the Ministry for Finance and a representative of the People's Council in the district in which the property is situated. The decisions of the Committees may be appealed against before the district court, whose decision is final.

Article 22:

The churches may maintain connections with churches, institutions, organizations or official persons who have their headquarters or domicile outside the boundaries of the country, only with the previous permission of the Minister for Foreign Affairs.

Article 23:

The churches or their branches (orders, congregations, missions, etc.) which have their headquarters abroad, cannot open up any branches, missions, orders, or charitable or other organizations in the People's Republic of Bulgaria.

Those which already exist in the country shall be closed down within a month of this Law coming into force.

All property of such institutions which have been closed according to the above paragraph (missions, orders, charitable or other organizations) becomes State property, with the just compensation of the former owners. The amount of compensation is fixed according to the procedure provided for in Article 21.

Article 24:

The churches may receive material support and donations from abroad only with the permission of the Minister for Foreign Affairs.

Article 25:

The churches which have property abroad are represented in any transactions concerning this property by the Ministry for Foreign Affairs of the People's Republic of Bulgaria.

The latter also defends the religious interests of Bulgarian citizens abroad.

Article 26:

Any incitement to hatred on religious grounds by speech, press or action, or in any other way, is punishable by imprisonment and a fine up to 10,000 leva.

Article 27:

Whoever, by force or threat, prevents citizens of the recognized churches from freely practicing their religious beliefs and from performing their religious rites and services, which are not contrary to the laws of the country, public order and public morality, is punished by imprisonment up to one year.

Anyone who in the same way forces anybody to participate in the religious rites and services of any church is liable to the same punishment.

Article 28:

Whoever organizes political organizations on a religious basis, or whoever, by speech, press or action, or in any other way, makes use of the church and religion for propaganda against the People's Government and its undertakings, is punished by imprisonment, if not liable to a heavier penalty.

Article 29:

Failure to comply with the provisions of this Law, apart from the punishment imposed by other laws, makes the offender liable to a fine of up to 10,000 leva, which is imposed by order of the Minister for Foreign Affairs.

Said order can be appealed against according to Book Six, Chapter Five, of the Law on Criminal Procedure.

Article 30:

All questions connected with the material support and with the internal organization and self-government of the different churches, inasmuch as they are not regulated by the present Law, are regulated in detail by special statutes for each church. These statutes are made by the leaders of the various churches in accordance with the Laws of the Republic, and are sent for approval to the Ministry for Foreign Affairs within a period of three months, as from the day of the coming into force of the present law.

If the statutes sent for approval contain provisions which are contrary to the law, public order and public morality of the country, the Minister for Foreign Affairs may ask for their removal. In cases where the church does not comply with such requests, the Minister for Foreign Affairs may refuse to recognize the statutes.

Article 31:

Within a period of one month from the coming into force of the present Law, the central leading organs of all churches are required to present to the Ministry for Foreign Affairs, lists containing the names of their religious representatives and ministers. These can remain in office if the Minister for Foreign Affairs does not object. Objections can be made against ministers who do not meet the requirements of the present Law.

Article 32:

The present Law abolishes all laws, statutes, regulations, decrees, etc., which are contrary to it.

(Press Service of the Bulgarian Legation, 12, Queen's Gate Gardens, London)

Appendix X

KOLAROV INTERPRETATION OF LAW ON THE CHURCHES (Excerpts)

February 17, 1949

Speaking on the Draft Law on Creeds which was on the agenda at today's session of the Grand National Assembly, the Vice-President of the Council of Ministers, Minister of Foreign Affairs and Creeds, Vassil Kolarov, said among other things . . .

"The People's Democracy would not be a real People's State, a Workers' State, if it had not observed and assured liberty of conscience and religious freedom, if it had not put on a lasting, democratic basis the relations between the Church and the State, and if it had not put an end to the practice of using the Church for aims which have nothing in common with the interests of believers. When I say this I have in mind particularly the practice of using the Church for imperialist, expansionist aims and its attempts at world domination."

Kolarov explained the three fundamental principles laid down in the Constitution of the Republic, which govern the relations between State and Church. The first principle is liberty of conscience, of creeds and of religious rites.

"The laws of the Republic forbid, and punish as a crime, any sermons which propagate hatred on racial or religious grounds, any attempts to prevent by force or threat the practicing of one's own religion quite freely, or of observing one's own religious rites. Religious tolerance is a tradition of the Bulgarian people, and they maintained this virtue during the darkest years of fascist fanaticism. The Bulgarian people have never supported and have always firmly rejected any attempt at oppression of freedom of conscience and religion in our country. The People's Republic of Bulgaria will never allow the slightest deviation from this important principle of modern civilization."

The second principle in the Constitution is the separation of the Church from the State.

"But the separation of the Church from the State," explained Kolarov, "does not mean either that the Church is left outside the State, or that it becomes another State within the State. The separation of the Church from the State means that the Church in its organization, in the choice of its servants, in its rites and services, is directed only by its statutes, canons and tenets—where these are not contradictory to law, to public order and the moral code."

Kolarov pointed out that the Church also submits to the supreme power of the Constitution, the law, and to the moral code.

"Bulgaria is not a no-man's land. It has a responsible government, and that is why no servant of the Church nominated by an organization having its center abroad, can take up his position without the consent of the Bulgarian authorities. This is so not only in Bulgaria but in all bourgeois and democratic states.

"We cannot allow any church or any servant of the church in Bulgaria to preach against the principles of the people's democracy, lead an open or secret struggle for the restoration of the former regime, serve as an agent of the imperialists, plot with the remnants of capitalism against the building of socialism or support those who are working towards a new world war and plotting against the liberty, independence and territorial integrity of our Republic. Equally inadmissable is activity by the Church in the education of Bulgarian citizens, which, according to the Constitution, is 'secular in a democratic and progressive spirit.' "

Kolarov pointed out the danger of Catholic Church servants becoming agents of a foreign intelligence service, and under the veil of religion supplying a foreign political center, such as the Vatican, with information which, according to the laws of all countries, is considered a State secret.

"It is well known that the Catholic bishops in the countries of the Orient (and Bulgaria is considered to be such a country) are obliged to proceed periodically to the Vatican and give details about the situation in the countries in which they serve—not only religious situation but also the economic, social and political.

"Our Law on Religious Creeds is aimed at preventing the Bulgarian servants of the Church from becoming agents, who, under the veil of religion, can supply foreign political centers with information which, according to the law of all countries is considered a State secret."

Pointing to the fact that Bulgaria has no diplomatic relations with the Vatican, Kolarov stated that the practice of sending to Bulgaria an Apostolic Mission from the Vatican was always of temporary nature, and that the existing Apostolic Mission in Bulgaria should now be considered to be definitely at an end.

"This measure was taken in order to protect the Catholic believers in Bulgaria from the danger of being caught up in the network of anti-democratic, anti-national, and anti-Soviet policy."

In conclusion, discussing the trial of the fifteen pastors, members of the Supreme Council of the United Evangelical Church, Kolarov said . . .

"Bulgarian citizens, including our co-citizen Evangelists, regardless of religion or nationality, are indignant at the fact that certain pastors, with no conscience, forgetting their duty and serving God and Mammon at one and the same time, have converted religion into a commercial undertaking, and have become traitors to their country.

"Relying upon the patriotism of the enormous mass of believers, and on the patriotism and honesty of the church servants, whose name cannot be tarnished because of the crimes of certain shameless pastors, our State will help all creeds in the country whose actions are in conformity with the Constitution, and who co-operate loyally with the People's Government."

(Press Service of the Bulgarian Legation, 12, Queen's Gate Gardens, London)

Appendix XI

ORTHODOX HOLY SYNOD COMMENT ON NEW LAW

February 19, 1949

Extract from the Minutes of the Plenary Session of the Holy Synod of the Bulgarian Church, dated February 18, 1949:

Under the terms of Article 78 of the Constitution of the People's Republic, the Church is separate from the State, but this attitude is not in any way dictated by a feeling of hostility to worship, and the enforcement of this principle does not in any way diminish the autonomous administration of the Church, a privilege expressly sanctioned by the Constitution.

The Grande Assemblee Nationale has now to sanction a special law concerning worship services. The outline giving reasons for this calls attention to the rights guaranteed to religious communities by the Constitution, especially to those of the Orthodox Church, which is the traditional church of the Bulgarian people, and whose history is closely tied up with that of the country.

It is quite obvious, in view of the great masses of citizens who fill our churches each Sunday, and the zeal with which religious traditions are maintained by us, that freedom of worship exists in our country. The Orthodox Church enjoys this liberty without any kind of restriction. The new law concerning worship provides means of dealing with any who attempt to interfere with religious liberty; Article 29 states in effect: "Anyone who by force or threat impedes the holding of services, or prevents citizens freely to practice their religion, or to hold services and perform rites which do not prejudice the law or public order and good behaviour, shall be punished by imprisonment for a period of up to one year."

In accordance with the traditional attitude of our Church in its solicitude for nurturing popular aspirations, and in its loyalty to the State, the Holy Synod has always exhorted its clergy to regard themselves bearers of the Divine Word, and guardians of the Holy Spirit, and to keep aloof from all political influences hostile to the country and its people. We may add that the pastors of the Holy Orthodox Church have conscientiously obeyed our advice. None of them has been persecuted by the authorities for their religious activities.

The Holy Synod strongly condemns all subversive activity carried on by the faithful, even more strongly condemning it when carried on by those of other creeds, all action to the detriment of our People's Republic, and any deeds which are liable to threaten the independence and liberty of our people.

Paissy, Metropolitan of Vratzy,
President of the Holy Synod
Archimandrite Simeon,
Secretary of the Holy Synod

Appendix XII

UNION OF ORTHODOX CLERGY POSITION ON NEW LAW, RELIGIOUS FREEDOM AND EVANGELICAL PASTORS

The Executive Board of the Council of Direction of the Union of Bulgarian Orthodox priests met on February 19, 1949.

In view of the fact that the constitutional principle of the separation of Church and State had been approved both by the 30th National Clergy Congress and by numerous regional gatherings of the clergy,

and that since this separation of the Church from the State had in no way affected either her moral strength or her material position, since financial aid had been allowed for in the civil estimates; and so that the grateful clergy should not forget the line taken in the circumstances by our national leader, President George Dimitrov,

and that since the Bulgarian clergy had prayed incessantly for the coming of God's Kingdom, a Kingdom of peace and justice, of love and brotherly feeling towards one another, and that this activity is jointly liable for the socialist legislation and work of reconstruction in our country,

it was unanimously greed that

the Bulgarian Orthodox clergy will continue, as in the past, to give its support to the common good, and to work for the advancement of socialism in our country, to the glory of God in our land;

the Bulgarian Orthodox clergy declare resolutely that our people, regardless of nationality, religion, or civil status, enjoy freely their civil and political rights, which the clergy would do their utmost to defend by backing up the civil authorities against any threats from whatever source;

the Bulgarian Orthodox clergy hereby express disgust at the traitorous and criminal activity of the Protestant pastors, who are but docile instruments of the Anglo-American Imperialists, and they would gladly see them suitably punished;

we exhort the Bulgarian people to rally themselves staunchly around the Party Front, so that liberty and independence may be safeguarded, for the furtherance of socialism and for the good and well-being of our country.

C. Bogdanov (President)
D. Kotzarov (Secretary)
D. Tederov, F. Pilkov, A. Tebemchirev (Members)

(Press Service of the Bulgarian Legation, 12, Queen's Gate Gardens, London)

ALBANIA

Introduction

The Christian faith was introduced into Albania, if not by St. Paul or other early apostles, in connection with the missionary effort of Orthodox Christianity in the ninth century. In the fifteenth century, with the advent of the Turks and Mohammedanism, the Christian religion was all but wiped out. Even before the liberation of Albania from the Turks, Roman Catholicism sent missionaries to teach and minister; the Franciscans since the time of St. Francis himself, the Jesuits in 1812, nuns of the order of St. Vincent in 1919. Catholic missionaries organized the first primary and secondary schools, and issued the first periodical in Albania in 1891. By the time Mussolini occupied Albania in 1939, there was a Catholic lyceum, a Jesuit institute, a training college for women teachers, elementary schools and a children's home with one thousand children (Gary MacEoin, *The Communist War on Religion*, pp. 166-167). The Orthodox Church has been autocephalous under the Archbishop of Tirana since 1927.

In 1933 the Government nationalized all schools. Some elementary and secondary Catholic Church schools were closed because they would not accept State control and supervision. With the Italian occupation, the Catholic institutions were treated more favourably, and vacancies in the hierarchy and the parishes were filled with Italian sympathizers. Roman Catholic Priest Anton Harapi became Regent of the Regency Council (Barron and Waddams, *Communism and the Churches*, p. 34).

1944:

Population	1,150,000
Moslems	688,280
Orthodox	210,000
Roman Catholic	104,184

Chronicle of Events

Post-War Period

November, 1944—

The country was liberated from Fascist occupation and a "Democratic Front" formed.

The Anti-Fascist Council in a proclamation guaranteed freedom of worship and press.

December, 1944—

The Roman Catholic press was nationalized (*News Behind the Iron Curtain*, Feb. 1953, p. 36).

March, 1945—

The Government requested the Papal Representative, Msgr. Nigros, to go to Rome to obtain recognition of the Albanian Government. When his mission failed, he was refused re-entry into Albania (Gary MacEoin, *The Communist War on Religion*, p. 167).

Communist instructors were appointed to teach in the Catholic Jesuit Institute at Scutari. Catholic leaders resisted the appointments and their teaching (*Ibid.*, p. 167).

1945—

Catholic Church buildings in Scutari were searched and Catholic printing establishments suppressed. All Catholic organizations were outlawed and many members of the clergy charged with Nazi collaboration and Fascism. Franciscans and Jesuits were ordered to leave the country (*Ibid.*, p. 167).

May, 1945—

Catholic children's homes were closed and Catholic orphanages placed under control of a Moslem youth organization. The nuns were shortly expelled (*Ibid.*, p. 167).

August 29, 1945—

Land Reform Law No. 108 provided for the nationalization of Church and other lands.

End of 1945—

By the end of 1945, 80 Catholic leaders had been sentenced to death on charges of war crimes, Fascist collaboration, or sabotage. Among them was the former regent, Priest Harapi (*Ibid.*, p. 167).

January, 1946—

By Governmental decree all Italian property was confiscated, presumably including church property (Barron and Waddams, *Communism and the Churches*, p. 34).

Various properties were used for a refugee center, a youth rest center and the Communist propaganda office.

The Constitution of 1946 was adopted. It states, *inter alia*:

Art. 16

"All citizens have religious liberty. The Church is separated from the State. Religious communities are independent in questions concerning faith and in practicing their religion.

"It is forbidden to use religion and Church for political purposes. Political organizations formed on religious grounds are also forbidden.

"The State may give material aid to the religious communities."

Summer, 1947—

The Education Minister decreed that the educational system should be run on Lenin-Marxist principles. Religious instruction was abolished (Gary MacEoin, *The Communist War on Religion*, p. 168).

January, 1948—

A delegation from the Albanian Orthodox Church visited Moscow with the following purposes:

(a) "Whereas all the other Churches, and especially the Vatican, wanted to put an end to the existence of the Albanian Church, the Russian Orthodox Church is its great defender.

(b) "The Russian Orthodox Church is national and patriotic. The emancipated Albanian nation is moving rapidly along the path of progress and wishes its Orthodox Church to be likewise national and patriotic. In this connection the experience of the Russian Church provides a valuable lesson.

(c) "In the common struggle against Fascism the Albanian nation has come close to the Russian people and wishes to be in close relationship with its Church" (Barron and Waddams, *Communism and the Churches*, p. 35).

Russian Bishop Nestor visited Albania.

January, 1948—

All schools were nationalized.

January-March, 1948—

Five members of the Roman Catholic hierarchy were executed on charges of war-crimes and Fascist collaboration.

July, 1948—

The Albanian Orthodox Church sent a delegation headed by Archbishop Paisi to the Pan-Orthodox Congress in Moscow.

August, 1949—

Orthodox Archbishop Kissi was deposed for engaging in "activities harmful to the Albanian people and to the church" (*Ibid.*, p. 35). He had also opposed submitting of the Albanian Church to Moscow jurisdiction. The Tirana journal, *Bashkini,* stated that he "was working against our interests . . . by his activity with the Unitarian Church during the Fascist occupation" (*News Behind the Iron Curtain*, Feb. 1953, p. 37). He was succeeded by Archbishop Paisi. Two other bishops were also arrested at the end of 1948.

November 26, 1949—

A draft law (no. 743) on religion containing 37 articles was published, similar to those of Rumania and Bulgaria. Liaison between Church and State was to be effected by the Council of Ministers, rather than the Minister of Foreign Affairs. The Orthodox Church was not given a privileged position. However it did receive State subsidies (Albania, Appendix I).

July, 1950—

The Government charged that Italy and the Vatican were organizing spy and sabotage units within Albania to overthrow the Albanian Government (*N. Y. Times*, July 2, 1950, 4:7).

August, 1950—

The Government announced a law severing relationships with the Vatican, and providing for subsidies for the Catholic Church in Albania from the Government. The law would permit Catholics to follow "the established world Catholic code" as long as this "does not conflict with the laws of the Albanian people's Republic, public order and good customs." Catholic priests were to be trained in seminaries "created and administered" on Government approval (Associated Press, August 3, 1950).

December 10, 1951—

The Albanian Orthodox Church sent a delegation to Czechoslovakia for the investiture of Orthodox Archbishop Eleutherios as Metropolitan of Prague and all Czechoslovakia.

Appendix I

CHURCH LAW NO. 743, NOVEMBER 26, 1949

Articles 13 and 15:

. . . All the elected and nominated personnel of Churches must be approved by the Council of Ministers . . . Those who act against the laws of the state . . . must be immediately dismissed from service . . . If the religious organ does not take action . . . the state acts itself . . .

Article 18:

. . . All religious communities are obliged to send immediately to the Council of Ministers pastoral letters, messages, speeches, memoranda and everything to be printed or made public. The Council of Ministers has the right to annul, if it does not agree . . . with them . . .

Article 23:

. . . The education of youth is conducted by the State, and religious institutions have nothing to do with it. . . .

Article 24:

. . . Religious communities cannot have hospitals, orphanages, institutions of welfare, real estate . . . All these institutions which still exist at this proclamation are immediately nationalized. . . .

(As quoted in *News Behind the Iron Curtain*, February 1953, Vol 2, No. 2, p. 36)

POLAND

Introduction

Poland officially "became Christian"—and Catholic—when Prince Miezko in 966 married the daughter of Catholic Prince Boleslaw of Bohemia. Contacts of a religious, cultural and political nature with other Slavic peoples have continued to the present time, occasionally resulting in the resistance of the people to Germanizing, "Protestantizing" and "Westernizing" influences. In the 13th Century Poland was invaded by the Mongols, then by the Teutons. In the 15th Century Poland became the dominant power of the East Central European area, extending her political and religious (Roman Catholic) influence into the neighboring Baltic area, especially Lithuania, the Ukraine, and West Russia. In 1722 Poland was partitioned between Russia, Prussia and Austria, and did not regain political unity until her re-creation as an independent nation after the First World War.

Polish church history records not so much a struggle between Church and State, as between nationalistic Catholicism and liberal non-Catholicism, or between Church-State and Free Church. During the Middle Ages, Jews, Christians fleeing the Inquisition, and various groups of reformers and religious dissenters found refuge in Poland. Poland came to be known as the *silum haereticorum*. These elements, combined with the influence of Luther, with that of Polish students who had espoused the Reformation while studying abroad, and with the growing liberal tendencies of the Polish intelligentia stimulated the beginnings of what might have become a general reformation in Poland. Freedom of conscience and of speech were realized well in advance of other countries. In 1563 the Bible was translated by the "reformers." The Polish language was systematized and a national literature developed. Protestant churches were soon established among the bourgeois and the intelligentia. This "reformation," however, never got beyond its embryonic stage.

By the end of the 16th Century Catholic leadership became aware of the dangers of the Protestant "heresy." During the following two centuries, aided by the influx of Jesuits, and by the dissensions and conflicts among Protestants themselves, the Catholic Church succeeded periodically in having Protestants either expelled from the country, or forbidden to preach, excluded from public office, and prohibited from worshipping except in private homes.

In that part of Poland partitioned among Russia, Prussia and Germany in the 19th Century, and in the territories affected by the Austrian occupation, Church-State patterns prevalent in those countries were imposed, e.g.,

"the regulations laid down by the Russian authorities . . . made encroachments on Church autonomy and established the influence of the State even in purely internal Church affairs" (*Religious Life in Poland*, Polish Research and Information Service, N. Y., p. 16).

Except for that period, the relationship established in the Middle Ages between Catholic and non-Catholic Churches, or between Catholic-State Church

(383)

and Free Churches, prevailed with some modifications until the present decade.*

As an independent nation between the two wars, Poland established obligatory religious instruction for children up to the age of 18. Catholic institutions, schools and other works grew rapidly. 17,000 nuns, 1,800 monks, 12,000 priests, 49 bishops and 2 cardinals constituted the ordained leadership of the Catholic Church.

The Churches During World War II:

In September, 1939, Poland was partitioned between Germany and Russia. In German-occupied Poland, on orders from the Foreign Office of the German Evangelical Church, the churches were reorganized: Lutherans were to be assimilated into the German Church. Polish literature and Bibles were destroyed and the theological faculty closed. When Lutheran Bishop Bursche and others protested, they were imprisoned. Under the leadership of Dr. Blau the United Protestant Church welcomed the Germans as "saviors out of twenty years of oppression" (*Religious Life in Poland*, p. 18).

The Reformed Churches were also aligned toward Germany. Two pastors who protested were imprisoned. The Orthodox Churches' administration was transferred to the jurisdiction of Archbishop Seraphim in Berlin. Metropolitan Dionysius of Warsaw was forced to resign in January, 1940, but was reinstated nine months later, for which he thanked the German governor and the "great leader, Adolf Hitler." Roman Catholics reported the closing of many churches, the supervision of mass and confession by the Gestapo, and the forbidding of religious education.

In Russian-occupied Poland much church property was immediately confiscated and some monasteries were stripped (Appendix XI). After the incorporation of Eastern Poland into the U.S.S.R. as a republic, the Orthodox Church was temporarily protected from the oppression of the former Roman Catholic Church-State. With regard to Roman Catholicism, *Bezboznik* (Moscow "Godless" magazine) stated in issue No. 29, 1939, "Everything that happened in Russia during the Revolution reappeared. Catholic priests with guns in hand tried to save the Capitalist enslavement of the workers" (Timasheff, *Religion in Soviet Russia*, p. 132). In October the *Anti-religious* journal reported in Moscow that Red troops were killing Roman Catholic priests (N. Y. Times, Oct. 12:8:2, 1939).

During the German occupation of all of Poland (1941-1944) there were few major developments in Church-State relations. Although Ukrainian Archbishop Polycarp declared himself ready to cooperate loyally with the German Government, the Germans also appointed an Archbishop, as did Metropolitan Sergius of Moscow. The Ukrainian Orthodox Church declared itself independent of Moscow and accused Russia of desiring the soul of the Ukrainian people for "traditional and imperialistic . . . and not religious reasons . . ." There were some conversations between Ukrainian Orthodox and Uniates with a view to establishing a united Ukrainian National Church. Following the death of Roman Catholic Archbishop Gall, the Vatican appointed a German as Archbishop, a group of Catholics in Poland appointed a Polish Archbishop.

In April 1944, just before the German collapse in Poland, a number of

---

* However, the Concordat between the Polish Government and the Holy See was not officially confirmed until February, 1925. The Evangelical Lutheran Church was formally granted freedom of belief and worship in 1936.

Polish bishops refused to sign a German appeal to the Polish people to hold back the Russians (N. Y. Times, April, 1944, 3:3:8).

The Churches at the End of World War II:

Some measure of the effect of the War on the churches, and on their postwar attitude may be indicated in the following figures:

	1939	1949
Total Population of Poland	32,000,000	22,000,000
Roman Catholic	22,900,000	19,500,000*
Orthodox	4,000,000	430,000
Jewish	3,500,000	100,000
Lutheran	500,000	100,000
Reformed	40,000	5 to 8,000
Evangelical Christian	30,000	10,000
Baptist	10,000	13,000
Methodist	Unrecognized	14,000**
National-Catholic, Old Catholic, Mariavite and others	?	50,000
Mohammedan	12,000	10,000

* 70% of total population in 1939 as compared with 90% now.
** Government sources report 80,000.

The positions taken, or seen to be taken, by the churches during the War have affected subsequent events. The Evangelical Lutheran Church was of German origin. The Germans attempted to use it as an avenue of infiltration, and although Polish Lutherans gave strong opposition, Lutherans became suspect by other Poles. The Methodists were of American origin and were therefore persecuted by the Nazis and their collaborators as American spies. The Catholic Church had its center of authority abroad which, though it may have been some consolation to Catholics during the occupations, was a reason for suspicion on the part of the occupying powers. 2,500 priests were killed by those powers. The Vatican's appointment of German bishops for German-occupied territories was later to be used as an indictment against the Pope for "pro-Germanism."

On the whole, however, the main body of the churches remained Polish—Polish nationalist—and was destined to become the nucleus around which the nationalism of the common people gathered.

Chronicle of Events

Period under the Provisional Government

July 22, 1944—

In its first manifesto, the Polish Committee of National Liberation stated that the basic principles of the Constitution of March 17, 1922 (Text, Poland—Appendix I) would remain in force, including stipulations guaranteeing religious liberty (*Yearbook on Human Rights*—1947).

August, 1944—

Following the Warsaw uprising against the Germans, the property of pastors was expropriated, most of which was later returned.

September 23, 1944—

By decree of the Committee of National Liberation, prison sentences were to be given for instigating riots or strife, or for being involved in same (Appendix II).

November, 1944—

The Ukrainian Uniate Church again invited the Ukrainian Orthodox Churches to unite with them and support an independent Ukraine (*ICPIS*, No. 45, Dec., 1945).

January, 1945—

The Polish Roman Catholic Church praised the attitude and dealings of the Lublin Provisional Government with the Catholic Church (*N. Y. Times*, Jan. 11:5:2, 1945).

March, 1945—

Osservatore Romano criticized the Lublin Government for its proposed economic reforms, accused it of being too much under Russian influence, and of Russian terrorism. A Rome Socialist paper scored the Vatican for its opposition to the land reform; U.S.S.R. *Izvestia* denied the charges of "terrorism" and undue influence (*N. Y. Times*, March 14, 28, 31, April 3, 1945).

April, 1945—

Evangelical sources intimated that the Government was giving preferential treatment to the Roman Catholic Church in exempting its property from the agrarian reform and in assigning "ownerless" land to Catholic priests and churches. Priests were included in Government offices.

June, 1945—

The National Evangelical Council applied to the Ministry of Public Affairs to be recognized as the provisional Synod of Evangelical Churches (*ICPIS*, No. 22, June, 1945).

June, 1945—

At an educational congress in Lodz, several delegates called for the Government to suppress religious instruction in public schools. Shortly thereafter, the Government decreed that religious instruction could be given only by priests (MacEoin, *Communist War on Religion*, p. 199).

July 6, 1945—

Poland and Russia signed a treaty for an exchange of population in the border area. All persons of Polish or Jewish descent then residing in Russian-annexed Eastern Poland were free to return to Poland (*Yearbook of Human Rights, 1946*, p. 237).

August, 1945—

Many German-speaking pastors, both pro and anti-Nazi, were expelled from the province of Mazuria along with the German-speaking populace. Much of their property was taken over by Roman Catholics, including parish houses, churches and hospitals.

September, 1945—

Vice-Premier Nikolajczyk of the predominantly Catholic Polish Peasant Party charged that non-Communists were powerless in the Provisional Government, and confirmed reports of rioting against Communist reform measures.

September 14, 1945—

The Government attacked the 1925 Vatican Concordat with Rome, and accused the Vatican of violation of its articles by:

(a) appointing German bishops to Poland during the Nazi occupation;

(b) disregarding (by high church officials) the articles "guaranteeing the Government the right to exercise influence in the question of nominating bishops" (*Religious Life in Poland*, p. 9).

The Polish Government explained that the denunciation was in line "with customs prevailing in international relations," and that profound changes had resulted in Church-State relations as a result of the "evolution of society."

The Roman Catholic Church protested the loss of its special relationship to the Government, and reported the arrest and deportation of some religious leaders following the denunciation (*N. Y. Times*, Sept. 15, 16, 1945).

October 16, 1945—

By Decree No. 46, the Government recognized the Methodist Church and granted it full equality with all churches (Poland—Appendix VIII).

October 25, 1945—

Vice-Minister Chajn voiced the opposition of the Government to the Roman Catholic, or any other church receiving its directives from abroad (*N. Y. Times*, Oct. 26, 1945).

November 9, 1945—

The Conference of Catholic Bishops issued a statement urging broad participation of the Catholic Church in the Polish Diet.

December 9, 1945—

Though the Polish Government declared that the Concordat with Rome had been violated by the Vatican and that it was therefore no longer considered valid, the Catholic Church's program of religious education in public schools, Catholic lands and institutions, theological training and publications were not affected. The Government continued support for the Roman Catholic Church in reconstruction, religious education and securing of "unclaimed" properties (*Religious Life in Poland*, p. 9, and Evangelical sources).

January 1, 1946—

By Governmental decree, marriage and divorce were to be considered legal only if performed by civil authorities. Records of births and deaths were to be kept by the Government. Church records, when approved by the Government, were considered valid for births, marriages, and deaths prior to January 1 (*Yearbook on Human Rights*, 1947, p. 272). The law met with some Roman Catholic opposition.

February, 1946—

The Council of Protestant Churches was acknowledged by the Government as the official organ of the Protestant Churches (applied for recognition in June, 1945).

February, 1946—

The conviction of Catholic Msgr. Splett as a German collaborator was strongly attacked by *Osservatore Romano*. Vatican-Polish Government relations were reported greatly strained (*N. Y. Times*, Feb. 3, March 17, 1946).

March, 1946—

Evangelicals reported that the Roman Catholic Church expropriated more than 75% of the Protestant Churches, and more than 200 Orthodox Churches, plus vicarages and hospitals in the Lublin district without

forewarning. Czechoslovakian Protestants fled, while Catholic sources spread propaganda that Protestants were "Germans" and therefore suspect.

In a letter to the Evangelicals, the Prime Minister assured them that their property rights and privileges would be respected, and that gifts from abroad for rebuilding could be received without Government interference. The Government provided the Methodist Church with two hours' radio time for the dedication of a chapel in Warsaw.

May, June, 1946—

Negotiations between the Roman Catholic Church and the Government over various points of difference and the proposed referendum on social reforms were abandoned (*N. Y. Times*, Sept. 18, 1946).

June, 1946—

Extensive social and institutional reforms were adopted by public referendum (*Yearbook on Human Rights* —1947). Articles dealing with "Offences Particularly Dangerous during the Period of the Country's Reconstruction" elaborated on the Decrees of September 23, 1944 and November 16, 1945, prescribing heavy punishment for inciting to riot or conspiracy (Poland—Appendix III).

July 21, 1946—

Minister Radkiewicz denounced the Roman Catholic Vice-President, Mikolajczyk, and attacked the Roman Catholic Church for its sympathetic attitude toward the underground opposition. He warned that he would use force if necessary to crush the "Fascist underground." The Papal Secretary of State admitted that the Pope had interceded for Roman Catholic Greiser who was on trial for war crimes in Poland (*N. Y. Times*, July 22, 23, 1946).

July 30, 1946—

The journal of the Polish Workers' Party, *Glos Ludo*, attacked Catholic Cardinal Griffin for his reactionary political role, and referred particularly to a message sent to Cardinal Hlond encouraging a stronger anti-Government policy (*N. Y. Times*, July 31, 1946).

September, 1946—

Negotiations between Cardinal Hlond and President Bierut to improve Church-State relationships (broken off after an impasse in June) were resumed (*N. Y. Times*, Sept. 18, 1946).

October 20, 1946—

In a pastoral letter, Cardinal Hlond indicated that he expected strong Catholic support for the Peasant Party in the forthcoming elections, and urged the people to cast a strong vote in opposition to Communist elements in the Government (*N. Y. Times*, October 21, 1946).

November 12, 1946—

Polish observers noted that in the National elections the Communist Party retained its majority in spite of strong Roman Catholic pressure for Vice-Premier Mikolajczyk and the Peasant Party (*N. Y. Times*).

November 19-24, 1946—

Roman Catholic Priest Z. Jarkiewicz was tried for "terrorism" and sentenced to hang. President Bierut advised the Roman Catholic Church to stop its political activity:
"Stop using sermons for political activity . . . These attacks from the pulpit form one of the greatest barriers to good relations between the Church and Government . . . Feelings (of distrust) on the part of the Catholic Church . . . are groundless, because Polish democracy does not exclude the possibility of working together. . . . We (the Government) never avoided the discussion (of a concordat). . . . Naturally, before a concordat can be signed, there must be a resumption of diplomatic relations" (*Religious Life in Poland*, p. 10).
The President attacked the Catholic Church for its underground activity and its bias in favor of the Germans, called attention to the privileges the Church was receiving from the Government (*N. Y. Times*, November 20, 23, 24, 1946).
To the Evangelicals President Bierut expressed a hope that foreign churches would aid the Polish churches in their educational, cultural, youth and scout activities. Evangelicals noted that the Government, contrary to the tone of relationships at the beginning of the year,

was now kindly disposed toward Evangelicals, and annoyed with Roman Catholicism. The Methodist Church was receiving great numbers of new members, many from Roman Catholicism, partly because, being of Anglo-American rather than German origin, it was less suspect.

December 16, 1946—

Cardinal Griffin made an open appeal for free elections (*N. Y. Times*, December 17, 1946).

December 27, 1946—

Roman Catholic Rev. Stefanski was accused of leading an underground opposition movement, and sentenced to death. The Vatican reported that two Ruthenian bishops had been deported to Russia (*N. Y. Times*, Dec. 16, 28, 1946).

January 5, 1947—

The Government promised the Roman Catholic Church adequate constitutional guarantees of Catholic Church rights following the election.
Cardinal Hlond issued a statement regarding the proposed new constitution, and stipulating that
(a) it should be that of a Christian State, since the Poles were Christians, and should favor the exercise of the Catholic religions;
(b) it should safeguard human rights and dignity, ensure equality of citizens, encourage private economic initiative, and assure the right of private property;
(c) it should protect the family and provide for religious instruction for all;
(d) it should ensure freedom of worship, autonomy of church administration, and freedom for the churches to carry out educational, welfare and social tasks (Gary MacEoin, *The Communist War on Religion*, p. 197).

February 19, 1947—

The Constituent Diet in a "Constitutional Act" re-affirmed that the Constitution of March 17, 1921, the Manifesto of July 22, 1944, and the Reform Law of June 30, 1946, would remain in effect until the adoption of the new Constitution.

February 22, 1947—

The Constituent Diet in a "Declaration of Rights and Liberties" (Poland,

Appendix IV) listed fourteen liberties it would uphold, including equality of individuals, personal inviolability, freedom of conscience and worship, and freedom of speech, press, assembly and demonstration. The abuse of these rights to oppose the Government was to be prevented by law ("The Provisional Constitution," *Polish Research and Information Service*, N. Y.).

April, 1947—

In a public declaration, the Catholic Episcopal Council insisted that any new constitution should "respect the conscience of Catholics, and assist Catholic citizens in the practice of their religion," should provide for religious instruction in public and private schools, and should "create a legal basis for the establishment of relations between Church and State" (*The Tablet*, April 19, 1947).

June 30, 1947—

In cooperation with the Polish Government, the Catholic Church re-established five administrative districts, with churches, priests, seminaries, institutions and other Catholic practices in the "Recovered Territories" (from Germany). The Western Press Agency of Poland stated that "The Catholic Church has become one of the bonds which unite the Recovered Territories with the rest of Poland. Its existence and moral significance are generally appreciated and recognized" (*Religious Life in Poland*, p. 13).

June, 1947—

Government leaders attended an "Ecumenical Bible Week" organized by the Evangelical Council, and warmly accepted gift Bibles. Small subsidies were provided by the Government for Evangelical Church reconstruction plans, for the support of the Evangelical Theological faculty. An ecumenical journal was being published and circulated widely. The Government's intensive youth program caused some confusion in church youth work, but religious education in the schools was still compulsory.

July 4, 1947—

The Government recognized the Evangelical Lutheran Church by a special law which replaced the regulations of all previous governments with regard to Lutherans (Poland— Appendix V).

September 5, 1947—

The Government recognized the Evangelical Reformed, Mariavite and Old Catholic Churches by a special law which voided all previous restrictions and laws regulating these Churches (Poland — Appendix VI). There was some Roman Catholic opposition to the acceptance of the Old Catholics and Mariavites, who were considered by Roman Catholics as "immoral" and heretics (*Religious Life in Poland*, p. 9).

September, 1947—

In a pastoral letter, Roman Catholic bishops deplored the publication of anti-religious literature, the press attacks on church schools, the deceitful measures used to entice Christians into anti-Christian political parties, against their will and conscience, and the censorship of Catholic publications and pastoral letters. They accused the Government of forcing Catholics to sign petitions for the removal of Catholic layman S. Mikolajczyk from the leadership of the opposition Peasant Party. Premier Cyrankiewicz warned Catholic leaders that the Government would not tolerate the use of religious freedom for political purposes (*N. Y. Times*, Oct. 1, 30, 1947).

December, 1947—

Public statements were made by Government officers linking Catholic Cardinals Hlond and Sapieha with a reactionary underground movement. Three weeks later, the visit of Cardinal Hlond to Rome was interpreted as the first step in new negotiations between the Government and the Roman Catholic Church (*N. Y. Times*, December 7, 30, 1947).

December, 1947—

At a second "Ecumenical Bible Week" (see June, 1947), no Government representative was present. Old Catholic, Orthodox and Protestant representatives participated in a pastors' conference organized by the ecumenical council. Minister of Justice Swiatowski addressed the leaders of non-Roman churches, exhorting them to exemplify unity, praising religious freedom in Poland, and pointing out the need to relate the Polish ecumenical movement to ecumenical traditions of the past among Slavic nations.

January, 1948—

Catholic Church authorities opposed a Government plan to include the Catholic youth organizations in the Government-sponsored National Youth Association. In a pastoral letter, the bishops declared, "The Church cannot agree to the training of Catholic youth without God" (*N. Y. Times*, Jan. 26 and May 25, 1948).

February, 1948—

Catholic Church authorities submitted to the Government proposed terms for an accord which would include recognition of religious marriage as legally valid, an extensive Catholic religious youth training program, and no restriction on Catholic religious publications (*N. Y. Times*, Feb. 9, 1948).

Victor Grosz, Minister of Foreign Affairs, stated:

"We are determined on the separation of Church and State, and our laws in this respect are similar to those in all civilized countries. The Government does not consider the Church a political partner, but the Government is prepared to cooperate with the Church with perfect tolerance of all religions" (*Religious Life in Poland*, p. 1).

The Government further demanded that the Catholic Church support its reconstruction and reform program as a prerequisite to resuming Church-State negotiations.

February 29, 1948—

The Polish Workers' Party publication *Glos Ludu* stated:

"The solution of these conflicts (between the Catholic Church and the Government) would remove the 'pangs of conscience' of many . . . who want to be good Catholics and at the same time serve the new Poland. The solution . . . lies in the interest of the Nation and . . . the Church" (*Religious Life in Poland*, p. 11).

March, 1948—

Rev. K. Najder of the Polish Methodist Church, questioned in America, asserted that the Polish Government guaranteed and provided complete religious freedom, and that numerous Communist leaders were Church members.

March, 1948—

The Pope's March message of sympathy to German bishops, branding their ousting from the Polish "Recovered Territory" as "inequitable and unjustifiable," was interpreted in Poland as refusal to recognize the territorial changes (*Religious Life in Poland*, p. 12).

May, 1948—

The Catholic *Warsaw Weekly* (May) supported Poland's new western borders and the decision to expel all Germans. Cardinal Hlond and the *Weekly* asserted that the Government's interpretation of the Pope's message as opposing the changes and favoring new revisions was "without foundation" (*Religious Life in Poland*, p. 12).

May, 1948—

Orthodox Archbishop Dionysius, who during the German occupation had opposed the subordination of the Polish Orthodox Church to the Moscow Patriarchate, was deposed (at the end of April) by Government decree on charges of German collaboration, and confined to his Warsaw residence. He was replaced by the Archbishop of Bialystok, Timotheus. Other priests were said to have been so badly frightened by police questioning that they abandoned the Orthodox habit except in worship services (*EPS*, No. 20, May, 1948; *N. Y. Times*, June 11, 1948).

June 7, 1948—

Fifty-four Catholic leaders, lay and clergy, signed a letter to the Pope confirming Poland's right to the "Recovered Territories," the unity of the Polish people on this matter, and the devotion of Polish Catholics to the Holy See.

The non-Roman Catholic Ecumenical Council declared itself in favor of Poland's maintaining her present boundary (*Religious Life in Poland*, pp. 12, 17).

June, 1948—

A month after the ousting of Archbishop Dionysius, the Government ordered the Polish Orthodox Church to make its peace with the Russian Orthodox Church, and submit to the authority of Moscow Patriarch Alexei (*N. Y. Times*, June 11, 1948).

A delegation, led by Archbishop Timotheus, called on Patriarch Alexei. By August an agreement was reached guaranteeing the Polish Orthodox Church an independent (autocephalous) status within the Moscow jurisdiction (*Religious Life in Poland*, p. 23).

July, 1948—

Catholic Rev. J. Mix of Chicago, after a six-weeks' visit to Poland, reported that the Government did not interfere with the administration of Catholic institutions, and was tolerant toward religious processions. "At one (procession) the Government sent two State officials in uniform to escort Cardinal (Hlond)." Back in the U. S. he added that "the air you breathe (in Poland) is not free" (*N. Y. Times*, July 26, 1948) (*Religious Life in Poland*, p. 10).

September, 1948—

The director and editor of two Catholic publications were "detained," their publications suspended (*N. Y. Times*, Sept. 1, 3, 1948).

September-October, 1948—

Religious education in public schools was declared optional. At the Congress of Grammar School Teachers a resolution was adopted calling for the elimination of clerical influence in education, and the establishment of education on a Marxist basis (Gary MacEoin, *The Communist War on Religion*, p. 199). The Communist Party established a number of special schools in which religious instruction was forbidden.

The Government urged the Protestant Churches to unite in one church. A constitution for the Ecumenical Council was submitted to the Government, which returned it asking for a looser framework emphasizing the Council's religious and spiritual nature. "Direct relations with the head office in Geneva . . ." were broken off.

September, 1948—

Roman Catholic bishops, in the "Manifesto of Wroclaw," protested the Government's expulsion of priests from teaching positions, the removal of crucifixes from school rooms, the suppression of religious instruction and the introduction of atheistic teaching into the classrooms. They also declared that the Pope, in expressing his sympathy (in March, 1948) for German refugees expelled from the Western Territories had no desire to reflect on the position of the new frontiers (MacEoin, *op. cit.*, p. 198).

November, 1948—

Religious Life in Poland, a document of the Polish Research and Information Service, N. Y., stated that the territories recovered from Germany had belonged to Poland as far back as the 10th Century, when they were the "cradle" of Polish Catholicism, and that the territories had always retained a Polish and Catholic character through centuries of German rule (p. 12).

December, 1948—

The Polish Workers' Party Congress declared that children of nonbelievers must be protected from persecution in the schools. The Congress demanded the expulsion of priests from the schools and the abolition of private (Church) schools. It attacked the clergy for their opposition to the Government program on grounds of defending religious freedom and faith.

The attitude of the Party to the Churches was defined by delegate General Zawadski (Poland—Appendix XII) as one of tolerance and neutrality so long as the Church did not interfere in social or political affairs. He called on the clergy to support the Government in its social, progressive program (*Poland of Today*, Feb. 1949, p. 9).

"The Party . . . will not allow the State to interfere in religious matters of believing people . . . (but) the Party demands unconditional loyalty of the clergy of all confessions to the Peoples' State" (*N. Y. Times*, January 8, 1948).

January, 1949—

Premier Cyrankiewicz admitted that underground activities in opposition to the Government were growing stronger, and warned the clergy not to interfere in State affairs. He warned the churches to stop exploiting the people's religious devotion for anti - Government resistance. One Catholic priest and two aides were "detained" on charges of "agitation"; 100 other priests were reported by the Catholic Church to have been seized since October (*N. Y. Times*, January 12, 28, 1949).

February, 1949—

In a letter to President Bierut, Cardinal Sapieha urged that a joint Church-Government commission be set up to settle Church-State differences. Bishop Choromanski, secretary of the Roman Catholic Episcopal Council (Bench of Bishops), asserted that the Church was willing to cooperate with the State, but would fight to preserve its status (*N. Y. Times*, Feb. 3, 7, 1949).

February 6, 1949—

Bishop Wyszynski was installed as Catholic Primate of Poland. No Government representative attended the installation services. The Catholic publication, *Tygodnik Warsawski*, closed since September, printed a special edition on the installation (*N. Y. Herald Tribune*, Paris Edition, Feb. 7, 1949).

February, 1949—

Bishop Adamski addressed a pastoral letter to the Catholic Churches condemning the anti-religious activities of the Government. Catholic sources reported that twenty priests were held temporarily for reading the letter from their pulpits. The Government denied that it was engaged in an anti-Church campaign, but was simply prosecuting criminals. Ten days later (March) two priests were charged with blessing a group of underground terrorists and later sentenced to prison terms. Three other priests plead guilty to charges of cooperating with an illegal organization, and another was accused of misusing the funds of an organization of peasants (*N. Y. Times*, February 9, 10, 19, 27, 28, March 1, 2, 3, 12, 1949).

March, 1949—

Minister of Public Administration Wolski in a statement to Bishop Chor-

omanski, Secretary of the Roman Catholic Episcopal Council, defined the "present position" of the Government to the Churches (Poland, Appendix XIII). He accused some church leaders, "associates of criminal Nazis and foreign elements," of an increasing effort to stir up unrest among the people by claims of religious persecution. He stated that the Church had religious freedom, its institutions could function and that there was no interference in the inner life of the Churches so long as they abided by the law. He noted that a final settlement of Church-State relations would be made in the new constitution, and that an exchange of proposals on that subject would be welcomed.

March 14-29, 1949—

The statement (Poland, Appendix XIII) was published widely in the Polish press. Mass meetings were organized to discuss the statement and attitude of the Church, and new statements were made condemning the Roman Catholic hierarchy for its reactionary attitude and relation to "American imperialism" and the Vatican, and pointing out that the Roman Catholic Church alone had been unaffected by the agrarian reform, that the priests received special privileges, and that the Church had more advantages in education, publications, etc., "than in many capitalist countries." Care was taken to point out that many priests "were honest patriots." Demands were heard at meetings that the Church should cease its anti-Government activities (*Polish Facts and Figures*, March 26, 1949).

The Polish (London) Press Office, in an editorial, accused the West of first seeking to overthrow the Government through the Underground and Warsaw Uprising Movements, then through the Peasants, then through the Socialist Party—all of which had failed. Thereupon the West was seeking to overcome the Government through the last remaining force, the Church—"obviously contrary to the interests of the Catholic population" (*Ibid.*).

April, 1949—

"Irreproachable sources inside Poland" were quoted by the National Catholic Welfare Conference as stating that many Catholic schools had been closed, in many cases priests had been refused the right to give religious instruction in the schools, that crucifixes had been removed from classrooms, that Catholic young people had been compelled to join youth organizations hostile to the Church, and that Catholic publications were subjected to severe censorship (*Pilot*, April 16, 1949).

April, 1949—

Catholic Church leaders again openly accused the Government of using pressure on the Church and the priests, and expressed scepticism concerning the proposed new constitutional regulations. Archibishop Wyszynski said that the Government was trying to divide the people from the Church. Catholic Bishops urged the people to ignore the attacks of the press against the Church. Another priest, Danson, was sentenced to four years' imprisonment for preaching against the Government (*N. Y. Times*, March 26, 30, April 3, 25, 1949).

April 24, 1949—

An unidentified bishop sent a pastoral letter to his parishes exhorting priests, parents and youth to remain faithful and warned them against Godless gatherings, Godless publications, and education without religion. "The education of a Catholic nation cannot take place without the cooperation of the Church . . ." (Poland—Appendix XIV).

By the end of May, 50,000,000 revised textbooks had been issued (MacEoin, *The Communist War on Religion*, p. 200).

May, 1949—

The Polish Press Agency announced on May 11 that Catholic Msgr. Z. Kaczynski had been put under preventive arrest (as of April 3) as a "member of an anti-State organization," and for having an "anti-State attitude" (*East Europe*, May 26, 1949, p. 5).

May, 1949—

Archbishop Wyszynski, in a sermon delivered in Warsaw, stated:
"Once again we have concentration camps and the jails are packed to overflowing. The bricks and stones of war-damaged churches are being used to build penitentiaries. Many priests are in prison" (MacEoin, *The Communist War on Religion*, p. 202).

May 10, 1949—

The Communist *Trybuna Ludu* stated that the policy of the leaders of the Catholic clergy had nothing in common with the good of the country, religion, or the best interests of the Polish Church. The Army daily *Polska Zbrojna* stated:
"Instead of a settlement the Church hierarchy tries to inflame relations between Church and State . . . Despite the feverish attempts of the reactionary part of the hierarchy, they will not succeed in unleasing a Kulturkampf in Poland or creating an artificial division between believers and unbelievers . . . The continued persistence of the hierarchy in opposition to the State will bring about their complete isolation from the progressive part of the nation" (*Ibid.*)

May 26, 1949—

Polish newspapers reported that peasants on Church-owned farms were striking and charged that they were being exploited by the Church (*N. Y. Times*, May 27, 1949).
Non-Governmental sources stated that riots were a demonstration against the Government.

June, 1949—

The non-Roman Ecumenical Council's *Universal Church* publication was suspended June 1, but a mimeographed information sheet on ecumenical affairs in Poland was continued monthly.
A theological conference for pastors was held near Warsaw.

June, 1949—

Roman Catholic sources reported that the Government had seized several (nearly 20) Catholic printing establishments (*N. Y. Times*, June 20, 1949).

June 28, 1949—

Roman Catholic and Government representatives began talks to try to settle the Church-State conflict, and to arrive at a workable continuing relationship (*N. Y. Times*, June 29, 1949).

July, 1949—

Following the report of a miracle (that the statue of Mary had shed tears) in the Lublin Cathedral, great crowds of people sought to go to Lublin on pilgrimages. The Government closed the church, curtailed rail travel and forbade pilgrimages to Lublin. The press accused the Church of fabricating the story in order to gain money. A reliable observer reported that the people had given up hope of any help coming from outside to free them, and were now turning in their extremity to some supernatural intervention.

July, 1949—

In a radio address to a Catholic congress in Berlin, the Pope spoke sharply against the situation in Poland. Following the Pope's 9-point statement of accusation against the Government, especially that there was no longer religious freedom in Poland, and his decree that Communists and Communist supporters would be excommunicated, the Polish Government condemned the Papal decree and accused the Pope of supporting German imperialism and border revisionism. Protestant Church leaders were called to a meeting with Government representatives and were pressed to sign a statement that the Pope's 9-point statement was not true, that Christian people still had full religious freedom, and that religion was still taught in the schools. An unbiased observer reported that the Protestant statement was partly true, and the Government had recently obtained sanctions against over-enthusiastic Communist students in Warsaw who disturbed a Catholic procession on Corpus Christi Day.

The Pope's statement widened the breach between Catholic leaders who sought to be loyal to the Government, and those who were strongly opposed to it.

Roman Catholic Primate Archbishop Wyszynski, in a pastoral letter referred to by the *N. Y. Times*, October 12, stated that there were

"Many who have strayed . . . We are deeply grieved by so many tragedies of priests' souls that do not withstand the pressure of perplexing circumstances . . . The right of our youth . . . to accomplish religious duties is often violated."

July, 1949—

Polish Communists were quoted as saying:

"The Vatican's resolution, like the Atlantic Pact, is the work of the imperialist centers trying to conquer the world . . . Priests who perform their religious duties in accordance with the commands of patriotism and loyalty toward the Peoples' State will be surrounded by friendly protection from the authorities, but any violating the laws of the land will be punished" (Markham, *Communists Crush Churches*, p. 108).

July, 1949—

After denouncing the Pope's decree of excommunication and demanding the loyalty of the clergy to the State, the Government again moved to reopen negotiations with the Catholic Church. The Government particularly sought three changes: the Polish Church should be independent of Vatican directives, the Church should recognize the validity of the "Recovered Territories" and re-arrange the dioceses accordingly, education should come fully under State authority (*N. Y. Times*, July 27, 31, 1949).

July, 1949—

The Polish Miners' Union publication declared that Sunday would have to become a working day in order to fulfill the Three Year Plan (MacEoin, *The Communist War on Religion*, p. 201).

August 5, 1949—

The Government issued a decree of 17 articles (Poland—Appendix VIII) which would provide sentences ranging up to five years' imprisonment for priests who implemented the Papal decree excommunicating Polish Communists, and for anyone offending religious feeling by profaning religious objects. Government representatives read the decree to an estimated 6,000 priests, summoned to meetings throughout Poland, stating:

"Priests who perform their religious duties in accordance with the commands of patriotism and loyalty toward the Peoples' State will be surrounded by friendly protection from the authorities."

The Government attempted with little success to get statements from lower clergy endorsing the Government's position against the Vatican. Shortly thereafter, one priest was sentenced to die, and four others jailed on charges of anti-Government activities (*N. Y. Times*, August 7, 15, 1949).

August 11, 1949—

The Church's records of births, marriages and deaths up to 1945 were taken over by and incorporated into the Government's records of vital statistics (*News Behind the Iron Curtain*, Feb. 1953, p. 27).

August-September, 1949—

The Polish press warned that the Catholic Church must break its ties with the Vatican and the West. President Bierut warned anti-Government and underground organizations not to use the Church for their anti-Government activities (*N. Y. Times*, August 26, September 12, 1949).

August, 1949—

The Polish Labor Party passed a resolution condemning the Pope and expressing the hope that "patriotic Polish clergy would reject Vatican recommendations and follow the directions of the Polish Government (Markham, *Communists Crush Churches*, p. 13).

August, 1949—

A miracle was reported to have occurred in the Orthodox Church in Warsaw. The following day leaders of the church were arrested and the church closed.

September 1, 1949—

In a letter addressed to Cardinal Sapieha in Poland, the Pope charged the Polish Government with dissolving religious associations, obstructing religious education and the work of institutions, censoring Catholic publications, accusing religious leaders unwarrantedly, denying religious aid to prisoners and the sick, and prohibiting "free and secure" communication with the Vatican (Markham, *Communists Crush Churches*, p. 113).

September, 1949—

Following the Governmental decree "In Defense of Freedom of Conscience and Religion," non-Roman church leaders "belonging to nine different

confessions . ' . expressed to the Minister (Premier Cyrankiewicz) their firm intention to take part in a loyal manner in the life of the new Poland and to work honestly for the good of Democracy, Freedom and Peace" (*Luzerner Neueste Nachrichten*, March 25, 1950).

August-September, 1949—

Contacts with church groups abroad became increasingly difficult and the object of careful surveillance. Foreign church-affiliated relief agencies were requested (in March) to turn over their work to the Department of Social Welfare, and withdraw all foreign personnel. By September all were gone but three. The World Council of Churches was regarded as "the Little Marshall Plan," and its offices considered the seat of an international spy ring working in cooperation with the Western powers. Reliable observers advised that statements attributed to non-Catholic leaders which appeared in the Polish and, subsequently, international press, were "not to be believed if contrary to Christian principles," that the thought and spirit of the non-Catholics were not accurately represented therein, that signatures were frequently affixed to documents on quite another basis than that generally accepted in civilized nations.

Within Poland, the fellowship and confidence of non-Roman leaders had been broken upon into several fragments: those whom fellow pastors felt were spying upon them for the Government; those who tried conscientiously to be loyal to their faith and their Government; and those in opposition to the Government. Pastors were frequently questioned by the police, but none were in prison. There was, however, no direct persecution.

"We are ONE in Christ with . . . all, even if we must be sometimes elastic because of the situation. Most hearty greetings in Christ's Name," read a message from Poland.

September, 1949—

According to the Communist press, more than 1,000,000 Polish children received Communist indoctrination in summer camps (Markham, *Communists Crush Churches*, p. 102, 103). The Secretary of the Communist Youth organization stated in August that the organization had over 1 million members and would have 2 million by autumn. Mass recruitment was necessary, he said, in order to educate youth in the spirit of the People's Democracy and the principles of socialism. As the school year began, the Polish News Agency announced that the educational system was based on the most recent findings according to Marxist-Leninist philosophy, that particular emphasis would be given to studies in class warfare, the Soviet Union, Anglo-American imperialism, and the Russian language (MacEoin, *The Communist War on Religion*, p. 202). The Communist Party *Official Gazette* announced that every religious congregation, society, association, or order must register and describe in detail its membership, activity and property in order to "regulate the legal status (and recognition) of religious orders and congregations." Public processions without State permission were to be forbidden (Markham, *Communists Crush Churches*, p. 114).

September, 1949—

Justice Minister Swiatkowski, in a speech to a group of lawyers on the decree "In Defense of Freedom and Conscience" accused the hierarchy of crimes including spying and underground fighting. President Bierut was reported to have informed a group of priests that the Communist Party would give the Church peace on certain conditions:

"Complete support of all social, educational, economic and religious changes which the regime seeks to introduce; active support . . . for . . . socializing Poland; weakening of the ties with the Vatican; the use of the pulpit for propaganda of the great achievements of the People's Democracy: democratization of the Polish Church in such a manner that the priests and not the Hierarchy rule" (Markham, *Communists Crush Churches*, p. 115).

September 21, 1949—

The Government decreed the nationalization of church hospitals.

October, 1949—

Catholic "Youth Action" groups were formed, according to Catholic sources, to spearhead a movement against the Vatican and the Hierarchy. Members were expected to spy on their friends and denounce "reactionary" religious bodies. In a letter to leaders and teachers of youth, Primate Wyszynski exhorted the leaders to overcome the restrictions placed in their way and the violations against youth's religious feelings. He urged them to give special attention and love to the growing numbers of young atheists (Markham, *Communists Crush Churches*, p. 117).

October 3, 1949—

Government and Roman Catholic negotiators concluded a tentative draft for an accord which was to be presented to the Government and the Church for official ratification. It included:

(a) formal recognition of the Government and Constitution by the Church;

(b) revision of dioceses and permanent administrative set-up for the "Recovered Territories";

(c) retention by the Church of all land, properties and institutions except by mutual agreement;

(d) taxation of Church productive properties on an equitable basis;

(e) continuation of religious education in the public schools under Church supervision (*N. Y. Herald Tribune*, Paris Edition, October 5, 1949).

October 14, 1949—

Catholic sources reported that Catholic Church-State negotiations had again been broken off (*N. Y. Times*, October 15, 1949). Catholic bishops protested against the Communist Party's September directive requiring all religious organizations to petition the Government for legal status on the grounds that a non-religious or anti-religious organization had no right to sit in judgment on the religious validity of a religious organization and that the directive was not in keeping with the Constitution (*Pilot*, October 29, 1949). They further instructed the clergy not to obey the decree (Markham, *Communists Crush Churches*, p. 117).

October 16, 1949—

The Polish Y.M.C.A. decided to break off its ties to the international World's Alliance of Y.M.C.A.'s headquarters in Geneva, to change from "its absolute and harmful character," and to change its name to "Social Workers' Association Center" (*N. Y. Herald Tribune*, Paris Edition, October 17, 1949; Text of *Polish Journal* report, Poland—Appendix XIV).

October, 1949—

Thirteen hospitals operated by Roman Catholic orders were taken over by the Government (Markham, *Communists Crush Churches*, p. 101).

November, 1949—

A Government - sponsored Roman Catholic publication denied rumors that the Polish Government intended to sever the ties between the Vatican and the Polish Roman Catholic Church and establish an independent National Catholic Church (*N. Y. Times*, November 9, 1949).

November, 1949—

The Ecumenical Council held a theological conference for pastors of non-Roman Catholic Churches near Warsaw.

December, 1949—

Lutheran Church leaders in Germany charged that the Polish Government was oppressing Lutherans in the former German territories of West Poland (*N. Y. Times*, December 11, 1949).

January 23, 1950—

The Government seized the Roman Catholic CARITAS (international relief and welfare) offices on grounds of "fraudulent abuses (of their offices) for political purposes, hostility to the State," and "mishandling of funds (for anti-Government activity)." The organization was placed under the control of a Government-appointed board of trustees (*N. Y. Times* and *N. Y. Herald Tribune*, Paris Edition, January 24, 1950).

January 30, 1950—

Minister of Public Administration Wolski addressed a group of more than a thousand "patriotic priests" assembled by the Government (by force, according to Cardinal Sapieha) and charged that the hierarchy was blocking the possibilities of a Church-State agreement. He urged them to take the matter in hand, and to "make a concordat from the bottom

over the heads of the Episcopate" (*N. Y. Times*, February 2, 1950, April 8, 1950; *Tablet*, February 25, 1950).

February 12, 1950—

A pastoral letter re. religious liberty and the CARITAS seizure, prepared by the bishops, was read from Catholic pulpits. Priests were warned not to participate in "meetings of a political character . . . or directed against church institutions or aiming to weaken the unity of the Church hierarchy." Two priests who refused to read the letter were disciplined by their bishop, whereupon the Government started an investigation of the bishop for his anti-State activities (*The Tablet*, February 25, 1950). The Warsaw newspaper, *Trybuna Ludu*, replied on February 16:

"The Government cannot permit Church dignitaries filled with feudal haughtiness and acting on orders from foreign circles to wreak their anger on those clergymen who acted in accordance with their own conscience and the laws of the Polish Republic" (*N. Y. Times*, Feb. 17, 1950).

February 12, 1950—

The Government-appointed director of CARITAS, M. Tyminski, in a press interview stressed that CARITAS activities would not be reduced, and that future distribution was assured by a 100 million zloty gift from the Government. He appealed to Poles in the United States to continue their donations (*The Tablet*, February 25, 1950).

February 16, 1950—

In a sharp letter to President Bierut, Cardinal Sapieha and Msgr. Wyszynsky, Catholic Primate of Poland, charged that (Text, Poland—Appendix XV):

(a) the Government tried to pack the leadership of CARITAS in order to control it;

(b) the Government usurped the Church's right of discipline;

(c) the Government intimidated and forced the clergy to make decisions, attend meetings, accept offices, make statements, and recognize the Government against their will;

(d) the Government sought to make "a concordat from the bottom" over the heads of the bishops through intimidated "patriotic" clergy.

(e) the Government sought to incite the clergy against the episcopate, to disrupt and sow discord among the clergy, and make the clergy ridiculous in public eyes;
(f) the Government had persistently acted in bad faith through its representative, M. Wolski, in the Church-State accord conversations;
(g) the Bishops and people of Poland would not yield to intimidation.

February, 1950—

The Catholic Bishops' withdrawal of their support from the Government-controlled CARITAS was interpreted as a move to dissolve that organization rather than hand it over to the State. The Bishops issued a 6-point warning to the clergy on loyalty to the Church and called them to remain steadfast in spite of intimidation and persecution. The Government placed Bishop Kowalski under house arrest on February 16 for "anti-Government activities," i.e., for disciplining two priests for their participation in the reorganized CARITAS (see Feb. 12, above) and warned Church leaders to stop their "sabotage" or take the consequences of "acts directed against the Peoples' State, i.e., treason" (*N. Y. Times*, Feb. 28, 1950).
By the end of April, six priests were sentenced to die for treason (*N. Y. Times*, April 25, 1950).

February 28, 1950—

The Polish Press Agency in an official release (excerpts, Poland, Appendix XVIII) charged that the Catholic hierarchy hindered Church-State relations by the following:
(a) their hostility to the social system, the Government and its intentions;
(b) their execution of unfriendly orders from the Vatican;
(c) their opposition to the Government's re-organization of CARITAS;
(d) their disciplining of priests who refused to read an Episcopal letter condemning the re-organization of CARITAS.
The Agency warned that political reaction of the hierarchy would "encounter appropriate (Government) resistance" and would only further isolate the bishops, then asserted that Church-State relations would eventually become stabilized on the basis of "full religious freedom and on the full recognition of the State interests

. . . and the achievements of the Polish people" (*Poland Today*, April, 1950, pp. 16-18).

February-March, 1950—

In the absence of ordained clergy, laymen, women and deaconesses were conducting religious services among Evangelical Churches (*Evangelischer Pressedienst*, Bethel, Germany, February 22, 1950). Non-Catholic Churches began close cooperation in various types of religious work and laid an informal basis for spiritual unity. "A strong sacramental spirit" was felt among the groups, which extended beyond Polish borders. The Ecumenical Council (non-Roman Catholic) which had been functioning since 1945 was not recognized by the Government, and was to be discontinued at the end of March.

March 20, 1950—

The agrarian reform of Church properties introduced to Parliament by Premier Cyrankiewicz on March 6 became law. All Church lands and estates exceeding 250 acres were to be nationalized. Small farms (125-250 acres) for the support of priests and sanctuaries, or attached to inhabited convents and monasteries, were excepted. The Roman Catholic Church at one time owned 373,000 acres. The Premier declared that the Church had exploited the peasants and had used the income from estates for purposes harmful to the State. However,
"The undermining activities of reactionary priests have failed . . . The State respects religion and freedom and expects the priests to be loyal."
Proceeds from the nationalized lands were to go to a special Church fund "to ensure the material welfare of meritorious priests, the aged, charitable purposes, and other Church needs." The fund was to be subsidized by the State if it proved inadequate. It was to be administered by a mixed committee of priests and laymen. Roman Catholic Church circles denounced the measure as persecution, and complained that it deprived the Church of revenue for
(a) the maintenance of the life of the Church;
(b) the education of priests;
(c) the provision of homes and care for orphans and the aged;

(d) assistance to the needy;
(e) and for educational institutions conducted by the Church.

The Government announced that information on the activities of the Church Fund would be carried in a new bi-monthly journal, *Glod Kaplava,* "The Voice of the Priest" (*N. Y. Times,* March 7, 1950; *The Tablet,* April 8, 1950, p. 265).

March, 1950—

According to Catholic sources, three priests were sentenced to imprisonment for unfriendly acts toward the USSR and for an "anti-Communist attitude." Seven hundred priests had been brought to trial on various charges since the end of the war (*Tablet,* April 8, 1950, p. 266).

April, 1950—

Catholic News of April 8 reported that special Government police were investigating all income of, as well as instructions given by priests in relation to baptisms, marriages, confessions, etc.

April 14, 1950—

Negotiations between the Roman Catholic Church and the Government for an accord were consummated in an agreement signed by the representatives of the Government and three Bishops, not including Cardinal Sapieha (who left Warsaw for Rome on April 13), nor Msgr. Wyszynsky. The Vatican reported its fear that Sapieha would not be permitted to return (Summary, Poland—Appendix IX).

The three Bishops agreed to recognize the Government's authority in all matters but faith and ecclesiastical jurisdiction, to seek Vatican recognition and support of Poland's present boundaries, to support the Government in its efforts for peace and progress, not to oppose the development of rural cooperatives, and to oppose all anti-State and underground activities. The Government agreed to religious instruction in the schools conducted jointly by Church and State, and to give to the Catholic publications, assemblies, organizations and institutions the same rights extended to others.

April 16, 1950—

The Vatican expressed surprise and skepticism at the signing of the pact,

cited the presence of Cardinal Sapieha in Rome, and expressed the opinion that the Bishops allegedly signing the pact would not have changed their loyalty to an agreed-to Church position (*N. Y. Times,* April 17, 1950).

April 17, 1950—

Catholic Church leaders reported that there was a secret five-point annex to the Catholic-Government accord which the Government had not revealed with the rest of the agreement (*N. Y. Times,* April 18, 1950).

May, 1950—

In a letter to be read in the churches, the Catholic bishops announced to their constituency that an agreement had been signed by all bishops, but that some issues were still not settled.

"If not everything has been agreed upon it was because it constitutes a declaration and not a concordat, and many matters belong solely to the jurisdiction of the Holy See."

The letter confirmed that two annexes had not yet been made public, annexes probably dealing with the reorganization of the dioceses (*N. Y. Times,* May 4, 1950).

May, 1950—

Polish leaders expressed approval of the Church-State accord and commented as follows:

Parliament Deputy Jan Frankowski, Catholic Social Club: "Polish Catholics have accepted the social and political program represented by the People's Government."

Professor Leon Halban, Dean, Law School, Catholic University of Lublin: (the accord recognizes that) . . . "the new institutions of the People's State . . . are in full harmony with . . . . the principles of Christian ethics."

Jan Dobraczynski, Catholic writer: "Catholicism has always stood for peace . . . this agreement becomes a valuable contribution toward the maintenance of peace."

Rev. Jeremiasz, Bernardine Prior: "Nothing stands in the way of the clergy's religious influence . . . in the new social and political system."

Edward Ochab, Vice-Minister of National Defense: "We want this agreement . . . to be carried out in full by all affected parties . . . Our attitude toward the Church hierarchy will be measured by the sincerity with which the Episcopate and the individual bishops and priests will carry out their part of the agreement" (*Poland Today*, June, 1950, pp. 12, 18).

May 4, 1950—

A. Bida was named director of the new Religious Cults Office. A central office for anti-religious activity was reported to have been opened in Warsaw (MacEoin, *The Communist War on Religion*, p. 206).

May, 1950—

At a conference of Catholics organized by non-episcopal elements, strong support was urged for the Stockholm Peace Appeal (*Christian Century*, September 27, 1950).

May 29, 1950—

The Polish press assailed Bishops Skierski and Stepa for violating the Church-State pact in sending a pastoral letter to their Churches repudiating specific terms agreed to in the accord, namely, that
(a) they forbade priests to participate in local "peace committees" seeking signers for the Stockholm "Peace Manifesto,"
(b) they forbade priests to sign the "Manifesto," and thereby opposed rather than supported the Government's peace program as agreed in the pact (*N. Y. Times*, May 30, 1950).

June 20, 1950—

The Polish press accused other Catholic bishops of violating the Church-State agreement by not signing the Stockholm Peace Manifesto. Bishop Choromanski replied that the Roman Catholic prelates were supporting the Stockholm Appeal (*N. Y. Times*, June 21, 25, 1950).

June 29, 1950—

The Government accused four Roman Catholic religious orders of organizing underground activity, and jailed the monks pending further investigation.

June, 1950—

The Minister of Security stated that a U. S. spy ring operating through the Jehovah's Witnesses had been liquidated (*N. Y. Times*, June 30, 1950). *Trybuna Ludu* reported that the Jeho-

vah's Witnesses had refused to sign the Stockholm Appeal, along with 190,000 "Kulaks, urban speculators, and the episcopate, heading the reactionary section of the clergy" (*Christian Century*, September 27, 1950, p. 1131). In Plock, the nuns of St. Magdalen Convent refused to sign the Appeal and an hour later were taken away by Security Police (*Notes on Soviet Affairs*, June 23, 1952, p. 7).

August, 1950—

A. Kleszynski was jailed for copying and circulating a letter from Jehovah's Witnesses in the U. S. (*N. Y. Times*, August 1, 1950).

September 12, 1950—

At the conclusion of the Warsaw Peace Congress, 73 Polish Catholic delegates addressed an appeal to Catholic priests in other countries. The appeal was made public at a National Conference of CARITAS on September 12. It condemned the action of the U. N. in Korea, the sanction of churches in the West for that action, and appealed for disarmament and outlawing of atomic weapons and aggression (*An Appeal for Peace*, Polish Research and Information Service, N. Y.).

September, 1950—

Following a meeting of the Episcopal Council, Catholic Primate Archbishop Wyszynski and Cardinal Sapieha addressed an unpublicized "statement of grievances" to the Government, listing the following measures recently taken by the Government:
The concordat with the Vatican had been rejected.
Church hospitals and printing establishments had been seized.
Anti-religious propaganda and attacks on the hierarchy had been organized.
Attempts had been made to create division among Church leaders.
Since April, 500 priests had been removed from teaching positions for not signing the Stockholm Appeal.
Three seminaries had been closed.
"More than a thousand schools have unconstitutionally been handed over to the 'Children's Friends Association' despite the fact that only 'public schools' exist in Poland, and religion must be taught in public schools."

In these schools there was no religious instruction although the Government had agreed in the concordat to provide religious instruction.

Priests were constantly investigated, "imprisoned without trial, or sentenced to penal servitude."

The Polish press denounced the bishops as war-mongers, enemies of the people, supporters of German Territorial claims, and violators of their pledges (MacEoin, *The Communist War on Religion*, p. 210).

October 23, 1950—

The Government addressed a letter to Bishop Choromanski, Secretary of the Catholic Episcopate, pointing out that the Church had not yet converted its administration in the "Recovered Territories" to a permanent one, as agreed in the April accord, and added that it could not tolerate the existing state of affairs any longer. Subsequently several conferences of Catholic priests approved of the Government's action and sent messages to the Government and the Episcopacy. One delegation of 30 priests and four nuns carried to Archbishop Wyszynski's office a memo requesting immediate conversion of the Western dioceses to permanent ones, but were refused admittance (*Poland Today*, December, 1950, 19).

October, 1950—

Education Minister Jarosinski stated that the new school curriculum was based on the principles of dialectical and historical materialism, and called for the rooting out of the remnants of reactionary Christian and capitalistic influences (MacEoin, *The Communist War on Religion*, p. 209).

November, 1950—

Acting Catholic Apostolic Administrator Nowicki of Gorzow supported the Government in its position vis-a-vis the Catholic Church, against the wishes of the prelates. He was said to favor establishment of permanent dioceses in the area claimed from Germany, and to cooperate with the "patriotic priests" (*N. Y. Times*, Nov. 3, 1950).

November, 1950—

The Government took over the principal Lutheran Church building in Warsaw for State purposes.

November, 1950—

Catholic sources reported that all Polish bishops were to confer on what was interpreted as a growing crisis (*N. Y. Times*, November 9, 1950).

December, 1950—

In a pastoral letter to be read on Christmas Day, Primate Wyszynski begged the Polish people to devote themselves to God, and not to "the Party or worldly things" (*N. Y. Times*, December 26, 1950).

Summary of Situation—January, 1951

Worship:

Most churches are open and greater numbers of people are attending services than for many decades.

Religious Festivals:

Special services and processions are being held on special occasions. Christmas was observed as a religious festival. However, the restiveness of people seeks venting in public demonstration; mass pilgrimages have therefore been curtailed.

Religious Education:

Religious instruction in public and private schools is formally permissable. However, in some schools no religious instruction is given, in some it is *de facto* forbidden. The number of religious instructors has been greatly reduced because of "political activity" of the instructors. Textbooks for religious instruction, schedules and supervision are the "joint" responsibility of Church and State. Religious leaders urged parents to begin the religious instruction of their children at home.

Youth:

The number of young people in worship services is diminishing. Church youth groups are disappearing. Youth are encouraged to participate in officially approved non-religious groups. Religious leaders urged Christian young people and their leaders not to ridicule or offend atheistic youth, but to win them in Christian love.

Institutions:

Government agencies are gradually taking over responsibility for welfare and relief programs. More than 1000 educational institutions have been put under Government direction. The churches have had a small number of other institutions taken over, but continue to operate most of them, many with State support. The Catholic "Special Church Fund," created from proceeds of nationalized estates and CARITAS, is directed by a mixed lay-clergy committee, subsidized by the Government.

Estates:

Larger estates have been nationalized. Small farms of local parishes and inhabited monasteries remain at the disposal of those bodies.

Publications:

Approximately 15 of 35 Roman Catholic publications functioning in 1948 are operating, some under Government patronage, others directed by the Church. Restrictions on paper supply, rigid censorship and union decisions on religious printing limit output.

Church Administration:

Reports on church activities, offerings, and membership of churches and organizations must be submitted regularly to the Government. The Catholic Church faces the necessity of reorganizing its dioceses on a permanent basis, including the "Recovered Territories."

Training Leaders:

Three Roman Catholic seminaries are closed, but others continue. There is a greater number of applicants for the ministry, but increasingly limited teaching facilities.

Church Leadership:

Leaders report that there are constant investigations, jailing and imprisonment for "underground and anti-State activities" and now "treason." Over 700 clergy have been tried for various anti-Government offences since 1945. Many local civil authorities are in sympathy with religious leaders, and are apologetic about implementing their orders. Attendance is required at many meetings; statements must frequently be signed under pressure, or "in absentia," Roman Catholic leaders still openly criticize the Government. Within the Church the breach between the pro-Government and anti-Government factions is widening, but it is not yet completely separated. The first hint of a public show-down between the two factions came only in December. Most prelates are united, and are followed by the majority of the clergy. At the same time the clergy participate voluntarily or of necessity in Government-organized demonstrations, courses, etc.

Among Evangelicals, leaders, with few exceptions, are drawing closer together, in a spiritual and evangelistic fellowship. Where there is no ordained leader, laymen and laywomen continue the ministry and services.

International Contacts:

The Orthodox Church is under the patronage of the Moscow Patriarchate. Jehovah's Witnesses have been "liquidated." Theoretically, contact of other churches with religious colleagues and organizations abroad is permitted. However, there is no normal contact. Nonetheless, leaders report a deep sense of participation in the spiritual life and moral strength of the Church around the world.

Ongoing Witness:

There are many points where the churches are on the defensive, some of them scarcely related to the Divine Mission of the Church. There are other points where some leaders see possibilities of cooperation with the Government, without necessarily invalidating the rest of their ministry. There is a small, but increasing, number of points where Christians have abandoned what was being defended because they see positive ways of Christian witnessing. It is only a beginning, but it is a beginning which shows no signs of tiring nor of succumbing. Even the pastoral letters of those most stubbornly holding the line of defense are taking on more and more the character of affirmations of the "good news" and less and less denunciations of a situation of the world which could never be wholly sanctified.

Appendix I

THE CONSTITUTION OF POLAND OF MARCH 17, 1921

Article 110:

Polish citizens belonging to national, religious, or linguistic minorities have the same right as other citizens of founding, supervising, and administering at their own expense, charitable, religious and social institutions, schools and other educational institutions and of using freely therein their language, and observing the rules of their religion.

Article 111:

Freedom of conscience and of religion is guaranteed to all citizens. No citizens may suffer of limitation of the rights enjoyed by other citizens, by reason of his religion and religious convictions.

All inhabitants of the Polish State have the right of freely professing their religion in public as well as in private, and of performing the commands of their religion or rite, in so far as this is not contrary to public order or public morality.

Article 112:

Religious freedom may not be used in a way contrary to statutes. No one may evade the performance of public duties by reason of his religious beliefs; no one may be compelled to take part in religious activities or rites unless he is subject to parental or guardians' authority.

Article 113:

Every religious community recognized by the State has the right of organizing collective and public services; it may conduct independently its internal affairs; it may possess and acquire movable and immovable property, administer and dispose of it; it remains in possession and enjoyment of its endowments and funds, and of religious, educational, and charitable institutions. No religious community may, however, be in opposition to the statutes of the State.

Article 114:

The Roman Catholic religion, being the religion of the preponderant majority of the nation, occupies in the State the chief position among enfranchised religions. The Roman Catholic Church governs itself under its own laws. The relation of the State to the church will be determined on the basis of an agreement with the Apostolic See, which is subject to ratification by the Sejm.

Article 115:

The churches of the religious minority and other legally organized religious communities govern themselves by their own laws, which the State may not refuse to recognize unless they contain rules contrary to law.

The relation of the State to such churches and religions will be determined from time to time by legislation after an understanding with their legal representatives.

Article 116:

The recognition of a new, or hitherto not legally recognized religion, may not be refused to religious communities whose institutions, teachings, and organizations are not contrary to public order or public morality.

Article 120:

Instruction in religion is compulsory for all pupils in every educational institution, the curriculum of which includes instruction of youth under eighteen years of age, if the institution is maintained, wholly or in part by the State, or by self-government bodies. The direction and supervision of religious instruc-

tion in schools belong to the respective religious communities, reserving to the State educational authorities the right of supreme supervision.
(*Yearbook of Human Rights*, 1946, p. 235)

Appendix II

POLISH MILITARY PENAL CODE

Decree of the Polish Committee of National Liberation of September 23, 1944

Article 102. Par. 1:

Whoever publicly incites to nationalistic, racial or religious strife, or whoever produces, distributes or keeps in custody publications, printed matters and graphics intended for the above purposes, shall be punished by imprisonment.
(*Yearbook of Human Rights*, 1946, p. 236)

Appendix III

OFFENCES PARTICULARLY DANGEROUS DURING THE PERIOD OF THE COUNTRY'S RECONSTRUCTION

Decree of June 13, 1946, replacing the Decree of November 16, 1945

Article 30:

Whoever publicly incites to nationalistic, religious or racial strife or approves of them shall be punished by imprisonment up to five years.

Article 31. Par. 1:

Whoever publicly insults, derides or traduces any group of the population, or any individual person because of nationality, religion or race, shall be punished by a penitentiary sentence up to five years or by imprisonment.

Par. 2:

The same penalty shall apply to anyone who bodily assaults or inflicts light bodily injuries on a person because of the latter's nationality, religion or race.

Article 32:

Whoever commits an offence against a group of the population because of nationality, religion or race, followed by death, or grave bodily injuries, or disturbance of, or danger to the public peace and order resulting from such offence, shall be punished by imprisonment for not less than three years, or for life, or by death.

Article 33:

Whoever participates in a conspiracy aiming at committing an offence as set forth in Paragraph 1 and 2 of art. 31 or who participates in a public riot which collectively commits such offence, shall be punished by imprisonment.

Article 34:

Whoever, contrary to his duty, fails to counteract offences as set forth in articles 30 to 33 shall be punished by a penitentiary sentence up to five years, or by imprisonment.

(*Yearbook of Human Rights*, 1946, p. 236)

Appendix IV

DECLARATION OF RIGHTS AND LIBERTIES

Approved by the Constituent Diet on February 22, 1947

The Constituent Diet, representing the sovereign authority of the Polish people, solemnly declares that in the exercise of its constitutional and legislative power and in the exercise of its supervision over the activities of the Government, as well as in its determination of the basic policies of the nation, it will continue to uphold such fundamental civil rights and liberties as:

(1) Equality before the law, regardless of nationality, race, creed, sex, origin, social status and education;

(2) Security of person, life and property;

(3) Freedom of conscience and of worship;

(4) Freedom of press, speech, association, assembly, public meetings and demonstration.

At the same time, the Diet goes on record in stating that the abuse of the civil rights on liberties for the purpose of overthrowing the democratic form of government of the Republic of Poland, shall be prevented by law.

Appendix V

LAW ON THE RELATIONSHIP BETWEEN THE STATE OF POLAND AND THE EVANGELICAL-LUTHERAN CHURCH

July 4, 1947

Summary

The law regulates anew the relationship between the State of Poland and the Evangelical-Lutheran Church (Augsburgian Confession), unifies several religious communities of this denomination inherited from the time of partition and existing before the Second World War in different parts of Poland, in one Evangelical-Lutheran Church (Augsburgian Confession) embracing the whole territory of the Polish Republic with a view to a reorganization in the near future of a separate Evangelical Reformed Church. The law regulates the succession of real and personal property of the several religious communities previously existing, transferring it to the Evangelical-Lutheran Church (Augsburgian Confession), and repeals the old statutes relating to the Evangelical-Lutheran, the Evangelical-Reformed and the Evangelical-Lutheran (Augsburgian Confession) religious communities, statutes which dated back to the time of Poland's partition.

(*The Yearbook of Human Rights*, 1947, p. 272)

Appendix VI

DECREE REGULATING THE LEGAL STATUS OF THE EVANGELICAL-REFORMED CHURCH, THE MARIAVITE CHURCH AND THE OLD-CATHOLIC CHURCH

September 5, 1947

Summary

Article 1 provides that the Evangelical Reformed Church, the Mariavite Church and the Old-Catholic Church whose legal status as religious communities within the territory of the Polish Republic was heretofore based on regulations which had been in force only in certain portions of the Polish Republic, are granted the status of religious communities recognized by law throughout the entire territory of Poland.

Article 2 provides that the internal matters of the aforesaid religious communities shall be controlled by their own regulations, which are subject to approval by the Council of Ministers.

Article 3 lists and repeals 13 different statutes, all dated prior to 11 November 1918 and relating to the aforesaid religious communities except three statutes which relate to the Baptist denomination. Any interference by State authorities in cases of change in religion by citizens is abolished and the pertinent statutes dating from the time of partition revoked.

(*The Yearbook of Human Rights*, 1947, p. 273)

Appendix VII

ON THE RELATIONSHIP BETWEEN THE STATE OF POLAND AND THE METHODIST CHURCH

October 16, 1945

As to the Methodist Church, its legal situation in the Polish Republic was regulated by decree of 16 October 1945 concerning the relation of the State to the Methodist Church in the Polish Republic (*Journal of Laws of the Polish Republic*, No. 46, item 259). By virtue of this decree, the Methodist Church in Poland achieved full equality with other religious communities and full liberty of worship. The Methodist Church was granted the right to govern its own affairs by its own regulations subject to the approval of the Council of Ministers. This Church achieved the right to acquire property, real and personal, to dispose of it and to manage its own property. Its vital statistics were granted recognition as fully valid legal documents until the date of the coming into force of the Polish law on civil marriages and vital statistics (1 January, 1946).

(*The Yearbook of Human Rights*, 1947, p. 273)

Appendix VIII

DECREE PROTECTING FREEDOM OF CONSCIENCE AND RELIGION

(Passed by the Council of Ministers, August 5, 1949)

I

The Polish Government guarantees freedom of conscience and religion to all its citizens.

II

Whosoever infringes on the rights of a citizen because of his creed or absence of religious affiliation is liable to imprisonment up to five years.

III

Whosoever forces a person to participate in religious worship or whosoever prevents another person from participating in such worship is liable to imprisonment up to five years.

IV

Whosoever misuses religious freedom by refusing to let another person participate in a religious ceremony because of his political, social or scientific activities or beliefs is liable to imprisonment up to five years.

V

Whosoever outrages the religious feelings of others by publicly desecrating religious objects or places of worship is liable to imprisonment up to five years.

VI

Whosoever publicly foments religious conflicts or sanctions them is liable to imprisonment up to five years.

VII

1. Whosoever publicly insults, scoffs at, or humiliates a group or an individual because of religious affiliations or convictions or because of absence of religious affiliations is liable to imprisonment up to five years.

2. Whosoever commits physical violence against a person because of his religious convictions or absence of religious affiliations is liable to the same punishment.

3. Whosoever commits any other criminal act against a group or an individual because of religious affiliations, convictions or absence of religious affiliations is liable to imprisonment.

4. If any action described in Paragraph 3 results in death, serious injury, disturbance of peace and order, or jeopardy to public safety, the person committing the act is liable to imprisonment for a period not less than three years, for life, or the death penalty.

VIII

1. Whosoever misuses religious freedom and freedom of conscience to pursue aims hostile to the form of government of the Polish Republic is liable to imprisonment for a period not less than three years.

2. Whosoever makes preparations to commit an act of violation of Paragraph 1 is liable to imprisonment.

IX

Whosoever misuses religious freedom for personal gain, takes advantage of human credulity by spreading false rumors, or by misleading others through deception and overt acts, is liable to imprisonment.

X

Whosoever takes part in an agreement, the purport of which is the commission of any crime under Articles 3 to 9, or whosoever deliberately joins a crowd which collectively commits such a crime, is liable to imprisonment.

XI

Whosoever contrary to his duty fails to intervene in the commission of such a crime is liable to five years maximum imprisonment.

XII

Whosoever in any manner instigates, encourages, recommends or publicly sanctions the committing of a crime defined in Articles 2 and 11 is liable to imprisonment.

XIII

Whosoever is found guilty under this decree may be deprived, by the court, of his public and civil rights.

XIV

All cases arising under this decree are under the jurisdiction of Courts of Appeal.

XV

The provisions of the Criminal Code of 1932 and the Decree of July 15, 1946, concerning crimes especially dangerous during the period of national reconstruction are set aside in cases arising under the present decree.

XVI

The Minister of Justice is charged with the execution of this decree.

XVII

The decree goes into effect upon the day of publication.

(*Religious Freedom and the State-Church Agreement*, Polish Research and Information Service, N. Y., pp. 1-3)

Appendix IX

AGRARIAN REFORM OF CHURCH PROPERTIES

March 6, 1950

The draft of the law proposed:

1. Transfer to State ownership of land now held by religious bodies, with the entire income from such estates to be earmarked through the Church Fund exclusively for church and welfare purposes.

2. Church lands farmed by parish priests and not exceeding 125 acres (250 acres in some cases) are not to be transferred; on the contrary, the State will guarantee these lands to the clergy to provide means for their personal subsistence.

3. Excluded from the transfer are sites used for religious worship, also buildings used as monasteries, convents and diocesan offices of bishops and archbishops, even though such buildings may be located on land to be taken over by the State.

4. Certain properties transferred to the State may, by decision of the Council of Ministers, remain under the administration and for use by those institutions now occupying them or may be assigned to other church institutions.

5. A Church Fund is hereby established, in the administration of which the participation of clergy and laity will be assured.

The Fund will be used for maintenance and reconstruction of churches, welfare benefits for the clergy, and charitable activities of the churches.

Premier Cyrankiewicz declared the new law a further step in the direction of stabilizing Church-State relations and expressed confidence it would receive wide support from the clergy and the people.

(*Polish Newsletter*, March 16, 1950)

Appendix X

ACCORD BETWEEN THE ROMAN CATHOLIC CHURCH AND THE POLISH REPUBLIC, AND ANNEX

April 14, 1950

For the purpose of assuring the People's Poland and its citizens the best opportunity for development and peaceful work, the Polish Government which advocates respect for religious freedom, and the Polish Episcopate which is concerned with the welfare of the Church and the interests of the State, agree to regulate their relationship in the following manner:

I

The Episcopate shall urge that in the course of the clergy's pastoral duties and in accordance with the teachings of the Church, the clergy teach the faithful respect for law and the authorities of the State.

II

The Episcopate shall urge that in the course of the clergy's pastoral duties, the clergy call upon the faithful to intensify their work for the reconstruction of the country and the advancement of the nation's welfare.

III

The Polish Episcopate states that economic, historical, cultural and religious reasons and also historic justice demand that the Recovered Territories should belong to Poland forever. Basing itself on the premise that the Recovered Territories form an inseparable part of the Republic, the Episcopate shall address a request to the Holy See that those Church administrations now holding the rights of residential bishoprics shall be converted into permanent episcopal dioceses.

IV

To the extent of its ability the Episcopate shall oppose activities hostile to Poland and particularly the anti-Polish revisionist actions of a part of the German clergy.

V

The principle that the Pope is the competent and supreme authority of the Church refers to matters of faith, morals and Church jurisdiction; in other matters, however, the Episcopate is guided by the interests of the Polish State.

VI

Basing itself on the premise that the mission of the Church can be fulfilled within various social and economic systems established by secular authority, the Episcopate shall explain to the clergy that it should not oppose the development of cooperatives in rural areas since the cooperative movement is based essentially on the ethical element in human nature directed toward voluntary social solidarity which has as its goal the welfare of all.

VII

In accordance with its principles and in condemnation of all acts against the Polish State, the Church shall oppose particularly the misuse of religious feelings for anti-State purposes.

VIII

The Church which condemns all crime in accordance with its principles shall combat the criminal activities of underground bands and shall denounce and punish under canon law those clergymen who are guilty of participation in any underground activities against the Polish State.

IX

In accordance with the teachings of the Church, the Episcopate shall support every effort toward strengthening peace and oppose, to the extent of its ability, every attempt to provoke war.

X

Religious instruction in schools:

A. The Government does not intend to reduce the present status of religious instruction in schools; the program of religious instruction will be worked out by school authorities together with representatives of the Episcopate; the schools will be supplied with appropriate textbooks; lay and clerical instructors of religion shall be treated on an equal footing with teachers of other subjects; supervisors of religious instruction shall be appointed by the school authorities in consultation with the Episcopate.

B. The authorities will not place obstacles in the way of students wishing to participate in religious practices outside the schools.

C. While existing schools which are Catholic in character shall be continued, the Government shall require that these schools carry out instructions loyally and fulfill the program as determined by State authorities.

D. Schools run by the Catholic Church will enjoy the privileges of State schools in accordance with the general principles defined by the appropriate laws and the regulations of the school authorities.

E. Where a school is established which provides no religious instruction or where a school is transformed into one which does not provide for religious education, those Catholic parents who so desire shall have the right and the opportunity to send their children to schools where religion is taught.

XI

The Catholic University of Lublin shall be permitted to continue the present scope of its activities.

XII

Catholic associations shall enjoy the same rights as heretofore after satisfying all requirements provided in the decree concerning associations. The same principle shall apply to the Sodality of St. Mary.

XIII

The Church shall have the right and the opportunity to conduct its activities in the fields of charity, welfare, and religious education within the framework of existing regulations.

XIV

The Catholic press and Catholic publications shall enjoy privileges as defined by appropriate laws and the regulations of the authorities, and on an equal basis with other publications.

XV

No obstacles shall be placed in the way of public worship, traditional pilgrimages and processions. In accordance with the requirements for maintaining public order, arrangements for such ceremonies shall be made in consultation between Church and administrative authorities.

XVI

The status of military chaplains shall be defined by special regulations to be worked out by military authorities in agreement with representatives of the Episcopate.

XVII

Religious ministrations in penal institutions shall be in the hands of chaplains appointed by appropriate authorities upon recommendation of the diocesan bishop.

XVIII

In State and community hospitals religious ministration for patients who desire it will be in the hands of hospital chaplains who shall be remunerated through special agreement.

XIX

Religious orders shall have full freedom of activity within the limits of their calling and within the framework of existing laws.

(*Religious Freedom and the State-Church Agreement*, Polish Research and Information Service, New York, pp. 4-8)

PROTOCOL TO STATE-CHURCH AGREEMENT

1. In view of the agreement reached by the representatives of the Polish Government and the Polish Episcopate concerning the activities of "Caritas" and in order to normalize relations between the State and Church, the Church organization "Caritas" is being transformed into the Association of Catholics for Aid to the Poor and Needy. The Association shall carry on its activities through branches corresponding to the administrative division of the country. In view of the charitable aims of the Association, the Episcopate shall make it possible for those members of the clergy who wish to do so to work in this Association in accordance with the principles and practice of the Catholic Church.

2. The Polish Government, in carrying out the law for "the transfer of Church lands to State ownership" within the framework of Article 2, Paragraph 3, and Article 7, Paragraph 1, of the law, shall consider the needs of the bishops and of church institutions in order to provide assistance for them.

3. The Church Fund shall place adequate sums at the disposal of diocesan bishops.

4. Implementing the law on military service, the military authorities shall make necessary arrangements for students of religious seminaries to enable them to complete their studies; ordained priests and monks who have taken their vows shall not be called to active military service, but will be transferred to the reserve corps and qualified for military service.

(Supplement to *Polish Newsletter*, May 17, 1950)

Appendix XI

NOVOYE SLOVE ON SOVIET-OCCUPIED POLAND

August 24, 1941

"Officially, the Soviet authorities did not carry on any fight against religion and did not decree the closure of churches; all they did was to impose heavy taxes on church buildings and make the priest responsible for paying these taxes—any failure being followed by the closing of the church and arrest of the priest. The tax for a village church might amount to as much as 25,000 roubles a year. For many parishes it was impossible to gather this sum, in spite of all the sacrifices of the faithful. For example, the priest of a parish in Volhynia was obliged to sell his personal effects to raise the amount of the tax, but even that was not enough, and he had to leave the village.

"Few changes were made among the leaders of the Church during the period of Soviet occupation. Nearly all the bishops remained at their posts, but since the beginning of the Germano-Russian hostilities they were constantly on the point of being arrested. Some of them succeeded in hiding; Bishop Simon of Ostrog fled to a priest in Polecia; Bishop Polycarp of Lusk hid in the catacombs of his cathedral. Archbishop Alexis of Bolhynia and Kremenetz was arrested the third day after the beginning of the war; his head was shaved and he was taken to the prison of Tarnopol. Before this town was taken by the Germans, a group of prisoners was shot and the others, including the Archbishop Alexis, were obliged to follow the army in its retreat. The Archbishop managed to escape on the way during an air attack. After wandering through the fields for several days he managed to reach Kremenetz, which was occupied by the Germans. Archbishop Alexander of Polecia and Pinsk continues to supervise his diocese. Three new bishops, Damasus, Pantaleon, and Benjamin, were introduced by Metropolitan Sergius of Moscow. They had been recruited from among the monks of the famous Abbey of Potchaiev. Damasus was nominated bishop of Cernowitz; his fate is unknown. Panteleon and Benjamin are in the Abbey of Potchaiev which has not suffered from the war. The monastery of Bogojavlinsk at Kremenetz has also remained intact. The convent of Cortze, at the old frontier between Poland and Soviet Russia, has on the other hand, suffered enormously."

(The Russian weekly *Novoye Slovo*, New Word, published in Berlin, August 24, 1941)

Appendix XII

POLISH WORKERS' PARTY CONGRESS ON CHURCH-STATE RELATIONS

December 17, 1948

The attitude of the new party with regard to religious freedom, as defined by Alexander Zawadzki, United Workers' Party:

"The United Polish Workers' Party does not oppose or combat religion. And what is more, the party stands for freedom of conscience and religious beliefs.

"This means that the party respects the feelings of those religiously inclined, it guarantees legal protection to their rites, and advocates non-interference on the part of Government with the religious concerns of the individual.

"Our party is fully aware that the majority of the Polish people are faithful members of the Catholic Church. We are sure that nothing separates us from these Catholic masses. On the contrary, we feel that we are linked with them by the unity of the working class, by the alliance of workers and peasants; by our common nationality, by our joint efforts to build a classless society, thereby attaining moral and political unity, and finally by the fact that we have thousands of believers within our own party ranks.

"The United Polish Workers' Party does not propose to interfere with the internal affairs of the Church, but at the same time it rejects interference on the part of the Church with matters pertaining to the state.

"Furthermore, the United Polish Workers' Party calls upon the clergy of all faith and denominations to stand loyally by the People's Government and to support it in all its measures aimed at full social liberation, prosperity, progress, and the happiness of all."

(*Poland of Today*, February, 1949)

Appendix XIII

THE GOVERNMENT POSITION ON CHURCH-STATE RELATIONS

March 14, 1949

On March 14, the Secretary of the Episcopal Commission, Bishop Zygmunt Choromanski, called on the Minister of Public Administration, M. Wladyslaw Wolski, to discuss questions connected with the settlement of relations between the State and Church. During their conversation, M. Wolski made the following statement concerning the whole question of relations between the State and Church:

"For several months now, there has been a noticeable increase in the activity of certain sections of the clergy, inimical to the Government and people's State. A part of the higher Church hierarchy have been trying, through pastoral letters and confidential instructions, to produce a state of unrest and agitation by claiming an alleged threat to religion, without any grounds whatever for such allegations.

"It is no accident that, in this anti-democratic campaign, which creates confusion, a leading part is played by those bishops who, during the occupation, were notorious for their conciliatory and even servile attitude towards the Nazi invaders—as for instance Bishop Kaczmarek and Adamski. Neither is it accidental that the majority of the Church hierarchy, in defiance of the general opinion of the whole patriotic community, has failed to resist the anti-Polish statements of official Vatican circles supporting German chauvinist claims to the Regained Territories. On the contrary, they even tried to justify this.

There are frequent cases in which priests endorse or even collaborate with various criminal and anti-State groups, agencies of Anglo-American imperialism. These facts have neither been condemned nor adequately resisted by the Church hierarchy and the Catholic Press which it controls.

"The Church authorities in practice do not oppose the infiltration of criminal underground elements into religious organizations and associations, elements which are making efforts to use those associations as a base for their activities.

"All this remains in obvious contradiction to the harmonious efforts of the overwhelming majority of society which is reconstructing a destroyed country, which wants order and welfare, which resists every attempt to bring discord into the country's development. As the guardian of peace and public order, the Government will tolerate no diversive activity, that is why only a change in the attitude of the Church hierarchy and its restraint from inimical acts against the people's State, can create a basis for settlement of relations with the Church.

"The Government states with the utmost firmness that it does not intend to restrain religious freedom. The clergy in Poland enjoys various prerogatives, to a far greater extent than in many Western European countries. All rumors of the liquidation of religious classes in schools are groundless, but while preserving the teaching of religion, the Government will stand firmly by the general constitutional principle that 'freedom of religion cannot be used in any way contradictory to the law,' and will not tolerate certain ecclesiastics abusing religion in order to sow unrest in the minds of youth and to incite against the State authorities. At the same time, the Government will firmly oppose excesses which might offend the religious feelings of believers or violate the existing laws.

"The monastic educational institutions which belong to religious orders or are controlled by the clergy, and which satisfy the requirements of the laws and regulations in force, will enjoy appropriate prerogatives. Also, charitable institutions belonging to religious orders or controlled by the clergy, will be able to continue their activities after adequate control and scrutiny of their activities on the part of the State authorities.

"The State authorities do not intend to interfere in matters of religion or in internal affairs of Church administration but will demand the settlement of the legal position of dioceses and their boundaries in accordance with the new laws and the frontiers of the State. All loyal representatives of the clergy and religion will enjoy the full protection of the law and of the authorities.

"A concrete settlement of relations between the State and the Church, which will find expression in a new constitution, will be shaped—as far as the rights of the Church hierarchy are concerned—on the basis of experiences resulting from the attitude of the clergy and Church hierarchy toward the People's State.

"The present attitude of the Government in questions of religion and towards the Church is a proof of the sincere endeavour of the Government to normalize relations between the State and Church in a spirit of loyalty and true concern for public welfare. Any steps taken by the Church hierarchy aiming at the regulation of relations according to the above principles can be sure of having the Government's support; an exchange of concrete proposals shaped in this spirit will be supported with complete good will."

(*Polish Facts and Figures*, March 26, 1949, issued by the press office of the Polish Embassy in London)

Appendix XIV

A PASTORAL LETTER ON CHURCH-STATE RELATIONS

April 24, 1949

"Because the situation of the Church is growing worse and the carrying out of its apostolic mission is becoming more and more difficult, and because the Hierarchy alone is blamed for this state of affairs, the truth must be told.

"Church and State can reach harmony in education, family life, training of youth, public life . . .

"Is it not urgent to unite all forces to fight the misery left by the war, to work together in rebuilding our country . . . After the moral destruction wrought by the war, what will help the country most: secularization or sanctification of the nation's spirit? Which is better for Poland: to break her up in rival sects or to strengthen her in one faith through one grace? Catholics, the critical hour for our Christian conscience has come.

"In the worst years of bondage, the people felt the priests standing by as almost unique defenders and teachers. Polish priests built the first schools, opened the nation's eyes, provided books, founded libraries, hospitals, orphanages, the first cooperatives and savings banks. They were the first to teach hygiene. They brought the hard working people in their Sunday clothing before the altars of the Lord. They were the first to teach the people of the freedom of God's children and the high dignity of every worker and plowman.

"Never before have the Polish people been closer to the priests, to the Church and to the altar. Their faithful eyes, prayerful lips, the over-flowing churches, the besieged confessionals, the great response to all that is good is evidence.

"Teaching the love of God, our clergy has not forgotten the love of its Country! They combined the first with the second in such a wonderful manner that when the time came they could take the cross and themselves show how to die for the nation. They have taken their place at the head of the exiles, strengthening their faith in a higher justice, that of God. Too many priests have laid down their lives in this land for Poland to entertain any doubts as to whether their hearts love the nation!

"When the enemy attacks, do not lose your peace of mind, remain at your posts as it befits you. Apply yourselves with zeal to teaching the Gospel, for that is your best and unique course of action. You know that you are not called upon to perform political work but to save human souls! Your works tend toward the country's peace, both when, at night, you go to the dying, when you strengthen the people in patience, as also when you defend the holy Faith from sectarians and blasphemers, when you take your stand in the defense of crosses, of the Catholic schools which are being closed down, of prayer in the kindergarten!

"You rightly believe that Poland does not need to be godless in order to be just to all! The defense of the Faith, therefore, is not a political activity but the fulfillment of the obligation of religious vocation! Never were you so distant from political matters as today.

"The church recognizes the right of the family and the State to direct education at school; it also takes the stand that the education of a Catholic nation cannot take place without the active cooperation of the Church and the securing of its rights in the school and toward the school.

"Catholic parents should have the right to choose their children's schools and should not be forced to send them to institutions where religion is altogether non-existent, or where education is based upon principles incompatible with Christian morality.

"Religion in school cannot be a mere secondary subject; it must be the center of education, as a force whose value has been proven through the centuries.

"The young Polish generation, which experienced the might of hatred in so many concentration camps, must believe in the values of the heart, for it must be prepared to build a just, loving Poland. Therefore, it should be educated in Christian principles of love and justice.

"We await with confidence, after so many fruitless attempts, the triumph of the respect of a child's rights to God, recognition of the Gospel's value, of the educational role of family and Church.

"Remember, you are children of God. Shun treason toward your Heavenly Father and your Mother—the Church. Do not attend godless gatherings, do not raise your voice against your Creator, do not renounce Him Who loved you to the death on the Cross.

"Face with courage and dignity the violent attacks against your conscience delivered by godless young elements, godless publications and associations! Do not mix with blasphemers and do not take part in their councils. Do not read godless literature and do not sing anthems which stir hatred, which are alien to our religious and national spirit.

"Read diligently the Holy Gospel, learn God's Truths with zeal, pray fervently, defend your chastity and sobriety. Perform your service to Poland in such manner as not to abandon God's service! Remember that you will never build a better Poland by betraying God!"

(Markham, "*Communists Crush Churches*," p. 104)

Appendix XV

PAPAL CHARGES AND POLISH DENIAL

July, 1949

(1) Papal accusation: The teaching of religion in Poland's schools has been prohibited.

Reply: Religious instruction not only has not been prohibited in Poland, but in contrast with other countries, including France and the United States, it constitutes part of the school curriculum, and the cost is defrayed by the government.

(2) Accusation: The extension of activities of institutions maintained by nuns and priests has been hampered.

Reply: Catholic nuns and priests maintain 300 homes for orphans with 15,000 children, 600 kindergartens with 22,000 children, 40 secondary schools with 900 students, besides the Catholic University in Lublin.

(3) Accusation: The Catholic religion is attacked and persecuted.

Reply: The number of monasteries and convents grew substantially in the new Poland. There are today 2100 convents and monasteries, as compared with the 1742 in 1939. The number of nuns has risen from 17,265 in 1939 (when Poland's population was 35,000,000) to 17,659 in 1949 (Poland's total population 25,000,000).

(4) Accusation: Censorship creates difficulties for all expression in the Catholic press.

Reply: The Catholic press comprises 63 papers and periodicals, with a total circulation of 700,000. It is not restricted by any special regulations, nor does it have any rights other than those of the press in general.

(5) Accusation: The prisoners and the sick are deprived of religious solace.

Reply: Not only are the sick not deprived of religious solace but in many hospitals religious services are held daily. This is a fact known to all invalids, all doctors and those who visit the inmates of hospitals. Prisoners also receive religious solace by priests—a service administered in all prisons.

(6) Accusation: The exchange of correspondence between the Holy See and the Polish bishops and faithful has been made impossible.

Reply: The Polish post office does not keep records of "faithful" and "nonbelievers" but delivers letters to all, irrespective of their religious beliefs.

(7) Accusation: Religious practices encounter increasing difficulties.

Reply: This charge does not square with the fact that the government has spent money for the rebuilding of many churches damaged and destroyed by the war and has turned them over for the use of the clergy and the public.

(*Poland Today*, New York, October, 1949, p. 22)

Appendix XVI

Y. M. C. A. DECISION

October 16, 1949

(From *Zycie Warszawy*, Oct. 25, 1949)

"The 21st General Meeting of Polish Y.M.C.A. delegates was held in Warsaw on October 22 and 23. Reports and discussions unanimously confirmed that, during the period between the two world wars, the Polish Y.M.C.A. had been promoting imperialistic ideology.

"It is considered that the old organizational forms of this Association are incompatible with the spirit, the duties and the aims of the Y.M.C.A. in People's Poland. It has, therefore, been decided to abandon these forms.

"By unanimous decision, the Charter was amended and the Polish Y.M.C.A. will now be called 'Ognisko.' The 'Association,' reads the amended Charter, 'is a social organization acting in accordance with the ideology of People's Poland and with the instructions and recommendations of the Central Council for Problems affecting Youth and Physical Culture.'

"The Charter describes the Association's duties. Polish citizens, both male and female, as well as legal entities may be members. The Central Trade Union Council, the Polish Youth Association, the Polish University Youth Association, the 'Service to Poland' organization, the Polish Scouts' Association, the Women's League, the Society of Children's Friends and various athletic organizations will automatically become members of the new Association.

"The Assembly unanimously adopted a resolution reading in part:

'The Y.M.C.A. was created because the rulers of capitalism wanted to hamper the process of consolidation of class consciousness among the working masses, because they wanted to reconcile them to capitalism and to counteract Marxist teaching, which was becoming increasingly popular among these masses. The American Y.M.C.A. and the World Y.M.C.A. organization are both harnessed by capital to serve American imperialism.

'The maintenance of the old organizational forms made it impossible, in spite of the attempts of the Association's progressive members, completely to liberate this organization from Y.M.C.A. traditions, or to safeguard it from the infiltration of hostile imperialistic ideology.'

"The Assembly further stated that the Polish Y.M.C.A. has now completely adopted the attitude of People's Poland and that it has irrevocably broken connections with the cosmopolitan Y.M.C.A. World Organization. The Assembly recommended that the National Council join the organizations fighting for social reconstruction.

"In conclusion, the Assembly elected officers of the Ognisko Association."

(Markham, *Communists Crush Churches*," pp. 99-100)

Appendix XVII

LETTER OF CARDINAL SAPIEHA AND THE PRIMATE TO THE PRESIDENT

February 16, 1950

(Extracts)

Mr. President, the fight against the Church, against religion and against God Himself in Poland is blatantly evident.

When we state this fact we desire one thing: that we shall not be asked to believe that this fight is not being waged at all. We ask at least this much of the consideration that is due to men: that the truth be told to them. Therefore either the deeds be openly acknowledged or the attitude adopted towards the Church should be changed. Should an acknowledgment follow, one would have to ask whether it is possible to take upon one's self the right to declare war on the Christian views and character of the nation. Poland never fought against the faith and religion of her citizens, or against the Catholic Church— which bears witness to one thing, namely, that the Church has never threatened the freedom of the national spirit.

The meeting at the Technical High School (in Warsaw), and the speeches delivered there by representatives of the Government and by various speakers, revealed the true intentions of the organizers of that meeting.

It is obvious that "putting an end to the abuses in CARITAS" was not what mattered. One does not achieve such an aim by means of chicanery, by lavish receptions, by plying the clergy with drink at parties in the offices of district governors and in the premises of the Council of State, by giving presents and similar bribery, for which so much money was spent that the limited budget of many a CARITAS institution could be sufficiently provided for years to come. Who is going to believe that this waste of public funds was caused by solicitude for the poor?

A much bigger issue was at stake, namely, to disrupt and to sow discord among the clergy, and to make the clergy ridiculous in the public eyes; to oppose the clergy to the Bishops and to create a jumping-off-board for detaching the clergy from the Holy See and from the unity of the Church, an objective to which much effort has been devoted for a very long time.

If these plans have not brought results, it is because you do not know the clergy. The clergy may have their faults, they may at first succumb to terror, but they will soon recognize violence and fraud and will turn their back on such behaviour.

Propaganda has taken the liberty of making a distinction between the "reactionary clergy" and the "patriotic priests." We wish to remind you that in the years 1941-44 the German propaganda machine placed its hopes in the so-called "patriotic priests," and the people of Warsaw still remember it. Today we note a singular innovation in the Press. We used to read about "the reactionary episcopate," but we read today about "the reactionary section of the episcopate." This is a new attempt, relying this time on "patriotic Bishops." All these attempts can be reduced to one common denominator: they reveal the true countenance of the anti-Church activities.

Who will profit by the disruption of the Church? Most assuredly not Poland, who so many times in her tragic history has found the strength to survive in the unity of the Church, which united the whole nation.

Could the Church harm the People's Poland? If that Poland is to be truly a commonwealth of people, just and loving towards its citizens, if she does not violate their conscience and if she halts the fight against God, then such a Poland will truly deserve the full respect and support of all citizens.

The attitude of the Church towards the State will depend on the attitude of the State towards religion. If the State respects religion, who will dare to oppose the State? The State's anti-Church laws are today a source of accusations against the Government; when those laws disappear the long-desired peace will return.

All sorts of attempts have already been made to force the Catholic clergy to yield to "the modern reality." The Bishops are being compelled to "recognize the People's Government"—as if the Episcopate were a parliament. The

Episcopate holds itself and its clergy aloof from participation in political contentions. It is not for us to give approval to the actions of the Government. We have never done that, and we see no reason why we should do it now. The field of our activities is clearly-defined and well known. We desire to remain within it, convinced that our work will serve the realities of Poland.

On the other hand, we are astonished at the attempt to drag the clergy into politics and mass meetings, in direct contradiction to the argument of the party, that "priests should abstain from politics." First this attempt was made to turn the military chaplains into political agitators. This attempt met with no success. Now the attempt is being made to bring the whole of the clergy into politics, in order to incite them against the Episcopate.

Minister Wolski had the temerity to appeal the "mixed commission" (Scilicet, of representatives of the Hierarchy and the Government, meeting in Warsaw) to the public meeting in the Technical High School on the question of an "agreement between Church and State," although he did not break off his negotiations with the Bishop's Committee. We are obliged to describe this unusual method of conducting negotiations as a demagogic move, prejudicial to the established method of conducting negotiations. At the same time it is an example of the lack of understanding of the internal life of the Church. The clergy may, by means of force, be brought to a mass meeting, as was done on January 30th, but they know well that nothing can happen in the Church through force.

Force was also used in appointing priests to offices in CARITAS, although the clergy know that they may not accept any office from a lay authority without the permission of their Bishops. Force was also used in trying to dissuade the clergy from obedience to the Bishops when the Bishops ordered the reading of their Statement on CARITAS.

The use of violence against the clergy is becoming an accepted method. Even if it should produce some results, it would hardly bring credit to the Government, for the Catholic people know their priests and are well aware to what elements the Government has appealed. It must be stressed that more than a thousand priests who were brought to the Technical High School were deceived and assembled by violence and coercion. Those who delivered the lectures imposed on them, and those who participated in the discussion are men who had suffered from their experience in the war and in concentration camps, and who now find themselves in conflict with the law of the Church, or who are being blackmailed by the police because of the punishments hanging over them. To seek to establish a new order with the help of such people would mean to alienate the Catholics who constitute a majority of the nation.

Assuredly modern States have powerful means for disrupting the Church. We see what has been attempted against the Church in Hungary or in Czecho-slovakia. Yet the outrages perpetrated there caused indignation through the whole of the civilized world.

The degradation of the high authority of the public administration became most evident when it was attempted to mobilize the clergy against the charitable activities of the Church. High Government officials were reduced to the role of agents for bringing the clergy to CARITAS meetings. The methods used were an insult to their human dignity and to the dignity of the State in whose name they were acting. County administrators, mayors of towns, and sometimes even the Governors of Provinces, ordered to bring priests to mass-meetings, would spend hours in irksome persuasion, often using threats and violence. What was most distressing was the obvious lies and blackmail used when other argument failed. All this was done to thousands of priests, all over Poland, often in the presence of the people, the servants of the Church and the domestic servants of the priests, who thus witnessed to what degradation the representatives of the State had sunk from their pedestal of authority. Even the men who carried out these orders did not always conceal their dislike of the ruthlessness of the orders. If today some priests are accused because, while defending their freedom against intruders, they used sharp words and, allegedly, "insulted the representatives of the State," one must take into account that these latter were insulted earlier, and a hundred times worse, by those who issued such instructions to them.

And what took place in Poland on the Friday and Saturday preceding February 12th, the day on which the Statement of the Episcopate on CARITAS was to be read, surpasses all notions of legality and public order. Before the spectacle of such terror one feels offended, not only in one's dignity as a representative of the Polish clergy, but even in one's basic dignity as a human being. This was no longer the exercise of official functions, but a noisy riot of which the memory alone produces a humiliating feeling of shame that the State can sink to treating its citizens in this manner.

And all this is not considered to be a violation of the human conscience; it is even announced as being in conformity with binding decrees. But when a Bishop exercises his authority with regard to the clergy and acts in defence of the discipline of the Church, the public prosecutor brings in legal actions and applies preventive measures against the Bishop for an alleged infringement of the decree "On the Protection of the Freedom of Conscience and Faith." There can hardly be an example of a more glaring confusion of ideas.

Minister Wolski, in negotiating with the Episcopate as your representative, Mr. President, is certainly aware of the nature of his actions. Being convinced that he acts in conformity with parliamentary procedures, we have refrained from appealing to you, Mr. President. Today, however, when the Minister has appealed to the clergy to make "a concordat from the bottom," over the heads of the Bishops, we no longer have any obligation to remain silent.

We therefore present our protests against the methods being used in conducting the negotiations. Minister Wolski, in spite of constant promises, never supplied in time the minutes of the meetings which had taken place. That delay hindered further discussions, and now the Minister has the audacity to charge the Episcopate with responsibilitty for their slow progress. Other protests are aroused by the singular methods of seeking to intimidate the Bishops. The Minister has admitted that he seeks to bring a decisive pressure to bear upon the Bishops by means of anti-Church laws. This method of constant intimidation has brought about an opposite result, and the Episcopate has been continually confirmed in its conviction that the Government has no intention of keeping its word, but wants rather to confront the Episcopate with *faits accomplis* against the freedom of the Church.

During the last conversation, on December 19th, 1949, Minister Wolski undertook to send the outstanding minutes within four days, and a meeting of the mixed commission was to be arranged immediately afterwards. This was never done, and instead, during that period, the whole campaign against CARITAS was prepared. Even on January 23rd, 1950, after that campaign had already begun, Minister Wolski received new proposals from the Episcopate, and promised that he would immediately, on the following day, arrange a meeting of the sub-committee. This also did not take place, and instead the mass meetings began.

We are of the opinion that intimidation cannot be applied between two negotiating parties. We are the representatives of the Church, which sometimes submits to persecution for the sake of the truth, but does not ever change under threats. Even the most painful threats and the most prejudicial laws, therefore, will have no effect on our attitude on matters on which, on doctrinal grounds, we cannot yield.

Other protests are called forth by another peculiar argument, which Minister Wolski has used much too frequently. "Regulations already published," he used to say, "will not be implemented if the agreement is signed." The question arises: What exactly is the law, in the hands of the State? Is it a means of maintaining public order, or is it a means of intimidation? If today a Minister of the Polish Republic proclaims that a law issued by the State may not be put into effect, what guarantee do we have that the Government will respect an agreement signed with the Bishops?

Is it possible, in the light of these facts, to accuse the Episcopate of delaying the negotiations and not desiring a real agreement with the State? And yet M. Wolski has had the audacity to do so. Although he knew only too well who was procrastinating and what was being prepared, he publicly accused the Episcopate, laying the blame on the Hierarchy of the Church.

Our letter on this occasion has not the character of a protest. It is not a declaration of grievances from the abused clergy or the slandered Episcopate. Nor does our letter contain any request. Our letter is the voice of the conscience of the Polish nation, which speaks through us; and that voice is addressed to you, as President of the Republic, and is compelled to regard you, Mr. President, and your Government as responsible before God and before history for the fight against religion and against the Church in Poland.

Appendix XVIII

POLISH PRESS AGENCY ON CHURCH-STATE RELATIONS

February 28, 1950

. . . "the Government respects freedom of religion and of religious practices and scrupulously adheres to this attitude. Catholicism as a religious denomination is protected by law.

. . . "In the interests of the State, and with the increasing support of the majority of the people and of the clergy, the Government has spared no effort to bring about a stabilization of relations with the Church through direct talks with the Episcopacy. An indispensable condition for this highly desired stabilization is the discontinuation of all acts hostile to the Government, and loyalty on the part of the Polish Episcopacy to the social system and the State interests of the People's Poland.

. . . "the leading circles of the Episcopacy failed even in such elementary loyalty as to consent to the use of the words 'People's Poland' in the projected statement on Church-State relations.

. . . "The Episcopacy refuses to reconcile itself to the fact that power in Poland is now in the hands of the masses, that the form of government in which a handful of capitalists and landowners exploited and dominated the nation has been eliminated once and for all, and that the medieval privileges of the Church hierarchy—which have long since been removed in many European countries—cannot be maintained.

. . . "The Government has never questioned the Pope's jurisdiction in matters concerning the Roman Catholic religion. At the same time the Government, obviously enough, cannot shut its eyes to the fact that while the Vatican has no diplomatic relations with Poland, it stubbornly fosters such relations with the handful of reactionaries who call themselves the 'London Government' and who are paid by foreign intelligence services.

. . . "The Vatican has taken political measures to back the revisionist tendencies of the imperialists in the Western Zones of Germany and these measures coincide with the activities of warmongers. They are, therefore, aimed at Poland's most vital interests. Clearly, under such conditions, the execution by the Polish clergy of foreign orders issued by the Vatican on non-religious matters cannot be reconciled with the interests and sovereignty of the Polish State.

"That is why in this matter the Government proposed the following formula to the Episcopacy: 'Recognizing the Pope as the competent authority of the Roman Catholic Church in religious matters, the Episcopacy will in other matters be guided by the State interests of the People's Poland." Although such an attitude in no way violates the principles of the Catholic faith, the Episcopacy rejected this proposition.

"The introduction of Government control into the Caritas organization in order to end abuses, the waste of public property and criminal negligence, is unanimously looked upon today by public opinion as a step in the right direction of putting the administration of Caritas on a sound basis.

. . . "The Episcopacy's leading circles have . . . taken a stand against the decrees of Government authorities and they have tried to liquidate Caritas in order to exploit this fact in a political campaign against the People's Poland.

. . . "priests who, following the dictates of their own conscience, raised their voices in protest against the abuses of the Caritas organization and gave their support to the initiative of the Government, found themselves exposed to threats and severe reprisals on the part of some bishops.

. . . "—a game against the people and the State, which is determined to take part in the charitable work of Caritas . . . (therefore) the great majority of the clergy refused to read from their pulpits the unprecedented statement on the Caritas affair released by the bishops.

. . . "The attempts of the reactionary group of the Church hierarchy to bring political reprisals against honest and patriotic priests will encounter appropriate resistance and . . . can only lead to further isolation of the leading circles of the Episcopacy.

. . . "The Government is convinced that with the active support of the faithful and the proper understanding and continued active support of the enlightened clergy, relations between Church and State will eventually become stabilized. These relations will be based on full religious freedom and on the full recognition of the State interests of the People's Poland and of the achievements of the Polish people."

(From *Poland Today*, April, 1950)

HUNGARY

Introduction

The Magyars are a people of Asiatic origin situated in the Western European community and living as a Western nation.

West vs. East: Around the year 950 two Magyar leaders, Gyula and Ajtony, were baptized Christians in Constantinople as one of several measures taken to resist Western Franconian influence. Twenty-five years later missionary activity began at the request of Prince Geza, later followed by the infiltration of German knights and monks. In Western Hungary, under the influence of Stefan the Pious in the 11th century, permanent Christian ties were established with Rome. The Eastern Magyars, however, reacted against and withstood Western missionary endeavor until the end of the 14th century, when the Christian impact came to them more acceptably through the Balkan Bogomil Christians.

Catholicism vs. Protestantism: By the time of the Reformation, both religiously and politically, the people were split between East and West, West Hungary being Catholic with spiritual allegiance to Rome, led politically by a foreign (called "German") nobility, East Hungary having an indigenous landed nobility. With the Reformation, Eastern Magyars, not wishing to ally themselves with the pagan Turks (they considered themselves as the frontier of Christianity against the pagan East), became "Calvinist," while Magyars of the West who came under the influence of the Reformation (largely through German reformers), became "Lutherans." The larger bloc of the West remained Catholic.

At the end of the 16th century, as the threat of Turkish occupation lessened and the Hapsburg-Catholic counter-reformation pushed eastward, Eastern Hungarians revived their nationalist traditions against the Hapsburg dynasty and Rome, and allied themselves with the Turks against 'papal' Vienna. This placed Protestants in West Hungary in a very difficult situation, and, though many by then were of occidental origin, because they were Protestant they were persecuted as traitors to the Western, Catholic cause, as allies of the Turks. Not until the Turkish siege of Vienna in 1683 did Eastern Magyar Protestants make common cause with Catholic Hungarians, when they broke their alliance with the Turks to help push them back from Vienna and West Europe. However, the fundamental tensions between Western-Catholic (and some Lutheran) Hungarians and Eastern Calvinist Magyars were not resolved. Confessional schools continued to promulgate confessional, national animosities.

During the Counter-Reformation of the 18th century, with the appointment of nobles as leaders and inspectors of the churches, political interests and controversies became even more firmly rooted in the churches. It was not until pan-Slavism, through the Slovak Christians, threatened the assimilation of the Magyar Lutherans and the conquest of Hungary that common Magyar ties of Lutherans and Calvinists superseded their Oriental vs. Western, Calvinist vs. Lutheran differences and they united to push back, and eventually to Magyarize the Slovaks. Hungarian Catholicism showed scant interest. For the next twenty years, Lutherans and Calvinists, stimulated by the awakening social conscience of the Eastern Calvinists, welcomed Western liberalism, began to see the need for social and political reform, and stood together against Rome.

In the middle of the 19th century, Hungary was over-run by allied Austrian and Russian troops, and through the naming of Emperor Franz Josef of Austria as King of Hungary, became firmly attached to the Western and predominantly Roman Catholic world.

Conservative Government, Church and the "West" vs. the Proletariat and the Reformers: At the end of World War I, with the loss of two-thirds of the territory formerly known as Hungary, Hungarians of all confessions felt that the whole nation had been betrayed by the West. At the same time, the agricultural proletariat and the laboring class felt they had been betrayed in a more particular way. Immediately after the war, under the leadership of the socialists and a number of well-known Protestants, a promising program of social and economic reform was initiated, a reform which, if successful, would have turned feudal lands of the churches and the nobility back to the people. When the leadership appeared to be increasingly in the hands of the Communists, particularly Lenin-trained Bela Kun, conservative elements in Hungary, including high Catholic and other church leaders, joined together with the West under the leadership of Horthy in a counter-revolution to overthrow the socialist reformers. Social reaction and a revived nationalism were the natural outcome. The "red terror" of three months duration was followed by the "white terror" of the Horthy regime. From conservative and government circles, fearful of Communist occupation, came strong anti-Communist, anti-Russian propaganda; among laborers and landless peasants there remained resentment towards the West. When, later, Germany intimated her sympathy for Hungary and suggested a possibility of territorial revision, industrialization and prosperity, proletariat Hungarians were ready to accept her proffered aid, without too much popular questioning about anti-Semitism, totalitarianism and imperialism.

Church and State: During this period, 1920-1939, except for a few "heretic" reformers, the Church was committed to the policies of the Government. The strength of the churches was thought to lie in their cordial relationship to the Government, their church-political leaders, their land holdings and school. The Catholic Bishop of Esztergom had the rank of Prince, and had been second only to the King in political power. The inspectors and leading laymen of the churches were cabinet ministers, members of parliament and landed nobility. The Catholic Church was the greatest landholder of Hungary, with 877,000 hold (over ten million acres) and tax-exempt privileges, whereas the peasants, 100,000 of whom tilled church lands, were land-hungry and tax-burdened. The Catholic Church alone controlled more than half* of all schools in Hungary, and in most church, as well as state schools religious instruction was obligatory for children of any or no faith.

---

* Church and State schools in 1949, according to *Nepszava*, May 1, 1948:

	Church	State
Elementary	1674	976
Secondary	2895	1952
Middle	108	260
Gymnasia	94	85
	4771	3273

According to Catholic sources, the R. C. Church had 4813 schools (*Four Years' Struggle of the Church in Hungary*, p. 127).

After 1848, the Hungarian laws guaranteed substantial religious freedom to almost all churches. The Roman and Greek Catholics, the Eastern Orthodox groups, the Reformed and Lutheran Churches, the Unitarians, and, since 1895, the Jewish congregations have enjoyed similar rights and privileges.

The State regulated the following:

(a)　the changing of church membership (1868);

(b)　the right to perform marriage services, not granted to any of the churches after 1894, unless performed first by civil authorities;

(c)　the religion of children: boys followed the confession of the father, girls that of the mother, unless another agreement was made prior to the civil marriage before the magistrate. If parents had no confession, they had to decide to educate their children in one of the above-mentioned religions, and when the children became 18, they could choose their own religion;

(d)　anyone who left one religious group without joining another had to pay church taxes for six years to his abandoned group.

The State granted:

(a)　freedom of worship, organization and administration, election of officers and leaders to these religious groups;

(b)　the right to maintain parochial schools and institutions of higher learning;

(c)　an opportunity for all churches to teach religion in the public schools, including those operated by the community and private groups: no pupil could enter a higher class without having attended religious instruction by his own pastor or by an instructor appointed by his church; funds to maintain religious instruction in state and community schools had to be provided by the State or community;

(d)　the above religious groups had the privilege of levying church taxes and either collecting them from their own members, or, with certain limitations, they were collected by the State together with the state taxes and paid to the respective churches. The law gave the churches the right to force everyone to pay church taxes.

(e)　After 1895, the pastors for the various religious groups received state help if the local congregation could not pay a proper salary. These churches also received state aid to maintain their parochial school systems and to carry out their administrative and cultural obligations.

(f)　According to a law of 1885 these religious groups also had the privilege of being represented in the Upper House of the Parliament through their leaders (bishops and laymen).

The churches were not obliged to carry out functions of the State, (i.e., keeping records, etc.) as in the Scandinavian countries.

These religious groups were the so-called "Accepted Religions," sometimes also called "Historic Churches."

Three other denominations were called "Recognised Religions": the Baptists, Methodists and Mohammedans. These groups had the same privilege as the others to organize themselves, elect their own officers and leaders, to conduct services and teach religion to their own children in public schools, but they did not receive state subventions and could not collect their church dues as state taxes.

No other religious groups could register their members as belonging to a specific religious group. Their members had to declare themselves as people "without religion." They could organize themselves as associations, but were controlled by the Ministry of the Interior like other associations and had to present their constitutions to the authorities.

Church leaders pre-occupied with government and administrative affairs observed the inherent pietism of the peasants, the vestiges of religion in folkways and national celebrations, the influence which, theoretically, the Church exerted through its compulsory religious education program, the official membership rolls of the churches, and assumed that all was well. By 1939 the Government was characterized as conservative and feudalistic, the "established" Church as conservative, feudalistic and bourgeois.

Social Unrest and Religious Revival: But there were already undercurrents of revolution, both within the Church and among the people. Sociologically the Church had become largely identified with the middle-class bourgeosie and the peasants. Church ties with a large part of the peasantry, however, had considerably weakened since the time when all Magyars were Christianized as peasants (but, significantly, at that time tilling their own or their nobles' land, not that of the churches). And the Church had little contact with the laboring class, which by now had grown to 50% of the population. There was much misery, but scant reference to such unpleasant matters in official circles.

Within the Protestant churches a small minority was seriously concerned about spiritual disintegration in high places. They espoused the forgotten working class and the pauperized peasants. In their deeper probing into theology and the Bible, their preoccupation with youth, social justice and evangelism, their proposals of separation of church and state, nationalization of church schools, land reform, and self-support of the churches they were to become the leaders of a revival movement which was to continue to the present time. At a critical time, when the official Church was unquestionably identified with conservatism, with the West, with indigenous and Western nobility, with feudal landholders and with oppression, it was significant that there was this beginning of a revival which should eventually weave through the whole fabric of chaos, destruction, uncertainty and reconstruction, and should, as a courageous prophet, call the Church to repentance and reform, to renewal and evangelism.

Religious Composition:

Total Population	9,316,000
Roman Catholic	6,120,000
Uniates	233,000
Reformed	1,934,000
Lutheran	557,000
Orthodox	37,000
Baptist, Methodist, Unitarian	26,000

Period of Alliance with Nazi Germany—1940-1944

In less than five years, 1940 to 1944, the thinking of responsible churchmen concerning the relation between the Church and the Hungarian State changed from "equation" and near-identity, to open hostility. With the deportation of the Jews by the Nazis, and the removal of Horthy, accepted political and theological ideas and administrative patterns were profoundly shaken. It was inevitable that the inner life of the Church and its relation to whatever government should come to power would be greatly effected.

Church and Nation: At the end of 1940 the churches were represented in Parliament by forty-eight religious leaders, of whom fourteen (archbishops) held their offices by "right of birth." The general secretary of the Reformed Commission for Foreign Affairs was also president of two Government offices. At a session of Government administrators organized by the Ministry of Interior he asserted that Protestants and Catholics must band together to save the Church of Christ from a poisonous third power (Socialism). In the autumn of 1940 the churches rejoiced at the annexation of Transylvania and the "return home" of Transylvanian Protestants.   Lutheran Bishop Turoczy, at a conference on "Nation and Society" early in 1941 equated the Church and the Nation, adding that neither is subordinate, independent or indifferent to the other.   Bishop Raffay (Lutheran), after the return of Yugoslavian-held territory, celebrated Easter proclaiming "not only the resurrection of our Redeemer, but also of our beloved Hungarian Fatherland" (*Protestant Churches in Hungary*, 1939-50, unpublished manuscript).

In the autumn of 1941, Secretary of State Szasz addressed the Reformed and the Lutheran assemblies: "(Side by side with) our mighty ally . . . Germany, with its Divinely-blessed weapons, (we) are bravely fighting to help the rule of Christ to victory over the paganism of . . . Bolshevism" (ICPIS, November, 1941).

Church and Government: Six months later the Reformed General Convention declared itself ready to cooperate with the State in improving living conditions, but asserted that it must go beyond the State in its exercise of Christian charity.   The convention prayed that God and the doctrine of Christ might be victorious in the war (ICPIS, May, 1941).

Nation and Russia: In August, 1942, the (Protestant) *Hungarian Press Service* announced that Hungarian (Nazi) troops invading Russia were leaving plaques and crosses entitled "Russians! The Hungarian Army has passed here and left you the cross, the earth and liberty" (As early as 1939 Protestant churches took up collections, sent messages of encouragement and held special days of intercession for their Russian-besieged Finnish brethren). Religious journals increasingly carried Germanophil slogans, and references to the anti-Soviet "holy war."   Pastors referred to the God-given task of Hungary to convert the Russian heathen.   Bishop Turoczy in his annual (1942) report to the Lutheran Church stated "it is impossible to thank God enough for the fact that the relationship (between Church and State) is so cordial . . . (especially in)measures which show clearly that the Hungarian State desires to build the work of the Church organically into its own activity" (ICPIS, August 1942).   The Church was reported in January, 1942, as collaborating with the State in the reorganization of society, youth work, social work, etc. State funds enabled the churches to maintain their schools and establish new educational institutions (ICPIS, January, 1943).   Public statements were characterized by appeals to "Christian National Unity" up to the winter of 1943-44.   One should not conclude that all people were in agreement.   But even public statements began to sound different after 1942.

Chronicle of Events

November, 1942—

Reformed Bishop Ravasz, who in July asserted "we are convinced we will win this war," stated in a published article that the Church is above political parties, that Christians must not disparage the value of their enemies, not calumniate them, but proclaim the sovereignty of God (*ICPIS*, November, 1942).

January, 1943—

The Church was reported as living and working "with almost entire freedom."

February, 1943—

At the turning point of the war, pastors spoke of repentance and faith through uncertain times.

February, 1943—

In a new catechism, the leader of the Hungarian Ecumenical Youth Council, Nicholas Makay, wrote, "world conflagrations denote a process of purification and open the way for the building of mighty new worlds" (*ICPIS*, February, 1943).

June, 1943—

The Lutheran Church held a "week of repentance" with daily communion (*Protestant Churches in Hungary*, 1939-1950).

Autumn, 1943—

The Reformed Churches formed a committee to aid Christian Jews and other persecutees of Nazism (*ICPIS*, September, 1943). Prior to the persecution of Jews and other excesses, Nazism had been welcomed as an ally which could help secure Hungary's territorial claims.

Autumn, 1943—

M. Gaudy, Inspector of Religious Instruction in Budapest, sent an urgent appeal to President Roosevelt to send missionaries to the U.S.S.R., ostensibly to "evangelize" Hungarians who were prisoners of war, but probably to ensure their good treatment (*ICPIS*, October, 1943).

Winter, 1943—

Reformed Bishop Ravasz, in an address before the General Assembly of the National Association of Reformed Pastors and the Association of Lutheran Pastors, identified the purposes of the Hungarian churches with those of the ecumenical movement, mentioning the Berlin International Protestant League, and the Geneva World Council of Churches. He asserted that any peace must be concerned with universal good. A few weeks later he exhorted the people to establish a one-class society, in which all people would be united in service (*ICPIS*, December, 1943, February, 1944). Bishop Béla Kapi, President of the Lutheran Church, warned the axis puppet Government not to be totalitarian in its attitude towards the Church, and cited the Norwegian Church example (*ICPIS*, December, 1943).

Winter, 1943-1944—

A Lutheran pastor who accepted election to the Nazi "Pfeilkreuzlerpartei" was expelled by his bishop (*The Protestant Churches in Hungary, 1939-1950*, p. 8).

December 31, 1943—

Lutheran Pastor Jarosi prayed for victims of Fascism and was subsequently court-martialed. Bereczky, Klada, Tildy and others participated in the anti-Nazi resistance movement (*Ibid.*, p. 8).

Spring, 1944—

Protestant churches established a relief committee for assistance to the homeless. Reformed Bishop Ravasz prepared his diocese administration for worse times, appointed a pastor for refugees in West Hungary (*Ibid.*, p. 9).

October, 1944—

Reformed Bishop Imre Révész denounced the puppet Nazi state's exploitation of the Church for political ends, stating that the Church preferred losing its position and subsidies to losing its independence (*ICPIS*,

October, 1944). The Reformed Church journal appealed to the churches and to Christians to do penance for the state of society and the Hungarian nation (*ICPIS*, October, 1944).

Roman Catholic Bishops Mindszenty and Shvoy were imprisoned for demanding that the Hungarian (Nazi) government issue a "cease-fire" order to Hungarian troops opposing the Allies (*Four Years' Struggle*, Mindszenty, p. 8). Mindszenty had also spoken out against anti-Semitism, as well as against Government leaders who refused to intervene with the Nazis on behalf of persecuted Jews.

By the end of the German-Hungarian alliance, Protestant and Catholic churches were surprisingly bold in opposing Nazi anti-Semitism, ghetto-ism, confiscation of properties, labor camps and trespassing of people's rights and liberties. In a number of instances the churches refused to participate in Government assemblies and celebrations.

The period 1939-44 was one of refining and renewal of the inner life of the Church. On the initiative of various revival movements, deaconess homes and ministries were founded, retreat and training centers established. Folkschools were opened, laymen were trained and ordained for religious work, evangelization was extended through preaching and publications, theological interest deepened and religious instruction was intensified (*Die Protestantischen Kirchen in Ungarn*, 1939-1950 unpublished). Nonetheless, there was ". . . anguish of heart . . . as the debacle ending the war was approaching . . . (churchmen) were awaiting the Divine judgment so well deserved by so much sinful omission, and how many had taken it for granted that all possibilities of our future activities would be lost to us owing to our unworthiness" (A. Bereczky, Radio speech, January 1, 1949).

"Liberation" and After

Winter, 1944-45—

A provisional government was constituted at Debreczen, December 23, 1944. Prof. Bela Zsedenyi, lay president of a Lutheran church, was elected president of the National Assembly. The Provisional Assembly proclaimed freedom of religion, press and organization. A Catholic priest proposed to the Assembly that Hungary make a declaration of "war of liberation," as an ally of the U.S.S.R. and the U.S.A. The proposal was adopted unanimously.

After the "liberation" and occupation of Eastern Hungary by U.S.S.R. troops, church leaders feared the fate of the churches. Catholic Bishop Apor of Gyor was killed by Soviet soldiers while trying to protect a group of women and girls (*Communists Crush Churches*, Markham, p. 80). Many spoke of penitence, and faith that after judgment would come a day of national resurrection. Thousands of Siebenburgers and South Hungarians were deported to Russia (*Protestantischen Kirchen*, 1939-1950, p. 11). Hungarian Nazi authorities advised pastors to flee with them Westward. Radio Moscow promised that there would be no intereference in church life and that pastors and priests would not be molested. The first law issued by the Soviets provided for opening of churches and holding services (*Ibid.*, p. 12).

Reformed Bishop Vasarhelyi of Cluj was asked by the Russian Army commanding officer to continue at his post, and Radio Moscow called on all clergymen to remain in their parishes and continue their work. The U. S. S. R. commander of Budapest received as his first guests, the Mayor, the Papal Nuncio and the head of the Free Churches (*Protestantischen Kirchen*, 1939-1950, p. 12).

February, 1945—

A group of pastors and priests met at Debrecen and issued a statement of guide-posts for Christians, including the following:

(3) There can be no effective reconstruction except that based on Jesus Christ.

(4) The greatest task of the clergy is to call the people to penitence in order that a renewal might be made possible.

(5) Re. Church and State, "Render to Caesar that which is Caesar's and to God that which is God's."

(7) An equalization of salaries and an agricultural reform are necessary to the welfare of the nation. In education, church schools have done and will continue to do most useful service.

March 18, 1945—

Nation-wide land reform was decreed by the Provisional Government, along lines requested by the National Peasants' Party (according to Catholic sources of information, under Russian orders). Pasturage would be on a communal basis, forests were to be nationalized, and estates of more than 1000 "hold"* were subject to confiscation, except church properties which would be reduced to 100 hold. Smaller estates would be expropriated on a compensatory basis and redistributed (*Communism and the Churches*, Barron and Waddams, p. 62).

The Roman Catholic Church possessed *ca.* 877,000 hold, of which *ca.* 12% was left to the Church.

In a pastoral letter dated May 24, the Catholic bishops, and particularly Bishop Mindszenty, expressed deep concern that they might no longer be able to cover administrative expenses of the Church without their lands, but added a hope that the happiness of the new land-owners would console the Church for her losses (*Four Years' Struggle*, Mindszenty, p. 17). *Magyar Kurir*, of February 8, 1949, stated that the bishops, who also lost their land, did not oppose the reform, in fact stated publicly "we are praying God's blessing on the new owners" (*Communism and the Churches*, Barron and Waddams, p. 63).

April, 1945—

The Hungarian Secretary of State praised Russian aid which had been extended to the Catholic Church, in contrast to the persecutions of the Nazis. He commended the attendance of Russian troops at mass, and added that he "feels no anxiety at all with regard to the U.S.S.R" (*ICPIS*, April, 1945). The Papal Nuncio was expelled (*Communist War on Religion*, MacEoin, p. 118).

May 9, 1945—

The new Government provided church building sites, materials and assistance to a number of congregations whose buildings had been destroyed (*Protestantischen Kirchen*, 1939-1950, p. 11).

In reply to Bereczky's appeal to the Reformed Synod for a statement re.

the Jewish question, Lutheran General Inspector Baron Radvansky denied the necessity of such a proclamation of guilt (*Ibid.*, p. 12).

May-June, 1945—

A pronouncement of the Hungarian Ecumenical Committee called the people to repentance and bold courage, and opposed all anti-Christian forces and alien teachings. It warned the people to expect great social changes. The first post-war edition of the weekly religious journal, *Life and Future*, was issued June 9, and carried articles by Bereczky and others on the repentance and regeneration of the Church (*Five Years of Hungarian Protantism* — 1945-1950, Hungarian Church Press, p. 18).

Lutheran Bishop Turoczy was sentenced to ten years' imprisonment for "supporting the (Nazi) war and anti-Soviet propaganda." After the Germans had re-captured Nyireghazas, he had held a special thanksgiving service, and had earlier fed the prisoners of the Russians (*Protestantischen Kirchen*, 1939-1950, p. 9).

Leaders of other Churches were tried on charges of Nazi collaboration or anti-Semitism and sentenced to imprisonment, later released. The churches urged the Government to release the churchmen, and strengthened their unity through this experience. Individual congregations were unhindered in their religious life and work (*ICPIS*, No. 38, October, 1945 and other sources).

August-September, 1945—

Hungarian Protestants reported that the Agrarian Reform would reduce church lands by 90%, or to a maximum 100 hold per church. No compensation was made for lands taken, except for those of the bishops, who subsequently received the salary of a Government minister (*Protestantischen Kirchen*, 1939-1950, p. 12). The churches became financially unable to maintain their schools and other obligations. Church taxes were no longer obligatory, so some congregations initiated free-will offerings. The Government provided temporary subsidies to enable some confessional schools to continue. A reporter urged that the churches be purged of collaborators and former Nazi govern-

---

* 1 hold equals 11.422 acres.

ment leaders so the whole church would not be attacked for their sins. Following the disillusionment of the people and the flight of 30% of the clergy, there was a general decline in the religious life of the people (*ICPIS*, No. 32, September, 1945).

September, 1945—

Though deportation without trial continued, people found themselves much better treated than they had expected; life and worship were possible. Baptist pastors stated, "Free church in a free state. What did the churches have to criticize? They had other things to do" (*Protestantischen Kirchen*, 1939-1950, p. 12).

September 23, 1945—

Catholic Bishop Mindszenty in a published article called Catholics to stand by the Church, the home, the family and the human person, to work for intensified evangelism, education and welfare (*Four Years' Struggle of the Church in Hungary*, Mindszenty, p. 24). He urged Catholic farmers not to accept lands confiscated from the Church.

September, 1945—

The Pope nominated Bishop Mindszenty as Archbishop (*N. Y. Times*, Sept. 25, 5:6). According to Roman Catholic sources, when sometime later he was to go to Rome to be invested as Cardinal, he was able to overcome Russian obstructions through the help of the American Military Mission. After his investiture Mindszenty paid courtesy calls on the leaders of the Protestant Churches.

October, 1945—

In preparation for the November elections, the Communist Party declared its intent to maintain friendly relations with the churches, and not to change the status of religious organizations. Additional support was granted to several churches for rebuilding purposes.

October, 1945—

In his first pastoral letter as Catholic Archbishop of Hungary, Mindszenty defined the ideals of democracy as freedom of conscience, the right of parents to educate their children, the right of working men to self-deter-

mination. He added that he had been patient with the present Government's excesses for many months, but that in view of coming elections he must clarify where the Government was democratic and where not. He accused the Government of being "one totalitarian dictatorship" after another, condemned the new marriage law as frivolous, condemned the agrarian reform as seeking the annihilation of one class and resulting in civil strife and hatred, condemned the Government for lawlessness and the wave of fear, and called on Catholics to work for candidates who championed morality, law, truth and order (*Four Years' Struggle of the Church in Hungary*, Mindszenty, p. 26 ff.). Conservative Protestants were prepared to join him. The Lutheran Pastors' Association urged the Lutheran bishops to issue a similar letter. *Elat 'es Jovo* called for courageous prophets to counteract the Government's methods (*Protestantischen Kirchen*, 1939-1950, p. 13). Leftist groups retaliated by attacking Archbishop Mindszenty as a reactionary interfering in politics, and warned other church leaders not to follow his example as it would only lead to catastrophe (*N. Y. Times*, Nov. 4:30: 4; 6:1:4). Whereupon a number of political parties in the "National Front" published a declaration in his defense (*Four Years' Struggle of the Church in Hungary*, Mindszenty, p. 37). The defeated Communist Party in the subsequent election charged that this was a Fascist underground conspiracy, and blamed Archbishop Mindszenty for their defeat (*Ibid.*, p. 46).

November 4, 1945—

The moderately Socialist Small Landholders' Party received a majority in the national elections. The Party promised, if elected, to divide large estates into small homesteads. The Red Army Command specified that the Communist Party should direct the Ministry of Interior which was under Lazlo Rajk (Ebon, *World Communism Today*, p. 82).

November 10, 1945—

Reformed Bishop Laszlo Ravasz called for "the removal (from church office) of all those (leaders) who were too intimately interwoven with the political life of the times past . . .

either voluntarily or involuntarily."
And later . . . "the Church cannot
become the illegal political party of
reaction" (*Five Years of Hungarian
Protestantism, 1945-1950*, pp. 18, 19).

November, 1945—

Finding the Church falling too
quickly back into pre-war patterns
and rigid ways, a group of Reformed
pastors led by Bereczky began the
weekly paper, *Hungarian Reformed
Awakening* (*Ibid.*, p. 19).

December, 1945—

According to evidence later introduced at his trial, Archbishop Mindszenty addressed a letter to Pres. Tildy
protesting the proposed dis-establish-
ment of the monarchial system (*Trial
of J. Mindszenty*, Hungarian State
Publishing House, Budapest, 1949, p.
69).

January, 1946—

The Government assumed responsibility for the support of many confessional schools. It further offered to
give additional subsidies in financial
difficulties. An attempt to interfere
in church autonomy was repulsed.
There was growing sentiment among
churchmen for a separation of Church
and State (*ICPIS*, No. 4, January,
1946).

February, 1946—

A demonstration was organized in
Budapest in opposition to Archbishop
Mindszenty's condemnation of the
agrarian reform (*N. Y. Times*, February 18:5:6).

February 16, 1946—

Magyar Kurir carried an article denying charges that Mindszenty had
been a member of the Nazi "Arrow-
Cross" (*Four Years' Struggle of the
Church in Hungary*, Mindszenty, p.
51).

April, 1946—

Soviet occupation authorities refused to grant (American) National
Catholic Welfare Conference clearance
for food shipments for Hungarian
groups (*N. Y. Times*, April 17:18:5).
In 1945 much of the harvest was tak-
en by Russian occupation troops, and
the Government had turned to the

West for aid, re-establishing friendly
relations, particularly through Protestant church contacts.

May, 1946—

The Government announced the un-
covering of a Fascist anti-Government
plot, the leader of whom was identified as a Catholic monk. Other
"plots" against the Red Army were
discovered (*N. Y. Times*, May 5:38:4),
usually involving some Catholic leader. A week later Roman Catholic
Bishop Coll forbade Catholic priests
to participate in political activities
(*Ibid.*, May 12:25:4).

May 20, 1946—

In a pastoral letter, Cardinal Mindszenty stated that parents and their
Church have a prior right over the
State in the education of their children, and that to fulfill this right
and God-given responsibility the
churches must have schools and compulsory religious education. He demanded that State subsidies be provided for the schools as a "right"
(*Four Years' Struggle of the Church
in Hungary*, Mindszenty, 55 ff. Appendix I).

June 20, 1946—

Cardinal Mindszenty protested to
the Prime Minister when the traditional Corpus Christi Procession was
not permitted (*Ibid.*, pp. 68, 69).

July, 1946—

According to Catholic sources of information, the Soviet authorities ordered the Hungarian Government to
suppress Catholic youth organizations
(*N. Y. Times*, July 8:5:5).

July, 1946—

The Hungarian Ecumenical Youth
Committee issued a statement of protest and appeal to the nations to take
a responsible attitude to the little
people who "cannot even complain effectively," warned that great future
catastrophies might be expected unless post-war anarchy, isolation, propaganda, and inadequate education
could be treated on a spiritual basis.

July, 1946—

The Government's Bill 7330 placed
all religious associations under the
Ministry of the Interior, in accord-

ance with a law dating from 1938 which empowered the Government to disband questionable organizations (*Communism and the Churches*, Barron and Waddams, p. 62). The Hungarian Government yielded to Soviet demands that certain Catholic opposition groups denounced by Russian Lt. Gen. Sviridov should be disbanded. The Catholic bishops sent a letter of protest to the Prime Minister asking that thorough investigations be made, in keeping with the law, before any associations were dissolved (*Four Years' Struggle of the Church in Hungary*, Mindszenty, p. 65). The Government appealed to the clergy to cease from anti-Soviet propaganda (*N. Y. Times*, July 20:9:5).

August, 1946—

Mindszenty's unanswered appeal to Premier Nagy for a general amnesty for political prisoners, including numbers of priests, many without trial, met with strong protests from the Leftist press (*N. Y. Times*, Aug. 2: 2:8).

August, 1946—

Protestant leaders in Budapest participated in the R. C. procession celebrating the feast of King Stefan (*Communist War on Religion*, MacEoin, p. 124).

At an unofficial Reformed Church gathering, the "Free Council of the Reformed Church" was created and approval was given to the Government's land reform program. An appeal was made that anti-Semitism be overcome, that the expulsion of Hungarians from Czechoslovakia be stopped, and that the Free Churches be granted equal rights (*ICPIS*, No. 31, September, 1946, and *Five Years of Hungarian Protestantism*, Hungarian Church Press, p. 19).

September, 1946—

The Hungarian Reformed General Convention addressed appeals to the Paris Peace Conference and other governmental and ecclesiastical authorities to preserve the confessional rights of Hungarian minorities outside Hungary proper ("Petition to Peace Conference," Budapest, September 10 ,1946).

September 6, 1946—

The Catholic Board of Bishops published a declaration that without ex-

ception they supported Mindszenty, and called on the people not to believe slanderous rumors concerning him or the unity of the bishops (*Four Years' Struggle of the Church in Hungary*, Mindszenty, p. 76). Mindszenty threatened Church retaliation if the Government maintained its ban on Catholic youth groups (*N. Y. Times*, September 6:8:5).

September, 1946—

The Reformed "Free Council" stated: "a faithful Christian cannot belong to the reaction." Whereupon a Lutheran bishop recommended a loosening of ties with the Reformed Church, and a strengthening of ties with the Catholics (*Protestantischen Kirchen*, 1939-1950, p. 13).

October, 1946—

President Tildy, one-time Reformed Church pastor, in a message addressed to world Christianity, stated: "The Church should lead civilization in new developments."

Some confessional schools were not able to begin the Fall term owing to church financial difficulties following the land reform. The Government assisted the churches by providing the salaries of bishops and many clergy. It further undertook to rebuild one destroyed cathedral for each major confessional body. The churches enlarged their social welfare programs. The Government recognized the Free Churches as churches, rather than associations, and their liaison with the Government was transferred from the Ministry of Interior to the Ministry of Cults.

November, 1946—

The President of the Reformed Church's Commission on Foreign Affairs stated that the Reformed Church stood for social reform, justice, and individual freedom. A month later the Reformed Churches proclaimed Hungary as the bridge between the East and the West (*ICPIS*, No. 33, September, 1944, December, 1946).

R. C. Bishop Romua was taken into custody by Soviet authorities (*N. Y. Times*, November 12:5:5).

November 6, 1946—

Magyar Kurir printed a protest of the National Association of Catholic

Parents against the Government's proposed monopolizing the printing of textbooks (*Four Years' Struggle of the Church in Hungary*, Mindszenty, p. 81).

December 31, 1946—

The Communist-controlled Interior Ministry announced that the Small Landholders' Party (which, as the majority party, was supposed to direct the Government) had conspired to overthrow the Government. Many Government leaders were arrested (Ebon, *World Communism Today*, p. 83).

January, 1947—

The Communist Party accused the Roman Catholic Church of plotting against the Government, and stated that the secretary to the Bishop of Szekestehervar had organized conspiratorial cells throughout the country (*N. Y. Times*, January 14; 15:1).

February, 1947—

With the signing of the Peace Treaty in Paris, the Control Commission of the Allied Powers left the country, with the exception of Russia which was responsible for disarmament (Appendix II).

March 12, 1947—

Right and Left wing political parties of the coalition Government agreed to introduce a bill which would make (formerly compulsory) religious education in the schools optional. The Small Landholders' Party, which claimed to be most friendly towards the churches, in introducing the bill pointed out that similar practices were current in Western countries. The Roman Catholic bishops stated that they could not agree to such a bill outside the framework of a total agreement (*Four Years' Struggle of the Church in Hungary*, Mindszenty, p. 95). Mindszenty threatened to excommunicate any Catholic members of Parliament if a bill to end compulsory religious education should be approved. Following a general protest against the bill, the bill was defeated (*N. Y. Times*, March 13:8:1; April 10:12:4 and *Communism and the Churches*, Barron and Waddams, p. 63). The Communist Party then stated that the Small Landholders' Party had introduced the bill only to

make the Communist Party hated, and added that the Communist Party had had nothing to do with it.

March 24, 1947—

Budapest Catholic Churches held a week's evangelistic mission which drew unexpectedly large crowds (*Four Years' Struggle of the Church in Hungary*, Mindszenty, p. 100).

March 26, 1947—

Addressing the Second Assembly of the Free Council of the Reformed Church, Rev. A. Bereczky stated that it was no longer a question as to whether church and state should be separated, but when and how. He recommended gradual separation over a period of ten to fifteen years, beginning with discontinuing tax support, following with liberty of conscience in matters of religious instruction in the schools, as opposed to compulsory religious education, and later questions of land reform and changes in education to be decided in relation to the spiritual mission of the Church.

He expressed regret that the Church had not, at the outset of the new Government, commended the land-reform and industrial justice (*Five Years of Hungarian Protestantism*, 1945-1950, p. 20) and called for the Church's recognition of the new Government (*Protestantischen Kirchen*, 1939-1950, p. 13).

May 7, 1947—

The Synod of the Reformed Church passed a resolution calling on Christians to "Offer their lives in the service of a radical and firm social and economic program," commended the separation of church and state and recognized the Hungarian Republic (*Five Years of Hungarian Protestantism*, 1945-1950, p. 21; *Protestantischen Kirchen*, 1939-1950, Encl. 30; Appendix III).

May 20, 1947—

Reformed layman Ferenc Nagy was replaced as Prime Minister by Soviet-nominated Lajos Dinnyes (*Four Years' Struggle of the Church in Hungary*, Mindszenty, p. 102).

July 25, 1947—

The Board of Bishops advised Catholics to vote in the Aug. elections for candidates who were conscious of their duty, respected human rights, and were devoted to their faith in God, church and country. In a stronger statement issued August 3, they advised Catholics not to vote for movements of "new oppression, despotism, and violation of law" (*Ibid.*, p. 106).

August, 1947—

Mindszenty, on behalf of the bishops, accused the Government of barring many Catholics from voting in the August elections by putting them under police supervision because of "immoral conduct," and urged the Government to cease its abuse of Catholic Church rights (*N. Y. Times*, August 20:10:6).

September, 1947—

After a visit to Moscow, Orthodox Archpriest Varju was appointed administrator of Russian churches in Hungary (A priests' training center had been established by the Hungarian Government and the Orthodox diocese in 1943. *EPS*, No. 42, November, 1947).

October 2, 1947—

After sending a letter of protest to the Prime Minister, Mindszenty sent a pastoral letter calling on Catholics to stop the expulsion of Hungarians of German origin (*Four Years' Struggle of the Church in Hungary*, Mindszenty, p. 116).

October 31, 1947—

Following the approval of Law 33, terminating the distinction between "introduced" and "recognized" confessions, the Methodist Church was included among "recognized" confessions (*Protestantischen Kirchen*, 1939-1950, p. 23).

November, 1947—

At the dedication of a Lutheran village church, rebuilt in part by Communist subsidies, Bishop Ordass and others spoke favorably of the cooperation of the Church, Communists, laborers and the poor in building the church (*EPS*, No. 43, December, 1947).

November 12, 1947—

Archbishop Mindszenty in a pastoral letter announced his refusal to comply with Bill 16 T.C., which would require all printed matter or form letters to be approved by the Government before circulation. "We are compelled to descend into the catacombs . . . we shall henceforth speak less frequently and only briefly."

He denounced the Government's textbook entitled *Life of Man* and forbade Catholic parents and teachers to use it (*Four Years' Struggle of the Church in Hungary*, Mindszenty, p. 122 ff.).

December, 1947—

President Tildy warned the churches against interfering in economic reforms (*N. Y. Times*, Dec. 25:14:7).

January, 1948—

A Government spokesman reported that Archbishop Mindszenty rejected all communications from President Tildy (*N. Y. Times*, January 10:4:5).

January 11, 1948—

Addressing the National Congress of the Communist Party, Matyas Rakosi stated: "The task of our Party this year is to settle the relationship between the Church and the Republic. It cannot be tolerated that the majority of the enemies of the people should hide in the shadow of the Churches, especially the Catholic Church" (*News Behind the Iron Curtain*, February, 1953, p. 18).

January, 1948—

The Government temporarily suspended radio broadcasts of Protestant religious services after the churches refused to submit their programs and sermons to Government censorship in advance. A partial compromise was later reached whereby the senior church authority would be personally responsible for the broadcasts. When the Government could no longer accept the arrangement, Lutheran Bishop Ordass declared in a sermon that the Government, following the Nazi pattern, had sought to censor the churches' radio programs, but that this had proved impossible, and the programs would therefore be cancelled.

January 14, 1948—

After Lutheran bishops protested against the censorship of press and radio, the State monopolization of schoolbooks, the use of Christian symbols for propaganda (*Protestantischen Kirchen*, 1939-1950, p. 14), the pastors' convention requested the Church authorities to clarify relations between Church and State (*Ibid.*, Enclos. 31).

February 23, 1948—

Minister of Religion and Education Ortutay, addressing the National Assembly, praised the Catholic Church for its contribution in the educational developments of the country, and asserted that the Hungarian democracy did not wish to deprive the denominations of their schools (*Four Years' Struggle of the Church in Hungary*, p. 141). Lutheran layman Reök, delegate in the house of deputies, asserted that there could be no conflict between the Church and State (*Protestantischen Kirchen*, 1939-1950, Encl. 32).

February, 1948—

The Catholic journal, *Magyar Kurir*, charged that Mindszenty's speech on February 15 was falsely interpreted and quoted by the local press to make him appear unpatriotic and opposed to peace (*Four Years' Struggle of the Church in Hungary*, Mindszenty, p. 130).

March 7, 1948—

The Government again invited the Reformed Church to collaborate with the Government in its social program, and to receive Government subsidies.

The Government indicated its willingness to pay pastors' subsidies retroactively to August 1, 1947, to those whose income from local sources was under 20% of their total income (*Protestantischen Kirchen*, 1939-1950, p. 12).

March 17-18, 1948—

E. Mihalyfi, an Evangelical pastor's son and chief of the President's Cabinet, in a speech to the Association of Lutheran Pastors during Lutheran Ordass' absence abroad, indicated that the Government desired to clarify its relationship with the Lutheran Church, and expected Lutheran co-operation. He attacked the leaders of the Church and urged the pastors to elect new men who sympathized with the new order in the People's Democracy.

The Lutheran Church had been put in an increasingly difficult position by its early sympathy toward the Roman Catholic position, and the fact that Mindszenty was being driven by his advisors to an extreme "overthrow the Government" position. Deszéry, who established his own journal after the official Lutheran journal refused to publish his writings, and his followers sought to swing the Church away from ties with the Catholics and their position, and towards that of the Reformed Free Council.

On his installation as Lutheran Bishop (successor to Kuthys), Szabos stated, "Those who speak of church persecution in Hungary are mistaken or intend to mislead others." Mr. Mihalyfi, representing the Government at the installation, spoke as he had at the "Pastors' Association's" meeting. Bishop Ordass answered the accusations against Lutheran leaders, pointing out that even under Nazi occupation the Church had guarded her administrative independence, but that the Church would be willing to discuss relations with the Government on equal terms.

March 19, 1948—

Minister of Education Gyula Ortutay proposed a 4-point program for elimination of religious influence in church schools including the nationalization of church schools (*News Behind the Iron Curtain*, February, 1953, p. 19).

March 20, 1948—

At the centenary celebrations of the Hungarian War for Independence, and in the presence of Hungarian President Tildy, Minister of Religions Ortutay, and others, Lutheran Bishop Ordass stated, "We . . . desire a regulation of the regretable tension . . . between Church and State. Our conditions are unhindered freedom of faith, free exercise of religion, maintenance of our schools, religious education of youth in Church and State schools, assurance of freedom for youth work outside the school, and assurance of freedom for welfare and social work." Another statement which had been prepared by Dr. Reök indicating that the Church was entirely happy with the Government's position towards the Church was not read (*Protestantischen Kirchen*, 1939-1950, Encl. 36). In a press interview, Ordass stated that the Church had no complaints against the State, but expressed regret at the "local character" of obstructions to social welfare work, youth work, extra curricular religious instruction, and restrictions on Good Friday religious celebrations at a time when relations were otherwise improving (*Ibid.*). The Hungarian press published Ordass' statement as an example of the position of the reactionaries, and the friendly statements of Bishop Szabo (above) and Béla Kapi as reality.

At the same time, the association of Lutheran pastors urged church leaders not to allow discord to grow among the pastors, and asked that desires of younger churchmen for reform be considered (*Protestantischen Kirchen*, 1939-1950, p. 15).

Imre Veöreös, in *Uj Harangszo*, April 25, noted many Lutherans' concern "that our church leadership is adopting a different (friendly) tone with the State," and gave the desire for improving relationships as the reason (*Ibid.*, Encl. 37). He criticized those in the Church who emphasized "by all means say no clear word," and called for clarity and understanding in stating the Church's dialectic position (*Ibid.*, Encl. 38).

April 2, 1948—

The largest Catholic printing establishment was nationalized. Many Catholic leaders and associations protested (*Four Years' Struggle of the Church in Hungary*, Mindszenty, p. 132).

April 5, 1948—

Following a visit of the Senior Bishop of the Lutheran Church to the Ministry of Cultural and Religious Affairs to express the willingness of the Church to discuss Church-State relations, Dr. Reök indicated to church leaders that the Government expected a declaration from the Church expressing its agreement with the agrarian reform, the nationalization of industries, banks, etc., and warned that the Church might otherwise suffer persecution.

When Lutheran Church leaders asked Deputy Prime Minister Rakosi about Reök's demands, he replied that Reök had promised such a statement, that the leaders of the Church should have been ready to adjust to new po-litical developments, and advised them to elect new leaders, to give up, voluntarily, schools, institutions, welfare and social work, and the privilege of compulsory religious education.

April 10, 1948—

The Reformed Church Synodical Council considered a series of proposals on Government relations. The Council

(1) stated its readiness to cooperate with the Government insofar as such action was in keeping with the spirit of Jesus Christ;

(2) acclaimed the provisions the Government had made for the equality of religions;

(3) recognized the Hungarian Republic as Hungary's legal Government (after many earlier invitations to do so were unanswered);

(4) approved the agrarian reform and the nationalization of industry as being in the interests of social justice and consistent with the Holy Scriptures;

(5) stated its readiness to discuss Church-State relations with the Government;

(6) asserted its conviction that the Church's liberty to preach, teach, and carry out missionary and charitable activities and self-government would be safeguarded;

(7) proclaimed the solidarity of the Reformed Church with the Hungarian people;

(8) demanded the right of performing works of mercy among the oppressed without being accused of, or turned to political strategems;

(9) warned the people to seek peace, and not to follow after specious slogans and promises;

(10) exhorted its members to work diligently and to press forward (*EPS*, June 4, 1948).

The proposals were accepted on April 30, after the resignation of Bishop Ravasz on April 28 (*Protestantischen Kirchen*, 1939-1950, Encl. 40; Appendix IV).

Bishop Ravasz had resisted pressure to resign for some time, finally resigned, according to one source, in protest against pressure to make the Reformed Church into a political tool of the Government. According to another source, he resigned only after the Government had threatened first to condemn him for relationships to former regimes, then to deport his family, and finally Rakosi himself threatened to cut off the salaries of all Reformed teachers (Markham, *Communists Crush Churches in Eastern Europe*, p. 87). At the same time he resigned as Bishop of his diocese, declaring that as one of the world past he hadn't the "Pentecost ecstasy of a hot, passionate, trustful, juvenile and victorious regeneration" necessary for the tasks before the Church (*Five Years of Hungarian Protestantism*, 1945-1950, p. 22).

April 22, 1948—

Bishop Béla Kapi, Senior Bishop of the Lutheran Church, resigned as President of the Church's Executive Council. Bishop Turoczy, next in line for the office, refused to accept the position, and it fell to Bishop Ordass. The Church again expressed its willingness to discuss Church-State problems with the Government, adding that the Church must have freedom to preach, to give religious instruction, to operate its schools and institutions, to organize its various groups and activities and to print.

April, 1948—

Lutheran Bishop L. Ordass indicated that the Central European Lutheran Convention could not be held in Hungary in June as planned (*LWF Newsbulletin*, May 1, 1950).

May 1, 1948—

The Communist paper, *Népszava*, announced that the church directed 1674 of 2650 elementary schools, 2895 of 4847 secondary, 108 of 368 middle, and 94 of 179 gymnasia, taught 666,-836 of 1,155,216 pupils. The Peasant Party announced (May 11) its belief in the mission of the church, in cooperation between Church and State, and the Peasant Party's intent to "press back the reactionary forces which have collected around the church. Therefore it finds the nationalization and unified democratic establishment of schools correct" (*Protestantischen Kirchen*, 1939-1950, Encl. 35).

May 11, 1948—

Mindszenty threatened to excommunicate any Catholics supporting the nationalization of church schools, forbade teachers to participate in conferences on the subject organized by the Government (*Protestantischen Kirchen*, 1939-1950, p. 16). In a pastoral letter he condemned the proposal as endangering the right of parents to education their children. The Pope called on faithful Hungarian Catholics to continue their fight against "the Government's anti-church policy" (*Four Years' Struggle of the Church in Hungary*, Mindszenty, p. 136; *N. Y. Times*, May 16:31:5; 17:4:7; 24:9:2; 31:6:2).

May, 1948—

Leaders of various movements in the Student Christian Association adopted a resolution condemning the Church for its adherence to the class system and to earthly power, and asserted that Christian youth should collaborate with "democratic, progressive youth" to eliminate social injustice and reconstruct the country.
A similar alleged declaration from Catholic students of Pápa was denied by the students (*Four Years' Struggle of the Church in Hungary*, Mindszenty, p. 151).

May, 1948—

Clergy were asked to make formal declarations of loyalty to the Government.

May 14, 1948—

The Government appointed a committee in the Ministry of Cults to study the nationalization of education.

May 15-16, 1948—

Minister of Cults Ortutay, in a conference with Protestant school representatives, announced that legislation was pending which would nationalize the educational system, combine confessional schools (*Protestantischen Kirchen*, 1939-1950, p. 16). According to one Catholic priest, the Government had proposed joint Church-State editing of school books earlier in the year, but the Roman Catholic Church had refused to collaborate (*State and Church in Hungary*, Hungarian News and Information Service, October, 1950). The Minister of Cults stated that the Nationalization of schools could not be used to attack freedom of religion. He stated that the purpose would be to provide better educational facilities and to help many confessional schools which had appealed for help. He promised that after nationalization, religious education would be obligatory, that church schools, historic centers of education, and church colleges would have special consideration (*Protestantischen Kirchen*, 1939-1950, p. 16 and Encl. 35).

May 19, 1948—

In reply to Minister Ortutay's invitation of May 9 to enter into negotiations for a Catholic concordat, Mindszenty stated that the Bishops were ready to discuss an agreement on certain conditions:

(1) that the proposed nationalization of schools should first be abandoned;

(2) that the dissolved Catholic associations should be re-established, with their property;

(3) that a Catholic daily journal (there had been 16) could be issued without restrictions.

On several occasions the Government sought to establish a "National (Catholic) Church" liberated from Rome. A few leaders wished to accede, but Mindszenty was adamantly opposed.

May, 1948—

Vice-Premier Rakosi stated that the time had come "to purge the educational system of reactionary elements, (and) to stop the intolerable situation where the core of the enemies of the Hungarian people hides behind the church, and first and foremost the Catholic Church" (*The London Times*, May 22, 1948).

May 23, 1948—

In a pastoral letter, Cardinal Mindszenty called on all Catholics to stand by the Church and oppose nationalization (*Four Years' Struggle of the Church in Hungary*, Mindszenty, p. 140 ff.).

May 29, 1948—

In a pastoral letter, Cardinal Mindszenty denied that prevalent rumors and publicized statements were true, namely:

(1) that the Bishops fail to agree among themselves;

(2) that local priests oppose the bishops and do not read pastoral letters;

(3) that where pastoral letters are read, they are interrupted by shouts of protest from the congregations;

(4) that teachers desire the nationalization of the schools;

(5) that the only step blocking national prosperity is the nationalization of schools;

(6) that the Church and Government have begun negotiations for a concordat (*Four Years' Struggle of the Church in Hungary*, Mindszenty, p. 148 ff.).

June 6, 1948—

Lutheran Veöreös wrote (*Uj Harangszo*) that while the Lutheran Church did not wish to give up its schools, "if the legislation . . . takes them from us, we bow before it. . . . The boundary line (of martyrdom) is not the school question" (*Protestantischen Kirchen*, 1939-1950, Encl. 42).

June, 1948—

Cardinal Mindszenty accused the Hungarian Government of being the worst in history, and denied that there was any rapprochement between the Catholic Church and the Government. He forbade Catholics to read Government publications or to listen to Government broadcasts (*N.Y. Times*, 7:1:6).

June 7, 1948—

Following a number of protests against nationalization in the provinces, and an attack on the police station of one village, Minister Ortutay addressed a letter to Cardinal Mindszenty demanding that these anti-Government demonstrations be stopped.

June 10, 1948—

Cardinal Mindszenty and the Board of Bishops replied by protesting the nationalization and demanding that the proposed order be rescinded.

June 12, 1948—

Cardinal Mindszenty warned by pastoral letter that anyone contributing to laws which would infringe on the rights of the Church would be excommunicated (*Communism and the Churches*, Barron and Waddams, p. 65). The Cabinet approved the bill nationalizing schools (Appendix IV; *N. Y. Times*, 12:16:7). Additional protests and riots broke out in other villages, and a Catholic priest was held for organizing a demonstration in Budapest. Priest Asztalos and five villagers who led the attack against the Pocspetri police station in which a policeman was shot, were sentenced to death. Rev. Asztalos plead guilty and claimed that the riot had been instigated by higher authorities. President Tildy commuted Asztalos' sentence to life imprisonment. The others were hanged (*N. Y. Times*, 11:15: 4; 12:16:7; 13:30:1).

June 13, 1948—

Deputy Premier Rakosi warned the Catholic Church against opposing the Government, and to make an early pact with the Government. "Anyone who opposes the democratic laws of the country will be smashed by the fist of democracy" (*London Times*, June 14, 1948).

June 13, 1948—

Lutheran Bishops in a pastoral letter mentioned that teachers and parents had been forced to vote for nationalization, that the Government would apparently nationalize schools regardless of the Church's position, that the Government and Church were discussing a contract which would provide for obligatory religious education, freedom to preach and carry out welfare work, financial subsidies on a diminishing scale, pensions for retired religious workers, assimilation of church-employed teachers in the State program. The letter assured the people that a conventus and synod were being called to decide the matter and asked the congregations to discuss it and inform the church leaders. The Synod appointed Bishop Kuthy chairman of the schools commission. The Association of Pastors requested the Government not to nationalize the schools (*Die Protestantischen Kirchen*, 1939-1950, p. 17).

June 14, 1948—

A special session of the Lutheran General Conference was called and protested against any attempts to nationalize church schools, after Hungarian President Tildy had called the bishops together urging them to come to an immediate, peaceful settlement with the Government on the school question.

June 14, 1948—

Cardinal Mindszenty, in a pastoral letter, ordered that special masses be held and church bells be tolled on June 18 in protest against the nationalization and actions against the anti-nationalization demonstrators. The following day one hundred Catholics were held for demonstrating in Budapest (*N. Y. Times*, 14:15:5; 15:23:5).

June 14, 1948—

The Reformed Synod, while upholding the right of the Church to maintain and establish schools, counselled autonomous bodies responsible for the schools "to proceed quietly and intelligently in the interest of peace," inasmuch as it seemed to be the firm intent of the Government to nationalize the schools (*Protestantischen Kirchen*, 1939-1950, Encl. 45).

June 14, 1948—

The National Synod of the Reformed Church approved the draft of the agreement between the Reformed Church and the State (Adopted October 7; *Five Years of Hungarian Protestantism*, 1945-1950, p. 23; Appendix V).

June 16, 1948—

The Hungarian Parliament approved the bill nationalizing confessional and private schools and all hostels and kindergartens related to them. Buildings, equipment, and funds became the property of the State, though exceptions might be granted by the Minister of Public Instruction. Institutions serving exclusively church purposes, e.g., theological colleges, were exempted. From July 1, 1948, all teachers would be State employees. No new schools could be established without specific approval of the Cabinet. The State was to be responsible for supervision of the schools and for preparation of new textbooks. Religious instruction would remain in the hands of the clergy (*Communism and the Churches*, Barron and Waddams, p. 64).

June 16, 1948—

In reply to Minister Ortutay's repeated invitation to discuss an agreement, Catholic Cardinal Mindszenty stated that the nationalization of schools would have to be rescinded first (*Four Years' Struggle of the Church in Hungary*, Mindszenty, p. 155).

June 19, 1948—

Bishop Kovacs, in a pastoral letter, stated that Catholic teachers themselves must decide whether they could continue to teach under the new system. A month later, Vatican sources reported that 600 teachers had been ousted for their opposition to the nationalization (*N. Y. Times*, June 19:4:8; July 18:17:4).

June 25, 1948—

Catholic deputies who supported the nationalization program were ordered to be excommunicated; Mindszenty enforced the order on certain leaders (*N. Y. Times*, 25:19:3).

June 29, 1948—

The Government forbade Mindszenty to speak against nationalization, and threatened the arrest of his followers; Mindszenty excommunicated all Roman Catholics who approved the nationalization program.

July, 1948—

Cardinal Mindszenty instructed Catholic priests to refrain from teaching in Government schools, and advised teachers and nurses (priests and nuns) to leave Hungary unless their presence was essential to the life of small communities (*Communism and the Churches*, Barron and Waddams, p. 66).

July 3, 1948—

The Government arrested 5 Roman Catholic priests on charges of being connected with an alleged Vatican-U. S. plot against the Government. The Communist press accused the Church of using its clergy as agents to distribute funds to support anti-Government activities, and to incite peasants against the Government (*N. Y. Times*, 3:2:2).

July 12, 1948—

The director of the Roman Catholic "Catholic Action" and others were mentioned in charges against three priests detained for "agitating against the Government" (*N. Y. Times*, 12:10:4).

July 14, 1948—

Catholic Church radio services from Rome were reported jammed by Government-controlled interference (*N. Y. Times*, 14:19:3).

July 16, 1948—

After two months' indecision and struggle, the Reformed Church elected Albert Bereczky bishop to succeed Bishop Ravasz (*Five Years of Hungarian Protestantism*, 1945-1950, p. 23).

July, 1948—

In the Reformed Church a central "missionary work group" was formed to coordinate and stimulate the evangelistic impact of 13 departments: Sunday Schools, Youth, Women, Evangelism, *Gemeinde-Aufbau*, Social Ministry, Diaconate, Jewish Mission, Foreign Missions, Pastors, Presbyters, Press, Extra-School Education. Evangelistic campaigns were held in the villages, largely by laymen.

July 24, 1948—

A People's Court sentenced Roman Catholic Canon Mihalovitch and others to serve jail terms (*N. Y. Times*, 24:5:4).

July 30, 1948—

President Tildy (a Reformed Minister) resigned after accusations were made against his son-in-law (*Information Service*, FCCC, March 19, 1949).

August 1, 1948—

In a pastoral letter Mindszenty called on Catholic families to receive into their homes and occupations the 4,500 Catholic instructors whom he expected to give up teaching. 600 had already been ousted or resigned (*Four Years' Struggle of the Church in Hungary*, Mindszenty, p. 160).

August, 1948—

During the year loudspeakers were banned for church use and processions and pilgrimages forbidden (*The Communist War on Religion*, MacEoin, p. 125).

August 12, 1948—

The Government advised the Lutheran Church to nominate another representative to the World Council of

Churches' Assembly in Amsterdam since Bishop Ordass would not receive a passport. The Church leaders decided not to nominate another delegate, but to make a new application for Bishop Ordass.

August 14-27, 1948—

A number of prominent Lutheran leaders were arrested and their offices searched. Among them were the lay president, A. Radvansky, and the General Secretary, S. Varga. Bishop Ordass, after police questioning, was told to consider himself under house arrest.

August 29, 1948—

Propaganda Minister Mihalyfi, in a speech in the town where his father was pastor, attacked the "reactionary" leaders of the Lutheran Church, and spoke of alleged infringement of currency regulations and activities against peace and democracy. He proposed that a "Democratic" Synod be called to lead the Church and work out relations with the Government.

August 30, 1948—

Representatives of the Lutheran Church, in a meeting with Government representatives, presented the resignations of almost all lay leaders of the Church and of Pastor Varga, General Secretary. Bishop Ordass refused to resign. Rakosi gave orders that he would consider the matter 8 days, during which time the Bishop was to be free.

September 1, 1948—

In a pastoral letter, Cardinal Mindszenty appealed to Christian families to give their children religious training in the home (*Fours Years' Struggle of the Church in Hungary*, Mindszenty, p. 163).

September, 1948—

Propaganda Minister Mihalyfi, at a meeting of Lutheran politicians and churchmen which he had called to discuss Church-State relations, accused Bishop Berggrav (Norway) of advising the Hungarian Lutheran Church to resist Communism in the same way as Nazism (LWF *Newsbulletin*, May 1, 1950). Mihalyfi urged dissatisfied Lutherans to form an "action committee" to visit Lutheran leaders and ask their resignations. The committee visited Ordass, but he again refused to resign.

September 4, 1948—

In reply to an enquiry from Lutheran World Federation, Geneva, Prime Minister Dinnyes stated that Ordass was free.

September 6, 1948—

The Central Committee of the World Council of Churches addressed a letter expressing solidarity with the Hungarian Lutheran Church and labeled the arrest of Bishop Ordass an "attack on the freedom of the Church." In another letter addressed to the Prime Minister, the Central Committee stated that Bishop Ordass had the full support of the World Council of Churches, and demanded his release without delay.

September 10, 1948—

The Government announced that Lutheran Bishop Ordass, General Inspector Radvansky and General Secretary Varga were arrested on charges of illegal currency dealings with the Lutheran World Federation, involving the importation of funds for the Church. Leaders abroad and Ordass pointed out that all transfers came via the National Bank. A bishop appealed for prayers from churches abroad saying the Church was ready for martyrdom though not seeking it (Lutheran World Federation *Newsbulletin*, May 1, 1950). Retired Bishop Kuthy was called to serve as acting Secretary of the Church.

September 10, 1948—

In an "Open Letter," Lutheran student-Pastor Dezséry called for a change to younger church leadership, for cooperation with the Government, closer ties with younger leaders in the Reformed Church, and withdrawal from Catholic ties. In December he received permission to publish a weekly, *Evangélikus Elet*. Three leading Lutheran laymen resigned their offices. Both Lutheran periodicals were suspended until December and Veöreös was instructed "to inform the people . . . in compliance with the official ecclesiastical viewpoint." In October Bishop Kapi retired, in December Bishop Turoczy became Bishop of Transdanubia and was succeeded by laborer-pastor Vetö; Inspector Radvansky was replaced by layman Mady, later by Reök (*Protestantischen Kirchen in Ungarn*, 1939-1950, p. 18 a, Encl. 49).

September 17, 1948—

In a reply to the Central Committee of the World Council of Churches, Hungarian Council President Lajos Dinnyes asserted that Ordass' detention was because of illegal currency activities and had nothing to do with his religious position.

September, 1948—

Catholic circles reported that obstruction had been put in the way of holding a number of traditional and religious festivals (*Four Years' Struggle of the Church in Hungary*, Mindszenty, p. 164 ff.).

September 29 to October 1, 1948—

Lutheran Bishop Ordass was sentenced by a "Working Man's Jury" to two years' imprisonment, five years' loss of office and civil rights, and was fined for alleged illegal traffic in foreign currencies. Lutheran leaders were reported to have expected much more severe persecution.

October 7, 1948—

An agreement was concluded between the Government and the Reformed Church. The Church agreed to

(1) recognize the Government of the Republic;

(2) pray for the head of the State and the welfare and peace of the Hungarian people;

(3) accept the nationalization of confessional schools and taking over of all personnel by the State schools (A measure sought by some Reformed leaders for 30 years).

The State

(1) accepted and agreed to further the free exercise of religion including services and Bible classes in church, public buildings, homes, schools, parish houses, missionary activities in religious journals and books, distribution of Bibles and literature, holding conferences and retreats, compulsory religious education in the schools, and charitable activities;

(2) left six educational institutions under Church control;

(3) acknowledged the right of the Reformed Church to give (compulsory) religious instruction in State schools;

(4) guaranteed the support of the Reformed Church on a decreasing scale until 1968 at which time the Church was expected to be self-supporting (Appendix V).

By December it was seen that serious difficulties would be encountered in implementing the agreement; e.g., local government authorities "discouraged" house meetings, provided no school rooms for religious instruction or Sunday schools (or only once a year to obey the letter of the law), censored, overtly or by intimidation, preaching and public demonstrations of a religious character.

Shortly after the agreement was signed, the Minister of Cults demanded that the churches prepare new textbooks for religious instruction before September, 1949, which would take into account new economic, social and political realities. Lutheran and Reformed Churches complied.

October 23, 1948—

The Hungarian Cabinet accused Mindszenty of meddling in official affairs of the Government (*N. Y. Times*, October 23:5:6).

October 26, 1948—

On behalf of the World Council of Churches, the Bishop of Chichester addressed a letter to Council President Dinnyes denying that Bishop Ordass had engaged in illegal currency exchange or had secret funds abroad, and accused the Government of hostility to Ordass because of his lack of support of the Government and his opposition to the nationalization of the schools.

End of October, 1948—

Special evangelistic campaigns were conducted by Protestants to create "evangelizing groups" within the "statistical" church. These groups were expected to be the units of Christian life "when the official church becomes an instrument of the State, . . . functioning as house congregations, Bible circles, etc., without clergy."

November 3, 1948—

Roman Catholic Bishops denounced the Government's attacks on Mindszenty for his alleged political meddling and asserted their confidence in him and support of him (*N. Y. Times,* 6:6:1; *Four Years' Struggle of the Church in Hungary,* Mindszenty, p. 181).

November 18, 1948—

In a pastoral letter Mindszenty denounced the Government as undemocratic, permitting no differing opinion, and silencing any criticism (Text, App. IV).

November 22, 1948—

Minister Gero stated that the "clerical reaction" led by Mindszenty must be liquidated (*N. Y. Times,* 22:10:3).

November 28, 1948—

Vice-Premier Rakosi made a strong attack on Mindszenty, and on the Roman Catholic Church as the center of reaction, and intimated that severe measures were to be taken against the Church (*N. Y. Times,* 28:1:4) and against Mindszenty (Appendix VII). In a letter to Mindszenty he wrote, "If the head of Hungary's Roman Catholic Church were as peaceloving a man as . . . Archbishop J. Grösz, who does not concern himself with politics but exclusively with the affairs of his church, there would be no trouble between the State and the Church in Hungary" (MacEoin, p. 139).

December 7, 1948—

An agreement was signed between the Hungarian Government and the Orthodox Church, similar to that between the Government and the Reformed Church (*Communism and the Churches,* Barron and Waddams, p. 67).

December 14, 1948—

A concordat was signed between the Government (Minister of Religion and Education Ortutay) and the Lutheran Church (Bishop Zoltán Turoczy). It included guarantees of freedom of worship, of church press, of distribution of the Bible and religious literature, of assembly, religious instruction in the schools, and charitable works. The Church agreed to the nationalization of the schools with the exception of the seminaries and schools for training specialized religious leaders. State support was to be diminished on a gradual scale

(Summary Appendix VIII). Two days later Bishop Turoczy at his installation appealed to Church and Government to have trust in one another and in their mutual dealings, and reminded the Church again that it was not yet time for martyrdom (*Die Protestantischen Kirchen in Ungarn,* 1939-1950, Encl. 51). Bishop Ordass was not immediately released after the agreement was reached, as church leaders had been promised.

December 15, 1948—

The Hungarian Premier attacked Mindszenty for his political activity (*N. Y. Times,* 15:19:3). In a letter to the priests, Mindszenty called for faithfulness in the face of persecution and possibly death (*Four Years' Struggle of the Church in Hungary,* Mindszenty, p. 185).

December 18, 1948—

The Vilgossag newspaper reported a demonstration by students and workers against Mindszenty. The Roman Catholic Board of Bishops announced that a consistory might be called to settle the Church-State dispute (*N. Y. Times,* 18:6:2).

December 23, 1948—

The Government discovered Cardinal Mindszenty's allegedly concealed private files (*Hansard,* British House of Commons Reports, April 4, 1949).

December 24, 1948—

The Pope's Christmas message was interpreted in Hungary as a declaration of all-out religious war against Communism.

December 27, 1948—

Roman Catholic Cardinal Mindszenty was arrested on charges of treason, espionage and black-marketing. A half-hour before his arrest he wrote that he had taken part in no conspiracy, that he would never resign, that he refused to give evidence, and that any alleged confession or resignation should be considered null and void (*Four Years' Struggle of the Church in Hungary,* Mindszenty, p. 188 and *N. Y. Times,* January 7, 12:8). The Hungarian Government reported that it had documentary proof of Mindszenty's activities, including his own confession. Other Roman Catholic leaders were also apprehended (*N. Y. Times,* 28:1:6, 28:8:4).

December 28, 1948—

The Roman Catholic Church concluded an understanding with the Government which would provide for financial support of the Church.

December 30, 1948—

The Government intimated that Mindszenty was linked to a Nazi royalist plot (*N. Y. Times*, 30:6:3).

January 1, 1949—

A delegation from Roman Catholic, Protestant and "Free" churches visited the President and expressed their desire for "peaceful cooperation" with the Government and for abstaining "even from the appearance of meddling in affairs not their own . . ." Reformed Bishop Bereczky described the Church's affairs as reconciliation between man and God, and stated that freedom for such work had been assured by the State. The President replied that "from the example of the Protestant Churches it can be seen clearly that to come to an agreement with the Hungarian democracy is not only possible but also necessary." In a later speech (Jan. 8) Bereczky stated that the Church should not become a "bulwark and instrument of antiquated aspirations." *Time* reported that through mass meetings, and individual solicitation people were urged or compelled to sign petitions denouncing Mindszenty (*Time*, January 24, 1949).

January 2, 1949—

President Szakasits stated that the Hungarian Government desired a concordat with the Roman Catholic Church in spite of the arrest of Mindszenty. The Government offered to negotiate with the bishops on major issues if they would denounce Mindszenty (*N. Y. Times*, 2:4:2). The Vatican rejected the offer (*N. Y. Times*, 3:1:2).

January 5, 1949—

The Government charged publicly that Mindszenty had favored the restoration of large estates. Representatives of the Government and Catholic bishops met to discuss an agreement (*N. Y. Times*, 5:18:4).

January 8, 1949—

The Government reported that Bishop Ordass was to have a new

trial (*N. Y. Times*, 8:13:4). It was reported that he was offered immediate release if he would sign a statement denouncing Mindszenty. Vice-President Rakosi demanded his resignation as Bishop, and Bishop Turoczy visited him in prison, unsuccessfully urging him to resign (L.W.F. *News-bulletin*, May 1, 1950).

January 10-11, 1949—

In Poland, Austria, Hungary and other Cominform countries, Mindszenty was denounced as an imperialist seeking to restore the Hapsburg monarchy (*N. Y. Times*, Jan. 10, 11).

January 11, 1949—

Conversations between Government representatives and the Roman Catholic Church towards an agreement were suspended. The bishops stated that further discussions "require the participation of a consistory at Rome" (*N. Y. Times*, 11:7:2; 13:3:2; *Communism and the Churches*, Barron and Waddams, p. 68).

January 15, 1949—

Petitions were circulated among the people demanding the death penalty for Mindszenty (*N. Y. Times*, 15:18:5).

January 16, 1949—

Hungarian Protestant church leaders, representatives of the Reformed, Methodist, Baptist, Adventist and Free Brethren Churches, denounced Mindszenty for his political activity and declared that there is "full freedom of religious worship in Hungary" (*Four Years' Struggle of the Church in Hungary*, Mindszenty, p. 121; Appendix IX).

January 20, 1949—

The Government published a *Yellow Book* linking Mindszenty with a Royalist plot and charged that U. S. Minister Chapin conspired with Mindszenty and that the latter took gifts from Cardinal Spellman (*N. Y. Times*, Jan. 20, 20:1).

January 23, 1949—

The Roman Catholic Bishops' Board pledged themselves to uphold Roman Catholic Church laws and dogmas and asked Hungarian Catholics to remain calm (*N. Y. Times*, Jan. 23, 46:5).

January 26, 1949—

Following charges abroad that the Government would use drugs (Scopolamin)to extort a confession from Mindszenty, the Government denied the use of any drug (*N. Y. Times*, Jan. 26, 5:6).

February 2, 1949—

The Government pledged itself to grant religious freedom if the churches would not interfere in politics (*N. Y. Times*, Feb. 2, 12:1).

February 3, 1949—

At his trial before a "People's Court," Mindszenty denied complicity in any plot to overthrow the Government, but confessed being guilty in general and admitted to currency speculation; the court rejected a plea for a separate trial (*N. Y. Times*, Feb. 4, 1:1).

February 4, 1949—

Prior to the trial the court president read a letter to the Minister of Justice in which Mindszenty stated his willingness to give up his church position if that would ensure a Church-State agreement (*N. Y. Times*, Feb. 4, 4:2).

February 5, 1949—

Mindszenty retracted his pre-trial letter discrediting any future confession, and denied that any duress had been used (*N. Y. Times*, Feb. 5, 1:8).

February 6, 1949—

The Government asked for a death sentence for Mindszenty (*N. Y. Times*, Feb. 6, 1:4).

Mindszenty and six others were convicted and Mindszenty was sentenced to life imprisonment for treason, currency offenses, and leading an organization aimed at overthrowing the Government (*Trial of Mindszenty*, p. 6).

February, 1949—

The director general of the Catholic People's League, Dr. Jaszovsky, escaped to Austria and declared that the Secret Police had tried to force

him in 1947 to publish denunciations of Mindszenty and accept Government-nominated persons in the executive committee of the League. He was asked to spy on the Cardinal, and in April and May, 1948, was informed of "conspiracy" plots and ordered to be prepared to testify against the Cardinal (*Four Years' Struggle of the Church in Hungary*, Mindszenty, p. 190). Following messages of sympathy, etc., from various British, German, American and other church leaders for Mindszenty, Hungarian Protestants expressed surprise that Protestants abroad should mix concern for Mindszenty with concern for Hungarian Protestants.

February 10, 1949—

The Hungarian Political Refugees' Relief Committee secretary reported that 250,000 people, including 1,400 clerics had been seized for political reason (*N. Y. Times*, Feb. 10, 15:1).

February 10, 1949—

The Minister of Education reported his expectations for an eventual Roman Catholic Church-State agreement (*N. Y. Times*, Feb. 10, 4:3, 4).

February 11, 1949—

Minister of Cults* Ortutay announced a law implementing articles of the Protestant-Government agreements; religious educators and cantors were to exercise their religious interests and duties only during free time from their State school responsibilities. Through intimidation or fear a number of church-educators resigned from their church work; others quit appearing in church at all. Some quit their educational work (*Die Protestantischen Kirchen in Ungarn*, 1939-1950, p. 23; Appendix X).

February 11, 1949—

Roman Catholic leaders were reported divided on the Church-State agreement issue, some former bishops now in the Government desiring to create an independent National Catholic Church (*N. Y. Times*, 11:2:2; 4:6:8).

---

* A provisional State Office for Church Affairs was established in 1949 and was responsible for all church income. The office also held the episcopal seals and could send out circulars with the bishops' consent.

February 12, 1949—

The Vatican excommunicated all Catholics connected with the Mindszenty imprisonment (*Communism and the Churches*, Barron and Waddams, p. 68).

February 12, 1949—

Bishop Ordass refused to resign as Lutheran Bishop.

February 16, 1949—

J. Revai, Minister of Education, reported on behalf of the Government (and the Vatican confirmed) that the Vatican had rejected the Government's request that Mindszenty be transferred out of Hungary before the trial and that an agreement be negotiated (*N. Y. Times*, 17:5:6).

February 17, 1949—

Handwriting experts F. Szulner and his wife fled to Austria and claimed that they had forged documents presented as Mindszenty's at the trial, and that Mindszenty had been drugged (*N. Y. Times*, 11:2:2; 17:5:6).

February 24, 1949—

Minister J. Darvas, member of the Peasant Party, was elected chairman of the Luther Society, publishers of Lutheran literature. In a speech on the occasion of his introduction to the conventus as inspector (Feb. 21) he lauded the peace efforts of Bishop Vetö and the Soviet Union, called on Lutherans to be progressive Christians, opposing all reactionary efforts (*Hungarian Church News Service*, March, 1950).

On the initiative of one pastor the conventus voted their fidelity to Bishop Ordass (*Die Protestantischen Kirchen in Ungarn*, 1939-1950, Encl. 59). The conventus of the Lutheran Church, which had only one school, asked the Government for another school for religious purposes, and for confirmation that religious education of youth outside school was within the agreed "free activity of the church" (*Ibid.*, p. 22, Encl. 66a).

March, 1949—

Ex-Prime Minister F. Nagy (in America) reported that agents kept lists of names of church-goers, and that students and civil servants were promoted or ousted depending on their religious interest (*Information Service*, FCCC Am., March 19, 1949).

March, 1949—

The Lutheran General Synod elected Ivan Reök as lay inspector to replace Baron Radvansky (L.W.F. *Newsbulletin*, May 1, 1950).

March 27, 1949—

Lutheran and Reformed Churches joined the Soviet-sponsored peace movement. A special call to pray for peace on Palm Sunday was sent by the leaders to all Protestant Churches (*Lelki Pasztor*, Ap. 1949, p. 156).

April 2, 1949—

A reference of Lutheran Pastor Deszéry in *Evangélikus Elét* to the long-awaited resignation of two presbyters was interpreted as meaning Ordass (*Die Protestantischen Kirchen in Ungarn*, 1939-1950, p. 20).

April 17, 1949—

At Debrecen, Reformed Bishop Révész, on the occasion of the centenary celebration of the Hungarian Declaration of Independence, praised and blessed the Government for its assistance in rebuilding the church of Debrecen and for all aid given to the churches (*Five Years of Hungarian Protestantism*, 1945-1950, p. 23).

April 28, 1949—

Lutheran Church leaders exhorted Lutherans to fulfill their civic duties in the coming elections: "We must stand by the forces of reconstruction, work, peace. Because it is God's will that we lead a quiet still life in worshipping Him" (*Die Protestantischen Kirchen in Ungarn*, 1939-1950, Encl. 82).

April 30, 1949—

At the "Peace Partisans' Congress" in Paris, Reformed Bishop Bereczky appealed to Western churches to open their eyes and hearts to the countries on the road to socialism and to the churches which "fight for peace together with socialism."

May, 1949—

Lutheran Bishop Turoczy, in a circular letter, exhorted the people to become stewards of God's gifts, supporting the works of God and His church with contributions direct to the churches (*Lelki Pasztor*, June, 1949, p. 27).

May, 1949—

In connection with the May elections Vice-Premier Rakosi stated that all who did not vote for the Front "would be his own enemy, the enemy of his family and of his fatherland." Protestant churches advised their members to vote for the Front. Catholic leaders urged Catholics "to vote and use their rights as citizens as their conscience dictates" (*Communism and the Churches*, Barron and Waddams, p. 69).

June 12-17, 1949—

Protestant church leaders participated in the Hungarian Peace Congress and assured the Congress of the churches' concern and work for peace.

June 15, 1949—

Lutheran Pastor Szimonidesz, onetime renegade leftist, was appointed field bishop of the Hungarian Government.

July 17, 1949—

The Government agreement to support Catholic clergy was extended to 1950 (*N. Y. Times*, 17:19:6).

August 17, 1949—

Deputy Premier Rakosi stated that the Government desired a concordat with the Catholic Church, but that the clergy was blocking it (*N. Y. Times*, 18:13:5).

August 18, 1949—

The new constitution declared Hungary a People's Republic of workers and working peasants. The constitution was patterned after the Soviet model but established in addition a Praesidium of 21 members which would govern the country between semi-annual meetings of Parliament. The Praesidium was empowered to dissolve Government bodies or annul legislation which violated the constitution or the interests of the working people. The Church was separated from the State.

Freedom of speech and of assembly "in the interests of social, economic and cultural activities" were guaranteed (Excerpts. Appendix XI). Vice-Premier Rakosi, in presenting the constitution, stated that under the Hungarian People's Republic no one had been and no one would be persecuted for his religion. The Reformed Church replied: "We accept our new situation as the sign of God's mercy on us, and we seek for guidance in His Word for what is to be done by us" (*Five Years of Hungarian Protestantism*, 1945-1950, p. 26).

August, 1949—

The Lutheran World Federation, following a visit to Geneva of Bishop Vetö and Inspector Reök, advised the Hungarian Lutheran Church that aid would be sent if the Hungarian Church

(a) would provide an accounting of the use of all aid sent;

(b) would secure an official statement of Government approval to receive aid;

(c) would provide a plan for future aid;

(d) would arrange for an official visit of U. S. Lutheran representatives.

On their return to Hungary, Reök declared "also abroad I have become convinced of the correctness of our Church policy" (*Die Protestantischen Kirchen in Ungarn*, 1939-1950, p. 26).

Bishop Vetö and Inspector Reök sent Pastor Ruttkay-Miklian to see Ordass in prison to urge him to resign, pretending that Lutheran World Federation leaders in Geneva had agreed. Bishop Ordass refused (*Luth. World Federation Newsbulletin*, May 1, 1950). Six months later, in a message to Lutherans in the West, Hungarians expressed their desire to receive fraternal gifts of love, if no conditions were attached (*Die Protestantischen Kirchen in Ungarn*, 1939-1950, Encl. 84).

September 5, 1949—

The Pope ordered that all practising Communists be excommunicated (order actually in effect in July; *N. Y. Herald Tribune*, Sept. 5, 1949).

September 6, 1949—

By Government decree, compulsory religious instruction of children was abolished; religious education was declared optional. Parents might apply to local schools before September 15 if they desired such instruction, which would be provided at Government expense (*Die Protestantischen Kirchen in Ungarn*, 1939-1950, Encl. 69; Appendix XII).

The Catholic Board of Bishops sent out a pastoral letter telling Christians it was their duty to God to apply for religious instruction for their children, and simultaneously protested to the Government that religious instruction should be restored to its former place in the schools.

Protestant leaders sent out no instructions. In rural areas it was estimated that nearly 100%, and in industrial areas nearly 70%, applied. Deputy Premier Rakosi called the Catholic pastoral letter "bellicose" and accused the Church of persecuting parents and children. Nineteen teachers were removed on charges of bringing pressure on parents and children to receive instruction. Rakosi asserted that since religious freedom was used "to terrorize the conscience . . . by the reactionaries . . . (the Government would) . . . fill in the gap on the spiritual front as well" (*London Times*, 5:10:49). Parents were then asked to withdraw their children from religious instruction classes.

September 16, 1949—

Former Foreign Minister L. Rajk, on trial for treason, stated that Mindszenty had been inspired by the Vatican and "the Great Powers to instigate uprisings through the country" (*N. Y. Herald Tribune*, Sept. 17; *L. Rajk and His Accomplices*, Budapest Printing Press).

September 16, 1949—

The reorganized ecumenical committee of Protestant churches, Reformed Bishop Bereczky and Lutheran Inspector Dr. Reök presiding, decided to continue extensive evangelistic campaigns, to hold an ecumenical conference of ministers in November, and to organize united Bible weeks in the churches.

The *Hungarian Church Press* reported the organization of lay and clerical groups in Reformed parishes for Bible and theological studies, for prayer and evangelism. The four Reformed theological faculties opened the Fall term after a retreat for their leaders with increased enrollment throughout (*Hungarian Church Press*, Oct. 4, 1949, p. 6).

September, 1949—

Reformed Bishop Révész resigned, stating "my conscience forbids me to do otherwise.

October 1, 1949—

Matyas Rakosi declared that in view of the number of children still receiving religious instruction "we Communists shall change our methods." The Ministry of Public Enlightenment was charged to overcome this work "of our enemies" (Christians) and see that the working class "takes a correct attitude" (*Communists Crush Churches in Eastern Europe*, Markham, p. 84).

October 8, 1949—

The Communist daily *Nepszava* quoted worker parents: "We will not permit our children to be set against the People's Democracy under pretext of religious instruction," and added that activities of nuns, teachers, clergymen in distributing printed forms and urging parents to apply for religious instruction for their children was a violation of freedom of conscience and religion. A priest was accused of scheduling masses simultaneously with "Pioneer" (Communist children's organization) activities "to confuse the children" and thereby violating religious freedom (*Communist Crush Churches*, Markham, p. 91). Courses in Marxist-Communist doctrine subsequently became obligatory (*Die Protestantischen Kirchen in Ungarn*, 1939-1950, p. 23).

October 14, 1949—

The Government issued a decree requiring all citizens who received salaries or subsidies from the Government to sign loyalty oaths (*N. Y. Herald Tribune*; Appendix XII). This would include clergy and religious educators. Many teachers resigned "voluntarily" from giving religious instruction, and as loyal Party members, were to take children from religious courses (*Die Protestantischen Kirchen in Ungarn*, 1939-1950, p. 23).

October 14, 1949—

The printing of religious textbooks was begun after the texts were approved by the Ministry of Religion (*N. Y. Herald Tribune*, 14:8:6).

October, 1949—

Lutheran Bishop Kemeny, in his annual report, called on the Government to observe the constitutional rights of religious freedom in implementing the "optional religious instructions" ruling and spoke of a deepening of the inner life of the Church (*Die Protestantischen Kirchen in Ungarn*, 1939-1950, Encl. 72a).

November, 1949—

The Protestant Pastors' Union met to discuss questions of lay cooperation and church instruction. Controversial subjects were avoided because of increasing tensions and disagreement among the churchmen (*Ibid.*, p. 27).

November, 1949—

All independent youth organizations were dissolved. In the Protestant churches youth activities were assimiliated as a part of the total church life.

November 11, 1949—

After a "violent struggle," Pastor János Péter was elected to succeed Imre Révész as Reformed Bishop of Tibiscian Diocese. Péter was of the Free Council (*Five Years of Hungarian Protestantism*, 1945-1950, p. 26).

In his annual report, Bishop Turoczy spoke with measured appreciation of the Government's attempts to arrive at a working understanding with the Church, and asserted that the new constitution would not alter the agreement reached in 1948. With regard to the new ruling re. optional religious education, he emphasized that responsibility would now be placed wholly on parents, then godparents and teachers, all of whom must become missionaries and shepherds vis-à-vis children and youth (*Die Protestantischen Kirchen in Ungarn*, 1939-1950, Encl. 72).

December 6, 1949—

Reformed Bishop Bereczky announced that Protestant pastors would sign loyalty oaths to the "People's Republic, its peoples and its constitution." He stated that the wording of the oath was "unobjectionable" (*N. Y. Herald Tribune*, Dec. 7, 1949; Appendix XIII). Roman Catholic priests and Lutheran pastors also signed.

December 13, 1949—

State subsidies for church work were reduced in accordance with a prearranged scale of diminishing support (*N. Y. Times*, Dec. 13:3:5).

December 20, 1949—

The Minister of Religion, Ortutay, following Catholic opposition to the loyalty pledge and to the obligatory teaching of Marxist-Leninist doctrine in the schools, warned Catholic leaders that it was "time they supported the cause of the people."

Subsequently the bishops approved of lower clergy taking the oath with the reservation, "insofar as it is not in conflict with the laws of God and the Church, and the rights of man," but refused themselves until approved by the Vatican (*N. Y. Times*, 21: 11:2; *N. Y. Herald Tribune*, 20, 23).

December 21, 1949—

On the occasion of Stalin's 70th birthday and the introduction of courses in *Weltanschauung* in the theological faculties of Sopron and Debrecen, Lutheran Inspector Groo equated Communism and Christianity in an evaluation of their practical works. Lutheran Pastor Dezséry referred to the necessity of the Church's being familiar with its environment (*Die Protestantischen Kirchen in Ungarn, 1939-1950*, p. 24).

December 24, 1949—

The Government forbade traditional Christmas celebrations and extended the observance of Stalin's birthday through Christmas eve (*N. Y. Times*, 25:8:5). According to MacEoin (*The Communist War on Religion*, p. 130), the Communist publishing house distributed thousands of cards depicting the Holy Family with the text overprinted in red "Christmas is their holiday, ours is the First of May. Christ is their superstition, our hope is Socialism."

December 24, 1949—

A training course for church organists was organized by the Lutheran Church in the Martin Luther Institute (*Hungarian Church Press*, Oct. 1, 1950).

December 28, 1949—

All trade and industry in private hands were nationalized by Government decree (*Communism and the Churches*, Barron and Waddams, p. 70). Both printing offices of the Lutheran Church were nationalized. A committee under Bishop Vetö was formed to promote new publications and negotiate with the Government. Regular press conferences were introduced (*Protestantischen Kirchen in Ungarn*, 1939-1950, p. 24).

December 31, 1949—

The Lutheran Church and the Government entered into an agreement whereby the churches would sell to the Government, at an advantageous price, land and other property in areas being developed by the Government (Appendix XIV).

January 1, 1950—

A special decree forbade the employment of Catholic nuns in State or municipal hospitals. The ruling was not effected immediately owing to the shortage of nurses (MacEoin, *The Communist War on Religion*, p. 134).

January, 1950—

In a New Year's message, Bishop Veöreös called on the Church to follow a New Way, breaking from worldly ties and material comforts originating in Constantine, and becoming a missionary movement (*Lelki Pasztor*, Jan. 1950, Encl. 90a).

January, 1950—

Lutheran Bishop Vetö exchanged New Year's telegrams with the Patriarch of Moscow (*Die Protestantischen Kirchen in Ungarn*, 1939-1950, p. 27).

February 18, 1950—

Hungarian Church Press published a message from Hungarian Lutheran leaders to Christians in the West. In it they denied having any part in, or need for a "so-called resistance" against restrictions on church functions. They characterized the Church as being awakened and renewed by the Gospel since the removal of human and worldly assurances, appealed to Western Christians to be more responsible and loving towards them, and welcomed gifts of love if no obligations or conditions were involved (*Hungarian Church Press*, March 1, 1950).

February 23, 1950—

The Ministry of Religious Affairs advised the churches that April 4 would be remembered as the fifth anniversary of the liberation, and that in keeping with their agreements with the Government, the churches should celebrate and offer appropriate prayers (*Protestantischen Kirchen in Ungarn*, 1939-1950, Encl. 92; Appendix XV, Encl. 92).

March, 1950—

The Council of the Reformed Church approved a plan for the reorganization of all missionary work of the Reformed Church under the central administration of the Church, and locally related to the pastor and parish (*EPS*, March 31, 1950).

March 3, 1950—

The Lutheran General Convent, after considerable dissent, voted to hold new elections in all presbyteries, courts and committees (*Die Protestantischen Kirchen in Ungarn*, 1939-1950, p. 21).

April 1, 1950—

"On request of the Minister of Public Worship and Education (Lutheran Darvas) . . ." a special disciplinary Judiciary Commission of the Lutheran Church of Hungary was convened and deposed Bishop Ordass (*EPS*, April 21, 1950). Owing to the fact that "the grave situation due to the sentence passed by the Usury (Civil) Court . . . prejudices the interest of the church . . .", the Lutheran World Federation asked for an explanation as to judges, reasons and punishment (*Newsbulletin*, LWF, May 1, 1950. According to the Lutheran constitution any official condemned by a civil court must appear before an ecclesiastical disciplinary court. *Die Protestantischen Kirchen in Ungarn*, 1939-1950, p. 21). The special court arrived at its decision after a new court had been elected, and five pastor-members imprisoned.

April 4, 1950—

At a service commemorating the five years of Hungary's liberation, Reformed Bishop John Péter called on Western churches to be more specific in their programs for peace, and commended to them points defined at the Paris and Stockholm Peace Congresses.

April 14, 1950—

Dr. Ivan Reök, Inspector General of the Lutheran Church, presented to the Government a petition for amnesty or release for Bishop Ordass and former Lutheran Secretary General Varga (LWF, *Newsbulletin*, May 1, 1950).

April 19, 1950—

Lutheran Bishop Josef Szabó resigned as representative for foreign affairs of the Hungarian Lutheran Church. Bishop Lajos Vetö succeeded him (LWF *Newsbulletin*, May 1, 1950).

April 26, 1950—

Forty-five leaders of Roman Catholic religious orders, in a memorandum to the Government, accused the Government of violating the basic precepts of religious freedom by depriving monasteries of all their property, forcing their members into ghetto conditions and separating them from contact with the people, forbidding them to teach or to minister in hospitals, and confiscating their theological schools and training centers.

The Minister of Education replied by calling the 45 leaders imperialist agitators and reactionary newsmongers (*New York Times*, 25:22:3).

April 26, 1950—

The Comenius celebrations planned by the Reformed churches for May, 1950, were taken over by the Government as a cultural festival.

May 2, 1950—

The Lutheran Executive Committee of the Montana (Banyai) District, acting Bishop Kemény and Inspector J. Darvas presiding, voted to recommend to the churches that Student Pastor Láslö Dezséry be elected bishop to replace L. Ordass (LWF *Newsbulletin*, June 1, 1950).

May 21, 1950—

Lutheran Secretary J. Groo expressed alarm that the World Council of Churches was becoming a Western political body and called on churches to listen and speak to each other. "We (Hungarians) must show that Christ has His Church (also) in Socialism." Mr. Groo regretted that the World

Council had not clearly repudiated the idea of a common Catholic-Protestant-Moslem front against Communism (*Evangélikus Elét*, May 21, 1950).

May 30, 1950—

The Minister of Justice ordered the release of Bishop Ordass, said he, because the former Bishop asked that the remainder of his sentence be commuted (LWF *Newsbulletin*, June 1, 1950).

June, 1950—

Rev. L. Dezséry was elected Bishop of the Montana (Banyai) Lutheran Diocese, succeeding Bishop Ordass (*EPS*, June 30, 1950). Pastors Keken, Kendeh and three others who allegedly opposed Deszéry disappeared from religious activity (*Die Protestantischen Kirchen in Ungarn*, 1939-1950, p. 22).

June 7, 1950—

Education Minister Revai, in a report to the Workers' (Communist) Party urged the Party to launch an all-out drive against the Roman Catholic Church. He charged that the bishops were still acting in opposition to the Government, attacked them for their refusal to sign the pledge of peace outlawing the atomic bomb and disapproved their teaching of miracles. He proposed that in reprisal many monasteries and religious orders be dissolved. He attacked the bishops for their refusal on grounds of Vatican non-approval to take the oath of allegiance to the State, noting that they had taken the oath under the Horthy regime without Vatican permission. "We will no longer tolerate the Vatican's nominating Bishops without consulting the Government. We will use our rights in connection with the appointment of Bishops in the future." After accusing the bishops of sabotaging popular holidays by organizing masses and religious ceremonies as counter-attractions, he added, "clerical reaction tries to discourage workers and peasants from sending their children to school and oppose our teachings of science to the peasants . . . The Government would welcome an agreement with the church as was reached in Poland." Minister Revai called for stronger anti-religious propaganda, forbade that children of Party officials should have religious instruction, instructed officials not to take part in church ceremonies and to educate their wives in the spirit of the new world view (*N. Y. Times*, June 7:7:2; Appendix XVI).

June 12, 1950—

The Catholic bishops issued a pastoral letter in reply to Revai's charges, defending the religious orders and contending that recent measures against some cloisters were frequently arranged by irresponsible non-official elements. They noted that there was as yet no new regulation regarding the non-compulsory system of religious education (*N. Y. Times*, 12:3:4).

June 22, 1950—

Following the disclosure of the first mass arrests of monks and others connected with the Roman Catholic Church, the Government reported that the bishops made overtures towards the Government for a new accord. The Vatican charged that ca. 1000 members of religious orders were deported or interned, according to one writer, because of opposition to the Stockholm Peace appeal (*N. Y. Times*, 22:1:3; 27:21:15). The Government revealed that shortwave transmitters, buried money, espionage supplies, immoral books, and corpses had been found in the monasteries (MacEoin, *The Communist War on Religion*, p. 135).

July 8, 1950—

The Government reported that negotiations for a Church-State agreement were underway between the Government, represented by Rakosi, and the Catholic Church, represented by Jesuit Horvath. The first session was described as a heated one involving demands on the part of the Church for Mindszenty's release, the return of church schools, religious education in the State schools, and on the part of the Government, the dissolution of the religious orders, the placing of theological studies under the Ministry of Religions (Text—Appendix XVII).

July 28, 1950—

The journal *Szabad Nep* charged that three bishops were blocking the Church-State pact. The creation of a national independent church was suggested (*N. Y. Times*, 28:6:7).

August, 1950—

The Catholic bishops elected Mgr. M. Beresztoczy as Vicar-general of the archbishopric of Esztergom to replace Mindszenty, after, according to several reports, two elected candidates were imprisoned by the Government. Beresztoczy had been appointed by Mindszenty to the Catholic Affairs Department of the Ministry of Cults, and later head of Catholic Action. He was convicted with Mindszenty but later pardoned. The Vatican declared the election void because it was allegedly conducted under duress (*Christian Century*, Sept. 6, 1950, p. 1035; *N. Y. Times*, 2:21:6).

August 1, 1950—

A meeting of lower Catholic clergy was held in Budapest to "declare that the attitude of our church towards the People's Republic has to change, in order to get it out of the cul-de-sac into which some of the bishops have got it as a result of . . . their prejudice against progress and their desire for the older order to return." Speeches were made by a priest, a monk and József Darvas, Minister of Religion and Education, denouncing the misleading political attitude of the Bench of Bishops, scolding Rome for getting its information from refugees, praising the understanding between the Polish Government and Polish Catholic Church, and assuring the priests of the approval and support of the Government for their movement.

The priests passed resolutions
(1) declaring their fidelity to the Catholic Church;
(2) declaring their fidelity to the State and its five-year plan (one speaker noted that the Bench of Bishops had approved the five-year plan prior to the election of the People's Front);
(3) promising their support in the fight for peace;
(4) condemning the war-mongering imperialists, their action in Korea, and the atom bomb;
(5) expressing the desirability of the State's supporting those clergy "true to the people" (Appendix XVIII).

August 12, 1950—

The National Peace Committee urged that Roman Catholic Bishop Peteri be tried for violating constitutional guarantees of freedom of conscience and worship. According to the committee, Catholic priests had protested against Peteri's threats of excommunication for participating in the "National (peace) Congress" of Catholic Clergy on August 1. "Besides unlawful and war-mongering activities" he had opposed "the peaceful interests of the Hungarian people" (*N. Y. Times*, 12:3:5). He had also refused to receive a workers' delegation seeking his signature to the Stockholm Peace Appeal (*Christian Century*, Sept. 27, 1950, p. 1131).

August 19, 1950—

Catholic priests were asked to devote special sermons to praise of the Constitution (*Ibid.*, 19:4:6).

August 31, 1950—

The Foreign Ministry announced the conclusion of an agreement between the Catholic Bench of Bishops and the Government following discussions begun June 22. The agreement provided for the setting-up of a special committee of representatives of the Church and Government to make necessary future adjustments. The Bishops agreed to support the constitution, to counter-act clerical anti-Government and anti-collectivization activities, to condemn subsersive activities, to request Catholics to support the five-year plan, and to support the peace movement. The Government agreed to return eight nationalized Catholic schools (of 2992) and permit religious orders "to work in sufficient numbers to perform their teachings," to subsidize the Roman Catholic Church through 18 years, to guarantee complete freedom of religion (Text—Appendix XIX). The Vatican refused to recognize the episcopal signature as legal (*News Behind the Iron Curtain*, Feb. 1953, p. 20).

September 11, 1950—

The Vatican radio reported that 300 monks were removed from border provinces; a pastoral letter indicated that all but four religious orders were banned. The Catholic bishops were reported to be in disagreement over the concordat with the Government (*N. Y. Times*, 11:13:1).

September 19, 1950—

The Ministry for Religious Affairs issued a decree regulating religious instruction in public schools (Text—Appendix XX). Religious teachers would be employed by the school authorities, and could have no other gainful occupation; they must be qualified dogmatically and could not be hostile towards the Government, or its decrees; instruction would be from the Ministry's textbook; teachers could have no other contact with pupils than in the religious education class, and could not participate in faculty meetings; attendance of pupils at class was not compulsory; class work would be supervised by the school director with the help of pupils, parents and others. Nearly 60% of all pupils in the schools had asked for religious instruction, as against 70% in 1949.

September, 1950—

The *Hungarian Church Press* (Oct. 1, 1950) reported that the Reformed Church was planning for the annual "Protestant Festival" the last week of October, with special evangelistic services on the theme "Peace on Earth." A special conference of Lutheran pastors was to be held in preparation for evangelistic work. A special theological conference was organized at Debrecen in September by the Reformed churches on questions of training for the ministry. Simultaneously, a student conference and evangelistic talks were arranged for the 100 students of this Reformed seminary. The *Hungarian Church Press* published and circulated the book *Five Years of Hungarian Protestantism* "to maintain spiritual fellowship and to pass on messages . . . received from God during these years of radical social transformation."

September, 1950—

At the annual meeting of the Hungarian Lutheran Church it was reported that the Theological Faculty of Sopron, formerly a department of the University of Pécs, would be operated as an independent church school supported by the State. Plans were made for the eventual self-support of the Church, in view of the reduction of State subsidies by 25% every 5 years. The work of home missions, laymen's training, Bible schools, choral training and family care were re-organized as an integral part of church life. Charitable institutions were to be recognized by the Government (*Hungarian Church Press*, October 1, 1950). By September, 12 organists had received diplomas in organists' training from the Martin Luther Institute since the opening of the courses in December, 1949 (*Ibid.*).

Sepember 29, 1950—

The Government invited Roman Catholic priests to run in the October 2 communal elections (*N. Y. Times*, 29:10:7).

October 20, 1950—

The Vatican charged that the Hungarian Government was seeking a new concordat with the Hungarian bishops which would include breaking ties with the Vatican.

December, 1950—

Four Lutheran bishops circulated a pastoral letter exhorting Lutherans to face the tensions and issues of the world with the love of peace and the will to make peace as revealed in the Gospel of Jesus Christ, and urged pastors to support the peace movement of the people (*EPS*, December 22-29, 1950).

Catholic leaders in two pastoral letters urged the faithful to pray for peace and replacement of "the reign of violence by the Kingdom of God."

December, 1950—

The press and radio urged the substituting of the Soviet mid-winter celebrations for the "Capitalistic and superstitious conception of Christmas." School children were told that midwinter gifts came from a real Father Frost and not from a legendary Baby Jesus.

Summary of Situation—January 1, 1951

Repentance:

The most distinguishing and significant single factor affecting post-war life in the Hungarian churches was the extensive spirit of repentance among conscientious Christians. Shocked at their nation's involvement in Nazi crimes, many anxiously awaited annihilation. When the expected destruction of church life, the closing of churches and the mass expulsion of pastors did not come it was as a resurrection from the dead.* The possibility—and Russian encourage-

---

* "All we went through, we had deserved it on account of the many faults committed. We have also deserved the nationalization of our lands, as we made idols of our land, sacrificed our descendants to it in order to prevent its being split. And it was God Himself Who pulled down this idol.

"We had our schools which were our pride and we made them and their system a question of prestige towards the Roman Catholic Church. They were a part of our Church policy. And it was again God Who destroyed also this other idol, giving instead a hunger and thirst for the Word of God to our youth.

"And what about the Jewish question? We tolerated the petrification of Jewish persecution and thus we brought upon ourselves God's well-deserved punishment. And yet we were alive. God permitted a new life to spring up out of our churches, where His Word can be freely proclaimed.

"The fruit of repentance is manifest in the Church in a wonderful revival. Sunday became the Lord's Day again. Everywhere Bible classes are started which are attended by many, after the hard work of the day. These Reformed Hungarian Christians do not mourn for their past prosperity, but are looking ahead with a firm faith in God, a God, Who is not confined to the vestry or the quiet room, but Who upsets the power of the mighty to build up His Kingdom" (Hungarian churchmen, as quoted by Prof. Thurneysen and Rev. Luthi of Switzerland, *Hungarian Church Press*, No. 12, Oct. 4, 1949).

ment—of continued and renewed church life was received as a special act of grace. And, by comparison with people's fears, the early changes in economic and social spheres were as the mildest judgment of an over-indulgent God. Repentant for past mistakes, many Christians felt too guilty or too relieved to prophesy over the new social reform; others espoused it.

But a great number lost themselves in inner searching and in penitence before God. The mistakes the churches had made in the past temporarily dimmed their prophetic vision and muffled the prophesying of the detached spokesmen of God over the new situation. Many were temporarily either satisfied with strictly religious considerations of their new spiritual situation, or else were so compromised that they were forced to become as intimately involved with the new regime as with former regimes. Only some time later did the unmistakable voice of aggressive resistance partially supplant the almost total repentance of the people.

By 1951 the spirit of repentance is not lost, but confessions of guilt are directed more God-ward and less regime-ward. The new Government and its reforms are no longer regarded as the wrath of God, but also as the instruments of mortals, which must have the word of God pronounced over them. Those churches which have undergone a spiritual renewal are in a better position spiritually, and less vulnerable materially, to speak with authority about the meaning of judgment, God's love and resurrection.

Church Properties:

The churches, technically, may own 100 hold (1100 acres) each, or something under 10% of former holdings. The churches, therefore, are no longer landed organizations. Other profit-bearing holdings have been nationalized. The churches' support must come from other sources; their energies may be directed towards other opportunities.

State Support:

Immediately after the land reform and the cessation of obligatory church taxes, congregations began partial support of the churches through free-will offerings. The present agreements of the churches with the Government provide that the Government will support the churches, their administration, repairs, rebuilding, salaries, etc., on a diminishing scale for twenty years (until 1968). Joint Government-church committees supervise implementation of the agreements. Congregations are providing increasing support. Some leaders expect the agreement to be changed to conform with the Czechoslovakian pattern—i.e., the Government will eventually support the administrative costs and salaries of approved churches and pastors.

Reconstruction:

The Government rebuilt one principal structure for each major religious body. Local Government-related organizations have cooperated in some local church rebuilding programs depending on the degree of cooperation of the church leaders. There is currently no major program of rebuilding or of new construction, although the Government expressed its willingness in the agreements to help with rebuilding of strategic centers.

Social Welfare and Religious Orders:

Relief, welfare, health and hospitalization programs are organized on a national basis by the Government. With few exceptions church institutions or agencies serving these purposes have been nationalized or liquidated. Members of religious orders, again with some exceptions, have been absorbd into other activities of the church or are "in useful occupations." Several hundred are supported by the Government as teachers in schools, and in various ways continue Christian work there. Technically, the churches may continue their ministries of welfare and relief, but on a more localized, individual and limited scale. In that framework they effect a noble service of love and mercy. Limited gifts of food, clothing and of funds may be received by the churches from abroad.

Church Schools:

All church schools, with the exception of a limited number of higher schools for the training of religious leaders (defined in the Church-State agreements), were absorbed into the over-all Government educational system. Though the number of candidates seeking to enter the church seminaries is increasing, the practical possibility of their continuing formal theological studies is decreasing. Many therefore receive special training in shorter institutes, or in locally tutored groups. The Ministry of Public Worship has stated that there is no longer any room for a theological faculty in a progressive university.

Religious Education:

Facilities for religious instruction of children are theoretically provided by the State at the request of the parents. The Government supports some instructors and provides some class room facilities for such purposes. However, difficulties encountered in securing adequate instruction have led the churches to make special efforts to provide religious instruction in the homes, or in church buildings. There is a special children's missionary work; volunteers receive special training for children's work. Parents come together to prepare themselves for the religious training of their children. The conduct of Christians teaching in State schools is not without its influence. The interest of wives and children of Party members is such that Party leaders threaten expulsion of fathers, and seek to outlaw "optional religious instruction." One should not conclude, however, that the majority of the children are receiving religious instruction.

Youth:

All organized youth work is controlled by the Government or its agencies. The Y.M.C.A. has become part of the national youth organization. Church youth work has been absorbed into the broader activities of the local parishes. Confirmation classes are held, and youth participate in evangelistic activities. Special religious publications for youth and youth leaders were prepared in the last three years. However, the masses of high school youth have a weak tie, if any, with the Church. On the whole, the minority of those who are in the Church are devoted to it; those not in it have nothing to do with it.

Religious Publications:

Religious copy, in quantity and subject matter, is influenced by the fact that printing facilities and paper supplies are controlled by the Government. The Reformed Churches have a popular weekly, a pastors' bi-weekly, a bi-weekly for church workers, a news service, and a monthly journal. In addition, they have been able to print a new hymnal, calendars and several theological works, including those of Karl Barth, and Calvin's Commentary on the New Testament. Lutheran Churches have a committee which oversees and stimulates publication of two regular journals and other religious materials. The Catholic Church has an occasional official publication plus the works of the Catholic "Union." A revised edition of the New Testament was published in 1950, and scholars are working on the Old Testament. The demand for Bibles and religious literature is increasing. In comparison with the amount and variety of material issued prior to the war, present publications are miniscule and unvaried, either evangelistic, exclusively religious or pro-Government.

The Church's Social Message:

To all external appearances, the churches do not "prophesy" or express their evaluation of political actions; they accept them, or are silent—"abstain even from the appearance of meddling in affairs not their own."* The churches are all actively involved in the Hungarian Peace Movement; they preach, and some are convinced, that the greatest menace to world peace is Western imperialism. There is much discussion of the place of the Church in the new State. Churches may preach and work to overcome the economic injustices and social ills of the former "capitalistic-feudalistic" society, and engage in programs of reform and reconstruction alongside the Government.

This is not to say that they do not affect domestic political and social issues; where the churches have shown a concern for reform and willingness to cooperate, Government measures have been tempered and humanized. Through constant conversations with high Government executives, much unnecessary suffering has been avoided, many abuses have been rectified, and local frictions dealt with as calmly and temperately as possible. Discerning sermons on spiritual issues, exhortations to confidence and moderation, exegesis on the meaning of judgment and resurrection have affected social readjustments in helping parishioners respond positively and religiously to Government measures. Though the voice of the Church may be less clear, it is no less alive socially and spiritually for the fact that the churches now have active exponents of the "democratic" laboring class as well as the bourgeosie in their membership.

Leadership:

The former conservative leadership of the churches which helped put down the post-World War I socialist revolution and its religious leadership, has largely been replaced (a) by those same "radical" or "liberal" social reformers who, now that social reform has come, are preoccupied with the spiritual revival of the churches, (b) by some more recently "converted" former Nazi or Horthy collaborators, and (c) by Christians of a genuine proletarian background.

---

* A. Bereczky, *The Church and Churches in Hungary*, Jan., 1949.

Church leaders do not necessarily have the full support of their churches behind them, though most churchmen would recognize that there is no alternative. Conservative churchmen tend to look on the new church leaders as being Communist or Communist colalborators, and to regard social "conversion" or repentance for former errors as opportunism. Though the official position of the churches is now one of cooperation with or neutrality toward the Government, there are, among pastors and lay leaders, several bodies of opinion with regard to Church-State relations which overlay one another:

(a)   the Government-sympathizing "Unions" of lower clergy, e.g., the "Progressive Catholics";

(b)   the "prophetic-progressive" theologians and former activist social reformers who now seek to renew the churches as the Church;

(c)   those who conclude that Communism and Christianity must ultimately lock in battle, that the Church must be martyred, that that time is not with the nationalization of schools, but is yet to come;

(d)   the aggressive resisters who follow Mindszenty's lead, among them a number of Protestants as well as Catholics;

(e)   the pietists who may combine with their gospel of individual salvation a revived nationalism, of Communistic or anti-Communist flavor.

Present church leadership comes from the first two groups, with the "progressive" theologians in first place. Obviously, the best efforts of these leaders to renew the churches along churchly lines are made more difficult by the presence of those who have Western ideas of resistance. The proximity of the Government sympathizers to the central control of the Church may be seen as a counter to that opposition. It has been observed that the numerous pastors and theological conferences look very much like political instruction meetings for the pastors.

On political issues, relations among church leaders are strained. In formal meetings, discussion of controversial political subjects is avoided. Differences do not adhere closely to confessional lines, since there are shades of every opinion in every church; the churches are not therefore tempted to exploit one another for political advantages, although some Protestant leaders have denounced Catholicism *en bloc*, and Free Churches which have historically been kept at a distance, reciprocated when "established" churches were in trouble over nationalization of schools or other issues. Catholics shared in the denunciations of Archbishop Mindszenty, and serious churchmen made an attempt to distinguish between the ideas of "political Catholicism" and Catholicism.

International ecumenical contacts are limited, and correspondence greatly restricted. Theological students do not get passports to study in the West. There is a little contact with sister churches in other countries of East Europe. On the other hand, contacts with the Orthodox Church in Russia are being developed, through exchanges of literature and greetings, and through visitors. Within Hungary a real effort is made to maintain the ecumenical fellowship of the churches. Pastors, often with laymen, come together on an ecumenical basis for Bible study, study of the renewal of the Church, the Reformation, theological topics, the ecumenical movement and unity of the churches.

Renewal, Evangelism, Missions:

The significant fact in the Hungarian church situation is that the Church has been renewed in these areas where the Church has its primary concern.

The churches have changed in character from formal administrative agencies to missionary movements. Mission, evangelization, Bible work, religious publications and charities were formerly private, independent endeavors; today they are at the heart of the Church. Congregations have become living fellowships of believers. Sunday preaching and week-day services are attended by increasing numbers. Adult Bible classes for after-work hours, theological studies and prayer groups in homes and small meeting-places have enthusiastic participation. Deep discussions center around the purposes of God, the meaning of "church membership" and the nature of the Church.

Evangelization and missionary work set the temper of the parishes. "A group of villages is intensively evangelized through a team of evangelists (representing—if possible—all the different branches of the church). After this concentrated attack on the 'statistical' church the follow-up work is done by 'Congregation-builders,' who try to gather the 'awakened' in dynamic, evangelizing groups. It is generally held that these groups will be the units of Christian life in the church of tomorrow, when the official church will be an instrument of the State. These cells are formed all over the country already (house congregations, Bible circles, etc.) and they function (as in the future they will have to) without clergy—'We cannot sleep further on the soft cushions of the institutional church, but have to change our church radically into a missionary and evangelistic force. Our device should be: the 'missionary-transqualification of the church must begin with me and through me.'" Not only in teams, but as individuals many have a new boldness to bear witness to their faith in work and social contacts.

A basic change is in the extent to which laymen sense that they are the Church. Responsibility for much of the leadership, Bible studies, evangelization, training of church workers, choir masters, children's workers, rests with laymen. And in material ways they are beginning to provide for the future requirements of their ministry, worship and missions.

The churches have lost a great deal in political influence and prestige; they have gained very much in nearness to God and in His calling. Few church leaders have any illusions about the future. In the long run, yes, it is in God's hands and He will not be mocked; but many who feel they have little freedom of religion now expect the situation to worsen before it gets better, that ultimately the official church may become entirely a department of the Government. Others feel that they have more opportunities for Christian work than they can exhaust, and that they should be about God's business today, letting "tomorrow worry about itself."

Appendix I

CARDINAL MINDSZENTY ON CONFESSIONAL EDUCATION

(Excerpts)

May 20, 1946

The Catholic Church founded the schools in this country which are the predecessors of the present schools. It was the Church which instituted schools of her own as early as the first centuries in the ancient Roman Empire in order to protect the children from pagan influences by which they were taught idolatry and immoral mythological tales.

While the Church was most progressive in the matter of education, the State was slow in this activity and failed to establish schools until much later —in Hungary in the eighteenth century.

The Church has, however, still another much more compelling right to the education of youth than her historical right. Her educational mission springs from God Himself. Perhaps this right is not acknowledged by those who do not believe in God and do not accept Christ and His Gospel. For you Catholics, however, it is an irrefutable law, since you have entered upon the inheritance of Christ. Before the Ascension, the Lord said to His disciples: "Go ye therefore, teach ye all nations" (Matthew xxviii. 19). In the spirit of this commandment, the Church professed herself as the teacher of nationals.

The right of the Church to schools is entirely in concord with the right of parents to educate their children. What is incumbent upon the parents in all questions of natural life is incumbent upon the Church with regard to the supernatural life. Parents are prior to the State, and their rights were always and still are, acknowledged by the Church. The prerogative of parents to educate their children cannot be disputed by the State, since it is the parents who gave life to the child. They feed the child and clothe it. The child's life is, as it were, the continuation of theirs. Hence it is their right to demand that their children are educated according to their faith and their religious outlook.

It is their right to withhold their children from schools where their religious convictions are not only disregarded but even made the object of contempt and ridicule. It was this parental right which German parents felt was violated when the Hitler government deprived them of their denominational schools. The children came home from the new schools like little heathens, who smiled derisively or laughed at the prayers of their parents.

You Hungarian parents will likewise feel a violation of your fundamental rights if your children can no longer attend the Catholic schools solely because the dictatorial State closes down our schools by a brutal edict or renders their work impossible.

(Mindszenty, *Four Years' Struggle of the Church in Hungary*, p. 55 ff.)

Appendix II

HUNGARIAN PEACE TREATY

February, 1947

Article 2:

Hungary further undertakes that the laws in force in Hungary shall not, either in their content or in their application, discriminate or entail any discrimination between persons of Hungarian nationality on the ground of their race, sex, language or religion, whether in reference to their persons, property, business, professional or financial interest, status, political or civil rights or any other matter.

Appendices III and IV

THE DECLARATION OF THE COUNCIL OF THE SYNOD OF THE HUNGARIAN REFORMED CHURCH CONCERNING CHURCH AND STATE RELATIONSHIPS AND OTHER CONNECTED ISSUES

April 30, 1948

The Council of the Synod of the Hungarian Reformed Church considers it to be necessary that, arriving at a historic turning point in the church and state relationship, the legislation, or, the Parliament and the Government of Hungary on the one hand, and our congregations and their responsible leaders on the other hand, should fully and completely be informed how the Council looks upon the situation of the Church and what attitude it thinks to be desirable in such a situation.

The 1946 Act of the Hungarian Parliament, which has assured the fullest measure of religious liberty among other human liberties, has made a reassuring impression not on the Hungarian churches only, but all over in world Christianity as well.

According to the practice and principles of our Church, the freedom of religion involves the free activity of church life: the freedom of preaching and teaching, of all missionary and charity work, and self-government of the church.

We must state that the Hungarian Government not merely has not prevented or impeded our Church in whatever respect in the exercise of these fundamental liberties, but it surely has given help and assistance by granting considerable sums, during the post-war financial and economic crisis and difficulties. The Government has given our Church essential material support to be able to pay the stipends and salaries of our pastors and educators, and the pensions of their widows and orphans, lastly it has granted considerable sums to the rebuilding and restoration of war damaged church buildings.

Partly this praiseworthy effort on behalf of the Government, partly a love of freedom inborn in the evangelical confession of our Church, based upon the free and full Word of God, has moved our Church to give expression to a positive standpoint towards the present constitutional and social order of our country.

We want to point out that memorable declaration which has been issued by the Presidency of the Synod concerning the reformation of our church life, after a consensus of the four bishops and four chief curators of the Church Districts, at the session of the Synod, held on May 7th and 8th, 1947. This declaration has given general directions to the further work and deliberations of the Synod. The Council of the Synod want now to quote and underline the following important statements, included in the above mentioned declaration:

"We must take our stand as new men, facing new tasks in a new world."

"The old forms and ways of life, both of the community and of the individuals, have disappeared, and we don't feel at all sorry about it. They have disappeared out of the will of God. We confess that the forms of life in present day Hungary are not alien to our innermost hearts, and we discover the framework of a juster and happier life in them, as ordered by God Himself.

"We confess that we find the essentials of democracy as expressed in the human liberties, contained in the above mentioned 1946 I. Act of the Hungarian Parliament, are not only in concordance with the spirit of evangelical Christianity, but we also recognize the achievements of the Reformation and the noblest traditions of our church history in them.

"We, all of us, do feel that the relationship between our Church and the Hungarian State needs a thorough revision.

"The Hungarian Reformed Church has chosen, as its ideal, a free church living out of its own efforts, supported by free will offerings of its members, obeying its heavenly Lord, to Christ only. We proclaim therefore that a moral independence of the church involves full material independence from state, politics, and all worldly potentates as well.

"Social revolutions, class struggles, have arisen only because men have not put into effect the divine programme of our Lord Jesus Christ. This has been the greatest responsibility and severest judgment the church had to bear. It has proved to be fatal for the Church, that it has not taken the part of the poor and the oppressed radically in the fearful economic struggle. The Church has not given the world a deeply-going, all-embracing social programme which would have prevented the wrongs eventually committed and would have built a better world. It has been a judgment bearing upon the Church that such programme had been realized not only without, but against the Church by men who were convinced that the Church opposed social reform, and when they started a fight against the existing social and economic order they became openly hostile towards the Church as well.

"It has become therefore necessary that the Christian Church should draw all the consequences of the social teaching of the Gospels. The churches must proclaim a radical and courageous social and economic programme giving all their energies to the services of such a programme.

"Our greatest shortcoming, as well as chastisement in the latest years has been that there have been so many who called things Christian which had nothing to do with Christ, but were quite contrary to it. The Reformed Church would deny itself, if it would use its members for experiments in party politics. The Hungarian Reformed Church would forget its substance, if it would conceal the commandments of the laws of God in the great problems of the individuals, the community, the nation and humanity, and would not preach constantly of what it had been taught by its spiritual mother, the Church of Christ."

Considering all that has been said above, the Council of the Synod, using the jurisdiction of the Synod, assigned to it by the 3 paragraphs of the VII Act of the 1942 Church Laws, declares the following:

1. It offers every service to help the new constitutional and social order of Hungary, inasmuch as such services can be rendered in the name of our Lord Jesus Christ through the power of the Holy Ghost.

2. It approves and welcomes the efforts of the Hungarian Government and Parliament to accomplish the fullest measure of religious liberty, and it considers as a logical consequence of these efforts, that the free joining to the various churches should be assured, abolishing the still prevailing legal restrictions. In this way, many bitter controversies, now so frequent, could be done away with for once and all; thus e.g. the quarrels about religious education of children born out of mixed marriages and the abolishing of the presently prevalent and legally fixed rules, commonly called reversions, deciding in advance the religion of children born out of mixed marriages.

3. The Synod recognizes the constitution, legislation, and various institutions of the Hungarian Republic, declaring at the same time that it considers the republican constitution as particularly suited for the raising of free society of free men.

4. The Synod considers the breaking up of the big-landed estates and their distribution amongst the peasants, similarly the nationalization of the greater industrial undertakings in harmony with the spirit of the Scriptures, insofar as these measures have been taken in the interest of a better and juster social order. Our Church will always be ready to serve in a society which has been built with the cooperation of workers, peasants, and the educated classes. It regards such a society suited for a better assertion of the spirit of the Gospels, though necessarily not even such a society can be free of the temptations of human sinfulness.

5. The Council of the Synod expresses its readiness to start negotiations concerning a thorough revision of all aspects of state and church relationships.

6. The Council of the Synod is aware of the fact that the Church must make sacrifices in the new world and among changed conditions. But it believes that our Church will be able to fulfill the tasks given to it by its Lord, the preaching and the teaching of the Gospels, the mission, the care of the poor, and the administration of the Church, notwithstanding changed conditions.

7. The Council of the Synod remembers with gratitude to God all working people of Hungary, the peasants, the workers, both in the industrial undertakings and in the transportation system of the country, the black-coated labourers, and last but not least, the women who in extraordinarily difficult circumstances and with superhuman effort and sacrifice have started new life and rebuilt the ruins, after the terrible destruction caused by the war.

8. Such an immensely great revolutionary change of which we are the witnesses presently cannot run its course without great and many sufferings. The Church would betray itself and its heavenly Lord, if it would not praise God for His mercy towards all who have become victims of all these changes, either out of their own or of others' faults. We must share their sufferings as

the weight of a judgment deserved by all of us. When the Church, however, acts in the role of the good Samaritan among these wounded souls, it strongly objects that any acts of mercy should be exploited for purposes of political experimentations.

9. It was our divine Master who ordered us to seek peace among men; we therefore call upon all our church members, but also the other churches, the responsible political leaders of our country, and all men of goodwill as well, to preserve the peace, this greatest of all God's presents, making even the greatest sacrifices. Nobody must be misled by tempting slogans or alluring phrases in order that any man should promote war and bloodshed. Nay, all men must do everything they can to assist the cause of peace, receiving the Prince of Peace into their hearts, and confessing the Lord Jesus courageously.

10. Lastly, we call upon all members of our Church that, leaving behind hesitation and idle waiting, they should put their hands to the plow, not looking back. They must have their share in the great task of rebuilding our country, bearing responsibility before the face of God, and be with good hope.

"Wherefore lift up the hands which hang down, and the feeble knees; and make straight paths for your feet, lest that which is lame be turned out of the way: but let it rather be healed. Follow peace with all men, and holiness, without which no man shall see the Lord: looking diligently lest any man fail of the grace of God; lest any root of bitterness springing up trouble you, and thereby many be defiled." Hebr. 12.12-15.

(*Die Protestantischen Kirchen in Ungarn*, 1939-1950, Encl. 30, 40.)

Appendix V

AGREEMENT BETWEEN THE HUNGARIAN GOVERNMENT AND THE SYNODICAL COUNCIL OF THE REFORMED CHURCH IN HUNGARY

June 14, 1948

The Commission established by the Government of the Hungarian Republic and the Synodical Council of the Reformed Church in Hungary has come to the following agreement in order to achieve a peaceful and correct understanding between State and Church as desired by both parties:

1. In order to regularize the situation of the Church in the Hungarian Republic, the Government of the Hungarian Republic and the Reformed Church in Hungary have appointed a standing common committee to work out proposals for the new religion rules, among them in the first place one on the religion of the children. The changes—in accordance with the State religion rules (in the church rules) will be made by the church legislature.

2. The Government of the Hungarian Republic also at this occasion expresses the fact that it recognizes the full freedom in the exercise of religion and assures it with all possible and necessary means. The Hungarian Reformed Church however also at this occasion establishes the fact that the legislation of the Government of the Hungarian Republic has also so far assured, protected and in accordance with Article XXXIII, 1947 even greatly expanded,

the full freedom in faith, and with the contribution toward personnel and material expenditures of the Church has made possible the maintenance of church life within the hitherto existing frame.

3. The Government of the Hungarian Republic in accordance with existing legal principles considers the following points as being within the circle of free exercise of church life: Holding divine services in churches, other suitable public buildings, private homes and out of doors; holding Bible classes in churches, schools, private homes, community houses; the mission work of church papers and independent press productions; distribution of Bibles and periodicals (pamphlets), holding community and church conferences and retreats; obligatory religious instruction at school and the exercise of welfare work. To this end, it permits the Church free of charge the use of school halls and other suitable rooms of State schools, wherever the Church finds this necessary, outside the normal school time, in agreement with the school authorities and against a promise to pay for any damage made during the use, for divine services, Sunday Schools, Bible classes, choir practice and other religious and church meetings and gatherings until such a time when the church communities can supply other buildings for this purpose.*

The Government of the Hungarian Republic furthermore regards as part of the free exercise of church life: church jurisdiction within the frame and in a manner in which this activity controls church laws which are approved by the head of the State.

4. The Government of the Hungarian Republic takes note of the obligation of the Reformed Church in Hungary which has been given to it according to the command of Christ and the confessions of the Church in order to stimulate her believers to good works, especially to care for the poor, destitute, orphans and old people, honours this and allows it to be honoured. Therefore it assures within the frame of existing legal rules the right to maintain and develop welfare agencies and the collection of gifts.

5. The Government of the Hungarian Republic takes cognizance of the desire of the Reformed Church to realize the principle "Free Church in Free State."

During the interim period in which the Reformed Church can gain material strength, the Government of the Hungarian Republic states its willingness to grant the Church State aid in the following manner:

a) The Hungarian Republic assures a personnel State contribution in accordance with the hitherto existing functionary salaries for the period June 30 to December 31, 1948 and from that date for five years. This sum for personnel payments decreases on January 1, 1954 by 25%. The Government assures payment of the remaining sum of 75% until December 31, 1958. From January 1, 1959 to December 31, 1963, 50% of the present State contribution must be paid, from January 1, 1964 until December 31, 1968, 25%. All State contributions will cease on December 31, 1968.

b) As contribution toward extraordinary expenditures the Government also assures yearly 10% of the future annual sum for personnel State aid.

---

* It must be mentioned here that this is a reference to schools a larger number of which were formerly in the possession of the Church and given to the State, which schools replaced in smaller communities the community hall and often also the Church (Part of original text).

c) The Government of the Hungarian Republic assigns furthermore exclusively for the reconstruction, new building and maintenance and repair of church buildings, i.e. of churches, community houses, rectories, one year's allocation of the State aid for the period August 1, 1946 and July 31, 1948, for material aid to maintain, equip and erect church buildings of the Reformed Church. The State contribution will also decrease as indicated above every 5 years and ceases on December 31, 1968.

d) All State payments hitherto made under different titles must in accordance with the above principles be decreased gradually.

e) The State will take over the support of members of the Reformed Institute for retired pastors, their widows and orphans also in accordance with payments of functionary pensions, as well as pensions of pastors retiring before December 31, 1953.

6. The Hungarian Reformed Church will in its order of worship in accordance with the clear command of the Gospel pray for the Hungarian Republic, the State head, the Government, the prosperity and peace of the Hungarian people, and conduct divine services on State holidays in accordance with the confession of the Church. At the same time, it makes known that the hymn book which is about to appear, contains hymns suitable for such occasions.

7. The Reformed Church in Hungary takes cognizance of the decision of the Government of the Hungarian Republic to nationalize non-State schools and annexed internats. During the nationalization period of Reformed schools, the followig agreement will be followed:

a) The Government takes over all teaching and other personnel of the schools in question and the annexed internats into State service with effect from July 1, 1948.

b) The buildings and sinecures of the schools and annexed internats taken over by the State become possession of the State, with all debits per May 15, 1948. Any unclear points will be decided by the Minister for Worship and Teaching following a hearing of the committee formed in accordance with point 1.

c) The Government agrees that the teaching personnel exercise the function of a cantor and continue their cantor service for two years after the agreement on hitherto existing conditions. The sinecures intended for cantor service remain possession of the Church.

d) The nationalization does not affect the teaching institutions of exclusive ecclesiastical purpose which do not serve for general education, e.g. theological academies, preaching seminaries, deacon homes and deaconess homes, mission seminars and any other eccleiastical institutes for the training of workers. The present legal situation between the Debrecen theological faculty and the ministry for Worship and Teaching remains unchanged.

e) The Government agrees that in view of the merits of the Reformed Church on the field of Hungarian school education and in order to secure the training of future pastors, of the Reformed colleges with great historical tradition the folowing may remain church schools—but not on a larger scope:

The Gymnasium, Lyceum and teachers seminar, belonging to the Reformed Collegium in Sarospatak,

The Gymnasium, Lyceum and teachers seminar of the Reformed Collegium in Debrecen, and the girls lyceum and teachers seminar of the Doczy Institute,

The Gymnasium of the Reformed Collegium in Papa, the Reformed

Gymnasium in Budapest IX, Lonyay Utca and as part of it the Reformed Baar Madas girls gymnasium.

Any suggestions for the expansion of the hitherto existing frame within the coming years must be made to the Government through the committee mentioned sub. 1.) The Government of the Hungarian Republic assures the maintenance of the above colleges during the period of State contribution in the same manner as indicated sub point 5.) a) of the agreement regarding personnel State maintenance: when State contributions cease, their maintenance is full responsibility of the Church.

f) The Government of the Hungarian Republic recognizes and assures the right of the Reformed Church that in the State schools the obligatory religious instruction will continue to be freely exercised. The question of religious instruction is to be newly organized especially in consideration of members of free churches and those who are without confession.

g) The personnel in schools which are to be dissolved (public schools, teachers seminars) will be taken over by the State to join the ranks of other teaching personnel taken over by the State in accordance with their rank, and will be employed accordingly.

h) If the Kecskemeter Law Academy should be dissolved, the State will see that the professors teaching at the present time are employed in a manner corresponding to their present position.

i) The Government of the Hungarian Republic will see that where children of non-Hungarian language (Rumanian, Serbian, Ruthenian, Slovakian and German) attend, the teaching will take place in accordance with the parents wish in their mother tongue. At the same time, the Government will endeavor to achieve a similar arrangement for the school youth living in neighboring states (parity principle) whose mother tongue is Hungarian.

8. The Church will alter its laws regarding teaching in accordance with the new State laws.

9. The discussion of proposals for any further unsettled questions will be conducted by the committee formed, sub-point 1.)

Budapest, October 7, 1948

In the name of the Government
of the Hungarian Republic:

Ortutay Gyula e.h.
Minister for Worship and Teaching.

In the name of the Synod of
the Reformed Church in Hungary:

Dr. Révész Imre e.h.
Ref. Bishop, spiritual chairman
of the Synod

Dr. Balogh Jeno e.h.
Worldly Chairman of the Synod.

(*Five Years of Hungarian Protestantism*, 1945-1950, p. 23 ff.)

Appendix VI

LAST PASTORAL LETTER OF MINDSZENTY ON GOVERNMENT ABUSES

November 18, 1948

Reference No. 8021.   No. 104

Beloved in Christ,

For many weeks attempts have been made to state "resolutions" directed against me in all the townships and village communities of Hungary. I am being blamed for counter-revolutionary plots and activities hostile to the people, because of the Marianic Celebration in 1947-48. It is complained that reconciliation between the Church and the State was frustrated and the demand is made that these "activities obnoxious to the people" should cease.

The goal of those "Days of Mary," celebrated in the Marianic Year, was the deepening of the traditional Hungarian devotion for the Holy Virgin and the strengthening of faith. Never were purely political matters made the subject of speeches on those occasions. The subjects were the Virtues of the Mother of God, the Ten Commandments, human dignity, love and truth.

Those Marianic days attained their ends. The Bishops of Hungary, who are the competent judges, testified to this in their letter of November 3rd. They identified themselves with me against those attacks which were launched against the Marianic days. This same testimony is given also by the millions who represent public opinion on this country and against whose heroic patience, means had to be adopted which degrade those who employ them and which are in opposition to the principle of religious freedom guaranteed by democratic laws.

As to the legal significance of these "resolutions," it should be noted that no elections of local autonomous administrations have been held, in spite of many official promises, except in Budapest. Consequently all those decisions or "resolutions" which have been staged in counties, townships and villages lack any legal basis. The signatures to them are extorted by threats of loss of livelihood and freedom. The country is condemned to silence and public opinion has been made a mere frivolous jest. Democratic freedom in this country means that any opinion that differs from the official one is silenced. If a man dares to raise his voice in contradiction he is dismissed from his post because of his criticism of democracy, as many examples show, or he is punished in other ways. I feel the deepest sympathy with the sufferings of these people and compassion for every man who has fallen a victim of these measures. I was greatly impressed and deeply moved by many wonderful examples of unflinching courage and loyalty.

We asked the Government to publish those letters of mine to which such strong exception has been taken and to submit them to the judgment of public opinion in the whole world. But this has not been done. They continue to indulge in defamatory generalizations.

With regard to the fact that between Church and State—or perhaps we should say "Parties"—no agreement has yet been reached, it is well known that the Church was invited to negotiate an agreement only after a delay of three months, although she had publicly declared her willingness to enter into negotiations. At first it was announced that the questions pending between Church and State must be settled by mutual agreement. When, however, the Church was at last invited to negotiate, the main point—the problem of the schools—had been settled already by the State and the Church had to play the role of scapegoat.

I am looking calmly at this artificial whipping up of the waves. In the place where I stand, not by the grace of any party, but by the grace and confidence of the Holy See, such troubled waters are not an extraordinary phenomenon. This history proves.

Of my predecessors, two were killed in action: two were robbed of all their possessions: one was taken prisoner and deported: one was assassinated: one exiled and one died after visiting and nursing victims of an epidemic.

Of all my predecessors, however, not one stood so bare of all means as I do. Such a systematic and purposeful propaganda of lies, time and again disproved but time and again repeated, has never been organized against the seventy-eight predecessors in my office. I stand for God, for Church, and for Hungary. This duty was imposed upon me by the fate of my nation which stands alone, an orphan in the whole world. As compared with the sufferings of my people, my own fate is of no importance.

I do not accuse my accusors. If I am compelled to speak out from time to time and to state the facts as they are, it is only the misery of my people which forces me to do so and the urge for truth.

I am praying for a world of truth and love. I am praying for those who, in the words of our Lord, "know not what they do."

I forgive them from the bottom of my heart.

Josef Mindszenty,
Cardinal,
Prince Primate of Hungary,
Archbishop of Esztergom.

Esztergo, November 18, 1949

(Mindszenty, *Four Years' Struggle of the Church in Hungary*, p. 182)

Appendix VII

SPEECH OF DEPUTY PRIME MINISTER RAKOSI AGAINST THE CATHOLIC CHURCH

November 28, 1948

(Excerpt)

Now there can no longer be any political tolerance. This tolerant policy, which used kid gloves for dealing with spies, traitors, smugglers, adherents of the royal Hapsburgs and other reactionaries moving about in the gowns of priests or those of a cardinal, is over and done with forever. The law must be applied, not only to small clerical criminals. We cannot allow such organized shock troops of Fascism as clerical reaction to disturb any longer our reconstruction and stabilization.

(Barron and Waddams, *Communism and the Churches*, p. 66)

Appendix VIII

CONCORDAT BETWEEN THE STATE AND THE LUTHERAN CHURCH

December 14, 1948

(Full Text, Lutheran World Federation *Newsbulletin*, Vol. IV. 2)

The Church and the State will form a common commission to issue new laws concerning the religion and especially the religious education of children.

The Government declares that it will in every way assure full freedom of religion. The Church for her part acknowledges that the State has up to now maintained and protected the freedom of religion and even supported the efforts of the Church.

The Government guarantees to the Church freedom of worship in churches and official buildings, in homes and open places, freedom of the church press, of spreading the Bible and religious literature, holding conferences, religious instruction and the ecclesiastical work of mercy . . . The Government guarantees her the right to maintain social institutions . . .

The State will reduce its financial support on a sliding scale. After December 31, 1968, all support will cease.

The Church yields to the decision of the nationalization of church schools. The teachers will be employed by the State. All school-buildings with their equipment and funds as well as the territories belonging to them, will become property of the State. However, this nationalization does not refer to theological seminaries and departments, deaconess institutions, and schools training voluntary workers for the Church. The Church will continue to have the right to give religious instruction in the schools taken over by the State.

The Church will also in the future offer prayers on behalf of the Hungarian Republic, its President and the Government.

(Ecumenical Press Service, January 21, 1949)

Appendix IX

HUNGARIAN PROTESTANTS' STATEMENTS ON MINDSZENTY

I.

January 16, 1949

The Hungarian Reformed Church could not remain silent in the various questions concerning the churches, brought forward by the so-called "case of Mindszenty." A statement was broadcast in this matter already by Bishop Albert Bereczky under the title: "Church and the Churches in Hungary." We feel that we must draw our conclusions in three particular points.

We want to point out, from this radio statement, the following words, addressed to Christian world public opinion: "We were led by sincere desire for peace and tranquillity to recognize the authorities ordered by God in a country recovering from wounds caused by the last war, and to conclude an agreement which assured religious liberty and the free possibility of church activity." The representatives of Western Christianity who had visited us frequently recently—among them many outstanding personalities—were able to assert that our Church has been in the possession of both inner and outer liberty to accomplish its work according to the Gospels. We have emphasized, therefore, over and over again that the Archbishop of Esztergom has not been fighting for religious liberty, for the simple reason because such a fight has not been necessary at all, but he has fought for political ends. Whatever opinion should be formed on such a fight by men and churches, we Hungarian Protestants do know that we definitely reject all attempts to restore the rule of the Hapsburgs, a dynasty of most evil memories, and a feudalistic regime, a logical outcome of the former. We beseech the leaders and members of sister churches in foreign countries to believe, all of them who truly live in faith and with responsibility for the welfare of the Church—that they serve the cause of the Church in Hungary best, if they help us to separate the "case of Mindszenty" from the vital interests of the church.

We ask members of other churches in Hungary to do everything possible not to mix up political experiments with the cause of the Church. All this logically means to have our peace with the Hungarian Republic, an authority ordered by God. We must have no doubt that everybody who unwittingly identifies any political experiment with the cause of the Church endangers it with unfounded suspicions.

Lastly we feel it necessary to apply to the Hungarian Government, asking its responsible members that in the future as in the past, they should not identify the Church and its manifold activity in the service of the Gospel with any kind of political activity, including the present one, which only appears of ecclesiastical character.

Signed by:

Dr. Eugen Balogh,
Lay President of the Synod and General Conventus:
Bishop Emergy Révész, D.D.,
Ministerial President of the Synod and General Conventus.

The same statement was agreed to and seconded by Prof. Francis Kiss, President of the Hungarian Federation of Free Churches; Rev. Dr. Emery Somogyi, President of the Hungarian Baptist Union; Rev. John Szécsey, Deputy Superintendent of the Hungarian Methodist Church; Rev. Ladislas Mishnay, President of the Adventist Church in Hungary.

(Mindszenty, *Four Years' Struggle of the Church in Hungary*, p. 121.)

II.

January 18, 1949

The bishops of the Hungarian Evangelical (Lutheran) Church do not want to interfere with the internal affairs of another church, neither to criticize the standpoint of another church in the matter of a conclusion of an agreement with the State, and still less to express an opinion about a matter to be tried in court, knowing the command of the Apostle, I Peter iv, 15, "None of the Christians busybody in other men's matters," and also what Romans xiv, 12, said: "Every one of us shall give account of himself to God." Nevertheless we feel that evidences published in the case of Joseph Mindszenty, Archbishop of Esztergom, have drawn attention to such questions, and may lead to consequences that it is not only our right, but our duty to say what we are thinking.

We have heard therefore gladly of a statement made by representatives of other Hungarian Protestant denominations in this matter, in approvement of which, we, as the spiritual leaders of the Hungarian Evangelical Church, state, being anxious to say the full truth of our own accord, that pastors are not restrained in any way to render spiritual services which belong to the essentials of church life. They preach in churches filled with the faithful, and administer sacraments freely.

It is the consequence of misinformation or political partiality to say not a word about religious persecution in Spain, and to speak of the suppression of churches and religion in Hungary, when there is no foundation whatever for it.

The Government of Hungary gives substantial financial aid to all churches in just proportions and the free preaching of the Gospel is assured. It is political Catholicism which has come into conflict with the State; Joseph Mindszenty, Archbishop of Esztergom, has been a typical representative of political Catholicism. We believe an activity which has had nothing to do with the functions of the church as it is understood by the substance of the Gospels, would have been deemed contrary to the existing laws, in the judgment of all governments. As against this, there are followers of spiritual Catholicism in Hungary too, among the bishops, members of the lower clergy and naturally simple members of the Roman Catholic Church, all of whom are urging an honest agreement with the State.

We are convinced that God has not entrusted the care of the royal crown to the Church, but the peace of men's souls, and our duty is not to restore the throne of the Hapsburgs, a dynasty of evil memories to all Hungarians, but more especially to all Protestants, but to serve the Kingdom of God. This can be done in Hungary freely, which can be testified by all unbiased visitors arriving in our country from abroad.

Signed by:

> Bishop Joseph Szabó
> Zoltan Turoczy
> Louis Vetö
> Deputy Bishop Daniel Benkoczy

Appendix X

GOVERNMENT DIRECTIVE TO EDUCATIONAL LEADERS CONCERNING RELIGIOUS ACTIVITIES

February 11, 1949

No. 64293/1949 III.

To all directors, school circles and school inspectors:

I draw your attention to the fact that the Government of the Hungarian Republic has made an agreement with the Reformed, United and Evangelical

Church and with the Israelite community in order to peacefully and correctly regularize the relation between State and Church.

I lay great stress on the keeping and exercise of the obligations taken over in the agreements on behalf of the Government, and request you to carefully and thoroughly carry them out and to see to it that your orders comply with the agreement.

I. In accordance with point 3 of the agreement, the churches and the various church communities, respectively, will submit requests for school rooms for divine services, Bible classes, choir practice and other religious meetings. These requests refer partly to individual cases, partly to the use of school rooms for a longer period. In accordance with the agreement, the school rooms are given for these purposes on condition that the Church supplies the heating, lighting and cleaning and is obliged in writing to take over the material responsibility for any damages. The use of the school rooms, however, is permitted to the churches and church communities, respectively, only within the frame and manner in which they were used for church purposes before the nationalization of the schools. A school room cannot be used therefore if it was not used for the above purposes before the nationalization of the schools, or if church meetings were not held in the schools; but where before the nationalization of the schools a meeting took place in a school room once a month, it may be used once a month now but not once a week.

II. In accordance with the agreement, the teaching personnel, who are cantors, can exercise their service on the same conditions for two years after the agreement. In this respect I must determine that the State teachers are obliged to fulfill their duty within the prescribed period, and may exercise the cantor service or secondary occupation in their free time only. If therefore the cantor service falls within the hours of classes during this period, the teacher cannot be freed from the fulfillment of his school-obligation, but no change is allowed in the period set for his school-obligation.

III. The agreement assures everybody, "also members of the teaching personnel," full freedom in the exercise of religion, and considers as being within the free exercise of church life the participation or activity (levity service) in divine services, Bible classes, choir practice and other church meetings. Therefore this kind of activity of teaching personnel requires no special permission. No permission need be requested or given for this. But this religious activity of teaching personnel may not be carried out within the period of their obligation as State employee, but outside this duty. Therefore, for this reason no release from duty connected with the main occupation and in general with its activity will be given.

In connection with this, special attention must be given to the fact that such an activity of the State teaching personnel with regard to the People's democracy should cultivate the peaceful spirit, and not present conduct not in agreement with the State appointment.

Budapest, February 11, 1949   Ortutay Gyula e.h.

(*Die Protestantischen Kirchen in Ungarn*, 1939-1950)

Appendix XI

EXCERPTS OF THE HUNGARIAN CONSTITUTION

August 18, 1949

(*Uj Harangszo* of August 21, 1949)

Paragraph 54 of the Hungarian Constitution

1. The Hungarian People's Republic assures conscience-freedom for the citizens and the right to freely exercise religion.

2. In the interest of the assurance of conscience-freedom, the Hungarian People's Republic separates the Church from the State.

(*Die Protestantischen Kirchen in Ungarn,* 1939-1950.)

Appendix XII

RULES OF THE PRESIDING COUNCIL OF THE HUNGARIAN PEOPLE'S REPUBLIC CONCERNING RELIGIOUS INSTRUCTION

September 6, 1949

(*Magyar Kozlony* of September 6, 1949)

Paragraph 1. According to the rules in paragraph 54 of the constitution of the Hungarian People's Republic regarding separation of Church and State, religious instruction in the schools is not compulsory.

Paragraph 2. This rule comes into force on the day of its announcement. The minister for Religious Affairs and Teaching will attend to its carrying out.

Instructions for the Minister for Religious Affairs and Teaching:

The minister for Religious Affairs and Teaching is authorized by the Rule No. 5, 1949 of the Presiding Council of the Hungarian People's Republic to order the following:

Paragraph 1. Beginning with the school year 1949/50, religious instruction is not compulsory.

Paragraph 2. Those parents who desire religious instruction for their children, must submit their wish before September 15 verbally or in writing to the school.

Paragraph 3. The minister for Religious Affairs and Teaching will supply the funds for religious instruction.

Paragraph 4. The present ruling comes into force on the day of its announcement.

(*Die Protestantischen Kirchen in Ungarn,* 1939-1950)

Appendix XIII

OATH FOR PASTORS AND CHURCH EMPLOYEES

December 6, 1949

(*Uj Harangszo* of Dec. 18, 1949)

In accordance with the ruling of the ministerial council 4288/49 of Oct. 14, 1949.

I, ..., swear that I will be true to the Hungarian People's Republic, its people and constitution, will keep to the rulings, will maintain State official secrets, serve the interests of the people within the scope of my office, and in all things look to develop the Hungarian People's Republic to strengthen and expand.

Common statement of the Reformed and Lutheran Church leaders of Dec. 6, 1949:

The contents of the oath formula for church employees are according to the viewpoint of Christian conscience unobjectionable. No word is contained in it which a faithful servant of the Church of Jesus Christ cannot accept with a free and good conscience.

(*Die Protestantischen Kirchen in Ungarn*, 1939-1950)

Appendix XIV

AGREEMENT BETWEEN THE GOVERNMENT AND THE EVANGELICAL LUTHERAN CHURCH LEADERSHIP REGARDING THE NATIONALIZA-TION OF CHURCH PROPERTY OF DEC. 31, 1949

(*Uj Harangszo* of Feb. 5, 1950)

Agreement between the presidency of the Evangelical General Convent as representative of the autonomous bodies (church communities, senior councils and church districts) of the Evangelical Church in Hungary, as well as the church foundations, offices, institutes, organizations and unions under their control—as sellers, and the Hungarian State as buyer, based on the following conditions:

1. The presidency of the Evangelical General Convent sells for always and irrevocably, and the buyer buys the sites with buildings etc. under the control of the sellers.

2. The conditions of sale and purchase are as follows:

(Extract)

The owner of the church sites (church community etc.) can offer these until latest December 31, 1952. From the offered sites, the State will take over those which are to be used for agriculture. The purchase price is in accordance with each "Kataster"—crown; of the sites offered in 1949, 70 guilders, of sites offered in 1950, 65 guilders, sites offered in 51 and 52, 60 guilders. For the building on the sites in accordance with each Kataster-crown of the area belonging to the independent economy-unity further 5 guilders. An independent economy-unity is the area which officially serves the farm-building.

The state pays the price during 20 years from the first day of the year following the acceptance of the offer, without interest in such a way that in the first five years 40, in the second, third and fourth year each 20 percent of the purchase price are paid out in quarterly equal sums.

The State acquired the right of possession of the site on the day the offer is accepted, but the selling church body enjoys during the year of acceptance of the offer the benefit of the sold site and bears until the end of the year the taxes.

———

Information from the church leadership to the communities.

The presidency of the Evangelical General Convent informs the communities of its joy in succeeding in making an agreement with the Hungarian State regarding church property. This agreement has the approval of the General Presbytery.

The above agreement does not affect the free disposal of church property as set forth in the church constitution. This agreement determines that if any church property owners (church communities etc.) wish to offer their property, the transfer of the site takes place on the following conditions:

The agreement does not make it necessary for church property owners to offer their sites, but renders a possibility for them to do so on conditions which are more favorable than usual. If the competent organs of the Agricultural Ministry work out a soil reform program of an area, the Agricultural Ministry informs the church authorities accordingly. The plan is then sent by the church authorities to those who are interested, and any autonomous church body that owns property can decide freely in accordance with the church rules whether it will avail itself of the offer on the given conditions.

The buildings on a site with the vicarage are not part of the independent economy-unity and not considered as part of the fields to be transferred with the farm-building.

(*Die Protestantischen Kirchen in Ungarn*, 1939-1950)

Appendix XV

CIRCULAR LETTER OF LUTHERAN BISHOPS TO THEIR PASTORS

February 23, 1950

(*Uj Harangszo* of April 2, 1950)

The minister for religious affairs informed our General Inspector on February 23 that the Government of the Hungarian People's Republic and Hungarian people on April 4 of this year will remember in special gratitude the fifth return of the day on which the war ended in our country, and our people could commence the great work of removing rubble and the reconstruction of the new life.

The agreement of our Church with the State commits us in point 7 to remember the State celebrations in a way which is in agreement with God's Word and the confession of our Church at our divine services.

God's Word commits us theologically to consider all authorities so that we may lead a quiet life in all godliness and honesty.

But our unity with our people commits us to thank God this day that the bloodshed of war has ceased, to thank Him for each ruin that is removed and for each new spring in life, and to ask for His peace-preserving mercy.

Our church remembers the celebration in prayers at the morning service on Palm Sunday. We ask you to think of the above in repentance and gratitude to the Prince of Peace in your prayers at the Palm Sunday worship service.

(*Die Protestantischen Kirchen in Ungarn*, 1939-1950)

Appendix XVI

EXCERPT FROM AN ADDRESS GIVEN BY THE MINISTER OF PUBLIC
WORSHIP AND INSTRUCTION TO THE PARTY COMMITTEE

June 7, 1950

(*Uj Harangszo* of June 18, 1950)

We must start a vast work of enlightenment, and in the first place explain to our party colleagues and also to all workers that any father who sends his child to religion classes, places it in the hands of the enemy and entrusts his soul and thinking to the enemies of peace and imperialistic warmongers.

A part of our working people believes that participation of children in religious instruction is a private matter which has nothing to do with the political conviction of their parents. They are wrong. To send children to a reactionary pastor for religious instruction, is a political movement against the People's democracy, whether intentional or not. Optional religious instruction in the schools is in this connection not yet the last possibility of realizing the democratic principles. We do not wish to change anything yet in the present order of optional religious instruction, but we emphasize that this order cannot present the clerical reaction with a free hand to agitate the children against the People's democracy, to influence the children in the schools in a reactionary manner. So far, we have applied the principle of optional religious instruction too liberally, and this we shall also alter. Optional religious instruction cannot apply to technical and similar schools, even less so because the youth at these schools, if they wanted to, did attend religious instruction in the lower classes. No university has room for theological faculties any longer.

Logical consequence of the separation of State and Church is that the theological training of pastors is solely a Church concern and no responsibility of the State. The theological faculties must therefore be handed over to the churches . . .

Already now I warn against any exaggeration, i.e. removing or branding every working person who sends his children to religious instruction in spite of our enlightenment. Probably we shall have to commence some propaganda against the participation of children in religious instruction, but we must not take administrative steps, and any threat of material disadvantage is not allowed.

The agreement with the Protestant churches is still in force and is working well. This agreement proves that the People's Republic assures complete religious freedom and that the churches, if they do not turn out to be accomplices of foreign and native reaction, can live in peace and fulfill their responsibility in the People's Democracy. But even in the Protestant churches there are reactionary efforts. In presbyteries in very many places 'Kulaks' are in the majority; a few Protestant pastors follow the Catholic reaction in connection with April 4th as their example, and the election of reactionary, formerly Horthy politicians, for leading offices of the Protestant churches shows that the reaction is still struggling to put its foot on these churches.

In carrying out the basic principles, religion within the party is no private matter, but we must make a difference between plain party members and party officials, and must not in any case make party membership dependent on the fact whether our party members are religious. In the first place, we must expect from our party officials, our leading men, that they do not send their children to religious instruction courses, do not take part in religious ceremonies and train their wives in the spirit of communistic conception.

Also, we must patiently endeavor to enlighten our members, and ensure through training and propaganda that they realize: "In going to Church, taking part in processions, sending our children to religious instruction, we unconsciously further the efforts of clerical reaction."

(*Die Protestantischen Kirchen in Ungarn*, 1939-1950)

Appendix XVII

NEGOTIATIONS BETWEEN REPRESENTATIVES OF THE ROMAN
CATHOLIC CHURCH AND THE STATE
at the Ministry of Education, Budapest

July 8, 1950

Representatives: Rakosi for the State; Rev. Ferenc Horvath, Jesuit, for Archbishop Grösz.

Horvath opened the conversation by demanding the release of Mindszenty.

Rakosi: "Please, no arguments. The people decided that."

Horvath: "You know as well as I do who really decided that. It was anything but a people's decision."

Rakosi: "It's no use. We can't turn the clocks back."

Monasteries:

Rakosi promised to return 8 of 157 church schools seized two years earlier, and to include religious courses in the curriculum of the Hungarian schools. But he insisted that the monasteries must go (By September all were emptied).

Monks and nuns might work with priests and in the villages, teach in Communist-run schools, or become itinerants. But there could be no organized orders, and no habits.

Horvath: "How can you expect monks to teach against their principles, from Communist textbooks?"

Rakosi: "I made you an offer. Take it or leave it. If you leave it, you openly admit that you refuse to educate Hungarian youth, the right to which you demand."

Bishop Czapik: "In four years, you people in the Government haven't kept one of your promises. What assurance have we that you will keep the new ones?"

Rakosi: "Very well. You don't believe us. What are you going to do about it?"

(*Time* Magazine, Oct. 9, 1950)

Appendix XVIII

THE DECISION TAKEN AT THE NATIONAL CONFERENCE OF CATHOLIC PRIESTS

August 1, 1950

The participants of the conference, Catholic priests and monks, belonging to all ecclesiastical districts of the country, declare that they are faithful priests of the Roman Catholic Holy Mother Church and Her Head, faithful citizens of the Hungarian People's Democratic State. They regard it as their duty as priests and citizens to fulfill their vocation as pastors of the soul, and to support the great work of the Hungarian people in building their country, and active participation in the fight to ensure a lasting peace. They decided therefore:

1. They wish for an urgent and complete agreement between Church and State which mutually respects the laws of Church and State. They, therefore, greet with pleasure the discussions which have started between the representatives of the Bench of Bishops and the representatives of the Government of the people and they wish to promote these discussions on their part with all their strength.

2. In order to re-create confidence between the clergy and the working people they express their fidelity towards the State of the People's Democracy, the Hungarian People's Republic. This they regard even more as their patriotic duty, because the People's Democracy considers the social liberation of the Hungarian people and its raising to a human level as its main task, and proclaims that the clergy believe to be according to its Christian creed: "The greatest value is man." They declare that they will do all in their power to implement the Five-Year Economic Plan in order to contribute to raising the material and spiritual standard of life of the Hungarian people. They oppose every internal and external reactionary aspiration; first of all, of course, all

reaction within their own ranks which endeavours to hinder and sabotage the implementation of the Five-Year Plan and the construction of socialism. They do not want reaction to use the Holy Catholic Mother Church for its own ends. They do not lament the social injustices of the past. They want to progress welded together with the people in patriotism, love and work.

3. They support without reservation the fight for peace of the Hungarian people and they want to take part actively in it, keeping in mind the following sentence from the Sermon on the Mount of our Lord Jesus Christ: "Happy are the peace-makers, for they shall be called the sons of God." That is why they support unanimously the Stockholm Peace Petition and appeal to all those brother priests who have not yet signed the Petition that they should regard the signing of it as their urgent Catholic duty.

4. As the defence of lasting peace is in the interests both of Church and State, and both the clergy and the working people, they condemn the war-mongering of the imperialists and the imperialist interference through war aimed at the suppression of the struggle for freedom of colonial and semi-colonial peoples. In the name of true Christian humanism they protect against the publicizing and use of the atom bomb. They stigmatize those who, in connection with Korean war, demand the use of the atom bomb. They protest against bombing attacks on the Korean population, on defenceless towns and villages.

5. In the interests of peace between State and Church, cooperation between the working people and the clergy, they believe it to be desirable that the State power should with all its strength support the clergy and monks true to the people in the fulfillment of their vocation and in their work for the reconstruction of the country and for lasting peace.

("State and Church in Hungary, Catholic Clergy for Peace," *Hungarian News and Information Service*, 33 Pembridge Square, London, October, 1950)

Appendix XIX

AGREEMENT BETWEEN THE GOVERNMENT OF THE HUNGARIAN PEOPLE'S REPUBLIC AND THE CATHOLIC BENCH OF BISHOPS

August 31, 1950

Inspired by the wish to ensure the peaceful coexistence of the State and the Catholic Church and thereby to promote the unity and constructive work of the Hungarian people and the peaceful development of our country, the Government of the Hungarian People's Republic and the Hungarian Catholic Bench of Bishops conducted negotiations and concluded the following agreements:

I.

1. The Bench of Bishops recognizes and supports, in accordance with the duty of its citizens, the State order and Constitution of the Hungarian People's Republic. It declared that it will take action, according to the laws of the Church, against persons in the Church who act against the lawful order of the Hungarian People's Republic and the constructive work of its Government.

2. The Bench of Bishops definitely condemns all subversive activities, from whatever quarters they may come, directed against the State and social order of the Hungarian People's Republic. It declares that it will not permit the exploitation of the religious sentiments of the believers or the use of the Catholic Church for political purposes against the State.

3. The Bench of Bishops calls upon all faithful Catholics, as citizens and patriots, to participate with all their strength in the great work which is being done, under the leadership of the Government of the People's Republic, by the entire Hungarian people in order to raise the living standard and secure social justice through the realization of the Five-Year-Plan. The Bench of Bishops appeals to the clergy with the particular request not to put up any resistance against the agricultural producers' co-operative movement which, as a voluntary organization, is founded on the moral principle of the solidarity of man.

4. The Bench of Bishops supports the peace movement. It approves the endeavours of the Hungarian people and the Government of the Hungarian People's Republic in the defence of peace; it condemns all warmongering and the use of atomic weapons, and therefore will consider the first government to use the atom bomb, guilty of a crime against humanity.

II.

1. The Government of the Hungarian People's Republic guarantees, in accordance with the Constitution of the People's Republic, full freedom of religious worship for Catholics and freedom of religious activity for the Catholic Church.

2. The Government of the Hungarian People's Republic agrees to return eight denominational schools to the Catholic Church (six boys' and two girls' schools), furthermore it agrees that in the schools of the Catholic Church the necessary teaching staff to be composed of the required number of persons, male and female, from the Catholic teaching orders.

3. The Government of the Hungarian People's Republic, in the spirit of the agreement already concluded with the other denominations, is ready to provide for the financial needs of the Catholic Church. For 18 years, that is, until the Catholic Church shall be able to finance itself from its own resources, it will remit an adequate sum, to be proportionately reduced every three or five years, for the requirements of the Catholic Church. Within these financial provisions, the Government of the Hungarian People's Republic pays special attention to ensure an adequate subsistence for the parish clergy.

For the practical execution of the above agreement a committee with equal representation from both sides is to be formed from representatives of the Government of the Hungarian People's Republic and of the Bench of Bishops. Budapest, August 30, 1950

In the name of the Council of	In the name of the Hungarian
Ministers of the Hungarian People's Republic	Catholic Bench of Bishops
Signed by:—	Signed by:—
József Darvas	József Grösz
Minister of Religion and Education	Archbishop of Kalocsa

("State and Church in Hungary, Catholic Clergy for Peace," *Hungarian News and Information Service*, 33 Pembridge Square, London, October, 1950)

Appendix XX

DECREE REGARDING TEACHERS OF RELIGION

of September 19, 1950

The Minister for Religious Affairs orders the following:

Paragraph 1—

Religious instruction will be given in the schools by full-time teachers or teachers paid by the hour.

Paragraph 2—

1. A "full-time" teacher is one who teaches religion in the towns or in schools at which the obligatory number of hours for general education at the school in question is fulfilled.

2. The full-time or independent teacher conducts the instruction of religion as his sole responsibility and may not accept another gainful employment which would secure his living.

3. The independent teacher receives pay and family allowance in accordance with No. 4 of the tables attached to the ruling No. 8250/1948. VIII.1./Kor: regarding social security and vacation; he has the same privilege as the employees in public service.

4. The Executive Committee of the Committees of Counsellors are instructed to submit before September 15 of each year to the Minister for Religious Affairs the number of pupils attending religious instruction, divided according to towns and schools as well as denominations.

Paragraph 3—

1. In towns or schools where no "full-time" teacher of religion functions, a religious teacher will attend to the instruction, paid by the hour.

2. The teacher who is paid by the hour, receives payment in accordance with the number of classes given by him; the hourly fee is the same as that paid to all teachers at the school in question. Church employees, who receive a salary-supplement for their activity as pastor, receive payment for the teaching of religion only for classes in excess of 8 weekly classes.

Paragraph 4—

1. The full-time teachers of religion and those paid by the hour, are, following recommendation of the competent ecclesiastical body, employed by the Executive Committee of the Committee of Counsellors.

2. Employment as full-time and as hourly-paid teachers of religion can only be given to such persons who possess the required knowledge of dogmatics. In the event that this knowledge is not certain, the Minister for Religious Affairs will decide.

3. The Executive Committee of the Committee of Counselors can refuse employment as full-time and hourly-paid teachers of religion to any religious instructor who adopts a hostile attitude towards the People's Democracy or its decrees, or can at any time cancel the appointment. One who has been relieved

of employment as a religious instructor, cannot be entrusted with the teaching of religion at any other school.

Paragraph 5—

1. The religious instructor is obliged to follow the teaching plan and book as approved by the Minister for Religious Affairs.

2. The religious instructor may not be used for any other educational activity at the school (deputizing, supervision during excursions or in recreation breaks, etc.) apart from the teaching of religion. The religious instructor cannot attend conferences of the teaching personnel, and may remain in the school building only during the teaching of religion.

Paragraph 6—

1. Religious instruction must follow the last teaching class. Religious instruction may only be given in the school building. The teacher cannot assemble the pupils outside the school for any other occupation.

2. The pupils attending religious instruction must be grouped in such a way that the number corresponds to the average number of other classes at the school; in this frame, religious instruction is to be carried out in accordance with the order of undivided or partly divided schools.

3. Pupils receive no grades (marks) for religious instruction. The pupils cannot be given any disciplinary punishment for not attending religious instruction.

4. The teacher's work for the classes, his plan of work and his class outlines are controlled by the teaching authorities in accordance with the rules regarding all other educators. The director is responsible for supervision and, to assist him in class supervision, he can call upon the general supervisory authority for teaching, the head of the class, the president of the parents' union and the competent representative of the educational organization.

Paragraph 7—

This ruling is to be applied from the beginning of the school year 1950/51. At this time all former rulings become invalid.

(Taken from *Reformatus Egyhaz*, II issue, No. 20, October 15, 1950)

CZECHOSLOVAKIA

Introduction

In the ninth century, hard-pressed by nationalist missionaries from Germany, Duke Ratislav of Moravia sought to create an independent Christian movement loyal to Slav, and not Germanic political leadership. Knowing that Pope Nicholas I would not permit the establishment of an autonomous Catholic Church, Ratislav requested Orthodox Patriarch Photius of Constantinople to send Slavic missionaries. Methodius and Cyril were commissioned to the task in 863 (Spinka, *Christianity in the Balkans*, pp. 17, 18). There followed more than a thousand years of struggle for religious independence from political and papal domination.

Revolution, 1350-1450: A violent revolution, moral, religious and political, carrying through a hundred years and affecting the whole continent began in the middle of the 14th century. There were anti-clerical riots followed by suppression and beheading of rioters. It was essentially a people's revolt against clerical extortion and superstition, against a Papal bull selling indulgences to finance the war against Ladislos of Naples, (said the reformers) against levying of burial taxes and fees for sacraments, against benefits accruing from relics, and so on. It was a protest "against the materialization of religion and the cult of *adinvenciones hominum*, and in part the revolt of the townsmen against exploitation by a clerical caste whose functions were becoming stereotyped and of a value that was decreasingly apparent. The same can be said of the protests . . . (of) Hus against the feudal legal system. . . ."

The revolutionaries sought salvation "not by works alone; not by absolution and penance, not by indulgences or miracle-working relics and images . . . but by a change of heart, penitence and not penance, by the indwelling of the Spirit" (Matejz Janova, Regulae, ed. Kypal, IV, 222-24, quoted by R. R. Betts, *The Place of the Czech Reform Movement in the History of Europe, The Slavic Review*, p. 377, Vol. 25, 1946, 1947).

Counter-reformation, 1621-1781: At the Battle of White Mountain, November 8, 1620, Protestant Czechs were overcome by the Hapsburg forces, and for the next 150 years were forced to profess Roman Catholicism. The destinies of the two, Hapsburg dynasty and Roman Catholicism, were so closely identified that an enemy of one was considered the enemy of both. The monarchy supported the Jesuits in extending the Catholic domain; the power and wealth of Roman Catholicism in Czechoslovakia is from that era, an era characterized in Czechoslovakian history as "The Time of Darkness."

By 1781, after a number of reprisals of a religious nature, Josef II granted the "Patent of Toleration." Protestants of "Helvetic" or Reformed faith could again hold services, but they never regained a position of equality until the creation of the Republic of Czechoslovakia in 1918.

Czechoslovakian Republic, 1918-1938: In 1868, by imperial decree, Protestant churches were given the possibility of receiving State subsidies. This was extended to equal recognition as well as support (except for Free Churches) in 1918. In addition, Catholic churches continued to enjoy the proceeds of vast land-holdings and other properties. With the post-war renaissance of a liberal spirit and freedom of expression, nearly a million Roman Catholics broke away from Rome to form the Czech National Church.

During Czechoslovakia's history, Roman Catholicism has always played an active part. Three Catholic parties—the German Christian Socialist Party, the Slovak People's Party and the Czechoslovak People's Party, were represented in the republican Government. Protestants in Czechoslovakia still find it difficult to discern where the religious and the political start and end in manifestations of Catholic power. At the same time Protestants claim that Czechoslovakia's enlightenment, indeed all her greatest spiritual leaders (Hus, Blahoslav, Comenius, Palacky, Masaryk), sprang from Protestantism. "The early translation of the Bible had an immense influence on the cultural development of the country, and the heroic and tragic story of the Czech Reformation became an inspiration in all later strivings for liberty and independence. . . . The spiritual regeneration and purification of Roman Catholicism is a fact of recent years and its effects are not yet fully seen."

Nazi Occupation, 1939-1945: Political Catholicism became influential again during the Nazi occupation. A devoted Catholic, Dr. Hacka, was "president" of the German-protectorate of Bohemia-Moravia, and in Slovakia, the Roman Catholic Tiso regime was in control. The Slovak President, Roman Catholic Msgr. Tiso, asserted in 1940 that the Slovak State would be "Christian-Catholic." During the period of his leadership, nearly thirty Protestant periodicals were forbidden, including the Lutheran home missions journal; several Protestant pastors and bishops were imprisoned or ousted; all schools were made confessional and textbooks were revised by the Catholic-State. In 1943 an uprising of Slovak Protestants against the regime was quickly suppressed. At the same time, many Roman Catholics fought loyally for the liberation of Czechoslovakia, notably Rev. J. Sramekwas, head of the government in exile in London, and Archbishop Beran, later head of the Catholic Church in Czechoslovakia, who spent nearly three years in the Nazi concentration camp at Dachau. After the liberation Slovak Protestants sought, along with many Catholics, to hold back the advance of Communism.

In Bohemia and Moravia where Protestant churches were much weaker, they played a minor role. Some, especially in the region of Silesia, were incorporated into the German Church. Others, when their halls, chapels, and institutions were confiscated, continued their ministry in private quarters and organized intensified lay activities to provide leadershp. Dr. Krenek, leader of the Czech Brethren, was decommissioned by the Nazi puppet Government for refusing to sign an appeal to found a League against Bolshevism. By early 1945, pastors in East Czechoslovakia were joining in the "Movement of Liberation" against the puppet Government and the Nazi occupation forces.

Among Christian groups, the small Orthodox churches probably suffered in the greatest degree: five leaders were shot, their churches dissolved.

The Czech National Church was ordered to change its name.

Social Conditions—1945: At the end of World War II, the republic of Czechoslovakia was re-established as a social liberal democracy. A National Front government was appointed with President Benes at its head. There was no race problem, though in many parts a strong antipathy towards all things German, very limited poverty or "slum" conditions, workers had the highest standard of living in East-Central Europe. An excellent social security system was soon created, and there was a high degree of political freedom. Post-war problems of supply and reconstruction were enormous, but not overwhelming.

The moral and spiritual indifference and lack of a clear sense of purpose of the pre-war period had been largely overcome during the resistance against Nazism; there was a renewal of national unity (at least among Czechs), and of spiritual interest and activity.

Nonetheless, caught in the stresses of international politics, Czechoslovaks still felt uncertain about their "friends" abroad. In 1939 they had been betrayed by the West. They had become disillusioned with Roman Catholicism politically since the First World War.* And they had no great love for the Soviet system. If Czechoslovakia must choose among foreign powers, what alternative would be the least evil? Here was a problem Czechoslovakia had to face, with growing "distrust as to the ultimate value or permanence of moral values and particularly as to the reliability and rationality of world politics" (*The Evangelical Church of the Czech Brethren*, report of July, 1945).

Population and Religious Composition, 1950:

Total Population—(Pre-war 15,250,000)	12,000,000
Roman Catholics	10,000,000
Czechoslovak (National) Church	1,000,000
Evangelical Lutheran, Slovakian	430,000
Evangelical Church of Czech Brethren	380,000
Reformed Church in Slovakia	150,000
Congregational, Methodist, Baptist, Old Catholic, Orthodox, Moravian, Salvation Army, Mormon	50,000

Chronicle of Events

Period under Coalition Government— to Feb. 28, 1948

April 4, 1945—

Article 5 of the "Program of Kosice," issued by the Parties of Liberation, guaranteed freedom of religion and conscience for all citizens (MacEoin, *The Communist War on Religion*, p. 25).

May 16, 1945—

In the former Catholic-led Nazi puppet State of Slovakia Roman Catholic schools were nationalized. By special decree of the Slovak National Council a similar bill in Bohemia was defeated. Dr. Paulik, Slovak Minister of Education, in a book on education in the U.S.S.R., pointed to the Russian education system as the pattern for Czechoslovakia, and praised the "spirit of fighting atheism" as an organic element of education (*Ibid.*, p. 25).

May 22, 1945—

Roman Catholic associations in Slovakia were dissolved by decree of the Slovak National Council (*Ibid.*, p. 25).

January, 1946—

A Czechoslovakian Orthodox delegation visited Moscow seeking admission to the Moscow Patriarchate. Eleutherius, who earlier succeeded in uniting Far Eastern Orthodoxy to Moscow, was named Exarch (*ICPIS*, No. 3, Jan., 1946).

---

* And perhaps religiously: "Many find no satisfaction in modern secularism, but are unable to return to the Roman Catholic Church, with her unspiritual concept of authority and her equally unspiritual relapses into superstition" (*The Evangelical Church of the Czech Brethren*, Report of July, 1945, Prague).

March, 1946—

The Czech National Church condemned the World Council of Churches for alleged sympathy towards Germans being evacuated from Bohemia, and for disinterest in problems of Slavs who suffered at German hands. The Church refused to receive assistance from occidental churches until the rights and needs of Slavonic nations were considered.

March, 1946—

Slovak members of an underground movement were arrested for attempting to revive the outlawed Hlinka Catholic Party (and Hitler Jugend) in Slovakia (*N. Y. Times*, March 25: 11:2).

April 8, 1946—

Bratislava students demonstrated against the Communist ideology on the first anniversary of the liberation. Catholics were particularly outspoken against Marxist tendencies in the new Government. Three priests were arrested on charges of conspiracy (*N. Y. Times*, April 8:8:2).

May, 1946—

The Vatican-appointed Internuncio to Prague was not recognized by the Czechoslovakian Government (*N. Y. Times*, May 15:3:5).

June 18, 1946—

At the first assembly of the reconstituted National Council, the nationalization of industries, banks and agricultural exploitation was proclaimed.

June 29, 1946—

The Church of Czech Brethren General Assembly, reviewing the resolutions of the Oxford inter-church theological conference, subscribed to various theological points, emphasizing in addition:

1) the need for the church to identify itself with the masses;

2) its support of the Czechoslovakian Government in realizing a progressive and socialist democracy, reserving the right of criticism at any and all points;

3) the duty of the Church to assist in eliminating class privileges and nationalizing the means of production, industry and natural riches;

4) the responsibility of the Church to bring a Christian spirit to bear on the socialist movement.

August, 1946—

The Chairman of the Russian Commission on Religious Affairs for Orthodox Churches visited Czechoslovakia (*EPS*).

September, 1946—

The General Assembly of the Czech National Church stated that it would regard nationalization of production favorably and would support the transformation of the Republic to a Socialist Democracy (*EPS*).

September, 1946—

The Communist Party stated that it had no objection to social justice being preached with a religious bias (*EPS*).

December, 1946—

Evangelical Church leaders spoke of their "complete religious liberty" and of best cooperation between churches and Government. President Benes called the churches to cooperate in the reconstruction of the country and to give moral leadership to Czech youth (*EPS*, No. 3, Jan., 1947).

December, 1946—

Roman Catholic Msgr. Beran, newly appointed Archbishop of Prague, protested to the Government re. the nationalization of schools in predominantly Catholic Slovakia and expressed the hope that the Government would confer with church leaders re. education and land reform.

February, 1947—

The Roman Catholic Church and the Catholic "People's Party" opposed the emphasis on "dialectical materialism" in the proposed educational reforms (*N. Y. Times*, Feb. 23:36:4). Pictures of Stalin had been introduced into all schools, and "Civics" courses on the U.S.S.R. were given to secondary and high school students (MacEoin, *The Communist War on Religion*, p. 26).

On Archbishop Beran's return from his consecration, M. Nosek, Communist Minister of Interior, pinned a wartime decoration on Beran, saying he merited the honor "not only because he had been a political prisoner, but also for his indomitable faith that the country's freedom would be restored —a faith he imparted to others."

May, 1947—

A National Council of Evangelical Churches was formed, including all but Unitarian and Czech National Churches (*EPS*, No. 19, May, 1947).

July, 1947—

The Government approved an agrarian reform law which would re-distribute all estates exceeding 200 acres, including church lands.

July, 1947—

Roman Catholic Priest Straka supported the inclusion of Catholic lands under the law, and denied that his Communist Party membership in any way violated the Church's dogma (*N. Y. Times*, July 22:9:6).

September, 1947—

The General Assembly of the Czech National Church reiterated its 1946 statement of support for the transformation of the Republic to a Socialist Democracy.

October, 1947—

The Czech Ecumenical Council stated that it would be impossible to have peace based on the worship of materials; that "political freedom is of value only if accompanied by spiritual renewal and eternal purpose."

October 30, 1947—

Roman Catholic bishops protested to the Allied Control Commission that Russia was making political arrests in Czechoslovakia, and had kidnapped more than 2,000 children of German origin (*N. Y. Times*, Oct. 30:12:3).

November, 1947—

Returning from a visit to Moscow, Protestant Professor J. L. Hromadka spoke appreciatively of the unification of the country (USSR), of the intellectual, cultural and moral renewal; of the possibility of religious renewal through cultural emphasis on history, or through present religious movements (*EPS*, Dec. 19, 1947).

November, 1947—

The Roman Catholic "People's Party" joined with the National Socialist and Slovak Democratic Party to block an attempt by Premier Gottwald and the Communists to bring Slovak trade unions into the National Front coalition. A serious cabinet crisis followed (*New York Times*, Nov. 5:14:4).

February 2, 1948—

Roman Catholic, Orthodox, Protestant and Czech National Churches held a mass meeting in Prague to launch an appeal for peace; to the Czech Republic said, "be responsible for every word (you) utter"; to Christians of the world, "(break down) the barriers dividing nations and social classes"; to statesmen, "overcome suspicion" and be patient in negotiations. Czech Government leaders were present (*EPS*, Feb. 6, 1948).

February, 1948—

Catholic leaders proposed the formation of a non-political inter-church body to protect religious life and rights, and to represent all churches before the State (*EPS*, No. 8, Feb., 1948).

In a pastoral letter, Roman Catholic bishops protested against the enactment of the proposed land redistribution law, on the grounds that the Church required land to maintain its institutions and welfare programs, and that the law violated the extant concordat with the Vatican which provided that no Church property could be taken without mutual agreement (MacEoin, *The Communist War on Religion*, p. 35).

The Roman Catholic Church was allegedly offered the support of the Government if it would break with the Vatican and establish a National Catholic Church (*The Tablet*, Jan. 15, 1949).

February 25-28, 1948—

Establishment of Communist Party majority rule in the Government. The reorganized National Front was to have central and local action committees comprising representatives of the unions, political parties and churches.

The Churches Under Communist Rule

February 28, 1948—

The Central Council of the Czech National Church sent a resolution to the Government, expressing its continued support for the reorganized Gottwald Government; its intentions to stay outside party politics (Open Letter of the Czech National Church).

February 28, 1948—

Protestant Prof. Hromadka characterized the *coup d'etat* as an indigenous social revolution, called on Communists to fulfill responsibilities now falling on them, noting differences of opinion and conflicts with churches, urged Christians not to be resentful of the loss of bourgeois comforts, not to withdraw into pietistic solitude, but to bring the most creative force of their faith into the situation to save the noblest aspirations of the new order from materialistic corruption.

March, 1948—

The Czech Brethren Church pledged itself to aid the new Communist Government insofar as it would abide by, and abet Christian principles (*EPS*, No. 12, March, 1948).

March, 1948—

The Roman Catholic hierarchy met and sent a declaration of loyalty to the new Minister of Justice, A. Cepicka, avowing that the Catholic Church was tied to no particular regime and would cooperate with any government allowing the essential minimum freedom of religious practice. They promised that the Catholic Church would scrupulously abstain from political activity.

March 16, 1948—

Czech National Bishop Novak stated that the National Church would fully support the new Communist Government (*N. Y. Times*, March 16:10:3). Patriarch Kovar urged all Czech National believers to support the Communist Government in its fight against American imperialism (Markham, *Communists Crush Churches in East Europe*, p. 33).

March 18, 1948—

The Government's Central Action Committee created an Office for Religious Affairs to regularize Church-State relations, prepare a new Church law, and consider State subsidies for church administration, salaries, etc.

The land reform law was enacted. All holdings of more than 50 hectares (125 acres) would be nationalized against compensation.

Six Catholic weekly publications and *Katolik*, journal of Catholic action, were banned by order of the Ministry of Information.

April 21, 1948—

According to a new law for State education, religious instruction would be obligatory for children in State schools from 6 to 15 years of age, as long as parents of the children did not object. Religious instruction would be supervised by church authorities (*EPS*, No. 14, April, 1948).

The churches appealed to the Central Action Committee to excuse religious objectors from "voluntary" reconstruction labor on Sundays, and proposed week-day service as an alternative (*EPS*, No. 16, April, 1948).

The Hungarian language was forbidden to be used in worship services in Slovakia. The churches appealed to the Central Action Committee (*EPS*, No. 17, April, 1948).

Dr. Husak, Chairman of the Slovak Board of Commissioners, stated that "nobody, not even the churches, dare hinder the development of the Czech people or the People's Democratic regime" (*Glasgow Herald*, April 8, 1948).

May 7, 1948—

Archbishop Beran forbade Catholic clergy to take any active role in politics except by permission of their bishops (*N. Y. Times*, May 7:9:2).

May 26, 1948—

Archbishop Beran again forbade Catholic priests to participate in politics or to be candidates for coming elections. Roman Catholic priest Plojhar was acting as Premier Gottwald's aide (*N. Y. Times*, May 26:11:1).

The Czech Brethren Church urged members to discharge their duties as Christian citizens, bearing in mind the Christian's responsibility for unity, peace and for fellow man.

May 27, 1948—

In an interview with the editor of *Rude Pravo*, Minister of Justice Cepicka explained that statements of the Central Action Committee regarding religious liberty should not be interpreted as an opportunist maneuver, that "the National Front realizes that religion has its function in society during a certain stage in the development of human society and knows that religion will continue to have that function. That is why we do not consider religion a private matter, but a public affair . . . Freedom of religion and worship (are) clearly stressed as one of the leading principles of our regime . . ." (*N. Y. Times*, May 28:8:3).

The national elections went "by overwhelming popular vote" to the leftist coalition. President Benes shortly resigned, and Catholic prelates visited his successor, M. Gottwald, to pay their respects and assure him that they would faithfully fulfill their duty towards the State (*Everybody's*, London, 9/7/49). They asked that relations with the Vatican be clarified, and that attacks on the Vatican be stopped (MacEoin, *The Communist War on Religion*, p. 41).

June 9, 1948—

On the third anniversary of the liberation of Prague, the last meeting of the National Council proclaimed the new constitution, which included clauses guaranteeing

1) equality of religious groups;
2) freedom of religious practice in public or in private, subject to public order and good morality;
3) freedom of belief or non-belief (and punishment for any undue pressure to force religious decisions);
4) freedom of conscience within the limits of responsible citizenship (no special privileges);
5) and provided for compulsory religious education under church direction for children from 6 to 15, except when objected to by parents. The curriculum for religious instruction was to be prepared by the Minister of Education (Appendix I).

June 15, 1948—

Premier Gottwald was received and welcomed by Archbishop Beran at a Te Deum in the St. Vitus Cathedral in honor of the new regime (*N. Y. Times*, 15:22:2). Archbishop Beran had agreed to have the Te Deum on the condition that Catholic schools

would be excluded from nationalization (MacEoin, *The Communist War on Religion*, p. 31).

Fifteen months earlier, Gottwald had attended the consecration of Beran as Archbishop and asked for a copy of the ritual in advance in order to follow it (*Everybody's*, London, 9/7/49).

June 20, 1948—

Roman Catholic Priest Plojhar was suspended from the priesthood by Archbishop Beran for his political activity (as secretary to Gottwald; *N. Y. Times*, 20:33:3).

July, 1948—

The Catholic "People's Party" and a peasants' group protested to the Pope against the suspension of Rev. Plojhar from the priesthood (*N. Y. Times*, 29:4:8; 30:5:3).

An agreement was reached between the Government and the Catholic Church that matters of controversy would be discussed between them before public airing or action (*Orbus Catholicus*, No. 3, March, 1948).

July, 1948—

Orthodox Archbishop Eleutherius attended the Pan-Orthodox conference in Moscow and signed the Orthodox declarations against the World Council of Churches. By special decree he was elevated by Moscow Patriarch Alexei to Metropolitan for Czechoslovakian Orthodoxy (*EPS*, No. 43, Oct., 1948).

A document of "instructions" to Communists was brought out of Czechoslovakia. Vatican authority was to be undermined, lower clergy separated from higher clergy, church honor discolored. The Czechoslovakian National Church was to be commended and supported, later the Moscow-linked Orthodox Church (Appendix II).

August 19, 1948—

Prof. Hromadka, visiting in America, reported that there was freedom of religion in Czechoslovakia, and mentioned a bill under discussion which would provide State salary grants for clergymen (*N. Y. Times*, 19:15:3).

August 28, 1948—

Catholic Rev. Zemek and other priests and laymen were arrested for assisting political refugees. Roman Catholic Monastery Znojmo was named as a center of anti-Government activities (*N. Y. Times*, 28:16:6).

August 30, 1948—

Catholic bishops issued a pastoral letter accusing the Government of conducting an anti-church campaign, of breaking its promises to reach an agreement on religious questions, and reported Government restrictions against religious publications and meetings, charitable works and institutions (*N. Y. Times*, 30:1:4).

August, 1948—

Evangelical leaders reported a new impetus and interest in Sunday Schools. The churches held special summer training courses for teachers and religious educators (*EPS*, No. 40, Oct. 1948).

September, 1948—

In a pending legislative bill on religious affairs the Government proposed
1) equal suport for church administration and leaders, and for the association of atheists;
2) obligatory approval of the Government for ministerial candidates;
3) cessation of voluntary church contributions.
The Czech Brethren Churches protested against the bill, and stated they could not accept State support on those conditions.
Other churches to object:
Slovakian Lutherans, Methodist, Congregationalists, Baptists, Mormons, and Roman Catholics.
To approve:
Czechoslovak National Church, Czechoslovakian Orthodox Church, Unitarian Church, Jewish Council of Moravia and Bohemia, Lutheran Church of East Silesia (*Neue Zürcher Zeitung*, May 16, 1949).
The Roman Catholic Church, in a pastoral letter (August 30) stated:
"We are criticized for not having put forward an absolute endorsement of all that was being done like the other churches have done . . . we had evidence that even in our country a hidden anti-church and anti-religious fight has started . . ." (Barron and Waddams, *Communism and the Churches*, p. 51).

September 13, 1948—

Archbishop Beran was expelled from the Union of Anti-Nazi Resistance Fighters for his action against Gottwald's assistant, Rev. Plojhar (*N. Y. Times*, 23:13:2). A declaration (followed by press statements) attributed to Catholic leaders deplored the Catholic attitude towards the Government, and the interference of the Church in public affairs (*The Tablet*, January 15, 1949).

October 6, 1948—

The Government approved a bill providing punishment for the misuse of any position, "spiritual or otherwise," for political purposes (*EPS*, No. 46, Nov., 1948 and *Dokumente; Appendix III*).
In a pastoral letter, Roman Catholic bishops indicated that theirs "alone (is) the true church," referred to non-Catholics as "sects." Orthodox and Czechoslovakian National Churches protested to the Government. Protestant churches refused to protest.
Slovak Baptist Churches which had been closed as "Western churches" were re-opened after a protest to the Government (*EPS*, No. 51, Dec. 1948). Czech Brethren Churches held a special training course for laymen.

November 17, 1948—

The Orthodox Church opened a seminary for training priests. Moscow Patriarch Alexei sent his blessing (*EPS*, No. 51, Dec. 1948).
Czech Brethren leaders expressed some anxiety that the Government was seeking a coalition of the Czechoslovakian National Church and the Orthodox Church as the National Orthodox Church under the jurisdiction of Moscow.

November, 1948—

Prime Minister Gottwald called church youth organizations "an obstacle" to social progress, and proposed the creation of one unified youth organization by Spring (*EPS*, No. 4, Jan. 1949).

November, 1948—

Roman Catholic printing establishments in Slovakia were nationalized by decree of the Ministry of Information (MacEeoin, *The Communist War on Religion*, p. 36).

December 5, 1948—

The Resistance Movement press warned the churches not to defend the old order of society (*N. Y. Times*, 5:16:1).

On the 30th anniversary of the establishment of the Church of the Czech Brethren, Prof. Hromadka and M. Bohac, lay president of the Czech Brethren Church, exhorted the churches to fulfill their non-political spiritual mission of proclaiming God's message of truth, justice, love and mercy, "the standards by which all is to be estimated" (*EPS*, No. 7, Feb. 1949).

December, 1948—

Minister of Education Nejedly stated:

"As the Catholics have the Vatican, the Evangelical Churches have their next of kin, especially in the Anglo-Saxon World. This world is not against us, and it is evident that the Evangelical circles do not find everything good in our regime. Now is the time for them to put order in their ranks and in their relations with the Republic. The path of every anti-State act leads to a monastery, church or priest, and it appears these acts must be co-ordinated in high places. Catholics may yet be forced to a test whether they are good citizens or whether they condone treacherous acts against the Republic" (*Manchester Guardian*, December 30, 1948).

Christmas, 1948—

The last issue of the youth publication *Bratistvo* was distributed before being banned.

January 1, 1949—

Vice-Premier Siroky announced the Government's decision to unify all youth organizations. Church youth groups "are unnecessary and indeed undesirable." Lutheran youth organizations in Slovakia were dissolved. Religious youth publications were banned. Siroky referred to some opposition, and cited the religious instruction in the schools and seminary training as being adequate for the religious needs of youth without con-

fessional youth organizations (*EPS*, No. 4, Jan. 1949).

January 1, 1949—

Pastors were excluded in the distribution of clothes ration cards in some areas as "non-essential laborers." After appeals had been made, the Official Trade Unions on Feb. 9 stated that ration cards should be delivered to clergy in active public service. Ten of twelve Baptist churches were requisitioned (*Neue Zürcher Zeitung*, May 16, 1949).

January 8, 1949—

The Roman Catholic hierarchy warned against any attempt to form an independent Czechoslovakian Catholic Church, after reports that the Government was moving in this direction (*N. Y. Times*, Jan. 8:5:6).

End of January, 1949—

Archbishop Beran and the Council of Catholic Bishops addressed a protest to the Government that "in spite of promised religious freedom, an attack has been initiated against the church and religion . . . like the well-known attacks in other countries." The bishops reminded the Government of the July, 1948, agreement that all matters of controversy should be discussed before action was taken, and charged that—

(1) Church officials were prevented from carrying out their duties;

(2) clergymen not participating in political demonstrations were considered as suspect;

(3) Catholic schools, institutions, organizations, press and meetings were being unduly restricted;

(4) Catholic property was being confiscated without compensation;

(5) attacks were being made on the Holy See, and attempts made to split the hierarchy from the people (*Orbis Catholicus*, No. 3, March 1949, p. 119 ff.).

February 10, 1949—

A Czechoslovakian news bureau reported that the people were urging the Government to take action against priests accused of anti-Government activities, and that they protested the Catholic Church's defrocking of two priests who were active in politics (*N. Y. Times*, Feb. 10:6:5).

February 17, 1949—

Following a preliminary meeting between Gottwald and four bishops in January, Government and Roman Catholic Church representatives began conferences with a view to settling Church-State disagreements (*Orbis Catholicus*, No. 3, March 1949, p. 119 ff. and *N. Y. Times*, Feb. 18:13:6).

February, 1949—

Education Minister Nejedly, in a radio speech, attacked Czech Brethren, Baptist, Mormon, Methodist and Congregational minority churches for their "Western orientation" (*Neue Zürcher Zeitung*, May 16, 1949).

February 22, 1949—

The Czech Brethren Synodical Council proclaimed the solidarity of the Czech Brethren Church with the people, and exhorted members "to cooperate everywhere there is a question of common interest and welfare of the people." A similar message was sent by the Czechoslovakian National Church to President Gottwald, adding that reactionary tendencies would be prevented from establishing themselves within the Czechoslovakian National Church (Barron and Waddams, *Communism and the Churches*, p. 52).

March 15-16, 1949—

Leaders of the Hungarian Reformed minority in Slovakia formed a "union of clergy of the Reformed Church" (*Neue Zürcher Zeitung*, May 16, 1949).

March 17, 1949—

A Prague journal reported that Roman Catholic leaders slandered reformer Jan Hus (*N. Y. Times*, 17:3:6).

March 19, 1949—

The formation of a Czechoslovakian Church Union was announced, with implied approval from the Government (*N. Y. Times*, 19:4:2).

Ten Baptist churches requisitioned in January, were freed for religious services.

The Salvation Army building in Bratislava was requisitioned (*Neue Zürcher Zeitung*, May 16, 1949).

The Salvation Army had received no paper for its publications since January.

March 23, 1949—

Negotations between the Government and Roman Catholic leaders begun in February were abruptly broken off after the bishops reported finding a secret microphone hidden in the conference room (*Everybody's*, London, 9/7/49).

March 24, 1949—

The National Assembly issued a law on the control of book printing. The State would become sole publisher and printer although the churches might continue to publish books on the condition that printing would be done by the State (*Dokumente*).

Shortly thereafter the Government issued the *Gazette of the Catholic Clergy*, which Archbishop Beran forbade Roman Catholics to read. The Government banned the official Catholic bulletin, *Acta Curiae*, and declared that no ecclesiastical instructions would be considered valid unless and until they were printed in the Gazette (Barron and Waddams, *Communism and the Churches*, p. 53; and MacEoin, *The Communist War on Religion*, p. 37).

April 1, 1949—

Reformed Church leader Rev. J. Tomasula was held by the Government for alleged treasonable contacts with the West (*N. Y. Times*, April 1:8:3).

May 15, 1949—

An anti-church press campaign indicated that Church-State negotiations re. an agreement had again reached an impasse (*N. Y. Times*, 15:16:1).

May 21, 1949—

In a pastoral letter to Roman Catholic clergy, Archbishop Beran accused the Government of intensifying its anti-church activities, and disclosed that hidden microphones had been found where the bishops were in session in March (*N. Y. Times*, May 21:1:6).

May 25, 1949—

Archbishop Beran accused the Government of trying to form a separate, National Catholic Church, and threatened excommunication of any Catholics aiding the Government in such plans. (The Independent Czechoslovakian National Church of some million members had come largely out of the Roman Catholic Church after World War I. *N. Y. Times*, May 25: 1:3).

May 29, 1949—

The Roman Catholic Bishops' conference denounced the Government for its intention to require pledges of loyalty from religious leaders (*N. Y. Times*, 29:1:6).

June 4, 1949—

Premier Zapotocky indicated to the Czechoslovakian Communist Party Congress that the dispute between the Church and State was the key issue of the day, intimated that the Government was friendly towards Roman Catholic priests (*N. Y. Times*, June 4:4:8).

Vaclav Kopecky, Minister of Information, speaking before the Communist Party Congress, accused the Roman Catholic Church of being responsible for present bad relations with the Government, of mobilizing reactionary forces in league with foreign powers against the Government, and of claiming that religion is contrary to the Communist efforts to create a just social order, "We can leave nobody in any doubt that traitors will not be tolerated or spared, even if they wear priestly robes" (*The Daily Worker*, London, 13/6/49).

Justice Minister Cepicka added: "It is quite natural that we claim for the State the right that only the State should educate all the children, that the State should direct every school without exception, and that every kind of education inside and outside the schools should be conducted in accordance with the scientific truths that constitute the spirit of Marxism-Leninism. We deny and reject with the utmost determination the claims of the Vatican to interfere in this purely internal matter" (MacEoin, *The Communist War on Religion*, p. 31).

Statements at the congress were considered by the Catholics as the signal to open conflict (*Everybody's*, London, 1/7/49).

June 5, 1949—

In a pastoral letter, the Roman Catholic Archbishop protested against Government action which, he said, would make Christian educational work impossible and illegal. He accused the Government of forcing lectures in political science on theological students, and of making it impossible for the clergy to maintain contact with the people outside the church buildings. Three theological seminaries had been sequestered (MacEoin, *The Communist War on Religion*, p. 31).

June 11, 1949—

The Government assigned special instructors to Roman Catholic seminaries to give lessons on history and politics (*N. Y. Times*, June 11:1:7).

June 12, 1949—

Archbishop Beran instructed Roman Catholic clergy to boycott Government sponsored organizations and publications. The Government was said to have taken over the Roman Catholic Church's "Catholic Action" organization with a handful of "apostates," after arresting the former secretary, subsidizing the new leadership and providing them with a journal, *The Catholic Gazette* (formerly the weekly journal of the Slovak Catholic Church). Mass meetings were held and a long list of names of "new members" of Catholic Action was soon published (Markham, *Communists Crush Churches in East Europe*, p. 23). Archbishop Beran reasserted the Church's supremacy over worldly powers (*N. Y. Times*, 12:8:1).

June 15, 1949—

The Roman Catholic hierarchy sent out a pastoral letter indicating:

a. that the Roman Catholic Church would accept no subsidies which enslaved and deprived it of its freedom;

b. that any renewal of discussions for a Church and State agreement must pre-suppose

(1) that the Christian concept of society would be respected and permitted in public, education, word, and deed;

(2) that the Government would acknowledge the supremacy of the Pope and hierarchy in Roman Catholic ecclesiastical affairs;

(3) that all limitations on religious freedom for Roman Catholics in Czechoslovakia would be withdrawn;

c. that the Ministry of Education's publication, *Gazette of Catholic Clergy* must be stopped;

d. that all restrictions or interference in Church life, administration and support must be stopped (Barron and Waddams, *Communism and the Churches*, p. 54).

June 15, 1949—

Czechoslovakian police searched the consistory premises of Archbishop Beran (*N. Y. Times*, 17:1:2).

June 18, 1949—

Archbishop Beran issued a pastoral letter urging priests not to sign any agreement which would violate the laws of God or the right of the Church and its bishops. He warned that any such confession or agreement bearing his signature should not be honored. The Government immediately issued a counter-order forbidding the clergy to read the pastoral letter, and stamped it with the Bishop's seal which had been taken from the consistory three days earlier (MacEoin, *The Communist War on Religion*, p. 42).

June 19, 1949—

In a service in St. Vitus' Cathedral crowds of people shouted down Archbishop Beran's sermon in which he criticized the Government-sponsored Catholic *Gazette* and Catholic Action Committee (*N. Y. Times*, 20:1:6). Beran announced also that he would "never conclude any agreement (with the Government) which infringes the rights of the Church or the bishops" (*London Times*, 20/6/49).

June 21, 1949—

Under instructions from the Vatican, the Roman Catholic Church excommunicated Government leaders and Catholic supporters of "Catholic Action." Numbers of Roman Catholic priests and laymen in Moravia were reported arrested (*N. Y. Times*, 21:1:6).

June 22, 1949—

Prime Minister Zapotocky in a radio broadcast declared that Catholic leaders were "victimizing and terrorizing" Government supporters, and asserted that such misuse of the Church

to promote disloyalty would be punished as treason (*Daily Telegraph*, London, 23/6/49).

June 24, 1949—

Some Protestant leaders were reported to be considering open support of Archbishop Beran and the Roman Catholic Church against the Communists (*N. Y. Times*, 24:9:3).

June 26, 1949—

The Government was reported to have seized nine Roman Catholic convents and monasteries in Slovakia.

June 26, 1949—

A pastoral letter condemning "Catholic Action" was reported by the Government to have been read by 90% of the Roman Catholic clergy (MacEoin, *The Communist War on Religion*, p. 43).

June 26, 1949—

Two Protestant ministers were arrested in Slovakia, where opposition to the Government appeared strongest (*N. Y. Times*, 26:2:4).

June 28, 1949—

Three decrees were published (issued on June 25):

The first decree forbade church leaders to have church conferences without the permission of the Government.

The second decree indicated that the Roman Catholic Church published pastoral letters "to cause unrest among the people" and that in future all pastoral letters, circulars, instructions, or any other publications should be submitted to the Ministry of Education before being sent out.

The third decree indicated that any punishment effected by the Church "for political reasons" was invalid and against the law, and that "the State would give its full support to every punished priest."

Subsequently, the regular weekly pastoral letters were smuggled when possible from town to town and read in various churches (Markham, *Communists Crush Churches in East Europe*, p. 27).

July 2, 1949—

Two policemen were reported killed in clashes with Catholics in Slovakia (*N. Y. Times*, July 2:5:5).

July 3, 1949—

Slovak peasants were reportedly armed to protect Roman Catholic clergy from the police. Some 25,000 laymen participated in a demonstration against the Communist Government in Trnva, Slovakia. Most of them carried clubs or pitch-forks (*N. Y. Times*, July 3:1:6, Markham, *Communists Crush Churches in East Europe*, p. 26).

July 4, 1949—

Several Protestant ministers were reported seized for "illegal activities." Minister Nejedly warned Roman Catholic clergy not to oppose the Government (*N. Y. Times*, July 4:3:6).

July 5, 1949—

At the Jan Huss Memorial Day services in Husinec, Deputy Premier Fierlinger declared: "Huss fought not only against the immorality of the Catholic Church but also against the increasing German influence in Bohemia which was backed by the corrupt Catholic hierarchy and the Pope. Now the battle between Czechoslovakia and Rome is renewed."

In similar services at Devin, Premier Zapotocky stated: "The Catholic Clergy are traitors and are in the pay of foreign Capitalism."

Education Minister Nejedly added at Sazala: "The Catholic Church is an enemy of socialism and of the Slav people. The State will deal with those bishops who are in the service of a foreign power as traitors. The clergy should not follow their bishops" (MacEoin, *The Communist War on Religion*, p. 40).

July 10, 1949—

At the World Council of Churches Central Committee meeting in England, Prof. Hromadka of the Czech Brethren Church spoke against the Committee's adopting a facile resolution simply condemning Communism and urged the Committee to consider the elements of God's judgment on the churches in relation to the revolution, adding that the churches should not become shelters for those who wished to retreat to an older social order, and urging the churches to consider ways in which they can "preach a potent and challenging gospel" (*The Scotsman*, 12/7/49).

July 11, 1949—

A Communist party circular assailed the Roman Catholic Church as the principal foe of the Czechoslovakian people (*N. Y. Times*). According to MacEoin (*The Communist War on Religion*, p. 41), Communist instructions stated that—

(a) the fight against the Church should be conducted openly,

(b) priests should be kept under constant survaillance,

(c) clergymen should be classified as progressive or reactionary,

(d) Church celebrations should be obstructed,

(e) the atheistic movement should be encouraged and supported.

July 13, 1949—

The Pope officially excommunicated Catholics who became Communists or who participated in anti-church activities (Markham, *Communists Crush Churches in East Europe*, p. 26).

A Government plan for expanding "Catholic Action" and suppressing Roman Catholic clergy was disclosed; priests who read pastoral letters were to be punished. Roman Catholic hierarchy were to be charged with treason (*N. Y. Times*, July 14:18:1).

Minister of Justice Cepicka replied to the Vatican decree: "Let no one doubt that anybody who tried to carry out that Vatican order commits treason against the principles of his own State and people . . . Anyone in our territory who tries to carry out the orders of the principal enemy of our State will be gambling with the right to call himself a Czech or a Slovak. If there is any fool who has confidence in the Vatican and its fellow-travelers, then the Vatican has taken care to make things clear. Even the remnants around Beran will disperse very quickly now" (*The Tablet*, July 23, 1949, as quoted in Barron and Waddams, *Communism and the Churches*, p. 10).

July 15, 1949—

Justice Minister Cepicka further accused the Roman Catholic Church of setting up an anti-State underground, and announced the draft of a new church law which would include provision for State control of church appointments, salaries, property and budget, seminaries, schools and charity organizations (see Appendices IV and V; July 15:1:1, *N. Y. Times*). He announced that 2,000 priests had joined "Catholic Action" (MacEoin, *The Communist War on Religion*, p. 39).

July 17, 1949—

The Catholic dean of Bratislava was imprisoned after announcing from the pulpit that all priests but one in Bratislava were faithful to the Church, and that that renegade had been excommunicated (*Ibid.*, p. 39). The Communist party called for an all-out anti-church drive. The "Citizens-Without-Religion Association" led off with an intensified propaganda program (*N. Y. Times*, July 17:1:3).

July 20, 1949—

The Government threatened mass reprisals if the Papal decree excommunicating Communists was implemented.

July 27, 1949—

Deputy Premier Fierlinger stated that the Government did not oppose religion, but would not tolerate Church interference in politics. He stated that the Roman Catholic Church would no longer need its big estates since the clergy would be supported by the Government. He accused the church-school system of being medieval in method and content (*N. Y. Times*, 27:1:2—1, 5).

July 29, 1949—

One Roman Catholic priest was tried and sentenced on charges of black-marketing (*N. Y. Times*, 29:6: 7).

July 31, 1949—

The Central Action Committee accused the Roman Catholic bishops of committing treason (*N. Y. Times*, 31: 18:4).

August 4, 1949—

A Roman Catholic priest, Rev. Fajstl, was sentenced to eight years in prison on charges of treason for refusing to administer the sacraments to a Communist woman (*N. Y. Times*, 4:5:5).

August 6, 1949—

Roman Catholic authorities warned priests to beware of Communists who sought the sacraments only to entangle them.

The Government offered pay raises to teachers of religion in the schools (*N. Y. Times*, 6:7:2).

August 14, 1949—

In spite of a Government threat, lack of required Government approval, and a sudden transport "breakdown," Roman Catholic bishops met in Trnva to consecrate Msgrs. Lazik and Pobpzni as bishops. Some 12,000 people (6,000, said the Associated Press) were reported present. The police took the names of visitors.

Re. Catholic Action, it was noted that less than 1% of 7,000 Roman Catholic priests had joined (only 13 guilty of apostasy) and even less than 10% of the workers in Government-controlled industries had joined.

August 17, 1949—

Archbishop Beran, under house arrest, addressed a letter to the Attorney-General accusing the Government of violating Article 18 of the new Constitution by posting a Government agent in his offices, by seizing his funds and estates, by withholding both personal and official correspondence, by depriving him of personal liberty without any investigation, or court trial or other official decision. He accused the Communists of organizing the demonstrations which interrupted the service in the Prague cathedral on June 19, which resulted in his enforced confinement (Waddams, *Communists Crush the Churches*, p. 23).

September 4, 1949—

Religious holidays were to be moved from week-days to Sundays (*N. Y. Times*, 4:10:3).

September 4, 1949—

A Slovak Roman Catholic bishop was accused of feasting the Nazis and boycotting his liberators (*N. Y. Herald Tribune*, Sept. 4, 1949).

September 6, 1949—

The Prague journal, *Svobodne Slovo*, charged that Roman Catholic bishops were not sending priests to vacant parishes in Sudetenland because they hoped for an early return of the Germans (*N. Y. Herald Tribune*, Sept. 6, 1949).

September 7, 1949—

A Roman Catholic source accused the Government of threatening to seize Church lands in order to provide more space for prisons (*N. Y. Times*, 7:15:6).

September 8, 1949—

70% of all Catholic priests and all the bishops were reported to have signed a protest to the Government against the proposed law to bring the Church under the control of a Government ministry. They rejected the idea of the Government's making or sanctioning Church appointments. A Vatican envoy was refused a visa to enter Czechoslovakia, thus leaving only one of four former Vatican representatives in Prague (*New York Herald Tribune*, Sept. 8; Appendix VI).

September 9, 1949—

Catholic lay teachers declared that they would refuse to submit to Government control. Some advised parents to withdraw their children from "controlled" classes.

Under instructions from the Vatican, priests were ordered to refrain from signing the Government's proposed oath of loyalty (*N. Y. Herald Tribune*, Sept. 9).

September 11, 1949—

The new Government textbooks for children were attacked by Catholic priests. A bishop in Bohemia and two nuns were arrested on charges of collaborating with the Germans (*N. Y. Herald Tribune*, Sept. 11, 1949).

September 12, 1949—

The Roman Catholic bishops submitted a seven-point memorandum to the Government as a proposed basis of agreement. The proposal was drawn up at the bishops' meeting in Trnva in August. It included demands for—

1) complete freedom for Archbishop Beran and the Church;

2) recognition of the Christian (Catholic) viewpoint and Vatican jurisdiction;

3) disbanding of the Government's "Catholic Action Committee";

4) and Catholic priests were not to be tried as traitors for executing the Vatican excommunication order.

They protested the planting of Communist spies in the churches, the closing of church schools, and the persecution of priests (*N. Y. Herald Tribune*, Sept. 12; Appendix VII).

September 13, 1949—

Fifteen priests were arrested on grounds of establishing an information link between Roman Catholic bishops and priests in defiance of Government orders. Roman Catholic printing facilities had previously been confiscated (*N. Y. Herald Tribune*, September 13, 1949).

September 14, 1949—

A Communist Party aide announced that "observers" would be sent to all religious meetings, including the confessional (*N. Y. Herald Tribune*, Sept. 14, 1949; *N. Y. Times*, 14:8:2).

September 15, 1949—

The Government announced that most priests agreed to the proposed law which would make them "civil servants" (*N. Y. Herald Tribune*, Sept. 15, 1949).

September 19, 1949—

Several priests were convicted allegedly of circulating illegal religious instructions and of encouraging Government opposition. Slovak villagers who defended them from arrest were tried for "rebellion" (*N. Y. Herald Tribune*, Sept. 19).

The Central Action Committee of the National Front accused the Catholic hierarchy of telling a "pack of scandalous lies" and of trying to "stir up the people against the regime" (Markham, *Communists Crush Churches in East Europe*, p. 25).

September 20, 1949—

Special lectures in socialism were introduced into theological faculties (*N. Y. Herald Tribune*, Sept. 20).

The Minister of Health, former Roman Catholic priest Plojhar, before a public gathering praised the Soviet Union as the world's greatest champion of freedom, and condemned the churches, "above all the Catholic Church (as the agents of) world imperialism and capitalism" (Markham, *Communists Crush Churches in East Europe*, p. 25).

September 22, 1949—

The Government began collecting full information as to the political belief of all priests (*N. Y. Herald Tribune*, Sept. 22, 1949).

September 26, 1949—

The Vatican reported that the Government had arrested 35 priests in Prague (*N. Y. Times*, 26:10:4).

26 priests were reported in jail in Bohemia (some in spite of peasant armed protection); 200 priests and nuns in all of Czechoslovakia (*N. Y. Herald Tribune*, Sept. 20, 30).

October 4, 1949—

The Government announced its intention to create a new ministry to cope with church problems and to administer the proposed law. The ministry would

a. supervise the finances and administration of the churches;

b. investigate the eligibility of church leaders and candidates;

c. secure inventories of all church property.

The Government would also require an oath of loyalty from all clergy (*N. Y. Herald Tribune*, Oct. 4, 1949).

October 10, 1949—

Parliament member Dr. Havelka stated: "The new (church) law will create a perfectly new situation for clergymen of all denominations. Clergymen who go along with the Church Administration will above all receive a basic salary from the State. A proficiency bonus will also be given."

Said another parliamentarian: ' 'Before our coming to power, it was impossible to follow the activities of individual churches. It took our regime to put things in order. All honest clergymen sincerely devoted to the people's order are now provided with perfect social independence" (Markham, *Communists Crush Churches in East Europe*, p. 19).

October 14, 1949—

Parliament approved two laws—one effective on October 14 establishing a Government ministry for church affairs, a second effective November 1, defining the terms of church administration and support under the Government ministry* (Full text—Appendices 4 and 5).

1. Government-approved clergymen and parish leaders would receive their salaries from the State. The rule that only citizens who had given the oath of allegiance could be approved might be waived by the Ministry in exceptional cases.

2. Vacant positions must be occupied within 30 days or the Government would take independent measures to secure leadership.

3. Church budgets must be approved by the State before payment of support.

4. All church property would become the property of the State.

5. All previous ordinances governing church recognition were repealed and churches must be recognized as such under the new regulation.

In final discussions of the law before the Church Commission of the Central Action Committee, Minister of Justice Cepicka (later also Minister of Religious Affairs) stated: "We want living churches. We want them to grow." He added that "resisters will be broken as enemies of the State."

October 15, 1949—

Czech Brethren leaders indicated that they could see positive possibilities in the new laws, though they were not happy about obligatory State support. They added that the effective aid of the State would help the Church fulfill its mission. The legal equality of all religious groups was received with appreciation, and churchmen felt that the "present structure and activities of the Church would undergo no modification."

Prof. Hromadka stated that while "representatives of the State gave

---

* Re. support and salaries: The Roman Catholic Church, Slovak Lutheran and Slovak Reformed churches had for many decades received some support from the Government.

Re. election of church leaders: Qualifications were unchanged, i.e., citizenship, civic reliability, moral integrity. Previously, however, church appointed leaders were approved if the Government raised no objection within four weeks after appointment. Hereafter, they must be approved in advance.

their solemn promise" that the purpose of the law was that the churches "might freely and fully develop their activity and thus concentrate on their religious and moral mission, from which they were in the past led away by their material worries, the laws themselves do not yet solve anything; the laws form only a legal basis for an effective solution—or they remove those obstacles from the past which prevented the right course of social development" (*Krestanska Revue*, Oct. 1949).

The general council of the Lutheran Church in Slovakia in a memo to the Government opposed the law (Markham, *Communists Crush Churches in East Europe*, p. 32).

The Silesian Lutheran Church approved the law, as did the Orthodox and smaller Protestant groups.

Dr. Svetly, Secretary of the Prague Diocesan Council of the Czechoslovakian National Church, considered the law as a fulfillment of the Premier's earlier pledges that the State would safeguard the welfare of religious bodies (Markham, *Communists Crush Churches in East Europe*, p. 33).

October 16, 1949—

Jesuits and American Catholicism were accused of inspiring an anti-socialist plot and the establishment of an anti-Government "third order" among industrialists, bankers and high officials (*N. Y. Herald Tribune*, October 16, 1949).

October 17, 1949—

The Vatican denounced all priests who participated in ceremonies celebrating Parliament's approval of the church laws of Oct. 14 (*N. Y. Herald Tribune*, Oct. 17).

October 18, 1949—

The Government announced that all clergy, in accordance with the law of October 14, would be required to swear allegiance to the republic and cooperate in the building of socialism (*N. Y. Herald Tribune*, Oct. 18).

October 25, 1949—

Roman Catholic bishops advised priests to accept State salaries and take the oath of allegiance, adding the phrase "provided that this is not in conflict with the natural rights of man." Priests would make a separate declaration to Church authorities:

"I declare that I accept the newly-arranged salary because it is decreed under a measure which became law. By accepting this salary, I do not assume any obligations which would violate my conscience as a priest nor the church laws. I proclaim again that I prefer the spiritual interest of the church and the unrestricted freedom of my priestly work to the material assurance of my existence" (Markham, *Communists Crush Churches in East Europe*, p. 28).

The bishops themselves refused to accept State salaries on grounds that there had been "no negotiation in advance" (*EPS, N. Y. Herald Tribune*, Oct. 25, *N. Y. Times*, 25:1:6).

October 25, 1949—

The Czechoslovakian National Church, Orthodox Church, Silesian Lutheran Church, and other small groups gave support to the law and oath. A newly appointed minister of the Czech Brethren Church was not approved by the State on the grounds that the congregation of some 100 people was too small to justify having a pastor. A Government officer expressed the opinion that only congregations of about 1000 members should have pastors.

October 29, 1949—

In a public statement, Gottwald declared that the Church-State issue had been solved and announced the release of *ca.* 100 Roman Catholic priests and laymen who had been sentenced for minor offenses (*N. Y. Times*, Nov. 3:11:2). One Roman Catholic professor, on his release, declared by radio that "I shall comply with the wishes of the Government. I am not against anything, I am not against the law. As soon as it is passed, I accept it" (Markham, *Communists Crush Churches in East Europe*, p. 16).

November 1, 1949—

Parliament effected the law of October 14 concerning Government administration of church property, elections, etc. (*Ibid.*, p. 17). Minister of Justice Cepicka became Minister of Religious Affairs, with 19 regional sub-offices (Markham, *Communists Crush Churches in East Europe*, 29).

According to Catholic sources, the Roman Catholic hierarchy returned their Government-paid salaries to the Government. A compromise oath for the clergy was agreed to. The agrarian reform was now to be extended to all church farms and properties (*The Tablet*, April 8, 1950).

November 2, 1949—

The Government announced that archbishops, bishops and apostolic administrators would take the oath of allegiance before Premier Zapotocky with the clause—"since I am convinced that the Government will never ask anything which would be contrary to the laws of God or human rights" (*N. Y. Herald Tribune*, November 3, 1949).

November 5, 1949—

President Gottwald announced that with the enactment of the law governing control of church property and administration, problems in Church-State relations had been solved (*The Economist*, 5/11/49).

November 10, 1949—

Religious publications, educational and charitable activities were placed under the Ministry of Church Affairs (*N. Y. Herald Tribune*, Nov. 10).

November 10, 1949—

The Roman Catholic seminary in Moravia was closed. 130 students were to take up work in mines and factories (*N. Y. Herald Tribune*, Nov. 10, 1949).

November 12, 1949—

The Communist Party of Slovakia announced that "the policy of the People's Democracy has brought many Roman Catholic priests into the camp of the Friends of the Soviet Union" (Markham, *Communists Crush Churches in East Europe*, p. 29).

November 13, 1949—

Interior Minister Nosek rejected the Roman Catholic bishops' proposed modifications of the loyalty oath and stated that no salaries had been returned to the Government. On the contrary, the Government had received thousands of letters of thanks (*N. Y. Herald Tribune*, Nov. 13, 1949). He added that anti-Communist activities on the part of the clergy would be punished (Markham, *Communists Crush Churches in East Europe*, p. 29). The Interior Minister also stated that after January 1, 1950, only marriages performed before civil authorities would be recognized (*N. Y. Times*, Nov. 13:1:4). Following their "repentance," Gottwald issued pardons to 153 Roman Catholic laymen who had been sentenced for violating Church laws (*N. Y. Herald Tribune*, November 13).

November 17, 1949—

Roman Catholic bishops addressed a 2200 word letter of defiance to the Government, attacking Premier Zapotocky for refusing their request to reconsider the church law, stating that they would not obey laws which destroyed religious freedom and are against the laws of God, and warning that the Government would be responsible for any subsequent holy war against the Government (*N. Y. Herald Tribune*, December 4, 1949).

November 17, 1949—

The Government ordered eleven U. S. Mormon missionaries to leave the country (*N. Y. Times*, 17:17:4).

The representative of the Lutheran World Federation was given three days to leave, he being considered "a threat to national security and social welfare." He stated that Czechoslovakian churches could receive help from abroad only after Government approval, and did not have possibilities of free communication with churches abroad.

November 22, 1949—

The Cabinet approved a law making civil marriage compulsory after January 1, 1950. Religious ceremonies would be permitted in addition to the civil vows (*N. Y. Herald Tribune*, November 22).

November 23, 1949—

168 priests were granted pardons in Slovakia (*N. Y. Times*, 23:12:3). In announcing their release, the Czechoslovakian radio stated that the priests had been imprisoned because they "had found themselves faced with two authorities and chose the foreign (Vatican) authority" (Markham, *Communists Crush Churches in East Europe*, p. 13).

November 25, 1949—

Roman Catholic bishops warned the clergy that they would be unfrocked if they violated Roman Catholic principles (*N. Y. Times*, 25:17:2) and appealed to them not to let Communist officers censor their sermons or direct their religious activity (Markham, *Communists Crush Churches in East Europe*, p. 30).

The Czech Brethren lay movement set forth directives and plans—
1) to intensify the training of lay, youth, Sunday school, and women parish leaders,
2) to study and understand "today's official ideology" in order to render better spiritual services,
3) to give a clear witness of service, love and mercy,
4) to be ready to speak forth judgment or consolation (*EPS*, No. 40, Nov. 1949).

The Czechoslovakian Y.W.C.A. announced that it was making preparations for special celebrations of the Week of Prayer and World Fellowship.

December 2, 1949—

The Vatican radio charged that 250 Roman Catholic priests had been seized in spite of the Government's amnesty pledge (*N. Y. Times*, 2:21:1).

December 5, 1949—

A Czechoslovakian army publication attacked the Roman Catholic hierarchy as enemies of the State (*N. Y. Times*, 6:15:1).

December 7, 1949—

The Minister of Justice attacked the Roman Catholic hierarchy for refusing to sign birthday greetings to Stalin (*N. Y. Herald Tribune*, Dec. 7).

December 21, 1949—

Roman Catholic Archbishop Beran's legal advisor fled to Western Germany (*N. Y. Times*, 21:21:5).

January 1, 1950—

The new marriage law making civil marriage compulsory, religious ceremonies optional, was enacted.

According to Catholic sources, a Government directive ordered Communist leaders to "take care that the churches keep a loyal relation towards the . . . regime." There must be an intensive propaganda campaign to popularize the Government's position on the religious issue. Local officials were to see that all priests took the oath of loyalty, and to insure that only trusted men were employed in religious institutions. Catholic sources also reported the promulgation of a law requiring priests to divulge secrets of the confessional to the Government (*Catholic Herald*, 10/2/50).

January 1, 1950—

C. Gottwald, in a New Year address, claimed victory for the Government over the Roman Catholic clergy "in spite of the Bishops' reaction" (*N. Y. Herald Tribune*, January 1; *N. Y. Times*, 2:5:3).

January 4, 1950—

The Government announced that church records would henceforth be considered as State property.

The Government indicated that permits would not be given for "Holy Year" pilgrimages to Rome (*N. Y. Times*, 4:22:5).

January 13, 1950—

A Prague paper labeled Archbishop Beran a "tool of the Vatican," and accused the Church of using its monasteries as centers of hiding for spies (*N. Y. Herald Tribune*, January 13).

40 youth leaders of the Czech Brethren Church held a five-day conference to study problems of ecumenical work. Speakers included delegates to the World Youth Conference at Oslo (1947) and at the World Council of Churches' Assembly at Amsterdam (1948; *EPS*, Feb. 24, 1950, No. 8).

January 25, 1950—

Rude Pravo reported that most priests were signing the oath of loyalty after unsuccessfully attempting to add the phrase—"If it does not violate the laws of God, the Church, and the natural rights of man" (*N. Y. Herald Tribune*, January 25).

Roman Catholic sources reported that the Government was continuing to arrest clergy who read pastoral letters or refused to sign the loyalty oath (*N. Y. Times*, 25:8:4).

January 30, 1950—

257 of 269 Prague priests took the oath of loyalty to the Government in

a mass ceremony (*N. Y. Herald Tribune*, Jan. 30).

February 1, 1950—

The *Lutheran World Federation Newsbulletin* (Geneva) reported that the Blue Cross (anti-alcoholic) movement was incorporated into the Lutheran Church in Slovakia. Catechetical schools and Bible courses for post-confirmation youth continued with great interest.

February 7, 1950—

The Government and press of Czechoslovakia denounced reports that alleged miracles in Bohemia (Cihost) implied Divine censure of the Communist Government. The priest whose congregation claimed to have witnessed the miracle was seized (*N. Y. Times*, 7:8:5).

February 8, 1950—

Two Mormon missionaries from America were imprisoned. They, with twelve others, had been ordered to leave Czechoslovakia for "endangering the safety and security of the State" (*New York Herald Tribune*, Feb. 8).

February 13-15, 1950—

The Synod of the Czech Brethren Church passed a resolution calling on Christians in hope and love and intercessory prayer to help "in the building up of juster social institutions . . . Though this is being done on a basis differing from the ultimate truths of our faith, we should for the sake of that very faith, set its true value on the positive side of this effort. We must return to the beginnings of the church, to apostolic times . . . We don't know what will happen tomorrow" (*EPS*, March 10 and October 13, 1950).

February 16-19, 1950—

When the Roman Catholic bishops appointed Vicar Brieden to succeed Bishop Skrabik in Slovakia, the Government overruled the appointment, and appointed Dean Dechet. The Vatican thereupon excommunicated Dechet (*N. Y. Times*, 16:18:4; 19:1:2).

February 21, 1950—

13 Mormon missionaries, including two earlier imprisoned, left Czechoslovakia at the Government's orders. The Government refused to approve a request from the Mormon Church to waive the regulation that all clergymen must be Czechoslovakian citizens (*N. Y. Times*, 18:14:2).

February 22, 1950—

The Government arrested three Roman Catholic abbots and accused them of concealing arms in their monasteries (*N. Y. Times*, 22:17:2:4).

February 24, 1950—

Two Roman Catholic priests in Slovakia were sentenced by a court for refusing the sacraments to Communists, advising parents not to select Communists as Godparents of their children, and advising parishioners not to buy or read the Government-sponsored *Catholic News* (*N. Y. Herald Tribune*, February 24, 1950).

March 1, 1950—

Catholic sources reported that fifty priests had been imprisoned since January 1, and that churches and monasteries had been searched by the police (*N. Y. Herald Tribune*, March 1).

Archbishop Beran and the Roman Catholic bishops circulated a pastoral letter forbidding priests to accept Government appointments without prior episcopal approval, or to take part in discussions with Government representatives, under penalty of excommunication (*N. Y. Herald Tribune*, March 1).

March 3, 1950—

Priest Dechet, who was excommunicated by the Vatican following his appointment by the Government to a Slovakian diocese, remained as Government administrator of the Catholic diocese. His installation took place after the Government ousted the Church's appointee to the office (*N. Y. Herald Tribune*, March 4).

March 3, 1950—

Minister of Justice and Church Affairs Cepicka, in an open letter to Archbishop Beran, accused Beran of inciting the priests to oppose the new church laws and to carry on anti-Government activities, and warned him that the State would not tolerate such "acts of provocation" (*N. Y. Herald Tribune*, March 7).

Excommunicated priests were offered special support by the Government and acclaimed as "patriots in the direct line of Jan Hus, who defied the Pope in the early New Era" (*The London Times*, 25/3/50).

March 4, 1950—

The Protestant and Orthodox Inter-Church Reconstruction Committee voted to disband allegedly "because no more support is coming from abroad."

March 6, 1950—

The Ministry of the Interior declared that the Roman Catholic priest who had reported a miracle in his church in Cihost admitted that the "miracle" was a fake. The Ministry accused the Vatican of instigating the hoax (*N. Y. Herald Tribune*, March 7).

March 10, 1950—

The Communist youth paper *Mlada Fronta* charged that the one remaining Vatican representative in Prague, Msgr. de Liva, was "executing medieval terror against progressive priests (by organizing) a court tribunal to judge the patriotic priests," and was "trying to organize unrest." The paper accused the Vatican representative of participating in the "faked" miracle of Cihost (*N. Y. Herald Tribune*, March 10).

March 13, 1950—

The Government ordered the last of 39 Mormon missionaries to leave Czechoslovakia, noting that he "constituted a danger to the safety and security of the State." 250 Czechoslovakian Mormons petitioned the Government for recognition as a religious institution (*N. Y. Herald Tribune*, March 13).

March 16, 1950—

The Ministry of Foreign Affairs requested the Vatican representative, Msgr. Ottavia de Liva, to leave Czechoslovakia, and accused him of abusing his office and interfering in internal affairs by directing the subversive anti-State activities of the bishops (*N. Y. Herald Tribune*, March 16, 1950).

March 19, 1950—

Minister of Justice Cepicka, in a speech to the National Assembly, charged that the "bishops, in obedience to hostile orders from the Vatican, engaged in activities of high treason in the hope that a new world war would make possible the establishment of the capitalist system . . . They will receive their reward" (*N. Y. Herald Tribune*, March 20, 1950).

March 20, 1950—

A Catholic priest was included among a group sentenced for "plotting rebellions against the State"—a revolution reportedly to be signaled by the reading of a pastoral letter from the Roman Catholic bishops (*N. Y. Herald Tribune*, March 23).

March 23, 1950—

Minister of the Interior Nosek, in a speech before Parliament stated:

"In the old days we used to read that missionaries circulated their faith among the colonial nations. Today they do not succeed in circulating their false Christianity in Asia, Africa or Australia.

"Therefore, these (Mormon) 'missionaries,' hardened not by the study of Christ's teachings but by training in the military or naval academies of the United States or in courses for spies, began a pilgrimage to our country.

"Their activities, of course, had absolutely nothing in common with Christ's teachings and therefore we had to send them back where they came from" (*N. Y. Herald Tribune*, March 24).

March 23, 1950—

The Communist weekly, *Tvorba*, accused the Roman Catholic Church of going underground to continue its battle against the Government. The journal labeled the "miracle" of Cihost as a hoax designed to propagandize the people and stir up mass rebellion, and asserted that monasteries were being used for "anti-state activities." According to *Tvorba*, Roman Catholic bishops ordered priests to meet in three man sessions, to hold conferences of Catholics behind closed doors and to visit families of believers frequently in order to organize the Underground (*N. Y. Herald Tribune*, March 24).

March 31, 1950—

Ten Roman Catholic abbots and monks from five Catholic orders were placed on trial in Prague charged with high treason, espionage for the Vatican and anti-State activities. The accusation stated that the leaders held obedience to ecclesiastical law and the Vatican above the laws of the State, formed a network of spies and agitators directed by the Vatican, and stole jewelry from the monastery of Brounov in order to smuggle it out of Czechoslovakia. Five priests pleaded guilty, two partly guilty and two innocent (*N. Y. Times*, April 1:1:4). The Vatican interpreted the trial as a step towards the outlawing of Roman Catholic orders (*N. Y. Times*, April 2:26:2).

April 4, 1950—

In a definition of the legal relationship between the Church, the State, and the clergy, Mr. Hobza, Prague University professor of law, denied the right of the Papal Internunciataire to have "official" contacts with Czechoslovakian bishops or to exert any authority over them other than religious. "The Catholic Church is not organized according to international law and therefore relations between the Pope, his representative and the bishop can have only a purely ecclesiastical character. While a Papal representative could not be brought to court for attempting to instruct believers how they should believe in regard to civil law, a Czechoslovakian church functionary who instructs his subordinates to obey the representative against civil law commits a crime" (*N. Y. Times*, 4:19:1).

April 5, 1950—

In the trial of ten Roman Catholic leaders, the Government prosecutor accused Jesuits of being Vatican spies, and defendant Jesuit Silhan as their leader. However, the prosecutor did not request the death penalty (*N. Y. Times*, April 5, 5:3:1).

Nine of the clergymen were convicted, one for life imprisonment, two for 25 years. Three appealed for another trial.

Roman Catholic priest, E. Duff, associate editor of *America*, in a letter on the background of the trials of the ten Catholic leaders, noted that five had been active anti-Nazis. He compared the questions put to the leaders to those put to U. S. citizen Vogeler in Hungary, e.g., Abbot Machalka was asked: "Are you faithful to the Vatican?" Reply, "Yes." "You confess therefore of having relations abroad, and with adversaries of the regime." Jesuit leader Silhan acknowledged discussing prospects for opening Roman Catholic schools with the Papal Internuncio, and was therefore charged with indulging secrets to an enemy government. According to Duff, these were the only remaining Roman Catholic leaders at liberty who refused to take the oath of allegiance without the reservation "unless it is in contradiction to the laws of God and the Church and the rights of man" (*N. Y. Times*, April 6:6:3, 7:24:6).

April 10, 1950—

New York Times correspondent D. A. Schmidt labeled as "imaginary" the alleged talks between him and Vatican representative Msgr. de Liva referred to in *Rude Pravo's* booklet, *Excommunication, Miracles, Sabotage.* In the booklet Schmidt was said to have plotted with de Liva to publicize the Cihost "miracle" (*N. Y. Times*, April 10:10:2).

April 18, 1950—

Prague journals reported that Roman Catholic monasteries were spy centers. Forty monks were reported arrested and moved to other monasteries (*N. Y. Times*, April 88:17:4). Catholic sources reported the Communists took photographs of nude women whom they had brought to the monasteries, which were later published as evidence of immorality among the monks. The official Government news agency announced that the Government was to convert many monasteries into hospitals, social institutions, and workers' apartments as a result of the facts revealed in the recent trial of ten leaders of Catholic orders. Monks and nuns would be concentrated in a smaller number of monasteries and given employment by the Government. The purpose of this step was "to stop the hostile activities of the orders that had sheltered agents, spies, etc., and concealed weapons and broadcasting apparatus." The monasteries should revert "to their original and truly religious mission." The report stated that only a few monks and nuns remained in Czechoslovakia, many having been deported to Soviet Russia (*N. Y. Times,* April 19:1:17).

April 20, 1950—

The seizure of Roman Catholic monasteries and the arrest of monks in Slovakia reportedly provoked public protests from the people (*N. Y. Times,* April 20:2:2).

April 26, 1950—

Minister Cepicka was appointed to the Ministry of Defense and succeeded in the Ministry of Church Affairs by Vice-Premier Fierlinger. Catholic sources interpreted the move as indicating completion of Government steps to control the Church (*N. Y. Times,* April 26:1:6).

April 30, 1950—

The Government was reported to have closed its legation to the Vatican in Rome.

May 3, 1950—

L'Osservatore Romano (Roman Catholic publication in Rome) editorialized that the Czechoslovakian Government was getting uneasy over its excessive anti-church drive (*N. Y. Times,* May 3:10:5).

May 27, 1950—

By a decree published on May 27, the Government gave to district civil authorities the right to supervise all religious activities, societies, orders and monasteries "to see that church life should develop in each district in accordance with the Constitution and the organization of the People's Democracy" (*N. Y. Times,* May 28:19:2).

June 9, 1950—

At a conference of priests in Moravia, Health Minister, Rev. (Roman Catholic) J. Plojhar denied that Roman Catholics in Czechoslovakia intended to set up a new Catholic Church (Ceteka News Agency, Prague, June 8, *N. Y. Times,* 9:11:6).

June 17, 1950—

By decree of the Government, the Salvation Army was dissolved, its property confiscated and two officers imprisoned on charges of subversive political activity (*N. Y. Times,* August 4:7:4; *EPS,* Oct. 27, 1950).

June 22, 1950—

Parliament discussed a new penal code which would provide for prosecution of "persons working as priests or appointing others for such work without state approval." Under the previous law, the clergy would refuse to take the oath and remain in office, but not receive State support. The Roman Catholic Church had permitted priests, but not bishops, to take the oath and receive support (*N. Y. Times,* June 23:12:4).

July 1, 2, 1950—

Representatives of churches in Czechoslovakia, U.S.S.R., Hungary, Rumania, Poland, Bulgaria, East Germany, and the Dean of Canterbury met under the presidency of Minister of Health Rev. Plojhar at Luhacovice, in a conference of "church leaders for peace." A resolution was adopted calling on Christians all over the world to fight for peace according to the Stockholm Manifesto of the Partisans for Peace, under the protection of the Soviet Union. The resolution condemned Marshal Tito (*L'Eglise en Lutte Pour La Paix,* Preparatory Committee for Conferences of Christian Churches, Prague).

The General Secretary of the Reformed Church of Slovakia indicated his approval of the fact that "churches with reactionary political aims had no decisive majority" at the Amsterdam Assembly of the World Council of Churches owing to the presence of the representatives of the younger churches and those of democratic countries. He pledged support for the World Council of Churches so long as it contributed to the creation of a new society, and said the Reformed Church of Slovakia would be the first to withdraw if the World Council of Churches should become a reactionary tool.

July 7, 1950—

A group of Roman Catholic priests was reported to have criticized the Vatican for its attacks on the Czechoslovakian Government (*N. Y. Times*, 7:5:1).

July 14, 1950—

Antonin Zapotocky and Zdenek Fierlinger, head of the State church office signed a decree (No. 112) abolishing all independent theological training, and providing for theological training and selection of students under official Government administration.

The decree ordered the establishment of a theological school for the Orthodox Church in Prague.

Roman Catholic schools were to be replaced by two in Prague. The former Protestant Theological Faculty was to become the Comenius Faculty with Prof. Hromadka as Dean. Jan Hus Faculty would continue but exclusively for the Czechoslovak National Church. Rectors appointed by Fierlinger were to "have power of decision in all matters pedagogical and theological" and would head faculty councils. Instructors would also be appointed by Fierlinger who would decide "spheres of work." Fierlinger was also to decide who would be admitted to the schools. Students were to "work to become patriotic priests or preachers, who would sincerely help the population" (*N. Y. Times*, August 6:34:5).

July 25, 1950—

Roman Catholics in Vienna interpreted the Government's intention to set up two new Roman Catholic theological schools, unrecognized by the Roman Catholic Church, with power to ordain priests, as a step towards the establishment of an independent Czechoslovakian Catholic Church (*N. Y. Times*, 25.15:1).

August 1, 1950—

A new law prescribed punishment by imprisonment from one to five years and fines for religious leaders refusing to perform religious functions when requested, or for performing them without Governmental approval, or for obstructing State officers charged with functions related to the churches (Appendix VIII).

August 20, 1950—

Catholic sources reported that Suffragan Bishop Buzalka was held by the Government for opposition to the Government-sponsored "Catholic Action" and for preventing Roman Catholic clergy from joining "Catholic Action." Vacancies caused by arrests of priests were being filled by Government appointed men (*N. Y. Times*, August 23:32:2).

September 7, 1950—

A new law being prepared would give the Government custody over all religious and other church treasures, relics, paintings and statues, according to the Czechoslovakian writers' publication, *Lidvoc Noving.* Indemnities would be paid in the form of support for the clergy and the churches. Of 800 historic church castles, 100 would be kept by the churches. 200 would be used as hostels, factories and storehouses (*N. Y. Times*, September 8:17:1).

September 8, 1950—

Following a Vatican accusation that Roman Catholic priest Kolarik had died a violent death at the hands of the Government, official Government sources denied that the charges were true (*N. Y. Times*, Sept. 9:5:3).

September 27, 1950—

According to *Svobodne Slovo* and *Catholic Action*, the Roman Catholic hierarchy, including Archbishop Beran, had reached full agreement with the Government on closing all but two Roman Catholic theological schools, one in Prague and one in Bratislava, which would henceforth be operated by the Government (*N. Y. Times*, September 28:24:4).

October 10, 1950—

Msgr. Peter Gojdic, Uniate Bishop of Presov, Slovakia, was reported by the Vatican as missing. 100 Uniate priests were also arrested.

The Vatican report stated that the Kremlin was training Communists in satellite states in two seminaries and 10 special schools under the leadership of an apostate priest Kraslin to organize religious activity in conformity to the Marxist creed (*N. Y. Times*, Oct. 11:15:3).

October 15, 1950—

The Comenius Theological Faculty (Protestant, Reformed) opened with 150 students, the greatest number ever enrolled in a Protestant faculty in Prague. This was due partly to the fact that smaller churches no longer had their own seminaries. Contrary to earlier specifications of Law No. 112 that Protestant students in Slovakia must study in Bratislava, Reformed students from Slovakia were permitted to go to Prague (*EPS*, No. 44, Nov. 1950). The Roman Catholic faculty, still larger, reported many more enrolled than expected.

According to Radio Vatican, 800 young workmen of the Communist party had entered the two Roman Catholic seminaries because salaries were four times that of workmen, they might acquire a car, and theological studies were reduced from six to two years (*Tribune de Genève*, Jan. 9, 1951).

October 27, 1950—

In reply to charges that Archbishop Beran was in prison, a Government spokesman reported that he was writing a book in his palace (*N. Y. Times*, October 28:4:2).

October 31, 1950—

Peace, a Prague daily newspaper, reported that Prof. Hromadka had written to the United Nations Security Council to protest against United Nationals police action in Korea as a "fatal decision" and accused America of aggression (*Christian Century*, December 20, p. 1535).

The National Union of Czechoslovakian Protestants in North America subsequently declared that Hromadka's views as reported did not represent Czechoslovakian Protestantism.

November 28-December 3, 1950—

After five days' trial, nine Roman Catholic leaders were sentenced to prison terms ranging from ten years to life plus fines, loss of civil rights for ten years, and of all property. The clergymen, including Msgr. Bou-

kal, first secretary to Archbishop Beran, abbots of two monasteries and one bishop, plead guilty to charges of espionage, treason and anti-State activities. Five of the prelates accused the Czechoslovakian hierarchy and Archbishop Beran and the Pope in particular for mis-directing them. Bishop Zela, who confessed to collaboration with the Nazis, had been interned by the Nazis in Dachau and Buchenwald for his opposition to them. In passing judgment the court condemned the "inciting and slanderous pastoral letters of Archbishop Beran" and his "secret and conspiratorial orders and espionage reports." The Vatican was denounced as Fascist; the Oriental Institute in Rome was called a school for spies, saboteurs and murderers (*RNS*, December 4, 1950; *N. Y. Times*, Nov. 28, 1950).

December 15, 1950—

A refugee student reported that the Roman Catholic Bishop of Spis was shortly to be tried for anti-State activities in Slovakia (*N. Y. Times*, December 16:2:2).

December 19, 1950—

The Vatican estimated that 2,000 Czechoslovakian priests were in jail or had been deported to concentration camps or were in forced labor (*N. Y. Times*, December, 20:6:4).

December 19, 1950—

Vatican radio reported that two priests had died in prison (*N. Y. Times*, December 9:44:6).

A prominent People's Party official proclaimed that "God has created the land and given it to mankind for use as a collective . . . Serve your own religion and God by helping the Government to build collective farms, collective cow-sheds, collective pig-sties" (*Ecumenical Courier*, November-December, 1950, Vol. 9, No. 7).

Summary of Situation—January 1, 1951

Worship:

Most churches are open and attendance is increasing. The pulpit may not be used to launch criticisms against the Government or provoke "unpatriotic" feeling.

Church Administration and Support:

There is no separation of Church and State.

All church property is now technically the property of the State and is administered under State supervision. Roll books, budgets and elections are supervised by the State. Church appointments must have Governmental approval. The State may appoint leaders to church posts. All church leaders must take an oath of allegiance comparable to that of a civil servant. All church salaries and pensions (except Roman Catholic prelates) are guaranteed and paid by the State. Private collections and other income is turned over to the Government. Among Protestants there is apparetly no real conflict over the arrangements for salary and administration. In principle they do not like it, and do not consider it gives them the freedom enjoyed prior to 1948, but they still consider it a framework in which they can still witness, teach and preach effectively.

Church Property:

All estates, palaces, institutions, according to law have become the property of the State. They are gradually being taken over by the Government and used for Governmental purposes, or collectivized. The churches have no private income from such sources. Since Protestant churches owned little more than the parish houses and pastors' gardens, this measure affects principally the Roman Catholic Church.

Church Leadership:

Probably a small minority of clergy has accepted the new economic and social order, and does not wish to turn back to the pre-1948 situation in spite of misgivings that the future may lead to a police-state control of the pulpit. Both church and Government leaders recognize that they have vastly different points of view and respect their differences, although the Government has evidenced its desire ultimately to make church purposes identical with those of the State.

Among Roman Catholics, some 2000 of a total 7000 clergy are estimated as being in prison, forced labor or sent abroad. While the remainder stick to their parishes, the bishops do battle with Governmental leaders. There is a strong organized resistance with an effective propaganda program. The Government-sponsored "Catholic Action" seems to have little success among the clergy, but is effective as an anti-Rome propaganda weapon.

Among Unitarian, Orthodox and Czechoslovak National churchmen there is little evidence that any considerable distinction is made between the ultimate purposes of the Church and those of the Government. There is some evidence that until very recently the Government hoped to weld these together in a national church. (On December 5, the Orthodox Church was declared autocephalous by a special act of Patriarch Alexei of Moscow, its journal changed from *The Light of Orthodoxy* to *The Messenger of the Orthodox Exarchate in Czechoslovakia of the Moscow Patriarchate.*)

Reformed, Lutheran, and other Protestants speak of serious difficulties, but real opportunities, of fear, but also of judgment and courage.

Training Leaders:

All seminaries have become State schools. There are two for Protestants, one for Orthodox and two for Roman Catholics. All others, of Roman Catholic and Free churches, have been closed. Directors of the seminaries are appointed by the Government. Support is provided by the Government. Roman Catholics have protested that the educational standard has fallen, that students come to get attractive salaries as clergymen, that the Government is simply training Marxists to infiltrate the Church. Protestants find that there are difficulties with the new administration, but possibilities to teach and prepare genuine church leadership. Attendance has increased in Protestant seminaries.

Confessional Schools:

All education is now administered by the Government, is free and compulsory.

Religious Education:

Optional religious instruction is given in the public schools, generally two hours a week, by teachers nominated by their own churches and supported by the Government. 80 to 90% of the children attend religion classes.

Youth:

Church youth groups have no publications, but Protestant youth groups meet regularly, and show increased interest and attendance. There is a national committee and secretary for Protestant youth groups. Christian youth are active in Sunday School work, also enter into secular youth movements to share their faith.

Publications:

Limited publications continue, after careful "editing." There are no church youth publications. Theological books and commentaries are being printed.

Theology, Evangelism and Missions:

Among Protestant churches, vague liberalism is disappearing, some former liberals having become humanists and Government officers, some profound Christians. In the formerly liberal Czechoslovak National Church, there is a real interest in solid theology. In an atmosphere of uncertainty and fear, there is a marked interest in eschatology.

Laymen and laywomen are very active in regular Bible study and evangelism, described as a "widespread revival." The Reformed Lay Training School is preparing men for church-community leadership, evangelism and preaching. There is a marked interest in missions abroad. In a public hall in Prague, popular lectures on religion from October to Easter are drawing overflow crowds. Though preachers may not criticize the Government from the pulpit, preaching is at a new high theologically.

Ecumenical and International:

Church contacts abroad have been severely curtailed, though not blocked. Foreign (Western) churchmen have been forced out of the country, and inter-church aid from the West has been suspended. The Orthodox Church has close contacts with Moscow and friendly relations are maintained between Protestants in Czechoslovakia and Hungary.

Some Czechoslovakian churchmen have indicated their fears that churches in the West have resigned themselves to blind participation in a political struggle against the political powers of Communism; on the other hand they are concerned about the blinding indoctrination which the Czechoslovakian people are being given concerning aggressive intentions of the West.

Appendix I

THE CONSTITUTION OF THE CZECHOSLOVAK REPUBLIC

June 9, 1948

Declaration:

The Czechs and Slovaks, two brotherly nations, members of the great Slav family of nations, lived already a thousand years ago jointly in a single State, and jointly accepted from the East the highest achievement of the culture of that era—Christianity. As the first in Europe they raised on their standards, during the Hussite revolution, the ideas of liberty of thought, government of the people and social justice.

Fundamental Articles of the Constitution:

Article 3:

1) The People's democratic Republic recognizes no privileges; work for the benefit of the community and participation in the defense of the State is the duty of all.

2) The State guarantees to all its citizens, men and women alike, freedom of the person and its expression and takes care that every citizen receive the same possibilities and the same opportunities.

3) All citizens have the right to education, the right to work, to a just reward for work done, and to leisure after work. National Insurance will provide for all citizens in cases of incapacity for work.

Part I—Rights and Duties of Citizens:

Section 13:

1) All schools shall be State schools.

Section 15:

   1) Freedom of conscience is guaranteed.

   2) No one shall suffer prejudice by virtue of his views, philosophy, faith or convictions; neither may any such views, philosophy, faith or convictions be a ground for anyone to refuse to fulfill the civil duties laid upon him by law.

Section 16:

   1) Every one shall be entitled to profess privately and publicly any religious creed or to be without denomination.

   2) All religious denominations as well as the absence thereof shall be equal before the law.

Section 17:

   1) Every one shall be at liberty to carry out the acts connected with any religious denomination or absence thereof. The exercise of this right shall not, however, be inconsistent with public order and morality. This right shall not be misused for non-religious ends.

   2) No pressure, direct or indirect, shall be put upon anyone to take part in such acts.

Section 18:

   1) Freedom of expression is guaranteed.

   2) Every one may, within the limits of the law, express his opinion by word of mouth, in writing, print, pictorially, or in any other manner whatsoever. No one shall suffer prejudice by virtue of the exercise of this right.

Appendix II

"INSTRUCTIONS TO COMMUNISTS"

July, 1942

   1. The Vatican. You are to undermine the authority of the Vatican by all means, especially by attacks in the press, compromising articles and news items.

   2. To break down unity among the clergy, separate higher from the lower clergy, drive a wedge between bishops and clergy, also between the priests and their parishes.

   3. Main principle: Do not deal directly with the higher clergy. This is reserved only to Dr. Cepicka, General Secretary, and the Secretariat of the Communist party. Our experience shows that negotiations by the district action committees lead to compromises, which must be avoided.

   4. The task of the Church Commission of the local committee of action is not to open co-operation or negotiation with the Roman Catholic Church, but to acquire authority to act without the Church and against the Church.

   5. Closest co-operation with the Czechoslovak Church. Praise their bishops and give them highest honours in all State functions and celebrations.

6. Emphasize the frustration in the religious situation of today and the necessity for unity. In the first phase use the Czechoslovak Church as the instrument for unity; the Orthodox Church will take this place later. (Prague will become a metropolitanate for the Russian Orthodox.)

7. Attack the Catholic Church with all the usual weapons: unreasonableness of celibacy, economic power and wealth of the Church, the Church as a capitalist institution, moral delinquents, homosexual trials, etc., etc. . . .

(Barron and Waddams, *Communism and the Churches*, p. 48-49)

According to Macoin (*The Communist War on Religion*, p. 30, cf. MacEoin, p. 139) the Central Committee of the Czechoslovak Communist Party sent out as follows the aims of the fight against the Church:

1. Archbishops and bishops should be prevented from communicating with the Vatican otherwise than through the Government.

2. Pastoral letters must always have previous Government authorization.

3. Sermons of priests and all addresses to church associations should be censored and kept under rigid control.

4. The Czechoslovak Church and the Church of the Evangelical Brethren should be made State churches. The Catholic Church's property should be seized and distributed among National churches.

5. The Catholic clergy should be forced to join the National Church.

6. The Catholic clergy should be morally compromised, if necessary by means of woman agents.

Appendix III

LAW NO. 231 CONCERNING THE DEFENSE OF THE PEOPLE'S REPUBLIC

October 6, 1948

A law was issued on October 6th, 1948. Article 28 of this law contains the following paragraph:

"Whosoever uses his religious or any other position for affecting the political development in a manner not compatible with the Constitution of the Republic, will be punished with imprisonment for from one to 12 months—if there are not reasons for even a more severe punishment."

(*Dokuments Zur Ordnung der Kirche*, July, 1951)

Appendix IV

LAW OF OCTOBER 14, 1949, WHICH ESTABLISHES THE
STATE OFFICE FOR CHURCH AFFAIRS

The National Assembly of the Czechoslovak Republic passes this law:

1. The state office for church affairs is established as a central office; it

is in charge of a cabinet minister, who is appointed by the President of the Republic.

2. The purpose of the state office for church affairs is to take care that the church and religious life should develop in harmony with the Constitution and principles of people's democratic order, and thus secure for everybody the right to freedom of confession guaranteed by the Constitution, founded on principles of religious tolerance and equality of all confessions.

3. The functions in all church and religious affairs, which until now were performed by other central offices, are transferred to the state office for church affairs.

4. In Slovakia, the minister who is in charge of the state office for church affairs, performs his functions in principle through the Slovak office for church affairs, which is in charge of a representative* appointed by the government.

5. The government shall disclose by a decree the detailed directions about the working and organization of the state office for church affairs, also about its functions.

6. This law shall become effective on the day of its publication; it shall be executed by all the members of the government.

(signatures)

Appendix V

LAW NO. 218 FOR THE ECONOMIC SECURITY OF THE CHURCHES AND RELIGIOUS SOCIETIES BY THE STATE

October 14, 1949

The National Assembly of the Czechoslovak Republic passed this law (Nov. 1, 1949):

1. *Personal salaries of clergymen.* The state grants, according to the subsequent ordinances of this law, their personal salaries to clergymen of churches and religious societies, who function with the consent of the state as parish leaders in church administration, or in institutions for the education of the clergy. The state office may in exceptional cases after the previous agreement with the Ministry of Finance grant the personal salaries of clergymen who are otherwise occupied.

2. The consent of the state may be given only to clergymen who are Czechoslovak state citizens, are politically reliable and blameless, and fulfill also otherwise the general requirements of acceptance into the state service. The state office for church affairs may in cases worthy of a special consideration forego the requirements of state citizenship.

3. (1) The personal salary of clergymen consists of: a. fundamental pay, b. additional salary for higher dignitaries, c. reward for special functions.

---

* Every ministry in Prague has an office for Slovakia in Bratislava. These offices are in charge of functionaries appointed by the government. They are called "poverenici," i.e. authorized persons, representatives.

(2) The government shall designate by a decree the sums of the fundamental pay, the methods and measures of its raising, the conditions of acknoledging the addition for higher dignitaries, and its limit, also the conditions for acknowledging the rewards for higher functions.

4. *Compensation for traveling, moving and other expenses.* Clergymen who have claim for personal salaries, have also claim for compensation on traveling, moving and other expenses according to the general directions.

5. *The duty to teach religion.* It is the duty of clergymen functioning as parish leaders to teach religion in schools without compensation, if religious instruction is not taken care of otherwise. The extent of this duty and its further arrangement shall be decided in agreement with the minister of schools, sciences and art, by the minister who is directing the state office for church affairs.

6. *Social allowances.* Social additions, especially additions for minor children, pensions for clergymen and the members of their families are given according to the periodical directions valid for state employees. The details shall be fixed by the government.

7. *Activity and appointment of clergymen.* (1) Spiritual (preaching, etc.) activity in churches and religious societies may be performed only by persons who have for it the consent of the state and who take the oath. The contents of the oath will be disclosed by a government decree.

(2) Every appointment (election) of these persons requires the previous consent of the state.

(3) Vacant places must be occupied at the latest within 30 days. If this is not done, the state may take the necessary measures for securing the orderly course in the parish leadership, church administration or education of the clergy.

8. *Material expenses.* (1) The state covers, according to their accepted budget, the regular material expenses of churches and religious societies connected with Divine service and other religious rites, also with church administration.

(2) The state gives in substantiated cases special help for extraordinary material expenses.

9. *Budgets.* (1) It is the duty of the representatives of churches and religious societies and the managers of church properties to prepare the budgets and financial statements, and present them for approval to the state office for church affairs.

(2) The budgets for regular actual expenses are prepared according to actual needs, following the principles of state budget; the details will be decided by the state office for church affairs after agreement with the ministry of finance.

10. *Property.* (1) The state supervises the property of churches and religious societies.

(2) The representatives of churches and religious societies shall prepare an account of all movable and immovable property and property rights of the churches and religious societies, their constituent parts, units, institutions, endowments, church buildings, benefits and funds and shall present it within three months from the day on which this law becomes effective to the state office for church affairs. The details shall be worked out by the state office for church affairs.

(3) Any selling or mortgaging of the property of churches and religious societies requires the previous consent of the state government.

11. *Elimination of obligations.* (1) All the private and public patronates (endowments, etc.) of church building, benefits and other church institutions are transferred to the state.

(2) All the obligations to contribute toward the purposes of churches and religious societies, their constituent parts, units, institutions, endowments, church buildings, benefits and funds based on patronates or some other legal reasons and long time customs, shall cease to exist, with the exception of the obligations of the members of the churches and religious societies, based on the order recognized by the state.

12. *Establishments for the training of clergymen.* The schools of learning and institutions for the education of the clergy are kept up entirely by the State.

13. *Penalties.* Actions or negligences contradicting the directions of this law or ordinances based on it are punished, if there is no question of criminal act, by the District National Committee as misdemeanors with a fine up to 160,000 Czechoslovak Crowns. In case of the impossibility to enforce the payment of the fine, a substitute punishment is meted out according to the degree of guilt, up to 6 months in prison.

14. *Repeal of ordinances.* All the ordinances which regulate the legal constitutions of churches and religious societies are repealed.

15. *Effectiveness and execution of the law.* This law becomes effective on November 1, 1949; it shall be executed by all the members of the government.

(signatures)

Gottwald	Kopecky	Siroky (also for Minister
Fierlinger	Petr	Dr. Clementis)
Dr. Gregor	Plojhar	General of the Army
Dr. Cepicka	Zapotocky	Svoboda
Krajcir	Dr. Dolansky	Dr. Nejedly
Erban	Kabes	Duris
Dr. John	Kliment	Dr. Neuman
Dr. Sevcik	Dr. Ing. Slechta	Dr. Srobar
Nosek	Ing. Jankovcova	

Appendix VI

STATEMENT OF ROMAN CATHOLIC CLERGY AGAINST THE PROPOSED LAW OF OCTOBER 14

With the consent of all the Bishops, the whole clergy state that they do not accept the proposed new law dealing with the payment of personal and material expenses of the church and religious organizations and that the entire Vicarate decided to publish and submit to the Government of the Republic of Czechoslovakia this declaration (in which we list only the outstanding points):

1. The clergy gratefully admits that the Government of the Republic of Czechoslovakia recognizes as a fact that the economic and financial position of

the clergy is not adequate to their education and their work for the common welfare and the supreme interests of the nation.

2. However, the suggested law aims to better the position of the clergy at the cost of their freedom and to bring the spiritual mission of the church into complete dependence on political agencies and interests. This can be seen in Paragraph 10 of the proposed law.

(Paragraph 10 of the proposed law reads: "The election or nomination of clergy receiving salaries or benefits in accordance with this law requires the prior approval of the state administration. The election or nomination of titular Bishops, diocesan Bishops, Archbishops, as well as their coadjutors, apostolic administrators, army Bishops and heads of individual churches requires prior approval of the proposed candidate by the Government. The Government may withhold approval on the ground of the political desirability of the candidates.")

Therefore the clergy declare that they will accept their church appointments only from the hands of free and unrestricted church superiors.

3. The proposed improvement in the position of the clergy and the material contributions to church objectives creates an unfavorable impression, as if the church were to be satisfied in receiving compensation for its estates and property, which it lost against its will. This happened by one-sided action on the part of the state, without preliminary agreement with the Holy See.

4. The salaries of the clergy are to be raised at a time when, because of various economic difficulties, it is being considered to lower the wages of the workers and the insurance benefits of pensioned people. Under such conditions the clergy voluntarily relinquishes the benefits of the increases proposed in the new law and respectfully requests that the incomes of the workers and pensioners be retained at their present levels or, better still, improved.

5. A law such as this—which, in Paragraph 17, threatens destructive sanctions even for small violations—is at the most anti-social and unfair, and therefore it is necessary to reject it under all circumstances.

(Paragraph 17 of the proposed law states: "Actions or omissions contravening the provisions of this law or regulations issued under it shall be punished, in so far as it is not a matter punishable by a court, by a district national committee as an administrative misdemeanor with a fine not exceeding 100,000 crowns ($2,000). An alternative sentence of imprisonment not exceeding six months shall be imposed simultaneously in case the fine is not collectable. Fines shall go to the state treasury.)

6. The clergy will be satisfied if, in agreement with the highest church dignitaries, the basic kongrua law be retained and in special cases adjusted, and if the repair of national church monuments will be financed and the church needs satisfied.

(This was a reference to the state-church agreement of the eighteenth century laying down the terms for state financial aid to the church in the old Austro-Hungarian Empire.)

7. It is particularly requested that the religious freedom of the people be completely respected and retained, as well as the freedom of priestly work and spiritual aims of the clergy, whose aim is the eternal and present welfare of our people.

(*New York Times*, September 8, 1949)

Appendix VII

STATEMENT OF ROMAN CATHOLIC CLERGY
AGAINST THE PROPOSED LAW OF OCTOBER 14, 1949

August 14, 1949

Summary of the main points of the bishops' peace condition:

1. All measures restricting Mgr. Beran's personal freedom should be removed.

2. Government plenipotentiaries installed in the bishops' consistories or, as in the case of Slovakia, in the bishops' offices must be removed. By the latter the State has assumed the right to decide in matters of religious rites and worship and in matters of morals and faith.

"Already the work of these plenipotentiaries shows clearly the extent of their illegal activities." In some dioceses they claim the right exclusively to decide in all business of the Church and they illegally use official Church seals for their personal instructions.

3. The Catholic Action movement which "under a veil of seeking agreement between Church and State was to bring disorder into the ranks of Czech and Slovak Catholics was rightly proclaimed by us as a movement of schism. We are of the opinion that a suitable moment has now come to stop this enmity against the Church.

4. The idea of the Christian world will be respected and recognized in public life and education by both words and deed.

5. The Government will recognize the spiritual authority of the Roman Pope as supreme head of the Church as well as the right authority of the bishops in their obedience to the Pope and Church orders.

6. All measures restricting and endangering religious freedom will be revoked.

"We demand further that interference, violating Church rights, with the education of priests and juniors of the orders must cease. We protest against the cutting of contact between the bishops and the believers, and we protest against the silencing of our just defence against untrue accusations and measures of persecution. We protest against the persecution of priests for reading pastoral letters and for faithfully fulfilling their priestly duties. We protest against the continued publication of the so-called *Gazette* of the Catholic clergy, and we demand renewal of full freedom for the Catholic Press which has been stopped.

"We call for a renewal of the freedom of meetings guaranteed by the constitution, and we especially protest against the fact that under various excuses priests are prevented from holding meetings among themselves and from making other expressions of religious life. We protest against the closing of Church schools, the requisitioning of Church and monastery buildings, and against all steps which limit religious freedom."

7. The bishops are willing to swear loyalty to the State on the terms of the existing arrangement between Czechoslovakia and the Vatican, provided the Government stops attacking the Church, guarantees religious freedom, and recognizes Papal authority in Church affairs.

(*The Times*, September 13, 1949)

Appendix VIII

PENAL JUDICIAL LAW RE: MISUSE OF RELIGIOUS FUNCTION

August 1, 1950

Article 123:

Anyone who misuses his position in the Church for the purpose of influencing political affairs in a manner injurious to the People's Democracy shall be deprived of his personal freedom for a period varying from three months to three years.

The perpetrator shall be deprived of his freedom for a period varying from one year to five years

(a)　if he refuses to perform a religious function to which he is called as a pastor (or in a similar capacity); or

(b)　if there are any other aggravating circumstances.

Article 173:　Interfering with supervision of churches and religious societies:

Anyone who performs pastoral functions in the church or religious societies without the consent of the State, shall be punished with the loss of freedom up to three years.

Similarly shall be punished anyone who performs pastoral functions in church or religious societies in a locality in which he was not placed with the consent of the State.

Whoever appoints any person to perform pastoral functions in a church or religious societies without the consent of the State shall be punished by loss of freedom for a period varying from one to five years.

Article 174:

Anyone who deliberately interferes with, or impedes, the authority of the state supervisor over a church or religious societies shall be punished by loss of his freedom for a period varying from one to five years.

The same penalty shall be meted out to anyone who, in any other way, deliberately infringes the law concerning the economic security of churches and religious societies.

Article 101:—Penal Administration Law: defence of order in matters concerning the Church.

Anyone who fails to keep the ordinances, or who infringes the law relating to the legal position of churches and religious societies, especially anyone who endangers or obstructs the functions of the state supervisor of property appertaining to churches and religious societies, shall be fined 100,000 Kc (Czech Crowns) or lose his freedom for a period up to three months.

(*Cesky Bratr*, October, 1950, as quoted by *EPS*, November 17, 1949)

EAST GERMANY

Introduction

Christianity was introduced into Central Germany (e.g. Saxony, Thuringia) at the turn of the Eighth Century as an integral part of Charlemagne's empire. In the following three centuries, as the Franks and Saxons pushed eastward, driving out or overcoming local Slavic tribes, they brought with them their Germanized version of the Catholic Christian faith. The spread of Christianity in East Germany did not therefore spring essentially from a missionary concern, though there were missionaries working among the peoples of that area as early as the Eighth Century. Rather, it represented an appendage of the social and political aspirations and customs of the people of present West-Central Germany as they expanded their boundaries Eastward.

At the time of the Reformation, East Germany became almost entirely Protestant and has remained so to this day. Compulsory religious education was introduced in the public school system; the Church took an active interest in ministering to the needs of the sick, the aged, orphans and children through an elaborate system of institutions, both church and private.

By the beginning of the Twentieth Century, certain aspects of German religious life had crystallized into relatively distinctive concepts:

(1) The Church was an established institution, with prescribed traditions and practices, whose existence and future were an accepted fact.

(2) Since the total culture was Christian, all people were born into the "Volkskirche" on entering into life in that cultural setting.

(3) The pastor was an expert in religion, who because of his scientific study was above contradiction—"Amt."

(4) Evangelization consisted of the proclaiming of the Word from the pulpit.

(5) The Church and the State were two kingdoms, with separate rulers, both ordained of God and both having a claim on the individual, who was a citizen of both kingdoms.

It was these concepts in addition to the tenets common to Christians in other lands which Communism faced in East Germany. Here for the first time Communism confronted religion where Protestantism, strong both in its Lutheran theology and its confessing spirit, was the majority religion.

Religious Composition:

Population	20,000,000
Protestants (including a very small number of Methodists, Baptists, Pentecostals, Christian Scientists, Jehovah's Witnesses)	16,500,000
Roman Catholics	2,500,000
Non-believers	1,000,000

Under The Nazi Regime:

Books by competent authorities are available on the struggle of the German Church under the Nazi regime; they need not be reviewed here. Listed below are only a few of the measures taken during that period which are relevant to later developments. The list could be readily expanded.

A Council for Spiritual Affairs was set up by the Nazi Government to oversee pastoral appointments and regulate church affairs. State support of the church depended on the church's attitude to the regime; church lands were administered by the regime. Obligatory religious instruction in the schools was discontinued. Education was distinctly materialistic. Organized Christian youth work was prohibited; Christian youth activities were absorbed into the life of the congregations. Laymen and laywomen began their role as leaders in congregational religious life. The social work of the church had a hard struggle to continue at all. Many religious journals were forbidden, others either continued as echoes of official Government policy, or went underground. Many Roman Catholic clergy supported the German war against Russia. Among Evangelical leaders, there was a distinct cleavage between the Bekennende Kirche (confessing or witnessing church) and the Nazi collaborationist "German Christian Church," with a great body of Christians between, who both wished to remain true to their Christian faith and to continue living as best they could. There were martyrs, some heroic Christian statesmen, many confused and oppressed, a good number who, under pressure, collaborated, and not a few who joined in leading the German culture-type church, propounded Nazi racial and social redemption theories. Ecumenical contacts were broken over several years.

Still, when the bombing and chaos, the killing and raping began to subside, people turned to the Church, among them many former soldiers, war prisoners, parents, teachers and laborers, for comfort, strength and guidance.

The Early Years of Allied (Soviet) Occupation:

The Allied occupation brought with it a blue-print for purported radical social reforms. Some were little different from those of the Nazis. Some were less radical. Implementation began slowly, and varied from place to place; laymen could sense little difference between the ideological and spiritual climate of the Nazi and the new regimes. Industrial reform put private business back in the hands of the authorities. Land reform was to have collectivized large private lands. The churches, however, did not relinquish their lands, a fact which they were later to regret. Separation of Church and State was more theory than fact as the Government continued to support the churches and to collect church taxes. Educational reform was to make education public, free and compulsory. Confessional schools, however, were not abolished in the East Zone until 1947, and in East Berlin in 1948. Religious education was struck from the public school curriculum, but churches were to have opportunity to arrange one or two hours weekly for religious instruction at their own expense and on their own responsibility. A sequestration act provided for Government ownership or control of public health and service institutions, but, facing overwhelming human need and physical destruction, the churches had unlimited opportunities for social and institutional work. Publications were started, subject to censorship by the occupying powers. In an unexpected way, the churches of East and West Germany were able to hold together, and the churches soon indicated that they were big enough to make room both for many former "German Christians" and the Resistance churchmen.

All in all, the immediate situation was not worse than East Germans expected. Some reported "unlimited tolerance," that openly anti-Christian and

anti-church bias was discouraged.   There were occasional attacks by "local
petty officials," but this did "not constitute martyrdom or persecution."   Religion was allowed for individuals.   Tension arose only when several such individuals came together to express their faith on current political and social
issues.   A prevue of what was to come, and what lay behind it, leaked out in
relation to the confiscation of the Salem Deaconess Orphanage at Klein Bies-
nitz in 1947.   When authorities were asked to explain their action, they wrote,
. . . "(this) . . . was an outcome of purely ideological concerns. . . . The
leadership and supervision of homes for children may be carried out only by
and through the Provincial government and in accordance with the lines
worked out by the Educational Administration in the Soviet Occupation Zone."

A year later, Bishop Dibelius and other bishops of the Evangelical churches
sent a letter to Russian Marshall Sokolovsky protesting against the East German authorities' attempts to use the churches to support their "people's petition for German unity."   They considered such attempts an interference in
church autonomy and an endeavor to involve the Church in political affairs
(*Daily Telegraph*, London, June 7, 1949).

Shortly thereafter the Soviet-controlled press complained that the German
pastors and priests were not supporting the "democratic reforms" introduced
in East Germany by the Communists.   By the time the new East German political leaders were ready to make their will known, the churches had already
implemented a great part of the variegated witness and ministry of the Church.

Chronicle of Events

The German Democratic Republic

March 19, 1949—

The new constitution of the East
German Republic was presented to
the People's Council.   Among other
provisions the constitution would:
1) abolish the State-Church, and
make churches legally responsible associations;
2) guarantee freedom of belief and
religious practices, but those leaving
the church must make a court or public announcement;
3) separate religious instruction
from the public school curriculum, but
allow churches to arrange instruction
on school premises;
4) make guardians responsible for
the child's religious instruction only
until the child is 14, at which time he
should decide for himself;
5) guarantee to the churches the
right to hold property and funds for
cultural, educational and welfare purposes (Appendix I).
Communist leaders invited Evangelical Church delegates to meet with

them to discuss questions of State policy, German unity, the Marshall Aid
Plan, atomic control and the Mindszenty case.   The conversation was to
be continued on the general theme,
"The Church and the Present Political Situation" (*EPS*, No. 11, March,
1949).

March 12, 1949—

Communists publicly assailed Bishop Dibelius for criticizing their system of having a Communist leader
responsible for political and other activities in each city block (*N. Y.
Times*, 12:5:1).

April 23, 1949—

Soviet occupation authorities placed a general ban on church publications (*N. Y. Times*, April 23, 4:4).
Some publications were simply forbidden.   Others had great difficulties
in getting paper.   *Petrusblatt*, Roman
Catholic weekly published in West
Berlin, was banned from East Germany since there was "no demand for
it."   Publishers were warned that if

they circulated the paper illegally, "addressees might find themselves in trouble" (MacEoin, *The Communist War on Religion,* p. 219).

June 6, 1949—

In a Whitsuntide letter read in most churches in Berlin-Brandenburg, Bishop Dibelius, after pointing out that during the past four years the churches had refrained from criticism of the occupying Government, stated that now with responsibility being laid on Germans the Church must speak frankly.

He called the K-5 department of the "people's police" a revival of the Nazi Gestapo, charged that judges had been instructed to practice a political "justice" which meant violence, stated that Divine Services, while not forbidden, had been made practically impossible because people were forced to work at the Sunday worship hour. He compared the falsehood of the recent voting methods to the pattern of Nazi elections, and added that whereas in the past he had felt it necessary to deny rumors of persecution of Christians in East Germany, he now found that clerical activity "was being hampered by measures of political violence" (*The Scotsman,* Edinburgh, June 6, 1949; *The Daily Telegraph,* London, 7/6/49).

June 11, 1949—

It was disclosed in Berlin that the Brandenburg People's Council was making plans to ensure adequate control and supervision of the churches (*N. Y. Times,* June 11, 2:2).

July 16, 1949—

East German journals attacked the Pope's decree excommunicating Communists (*N. Y. Times,* July 16:4:7).

July 18, 1949—

The Berlin *Neues Deutschland* assailed Bishop Dibelius for criticizing Communist policy and methods (*N. Y. Times,* 18:5:1).

July 20, 1949—

Catholics reported that the Catholic Christian Democratic Party sought to separate from the National front as a result of the Pope's decree (*N. Y. Times,* 20:10:4).

August 26, 1949—

The Communist East Berlin press announced that the Evangelical churches had rejected an invitation to participate officially in forthcoming "Peace Day" rallies (*N. Y. Times,* August 26:6:4).

September, 1949—

Bishop Dibelius in the *The Ecumenical Review,* Winter, 1950, reported on the church situation:

1. Very little literature was available on kiosks, but what was available did not include "sexy trash." Cinemas did not show trashy foreign films.

2. Where there had been interference from local German Communist authorities with church meetings or funds, Russian authorities had often intervened helpfully.

3. The State continued contributions to church expenses and some special aid for repairs.

4. Church services had not been interfered with except by what amounts to obligatory work programs. In some areas, however, "The Russian commandant can say, with some justice, that the people . . . would not go to church in any case!"

5. Religious instruction was technically permitted at church expense; Russian occupying powers attempted to see it carried out. The main difficulty was with local German authorities and materialist teachers.

6. The chief difficulty was where the church attempted to take up educational and social work.

7. It was difficult for children of educated classes (including pastors) to enroll in secondary school and universities, unless "in agreement with the new outlook. Education in politics begins at school, among quite small children." Church kindergartens were closed whenever a pretext could be found.

8. Theological schools continued in universities, but there was a reduction in numbers of theological students "because many students are excluded from the universities, owing to their origin, or for other reasons." It was increasingly difficult to find professors for faculties.

9. In youth work, there was considerable interference, except where confined to small local groups.

10. Difficulties were put in the way of training deaconesses as nurses.

11. What little literature was produced was subject to the censorship of the occupying powers (in all four zones).

12. Church life had improved, but people were too tired physically and morally for there to be a spiritual revival.

September 13, 1949—

Organized youth work was forbidden and subsequently absorbed into the normal church structure. Christian symbols worn by youth on the streets were forbidden (*Christian Century*, May 24, 1950, p 651).

September 21, 1949—

Communist families were instructed to keep their children away from church schools and to "agitate to hinder church education" (*N. Y. Herald Tribune*, September 21, 1949).

October 7, 1949—

The constitution of the German Democratic Republic was ratified by Parliament (Appendix I). The regulation requiring people quitting the churches to announce their intentions to an official court was looked upon by Evangelical leaders as a good thing. It would provide an opportunity to contact such people prior to final rupture with the church (*EPS*, No. 45, Dec., 1949). Less than 5% of the total Christian population had left the church (*Christian Century*, April 5, 1950, p. 426).

October 12, 1949—

The Evangelical Church Council issued a declaration to West and East German governments urging them to re-establish German unity, and to install church representatives with full powers in their respective governments (*EPS*, April 28, 1950).

November, 1949—

Taegliche Rundschau, Soviet military government journal, commented on the appointment of Archbishop Muench as Papal Nuncio as "significant for the alliance between American monopoly capitalism and the Vatican" (MacEoin, *The Communist War on Religion*, p. 218).

December 9, 1949—

The Government announced that special holidays and school programs celebrating Christmas would be forbidden (*N. Y. Times*, Dec. 9:12:3). Christmas vacation was renamed "Winter" vacation, and Easter was to be called "Spring" vacation. "Solimann" (a Communist version of Santa Claus) was to replace the Christ Child at the center of "Winter vacation" festivities.

December 20, 1949—

The Roman Catholic journal, *Petrusblatt*, denounced the use of Marxist history textbooks in the schools which on alleged scientific grounds denied the existence of Christ and described the scriptures as a collection of myths and legends (*N. Y. Herald Tribune*, Dec. 20, 1949). A Roman Catholic publication in West Berlin reported that young people in the East Zone were being forced to join Communist youth groups (*N. Y. Times*, December 21:23:1).

December 26, 1949—

Russian occupying authorities permitted Evangelical pastors to conduct Christmas services for Russian prisoners in former concentration camps. The Catholic Church also applied for, and received permission to hold similar services.

January 13, 1950—

Roman Catholic Bishop Von Preysing (of Berlin) severely criticized the condition of political and war prisoners in concentration camps after Evangelical Bishop Dibelius' and Dean Gruber's relatively favorable reports, as compared with the camps under Nazi rule, following their visits at Christmas to Sachsenhausen and Buchenwald (*N. Y. Times*, January 13:6:5).

January 22, 1950—

Cardinal Von Preysing protested to the East Zone Government that

a. freedom of religion and conscience was handled in such a way by the Government as to endanger or eliminate religious life;

b. children were forced to attend schools where they were educated "in the spirit of nihilism";

c. authorities had "persistently refused" to give permission to publish Catholic periodicals;

d. circulation of foreign periodicals had been banned;

e. religious rallies must be approved by the Government in advance (*N. Y. Herald Tribune*, January 22, 1950).

January 24, 1950—

M. Hickmann, leader of the Catholic Christian Democratic Union Party in Saxony was replaced for "opposing the National Front" (*N. Y. Herald Tribune*, January 24, 1950). Catholics interpreted his removal as the final step in "communizing" the party (MacEoin, *The Communist War on Religion*, p. 219).

February 16, 1950—

Cardinal Von Preysing in a pastoral letter to all priests forbade them to join the National Front or to cooperate with the Communists (*N. Y. Times*, February 17:1:7).

February 19, 1950—

The U.S.S.R. Berlin Army publication, *Tägliche Rundschau*, criticized Von Preysing for his pastoral letter "inciting priests to opposition" to the Government (*N. Y. Times*, February 19:28:5) and labelling him a "gladiator for American imperialism." The journal asserted that the cold war was being directed by the Pope.

February 27, 1950—

Bishop Dibelius, in a report on the church situation, reiterated that there was "no victimization of Christians," but that the churches were having serious difficulties with religious instruction of children, that "the church could never accept a curriculum 100% against Christian teaching," and that pastors were having difficulty finding academic openings for their children (*N. Y. Herald Tribune*, Feb. 27, 1950). On university campuses elections for student councils, though rigged for a Communist landslide, showed great student feeling against Communists. Christian students were being put through difficult questioning periods and some expelled. Student Christian associations were growing. Theological faculties showed a decrease in attendance, owing to the political screening of students. Theological lecturers were being replaced by men who were not approved by the churches. Hymns to Stalin were being sung in the schools, from which many Protestant students refrained. Roman Catholic students were able to join in by special dispensation of the Catholic Church. It appeared likely that Evangelical students would not receive State scholarships if they did not enter into such activities.

March, 1950—

Because pastors were being urged to cooperate with the "National Front," Evangelical Church authorities issued a statement advising pastors to "refrain from adherence to any association of a political, or even a pan-political nature, since your cooperation is capable of being interpreted as officially representing the church" (*EPS*, March 3, 1950).

At a Communist Party meeting in Thuringia, M. Hauschild, a high-ranking leader, stated that although the Party must ultimately do away with religion, it must for the moment protect religion. He warned that Roman Catholic priests must be watched with particular care and stated that a regular service for observing church activities had been established around experienced Communists. Emphasis was to be placed on training children so that when old people died, the Church would die with them (*The Church Herald*, March 10, 1950; Text, Appendix II).

In negotiations between Evangelical Church and Government leaders, Bishop Dibelius indicated necessary requisites towards avoiding eventual conflict:

(1) the Government must refrain from attacking Christian faith;

(2) pressure must not be applied concerning political decisions or affiliations, including youth groups;

(3) freedom of speech and conscience, legal protection upon arrest and other constitutional guarantees must be scrupulously adhered to by the Government (Letter of Bishop Dibelius to Grotewohl, Appendix III).

April 2, 1950—

The International Commission for Study of European Questions asserted that Communists were getting Lutheran Church support by emphasizing Roman Catholic strength and Lutheran weakness in West Germany, and pledging the rebirth of a strong German Lutheranism under a unified Germany (*N. Y. Times*, April 2:1:2).

April 16, 1950—

Protestant Church and Government leaders' daily discussions concerning the place of the clergy and the church in the new order reached a critical stage. The churches were said to have prepared a sharp letter to be read to all congregations on Good Friday. Plans of the Communist Party to require all functionaries to prove that they had no church connection by May 1 were delayed during the negotiations (*N. Y. Times*, April 16: 15:1).

April 18, 1950—

A report from Magdeburg stated that Christian youth being "attacked for their faith" were being advised by church leaders to contact local church authorities (*Christian Century*, May 29, 1950, p. 651).

April 20, 1950—

Bishop Dibelius, in a letter addressed to Prime Minister Grotewohl, pointed out that the Government had pledged that negotiations planned for Easter Tuesday were to discuss basic principles and not isolated incidents, and that only on that basis had the Church of Magdeburg agreed to set aside a proclamation critical of the Government, that children were being taught in compulsory schools an ideology contradictory to the faith of 9/10 of their parents, that people, and particularly students, were being forced to live a double life in public and at home, in violation of their faith and the constitution, that the State was only doing itself harm by undermining the people's respect in the integrity and authority of the State. He repeated the points of an earlier discussion concerning requisites for avoiding open conflict (Appendix III).

A Government official ordered all clergy to make public statements favoring the Communist-sponsored "National Front" (*N. Y. Times*, 24:1:7).

April 22, 1950—

In a letter to Prime Minister Grotewohl, Cardinal Von Preysing accused the Government of curtailing freedom of religion and of speech for individuals and the Roman Catholic Church:

1. The State supports the propagation of materialistic philosophy in schools, through the press, and through its officials and organizations;

2. State pressure has made church influence on public life impossible;

3. Christians have been forced to join organizations and advocate measures they know are wrong;

4. The Church has been forbidden to publish newspapers with which to counteract "countless attacks against the Church and false reports about the Church" (*N. Y. Times*, May 1:4:6).

April 23, 1950—

In spite of pressure from local Government officials, a message from the consistory of the Berlin-Brandenburg Church was read in all Berlin-Brandenburg churches, a similar statement in other churches of the East Zone. The message stated that members were besieging church leaders with pleas to "Help us! We are constrained to say things. . . . we cannot say . . . to engage in doings in which we cannot join with a quiet mind . . . to acquiesce in decisions we cannot approve. We are in constant peril of losing our liberty, our employment, our daily bread, if we refuse to do as others do." When these facts were presented to Government authorities, the reply was that such acts did not have Government approval and individual cases would be investigated. The message continued with a protest against the forcing of the materialist philosophy as the only valid truth into every level of life, and an appeal to public officials not to commit the sin of coercing men and children into believing falsehood, an appeal to Christians to stand together and resist in love the violence to which they were subjected, and an assertion that Christ came even to free those who despise Him (Appendix IV).

On the same Sunday a letter from the Roman Catholic bishops was read in the churches of East and West Germany. The letter, after condemning both capitalistic and Communistic materialism as atheistic, declared that any Catholic "consciously and voluntarily following and propagating the teachings of atheistic materialism is excommunicated" (*EPS*, April 28, 1950).

April 23-27, 1950—

At a meeting of the Synod of the EKiD (Evangelical Church in Germany), Bishop Dibelius noted that there had been opportunities for co-operation with Catholic authorities in matters requiring a church viewpoint as against the State or occupying powers (*Ibid.*).

April 24, 1950—

Prime Minister Grotewohl denounced the letters of the Evangelical and Roman Catholic leaders as an attack on the constitution, the Government and the Republic—"an illegal act, the more as it was undertaken while negotiations between the Government and the church on the subject of the church declaration had not come to an end yet." Grotewohl's denunciation went out in an official letter to the presidents of the five laender, their police chiefs and the laender church leaders (*N. Y. Times*, April 24:1:7).

April 27, 1950—

The formerly Catholic "Christian Democratic Party" warned Protestant and Catholic churches against mixing in politics and accused them of attacking the security of the State in their recent letters (*N. Y. Times*, April 28:7:3).

April 28, 1950—

After a six-hour conference, Prime Minister Grotewohl, Evangelical Bishop Dibelius, and Catholic representative Wesskamm released a joint communiqué: "Representatives of the churches gave assurances that the reconstruction of the German people's life in peace and freedom is their earnest desire. Representatives of the Government gave assurance that the churches can fulfill their work on the basis of the constitution as until now." Orally it was agreed that negotiations should continue and that in the future the churches would bring all complaints before the Government (*N. Y. Times*, April 29:6:4).

April, 1950—

A visitor to East Germany reported that among Protestants religious instruction was being given in improvised ways outside the schools and that most children were attending.

In villages where there were no pastors, laymen administered the sacraments and cared for the congregations. A renewed sense of God's concern and presence was found among those in worst conditions.

The Old Prussian Union approved the practice of lay administration of the pastoral office by "lay churchmen who possess a special aptitude . . . without receiving preliminary theological training . . ." (*EPS*, June 2, 1950).

May 14, 1950—

The EKiD, which had not subscribed to the Government's "Peace Appeal," in spite of heavy pressure, issued its own message on peace, adopted by the Synod (April 23-27) and read in all Evangelical Churches. The message included a statement that the laws of God stand against depriving a man of his liberty without fair trial, against coercion or terrorism in matters of faith or conscience, against persecution for his beliefs or coercion to act against his conscience (*EPS*, May 5, 1950).

May 14, 1950—

A four-page article in the Communist Party organ, *Neues Deutschland*, listed instructions to Communist Party members on their future tasks and focussed attention especially against the churches. Excerpts were quoted in other East German publications:

"Certain church leaders have undertaken one reactionary attack after another against the movement of the fighters for peace and against the democratic order of the German Democratic Republic. These are the same high church leaders who have consistently defended the domination of the monopolists and the Junkers, who approved the terror in the Nazis' time and blessed the arms for Hitler's predatory war.

"Today these same church leaders again stand in the front lines of the warmongers and reactionaries and fulfill the orders of the Anglo-American imperialists and their German tools."

The Politburo expressed resentment at the church leaders' protest against forced youth participation in Free German Youth (FDJ) and asserted that pastors who have affiliated with the National Front have been threatened with disciplinary measures by their church superiors (*N. Y. Times,* May 15:2:2; Excerpt, Appendix V).

June 3-5, 1950—

A "Youth Church" general conference and Bach festival in Leipzig was prohibited by order of the Government.

June 9, 1950—

In a letter to Prime Minister Grotewohl, Bishop Dibelius criticized the Government for its hostility to the Church and for supporting the anti-church resolutions adopted by the Socialist Unity Party of Germany (SED) (*N. Y. Times,* June 10:3:2).

June 17, 1950—

Government journals carried a declaration by Prime Minister Grotewohl that the Government would offer protection and support to clergy who suffered from their superiors because of cooperation with the Government and warned that anyone interfering with the political activities of such clergymen would be violating the constitution (Appendix VI).

In Thuringia, where an exceptionally high number of clergy had once joined the Nazi Party, some 120 of 200 had joined the National Front. In four other laender there was considerable joining, but less than in Thuringia. In other areas, practically none. Of 1000 pastors in the East Zone, probably less than 500 were members of the Front. In a lecture at the "House of Culture" in Berlin, H. Lehmann asserted that the June Congress of the SED (Socialist Unity Party of Germany) was the occasion for launching a full-scale attack against church leaders "who terrorize pastors and believers because they identify themselves with the National Front. They will suffer a set-back." He described the Church as the servant of the ruling class and the militarists, and accused the bishops of blessing "Hitler's Robber War" (*N. Y. Times,* June 17:4:2, 1950).

June 24, 1950—

Otto Nuschke, chairman of the CDU (Christian Democratic Union) in East Germany and deputy premier of the Government, in a speech at Dresden, charged that the Government was using "police measures" against the Church.

June 27, 1950—

The first of a series of conferences for pastors arranged by the Government was held in Dresden. 27 pastors attended (*Christian Century,* September 13, 1950, p. 1074).

June, 1950—

A reliable source reported that
(a) in the life of the congregations institutional "importance" had given way to simplicity, titles and prestige to simple love and solidarity.
(b) Prayer life and especially Bible-study had become of great importance.
(c) People felt isolated and longed for links with Christians "outside," but still experienced something real in the Church Universal.
(d) Church youth groups were alert—some 150,000 youth attended summer camps.
(e) Student Christian groups faced serious problems, but were very alive.
(f) Some 15,000 lay teachers were instructing children in religion.
(g) Pastors were concerned about whether to exclude from their youth groups young people with Communist affiliations, or whether this was an opportunity and responsibility for evangelism.
(h) The general situation in which people found themselves, economically and politically, was causing intensified interest in religious life.

July, 1950—

Following numerous church complaints to the Government, the sentence, "Jesus never lived," in the history textbook by Russian educator Michulin used in East German schools was deleted from all new editions.

At a meeting of 400 teachers in Berlin, Dr. Jacobi, General Superintendent of the Evangelical Church, stated that the Church would not look on "like a dumb dog" while intelligent pupils were excluded from examinations or even from secondary schools, on grounds of "economic-political immaturity" or membership in the youth branch of the Church (*EPS,* July 14, 1950).

July 22, 1950—

At the Congress of the Social Unity Party, Premier Grotewohl warned church leaders in the Soviet Zone that severe repressive measures would be taken if they continued to oppose East German Government policies. Further interference with curricula in schools would not be tolerated and only the State would dictate subjects and courses. From now on State funds will be withheld from clergy who oppose the administration, regardless of directives from their hierarchy. "Of course we do not put the pastors into the same kettle with Bishop Dibelius. Dibelius is not the church . . . he is a man who wants to disturb the peace of Germany" (*N. Y. Times*, July 22:5:5).

July 29, 1950—

In reply to Grotewohl's attack on Bishop Dibelius, Evangelical Churches of Germany told the East German Government that its attacks on Bishop Dibelius were regarded as attacks on the Church itself. "We shall not be separated from Bishop Dibelius by anything," said the church leadership of Berlin-Brandenburg. The accusations were called "a monstrous distortion of the truth" (*N. Y. Times*, July 29:4:1).

July 30, 1950—

Bishop Dibelius, in a detailed statement, denied Grotewohl's charge that he had been to see President Truman (on his visit to Toronto for the Central Committee of the World Council of Churches) where he received orders to intensify the churches' opposition to the East German Government (*N. Y. Times*, July 30:14:8). "We are a church, and a church does not recognize political orders. The information Prime Minister Grotewohl got from his agents is just another 'thriller' story" (*Christian Century*, September 6, 1950, p. 1056).

August 16, 1950—

Another of the Government's series of conferences for pastors was held at Potsdam. Berlin-Brandenburg pastors received invitations signed by high Government leaders and two former German-Christian pastors, as well as offers by local National Front leaders to provide free transportation and all expenses.

Legislature President Meier assured the twenty pastors present (of a total 1,500 in Berlin-Brandenburg)

that the Government would protect them and guarantee their positions and salaries if church leaders should discriminate against them for coming.

Brandenburg Prime Minister Jahn attributed the small attendance to the pastors' fear of reprisals from their church authorities. Former German-Christian Pastor Kehnscherper stated that very soon pastors who cherished the cause of peace would not be intimidated into abstaining from National Front peace rallies by . . . Bishop Dibelius and the *Potsdamer Kirche*, publication of the Confessing Church. He called for "ecumenicity" with the Orthodox Church of Moscow, and declared that "the National Front is a platform where socialism and Christianity can commune."

Resolutions against war, against the atomic bomb, for the Stockholm peace declaration and approving a common ballot for the October 15 election were signed by nine pastors. The following day East German papers declared, "Pastors of Brandenburg overwhelmingly approved the Stockholm peace declaration" (*Christian Century*, Sept. 13, 1950, p. 1075).

August, 1950—

Christian laymen in Dresden listed in a statement of "vows" that they would meet weekly for Bible study and lectures, they would read the Bible daily, they would each try to bring 10 to 15 neighbors to the Bible meetings, they would visit the sick and parents of children delinquent in religious instruction, and would meet each Sunday morning for prayer before worship (*EPS*, Sept. 29, 1950).

August 29, 1950—

The Government forbade the distribution of copies of Bishop Dibelius' sermons in East Berlin and East Germany.

August 30, 1950—

The *Tribune de Genève* published a "letter from Berlin" which claimed that many Protestants were becoming Catholics in East Germany because

(a) Roman Catholicism had taken a firm line against Communism, whereas Protestantism attempted to be neutral, i.e., "Let the church be the church";

(b) Roman Catholic leaders were suffering as martyrs while Protestant pastors retained their official status;

(c) the Roman Catholic Church has a uniform political line directed from one central authority whereas Protestants have no uniformity or authority (*Tribune de Genève*, 30/8/50).

August 29-31, 1950—

60 Jehovah's Witnesses were jailed and their group threatened with banishment (*N. Y. Times*, August 29:4:6, 31:16:1).

September 5-6, 1950—

The Jehovah's Witnesses groups were dissolved, their headquarters searched, and more than 1000 members jailed on charges of spying for a foreign power (*N. Y. Times*, September 5:10:6; 6:19:5).

In the following two months sentences were pronounced ranging up to life imprisonment for alleged espionage for America (*N. Y. Times*, October 5:19:5, November 27:4:3).

September 25, 1950—

Prime Minister Jahn of Brandenburg invited 950 Roman Catholic and Protestant clergymen to a conference to discuss the forthcoming elections. Church leaders were not consulted. 27 clergymen accepted the invitation. They were told that

(a) only "progressive" clergymen would thereafter speak on East German radio programs, and

(b) that church subsidies would be terminated and public collections banned.

Similar conferences were held in Saxony and Saxony-Anhalt.

September 27, 1950—

Protestant Pastor S. Ringhandt, Superintendent of the Church of Seelow district and member of the Confessing Church Fraternal Council was arrested, allegedly for carrying a heavy bag of nails into the East Zone for rebuilding purposes.

October 11, 1950—

Tägliche Rundschau called upon school children to make propaganda, distribute hand-bills, etc., for the October 15 elections (*Tribune de Genève*, October, 1951).

After two pastors, leaders of the "progressive" opposition against church authorities, had been asked to conduct the churches' regular morning radio services, the Evangelical and Roman Catholic Churches discontinued their cooperation with Radio Berlin and Deutschland-Sender in providing religious broadcasts (*EPS*, October 20, 1950).

In conferences in five cities of Saxony, pastors came together, under Church auspices, to discuss their problems and work. One particular emphasis was that the mission of the pastor is not to defend the tradition of the Church nor to develop its influence, but to make the Lordship of Christ visibly real in this world (*EPS*, October 27, 1950).

October 15, 1950—

Evangelical pastors in great numbers refused to vote in the Governmental elections. Roman Catholic priests were advised by the Bishop of Bautzen to vote for the National Front. Most did. West European and American officials advised East Germans that they should vote for the National Front, since all the world realized that the election was a hoax, and there was no wisdom in unnecessarily inviting trouble.

October 19, 1950—

According to East German sources, the Government intended to ask loyalty pledges from church leaders in return for continued freedom of worship (*N. Y. Times*, Oct. 19:3:4).

Secretary of the Interior H. Steinhoff declared that the "church problem" would be solved in six months (MacEoin, *The Communist War on Religion*, p. 227).

November 5, 1950—

Bishop Dibelius announced from the pulpit that the religious radio broadcasts now emanating from Radio Berlin and Deutschlandsender were being prepared by "progressive" opponents of the Church, that the Church had no responsibility for them and could not longer regard their contents as genuine preaching (*EPS*, November 17, 1950).

November 16, 1950—

Following the elections of October 15, Grotewohl, in a 2-hour address before the People's Chamber of Parliament, proclaimed the transition to a "workers' state," named the new cabinet, and threatened punitive measures against leaders of the Evangelical Churches in East Germany unless they admitted the authority and control of the State in public matters. He declared the clergymen friendly to the Government must be permitted and encouraged to continue their activities without instruction by "church leaders living in West Berlin" (*N. Y. Times*, November 16:14:2).

November 18, 1950—

The *Tägliche Rundschau* of Berlin editorialized that in principle the church must not provoke artificial opposition in relation to the State and constitution; difficulties could be overcome by an exchange of thought between church and Government; "but, when a group of Protestant church authorities . . . located in West Berlin . . . publicly promotes the re-armament of our Western homeland, and . . . clings to Western conceptions . . . organizes and carries through political and general disturbances (in East Germany), then it is the Government's duty to see to it that church and political life can continue side by side in a peaceful manner."

December 1, 1950—

Dr. S. Ringhandt, Evangelical Superintendent of Seelow, was released from imprisonment in Potsdam (*EPS*, December 1, 1950).

December 3, 1950—

Bishop Dibelius was labelled by the East German press as a "warmonger and an enemy of the people" (*N. Y. Times*, December 3:3:3).

December 5-6, 1950—

The Synod of the EKiD approved a message to the world warning that the situation in Germany could cause a world catastrophe in a very short time, asking the Government to take action to avert very likely war, and urging churches and Christians to pray and act for peace (*EPS*, December 15, 1950).

December 11, 1950—

The Brandenburg Ministerial Council passed a decree charging the Evangelical Berlin-Brandenburg Church administration with "illegal measures" against certain pastors for their National Front activities; approved the paying of stipends for such pastors direct from State funds, and advised the Church that unless the headquarters of the Church for Berlin-Brandenburg were moved from West Berlin to the Soviet Zone, State subsidies would cease as of January 1 (*The Christian Advocate*, December 28, 1950).

Protestant leaders replied that the Brandenburg Government had "seriously slandered" Bishop Dibelius and "interfered with church rights." They called Brandenburg Prime Minister Jahn's complaint that Dibelius' leadership was openly influenced by anti-German circles "a serious slander of our whole church" (*N. Y. Times*, Dec. 14, 1950). With regard to the removal of his offices to the East Zone, Bishop Dibelius in a letter (December 16) to Prime Minister Jahn, replied that no official stand could be taken until the meeting of the Synod in February. After discussion, the Government agreed to release certain church allowances which had been withheld for several months.

A Protestant weekly publication in Berlin, "not to leave anything undone which might contribute to peace," suggested that Bishop Dibelius invite the responsible leaders of East and West Germany (Chancellor Adenauer and Prime Minister Grotewohl) to meet in his home as a demonstration of good-will and to set up a three-man council to deal with practical problems (*EPS*, January 5, 1951).

December 12, 1950—

The minister of the Interior decreed that "the direct import of goods and objects of all kinds as charitable gifts is inadvisable," and added that the Church could make any distributions it desired through the Government's "Volkssolidaritat."

December 25, 1950—

Regulations prohibiting the public celebration of a religious Christmas were rigidly enforced. Religious Christmas carols were forbidden. The birthday anniversary of Stalin became the focus of public celebrations (MacEoin, *The Communist War on Religion*, p. 223).

Summary of Situation—January 1, 1951

General Atmosphere:

While the Government apparently seeks at an official and international level to use the churches for the "Peace," "De-militarization" and "German Unity" programs, local congregations and individuals are subjected to increasing pressure to join political organizations and participate in political activities. Fear and distrust are increasing. Communists have been required to give up their religious affiliations or be expelled from the Party.

Nonetheless, people look increasingly to the Church as the one place in which they can be individuals, where they can find trust and guidance. To the masses, the Church is still their minister: serving, healing, educating and nursing them. Less than 5% of their membership has left the churches.

Worship:

Regular worship in church buildings is permitted—though observed by Government employees. Other special meetings outside church buildings require police permits. Church buildings in some areas, particularly in villages, have been demolished since 1949, "to improve town planning or highways." Mr. R. Horn, member of the Socialist Union (Communist) Party declared, "When the time comes, the churches will be used as stables for the horses of the victorious Communist armies" (MacEoin, *The Communist War on Religion*, p. 221).

Christian holidays, including Christmas, were forbidden as "disturbances of the democratic order."

Church Administration and Support:

Technically, the churches are private associations, separate from the State, and must confine themselves to liturgical activities. In fact, church "taxes" are still optional to church members and can be paid through the Government. The churches receive subsidies from the Government for various expenses—differing in different laender. While legally no collections of funds are permitted outside church buildings, door-to-door collections are taking place.

The Government is seeking to have Evangelical Church headquarters removed to the East Zone, with a view to securing better control. Russian occupation leaders have appeared to be less fanatic than German officials and have occasionally intervened in disputes, in favor of the churches. Momentarily the Government's attitude seems to be less unfriendly, apparently with a view to winning support of the churches for the Government's German unity, de-militarization and peace campaigns.

Church Lands:

The land reform law of 1945 was not implemented. 95% of the arable land is still in private hands. The churches have had small holdings, and recently received more from private estates. Production quotas, however, cannot be met by the churches except by using church funds to buy goods in the expensive free-market "Handel's Organization" stores. The State refuses to take the lands even as gifts. The unfulfillment of quotas fixed by the State is a crime (sabotage of production) punishable by death.

Church Schools:

Confessional schools have been taken over by the State and are looked upon by many as confessional schools of the Communist religion. Church orphanages are now State institutions. The churches continue with nursery schools in many cities.

Youth:

Elementary Education:
The purpose of East German education is to train children politically, "to inculcate a burning patriotism." Every lesson is supposed to end with "die Nationale Front." Teachers must attend special courses on materialistic philosophy, history and politics. They may not present their own point of view, if divergent from the official point of view, to the children. Non-conformers are dismissed. Older teachers are gradually being replaced by younger, often very young, Marxists. Textbooks are frankly anti-Christian and materialist. Religious symbols have been removed from classrooms and replaced by Communist slogans and pictures of Communist leaders. Children have quickly grasped that they are expected to give prescribed answers in the classroom, and do so often knowing that the answers are untrue. Orphans are given particularly careful materialistic training. Children of parents considered "incompetent" to educate them have been taken away to State boarding schools. Children must attend extra-curricular excursions, demonstrations, and other functions even on Sundays. A new law prohibits the sending of children to the West to study—a law which even Government leaders do not obey.

Religious Education:
By decree of the Occupying Powers and later the constitution, religious education is excluded from the public school curriculum. Technically, churches may arrange with local school authorities for giving instructions two hours a week at the church's expense. Difficulties—unannounced changes in school programs, special school events, pressure on parents to withdraw their children—have only slightly affected attendance. Over the whole of East Germany, 95% of the children receive religious instruction, and in places where the situation is most difficult, oftentimes nearer 100% of the Protestant children. Instruction may be given in school rooms, church buildings, private homes, out-of-doors, or special circus wagons provided by the church. Financial support is provided through church budgets, special collections, gifts from parents and from churches abroad. The Evangelical Church has trained nearly 15,000 laymen to teach religion, many of whom also lead local youth groups.

Universities:
Before being accepted at a university, students must pass a rigid political examination including questions such as, "Are you willing to affirm the ideals of, and join the National Front?" "Do you accept all the legislation of the German Democratic Republic?" "Will you fight with weapons for peace?" In many universities candidates must appear before Vocational Guidance Commissions comprised of "Free German Youth" (Communist-led) students, faculty members and local political labor leaders. Before each term and during their

studies students must answer questions concerning one another. Before their final examinations and graduation, students must pass another severe political examination. Children of pastors are almost automatically ruled out of advanced study unless they have proved themselves politically loyal.

Student Christian groups (Studentengemeinden) continue to draw large numbers for worship, prayer and Bible study. New groups have been formed on several campuses. Where they cannot meet openly, they meet privately. It is expected that members of the Student Christian groups will soon all be members of the Free German Youth, as they cannot otherwise continue their studies.

Church:

Since separate Christian youth organizations have been prohibited, youth groups have been assimilated as part of local parish activities. Youth show increasing interest in the Christian faith, meet for Bible study, prayer and singing, have organized charitable work, evangelization and special retreats and public meetings. An increasing number of youth are pressed into joining the Free German Youth, some at the same time remaining faithful Christians. Young people must report on each other to higher Government authorities— which poses an acute problem in the Christian youth groups.

Social Work:

The Church is best known among the masses for its work through schools, orphanages, kindergartens, hospitals, homes and social welfare. Of these, only the work of the kindergartens, homes for the abnormal and social welfare work continue to any considerable extent. A Law of Sequestration enables the Government to take over institutions as quickly as expedient. By decree of the Minister of Interior, all relief work is to be done through the official "Volkssolidarität" (Community Chest). However, because this official organ is not able to handle all relief work, it seeks to maintain an advisory control over distribution. Goods from abroad designated for specific needs generally arrive, although a number of shipments are still held by authorities. Undesignated gifts may be shared between the "Volkssolidarität" and church agencies. Collections of relief for refugees, children and other needy are made within East Germany without difficulty. A special lay service has been organized in the Evangelical Church for this purpose. Catholic "Caritas" leaders have recently been accused of corruption. All church aid may soon be prohibited.

Publications:

Technically, religious publications have been banned. They do exist but in limited quantities owing to controls on paper, printing unions and censorship. Roman Catholics have no publications in East Germany, and virtually no copies of the West Berlin *Petrusblatt* arrive in East Germany. For Evangelicals some 100,000 copies of church publications are estimated to reach about 1% of the people by being passed from person to person. The future, from week to week, is uncertain.

Leadership:

Church leaders are carefully watched, their mail subject to censorship, their sermons audited. Criticism of the Government is sufficient grounds for arrest. However, few have been arrested, and they usually are not in prominent places. There have been no spectacular trials of the type of the Bulgarian pastors or Mindszenty. Leaders simply disappear.

Responsible church leaders have been attacked as "reactionaries," while the Government has made a friendly bid for the support of "progressive" lower clergy by using names like Niemoeller, Heinemann, and others in relation to the "Peace," "De-militarization" and "German Unity" programs (The East German Government switched in six months from calling Heinemann "a warmonger in the service of the Americans" to holding him up as an ideal Christian statesman). Church authorities have been threatened with severe penalties for standing in the way of 'Progressive" clergymen. Though less than 1% of the clergy have supported the National Front, the Government has made capital of their support in both domestic and international propaganda.

Life is extremely difficult for the pastors, partly because they are somewhat at the side of the stream of propaganda and coercion aimed at the people, but more because they feel how heavy is their responsibility when confused and tormented people come to them for guidance. There have been instances where pastors have been forced to spy on fellow pastors, but, while it has caused "serious concern," the number of instances is probably small.

Except for the ever-diminishing opportunities in university theological faculties, nearly all larger training centers for pastors, deaconesses, church teachers and organists have had to move to West Berlin.

Inter-Confessional Relationships:

At the episcopal-cardinal level there has been an exchange of views and some correlation of policy on Church-State problems. In individual cases in villages and towns there has also been some cooperation. On the whole, however, the policies and concepts of the Protestant and Catholic churches have been so divergent as to allow for little real ecumenical encounter in relation to existential problems. The fact that nearly all Roman Catholic priests, on the advice of the Bishop of Bautzen and of West European and American officials cast ballots in the October 15 (1950) election for the National Front, resulted momentarily in more favorable treatment. Protestants were astonished that they could do so in view of the Vatican order ex-communicating collaborators with Communism, and the fact that their fellow Catholics in neighboring Czechoslovakia were on trial for non-cooperation on a similar issue.

Roman Catholic students were also given special dispensation to participate in Communist youth organizations, e.g. to sing hymns to Stalin, while many Protestants faced expulsion for conscientiously refusing. At the same time a report published abroad claimed that only Roman Catholicism in East Germany had taken a stand against Communism and that Evangelicals, in trying to be "neutral," were in fact being weak.

Among Protestants, no comment was heard when the Jehovah's Witnesses were outlawed and many leaders imprisoned.

Ecumenical Relationships (International):

Between Christians in Germany and congregations in West Germany and abroad an intensive program of adoption and aid has indicated close solidarity and friendship. There is a growing expression of appreciation for the world-wide Christian fellowship.

However, several factors are leading towards deeper misunderstandings. Ministers from the West have visited East Germany with a view to taking up pastoral work there. The small number who have had the courage to endure the rigors of East German life as compared with those who have not stayed has not helped East Germans' respect for their Western colleagues. After East German-West German pastoral encounters, pastors of the East have been frank to say, "They do not understand us and they do not understand why we work the way we do." Further, Western advice to East Germans that they participate in the October 15 elections and vote for the National Front on the grounds that the whole world considered the election a hoax anyway, was hardly considered in the East as good advice or as a fair assessment of their own moral and spiritual concern in such matters. These are problems which presently push understanding farther into oblivion and will stand in the way of closer fellowship once East and West Christians can come again into close encounter. However, a recent "law against friendship with the West" directed against travel, correspondence and other contacts may result in a new, if inverse, stimulation of ecumenical interest and fellowship, though contacts may become increasingly risky.

Evangelization:

Observers note that the front lines of the church struggle are not where the official fencing between church administrators and Government officials takes place, but where the laymen and youth and parents reach out among fellow workers and students in an intensified evangelization program. All churches report increased attendance and the "Free churches" increased membership. Among Evangelical churches, the *Volksmission* organizes tours by evangelistic teams in pastorless areas. Courses have recently been started to train teachers for conferences on "Home Visitation." Emphases are on the Christian faith as related to work, political authority, peace and freedom; on the meaning of the Church, its structure, functions, etc.; on the Church and the world, ideologies, etc.; and on home conversation and pastoral help.

Laymen and laywomen in many parishes meet regularly for Bible study and serious consideration of present problems. Each layman seeks to bring ten neighbors! They read the Bible more, pray and seek to maintain brotherhood in everyday life, visit the sick, families with children having difficulties in school or in their religious instruction.

Christian youth are active in personal contacts, in small groups and public meetings to make known their faith and Christian teaching on problems their contemporaries are facing.

Preaching has also taken on more of a pastoral and evangelistic tone.

Ecclesiology and Theology:

As the material, political world closes in on the conventional church, it creates new problems and opportunities. Among new problems, that of living a double life and carrying a tortured conscience seems most acute. People in general appear to be more ready to bear that problem honestly than to organize some rationalization or "systematic" about it. Among students there has been some evidence of a tendency towards dualism—i.e., it is impossible to make a Christian witness in the present social setting, therefore write it off as of the devil, and draw back into a circle of the "saved" until the end comes. There is a general appreciation for the fact that physical life is not of greatest importance. Life is described as having become "genuinely simple" and real, and with that basic reality has come the realization of God's presence. Christians emphasize that their descriptions of the situation in East Germany are not intended as personal complaints, but as indications of how, in a very difficult situation, they have real joy.

Among pastors, confessional and theological argumentation holds little interest. Nor is there much interest in defending the tradition of the Church or developing its influence, but rather in making the Lordship and mercy and grace of Christ real to perplexed and tormented people. Institutional standing and titles mean very little. Pastors living in primitive quarters have, in the minds of their flocks, been transformed from theological scientists into fellow human beings and counselors. They have the respect and love of the people.

Many villages and towns have no ministers (the Evangelical Churches lack nearly 1000 pastors), but are ministered to by travelling pastors or lay elders. Consequently, new orders of "ministry" have appeared. Lay elders, neither ordained nor given special permission, administer the sacraments: "There is no other choice . . . In this situation we feel that we follow our Lord's command. The people hunger for God's grace. How could we turn them away?" There are also the "catechists" ministering to the children, and the lay "Home Visitors" doing pastoral work in thousands of homes. In reference to their life one again hears expressions like "priesthood of all believers" and "gathered churches."

Appendix I

CONSTITUTION OF THE GERMAN DEMOCRATIC REPUBLIC

(Introduced March 19, 1949; Ratified Oct. 7, 1949)

IV. *Education.*

Art. 40. Religious teaching is a matter for religious communions. Free exercise of this right is guaranteed.

V. *Religion and Religious Communions.*

Art. 41. Each citizen is given full freedom of faith and conscience. The undisturbed exercise of these religious rights is under the protection of the Republic.

Institutions of religious communions, religious rites, and religious teaching may not be used for unconstitutional or party-political purposes. However, the right of religious communions to take a stand concerning vital issues of the people is undisputed.

Art. 42. Private or civic rights and duties are neither dependent on nor restricted through exercise of religion. Exercise of private rights and admission to public services are independent of religious confessions.

No one can be forced to manifest his religious convictions. Administrative organs have the right to inquire as to one's adherence to a religious communion only insofar as rights and duties depend on it or it is made necessary for statistical recording under the constitution.

No one can be compelled to join in any religious rite or celebration, to participate in religious activities or to use a religious oath.

Art. 43. There is no State Church. The freedom to establish religious communions is guaranteed.

Each religious communion arranges and administers its own affairs in accordance with the commonly valid laws.

Religious communions are recognized by public law, as, heretofore, juridical bodies. Other religious communions are given equal rights at their request, on the condition that their constitution and number of members provide some guarantee of continuation. In the case of association of several such public and legal religious communions, such an association will equally be regarded a public and legal body.

Public and juridical religious communions are authorized to levy taxes on their members on the basis of the official taxation lists in accordance with general and public instructions. Associations which have a common concern and ideology are considered equal to religious communions.

Art. 44. The Right of the Church to give religious teaching on school premises is guaranteed. Religious teaching is given by personnel chosen by the Church. No one can be forced to or prevented from giving religious instruction. Guardians decide on participation in religious classes.

Art. 45. Public contributions to religious communions under previous law, treaties or special titles are replaced by the present law.

The right to hold properties and other rights of religious communions and religious associations in connection with their institutions, foundations or funds for cultural, educational and welfare purposes are guaranteed.

Art. 46. Insofar as there is a demand for divine service and pastoral care in hospitals, prisons, or other public institutions, religious communions are permitted to perform their religious activities therein. No one can be forced to participate in such rites.

Art. 47. Whoever desires to give up membership in a public and juridical religious communion has to make a declaration before court or an individual statement in publicly recognizable terms.

Art. 48. Decision on affiliation of children to a religious communion, until they are 14 years of age, is made by the guardian, thereafter the child decides on his or her affiliation to a religious or ideological organization.

Appendix II

"COMMUNIST LEADER MAKES FRANK STATEMENT ON RELIGION"

Berlin (RNS)

A cat-and-mouse policy toward religion is to be followed by the dominant Socialist Unity (Communist) Party in the German Democratic Republic, according to a blunt statement by a high-ranking party leader named Hauschild.

'To us Marxists-Leninists,' Hauschild said at a Communist party meeting in Thuringia, 'it is a matter of course that religion is only opium of the people, and we are going to stick to this traditional Communist principle. Time-conditioned aspects, however, demand that—on the surface—we shall have to deal with the religious question with diplomatic cunning. Funny as it may sound, we shall have to protect religion.'

Hauschild sounded the warning that 'it is only the priests we shall have to watch very closely,' and whoever is dangerous to our objectives must be done away with.'

He indicated that Roman Catholic priests will be especially watched. Declaring that church sermons will be supervised in the future by a regular "church service" set up by experienced Communists, Hauschild said that 'the fight against the solidly-organized Roman Catholic Church is more difficult than against the Evangelical (Protestant) groups which have no such strong coherence.'

According to Hauschild, aged people who cannot be remodeled anyhow 'will be left their religion, but we shall concentrate upon the education of the youth, which is our prime concern.' 'We have to see to it,' he said, 'that when the aged people die, the churches also will die. The school is, and must remain an institution of the State, into which the clergy must not stick their noses.'

(Extract from *The Church Herald* of March 10th, 1950.)

Appendix III

TEXT OF A LETTER SENT BY BISHOP DIBELIUS TO HERR GROTEWOHL, PRIME MINISTER OF THE SOVIET ZONE

April 20, 1950

(Copies are now in circulation, in the Evangelical parishes of the Eastern Zone, of a letter which Bishop Dibelius on April 20 addressed to Prime Minister Grotewohl, and of which he at the same time notified the pastors of his diocese of Berlin and Brandenburg, in order to nip in the bud certain misinterpretations of the Church's actions.)

Dear Mr. Prime Minister,

Thank you for your letter of April 18, whose explanations I am glad to note. I must, however, confess that I cannot regard these as altogether adequate. That the discussion agreed upon was to be an articulation of basic principles, and not the examination of material previously communicated and checked, is clear from the fact that the day proposed was the Tuesday after Easter. No-one could well entertain the idea that such material should be prepared, handed over and checked between Maundy Thursday evening and Easter Tuesday morning. Naturally, the stating of basic principles was not intended to be purely in the realm of the theoretical either: the points which we had at heart were to have been illustrated by examples. But what really concerned the governing bodies of the Churches was general principles, and not individual cases. It was only after a pledge had been given to arrange for a declaration of principles of this nature that the governing body of the Church of Magdeburg agreed to set aside its own proclamation.

I would now take the opportunity afforded by your letter of setting forth in writing what it is that is causing us to take up this attitude. We see the present situation in the following terms:

There are now living in the Eastern Zone of Germany some twenty million people. Of these, more than nine-tenths belong to a Christian Church.

The Church has baptised them, upon the promise, given before God, that they shall be brought up in the Christian faith. She bears a responsibility for seeing that this is in fact carried out.

This population of persons belonging to the Christian Church has now for five years had held up to it a propaganda on behalf of the materialistic conception of life and history. That this outlook on things is in direct contradiction to the preaching of the Church is obvious to all. We have only to glance at Michulin's history-book, in which it emerges from the materialistic view of history that Christ never lived at all, to realize this.

Now, it is indubitably the right of every citizen to adhere to that philosophy of life which appears to him the right one. And if combinations are set up which publicly maintain the materialistic philosophy, the Church may deplore it, but she cannot deny their right to do so. But the Church cannot keep silence where it is sought to enforce, through the powers at the disposal of the State, this philosophy which conflicts with the Christian faith.

It cannot here be objected that the State leaves the Church fully at liberty to bring the Christian Gospel to men in her services and in religious instruction. Anyone may hold aloof from the preaching of the Church. But no-one can withdraw from the State, and so long as the State denies us Christian schools for our children, no-one is in a position to stop his children from being influenced at school in a manner quite contrary to the faith prevailing at home —not to mention the other training bodies established, some by the State and some by the mass organizations.

It is this that is at the root of the inward distress which parents, and indeed the young people themselves, are suffering, and I ask you to believe me when I say that such distress reaches right down into the deepest depths of the human heart.

With this point there goes another. Materialism is not a theoretical affair: it has a fixed practical effect in the life of the individual and of the community. Since it knows nothing of God, it makes the earthly its summum bonum and its supreme value and obligation, and thereby inevitably comes into collision with the moral and ethical obligations of the Christian, which have their eternal basis in the commandments of God. It is no part of my duty to inquire how it is viewed from the materialistic standpoint when schoolboys writing political essays make statements contrary to their real convictions smply because they do not wish to throw away their chances of getting into the upper school of the University. According to the commandments of God, that is quite plainly a lie. Dialectical materialism may look how it likes on the constraining of people to take part in political demonstrations whch they consider wrong. For the Christian, it is an infringement of the God-given dignity of man. If a constitution solemnly declares that no injurious consequences shall accrue to anyone freely and openly stating his opinion and the manner in which that constitution is put into practice makes the exact opposite a daily occurrence, that is for the Christian conscience a breach of faith and belief. The leaders of the Christian Church cannot stand by while that Church's members gradually, under pressure from without, accustom themselves to living a divided life which can only end in universal deceit, and they cannot pass on unheeding while appeals come in to them daily from Christian people afflicted in their consciences.

What they now conceive it their duty to say and do in no way constitutes an attack on the State. For I say once again, Christianity is here on the defensive. Nor is it a political campaign or a deviation from the line which the Church's leaders have always drawn, to leave the political element to individual responsibility, and to refrain from meddling in the political decisions of the Government. But where we have to do with the faith of our children whom we have baptised Christians, and the freedom of our church members to act in accordance with their Christian consciences, the Christian Church is called to act in defence.

The Church is not desirous of a conflict with the power of the State, little though she fears this. In the course of conversation in March I took the liberty of indicating what possibilities might be said to exist of avoiding such a conflict. I should like to repeat certain of them here:

1. Something would have been done towards relaxing the atmosphere if the Government were to declare that neither in the schools nor in other gatherings was the Christian faith to be attacked, directly or indirectly, and if, for instance, the history book I mentioned were withdrawn from use in teacher's training. As I say, this would help relax matters, though it could not possibly satisfy the Christian of Eastern Germany. You cannot lay waste an orchard simply by pulling off the blossom and the fruit; you have to dig up the trees by the roots. What we as Christians are obliged to demand is that the State should, in all its organs, drop every kind of propaganda designed to mould people's outlook on life. Such an outlook is not the affair of the State; it is for each citizen of that State to decide for himself, and the Christian recognizes the commandment to obey God more than man.

2. The Government could declare that all kinds of pressure in political decisions were to be avoided, and that no one was to be forced against his will to join political organizations, including the Free German Youth.

3. The Government could in some way make it clear that it is, for its part, willing to carry out, in the most scrupulous manner possible, the provisions in the constitution regarding freedom of speech, legal protection upon arrest and so forth.

I am well aware that even such declarations as these would not alone suffice to allay the deep inward distress now being suffered by countless numbers of people. All that has happened has very seriously shaken public confidence in such pronouncements. But nevertheless they would serve to create a fresh atmosphere.

These were in effect the points which we wished to present to you by word of mouth, in that spirit of full openness and candour which to the Christian mind are an essential part of the dignity of man. We are convinced that we are by expressing our views, as we expressed them under similar circumstances to other Governments, doing a service to the State and its representatives. For none can with impunity set himself above the commandments, and no State can prosper if real authority is not inherent in it. And such authority will never come into being so long as nine-tenths of all the State's citizens are oppressed with the thought that they may be coerced with violence into actions they cannot in honesty approve. Even the services rendered by a State cannot be impartially reckoned up until freedom of conscience is guaranteed.

You will permit me to give a certain limited publicity to this letter, in order to nip in the bud the misinterpretations of the Church's actions which are becoming observable. You will always find the governing bodies of all the Land Churches in Eastern Germany ready and willing for oral discussion. As regards the proceedings of the Church in general, I would point out that every such governing body in Germany is independent and free to take its own decisions.

I remain, Mr. Prime Minister,

with kind regards,

Yours most sincerely,

(signed) DIBELIUS

Appendix IV

LETTER OF BERLIN-BRANDENBURG CHURCH TO ALL PARISHES

April 23, 1950

On Sunday, April 23, a Message was read from all the pulpits in the Berlin-Brandenburg Zone, which bore the signature of Dr. Otto Dibelius, Bishop of Berlin-Brandenburg, Dr. Albertz, Dr. Jacobi, Dr. Krummacher, Propst Gruber, Propst Böhm and others in the name of the Protestant Church leaders. All the signatories were members of the Fraternal Council of the 'Confessing Church.' The Message runs:

"Our Lord Jesus Christ speaks unto us, saying, 'The truth shall make you free.' And this truth is none other than He Himself, the Crucified and Risen Saviour. He is our comfort and our strength, and Him do we proclaim unto all men, even amid the great troubles of our time.

"Today more than ever before we find ourselves encompassed by oppressed and uneasy consciences. The people of our parishes cry without ceasing to their church leaders and pastors and elders, 'Help us.' We are constrained to say things that, out of regard for truthfulness, we cannot say. We are compelled to engage in doings in which we cannot join with a quiet mind. We have to acquiesce in decisions we cannot approve. We are in constant peril of losing our liberty, our employment, our daily bread, if we refuse to do as others do.' And this situation has grown sensibly more acute with the intensifying of the campaign on behalf of the National Front. Especially heart-rending are the appeals of parents who say that their children are becoming more and more accustomed, under the pressure of their schools and colleges and youth organizations, to say and write what they do not think, that the Christian faith is being made contemptible to them and teachers are seeking to persuade them that there is no God and that Christ never lived at all.

"Our people should know that the church leaders of the Eastern Zone have submitted these facts, frankly and seriously, to the highest authorities of the State. They were answered that many of these occurrences were not sanctioned by the Government, and that cases mentioned by name would be investigated and where necessary dealt with. But we are concerned not with individual cases, but with the whole set-up of public life. We feel obliged, therefore, to declare our views as follows:

"1. The Evangelical Church confesses to the truth that is Christ Jesus. This truth is not compatible with the materialist outlook on life. We protest, therefore ,against the propagation of this philosophy as the sole valid truth in schools, in colleges, in administrative bodies and in State-supported organizations. No governing power has the right to force upon anyone a philosophy that runs counter to his faith and his conscience. We call upon the members of our congregations to bear witness, gladly and resolutely, wherever their faith is assailed either overtly or covertly, that Christ is our Lord and that we are His, body and soul.

"2. Jesus Christ, Who is the truth, frees us from the power of the lie. It is a sin to coerce men by violence into falsehood, and to seduce mere children into the same. We most earnestly beseech all those now active in public affairs not to take on themselves the guilt of such a sin.

"3. Truth, which is Jesus Christ, likewise makes us free to love our neighbour even when he is our enemy. Where hatred is preached against nations, against races or classes, against individuals, the Christian is called upon to love. Whatever happens, he must not be accessory to acts of violence or to any propaganda of hate. And should he himself become the victim of such dealings, he must not answer force with force, but must seek strength from God to withstand through endurance.

"4. Truth, which we confess in our Lord Jesus Christ, binds us to one another in a fellowship of faith and charity. Where one falls victim to violence, it is the duty of the rest to come to his assistance, and to prove by their actions that he who suffers without cause is deserving of redoubled esteem and affection.

"5. Truth, in which we take comfort, is the voice of the Lord, Who will not break the bruised reed nor quench the smoking flax. We know how many have not the strength to resist pressure from without. And being men such as know their own weakness, we commend ourselves and you to the forgiveness of God. He is greater than our hearts. He can cancel all guilt ,and help us to begin anew, if we so ask Him. Only let none allow his conscience to lose its edge, and come to feel a life filled daily with falsehoods to be a thing inevitable and of no moment!

"6. Finally, we proclaim even unto them that still close their ears to the call of Christ that His truth is to make them also free. Without Him, we are one and all, even if we will not admit it, most poor and pitiable and troubled creatures. He alone makes us free to be fellow-beings and brethren one of another.

"Jesus Christ, Who rose from the grave, salutes His own with His Easter greeting, Peace be unto you. To that peace we commend ourselves and you. He is conqueror of fear, and of sin, and of death. He will forsake no man that puts his trust in Him. To Him be glory for ever and ever."

On the same Sunday, a pastoral letter drawn up by all the German bishops was read in the Roman Catholic Churches of Eastern and Western Germany. It was a declaration against materialism whereby any Catholic "consciously and voluntarily following and propagating the teachings of atheistic materialism is excommunicated." The letter goes on:

"Do not allow yourselves to be used for evil. Where materialism is concerned we have to do not with purely economic questions, nor with necessary social reform, nor with a more equitable distribution of property. Materialism is atheistic and anti-religious to its very roots, inimical to Christ and to the Church.

548 Chronicle—East Germany

"No-one can be at the same tme a true Christian and a genuine materialist. Materialism is not a political question. The Church refuses to take sides in the political and economic struggle between the Communist and anti-Communist Powers. It is untrue to say that it supports capitalism. Like Communism, materialistic capitalism runs counter to the Divine order of things. In condemning atheistic Communism, the Church desires solely to maintain the purity of the Christian faith, the administering of the Sacraments and the unity of the Church."

(*The Ecumenical Press Service*, No. 17, April 28, 1950)

Appendix V

POLITBURO STATEMENT ON THE
ROLE OF THE CHURCH IN THE GERMAN DEMOCRATIC REPUBLIC

May 15, 1950

The Constitution of the German Democratic Republic provides for any citizen complete freedom of conscience and free practice of their confession. It grants the Church complete freedom to carry out her confessional tasks. These regulations of the Constitution are strictly observed by all the official bodies of the Republic.

The bulk of the members of the Churches are as well members of democratic organizations and parties. Side by side with hundreds of their pastors, millions of members of the Churches are fighting within the ranks of the National Front of Democratic Germany for peace and for the democratic unity of Germany.

Nonetheless certain Church leaders undertook one reactionary attack after the other against the movement of those who are fighting for peace, and against the democratic regime in the German Democratic Republic. They are the same outstanding Church leaders who always fought for the regime of monopolists and "Junkers," who approved of Nazi terror and blessed the arms for Hitler's predatory war. At present these Church leaders have again taken their stand at the front of the war-mongers and reactionaries carrying out the orders of the Anglo-American imperialists and their German collaborators. They fulfill the orders given by the Minister Jakob Kaiser who is now trying in this way, on behalf of the Anglo-American monopoly-capitalists to disturb developments in the German Democratic Republic, after he has been cut off from this activity in this zone. The arguments of these reactionary Church leaders prove that they are not fighting for the justified interests of the Church, but that they intend to disturb the political development in the German Democratic Republic and to establish a monopolistic religious persecution. These Church leaders protest against the fact that the Univeristies of the German Democratic Republic are teaching dialectic materialism as the scientific ideology of the working classes. They have the benefit of the freedom of theological studies which is guaranteed for all the universities of the German Democratic Republic, whereas on the other hand they are not prepared to let the working classes have the same freedom in their activities according to their views (Weltanschauung) and are trying to persecute the working classes. These attacks made by these Church leaders have bearing upon all progress-minded people.

The reactionary Church leaders protest against pastors joining the National Front of the German Democratic Republic, they persecute these pastors with disciplinary punishments. On the other hand they have no objections to raise against pastors who misuse the pulpit for spreading reactionary propaganda. This means that they have no objections against political activities of pastors as a whole but against the political activities of those progress-minded, democratic pastors. Also here they want to exercise political coercion and deprive the progress-minded pastors of those freedoms which are guaranteed any citizen according to the Constitution.

These reactionary Church leaders protest against the fact that the young generation has formed a unified, democratic organization, the F. D. J., which is becoming more and more attractive to the majority of the young people. They also want to cut off the young generation from the privileges given by our Constitution to any citizen.

These reactionary attacks of the Church leaders have up to now been facilitated, because the Party and all the democratic forces so far have not paid sufficient attention to the work amongst the members of the Churches nor have they made sufficient efforts to support the progress-minded pastors and the democratic forces in the Church. The reactionary attacks have raised indignation amongst a great many of the democratic pastors who have been plunged into a grave conflict between their duty as pastors and their national duty. Hundreds of pastors have resolutely given evidence of their sympathy for the national struggle of their people and have joined National Committees of the National Front of the German Democratic Republic. These pastors must be supported and a broad movement of protest must be created within the Church itself, so that in future the Church members and the pastors are given full freedom to fulfill their national duty and to have the benefit of their privileges as democratic citizens.

(*Tägliche Rundschau*, May 15, 1950)

Appendix VI

GROTEWOHL DECLARATION CONCERNING POLITICAL RIGHTS OF CLERGY

June 17, 1950

According to the text and spirit of the constitution, every citizen not only has the right, but also the duty of cooperation and identification with the government of the German Democratic Republic, not only in his community, but also in his district and State.

This civil right and . . . highest duty, applies also for each clergyman and according to the constitution can be limited by no one.

Whoever tries to hinder a clergyman in the exercise of his legal rights and duty acts against the spirit and letter of the constitution.

Should accusations be made against any clergyman on account of the exercise of his basic civil right—especially in behalf of the "National Front" or the "peace movement," or should anyone attempt to hinder him in these activities, the government will protect him.

The government will utilize all measures at hand according to the factual situation to insure such clergymen constitutional freedom and to make amends to him for any material injury (e.g. loss of job).

(Quoted in *New York Times*, June 17:4:2, 1950)

EPILOGUE

Taking East Europe as a whole, developments between Church and State, or between Christians and Communists over the past two years have followed a course already apparent before the end of 1950. There is no indication of any underlying change of policy on the part of East European governments, nor is the writer aware of any strikingly new approach on the part of the Churches. Communist emphases have continued as at the end of 1950 on the "Peace" program, and on developing loyal, cooperative national Churches.

In various countries the situation has evolved—or deteriorated—at varying speeds, for example, East Germany appears to be arriving only this month at a situation somewhat comparable to that in Hungary in 1947-48. But little is happening there which has not already happened in Hungary, or Albania, or Russia. However, in each country the situation has moved farther along the way. It is worth summarizing a few outstanding developments in several countries.

A year ago the Patriarch of the RUSSIAN Orthodox Church appealed to all churches and religious bodies in the U.S.S.R. to join together in a peace campaign. A meeting was held in May last year with representatives from the various religious organizations. The alleged bacteriological warfare in Korea was condemned. Churchmen in Czechoslovakia, Bulgaria, Hungary and other East European countries echoed the Patriarch's message of condemnation.

In Cluj, RUMANIA, the "Catholic Action Committee" held a congress of 225 laymen and clergy on March 14, 1951. The congress established a "Catholic Council" of 27 members to create a national Catholic Church independent of the Vatican, in accordance with the "statutes" approved by the Committee in September, 1950. The "Council" was to take over the administration of all Roman Catholic property in Rumania. The Rumanian Government provided the "Council" with funds for the salaries of all priests who allied themselves with the National Catholic Church.

At the same time, a new greeting was introduced in the schools. Children were to greet their teacher: "There is no God." The teacher then replied, "And there never has been one."

In BULGARIA, after some revisions, the Orthodox Church statutes proposed at the end of 1950 were approved. The Patriarchal office has been established with great popular approval. Metropolitan Cyrill was elected Patriarch May 8-10, 1953. The small Roman Catholic Church, following the trial and conviction of 1 bishop, 27 priests and 12 laymen in September and October, 1952, has had to break ties with the Vatican.

In ALBANIA, a group of Catholic priests met at Shkoder on June 26, 1951, and voted to establish a "National" Catholic Church. On August 3, the Presidium of the People's Assembly approved the statutes submitted by the priests' "General Assembly," including the following:

"1. The Albanian Catholic Church has a national character, is a juridical person, and has no organizational, economic, or political ties with the Pope;

"2. Along with religious sentiments, the Catholic Church clergy must develop among the faithful a sentiment of loyalty toward the 'people's power,' the Albanian People's Republic, and the homeland;

"3. The Catholic Church must submit to the laws of God, the laws of the Republic, and also to the Canonic Code of the world Catholic Church provided the provisions of this code do not contradict the laws of the Republic, public order, and good customs . . .

"4. The Catholic Church is assisted financially by the Government, following the request of the Bishop and according to the possibilities of the Government. . . .

"5. Any nomination of clergy or their verbal or printed activity must be previously approved by the People's Government . . . and the training of the clergy can be carried out only in seminaries created and administered on the basis of rules approved by the Albanian Catholic Church upon request of the Catholic Episcopate and according to the abilities of the State; and

"6. Relations with foreign churches may be established only through official channels of the Albanian People's Republic and may be undertaken only to coordinate religious questions."

(*Notes on Soviet Affairs*, No. 138, June 23, 1952, p. 11, and *News Behind the Iron Curtain*, Feb. 1953, Vol 2, No. 2, p. 37)

In POLAND, the Government instructed the Catholic Church on January 26, 1951 to replace the Vatican-appointed temporary administrators in the 5 dioceses of former East Germany with a permanent administration. The Vatican had resisted establishing permanent dioceses pending signing of a German peace treaty. *Trybuna Ludu*, journal of the Polish Workers' Party, accused the "Vatican-Washington axis" of using the disputed territories to foster anti-Polish sentiment in Germany. The administrators were elected and Archbishop Wyszynski, following a protest to the Government for its interference in Church affairs, confirmed their appointments. (In September, 1953, Cardinal Wyszynski was arrested, and in Oct. acting Bishop Zink of the Western territories. On Oct. 15 a new organization of "patriotic priests and laymen" was established, called the "Committee of Church and Secular Catholic Activists affiliated to the All-National Committee of the National Front.")

Bishops of the Orthodox Church came together in 1951 to elect a new leader. Finding no satisfactory candidate in Poland they requested the Moscow Patriarchate to choose a suitable person. Archbishop Makary, influential leader in re-uniting the Uniate Church with the Moscow Patriarchate in 1947, was appointed.

A visitor to Poland a year ago reported that obligatory religious education continues, that confessional schools which still function receive State support. A catechism book in 400,000 copies was recently published, and a number of church structures have recently been rebuilt.

In HUNGARY, a special commission arrived in April, 1951, sent by the religious affairs department (Orginform) of the Cominform to speed up the liquidation of "Clerical reaction." (MacEoin, *Communist War on Religion*, p. 139). Roman Catholic Archbishop Joseph Grösz, who succeeded Cardinal Mindszenty as head of the Board of Bishops after the latter's imprisonment, was tried and condemned on charges of espionage, armed conspiracy, Nazi sympathies and black market currency dealings.

Janos Horvath, President of the Hungarian State Office for Church Affairs, in a speech to Reformed Church leaders, stated:

"The Church does her best (in the fight for Peace) when in her own way she explains to Church members that the individual's best contribution for the cause of peace is to do his work as conscientiously as possible" (EPS, No. 17, April, 1952).

Christmas, 1951, was observed as a religious holiday.

In CZECHOSLOVAKIA, Roman Catholic Archbishop Beran was banned from Prague on March 10, 1951, and fined the equivalent of $2,000 for his "uncooperative attitude" in the administration of the new Church laws. On April 12, *Rude Pravo* (Prague) reported that the last Slovakian bishop had sworn allegiance to the Government. *Parallel Fifty* (a Communist journal published in Paris) reported that the 4 leading bishops had replied to the Pope's latest excommunication decree: "We will not recognize the sanctions administered by the Church and we will not apply them to priests and laymen if they are imposed for political reasons."

At a peace congress of Catholic priests in October, 1951, Minister of Health Plojhar (a one-time Roman Catholic priest) stated: "We Czech Catholics completely differ with the Vatican's present policy which fully serves world capitalism and imperialism and supports the Crusade against the Soviet Union and the People's Democracies . . . We have full right as Catholic priests to disagree with Vatican policy . . ." (*News Behind the Iron Curtain*, Feb. 1953, Vol. 12, No. 2, p. 24). "Catholic Action" joined with churches of other East European countries in condemning the alleged bacteriological warfare in Korea. A Society for the Propagation of Political and Scientific Knowledge was created after the Russian pattern.

The greatest change since 1951 has taken place in EAST GERMANY. In October, 1951 visitors reported a growing spirit of optimism, of courage to speak out, of protest against the deplorable political situation. Christian students challenged materialist lectures openly. "Never since 1945 has the truth been spoken so openly in the market place," stated one observer. Communist Party functionaries were helping in the recruitment of theological candidates. The (Roman Catholic) Christian Democratic Union adopted a program ("Meissen Theses") for action which declared that Christianity and Marxist-Leninism were not incompatible, and that the Christian must support the struggle against "Capitalist imperialism." The 1950 ban on religious celebrations of Christmas was lifted, and Christianity was declared an important part of Germany's cultural make-up.

With the signing of a Peace Treaty between the West German Government and the Western Allied Powers in May, 1952, it became apparent that there could be no united Germany on East German or Soviet patterns. Almost immediately churchmen felt an intensification of the Government's hostility towards the churches.

Public parades included caricatures of leading Western political and Church personalities. There was growing distrust among churchmen following the use of the *Volkspolizei* and a small number of church leaders for secret service purposes. There was some breaking away from the Church, but more often people were breaking nervously, particularly young *Volkspolizei*, teachers and high school students. The measure of a man's worth was in technical and economic terms. Eastern pastors reported that an essential difference between this and the Hitler attack on religion was that the latter made a direct attack against pastors, whereas "the present regime attacks the individual believer," demanding rejection or acceptance of the new ideology and program. This month, however, church leaders stated that a deliberate attack was being launched against the Church.

The Ministry of Education in 1950 sent an explanatory circular to all teachers, which declared "the aim (of education) must be to instill into young people the love for the German Democratic Republic and for President Wilhelm Pieck" (*Tribune de Genève*, Oct. 1, 1951). Children were expected to participate in all school activities—week-day and Sunday. Extra-curricular excursions and mass demonstrations, special activities and demonstrations for election propaganda were organized. Emphasis was placed on peace, unity, friendship with the U.S.S.R. and other "peace-loving" countries, hatred of the enemy and disclosure of imperialistic war preparations. Slogans against Fascism and for "democratization" were said to become less meaningful as the Bolshevization program gained momentum. The Free German Youth had virtual control of most school systems through a small number of young teachers. Students' certificates indicated whether they were members of the FDJ (Free German Youth), whether they participated in propaganda and demonstration activities, and whether they identified themselves "with the inner life of the schools."

With the establishment of the equal status of women as workers and the subsequent "liberation" of mothers from home responsibilities, many children were put into State homes along with children of "incompetent" parents and of unmarried mothers. In institutions, prayers to God for meals were replaced by prayers to Stalin. Denunciations within families are said to be increasing. Parents' Advisory Councils were organized by local Governmental authorities to promote the "democratization" of the schools. Local pastors advised parents not to participate in the Councils unless they were in a position to be effective in them. In some instances parents' advisory committees were created by the churches. Churches and Christian families are making a special effort to keep teachers within the Christian fellowship. Some church kindergartens still function as private schools, but with many difficulties.

The Church seems ready to accept in principle that there should be no religious education in the schools but insists that if there is to be religious liberty according to the Constitution, religious education must not be replaced by religious materialism. Lay catechists still give religious instruction in East Berlin, but the number of teachers is falling rapidly. In the East Zone religious instruction is given but away from the public school, and even in many instances away from the churches. The work of the teachers is supported through church collections and by private donations of families. Some parents, themselves not Christian, want their children to know what the Bible says about the meaning of life and the destiny of man.

It is estimated that two-thirds of the youth in the Church are members of the (Communist) Free German Youth (FDJ). The FDJ has claimed that it has 121,882 propaganda groups and more than a million members. Activities of the FDJ include militaristic marches, repeating of hate-songs and slogans, and participation in propaganda programs. A resolution to stamp out the *Junge Gemeinde* (Christian Youth organization) was approved with great enthusiasm ,and the youth movement of the Church has since been declared illegal. It's leaders were attacked for their "methods of murder and agitation." The Christian Student Movement continues services on some campuses, but almost entirely in private. Great interest, however, has been shown by fellow-students.

The social welfare and charitable activities of the Church are reported as being almost entirely dissolved. The lack of replacements for deaconesses, the restrictions against training deaconesses, and the ban on private donations, has made institutional work almost impossible. The Church still cares for some abnormal children and old people; through the Volunteer Helpers' groups local collections are made for refugees and needy children. The Church's role is seen as being increasingly one of a pastoral nature. Welfare assistance from abroad was labelled "illegal Western propaganda" unless distributed via the official "Volkssolidarität." Roman Catholic CARITAS was accused of being corrupt. Some assistance, however, still gets through. When the Church requested amnesty for political prisoners who were ill, they were told, "Criminals cannot be released. You are agitating against the authority of the Government."

Church leaders are being arrested for criticism of the Government, for "inciting the people against the Government," for "sabotaging the economy or the farm quota system." Pastors believe that all their actions are watched as well as their services, and that they are classified "reliable," "improving," "unsteady," or "conscious opponents." Premier Grotewohl has written to Bishop Dibelius serving notice that all theological faculties of the universities should be dissolved. The Church was advised to find other ways to train its ministers. A number of theological students have been dismissed from the universities. Many went to Berlin to study until a new law established that anyone out of the East Zone for more than four weeks would lose his citizenship. A Christian Peace Action Committee (Christlicher Arbeitskreis für den Frieden) has established units all over East Germany. The organization has denounced pastors in some instances. The Church officially has resisted participation in the Government's peace programs and insists that it will work for peace in its own way. A central Department for Church Affairs was established by the Government in October, 1951.

Theoretically, approved religious documents can be printed and distributed. However, Foreign Minister Dertinger in 1951 stated that newsprint allocations for religious purposes would remain curtailed until leaders of the Church showed a more loyal attitude to the Government. A church calendar was banned in some areas, reportedly because the text for Pentecost was, "Not by might, nor by power, but by my spirit, said the Lord of hosts" (Zech. 4:6).

The *Volksmission* publications reach many people by passing from hand to hand. The Mission has conducted as many as two thousand "Bible weeks" in a year, attended by believers and non-believers, sometimes comprising as much as 90% of the local populace. Christian "shock troops" systematically visit every home in the villages for pastoral conversations. They leave helpful tracts and invite people to Christian meetings with their neighbors. The work of the "home visitors" has been expanded. The main problem which the visitors raise is, "How shall we advise families on matters of conscience?"

The concept of the Church moves increasingly in the direction of a gathered community. The *Volkskirche* idea "recedes into the romantic past." The growing sense of fellowship has brought with it new confidence and rejoicing in the Christian faith. To the people loyal to the Church, it is a place where they can speak most freely, a place where they can find their bearings through grace, renewal and real fellowship, and the only body which speaks up for the value and dignity of the individual and the sanctity of his convictions. Because of the increasing difficulties and dangers in having many church meetings, an attempt has been made to have less meetings of all groups but instead to hold annual conventions which break up into different functional or age groups.

Ecumenical contact has become increasingly difficult. Entrance into the East Zone, even for Berliners, is possible only by special permission. People feel isolated and desire closer fellowship and contact. The *Kirchentag* of 1951 was a great encouragement to East Zone Christians. Pastors report that the more people are afflicted, the more they are drawn to God, and the more aware they become of the reality of the universal Christian fellowship. Real understanding, however, becomes increasingly difficult in face to face confrontation.

Geneva, May, 1953

BIBLIOGRAPHY

Union of Soviet Socialist Republics

Books

Anderson, Paul, *People, Church and State in Modern Russia*, Student Christian Movement Press, 56 Bloomsbury St., London, 1944.

Berdyaev, H., *The Russian Idea*, The Centenary Press, 52 Doughty St., London, 1947.

Bolshakoff, Serge, *Russian Nonconformity*, Westminster Press, Philadelphia, 1950.

Curtiss, Jóhn Shelton, *The Russian Church and the Soviet State*, Little, Brown & Co., Boston, 1955.

Diem, Herman, *Die Kirche Zwischen Russland und Amerika*, Evangelischer Verlag, Zurich, 1947.

Fédorov, F., *L'Église et le Culte en U.S.S.R.*, Éditions Sociales, Paris, 1945 (Booklet).

Lauterbach, R. E., *These Are the Russians*, Harper & Bros., New York and London, 1945.

The Moscow Patriarchate, *Die Russische Rechtgläubige Kirche im Kampf um den Frieden*, Verlag des Moskauer Patriarchats, 1950.

The Moscow Patriarchate, *Proceedings of the Conference of the Heads of the Autocephalous Orthodox Churches*, (as reproduced by) Y.M.C.A. Press, Paris, 1952.

The Moscow Patriarchate, *The Truth about Religion in Russia*, Hutchinson and Co., London and New York, 1942.

Pares, B., *Russia, Its Past and Present*, The New American Library, 501 Madison Avenue, New York, 1949.

Rose, Karl, *Tychon Sergius Alexius—Oekumenische Profile*, Heimatdienstverlag, Berlin (Booklet).

Rose, Karl, *Predigt der Russisch—Orthodoxen Kirche*, Evangelische Verlaganstalt, Berlin, 1952.

Schuster, G. W., *Religion Behind the Iron Curtain*, Macmillan Co., New York, 1954.

Solovyev, V., *Russia and the Universal Church*, Centenary Press, London, 1948.

Timasheff, N. S., *Religion in Soviet Russia*, Sheed and Ward, 110 Fleet St., London, 1944.

Zernov, N., *The Russians and Their Church*, S.P.C.K., London.

Articles and Reports

Bennett, John, "Russia and Christians of the West," *Student World*, Geneva, Switzerland, Third Quarter, 1944.

Karpovich, Michael, "Church and State in Russian History," from *The Russian Review* (Semi-Annual Journal), 215 West 23rd St., New York, Spring, 1944.

Lefever, Ernest, "Religious Liberty in Russia" from *The Christian Century*, September 6, 1950.

Lowne, D. A., "Communist Morality," *The Christian Century*, May 24, 1950.

(557)

Niemoeller, Martin, "How Free is the Russian Church?", *The Australian Christian*, Melbourne, June 10, 1952.

Widdrington, P. E. T., "The Future of the Russian Church," *Christendom*, Vol. 14, No. 57, March, 1945.

Wight, Martin, "Die Kirche, Russland und der Westen," World Council of Churches Conference Report, Geneva, 1948.

Zernov, Nicolas, "The Future of Christianity in Russia," *Student World* (World Student Christian Federation), Geneva, Third Quarter, 1944.

"The Christian Approach to the U.S.S.R.," Study Department, World Council of Churches, Geneva, June, 1947.

"The Christian Cause in Russia," *The Australian Christian*, Melbourne, June 3, 1952.

"La Nature des Rapports entre l'Église Russe et le Kremlin," *Tribune de Genève*, Geneva, December 22, 1950.

"Religion in Russia," *Life*, New York, 1951.

"Soviet-American Relations," Federal Council of Churches of Christ in America, October, 1946.

Periodicals

The Current Digest of the Soviet Press, Joint Committee on Slavic Study, 413 W. 17th St., New York (Weekly).

The Eastern Churches Broadsheet, Monthly publication of Anglican and East Churches Association, London.

East Europe and Soviet Russia, 16 Chester Row, London, S.W. 1. (Weekly).

Intelligence Digest, Kenneth deCourcy, 14 Old Queen St., London, S.W.1 (Monthly).

Religion in Russia, Y.M.C.A. Press, Paris (occasional).

The Russian Review, 215 West 23rd St., New York (Semi-Annually).

The Slavonic and East European Review, "A Survey of the Peoples of East Europe, their History, Economic Development, Philology and Literature," Publication of the University of London School of Slavonic and East European Studies.

The Soviet Monitor, (Tass Agency News releases) Chronicle House, 72-78 Fleet St., EC4, London.

Baltics

Articles and Reports

C'Uibe, Leon, "The Lutheran Church of Latvia behind the Iron Curtain," *Olofssons*, Stockholm, 1948.

Kivirauna, Rudolf, "Fate of the Estonian Church" (News presented to Paris Peace Conference, 1946).

Perlitz, H., "The Fate of Religion and Church (of Estonia) under the Soviet Rule, 1940-41," London.

Rei, A., "Have the Baltic Countries Voluntarily Renounced their Freedom?", World Association of Estonians, Inc., 15 E. 125th St., New York.

"Close to Persecution," *The Christian Advocate*, Chicago, April 12, 1951.

Periodicals

Lithuanian Archives, a journal.

Lithuanian Bulletin, Lithuanian American Council, 233 Broadway, New York, 7 (monthly).

Rumania

Books

Beza, Marcu, *The Rumanian Church*, S.P.C.K., Northumberland Ave., W.C. 2, London, 1943.
Regime of Cults in Rumania, Rumanian Review Publications, Bucharest, 1946.
Rumania at the Peace Conference, Paris, 1946.

Articles and Reports

Markham, R. H., "Church Liquidation in Rumania," *Christian Century*, March 16, 1949.
"The Art of Dividing and Ruling—the Technique against Religions in Rumania," *The Tablet*, February 25, 1950.
L'Almanac des Emigrés Roumaine, Paris, Librarie Arsenie, 39 rue Delambre, Paris, 1952.
"Church and State in Rumania," *East Europe and Soviet Russia*, May 26, 1949.
"Communism vs. Christianity," unpublished document by a refugee, Geneva, Switzerland.
"Persecution of Religion in Rumania," Rumanian National Committee, Washington, D. C., November, 1949.

Periodicals

Biserica Ortodoxa Romans, (Official Bulletin of Orthodox Church) Bucharest.
Bulletins, Centre Roumain de Recherches, 28 rue Serpente, Paris.
Indrumatorul Pastoral, 1951 (Orthodox Patriarchate), Bucharest, (Orthodox Church Calendar and Devotional).
La Natione Roumaine (weekly), Societé Roumaine d'Editions, Paris.
Orthodoxia (Review of Orthodox Patriarchate), Bucharest.
Studii Teologice (Theological Studies, Orthodox Patriarchate), Bucharest.

Bulgaria

Books

Bojkoff, Liuben, *Bulgaria Is Not the Land of Roses Only*, Danoff Publishers, Sofia, 1946.

Articles and Reports

Tobias, R., "Fifteen Bulgarian Pastors," Unpublished report, World Council of Churches, Geneva.
"Missionary from Behind the Iron Curtain," *Boston Sunday Globe*, April 2, 1950.
"Religious Freedom in Bulgaria," *New Central European Observer*, London (Pamphlet).

Periodicals

Bulgarian Bulletin, Bulgarian Telegraph Agency, London.
La Bulgarie d'Aujourd'hui (bi-weekly), Bulgarian Legation, Paris, Sofia.
La Bulgarie Nouvelle (weekly), 12, Place Narodno Sobranie, Sofia.
Bulletin d'Information, Press Bureau of Bulgarian Legation, 1 Ave. Rapp, Paris.
Dimitrov Youth of Bulgaria (periodical), Committee of Dimitrov Youth, Sofia.
Free Bulgaria (bi-weekly), Sofia.

Free Independent Bulgaria, Bulgarian National Committee, 729 9th St., N.W., Suite 624, Washington, D. C.
Naroden Pastor, journal of the Association of Orthodox Priests, Sofia.
Nouvelles Bulgares (Bulletin), Information Bureau, Bulgarian Legation, Berne.
Press Service of the Bulgarian Legation, London.
Radio Bulletin (daily), American Legation, Berne.
Otechestren Front, periodical, Sofia.
Tzerkoven Vestnic, Journal of Orthodox Holy Synod, Sofia.
World-Over-Press (news release), Wilton, Connecticut.

Poland

Articles and Reports

Exbrayat, I., "Témoignage sur Varsovie," Chastanier Frères, Nîmes, 1950.
de Pury, R., "Carnet de route Polonais," *Viens et Vois* (journal), 27 June, 1952, St. Etienne, France.
"Appeal for Peace," Polish Research and Information Service, New York, 1950.
"Church Lands," *Polish Newsletter*, March 16, 1950, Polish Research and Information Service, New York, 1950.
"Loyalty in People's Poland," *Luzerner Neueste Nachrichten*, Luzern, March 25, 1950.
"Pattern of Persecution," *The Tablet*, April 8, 1950, London.
"Poland, Church and State," *East Europe*, May 26, 1949.
"Poland Today," Polish Research and Information Service, New York, February 1949; October, 1949; April, 1950; June, 1950; December, 1950.
"Protestant Churches in Poland" (Unpublished).
"Protestantism in Poland," *Polish Facts and Figures*, March 26, 1949, Press Office of the Polish Embassy in London, 47 Portland, Place, W.1.
"Protocol to State-Church Agreement," Polish Research and Information Service, New York, 1950.
"Recovered Territories and the Church," *Polish Newsletter*, January 31, 1951, New York.
"Relations between Church and State in Poland," *Polish Facts and Figures*, March 26, 1949, Press Office of the Polish Embassy in London, 47 Portland Place, W.1.
"Religious Freedom and the State-Church Agreement," Polish Research and Information Service, New York, 1950.
"Religious Life in Poland," Polish Research and Information Service, New York, 1948.

Periodicals

The Universal Church, Bulletin of Ecumenical Council, Warsaw.

Hungary

Books

Bereczky, Albert, *How Hungarian Protestantism Fought Anti-Semitism*, Budapest, 1945.
Evans, Rev. S. G., *The Trial of Cardinal Mindszenty*, Religion and the People Publications, Birmingham, 1949.

Mindszenty, Cardinal, edited by C. Hollis, *Four Years Struggle of the Church* (Catholic) *in Hungary*, Longmans, Green and Co., London, 1949.

Documents on the Hostile Activity of the U. S. Government against the Hungarian People's Republic, Information Department of the Ministry of Foreign Affairs, Budapest, 1951.

Documents on the Mindszenty Case, the Government's Yellow Book, Athenaeum, Budapest, 1949.

Five Years of Hungarian Protestantism, Hungarian Church Press, 1945-1950, Sylvester, N.E. Hermina-UT51, Budapest.

Laszlo Rajk and His Accomplices before the People's Court, Budapest Printing Press, Budapest, 1949.

The Trial of Jozsef Mindszenty, Hungarian State Publishing House, Budapest, 1949.

Articles and Reports

Bereczky, Albert, "Discourse d'Ouverture au Conseil Libre le 26 Mars, 1947" (Unpublished).

Evans, Rev. Stanley G., "Hungary's Churches Today," *Hungarian News and Information Service*, 33 Pemridge Square, London, W.2.

Nagy, Ferenc, "How the Russians Grabbed My Government," *Saturday Evening Post*, September, 1947.

"Barth to Bereczky," *Christian Century*, July 30, 1952.

"Declaration of the Council of the Synod of the Hungarian Reformed Church Concerning Church and State Relationships" (Unpublished), Budapest.

"The Hungarian Church Situation," *Information Service*, March 19, 1949, Federal Council of Churches, New York.

"Hungary," *Lutheran World Federation Newsbulletin*, May 1, 1950, Geneva.

"A New Development in the Mindszenty Story," *Christian Century*, Sept. 6, 1950, Chicago.

"Die Protestantischen Kirchen in Ungarn, 1939-1950" (Unpublished) Ostkirchenausschuss, Marienstr, 55, Hanover, Germany.

"Was it Justice or Expediency in Hungary," *Lutheran World Federation Newsbulletin*, May 1, 1950, Geneva.

Periodicals

Documents on Foreign Affairs by The Hungarian News and Information Service (bulletins), 33 Pembridge Square, London, W.2.

Hungarian Church Press, Editor Imre Kadar, Budapest XIV, Abonyi-u21.

News from the Hungarian People's Republic, The Hungarian News and Information Service, 33 Pemridge Square, London, W2.

Czechoslovakia

Books

Constitution of the Czechoslovakian Republic, Czechoslovakian Ministry of Information, August, 1948, Prague.

Articles and Reports

Betts, R. R., "The Place of the Czechoslovakian Reform Movement in the History of Europe," *The Slavonic Review*, Vol. 25, 1946, 47.

562 _Bibliography_

The Christian Newsletter, No. 311, 20 Balcombe St., Dorset Sq., London, N.W.1.
"L'Eglise en Lutte Pour la Paix," Preparatory Committee for Conferences of Christian Churches, Prague.
"The Evangelical Church of the Czech Brethren," Report of July, 1945, Prague (Unpublished).
"Der Kirchenkampf in der Tschechoslowakei," _Neue Zürcher Zeitung_, May 16, 1949, Zurich.
Orbis Catholicus (Journal), No. 3, March, 1949, Thomas-Morus Presse, Vienna.
"State Church Evolves," _Christian Advocate_, April 12, 1951, p. 481, Chicago.

Periodicals

Ceteka News Agency, Prague.
"Features and News from Behind the Iron Curtain," _Information Service of Free Czechoslovakia_, 37 Tregunter Road, London.
Krestanska, Prague.
Service de Press de l'Union Internationale des Etudiants, Voj Tesska 12, Prague.

East Germany

Books

Herman, Stewart, _Rebirth of the German Church_, Student Christian Movement Press, London, 1946.

Articles and Reports

Dibelius, Otto, "Church and State in Berlin-Brandenburg," _Ecumenical Review_, 1951, Vol. III, No. 3.
————, "The Position of the Church in the Eastern Zone," _Ecumenical Review_, 1950, Vol. II, No. 2.
Forell, F. J., "Germany's Fate is Ours," _Christian Century_, April 5, 1950.
Piper, O. A., "The Church in Soviet Germany," _Christian Century_, November 22, 1950.
Turner, E. E., "East German Church under Pressure," _Christian Century_, September 13, 1950.
"The Rôle of the Church in the German Democratic Republic," _Tägliche Rundschau_, May 15, 1950, Berlin.
"Soviet Zone Bans Youth Crosses," _Christian Century_, Sept. 6, 1950.
"Nazi Christians Regaining Posts," _Christian Century_, June 25, 1952.
"New East German Tension," _Christian Century_, July 23, 1952, Chicago.

General

Books

Armstrong, H. F., _Tito and Goliath_, Victor Gollancz Ltd., London, 1951.
Banning, W., _Der Kommunismus als Politisch-Sociale Welt-religion_, Lettner-Verlag, Berlin, 1953.
Barnabas, _Christian Witness in Communist China_, Morehouse-Gorham Co., New York, 1951.
Barron, J. B., & Waddams, H. M., _Communism and the Churches_, SCM Press, London, 1950.
Barth, Karl, _Die Kirche zwischen Ost und West_, Evangelischer Verlag, A. G., Zollikon-Zurich, 1949 (Booklet).

Bates, M. Searle, *Religious Liberty: An Inquiry*, International Missionary Council, New York, 1945.

Bennett, John C., *Christianity and Communism*, Haddam House, New York, 1949.

Berdiaeff, N., *De l'Esprit Bourgeois*, Delachaux et Niestle, Neuchatel, 1949.

Brunner, Emil, *Communism, Capitalism and Christianity*, Lutterworth Press, London, 1949.

Buber, Martin, *Paths in Utopia*, Macmillan Company, New York, 1950.

Butler and Devanesen, *Communism and Christianity*, Published for The Student Christian Movement of India, Pakistan and Ceylon by The Christian Literature Society for India, Madras, 1951.

Crossman, Richard, *"The God that Failed, Six Studies in Communism,"* Hamish Hamilton, London, 1950.

Desroches, H. C., *Signification du Marxisme*, Les Éditions Ouvrières, Paris, 1949.

Ebon, Martin, *World Communism Today*, Whittlesey House, McGraw Hill Book Co., Inc., New York, 1948.

Fischer, D. Martin, *Das Zeugnis der Verhafteten*, Lettner-Verlag, Berlin, 1953.

Forman, Charles W., *A Christian's Handbook on Communism*, National Council of Churches, New York, 1952.

Gollwitzer, Helmut, *Unwilling Journey*, Muhlenberg Press, Philadelphia, 1954.

Heimann, Edward, *Freedom and Order*, Charles Scribner's Sons, New York, 1947.

Hunt, R. N. Carew, *The Theory and Practice of Communism*, Macmillan Co., New York, 1951.

Hyde, Douglas, *The Answer to Communism*, Paternoster Publications, Ltd., London, 1949.

Hyde, Douglas, *I Believed*, The Reprint Society, London, 1950.

James, H. Ingli., *Communism and Christian Faith*, The Carey Kingsgate Press, Ltd., 6 Southampton Row, London, W.C.1., 1950.

Keller, Adolf, *Church and State on the European Continent*, London, 1936 (Willett, Harper and Brothers, New York, 1937).

Koestler, A., *Darkness at Noon*, Modern Library, Inc., 457 Madison Ave., New York, 1946.

Kohn, Hans, *Pan-Slavism, Its History and Ideology*, University of Notre Dame Press, Notre Dame, Ind., 1953.

Latourette, K. S., *A History of the Expansion of Christianity*, Vol. II, Harper & Brothers, New York, 1937-45.

Latu, *L'Eglise Derriere le Rideau de Fer.*

Lieb, Fritz, *Wir Christen und der Kommunismus*, Chr. Kaiser Verlag, München, 1952.

MacEoin, Gary, *The Communist War on Religion*, The Devin-Adair Company, New York, 1951.

Markham, R. H., *Communists Crush Churches in Eastern Europe*, Meador Publishing Company, Boston, 1950.

Miller, Alexander, *The Christian Significance of Karl Marx*, Macmillan Company, New York, 1947.

Niebuhr, Reinhold, *Christianity and Power Politics*, Charles Scribner's Sons, 1940. New York.

Northcott, Cecil, *Religious Liberty*, Student Christian Movement Press, Ltd., 56 Bloomsbury St., London, 1948.

Rehwinkel, A. M., *Communism and the Church*, Concordia Publishing House, Saint Louis, Missouri, 1948.

Schweitzer, W., *Eschatology and Ethics*, The Study Department of the World Council of Churches, 17, route de Malagnou, Geneva, 1951.

Sheen, Fulton J., *Communism and the Conscience of the West*, Browns and Molan Ltd., Dublin, 1948.

Spinka, M., *A History of Christianity in the Balkans*, American Society of Church History, Chicago, 1933.

Ward, Barbara, *The West at Bay*, Allen and Unwin, London (Ruskin House), 1949.

Weckerling, Rudolf, *Die Evangelische Kirche zwischen Ost und West*, Evangelischer Verlag A. G., Zollikon-Zurich, 1946 (Booklet).

Wood, H. G., *Religious Liberty Today*, Cambridge University Press, Cambridge, 1949.

Zankow, S., *Kirche und Staat*, Pyrsos, Athens, 1938.

————, *Nation, Staat, Welt und Kirche im Orthodoxen Osten*, Hofbuchdruckerei, Sofia, 1937.

The Church and the International Disorder, Student Christian Movement Press, 56 Bloomsbury St., London, W.C.1, 1948.

Charter of the United Nations and Statute of the International Court of Justice, New York, 1946.

World Christian Handbook, World Dominion Press, London, 1949.

Yearbook of Human Rights, United Nations, New York (annual).

Articles and Reports

Anderson, P., "Communism and Christian Education," *World Christian Educator*, 2nd Quarter, 1950, New York.

Barth, Markus, "The Mission and Misery of Europe's Churches," *Christian Century*, Nov. 11, 1953.

Bell, G. K. (Bp. of Chichester), "Communism and the Churches," *London Times*, 17 February, 1949.

Bennett, John, "The Christian Answer to Communism," *Social Progress*, January, 1951, Philadelphia.

————, "Can We Ever Support Communism?" *Christian Century*, June 11, 1952.

————, "Our Responsibility as Christians in Face of the Challenge of Communism," Study Department, 17 Rte de Malagnou, Geneva (Unpublished).

————, "Turn Communists to Christianity," *Christian Century*, April 18, 1951.

Brunner, Emil, "Our Attitude as a Christian Church to Communism," World Council of Churches Ecumenical Institute, Geneva, 1950.

Forman, C., "The Problem of Communism for Christian Missions," *Union Seminary Quarterly Review*, Nov., 1951, New York.

Garrison, W. E., "Free Church and State Church," *Christian Century*, November 5, 1952, Chicago.

Gollwitzer, H., "The Christian between East and West" (Unpublished), World Council of Churches Ecumenical Institute, 1950, Geneva.

Jackson, E., "Christianity and Socialism," *Christian Advocate*, April 26, 1951, Chicago.

Lefever, E., "The Church Has Five Choices," *Christian Century*, Feb. 7, 1951, Chicago.

————, "Religious Liberty in Soviet Satellites," *Christian Century*, December 6, 1950, Chicago.

Malik, C., "The Challenge of Communism," *Christian Century*, Jan. 17, 1951.

Mehl, Roger, "Is Political Action by the World Council of Churches Possible?" *Ecumenical Review*, Geneva.

Niebuhr, R., "Streaks of Dawn in the Night," *Christianity and Crisis*, December 12, 1949, New York.

————, "Two Forms of Tyranny," *Christianity and Crisis*, February 2, 1949, New York.

Olivier, P., "L'Eglise Derrière le Rideau de Fer," *Réforme*, February 12, 1949, Paris.

Oxnam, G. B., "How the Protestants Fight Communism," *Look Magazine*, October 11, 1949, New York.

Rohrbach, Heinrich C., "The Problem of Christian Illegal Resistance," *Union Seminary Quarterly Review*, Vol. VII, No. 4, June, 1952.

Root, Robert, "All in the Name of Peace," *Christian Century*, September 27, 1950, Chicago.

Shaull, M. R., "The Communists Face the Same World" (booklet), Division of Foreign Missions, National Council of Churches of Christ, New York, 1952.

Schweitzer, W., "The Church's Freedom and Its Responsibility in Eastern Europe and in the Western Orbit," World Council of Churches Study Department, 1950, Geneva.

Siedenspinner, Clarence, "Christianity and Communism," *Christian Advocate*, May 3, 1951.

Stowe, David, "Six Lessons from Red China," *Christian Century*, August 1, 1951.

Thomas, M. M., "Churches in the Political Struggles of Our Day," *Ecumenical Review*, Geneva.

Trevor-Roper, H. R., "Stalin Would Have Liquidated Marx," *New York Times*, January 30, 1949, New York.

Wagner, O. W., "The Either-Or Fallacy," *Christian Century*, April 12, 1950, Chicago.

West, C., "Christian Witness and Communist Society," World Council of Churches Ecumenical Institute, Geneva, 1950.

Zuurdeeg, W. F., "The Challenge of Communism," *Social Progress*, Feb. 1951, Philadelphia.

"Christianity and Communism, An Analysis," Garrett Biblical Institute, Evanston.

"Christianity and Social Work," Documents (unpublished) of the World Council of Churches Ecumenical Institute, 1952.

"Communism Exposed," *The Church Herald*, January 12, 1951, Grand Rapids, Michigan.

"Communist Inroads on the Roman Catholic Church in East Europe," *Notes on Soviet Affairs*, June 23, 1952 (U. S.).

"Die Kirche in der C. S. R., in Polen und Rumanien," *Orbis Catholicus*, March, 1949, Vienna.

"Green Europe, the Peasant Problem," *British Survey*, April, 1946, British Society for International Understanding, London.

"Green Europe, Behind the Iron Curtain," *Ibid.*, May, 1946.

"Lambeth and Communism," *The Bulletin* (Council for Social Service, Church of England in Canada), February 15, 1949, Church House, Toronto.

"On the Meaning of History," World Council of Churches Ecumenical Institute, Paper No. V, 1950, Geneva.

"The Red and the Black," *News Behind the Iron Curtain*, February, 1953, National Committee for Free Europe, New York.

"The Responsible Society," World Council of Churches Study Department, 1949, Geneva.

"Witness of the Imprisoned," Federation News Sheet, May-June, 1953, World Student Christian Federation, Geneva.

"The World Council of Churches and the Ideological Conflict of Our Time," Unpublished Documents of the World Council of Churches, Geneva.

BRIEF INDEX TO PART I